Global Subjects

Global Subjects

A Political Critique Of Globalization

Jean-François Bayart

Translated by Andrew Brown

polity

First published in French as *Le Gouvernement du Monde* © Librairie
Arthème Fayard, 2004

This English edition © Polity Press, 2007

Polity Press
65 Bridge Street
Cambridge CB2 1UR, UK

Polity Press
350 Main Street
Malden, MA 02148, USA

ISBN-13: 978-07456-3667-2
ISBN-13: 978-07456-3668-9 (pb)

A catalogue record for this book is available from the British Library.

Typeset in 10 on 11.5 pt Palatino
by SNP Best-set Typesetter Ltd., Hong Kong
Printed and bound in Great Britain by MPG Books Ltd, Bodmin,
Cornwall.

For further information on Polity, visit our website: www.polity.co.uk

This book is supported by the French Ministry of Foreign Affairs, as part
of the Burgess programme run by the Cultural Department of the French
Embassy in London. (www.frenchbooknews.com)

Liberté • Égalité • Fraternité

RÉPUBLIQUE FRANÇAISE

Contents

Translator's Note

I would like to thank Sarah Dancy for her scrupulous care in reading the typescript. Jean-François Bayart read the translation closely, at both typescript and proof stage: his queries, suggestions and improvements were invaluable. Needless to say, any errors that remain are my own.

Andrew Brown

Preface: Yours Globally

This book arose from the meditations that have been forced on me by airline companies ever since I first started to reflect on the historicity of political phenomena throughout the world. Globalization and air travel are more or less synonymous. The more or less frequent flights to which our way of life subjects us have to some extent become the equivalent of the pilgrimages discussed by the anthropologist Victor Turner. They are the peregrinations by means of which we produce our societies and give them meaning. Well then: on 25 June 2000, Air France, which wants to 'make the sky the most beautiful place on earth' – on condition that we actually leave the earth behind, as the advert ought to specify – was supposed to wing me from Venice to Paris, on flight AF1727, due to take off at 15:00 hours. On arrival at the airport, I learned, with another 50 or so passengers, that the flight had been cancelled. We would be departing from Milan, to which we would be taken by . . . bus, and from where we would be taking off for Paris at 20:20 hours on flight AF2215. The said bus broke down on the motorway, halfway there. Luckily another bus, which happened to be passing and was empty, enabled us to arrive at Malpensa in time. In very good time, in fact, since dear old flight AF2215 didn't take off until around 23:00 hours.

In spite of the kindness of successive Italian drivers, the journey from Venice to Paris and the interminable wait at Malpensa did not add up to 'the most beautiful place on earth'. We were not served any drinks. At check-in we had to ask firmly for vouchers that enabled us to obtain a sandwich and a soft drink (but not an espresso). So we had to pay for our own dinners. When, at the end of our tether, we took it upon ourselves to settle down in the waiting room of Air France, where in fact we had no right to be, the stopover manager, Franco Bassetto, threatened to call the police, and was dissuaded from doing so only by the indignation of the other passengers and the ridiculousness of the situation.

When it came to transparency, things were no less extraordinary. No fewer than six different explanations were given us in the course of those ten hours. From the point of view of governance, we were surprised to discover that the Milan–Paris crew was unaware that it had on board 50 enraged passengers who had come overland from Venice. As for commercial common sense, let's not even talk about it: no recompense was offered, not even in air miles. Obviously, on that particular day Air France was more at ease with the second sense of 'flight' ('a hasty retreat' – from its responsibilities, that is) than with the first ('the act or manner of flying through the air').

Air companies use and abuse the metaphor of freedom. And yet they are disciplinary institutions. The contrast between their superficial chilly affability and the authoritarian procedures by which they channel their passengers, assigned to ever more cramped spaces and forced to confront longer and longer queues, would have delighted Marcuse or Foucault. They have become a valuable source of assistance to the police, over and above the traditional relations that they always had with the secret services. As a result of Schengen, they themselves check the visas of their passengers wishing to travel to Europe, therefore rendering it de facto impossible to claim the right of asylum stipulated by the various constitutions, or by international law. They have been forced to open their files to the American authorities who trawl through them for personal information on the dietary preferences, modes of payment, state of health, and previous journeys of their passengers, all within an extended conception of the fight against terrorism. They denounce to the police those passengers who are guilty of making jokes – the fact that these jokes are not very good is irrelevant – or who linger in the toilets. They accept the discriminatory rules that, on entry into the United States, affect the members of their staff born in certain countries presumed to be suspect, even though they are not citizens of those countries. They transport people who have been expelled, often at the risk of losing their liberty or their lives, like the Cuban dissident Roberto Viza Egües, sent back against his will to Havana on flight AF3486 on 31 August 2000, without the captain protesting – even though he had the right and the duty to do so. They instruct their pilots to carry on flying when the presence in the undercarriage of an illegal emigrant is reported after an hour and a half's flight, as on flight AF897, Brazzaville to Paris, on 9 October 2003.

The air companies helped me to realize two things about globalization. By its standards, only waiting is an urgent matter. And private institutions, such as businesses or non-governmental organizations, now have the power of state that has been delegated to them in the shape of a diffuse system of indirect administration.

And yet this book is not a manifesto protesting on behalf of national sovereignty or anti-globalization. Its method is that of the historical

sociology of political phenomena, its aim is to problematize the period
in which we are living, and its conclusion will shock militants just as
much as its argument will dismay liberals: globalization is ours because
we have created it.

Liberals will be furious to see power at the heart of my analysis –
power in its crudest form. Anti-globalization protesters will be angry
at the importance I give to appropriation and desire in a period that
they feel is one of mortification. And supporters of national sovereignty
will be vexed by the persistent vigour that I find in the state. Specialists
in international relations will be cross at the amount of space I devote
to history. Economists will be filled with wrath at my ignorance. All
the same, my debt to all these groups is immense. A considerable
amount of research, conducted from every point of view, has over the
past 20 years been devoted to globalization. It is not my purpose to
show it any disrespect by placing it all under the generic notion of
'global studies', even though it may come from different traditions and
disciplines. I am simply trying to renew the framework of the discussion and reply to a thought-provoking question: what could an author
who had devoted the greater part of his research to the historicity of
the state have to say about a historical period that seemed to mark the
latter's decline?

It is not for me to decide whether this curiosity was unhealthy or
not. So that the reader can judge, I need to highlight two points. The
first has to do with method. These thoughts rest on a reading that is of
course not exhaustive, but still coherent, of the literature available that
I quote as fully as possible so as to fuel the debate. It is also based on
a careful reading of the press, which provides us with common raw
material on the basis of which we can develop different interpretations.
This should therefore make the critical use of this book easier. Finally,
the analyses in it have drawn on more or less extensive sojourns, of a
more or less scientific nature, in a great number of countries, and this
has made it possible for me to refine certain observations and to guide
my reading. They bear the mark of questions and domains shared with
me by real researchers and wonderful travelling companions: Fariba
Adelkhah, Romain Bertrand and Béatrice Hibou. Even if they turn out
to be perplexed at the fruits of their patience, my gratitude will still be
just as great. As for the rest, I am unfortunately too far advanced in my
professional itinerary to be able to thank everyone, or even the hard
core of those colleagues who have helped me think my way to where
I am now. I will try to give them due thanks at the right time in the
following pages.

The other point that deserves to be noted has to do with terminology.
The word 'globalization' has imposed itself *urbi et orbi*. The French are
more or less the only people to reject it and prefer the term *mondialisation*, not without arousing the irony of their European or American

neighbours. Since I'm not in the habit of being chauvinistic, I will comply with international usage. And I'm all the happier to do this since the purist insistence on referring to *mondialisation* – which is sometimes distinguished, in a rather redundant way, from 'globalization' – has in the course of time taken on an ideological connotation of a somewhat anti-internationalist nature from which I am keen to distance myself.[1]

The rest of the conceptual vocabulary to be found here is, for better or worse, that of the historical sociology of political phenomena. In the wake of my previous works, and drawing on the convenient formula of Bruce Berman and John Lonsdale, I draw a distinction between the 'construction' of the political, in so far as it is the deliberate creation of an apparatus of power, and its 'formation' as a historic, conflict-filled, involuntary, and largely unconscious process, conducted in the disorder of confrontations, compromises and imaginings by the mass of anonymous people. This second aspect of things and its paradoxes demand particular attention.

I have attempted not to abuse jargon. Rather, I have quoted concrete facts and reported the remarks of the agents themselves, since this globalization is ours. Nonetheless, the need to get away from commonplaces sometimes requires us to resort to a specialized terminology that, curiously enough, we find easier to take from our plumbers or garage mechanics than from researchers. In this jumble of words, two recurrent concepts call out for definition right from the start. The first is what is called 'evergetism', the 'ancient quest for personal reputation by means of gifts that are skilfully made public knowledge' to which the historians of antiquity, Peter Brown and Paul Veyne, have devoted some magnificent works. Rich or poor, globalization man is a zestful evergete.

The second key concept, one that is more off-putting, is that of 'governmentality', which I propose to substitute for the 'governance' that liberals are always going on about. I need merely point out for the time being that this notion is borrowed from Michel Foucault and refers to the way power is problematized as an 'action on actions'. What I mean by this is that globalization establishes relations of power without the latter excluding the practices by which we appropriate it for ourselves. More precisely – and I hope hereby to grasp more of the detail than do most authors who also interpret globalization in terms of governmentality – these relations of power on other people are simultaneously practices of the self, at the 'encounter between techniques of domination exerted on others and techniques of the self'. Globalization is ours because it is in the dimension of globalization that we fashion our ethics and bodies, that we imagine the way we conduct our lives, that we suffer and desire, that we submit others to ourselves and are made subordinate to them.[2]

1

Two Centuries of Globalization: The Changing Scale of State and Capitalism

As the well-worn expression has it, we are living through amazing times. In a mere two decades, the combination of spectacular techno-logical innovations, the collapse of the Soviet Empire, the rise of neo-liberal economic policies and 'mass international terrorism' have made the unity of our world a fact of life – a unity to which the expansion of world capitalism had been leading for four centuries. I use the term 'unity' of the world, *mutatis mutandis*, the same way that people used the word to refer to the 'unity' of Italy or Germany in the nineteenth century. Not, of course, that the phenomena are politically comparable. Even in the craziest dreams of our contemporaries, there is no question of a world state. But the spread of a world culture today and the forma-tion of the nation-states of yesteryear – apart from being the two sides of the same coin, as we shall be seeing – consist in the historical experi-ence of a change of scale in societies, without these societies thereby being unified. In both cases, we need to grasp simultaneously the coherence of the process and its heterogeneity, its totality and its incom-pleteness. It's an old problem that was already raised by any attempt to understand the state or culture, and it's one that we need to recon-sider from a new angle.

So I prefer to talk of the world's unity, not of its uniformization – as in the case of Germany or Italy: the latter combined their cultural and political diversity with the demands of a central government and a national economy that played a full part in the international system. Our own amazing period is experiencing a similar general metamor-phosis in its space-time. Its principles of sovereignty and legitimacy, its moral values, its modes of organization and the knowledge at its dis-posal are all being completely rejigged in the process. Keeping just to the essential points, we can mention, without any great risk of error, the integration of the capital market, the development of commercial exchanges, the improvement in means of transport, the acceleration of planetary communication in all its forms, the notable institutionalization of worldwide norms and mechanisms (including in the political and judicial domains), the increase in migration, the emergence of challenges to health and ecology which the whole of humanity has to face together, the persistence of tangible threats to peace, and even the survival of the planet as a whole. Most of these transformations deserve to be described in superlative terms. They result in perhaps even more profound changes in the social intelligence of mankind: in the way we perceive the collective or personal relations we enjoy with others, our past and future, our lives and our deaths.[1]

The characterization of each of these processes is a matter for debate. But you would have to be blind and deaf not to admit that our period is undergoing a remarkable 'time-space compression', in the now classic words of the Marxist geographer David Harvey.[2] And it would be better to keep silent rather than to propound the idea that this upheaval is somehow historically inconsistent. It has become common usage to call this upheaval 'globalization'. The concept's origin is rather vague. It appeared in the 1960s and 1970s, in English and French, in the bureaucratic language of the United Nations and of multinational corporations.[3] American Express turned it into an advertising slogan for its credit card.[4] In the social sciences, Marshall McLuhan ensured its runaway success in the book world when he announced, as early as 1960, the advent of the 'global village'. But the 1991 edition of the *Oxford Dictionary of New Words* still gives rather piecemeal definitions of the world 'global', associating it with 'environmentalist jargon' and an acquaintance with 'other cultures'. Then the term spread like wildfire through both everyday and scholarly language. Its (elusive) definition covers anything and everything, from the Internet to a hamburger.[5] Nonetheless, the term rose to prominence at the very heart of public debate and scientific thought, to such an extent that it became in itself an example of what it claims to be explaining: globalization needs a global concept!

This involved taking a few conceptual short cuts. In particular, the extension and intensification of social relations on a global scale (as Anthony Giddens puts it) are generally confused with the worldwide expansion of capitalism. Of course, the two processes have historically coincided, to such a degree that it is tempting to establish a causal relation between them, or to identify them with one another. This, after all, was the way Marx analysed the situation:

> The bourgeoisie has through its exploitation of the world market given a cosmopolitan character to production and consumption in every country. To the great chagrin of Reactionaries, it has drawn from under

the feet of industry the national ground on which it stood. All old-established national industries have been destroyed or are daily being destroyed.[6]

On the conceptual level, it is, however, preferable to distinguish between the two phenomena. The expansion and metamorphosis of capitalism – for instance, the conversion of Russia and China to a market economy, or the replacement of Fordist types of work organization by less hierarchical modes of business management which emphasize flexibility and the arrangement of production units in horizontal networks on a planetary scale – do not account for other forms of globalization, even if they interfere with them to a greater or lesser degree: the international communist movement, universal religions, scientific or cultural exchanges, war and political violence, migrations, climate change and epidemics are (or have been, in the recent past) vehicles of globalization which few Marxists these days would claim to be the simple harbingers or manifestations of capitalism. The present work will be mainly concerned with globalization as a change of scale, without necessarily identifying this change with any apotheosis, transformation or overcoming of the capitalist mode of production.

The limits of globalization

In any case, the inflation in the number of the things people say and write about globalization leads too frequently to the conclusion that the thing itself can be taken for granted. And yet there is something illusory or excessive about the term. *The Economist*, which can hardly be suspected of harbouring critical feelings on the topic, has no hesitation in claiming that 'globalization is not and has never been global'.[7] Thus the Internet – that 'technological basis for the organizational form of the Information Age: the network'[8] – affects only a minority of the inhabitants of the planet: 400 million in 2001, and probably a thousand million in 2005. In terms of users, URL names and broadband networks, its geography is extraordinarily concentrated around a few metropolitan areas, or even a few districts within them.[9]

Likewise, several authors have cast doubt on the emergence of an economy whose central elements can function as a unit in real time on a global scale, whether on the institutional, organizational or technological level, as Manuel Castells describes it.[10] They discern the systematization of the 'international open economy' that has been progressively built up since the Second World War, instead of a truly globalized economy within which national economies have melded together.[11] Authentically global companies are rare; multilateralism continues to lie in the domain of intergovernmental relations; the globalization of direct exchanges and investments is limited; the 'new economy', whose miraculous growth was supposed to herald a new age, rapidly went into recession and turned out to be a house of cards, if not a piece of over-creative accountancy; an insidious crisis of confidence spread through the money markets and within the multilateral institutions of Bretton Woods. In short:

> [E]conomists are not surprised by the intensity of integration – quite the contrary: what does surprise them is the persistence, in spite of the reduction of tariffs and fiscal or regulative barriers, of a definite fragmentation in the world economy, even between the countries and zones which have the strongest links with one another.[12]

Especially in the commercial domain, several invisible barriers continue to hamper international exchanges. Indeed, the liberalization of these latter is accompanied by the rise of a 'neo-protectionism' within the World Trade Organization (WTO), a protectionism which passes itself off as a way of safeguarding national industries, denouncing subsidies, engaging in anti-dumping actions and prescribing social, environmental or other kinds of norm. Entire sectors of activity are still being protected and regulated to a massive degree: they include agriculture, textiles, aeronautics, shipping, distribution and services. Even more fundamentally, the internationalization of the labour market comes with its political compartmentalization and the policing of immigration and emigration. As for the actual definition of property, it is to a very great extent determined by national juridical areas – including within the European Union – at a time when the increase in immutable contracts of a financial nature is conferring ever greater powers on the institutions of justice, and thus on their practices: this was illustrated by the way cases of bankruptcy were treated in Southeast Asia or Russia during the crises of 1997–8.[13]

In two of its constitutive dimensions (the circulation of the labour force, and the construction of property rights), contemporary capitalism is far from being 'global', even though the oscillations of the crisis it is undergoing are the product of powerful global interdependencies. Among these are the deregulation and growing integration of financial markets engendered by transactions in eurodollars, the collapse of the Bretton Woods system and the shocks and counter-shocks of the oil crisis in the 1960s and 1970s. These are all of the highest importance given the extreme volatility of floating capital and the opportunities for speculation.[14] However, it is a fairly widespread view that the rising power of multinational corporations, the increase in commerce within companies, and the assertion of an 'elective capitalism' between groups do not enable us to conclude that industrial production is completely globalized, whatever the advances being made in management, communication and transport.

Politically and socially, any judgement we may feel inclined to pass on globalization will be ambivalent. Its most obvious manifestations are counterbalanced by concomitant effects such as the erosion of certain forms of international solidarity, including public aid for development, the reinforcing of American 'unilateralism', and the loss of credibility of the United Nations or multilateral negotiations. It is significant that two of the most important treaties from the point of view of the integration of the international system – the Kyoto agreement regulating the emission of greenhouse gases and the Rome agreement that set up a permanent International Criminal Court – were immediately thrown into question by the United States, supposedly the paragons of globalization. At the same time, the fact that China has joined the WTO and the co-opting of Russia into the G7 (which thus became the G8) do of course attest to the way the great fault lines in the world system caused by the Cold War are now a thing of the past. But on closer inspection, a significant proportion of their population – in particular the vast majority of their peasantry or whatever has taken the place of the peasantry – seems to have been sidelined for an indeterminate period. Today, there are many places that resemble the Eboli where, according to Carlo Levi, 'Christ stopped', and beyond which the change of scale in globalization is barely in evidence.

This is true of what are called, by way of euphemism, the 'countries of the southern hemisphere', of course. But it is also true of the web of urban metropolises that form the fabric of the 'new geography' of centrality.[15] Marx had already talked of the '*little* Irelands' mouldering away 'in each of the industrial cities' of England or France.[16] Likewise, contemporary globalization establishes 'two-speed societies', to use an expression current in the 1970s, and an even more polarized international system, even though it may have been, at the end of the nineteenth century, a factor of convergence within the 'Atlantic economy', if we are to believe K. H. O'Rourke and J. G. Williamson.[17]

One of the urgent issues that needs to be addressed is indeed this very same question of these asymmetries or disjunctions. Are states, populations, poor and weak people actually protagonists of globalization (even if only as its victims), or are they merely its spectators, huddled outside its shop windows? Put this way, the problem is somewhat skewed, since it is in the very heart of the process that these dissonances are heard – for example after 1985, when the United States protested against direct Japanese investment in their economy, at a time when capital from their ally was financing their public debt and national deficit. From this point of view, 11 September 2001, which on many levels marked America's entry into the maelstrom of globalization (even if only to the extent that it put an end to the myth of the inviola-bility of its territory), drove a wedge through the transatlantic com-munity of interests and values, once the first upsurge of European compassion had died down. Such questions as Iraq, the conflict between Israelis and Palestinians, the humanitarian right to war, the death penalty and the fight against terrorism and ecology all became bones of contention that illustrate the gap between aspirations to 'global governance ' and the permanence of political societies.

Globalization: a concept and an event

However well-based these reservations may be, they do not annul the obvious fact that we have indeed been faced with a change of scale for twenty years. *Modernity at Large*: such is the suggestive title, with its many possible implications ('modernity in the long term', 'modernity out in the open', 'modernity at liberty', 'modernity in general', 'uncer-tain modernity') of one of the best attempts to encompass the trans-formations of our period.[18] The problem still needs, of course, to be correctly formulated.

It is far from certain that globalization constitutes a system, for example a qualitative and coherent transformation in the capitalist mode of production, or indeed its replacement, as has been suggested by Manuel Castells, Martin Shaw and Toni Negri, among others.[19] Nor is it certain that it is propelling us into a radically different period, not unless we subscribe to the platitude that every historical period is sin-gular and irreducible to the past. From this point of view, carrying out term-by-term comparisons between the 'first period of globalization', on the eve of the First World War, and contemporary globalization, in an attempt to discover whether we live in a world that is 'more' or 'less' unified than in 1914, leads nowhere. You can summon up the shades of the gold standard and point out that the volume of international savings transfers in proportion to GDP was almost twice as high at the end of the 1880s than it was at the start of the 1990s, or that the number of migrants was much higher in those days than now; you can object that this financial globalization was not accompanied by any world-wide integration of industrial units of production, concerned only the 'Atlantic economy' and the colonial empires, and had no proportionate commercial counterpart once exchanges are related not to the GDP but to the sector of exchangeable goods; you can talk about all these points until the cows come home, but the essential fact gets left out, namely the contingency of the complex event, and the way it is conceptualized by its contemporaries.

Roland Robertson adds a useful complement to the definition we have put forward: 'Globalization as a concept refers both to the compression of the world and the intensification of consciousness of the world as a whole.'[20] Thus the theorists of international relations or the international political economy are right to emphasize the turning-point that the last two decades of the twentieth century represented.

Many factors have created a sense of the world's unity both in people's minds and as an objective configuration. Among these factors are new technologies, the development of the mass media and transport, the extension of the market economy as a legitimate problematic (if not as a way of producing effective solutions), various ecological catastrophes, especially Chernobyl, the collapse of the Soviet Union, and the unprecedented fragility of the American territorial sanctuary. Étienne Balibar has remarked that:

> [T]he lightning speed at which the language of 'globalization' has spread, something which needs to be treated as a symptom, is linked to an *overdetermination of phenomena*. . . . The economic process has struck people as something radically new only insofar as it was combined with other novel phenomena. . . . Globalization has come to seem a structurally irreversible process *within a determinate set of political circumstances* that lies behind its obvious manifestations. Now this set of circumstances was the result of the convergence of several very different events which seemed to reinforce one another, and dramatically alter the previous shape of social life. Hence the impression of a turning-point in civilisation.[21]

And, in the eyes of the philosopher, the fall of the Berlin Wall had a specific repercussion in so far as it erased the global fault lines that had come into being as a result of the Cold War.

If the world had not first been sundered, there would have been no eventual sense of globalization.[22] Agreed. But the pet vice of the 'global studies' that have proliferated over the past twenty years is to exaggerate and reify one or other of these events by attributing to it an absolute catalytic virtue, constitutive of the new age, in the almost messianic sense of the term. Precisely because it is a complex and contingent event, globalization needs to be interpreted by the yardstick of its historicity. From this angle, we would be wise to emulate the caution of Roland Robertson: taking an interest in contemporary globalization must not lead us to postulate that it constitutes a recent event.[23] The great lines of force of the period we live in, and the awareness we have of them, are dependent on our past. They are the by-product of morphologies, interests, symbolizations and perceptions that are all constrained by the histories from which we have emerged. Any scrupulous analysis of the facts has always shown the error of sociologies or philosophies of the *tabula rasa*, whether they were colonial, communist or liberal. The same is true of the peremptory prophecies inspired by the disintegration of the Soviet Empire, the perfecting of the Internet or the mirages of neo-liberalism. Certain authors have been all too ready to invent their own Lisbon earthquakes. But not everyone can be a Voltaire, and we should be honest enough to admit that globalization will not actually be the end of anything at all: neither of history, nor of the philosophy of history, nor of national territories, nor of the state, nor of the past, nor of the future, nor of poverty, nor of sovereignty, nor of beef bourguignon. It will probably transform us, but it will not damn us any more than it will redeem us.

The propensity of global studies to hold forth, rather than to analyse, contrasts with the silence observed by two important approaches in the social sciences: the history and the historical sociology of the state. As we have seen, international political economy, the theory of international relations, the sociology of communication and postmodern anthropology have all seized on the theme of globalization and made their own contributions to the debate. Curiously, neo-Weberian or neo-Marxist historians and sociologists of state-formation have ignored this debate, even though they long ago came up with concepts that could help to extend it – they had after all worked on previous changes of scale.

In the 1960s, various notions started to flourish in the works of Fernand Braudel, Immanuel Wallerstein, Wolfram Eberhard, Perry Anderson, Charles Tilly, Theda Skocpol and others: the notions of 'global time', of 'world economy', of 'world-system'. The analyses of these different authors immediately brought out the close link, over several centuries, between world capitalism and the formation of a system of states. In Braudel, it was indeed this synergy that made capitalism the very opposite of a market economy. Its other decisive property, in his view, was its 'flexibility', its 'capacity for change and adaptation', its 'eclecticism': it 'does not invent hierarchies, it uses them, just as it did not invent the market or consumption. It is, in the long perspective of history, a latecomer. It arrives when everything is already in place.'[24] Marxists prefer to talk of the concatenation of modes of production: instead of effacing one another as they succeed each other, these modes of production are superimposed and overlap, so that, for instance, capitalism 'is interlinked' with hereditary societies or the system of castes that it encompasses.[25] If global studies had taken these works into consideration, the discipline would have avoided becoming entangled in the aporia of the zero-sum game between state and globalization (or between state and market) which has been such music to the ears, in quite contrasting ways, of liberals and sovereignty-mongers of every kind. Karl Marx and Max Weber had already linked the worldwide expansion of capitalism to the competition between states for control of 'mobile capital': in their works, the system of states, transnational flows of money and the change of scale attendant on globalization all go together.[26] Finally, the distinctions drawn by Weber and Braudel between, respectively, the 'creation' and the 'appropriation' of capitalism, between 'Civilization' and 'civilizations', should have killed off right from the start the recurrent confusion between westernization (or worse, Americanization) and globalization.[27] Series of events such as those comprised by the world economies of Mediterranean antiquity, Asia and the Indian Ocean, the conquest of the New World by Europe, 'transnational' movements[28] that were simultaneously political and cultural, the baroque and romantic movements, colonization, or indeed the diffusion of universal religions can, from this point of view, teach us many lessons. They are of a kind to exorcize the historical provincialism in which global studies have become entrapped and to moderate their over-prescriptive alarms (or exaggerations).

On one level, it is perhaps essential to relativize one of the features claimed as specific to globalization – a feature on which the theorists of international relations insist so much, as do those of postmodernism.[29] The blurring of the boundary between the 'internal' dimension of societies and their relations with their surroundings is by no means particularly contemporary. History, the historical sociology of the state, and anthropology too have amply demonstrated that all societies, however 'primitive', have always proceeded from their relation to the outside world. Max Weber, Otto Hintze, Reinhard Bendix and Perry Anderson on one side, Edmund Leach, Georges Balandier and Stanley Tambiah on the other, have written definitive studies of this subject. They need to be re-read – or read! And then let someone come up with the proof that a decisive break has been introduced by contemporary technological innovations in comparison with other episodes of 'time-space compression'!

Thus, several historians believe that the invention of the telegraph led to a more radical revolution in global consciousness than did the Internet. The expression 'real time' that is so much used and abused is obviously relative. When in 1871 the results of the Derby were transmitted in five minutes from London to Calcutta, people at the time felt the same sense of proud and rapturous vertigo as did the first users of the Internet. But the children of the latter now speak condescendingly of the pathetic slowness of their parents' computers. If there is one area where we should abstain from over-hasty judgements, it is that of the representation of time and space, especially when dealing with exchanges between societies. In reality, the theorists of international relations, who have long indulged in imagining the world system as a game of billiards in which different states are the billiard balls,[30] are the only ones to be surprised by the importance and acceleration of transnational flows in contemporary globalization. They suddenly feel hemmed in by their own axioms and rush feverishly to the doors that have long since been opened by their colleagues in other disciplines. We should not take their stupefaction seriously.

On a second level, it is important that we shift the debate outside a framework which leads us to make rash judgements. Global studies and journalistic commentaries are forever swaying between a gloomy twilight vision of the new age whose advent is being announced and a desperate optimism vis-à-vis the necessity of submitting that age to 'global governance'. For every Arjun Appadurai, who is delighted to see the social practices of mass consumption responding to the growing flexibility of the conditions of exploitation of the labour force,[31] how many other authors express alarm at the threats that globalization seems to bring! These threats, in their view, raise the spectre of 'barbarians' and other wild folk attacking the prosperous 'bourgeoisie' of 'market democracy'. One threat is the way the state is sidelined by transnational relations, torn apart by questions of identity politics, undermined by mafias, shaken by the markets, and supplanted by the arrogance and the financial power of multinational corporations. Another threat is the proliferation of weapons of mass destruction and of terrorism. And yet another threat weighs over the content and the boundaries of democracy or of the cultural and indeed genetic diversity of mankind. There is a threat hanging over the environment, the survival of different species, and plant life. Looked at this way, globalization is akin to an experience of dispossession and alienation that affects sovereignty, the exercise of citizenship, and identity. The most jaded observers trot out hackneyed ideas about the way we can oppose 'global turbulence' with an excess of 'governance without government' of 'worldwide public goods', the institutionalization of an 'international civil society', and the development of new forms of social integration. They hope to regulate, control and democratize globalization by building up a transnational public space on the same scale, reforming international institutions, creating ever more procedures for negotiation, compromise and arbitration, extending international law and regulation, and bringing 'rogue states' to heel. Some of them even mutter darkly about the dogs of war, the inevitable 'clash of civilizations', and the unacceptable nature of 'American unilateralism'. As for the organic intellectuals of globalization, they are positively thrilled by the 'state of emergency' in which globalization forces them to live.

None of these fears, none of these utopias, none of these sensationalist claims is absurd. But they are mostly pretty naive. It is gravely pointed out to us that globalization is velocity and leads to the universalization of western democracy as 'the final form of human government' (Francis Fukuyama). Let's keep a cool head about this. Didn't the 1990s represent a comeback on the part of history, freed from the corset of the polar confrontation between the West and communism, rather than its pre-programmed 'end'? 'The call of empire',[32] civil wars

rooted in the soil of historic territories, conflicts between states following the good old recipes of militarist nationalism: all of these marked
the period just as much as the 'merchandising' or the 'marketing' of
the international system. The 1990s marked the decade of the expan-
sionist temptations of China, the beginnings of rearmament in Japan,
the dramatic intensification of Indian-Pakistani and Israeli-Palestinian
territorial conflicts, nuclear proliferation on the part of states intent on
maintaining their sovereignty and the spread of international terrorism
in the service of fundamentally political causes. It was a decade that –
punctuated as it was by ethnic cleansing in Yugoslavia, the genocide
of the Tutsi in Rwanda, numerous mass massacres in Chechnya,
Afghanistan, Algeria, sub-Saharan Africa and various other places, the
events of 11 September 2001, the wars in Iraq in 1991 and 2003, the
spread of suicide attacks as a tactic of armed struggle, and the drown-
ing of thousands of clandestine migrants – was altogether tragic.

In other respects, some of the most prickly files on the 'international
agenda' are as often as not left to gather dust. This is the case with the
conflict in the Middle East, the constant irritant of Iraq, the situation in
Afghanistan once Soviet troops had withdrawn, the war in the Great
Lakes and the Congo basin, the convulsions in the Caucasus, the sub-
siding of sub-Saharan Africa into primeval stagnation, or the financial
crisis in Argentina. And I could go on. Europe itself is to some extent
created in this way – witness the weakening, in the 1990s, of Franco-
German relations (the importance of which was recognized by everyone, even though these relations seemed to be dying), the uncoordinated
extension of the Union to the East, the inconsistency of the Barcelona
process when it came to 'Mediterranean partner countries', the weakening of foreign policy and common security, the indefinite postpone-
ment of any reform to the Common Agricultural Policy, or the delays
in freeing up the international aid to which the Commission had agreed.
In 2000, it needed 1.8 years to set up food and humanitarian aid, 2.5
years and 3.8 years for aid to the Balkans and support of actions in
defence of human rights, 6.5 and 8.5 years for aid granted to Latin
America and the 'third-level Mediterranean countries'. Commissioner
Chris Patten felt in a position to state that the reduction in the average
wait for the provision of European aid from 4.1 to 3.7 years, in 2001,
was a great victory. Throughout the world, the only urgent thing is to
wait. First and foremost waiting for planes, as I have said, planes being
to contemporary globalization what steamboats and railways were to
the Industrial Revolution. Flight delays are now part of the system.

Furthermore, if we are indeed faced with the 'worship of the present'
or the 'effacing of the future',[33] this is only through the rear mirror. It is
easy to see globalization in a variety of past tenses, from the present
perfect, via the past continuous, to the pluperfect. It manufactures historical memory non-stop. We are witnessing a compulsive 'museifica-

tion' of the social landscape – at least in the West, there is not a village or a single activity that escapes it – a fetishistic (and self-serving) celebration of anniversaries, a generalized sense of debt and repentance. Furthermore, these give rise to institutional innovations that are some of the most tangible signs of the crystallization of a 'global governance' in the political dimension: a Permanent International Criminal Court has been set up in the wake of the international criminal tribunals of The Hague and Arusha, with responsibility for punishing crimes against humanity perpetrated in ex-Yugoslavia and Rwanda; ever since the interception of General Pinochet in Great Britain, national judicial systems are becoming less and less hesitant about putting people on trial for reprehensible political actions committed abroad, sometimes several decades previously; truth and reconciliation commissions are now part of the ordinary machinery of 'democratic transitions' and enjoy active international cooperation; the demands for 'reparations' or 'recognition' are becoming ever more frequent, and national parliaments and international conferences are taking up these demands.

Given these meta-discourses, which are often the product of the chattering classes, it is necessary – maybe urgent? – to return to the foundations of the social sciences. Globalization, which is extremely complex and contingent, as is worth repeating, needs to be grasped in its historicity, in other words in its banality, that of a 'rare form', in the Latin sense of *raritas*.[34] The oxymoron should be no surprise. Since globalization is a historical configuration, it is a singular phenomenon. It is a specific regime of power and accumulation, and it is as such that it requires to be treated as an ordinary matter. How has it 'emerged'?[35] In what social practices does it consist? What mechanisms of power and wealth does it constitute? What types of subjectivity does it engender? These are the main questions, apparently quite standard ones, that I will try to problematize, keeping in mind this common-sense observation: globalization is first and foremost a change of scale in time and space, and it is neither the first that mankind has experienced nor the last to which we will have to adapt. So my aim will not be to fix globalization in its 'essence' – a task which would be methodologically vain and philosophically dubious – but to understand it as an 'event' by means of which Being-in-the-world can be read as a production.[36] Unlike those who extol it or denigrate it, I want to recognize it first of all as a simple continuation of history, not in the geological terms of evolution or historicism, which would involve tracking down its 'origin', but by asking myself about its 'rise' in the 'singular chance of the event', by dint of random struggles, and via the 'interstices' of the social body, without anyone being able to claim responsibility for it.

Genealogy does not pretend to go back in time to restore an unbroken continuity that operates beyond the dispersion of oblivion; its task is not to demonstrate that the past actively exists in the present, that it continues secretly to animate the present, having imposed a predetermined form on all its vicissitudes. Genealogy does not resemble the evolution of a species and does not map the destiny of a people. On the contrary, to follow the complex course of descent is to maintain passing events in their proper dispersion; it is to identify the accidents, the minute deviations – or conversely, the complete reversals – the errors, the false appraisals, and the faulty calculations that gave birth to those things which continue to exist and have value for us; it is to discover that truth or being lies not at the root of what we know and what we are but the exteriority of accidents.[37]

In this respect, globalization opens as many opportunities as it imposes constraints. Toni Negri and Michael Hardt state this loud and clear from a revolutionary perspective that one is not forced to share, but which has the merit of breaking away from the morbid, circular millenarianism in which several of their militant anti-globalization friends still wallow.[38]

It is here that the study of previous changes of scale – the expansion of universal religions, the rise and fall of empires, the formation and crumbling of world economies, the creation of nations, colonization – turns out to be conceptually and methodologically useful. Analysing the event of contemporary globalization, its emergence as a historical configuration of power and the practices that constitute it, means that I need to stay close to the methods of historical sociology of political phenomena, thus extending my earlier work. This is not the place to repeat it. I will simply list three conclusions that directly concern the problematization of globalization.

1   The universalization of institutions and ideologies, both political and economic – the nation-state, the market, democracy – does not erode the historical trajectories of the societies that appropriate them, whether peacefully or not.
2   Cultural, political, and economic processes and representations are polysemic, and social change follows rhythms – Braudel would have called them *durées* – that differ from one domain to another; as a result this change often appears paradoxical.
3   Those who hold power do not have a monopoly on this social change, which comes just as strongly 'from below'; hence the usefulness of distinguishing between the 'construction' of civic life by means of the establishment of explicit public (or private) policies with the aim of building up an apparatus of control, on the initiative of the political elites, and its 'formation', as a contradictory and largely unconscious process of 'conflicts, negotiations and compromises' between different social groups[39] – or, in the words of Foucault, its 'emergence' in the 'interstice'.

From this point of view, it will be my aim to set out a few markers that should help us understand the alchemy of globalization on the basis of its effective practices, and not just in terms of the theory of international relations on the basis of deliberate discourses and policies as they are developed and pursued by the main agents in the international system: national governments (in particular those of the G8), multilateral institutions, independent regulatory authorities, multinational businesses, universal religious movements, international federations of various kinds, and the big NGOs.

The foundational nineteenth century

Our desire for historicity, and the very idea of a historical trajectory, mean that we need to periodize the process of relative unification of the world that we are trying to interpret. It should now be clear that globalization as a social phenomenon is 'neither entirely new nor fundamentally modern'[40] and that it is irreducible to the history of the West.[41] It needs all the more to be set back firmly within its historical field, since it has never proceeded by the effacement or substitution of its previous impulses, but by a real process of concatenation.[42] So there are surface discontinuities and, therefore, breaks. Fine – but in what sequence do they come? If the period from 1989 to 2003, or even from 1945 to 2003, generally picked out by the theorists of international relations, is obviously too short for my present purposes, my work would lose its focus if I included all the previous phases that historians indicate. For instance, using the terms put forward by the team of researchers working under A. G. Hopkins: the archaic form of globalization, before the appearance of industrialization and the nation-state; proto-globalization, which sees a reconfiguration in the system of states and the growth of finance, services, and pre-industrial manufacture between 1600 and 1800; or modern globalization, crowned by the rise of the nation-state and industrialization between 1800 and the 1950s.[43] The biggest lesson we can draw from these precocious sequences – and it is a lesson to which I shall be returning – already involves, in the long term, the interweaving of what political science now calls transnational relations (including the market of the economists) and the processes of state-formation: 'time-space compression' and the intensification of the awareness that we have of the latter.

In other words, globalization is not the product of the hypertrophy of transnational relations (or of the market) to the detriment of the state, as was at first stated by the theorists of international relations and of international political economy. It is the synthesis of each of these apparently contradictory principles. Now, this dialectic of movement becomes systematic during the 'long nineteenth century' – from 1776 to 1914 – which the work of Eric Hobsbawm has enabled us to pick out. So I will be taking it as the point of departure of contemporary, 'postcolonial' globalization.[44] More precisely, the nineteenth century remains foundational for our 'global' modernity for at least six reasons.

First, it sees the emergence of the architecture of the international system in which we continue to live. In 1757, the East India Company seized the rich province of Bengal from which the Mogul Empire drew most of its fiscal resources, and with this it also captured a strategic position lying between the sub-continent of India and China, a position that would be the commercial and financial launch-pad for British imperialism in Asia. Around 1800, the economic balance of strength between Asia and Europe was inverted.[45] But from 1913 onwards, the United States became the first worldwide economic power thanks in part to the organizational revolution that it underwent, especially in the railway companies from the 1850s onwards, and thanks to the British capital that was invested in them. The confrontation between Germany and Great Britain, culminating with the collective suicide of the First World War, left the way open to American hegemony at the end of this war. At the same time, the outsiders of globalization – in particular the Japan of the Meiji Era – took up their positions, as did most of globalization's losers, such as Russia, almost all Muslim societies, Latin America and sub-Saharan Africa. In very different conditions, India and China began a painful process of modernization, the difficulties or contradictions of which even now continue to constrain their international status and their insertion into the world economy.

Second, only in the 1830s did 'economic liberalism burst forth as a crusading passion, and laissez-faire become a militant creed', the utopia of which rested on a competitive labour market, an automatic use of the gold standard and international free exchange: the 'self-regulating market on a world scale' assures 'the functioning of this stupendous mechanism'.[46] Thanks to the Industrial Revolution and the new techniques accompanying it, the nineteenth century brought together means of communication and means of production. There followed a formidable expansion in world trade: this, which had not quite doubled between 1800 and 1840, increased by 160 per cent between 1850 and 1870, boosted by an improvement in transport, an increase in the number of means of payment, and the expansion of credit allowed by the discovery of new gold deposits in California, Australia and South Africa. Of course, commercial protectionism staged a come-back after 1879, but financial globalization became more intense, assuming unprecedented proportions up to the First World War, even if the market of capital was at this stage less complex, less autonomous and geographically less widespread than today. Furthermore, the establishment of private property and its commoditization became universal not only in western colonies but also in the political formations that had remained independent, such as the Ottoman Empire.

A third reason is that, from the end of the eighteenth century onwards, a new cosmopolitanism came into being, giving rise to an authentic awareness of the world as a whole, a *Weltgefühl*. Kant wrote his *Project for Perpetual Peace* and Schiller his poem *An die Freude*: 'Be embraced, ye millions! May this kiss go to the whole world . . .'. In his *Sketch of a Historical Tableau of the Progress of the Human Mind*, Condorcet saw men 'forming but a single totality, and aiming at a single goal'. Saint-Simonism, positivism, socialism and Christian missionary work exploited this vein in different ways throughout the nineteenth century. But even more importantly, perhaps, England's 'swing to the East', in the middle of the 1760s, after the humiliations which this colonial power had suffered in its American colonies, inspired marine exploration, cartographical research, ethnographic, archaeological and naturalist investigations, artistic fads, and outbursts of religious zeal which all constituted the prolegomena to the later imperial sciences.[47] The awareness of the world became scientific and fitted into the parameters of new disciplines such as meteorology.[48]

From the nineteenth century onwards, the construction of national, continental, and sometimes intercontinental railways, the establishment of worldwide telegraph systems thanks to the laying of submarine cables, the development of procedures of refrigeration, the appearance of mass publishing and a mass press, the invention of photography and, to a lesser extent, the progress of medicine all ensured that there was an unprecedented circulation, right across the planet, of information, ideas, goods and people.[49] In 1873, US President Grant could thus profess the advent of the single world: 'As commerce, education and the rapid transition of thought and matter, by telegraph and steam, have changed everything, I rather believe that the great Maker is preparing the world to become one nation, speaking one language, a consummation which renders armies and navies no longer necessary.'[50] The certainty that 'history from now on' would become 'world history'[51] spread from the circles of intellectual or political elites and became a matter of common sense. Children's books celebrated the prowess of explorers, military heroes of colonial conquest, and missionaries, making globalization an obvious fact in the eyes of young Europeans and Americans. In the same way, an increasing number of Asians or Africans entered into direct contact with the West through its persons and its ideas, the laws and the goods that they transported. From this process, early myths came into being, borne by the great waves of millenarianism, and the propagation of rumours on the traffic between the whites and the forces of the invisible, as well as various cults.

Fourth, the nineteenth century was that of great migrations, whose extent was only recently surpassed. The most spectacular movement of populations was across the Atlantic: around 44 million Europeans went to America (including 32 million between 1880 and 1915). To this we need to add migrations within Europe, preceding trans-Atlantic or similar migrations and often constitutive of the latter, as well as departures to Australia and other colonies designed to absorb excess populations, such as Algeria, South Africa and Siberia. Furthermore, the emigration to different parts of the world of between three and six million Indians from 1815 to 1914, some twelve million Chinese between 1815 and 1914 and a much lower number of Japanese contrived to make of this century an extraordinary moment in which populations were all flung into the melting pot – a moment that was brought to a halt by the spread of more restrictive legislation or regulation at the turn of the twentieth century, on the initiative of the United States.

But, over and above these figures, certain qualitative details in this great flow of peoples hold one's attention. These migrations were increasingly related to the phenomena of city life, mining activities and industrialization, and to some extent they reconstituted the multiculturalism of the merchant cities of the ancient world economies. Poles away from the imagery of the Far West, the gold rush in California took place against the backdrop of a certain city – more precisely the 'global city' that San Francisco rapidly became.[52] Furthermore, the lowering of seafaring transport tariffs facilitated seasonal or temporary migrations and the structuring of 'transnational circuits' with all the retroactive effects that these could induce between the country greeting the emigrants and the country they had left.[53] For instance, Italian 'swallows' (golondrinas) went to Argentina for the harvest at the end of the nineteenth century. And the rate at which migrants returned to their own countries was basically quite high – which was a determining factor in globalization: between a quarter and a third of those arriving in the United States between 1880 and 1930 returned to their countries of origin, the proportion varying markedly from one nationality to another;[54] 24.1 million of the 30.2 million Indians who left the subcontinent between 1834 and 1937 returned to it.[55]

Fifth, in the nineteenth century political experiences travelled right across the planet. Examples include the Napoleonic Wars, the repercussions of which were felt far beyond Europe – in particular in the Dutch Indies (as a result of the conquest of the Low Countries by France), in Latin America (with the emancipation of the Spanish colonies), in the Caribbean (with the independence of Haiti), in the Muslim world (with the occupation of Egypt by Bonaparte, the shockwaves this sent through Islamic societies, and the spread of republican or revolutionary ideas in the Ottoman and Qajar Empires), in Madagascar (where King Radama I, caught up in his projects of conquest and centralization, was a fervent admirer of Napoleon, in spite of being allied with England); the 'springtime of the people' in 1848, which Eric Hobsbawm described as the first virtually global revolution[56] and which reached as far as Pernambuco in Brazil, and Colombia; the multilateral or intergovernmental struggle against the slave trade and privateering, piracy and mercenary soldiering, a struggle with which the United States became involved; and colonial conquest, in which Japan now also took part, thus contributing to the universalization of imperialism. The way the colonial experience extended through almost all the societies in the world – including, indirectly, the states that preserved their formal independence, such as China, Siam, Persia, the Ottoman Empire or Ethiopia – was doubtless the factor of unification that would have the heaviest consequences during the second half of the century. It did not lead merely to the 'westernization' of Asia, Africa or Oceania, but also to several 'reverberation' effects between overseas possessions and the metropolitan societies or between the metropolitan societies themselves.[57] In this way, empires became veritable laboratories of political, social, urban, artistic and other sorts of modernity on a planetary scale. They contrived to spread the nation-state into societies that did not know this institutional form, or even the very principle of state centralization, and thus represented the triumph of 'the global ideology' of the nation-state system.[58] They crystallized the separation of the world into a 'North' and a 'South',[59] which is a salient feature of the period of globalization that I will be analysing. And if we follow Hannah Arendt, they led to the origins of the totalitarianism that was to disfigure the following century.[60]

A final reason that the nineteenth century remains foundational for our 'global' modernity is that one of the common political experiences of the century was the formation of what is these days called 'international civil society', whose agents laid down the bases of the contemporary themes of humanitarian rights and the duty to interfere. From the end of the eighteenth century onwards, the philanthropic movement to abolish slavery sparked off a transnational mobilization. It partly merged with the missionary zeal sometimes described as 'associative' that developed on the margin of the official churches or of groupings within the churches – especially among Protestants – and kept its distance from colonizing states and merchants. From this point of view, the contrast with the evangelization of Latin America, the Caribbean and Asia, in the sixteenth and seventeenth centuries, where evangelization was to a large extent in thrall to the absolutism and mercantilism of the Spanish peninsula, is very clear, even if preachers, traders and administrators did not fail to help each other along. Furthermore, the Christian missions, mainly those of the reformed churches, systematically translated the Bible into the vernacular or vehicular languages (there were 40 translations of the Scriptures between 1816 and 1845, 74 between 1845 and 1875, and 119 between 1876 and 1902) thereby 'glocalizing' their universal religion more than

Islam is able to do, in thrall as it is to its sacred language, Arabic.[61] In tandem with this, networks of political internationalism were established from the start of the nineteenth century onwards, after the epic of the French Revolution and the ambiguous adventure of General La Fayette in North America, either following national, religious or cultural sensibilities, favouring the Christian minorities of the Ottoman Empire or Italian unity, or following a socialist programme in the name of the workers' movement. It was also in 1863 that Henri Dunant set up the Red Cross for humanitarian action, and in 1904 Edmund Dene Morel founded the Congo Reform Association to denounce the exactions of the Congo Free State.

Naturally, I have no intention of reducing the complexity of the 'long nineteenth century' to these few sketches, or even of suggesting that this sequence is totally coherent. Karl Polanyi, for instance, has brought out the extent of the crisis of 1879, which led to a return of protectionism, the rise of imperialism and the impasse of the 1930s. But the picture I have drawn does bring out the historicity on which contemporary globalization depends. During this period, several main frameworks were set in place from which we have not yet emerged. To simplify, the nineteenth century established a 'governance without government'[62] dominated by 'high finance' and functioning from the 1870s to the crisis of 1929 as the main junction between global political organization and global economic organization,[63] in spite of protectionism. Paradoxically, this 'governance without government' was the result of the balance of European powers inaugurated by the treaties of Münster and Westphalia in 1648 and made more explicit in the Treaty of Utrecht in 1713, *ad conservandum in Europa equilibrium*. If we follow the analysis of Karl Polanyi, the existence of a European *directoire* in a very loose form guaranteed that the nineteenth century could enjoy a 'Hundred Years' Peace':

> Perhaps the strongest pillar of this informal system was the immense amount of international private business very often transacted in terms of some trade treaty or other international instrument made effective by custom and tradition. Governments and their influential citizens were in innumerable ways enmeshed in the varied types of financial, economic, and juridical strands of such international transactions. This silent pressure of private interest which permeated the whole life of civilized communities and transcended national boundaries was the invisible mainstay of international reciprocity, and provided the balance-of-power principle with effective sanctions, even when it did not take up the organized form of a Concert of Europe or a League of Nations.[64]

One of the symptoms of this western governance on a world scale was the multiplication of international organizations of standardization acting as so many independent regulation authorities: for example, the International Telegraphic Union was created in 1865, the Universal Postal Union in 1874, the International Bureau for Weights and Measures in 1875, the Meteorological Organization in 1878, the International Union for the Protection of Industrial Property in 1883, etc.[65] Another symptom was the birth of a whole swathe of global social institutions that are still alive: the International Bank, on whose importance Karl Polanyi insists; worldwide businesses of a rational-legal type (the essential feature of capitalism if we are to believe Max Weber); socialist Internationals and other international federations of different natures, such as the Olympic Committee; non-governmental universal organizations, of which the International Committee of the Red Cross and the International League of Human Rights are prototypes; transnational associative movements such as scouting, an offshoot of British imperialism and the Boer War; and international church organizations.

However, this configuration of institutions and private interests was inextricably interwoven with the interplay of states involved in the balance of power and, increasingly, the force-field of various types of imperialism whose interactions were the 'central factor leading to the chain of later catastrophes' given the 'increasing interdependence of internal and external social forces which defines the very notion of an Imperial Society'.[66] It should immediately be added that societies subjected to the worldwide expansion of this governance, in particular in the colonial context, were active protagonists of it, as has been frequently shown by historians and anthropologists: a large proportion of the colonial world was in fact a 'euro-Islamic condominium';[67] the previous universal empires continued to exercise power in Asia and Africa, such as the Ottoman Empire in the Maghreb and the Dutch Indies; and, apart from the genocides that happened in America and Australia, states or areas of dynastic power were, as they were conquered, 'enfolded' or 'incorporated'[68] rather than absorbed or annihilated by the occupiers. The combination of colonial powers – essentially the countries of Western Europe, the United States and Japan – and of their possessions or satellites was ultimately consolidated by the hegemony of the system of nation-states (or virtual nations), given that the 'colonial nationalisms'[69] played a part in the emergence of the latter on a world scale before decolonization could progressively ensure its real universalization. The nineteenth century conferred on this configuration of states the monopoly of sovereignty and exercise of legitimate violence by proscribing the private use of this violence, even by delegation.[70]

In short, the nineteenth century set up two political paradoxes that continue to perplex us if we are to judge by the number of absurdities to which they give rise. On the one hand, globalization goes with the formation of the state. On the other, the change of scale brought about by each of these two processes, the one contained within the other, entails a retraction of culture or identity. Indeed, the invention of modernity by the 'invention of tradition'[71] is at the heart of the unification both of the nation-state and of the international system: the crystallization of regional, ethnic or religious particularisms, the exacerbation of nationalisms, the generalization of culturalist ideology, the vogue for 'neo-'styles have all helped to spread both state centralization and globalization.[72] The history of communalism in India, religious affiliation in Lebanon, ethnicity in Africa and regionalism in France provides us with several examples.

The transnational and private logic of globalization has also constantly become interwoven with the logic of the public action of States. '*Laissez-faire* itself was enforced by the state', observes Karl Polanyi. 'The road to the free market was opened and kept open by an enormous increase in continuous, centrally organized and controlled interventionism.' And he goes on to remark that, under the guise of international principles, new bastions of nationalism were being established in the shape of central banks. The new nationalism was in fact a corollary of the new internationalism, and the gold standard could be maintained only in so far as the countries it was meant to serve could be protected from its dangers.[73] In fact, the succession of systemic cycles of accumulation, from the sixteenth century onwards, has constantly oscillated between two models in which finance and power were associated: the Venetian model of the capitalist state and the Genoan model of the deterritorialized 'nation' of merchants illustrated by the partnership between the *nobili vecchi* and the Spanish monarchy. The alliance between the merchants of Amsterdam and the house of Orange in the seventeenth century, the financial hegemony of England in the nineteenth century and its competition with Germany were merely variations on this alternative inherent in capitalism and its worldwide expansion. The distinguishing feature of the period under consideration – apart from the fact that it extended financial globalization to hitherto unequalled proportions – was that it brought together the territorial power, in the form of a huge colonial empire, and the industrial, commercial and financial power of which London was the epicentre.[74]

This synergy between apparently hostile principles could be found in every domain. Michael Mann has shown how production in the international system in the nineteenth century occurred at the intersection of social forces and state forces[75] – and it brought dissonances and conflict in its train. Nationalism contradicted and endangered the system of states that had created it. The philanthropic movement to abolish slavery, a movement that was religious and 'nongovernmental', gained the support of the Royal Navy, contributed to the creation of two states, Sierra Leone and Liberia, and was closely linked with colonial activity. The apogee of 'high finance' was concomitant with that of territorial imperialism. The conquest of the world by Europe was a kind of ideological cement for the nation-state facing the working-class movement.[76] International socialism was 'one of the main factors of the nationalisation of the habitus of workers' groups that had hitherto been particularist, localist and corporatist'.[77] The imposition of a global system of states was a condition of international investment, international trade, and the repayment of the international debt.[78] The *belle époque* was a period of unprecedented linguistic fragmentation, especially in Europe, but also the standardization of regional vehicular languages, the worldwide spread of European languages, and utopian quests for a universal language. It spread religious beliefs and universalist philosophies that often nourished excessive cultural, identity or political particularisms.

Throughout this foundational nineteenth century, the ambivalence of the relations between the global, the local and the state was unavoidable. It finally turned into tragedy when a transnational terrorist network, drawing on the help of the Serbian state, assassinated Archduke Franz Ferdinand in Sarajevo on 28 June 1914,[79] and when Turkish nationalism, imbued with the positivist ideology of the Sorbonne, exterminated hundreds of thousands of Armenians, thereby putting a dramatic end to the multicultural Ottoman Empire. Unity and prosperity in heterogeneity, confusion and blood: such is our lot, such was already the lot of our ancestors, who gave birth to us in the economic and political senses.

We still need to avoid two misunderstandings. The first would consist in seeing the minimal state of the neo-liberals at the end of the twentieth century as a pure resurgence of nineteenth-century liberalism. It would be easy to point out, detail by detail, the ways in which our world is different from that of our ancestors.[80] To put it briefly, BOTs (Build, Operate and Transfer) cannot be seen just as charter companies. Thinking the situation through in terms of historicity, of 'event', stops us imagining the resurrection of the Phoenix of the 'worldwide self-regulating market' or the vengeance of the 'essence' of global capitalism after the errings and strayings of the autarkical, *dirigiste* or Keynesian 'Great Transformation'.

The second error, one that is linked to the first, would be to identify this transformation with the regression of globalization, as several writers believe. Admittedly, the 1930s witnessed a drying-up of transoceanic migration, the political effacement of 'higher finance', the bankruptcy of the League of Nations, the spread of economic and financial autarky, the exit of the Russian Empire from the capitalist world economy and the victory of ideologies of exclusion and closure. But simply adopting these ideas without further ado would mean being satisfied with a highly normative and, to be frank, naive definition of globalization. By definition, the two world wars were 'global' – the second even more than the first – and had direct and indirect consequences that went far beyond the European battlefields. The sufferings they caused affected tens of millions of people on every continent, and the way the world viewed itself was completely shattered. Furthermore, the two conflicts led to technical innovations that intensified 'time-space compression'. They revived the demand for a 'global governance' that the systems of the United Nations and Bretton Woods put back on the agenda in 1945. They made it possible to imagine that mankind itself might disappear from the surface of the planet: *One World*, as Franklin Roosevelt proclaimed – for better and for worse, in the shadow of the atomic mushroom.

In a more selective way, the Nazi persecutions transformed the intellectual landscape of Europe and the Americas by driving several thinkers and artists, whether Jewish or not, into exile: American universities are still living off the benefits of this ostracism. The colonial pacts through which Great Britain and France endeavoured to replace a defunct international free exchange perpetuated the 'imperial societies' and conferred on them an extra integrative power. Even from a political point of view, things are more complicated than they seem. The commitment to fascism, as well as the fight against it, were both internationalist in scope.[81] In any case, Hitler aimed to establish a European order and not just a German regime. The case of Russia is just as ambiguous. According to Karl Polanyi, it was only reluctantly that Soviet Russia entered on the path of self-sufficiency, since it was unable to find external markets for its agricultural products: 'Socialism in one country was brought about by the incapacity of the market economy to provide a link between all countries; what appeared as Russian autarchy was merely the passing of capitalist internationalism.'[82] Eric Hobsbawm takes this line of reasoning even further, seeing the Russian Revolution as the saviour of liberal capitalism. It enabled the West to win the Second World War, but also forced capitalism to reform and throw off the shackles of market orthodoxy.[83] Be this as it may, 'the October revolution was universally recognised as a world-shaking event'.[84] And on many levels it contributed to bringing Russian society into the process of globalization.[85]

To summarize: the chain of events from 1760 to 2004, covering three periods that are often kept separate – the 'long nineteenth century', the 'short twentieth century' and the 'new world order', a neo-liberal order inaugurated by the fall of the Berlin Wall – forms an 'event' of globalization whose general dynamism leads to a coherent problematization.

Globalization: two or three things that we know about it

It would be amazing if, after twenty years of debate, the notion of globalization had not become more precise. Of course, we can decide to get irritated by the way it has become so trendy, seeing it as merely the effect of ideological fashion and deciding not to use it.[86] But we can also draw the conclusion that the scientific and philosophical critique of it is all the more necessary. We just need to 'problematize' it: not just as a historical sequence, as a regime of historicity, but also, more precisely, as a concept, analysing 'not behaviours or ideas, not societies and their "ideologies", but the *problematizations* through which being offers itself to be, necessarily, thought – and the *practices* on the basis of which these problematizations are formed'.[87] We need to attempt the hermeneutics of global man, if indeed the latter exists, seeking 'the forms and modalities of the relation to self by which the individual constitutes and recognizes himself qua subject'[88] in the context of globalization.

With this in mind, we need to take into account the far from negligible achievements of two decades' worth of thinking – without thereby repudiating the foundations of the social sciences. The world is perhaps not so very new as to justify excluding traditional approaches and concepts. It now seems well established that globalization, as a historical experience of 'time-space compression' and the awareness we have of this process, is not synonymous with westernization or Americanization. Rather, it establishes a 'generalized mutual interaction', an old Kantian formula that was taken up by Otto Bauer to conceptualize the nation, and one that is still valid to designate the supranational and supracontinental change of scale that has prevailed since the end of the eighteenth century. The phenomena of retroaction, appropriation and creative derivation are constitutive of globalization. In short, the latter, as a social fact, as an 'event', is a matter of *énonciation*, of utterance.[89] It thus consists of a 'reinvention of difference'[90] on a global scale – a reinvention to which postmodern anthropology has devoted much thought. Basically, it corresponds to the Christian paradigm of Pentecost:

> Now when this was noised abroad, the multitude came together, and were confounded, because that every man heard him speak in his own language. They were all amazed and marvelled, saying one to another, Behold, are not all these which speak Galileans? And how hear we every man in our own tongue, wherein we were born? Parthians, and Medes, and Elamites, and the dwellers in Mesopotamia, and in Judaea, and Cappadocia, in Pontus, and Asia, Phrygia, and Pamphylia, in Egypt, and in the parts of Libya about Cyrene, and strangers of Rome, Jews and

proselytes, Cretes and Arabians. we do hear them speak in our tongues the wonderful works of God. (Acts of the Apostles, 2: 6–11)

Thanks to the technology of transport and telecommunications, this generalized (and global) new dual interaction happens 'at a distance' by disconnecting the place of truth from that of experience,[92] in particular in the context of migrations. Globalization is television plus diaspora – this in substance is what we learn from Arjun Appadurai.[93] But thanks to its virtual dimension, it cannot be uniformization. This is how Gilles Deleuze puts it, picking up certain ideas of Gabriel Tarde:

> The actualisation of the virtual . . . always takes place by difference, divergence or differenciation. Actualisation breaks with resemblance as process no less than it does with identity as a principle. Actual terms never resemble the singularities they incarnate. In this sense, actualisation or differenciation is always a genuine creation. It does not result from any limitation of pre-existing possibility.[94]

Hence the importance of a critique of culturalism that ruins any attempt to think of globalization by reducing 'generalized mutual interaction' to a zero-sum game of identities:[95] if you are a democrat, you are less of an African; if you eat McDonald's burgers, you are less French; if you condemn torture, you are less Chinese; and if you are a Muslim, you beat your wife. Hence also the usefulness of returning to the definition of culture given by Michel de Certeau. He suggests that we see it as 'combinations of operations', including in the shape of a 'construction of one's own phrases with a received vocabulary and syntax'.[96] Globalization also includes those 'arts of doing', those 'tactics', in other words the use to which we put it and the practices in which we involve it, in negative counterpoint to the 'strategies' that are the 'real essence' of the dominant (or major) agents of the international system.

Globalization, when posited in this way as a historical regime of social practices, as an 'event', is a concept or, more precisely, an imaginary figure that refers simultaneously to its essential materiality and its fantasmatic developments.[97] To some extent it evokes the myth of autarky among the Romans: this myth shaped the moral economy of an empire that lived off trade and war.[98] Karl Polanyi has likewise shown that liberalism rested on the 'Utopia' of the self-regulating worldwide market – that 'Devil's factory' – and on the application of the fiction of merchandise to labour, the earth and money.[99] These fables were no less absurd, and no more innocent, than those of 'industrializing industry' and other forms of 'radiant future'. In an analogous fashion, we are delighted (or scared) by globalization, which in our heart of hearts we know does not correspond entirely to the realities of our time, but which provides us with an ideological or symbolic interpretation of our period.

Let us go further: globalization historically happens in this register of images, passions, hallucinations and utopias. Its ambivalence is a result of this. The statistics that economists and sociologists pore over do not exhaust the subject. We still need to understand millenarian risings, cults, rumours of spirits plotting and devouring, eschatological anxieties about the genetic mutation of mankind or the vertigo of fusion-acquisitions that have constituted the historical experience of globalization for two centuries. The question then arises for each of these actions in the imaginary domain. Does it consist of a refusal of globalization or an operation of appropriation, in other words of creation? It is not rare, as the cunning of history would have it, for protests, resistance and refusals all to turn out to be a form of consent. The spread and naturalization of the state 'imported'[100] into Africa and Asia thus happened through anti-colonial struggles: the white man has been chased away, but his ideological and institutional baggage has been kept. The century of liberalism too was imbued by this tension:

> For a century the dynamic of modern society was governed by a double movement: the market expanded continuously but this movement was met by a countermovement checking the expansion in definite direc-tions. . . . That system developed in leaps and bounds; it engulfed space and time, and by creating bank money it produced a dynamic hitherto unknown. By the time it reached its maximum extent, around 1914, every part of the globe, all its inhabitants and yet unborn generations, physical persons as well as those huge fictitious bodies called corporations, were comprised in it. A new way of life spread over the planet with a claim to universality unparalleled since the age when Christianity started out on its career, only this time the movement was on a purely material level.
>   Yet simultaneously a countermovement was on foot. This was more than the usual defensive behaviour of a society filed with change; it was a reaction against a dislocation which attacked the fabric of society, and which would have destroyed the very organisation of production that the market had called into being.[101]

In practice, we know what happened to it. So it is impossible to be content with a functionalist argument claiming that political and imagi-nary mobilizations hostile to globalization are akin to mere regulatory correctives, to vulgar 'rituals of rebellion', that ultimately endorse the reproduction of the social (and global) order, as Max Gluckman said of dramatized violence among the Swazi.[102] Indeed, the 'event' of global-ization, far from representing a coherent process of totalization, is composed of 'disjunctions'[103] that are not disconnections between the different areas (or 'landscapes') of human activity. On the contrary, they have a systematic coherence and can thereby turn out to be fateful. There is a disjunction between the liberalization of the financial market and the recurrence of a certain 'neo-protectionism' in the domain of commercial exchanges, under the cover of a liberalization that is being promoted simultaneously (or in competition with it) by organizations of regional integration and the World Trade Organization. There is a disjunction between the demands of financial, economic or technical globalization and the permanence of national sovereignties or political mobilizations. There is a disjunction, above all, between the desire to unify the markets of capital and merchandise and the wish to divide the labour force. From the point of view of capitalism – and *The Economist* makes no mistake about it, clashing swords as it does with restrictive legislations on immigration – globalization thus conceals a contradiction which already led to its being reversed at the end of the 'long nineteenth century'. Mass migrations that had made a decisive contribution to the convergence of Atlantic economies, by reducing social inequality in poor countries and increasing it in rich countries, finally led to a turn of the political wheel and the closing of the American labour market. The *belle époque* of globalization choked on itself rather than succumbing to blows from without.[104] These days, an explosive cocktail has been formed by adding the administrative and coercive regulation of the circulation of labour power across the globe, and the way that public opinion and political classes in the countries to which immigrants move tend to cling (in a populist way) to their own identity. Several processes of regional integration have been undermined by this, starting with the Euro-Mediterranean partnership and ALENA.[105]

A twofold frustration has arisen from this scissor effect: the rancour of the 'native' toward the 'foreigner' and the anger felt by the latter (and all virtual emigrants) towards the former. As Gilles Deleuze and Félix Guattari put it:

> The man of capitalism is not Robinson but Ulysses, the cunning plebeian, some average man or other living in the big towns, Autochthonous Proletarians or foreign Migrants who throw themselves into infinite movement – revolution. Not one but two cries traverse capitalism and head for the same disappointment: immigrants of all countries, unite – workers of all countries.[106]

International terrorism and the unconventional militarism of certain states are admittedly caused by other things than a global sense of responsibility towards the 'wretched of the earth'. But how can we fail to see that the sympathy they enjoy among the latter – in every sense of the word – is not unrelated to the torments of Tantalus that the majority of mankind is forced to endure? Globalization is something that you can contemplate and suffer from, but you must not touch its fruits. Furthermore, exclusion and subordination are capable of provoking the invention of new possibilities of life, as Nietzsche put it, or of new modes of existence, to use the terms of Michel Foucault and Gilles Deleuze.[107] It has often happened in history that such a production of unprecedented forms of subjectivity, such as 'subjectivation', occurs at the bottom or in the interstices of the social hierarchy: for example among the freed men of ancient Rome or in the nineteenth century among the slaves of Yoruba cities.[108] We will be seeing later how the condition of waiting, which goes together with a feeling of urgency, engenders liminal situations in the very heart of the process of globalization, situations that will eventually affect its running, in so far as they are centres of critical (or at least different) forms of subjectivation.

The main question then bears on globalization as an imaginary figure and configuration of power, in short as an imaginary configuration of power – this is a result of the fact that the imagination is 'constitutive'[109] and that the imaginary is not the unreal, but 'the indiscernibility of the real and the unreal'.[110] Understood this way, we cannot therefore think of the imaginary in abstraction from its materiality.[111] Contemporary fashionable political discourse exhorts us ardently to adopt a 'world governance': in the words of Pascal Lamy, a commissioner in the European Union, 'the set of transactions by which collective rules are developed, decided, legitimated, put into operation, and controlled'.[112] But the philosophical weakness of the concept lies precisely in the fact that it leaves out the dimension and the stakes of power, as well as the dimension and the stakes of subjectivation. In order to account for the heterogeneity, incompletion and contingency of the 'event of globalization', I will thus prefer, as I have already said, Foucault's notion of governmentality as a point of encounter between 'techniques of domination' applied to others and 'techniques of the self'.[113] Foucault's work, as is well known, focuses on the 'men's subjection: their constitution as subjects in both senses of the word',[114] in particular as 'moral subjects', not in the form of submission to an external rule imposed by an unequivocal relation of domination, but in the mode of 'belonging'.[115] It highlights 'the way in which the individual establishes his relation to the rule and recognizes himself as obliged to put it into practice'.[116]

The historic uncertainty in which we are living today is thus related to the emergence, or lack of emergence, of a global governmentality – rather than of a 'global governance' – as a 'set of actions on possible actions', following Foucault's definition of power:

> [The exercise of power] is a set of actions on possible actions; it incites, it induces, it seduces, it makes easier or more difficult; it releases or

contrives, makes more probable or less; in the extreme, it constrains or forbids absolutely, but it is always a way of acting upon one or more acting subjects by virtue of their acting or being capable of action. A set of actions upon other actions.[117]

Do our belonging to the world, our constitution as subjects, proceed from a global 'government' in this sense? Or is the process of globalization irreducible to any idea of belonging? Is it mere domination without action or subjectivation? Is globalization appropriation or dispossession? This is the alternative we need to explore.

2

The State: A Product of Globalization

In the historical sequence that we are surveying, the principle of the nation-state as a mode of territorial sovereignty in which the political sphere is made autonomous has been generalized to the global scale. We can agree with Max Weber when he says that the 'creation' of this 'rational-legal' state was the creation of the West alone, and was insepa-rable from the emergence of capitalism and its 'spirit'.[1] But only if we immediately add that this mode of organization of sovereignty has now spread throughout the world. Its vehicle was both European imperial-ism and also the struggle against the latter in the societies of Asia or Africa which it had subjected. However 'imported' it might have been, it then became the object of complex processes of 'appropriation', which rapidly conferred specific social and cultural foundations on it.[2] From this point of view, the state is an imaginary figure, as well as a mode of insertion into the international system and a structure whereby social inequality is produced, institutionalized and legitimated. It rests simultaneously on the exercise of coercion, fiscal extraction and the mobilization of symbolic or cultural resources. It is this ambivalence that the concepts of 'domination' (*Herrschaft*) in Max Weber, 'hege-mony' in Antonio Gramsci or 'subjectivation' in Michel Foucault aim to restore. And it is the same ambivalence that has made it possible to reproduce the 'imported' state once its 'creators', the Europeans, have withdrawn as a political force. It has not been emphasized sufficiently that the break-up of the Soviet Empire in Central Asia and the Caucasus has, from this point of view, corroborated the lessons learnt from the decolonization of former British, French or Portuguese territories. The artefact of the nation-state was imposed by violence and was perpetu-ated in people's minds as well as in the flow of economic and military resources. It was grafted onto the system.[3] The salient characteristic of

the last two centuries has thus been the universalization of the state –
an apotheosis which has been ratified by its proliferation: now there
are some 200 states in the world, 184 of them members of the United
Nations, as compared with 51 signatories to the Charter of San Francisco in 1945, and 29 members of the League of Nations between the
two world wars.

But a frequent objection is that this is merely a homage paid by vice
to virtue. This multiplication of different kinds of state, often without
content or substance – this proliferation of 'quasi-states'[4] without the
material and political resources of effective sovereignty – is merely a
metastasis. It carries malignant cells that spell doom for the legitimacy,
omnipotence and even the existence of the state itself, and entail other
disruptions to the international system. The paradox is thus that the
'end of the nation-state' (and that of its 'territories') is announced at
the very moment of its apparent triumph.[5]

Three sentences of death (or of life imprisonment) have been pronounced against the proliferation of the nation-state, even if some
people are quite ready to grant it a reprieve. To begin with, the state is
supposedly retreating under the blows of the deadlines imposed by the
market and the diffusion of power in the world economy, to repeat the
terms used in the classic analysis made by Susan Strange in *The Retreat
of the State*.[6] The extension of its field of intervention should not disguise the fact that its real prerogatives are in retreat, as a result of
technological transformations, their cost in terms of capital, and the
overhauling of international finance that ensues. At the same time,
transnational businesses are, it is claimed, playing an ever more important role as full-blown agents in the international system, which they
seem to be structuring to an ever greater degree, hand in hand with
independent regulatory authorities and the forces of 'civil society'. The
alienation of state sovereignty is apparent, it would seem, in the way
economic and monetary policy is defined and in the domain of fiscal
extraction. The rise of private protectionism at the behest of cartels or
alliances between transnational businesses, or more simply thanks to
technological monopolies, attempts at fiscal secession or dissidence on
the part of certain regions, certain agents or certain social categories in
industrial countries, the massive and recurrent flight of capital from
what used to be known as the Third World and the growth of the
international criminal economy – these are all, it is alleged, cruelly
revelatory of the 'retreat' of the state.

Second, the state is now included within a movement that is encouraging the 'new regionalization' of the international system, of which
the European Union is the most consummate example, but not the only
one: MERCOSUR and ALENA in America, ASEAN and APEC in Asia,
the Gulf Cooperation Council in the Middle East, the CEDEAO, the
free zone – mainly the UEMOA – and the SADC in Africa are all

groupings to which national political authorities need to pay attention, whatever may be the respective (very variable) performances of these different processes of regional integration. The perpetuation of the spheres of influence of the great powers in their immediate environment – their 'foreign neighbour', as they call it in Moscow – is also effected by the intermediary of regionalism, here too with a greater or lesser degree of success. The secret services and the Russian Army still constitute the backbone of the CIS (Commonwealth of Independent States), monetary integration in French-speaking Africa has since 1993 become a way for France to disengage from that area (contingent on the way the crisis in the Ivory Coast develops), the Euro-Mediterranean Partnership is an empty shell, while the ALENA and the growth of the European Union both represent consistent attempts on the part of the two main pillars of the international system to organize or absorb their periphery, notwithstanding their limits or their contradictions. State sovereignty is thus 'cut down by the daily effects of the interdependence of economies'[7] and, more broadly, by the effects of transnational osmosis, which is independent of intergovernmental efforts to manage it. The principle of 'dispersal' proper to neo-regionalism gives, it has been said, 'a patchwork configuration to the renascent international system':

> These many irregular forms inevitably become the antonyms of the idea of sovereignty. In particular they become, in the face of this slow retreat of the political sphere, the cause of a reduction in the number of communities emancipated from previous nation-state-type allegiances. . . . [The state] becomes a pole of interactions to the same degree . . . as . . . transnational agents and those who try to establish identities.[8]

In the long run, only the regional power is able to reconcile 'meaning and power' and to impose itself 'as the major reference point in the international system, the decisive unit in international competition'.[9] Its progress is all the more unstoppable in that it is apparently based on a 'logic of proximity' between neighbouring countries,[10] on the rise of city-states that are now 'global cities', and on the transformation of provinces into 'quasi-nation-states' within the existing nation-states.[11]

Finally, it is claimed, the increasing number of civil wars both permits and precipitates the fall of the state. It is revealing how these civil wars imply private armies, businesses or combatants, and their 'economic orientation' – as Max Weber would put it – is becoming ever more pronounced.[12] Unlike the conflicts between states that followed the Treaty of Westphalia, or the 'total wars' of the twentieth century, the wars of a 'third type' that we see these days flourishing across the face of the globe do not contribute to the formation of the state, as the classic doctrine of historical sociology or the theory of international relations would have it,[13] but quite simply to its destruction or to crisis within it.[14] This is because such wars now bear on the very definition of the state and on the nature of the political community that constitutes it rather than on 'international relations', as was once the case. Secession and ethnic purification are thus seen as the two favoured types which the tragedies of the late Yugoslavia and Rwanda have erected into ideal-types, officially recognized by the institution of ad hoc international criminal tribunals.

Dead man's reprieve

Globalization thus seems to provoke, *urbi et orbi*, the decline of the state, either by emptying it of its content, through terror, or by transcending it, through liberalization. Globalization is played out somewhere between parody (in which rump states indulge) and modesty (as proclaimed by minimal states). But in reality, things have turned out to be much more complicated. The authors who loudly proclaimed the death of the state are now being forced to admit that the patient is showing much more resistance than they had foreseen. And between remission and convalescence or cure, the difference is not always very great.

Not much of the idea of the 'death of the state' (and of its 'territories') is left, apart from the long complaint of the supporters of state sovereignty, the intellectual interest of which is in inverse proportion to its capacity to cause electoral damage. Each of the phenomena that are supposed to have delivered the *coup de grâce* has turned out to be a very inefficient executioner. We can, just for the sake of experiment, easily reverse the different arguments put forward by both sets of people, and cast doubt on whether the state is really soluble in market, region or war.

Thus, in industrial societies, economic and financial globalization has certainly dealt a blow to the welfare state in New Zealand and Great Britain, but it has not seen off the model found in Denmark, Sweden, the Netherlands, Germany, France or Japan. From 1985 to 1999, the proportion of tax and social security deductions in the GDP of thirty countries in the OECD rose by 3.5 points. Here and there, the grip of the state on societies and the market makes its presence felt by the recentralization of local and social finances, the increase in the proportion of social benefits and transferrals into the available income of households before taxation, the sly development of a commercial 'neo-protectionism', the bureaucratization of the peasantry through the intermediary of the handing out of subsidies or bonuses and an extensive effort to impose general regulation.

The case of East and Southeast Asia is equally eloquent: state interventionism has supplied the momentum that has globalized these national economies and has coexisted amicably with the working of family and diaspora networks; the financial and monetary crisis of 1997–8 ended in the spectacular, open and public ideological rehabilitation of state interventionism, with the full knowledge of multilateral institutions that all of a sudden turned out to be humbly forced to adapt to the re-establishment of the foreign exchange control in Malaysia, the maintenance of public subsidies in Indonesia, the non-convertibility of Chinese currency or the making public of private debts.

In short, nothing proves that globalization, and in particular the development of transnational economic and cultural relations, is resulting in a retreat of the state or the withering away of the nation that goes with it. Not without some plausibility, certain authors even demonstrate the exact opposite.[15] And in any case, questions of security have been the sea-wall against which the great wave of liberalization came crashing down at the turn of the century. While President Bush had already adopted a certain neo-Keynesianism by proceeding to a colossal increase in the military budget of the United States, the attacks of 11 September 2001 provoked or justified the comeback of the state in terms of the surveillance of air and sea transport, telecommunications and the capital market, a comeback that does not necessarily question the privatization of these sectors, but places them back under the vigilant guardianship of the administration.

In addition, one needs a considerable dose of angelic hope to grant more importance to 'neo-regionalism' than to militarist nationalism in East Asia, or to turn a blind eye to the way that regional organizations in Africa serve above all to institutionalize the way national political leaders are always trying to trip each other up, against a background of rivalries and wars. Furthermore, contemporary conflicts are perhaps not as much of an exception to Clausewitz's trinitarian scheme (resting on the distinction between government, army and civil population) as people sometimes say – no more than the wars of yesteryear corresponded all that precisely to it. The notion that the forms of belligerence at the start of this twenty-first century are completely unprecedented has been disproved.[16] Belligerence continues, in any case, to take national territory as its object, either in the form of rebellions that aim to capture the capital city and central power, or in the form of inter-state wars of the most classic kind – for instance, between Iran and Iraq, Iraq and Kuwait, Ethiopia and Eritrea, India and Pakistan, or else in the course of the perpetuation of struggles that are, after all, described as 'national', as in Palestine, East Timor, the Sultanate of Aceh or Western Sahara. As throughout the period of the Cold War, conflicts or tensions between states remain, at least in Asia and the Middle East, sources of state centralization.[17]

We thus need to raise the question of whether the classic contribution of war (even if it be 'civil' war or war of a 'third type') to the formation of the state is really obsolete. In Algeria, it seems indeed to have consolidated the regime that had been destabilized by the riots of 1988.[18] Likewise, in Afghanistan, it seems to have been the 'way in which the forms of organization were modernized' and 'power concentrated' by 'eliminating the weakest participants', just as the mechanism described by Norbert Elias would suggest; the 'clerical state' of the Taliban which emerged from it was, or so it has been claimed, 'progressively reconstructing institutions, in particular an administrative organization and a judicial system, on the basis of a fundamentalist vision of society', before being toppled by the intervention of the United States.[19]

As for the emblematic case of sub-Saharan Africa, it may well mean the opposite of what it is often said to mean. To be sure, the armed conflicts there seem to have been the pre-eminent mode of mobilization and political organization, extending progressively from the eastern and southern half of the sub-continent to its western hemisphere and assuming forms of alarming violence and disruption. But the most notable feature of this dramatic evolution is really the fact that the war has not destroyed the state as a sovereign entity. It merely impacts on certain of its administrative, social or economic capacities while reinforcing others, starting with the military power in countries such as Rwanda, Angola, Ethiopia or Eritrea.

Something that is quite unprecedented with regard to the conventional view of the artificial character of the frontiers inherited from colonization is the fact that secessions are pretty much absent from postcolonial history. If we leave aside the complex case of the rebellion in the south of Sudan, which kept voicing different demands, the two most notable separatist attempts, those of Katanga in 1960 and Biafra in 1967, do not disprove the rule, and we cannot even say that they are the exceptions that prove the rule, as the adage has it, since they are too ambiguous. Moïse Tshombe was acting on Belgian, South African and Rhodesian organizations and mandates, and could not claim to be incarnating any real national or proto-national aspiration. And General Ojukwu was, for his part, intent on preserving the autonomy (in particular the fiscal autonomy) enjoyed by the Eastern Region within a Nigeria that was more confederal than federal, constituted in 1914 by tacking together three distinct colonial possessions, and governed according to the decentralizing precepts of indirect rule. Basically, the secession of Biafra is more akin to those disturbing examples of the armed restoration of certain colonial territories such as Italian Eritrea, annexed by Ethiopia, or British Somaliland, 'reunited' with Italian Somaliland. As for the rest, the protagonists of civil wars strive to take control of the state, not to break it up. Neither RENAMO in Mozambique nor UNITA in Angola had nursed the hope that the country would be divided up in accordance with regionalist or ethnic bases, and, in the Great Lakes, the fantasy of a 'Hutuland' that germinated in the minds of certain foreigners or in the bloodstained pages of *Hutu Power* was unable to convince many of its viability.

In spite of the clichés, Congo-Kinshasa provides us with a superb counter-example. While all the conditions for its break-up are present, there is no question there of secession, but of occupation or annexation, even of 'colonization',[20] without the national sense of identity – still very strong – growing any weaker. In Kivu, the war is reproducing the mode of government that prevailed at the time of Mobutu.[21] Furthermore, the original causes of the war lay in something that had a direct link with the genesis of the state in question, namely the legal definition of Zairean-Congolese citizenship and the right to own property, and the exercise of universal suffrage that property granted (or denied) to non-indigenous persons of Rwandan origin.[22] Since 2001, exactly the same has been true in the Ivory Coast, where the rebels are demanding their return to the bosom of the state and claim to be the spokespersons of citizens from the *départements* of the north of the country, who have been excluded from the national community because their 'Ivoirean' identity has not been recognized. Here too, the key elements of the crisis were related to the area in which voting and property rights were granted. In order to seize power, these armed movements have of course reached a pact with Blaise Compaoré, the President of the adjoining Republic of Burkina Faso, always looking out for a crisis in which he can get involved so as to increase his regional influence. Nonetheless, until the contrary is proved, the latter intends in turn to base his hold over the Ivory Coast not on any 'Dioula Republic' in the north. He is endeavouring, of course, to divide so as better to rule. But he wants to rule in Abidjan, not in Bouaké.

Indeed, it is tempting to propose quite the contrary hypothesis to that of the state's demise. Is not the war in Africa, here too, yet again, part of the way the state (or system of states) is formed – by the development of armies, the interplay of regional alliances and the consolidation of the sense of national identities? Does it not allow the national political classes, subject as they are to the conditions laid down by financial backers, to free themselves from the latter and recover their sovereignty, as has been happening in Uganda and Angola over the past twenty years? Do not the multilateral peacekeeping operations transmit the liberal, Westphalian conception of the state?[23] Of course, the raising of a militia, the militarization of hereditary societies, the fissiparous adventurism of politico-military entrepreneurs and the predatory behaviour of foreign businessmen, firms or mercenaries may all go against this tendency, and make it less obvious, or even reverse it completely. Nonetheless, we cannot in principle exclude the idea that this kind of phenomenon can ultimately go hand in hand with such a tendency, as historians of the Thirty Years War have shown.[24] Indeed, surely Congo-Kinshasa occupies, *mutatis mutandis*, the (unenviable) place of Germany in the first half of the seventeenth century, a tragic epicentre both of a social violence that lacks not so much any definite aim as any coherent strategy of regional scope and also of large-scale manoeuvrings on the part of neighbouring states, intent on imposing their presence as a hegemon and feeding off the fatted calf.

We know that the invention of modernity is often paradoxical. In this case, cruelty is part and parcel of the paradox. In Sierra Leone, the rebels who offer their victims a choice between 'short sleeves' and 'long sleeves' are not questioning the way the state is envisaged, nor have they given up all hope of the advent of 'good governance'.[25] And in the south of Sudan, the time of 'government' (*kume*, from the Arabic *hakuma*) and that of the 'rifle' (*mac*) have coincided since the era of British colonization. The horrible civil war, which has claimed more than two million victims, to more or less general indifference (with the exception of the United States, Israel, Ethiopia, Eritrea and Uganda which financed or facilitated its continuation, so as to weaken the regime in Khartoum) has pulverized the different cultural representations of death, kinship and the social status of women and children, partly as a result of the introduction and generalization of firearms:

> Even for your mother, a bullet!
> Even for your father, a bullet!
> Your rifle is your food!
> Your rifle is your wife!

– words sung (in Arabic) by the young Nuer recruits of the Sudanese People's Liberation Army.[26] The local commanders of this army claimed, at the end of the 1980s, that the 'government war' (*koor kume*) in which they were engaged took precedence over the personal and social identities of the combatants, and thus over the ancient ethics of belligerence. The habitual forms by which violence was regulated were no longer to be observed; the massacring of women, children and old men, or the destruction of houses and harvests, would no longer be punished by divine vengeance; and no compensation in cattle would be able to pay the blood price any longer.[27] But the experience of the conflict also led the Nuer to distinguish between the 'government of the left' (*kume in caam*), identified with the regional administrative network of the leaders, law courts, police and civil servants of the territory, who 'want people to live', and the 'government of the right' (*kume in cuec*), the army, which brings death.[28] Naturally, there is nothing to say that a national consciousness or a civic space will emerge from these atrocities or these fine distinctions. We can even doubt as much, given the methodical destruction of education, which has made it inevitable that power be seen merely as the power to kill.[29] The terrifying mystery of war also stems from its futility. It is not my purpose to claim that it *is* the womb from which the state emerges in Africa, even less that it is a necessary and sufficient condition of its formation. This would require a gross simplification of European history and an evolutionary point of view of a kind familiar to followers of Barrès, both inept and revolting. It consists merely in *not entirely ruling out* this eventuality, not concealing the repugnant creative force of Mars, and not accepting taking for granted talk about the decline of the state.[30]

Not only is the state resisting the deleterious effects that would come with globalization; it participates in the process, even if only as a 'consenting victim'.[31] The celebrated 'technological foundation of the form of organization proper to the era of information',[32] i.e. the Internet, did after all develop at the interface of research programmes financed by the Pentagon, with the big markets' support, and its decentralized use by web-surfers and those putting the 'new economy' into operation. Now this example is highly symbolic, and constitutes the paradigm for a more general system. The regulation of globalization continues to depend, essentially speaking, on relations between states or the state sphere, even if it is being more and more systematically delegated to independent authorities that produce private laws which impose themselves on the states from which these authorities have emerged. Élie Cohen enjoins us to 'accept the fundamentally hybrid character of the independent regulatory authority as a public institution, making political choices, anxious to ensure that its decisions are well received in the short term but functioning as a private power of arbitration pursuing long-term objectives, producing its own laws in a definite limited area'.[33] This transfer of power has become widespread in the domains of telecommunications, energy, transport, commerce, banking, finance and currency, either to the profit of real multilateral organizations such as the IMF, the WTO and the ECB, or to the profit of mere authorities or commissions such as the Basel Committee on the supervision of banking, created in 1974, originally in order to manage the consequences of excessive risk-taking on the part of international financial establishments in a system of floating exchange rates, but whose mission has widened to the production of the prudential norms necessary for the security of the international financial system.

This last case shows clearly how collaboration between public power and the private sector – in this case central bankers and private financial agents – can definitively end up with the latter taking the place of the former, by creating an 'international zone of non-governance'.[34] The danger that lurks within this slippage is not insignificant, if we judge by the incompetence, irresponsibility or duplicity of the rating agencies as revealed by the Asian crisis of 1997–8 and the Enron affair in 2002. Or indeed by the self-serving approximations of the International Maritime Organization and the classificatory bodies which inspect merchant vessels and grant them certificates of seaworthiness as soon as they are in such good shape as the *Erika* or the *Prestige*. In Panama, it is thus the club of business lawyers, and not the maritime administration, which has real control of the national flag. The cabinet of Morgan & Morgan, which carries out 30 per cent of registrations there, has its own classificatory body, and is not in the least worried by this flagrant conflict of interests.[35] Likewise, the Cambodian state mandated the Cambodia Shipping Corporation, between 1994 and 2002, to register, online and without the least control, some 2,300 ships. The company acting as agent that took over in January 2003, Cosmos Group, already established in Panama, Belize and Bolivia, also prides itself on same-day delivery, via the Internet, of provisional certificates of seaworthiness.[36]

Nonetheless, the incoherencies or blind spots of the privatization of regulatory or jurisprudential activity should not lead to over-hasty conclusions tainted by populism. The fact that the state has delegated certain of its prerogatives does not necessarily entail any alienation of its sovereignty or any diminishing of its democratic credentials. It is indeed public institutions, and in most industrial countries institutions that are subject to the exercise of universal suffrage, that consent to this shift in the locus of decision even if the fact of the matter is that public opinion feels the need for a refoundation and change of scale in political representation.

Furthermore, the privatization of authority fits into the context of certain given historical situations. It remains dependent on their specific trajectories. Thus, in Morocco, the liberalization of telecommunications, at the time of the succession of Hassan II, was placed under the control of the Palace, behind the protective screen of an independent regulator with public status, the National Agency for the Regulation of Telecommunications. It serves the extended reproduction (and one that is to some extent transparent – as 'good governance' necessarily implies) of the Makhzen by proceeding to a simple 'shift in opacity' inherent in this type of government. It is finally of the same kind as other liberalizing reforms, wrapped in the finery of the 'Washington consensus', but subject to the purposes or force of gravity of the monarchy, for instance the 'clean-up' campaigns aimed at corruption and fraud, the privatizations of public enterprises, and the way customs regulations are moving towards free trade with the European Union.[37]

Likewise, the 'information era' has not shaken the power of the Chinese Communist Party. The privatization of the economy has not led there, any more than elsewhere, to a retreat of the state, but rather to a commodification of clientelism and of bureaucratic power and to the reconstitution of the 'overstretched Empire'.[38] In this case, the party keeps control of the communication sector and the unprecedented social practices which the latter engenders, for instance on telephone hotlines which lavish lifestyle advice on family and sexual relations, on satellite televisions or the Internet.[39] The increasingly blurred distinctions between state-controlled firms and the private sector, which the WTO confirms by agreeing to consider as 'private' the great public telecommunications monopolies so as to foster their partnerships with foreign investors, facilitate the perpetuation of the political surveillance of new technologies of information and communication. This is illustrated in an almost grotesque way by the Murdoch family (owners of *Star TV*), so very eager to oblige the regime, and the closeness of the personal relations that it has established with the latter. In the final analysis, the anxiety of the Red Hierarchs to ensure their control of the 'information era' no longer appears as bizarre and archaic as it did a few years ago. Technically, cable television makes possible a lucrative censoring of programmes.[40] Furthermore, the political authorities are in a position to control private operators via their financing, whether this rests on income from advertising or the subscriptions of viewers. The international obsession with security and the desire to fight 'cybercrime' will do the rest, and ensure that the economic and financial liberalization that China's joining the WTO is expected to bring about will not imperil the ability of the Communist Party to maintain its control of the structure of the World Wide Web and the airwaves, even if human rights should suffer as a result.[41]

This is one of the paradoxes of the last period of globalization to which some (but too few) analysts of economic reform draw attention. 'While a vast movement of convergence and homogenization has been described as leading to a unified global market, [the partial globalization of the 1990s] in fact makes the markets *much more vulnerable* to the failings and diversity of local economic institutions.'[42] This is all the more true in that it rests to a great extent on private participants and contracts which have the effect of fragmenting the management of financial flows, especially at times of crisis. The way the global power of the 'market' has been taken over by the national territory and its own particular political economy has been evident in sub-Saharan Africa, in the implementation of structural adjustment programmes, or in Asia and Russia, in 1997–8, for instance in the way the question of bankruptcies was tackled or the manner in which the biggest private financial institutions freed themselves from the prudential constraints of their countries of origin only to subject themselves to the opaque rules of the game enforced by local oligarchies. 'Opportunistic agents tend to adapt to the terrains in which they are intervening instead of causing an institutional adjustment of these markets.'[43] The convergence of national economies, confident in their own historicity, thus depends less on the methodical erosion of states than on multilateral negotiation between these states and their endorsement of new jurisprudential norms developing within independent regulatory authorities or the interstices of a 'capitalism of alliance'.

The privatization of states: hybridization and straddling

Béatrice Hibou has shown how 'privatizing the state', including certain of the state's sovereign prerogatives in the fields of tax collection, homeland security, diplomacy or national defence, amounts to a reinvention of the 'discharge' principle, whereby public power entrusts private agents with performing a select number of tasks that lead, in effect, to the privatization of sovereignty and coercion.[44] From this point of view, the contemporary era of liberalization comes at the end of a parenthetical period, that of the Great Transformation discussed by Karl Polanyi, although it is of course impossible to equate it simply with a revised version of the way war, fiscal extraction and capital mobility used to be leased out – a system that prevailed up until the nineteenth century, to the benefit of tax farmers, finance 'nations', pirates, condottieri, great mercantile companies or 'explorers'. Nor can it be seen as a resurrection of the liberalism of the 'Hundred Years Peace', and the golden age of banking. The conditions in which this contemporary 'discharge' is effectuated, its stakes, the interests which it serves, the values which it transmits, its quantitative, temporal or spatial scale, and those who participate in it – these are all obviously without precedent. Basically, the metaphor of K. H. O'Rourke and J. G. Williamson has some relevance here: they talk of the 'Renaissance' of globalization after 1950:[45] the relationship between this renaissance and its past is a creative one, less of a resurgence than an innovation.

The fact remains that the synergy between state-formation and the structuring of the international system is again experiencing an organic straddling between the traditional, nominalist categories of private and public. For three centuries, the interlacing of these latter categories sustained the centralization of political power – absolutist, then republican or democratic – the crystallization of civil society, the emergence of the 'European concert' in the alternating mode of war and diplomacy, the imperial expansion of the West, the establishment of the world market and international finance, the global influence of universalistic ideologies or beliefs, and the beginnings of their transformation into a transnational public space.[46] This principle of straddling has peacefully coexisted with a great diversity of institutional configurations, political styles and systems of economic exploitation; this took the form of the 'Colbertism' of the French seventeenth-century golden age, but also that of the Whig 'liberalism' of the English eighteenth century;[47] it was also found in the 'politics of the belly' in Africa, as well as in the reign of the 'oligarchs' in Russia, the rise to power of the 'children of party cadres' in China, the 'pastoral government' in

Indonesia and that of the Makhzen in Morocco. The classic interrelationship between tax farmer and monarch, or between privateer and Royal Navy, between 'explorer' and minister for the Colonies, between missionary or colonist and administrator, between banker and political authorities of the nation-state, sums up a more fundamental confusion of types and procedures than is conceptualized by the very notion of 'civil society', if one takes it in a precise philosophical sense: whether it be Lockean, 'Scottish', Hegelian, Marxist or Gramscian, the said civil society proceeds from its relation to the state, not from its exteriority to the latter, as the common neo-liberal vulgate would have us believe.[48]

Hence the need to reverse the usual argument (with all its naivety) of global studies when discussing liberalization. We should not take the classic route (accumulation of power and wealth, decision-taking, and the codification of positive norms) as something startlingly new. And if the 'discharge' has spread absolutism, why is it not these days the matrix of new and powerful, indeed extreme, forms of political subjection?

The same applies to the implementation of strategies of identity that, it is alleged, underlie the fall of the state. Let us pay the murderers the honour that is due to them, and consider the allegorical cases of Yugoslavia and Rwanda. The dismantling of the Yugoslav Federation and the operations of ethnic cleansing to which it led were brought about by the political class of the state, ex-communist (or socialist). The latter pursued a nationalist objective that was, in the final analysis, perfectly recognizable: the reconstitution of national states which Titoism had transcended, or at all events moved beyond and absorbed, and the reworking of the old dreams of grandeur of the nineteenth century and the first half of the twentieth; in short, a return to basics. In an abstract sense, we are now quite close to the example of Somaliland: secession as resurrection. But these nation-state-type projects were, for reasons of convenience and opportunism, contracted out to private operators, the militia. We might also point out that the crisis in Yugoslavia became internationalized almost immediately (albeit still belatedly), thanks to diplomatic and military intervention on the part of the European Union, the United States, NATO and the United Nations, as well as through the imposition of sanctions and the regional political economy to which they gave rise, and the factor of emigration, or else in the monetary form of the 'dollarization' and 'markization' of Serbian, Bosnian and Kosovar societies: we thus find this loose interrelationship between state and globalization which partly coincides with the intimate embrace of private and public, and with which we are starting to become familiar.[49]

Likewise, in Rwanda, the legitimacy of the genocide of the Tutsi – at least in the eyes of those who carried it out, of course – came from the fact that it was sponsored by state authorities, and is thus in some degree derived from its character as a public policy.[50] This needs to be highlighted, in particular because those who enacted it were on occasion able to refuse or get round the government's commands when they judged this to be desirable, especially in the economic field.[51] But, as it happens, they obeyed – which proves that state actions are not necessarily doomed to failure in sub-Saharan countries. This made it possible for the application of its public policy of extermination to be delegated, on the one hand to local collectivities and on the other to private initiative and the vital forces of civil society: local mayors were its coordinators, the logistical support of the Catholic Church was requested and often obtained, and the 'job' (to put it in crude terms) was entrusted to people of good will, more particularly to gangs of young unemployed men. In a symmetrical fashion, the Ugandan state supplied military support for the Rwandan Popular Front, incorporated as it was into its own national army, and probably to get rid of it more economically when it became too much of a nuisance. The genocide of the Rwandan Tutsis is equally instructive in that it was financed from above thanks to massive international aid that was bilateral, multilateral and private.[52] Non-governmental organizations in particular were to be found throughout the country. Quite unwillingly, they sanctioned the preparation for the butchery at the same time as they provided it with resources.

Thus the inactivity or disengagement of the Great Powers and the United Nations, in 1994, must not conceal the double way the tragedy formed part of contemporary liberal globalization. Its protagonists were two states, one of which, Uganda, was the model child of structural adjustment, and the other, Rwanda, was the spoilt child of 'international civil society'. But there is nothing in these false paradoxes that ought to shock us, since the *combinatoire* of state and globalization has, ever since the nineteenth century, fostered all sorts of particularist political mindsets, such as ethnicity, communalism or confessionalism.[53]

Nonetheless, the contemporary leasing out of force is a more general phenomenon. It applies equally to the harassing of opponents in processes of authoritarian restoration in the guise of 'democratic transition', the repression of separatists or autonomists, the fight against delinquency, the preservation of public and moral order – or more generally to the segregation of wealth and poverty, the regulation of migrations, the security of military and industrial installations or infrastructures and transport systems, national defence and military interventions abroad.

It is well known, for example, how people like Vladimir Putin, Daniel arap Moi, Paul Biya, or Laurent Gbagbo, in countries as different as Russia, Kenya, Cameroon or the Ivory Coast – or indeed how the

Indonesian Army in Java, Kalimantan, in the Moluccas, East Timor and Irian Jaya – hired the services of strong men to harass dissidents or troublemakers in the style of 'who's to know?', or to conduct real 'tension strategies' that led to massacres, assassinations and the destruction of property when delicate political deadlines were approaching.[54] The leaders of these regimes are indeed often shareholders in or owners of private security companies, and certainly mix with the underworld.[55]

In 1997, the Cameroonian Defence Minister, Philippe Menye me Mve, thus surreptitiously created a Rapid Intervention Service, of which he was the real owner, and at the same time passed a law on security firms that excluded foreigners from the protection market. He had chosen his moment wisely, since the construction of the Doha-Kribi pipeline was just beginning – and this would necessarily require contractors of this kind.[56] Interference in neighbouring states is also likely to be subcontracted out to politico-military entrepreneurs or local armed movements, as Uganda and Rwanda have done in the east of Congo-Kinshasa.[57] In extreme flare-ups of social violence, the distinction between troublemakers and agents of order becomes even hazier. In the north of Cameroon and in Chad, people talk of *douaniers-combattants* (literally 'customs officials-soldiers', or more prosaically 'fighting customs officials'), or in Sierra Leone of 'sobels' – soldiers by day and rebels by night.[58] And in Nigeria, 'private armies', such as the Bakassi Boys, with their sinister reputation, often provided with sophisticated equipment removed from arsenals, cheerfully meld together different activities: the struggle against banditry, creating the need for 'protection' in the market, resistance to the military dictatorship, the extortion of material benefits from foreign oil companies, the defence of 'natives' as opposed to non-indigenous persons within the framework of democratic reconstruction, or the vigorous (and sometimes forceful) promotion of the electoral campaigns of the governors of different federal states.[59]

Nonetheless, we should be wary of drawing the wrong conclusions. The privatization of coercion is characteristic neither of authoritarianism with its hankering for restoration, nor of the disintegration or the real or supposed weakness of state institutions. It is more fundamentally a way of reinventing the state and its intervention in the industrial heart of globalization. It is part of its new liberal theory.[60] It receives the blessing of multilateral organizations of development and non-governmental organizations.[61] 'Fortress Europe' is far from hostile when it imposes on air companies or Eurostar the task of ensuring passport control of their travellers and rests its immigration policy on the principle of the 'transporter's responsibility' should a passenger without the right papers be turned back at a frontier. Likewise, in the United States, the war on delinquents, clandestine operators or quite simply the homeless has been partly entrusted to private operators such as the Business Improvement Districts, charged with the social cleaning up of city centres, like the Grand Central Partnership round Grand Central Station in New York, or penitentiary enterprises such as Corrections Corporation of America or Wackenhut Corrections, who look after some hundred thousand detainees, in other words 5 per cent of the total prison population.[62] Finally, the United States and Britain have delegated some of their military interventions overseas to security firms, both in the hope that this will reduce costs, in conformity with the neo-liberal creed, and to get round the susceptibilities of their parliaments: the services provided by MPRI at the side of the Croatian Army, those of DynCorp in Columbia and Bosnia, or indeed the help given by Sandline to the government of Sierra Leone, have all given rise to endless comment ever since 1995.[63] At the same time, Washington and London were insisting in the Security Council that the Kroll cabinet, linked in particular to MI6 and the CIA, should be charged with the job of carrying out an inquiry into the holdings of the leaders of UNITA, to the great displeasure of French diplomacy, attached as it is to the state's sovereign prerogatives, anxious about powers of investigation being granted to a private operator and worried about the United Nations contracting with a western company at the risk of drawing the wrath of southern countries down on its head.[64]

The war on terrorism following the attacks of 11 September 2001 has naturally increased this association between the private sector and tasks of surveillance, repression and even belligerence, a collaboration which, we must emphasize, has been accompanied by a state come-back in the way the market operates. In particular, the American authorities have demanded from foreign banks information on the movement of funds, and have managed to gain access to the reservation systems of air companies landing in the United States to try and detect suspect passengers on the basis of their names, but also from the numbers of their credit cards, their dietary requirements, their previous journeys or where their journey was paid for.[65]

But fairness requires that we also mention the privatization of peace. The 'facilitation' of the negotiations between the protagonists of civil wars in which the Catholic community of Sant'Egidio, in collaboration with the Farnesina, the Curia and different Ministries of Foreign Affairs, have taken part, is a good example.[66] Several initiatives of this order have flourished on the outskirts of diplomatic and academic milieus, giving rise to new courses being taught (in particular at Harvard Law School, under the aegis of Roger Fisher) and to the creation of institutes or centres of a 'non-governmental' status such as the Henri-Dunant centre in Geneva, the kingpin of the precarious agreement between the Jakarta authorities and the national liberation movement of Aceh in 2002.[67]

The indirect and private administration of public force, or of the exercise of sovereignty is, however, irreducible to the neo-liberal times in which we are living. It has admittedly become more rarefied with the monopolization of war and violence by the state that occurred in the nineteenth century.[68] But it never disappeared, and has remained one possible mode in which the state can intervene. At the height of imperialist nationalism, at the end of the nineteenth century and the beginning of the twentieth, concessionary companies were entrusted with the task of colonization; the diplomatic and secret services of Israel, a strong state if ever there was one, operate at the interface of the private sector, especially in security services, armaments, the BTP, tourism and diamonds; the Second Bureau in France and the CIA in America have financed their covert actions in Indochina by the trade in heroin, in partnership with organized crime, what is left of the Kuomintang who have taken refuge in Myanmar, or the South Vietnamese air force of General Ky; and, during the 1970s and 1980s, the 'third force' in South Africa resorted to similar methods to counter the ANC or to destabilize the 'frontline countries'.[69] The 'Foccart networks' (and, later on, the 'Pasqua networks') in sub-Saharan Africa were merged with private interests and investments so as better to serve the grandeur of the Republic; and in Turkey, the 'deep state', soaked in a nationalist and centralizing ideology, did not hesitate to request the help of mafias and to rely on the militias of the 'village guardians' to repress the extreme left and Kurdish separatists.[70]

The contemporary phase of liberalization is thus limited to broadening and making more acceptable the degree to which the public power can operate repeatedly (if indirectly). Nonetheless, the public power holds the reins and is still in charge as a barely disguised protagonist if we consider, for example, the fact that many of the personnel of private security societies or peace institutes are ex-soldiers or diplomats no longer in full state service, who have gone on to work in the private sector. This is obvious in France, where private enterprises of protection increase and extend the grip of the police, to which they remain closely subject, in particular through the way the latter grants them authorization for their activities. And so it is actually less a matter of the privatization of public security than of the 'publicization' of private agents of protection assigned to tasks of public interest in accordance with the instructions, regulations and approval of the administration.[71] It is true that in the United States or Great Britain, the functions that are devolved to businesses (or elected citizens: the sheriffs) are more extensive, for reasons that stem from the history of government and the legal systems in those countries. Nonetheless, they are still limited by and subordinate to the law, although the practice of lynching or the effective conditions of detention in prisons managed by business have demonstrated that they were able to include the extra-judicial use of physical coercion on individuals.[72] In big firms and in western states, the subcontracting of security and protection is, these days, turning out to be more costly than was expected, and is therefore on the wane.[73] Great Britain, for its part, is returning to the radical deregulation of its economic sector, which it had experienced under Mrs Thatcher, and is restoring a system whereby the public power grants its approval to private security agents, as on the Continent. The increasingly hybrid quality of the private and public modes of policing is clearly in evidence when the insurance companies get the state to pass regulations that make it obligatory for certain 'at risk' professions or ordinary individuals to resort to forms of protection such as property security or electronic surveillance – services that are sold by companies which they themselves own or of which they are reference shareholders.[74]

Chancelleries have an expression to designate informal talks between experts, the representatives of 'civil society' and civil servants or politicians who constitute a significant proportion of international sociability and influence government action, in the shape of institutes or ad hoc conferences: 'track two'. This term deserves being extended beyond diplomatic activity, as this 'second track' principle shows how 'all the modes of interaction between public and private on which the welfare state rests'[75] are being systematically revised without the sovereignty of the state necessarily being impaired. 'In the western world', as Luc Rouban summarizes the situation, 'the "privatization" of the state designates less a disintegration or homogenization of the state than a transformation of power relations . . . [via] new technologies that allow one to accredit and involve social agents in a discretionary way, depending on the usefulness they are seen as having',[76] but also via a dilution of accountability that greatly boosts its absolute pre-eminence. 'Discharge' as a form of subjection: we will definitely need to come back to this theme, and take up some of Michel Foucault's ideas about the way the places of power are dispersed in liberal governmentality.

Meanwhile, we can follow those authors who, in growing numbers, are abandoning the sensational notion of the decline of the state and turning instead to the idea that it is being rebuilt and 'redeployed' in a 'new interventionism',[77] in the context of globalization. It is also plain common sense not to set up these two terms as if they were opposites or formed a zero-sum game, and to get away, once and for all, from the 'sterile debate of state versus globalization'.[78]

Finally, we need to remember that the way the state renounced certain of its prerogatives often preceded the big turn to liberalization of the 1980s and the fall of the Berlin Wall. The logic of 'blocs' in the Cold War had already eroded national sovereignty, and this process of the integration or internationalization of the state was even more marked in the western camp than in the Warsaw Pact countries, despite

what the 'Brezhnev doctrine' suggested: where the latter confiscated
sovereignty, the western bloc mutualized it.[79]

Likewise, the formation of the state in various Asian, African or
Latin American countries had long been based on private agents such
as businesses or religious institutions: the education system and health
service was often in the hands of the churches (or of those who played
the role of clergy in Muslim, Hindu or Buddhist societies); fiscal extraction or control, coercive if necessary, of the workforce, was left to multinationals, colonial companies or 'native' intermediaries – the so-called
'traditional' chiefs, for example – in particular in infrastructural projects, in plantation agriculture and in the mines; certain offices regulating the prices of agricultural products – such as the offices for the
stabilization of cocoa or coffee prices in the Ivory Coast and Cameroon
– brought together administration, producers and exporters; last, but
not least, given the emblematic character of the current civil war in
Sierra Leone, the repression of the diamond-smuggling trade in this
country had already been handed over to private security societies in
the 1950s, on the initiative of both De Beers and the British colonial
authorities.[80]

But having said this, we have not really said very much.[81] For who
could ever have imagined that the state, globalization or no globalization, would undergo historical change without a fuss? Global studies,
and the ideological chatter they foster, draw up the balance sheet of its
transformations with malevolent joy or open disquiet. The state no
longer does this; it no longer does that – so what? The discussion all
too easily gets dumbed down to the grave diagnosis offered by second-
ary-school teachers and pupils' parents: 'Standards are dropping.' In
spelling, they are probably right. But what about information technology? Let alone the fact that the sublimated model of the Westphalian
system of states, the yardstick of the theory of international relations
in all its glory (or terror), has failed to survive the scrutiny of
historians.[82]

If we are to delve deeper into the analysis of the composition of the
nation-state and its globalization, it will be useful to draw on a few
examples of the way these two things interact: the manufacture of historical memory; transnational trade; the constitution of international
civil society; the deregulation and indeed criminalization of political
power and the international economy.

The transnational production of national memories

Globalization, which people imagine as imbued by a sense of 'urgency',
as experienced by the 'man-living-in-the-present',[83] is often lived – as
we have pointed out – in the past. This was already the case in the

nineteenth century, which lies behind much of modernity – the invention of which was filtered through the invention of tradition, as in the now classic analysis of Eric Hobsbawm and Terence Ranger.[84] The contemporary phase of globalization has intensified this retrospective fever, giving it a tinge of 'nostalgia' which at times can be 'imperial'.[85] Museums have become major social institutions, perhaps even more than in the period when the nation-state was constructed and colonization was rife.[86] For the 'political museumizing' and 'logoization' of communal life that it facilitates is now accompanied by the economic activity, material culture and local historical heritage that are systematically put into the museum.

This museumizing concerns not only the 'imagination' of the civic community, but simultaneously two central processes of globalization to which we shall have to return: the commoditization of social life and the reactivation of the sense of locality. It is thus linked to the 'authentification of merchandise', which is one of the main modes of appropriation of globalization.[87]

If we stick to the purely political sphere, then the omnipresence of a past, which is sometimes envisaged in the shape of commemoration, sometimes in the terms of debt, repentance and reparation, goes far beyond the walls of the museum. Indeed, forgetting, concealing and denying have themselves become objects of polemic. The crystallization of the allegory of the Holocaust in the United States between 1970 and 1990;[88] the campaigns meant to sway opinion or, two decades ago, the actual attacks carried out to obtain Turkey's acknowledgement of the Armenian genocide under the Ottoman Empire; Japan's barely shame-faced flirtation with its militarism of bygone years; the elucidation of the fate of the 'disappeared' under the military dictatorships in Argentina, Uruguay and Chile, or during the last civil war in Algeria; the way the question of slavery took over the debates of the World Conference on Racism and Discrimination in Durban in 2001; the setting up of the international criminal tribunals in The Hague and Arusha and the establishment of the Permanent International Criminal Court; the spread of truth and reconciliation commissions; the law on the 'universal jurisdiction' of Belgian justice: these are just some of many examples of the proliferation of the politics of memory and its growing institutionalization. The relationship to the past is thus an element of 'global governance': it is one of the main themes of international relations in their two dimensions, transnational and intergovernmental; it gives rise to cooperation between NGOs or between administrations, and to effects of diffusion that contribute to the setting up of a new political machinery. They are narrow and dangerous waters that lie between 'negotiated transitions' to democracy, as in Spain, Argentina, Chile or South Africa, in the course of which the dismantling of authoritarian regimes is obtained in exchange for the impunity of those responsible for the repression which they had legitimized.[89]

What is interesting in this generalized memorializing experience is that it stems at one and the same time from the public policies of states, from the militancy or lobbying of non-governmental agents, from a worldwide circulation of information, images, know-how, experts, diplomats or committed citizens, and from the way that aid is made conditional on development or belonging to the European Union. So it is forged at the interface between the state and transnational movements, between the private and the public, with all the ensuing conflicts and arbitration between interests and ethics: under diplomatic pressure from Washington and Jerusalem, the Belgian government thus resigned itself to reducing the scope of the so-called law of 'universal jurisdiction'.[90]

But political memories remain national to an amazing degree even when they are borne by the movement of emigrants. 'Long-distance nationalisms'[91] – starting with extremist Armenian nationalism and Zionism, both dedicated to the commemoration of genocide – reveal the symbiosis between the idea of nation (or nation-state) and the social practices of globalization in this memorializing register. The posthumous celebration of the 75th anniversary of Beethoven's birth in his home town of Bonn, in 1845, had already constituted a most remarkable example of this. It brought together musical cosmopolitanism, German national sentiment, French and English chauvinism, the contradictory power games of the town councillors and the King of Prussia – all against a background of the commoditization of cigars, trousers and cravats 'à la Beethoven', and as a prelude to the 1848 'Springtime of the Peoples' (or indeed to the unleashing of the militaristic movements of the end of the 'long nineteenth century').[92]

A combination of circumstances of this kind acts as a vector for the way in which individuals are subjectivated, the way in which the political communities with which they identify are constituted, but also for the conditions of 'domination' (Herrschaft), of 'hegemony' or 'subjection' within them and within the mutual relations between them all.[93] From this point of view, historical memory is a complex and fallacious process whose emotional power is at least partly disconnected from the tangibility of facts. Without going as far as the grotesque consecration of Michael Jackson in the Akan village of Krinjabo in the Ivory Coast (his unconscious had suggested that his ancestors came from here),[94] the pilgrimages made to the island of Gorée by Afro-Americans with a hankering after 'roots' demonstrate it in an exaggerated way. It is not even certain that the famous House of Slaves actually ever was such a place, and it is certain that the majority of captives whose descendants people the United States did not come from Senegambia. Nonetheless, even if one needs to put a spin on the facts, it is easier and less dangerous to meet one's past a few cables' length away from Dakar than in

the delta of the Niger, in Fernando Po or Sao Tomé. The need felt by
Bill and Hillary (or by George W. and Laura) to have themselves pho-
tographed in the doorframe of the mythical door, which the ancestors
of their electors supposedly crossed, confirms that it is not actually just
a matter of cultural and family tourism, nor of any sorrowful or nostalgic contemplation of history, but rather of the self-expression of
contemporary power. In any case, one result of the Civil War, and the
massive European immigration and the social phenomenon of racism
that ensued, is that the memory of slavery in the United States assumed
a political importance out of all proportion to the slave labour that was
really transported there and to the effective conditions of its existence,
if we take as our measure the slave societies of the Caribbean or
Brazil.[95]

In its selective and deforming aspects, the memorializing narrative
is a relation of power, and the empty spaces left by what it forgets or
omits structures the usage of domination, as Michel-Rolph Trouillot has
shown in detail in his study of Haiti.[96] Ultimately, the narrative of
memory is the product of a rational transaction, as happens in 'negotiated transitions' – so it has been said of truth and reconciliation commissions, which have in fact brought neither truth nor, if we are to be
truthful, reconciliation.[97] The important point here is to see how the
global effects of historical memory – in other words, the transfers of its
political technology, the activism of emigrant communities, the intervention of the media worldwide or of the international community of
historians, and the pressure of NGOs – do not mark 'the crisis of the
national novel'[98] but quite the opposite: they participate in the production of 'domination', 'hegemony' or 'subjection' on the national scale.
And more fundamentally, we also need to grasp how the nation-state,
rather than the elusive dimension of global extent or the post-national
points of reference, remains the 'political site of the practices of
memory'[99] even though the latter are becoming globalized. The 'Grand
Narrative' – since there is such a narrative in postmodernity, *pace*
Derrida, *pace* Lyotard – of the Holocaust has thus legitimized Israel and
its conception of the 'national interest'. At the same time it has made
it easier to perpetuate a Jewish-American social identity within the
framework of the new multiculturalism and has led to a certain competitiveness (in more or less good taste) with Afro-Americans. As James
Baldwin wrote at the end of the 1960s:

One does not wish, in short, to be told by an American Jew that his suffering is as great as the American Negro's suffering. It isn't, and one
knows that it isn't from the very tone in which he assures you that it
is. . . . For it is not here, and not now, that the Jew is being slaughtered,
and he is never despised, here, as the Negro is, *because* he is an American.
The Jewish travail occurred across the sea and America rescued him from

the house of bondage. But America *is* the house of bondage for the Negro, and no country can rescue him.[100]

As an historical event that was both multinational and transnational, the extermination of the Jews and the way it is remembered have constantly been related to the state: to the idea of citizenship and nation, to its territorialization and to the social or foreign policy of governments, whether in Nazi Europe, America or Palestine.

Frontiers, smuggling and state-formation

We are forced to reach a similar conclusion if we consider the transnational commerce which, by definition, is reputed to betray and aggravate the state's weakness in a global situation, especially when it assumes the form of smuggling or customs fraud. A more subtle analysis of the flow of trade of this type generally leads one to qualify such assertions. Thus, the shady mass commerce that is practised from bases in the Kurdish provinces of Turkey, Iran and Iraq, from the port of Dubai, Afghanistan or indeed Pakistani Baluchistan neither weakens nor contradicts as much as is sometimes made out the different states that seem, at first glance, to be the losers as a result – and this is true from the viewpoint of both their tax revenue and their territorial sovereignty. We need to remember, first of all, that smuggling is the result of the institution of the nation-state, and in particular of the creation of frontiers, which are indispensable to generating the value of the products that are fraudulently exchanged. According to this tried-and-tested formula, the frontier is vital to the smuggler, and in all these countries of central or southern Asia Minor, he maintains relations with the public authorities which, although ambivalent, are nonetheless intimate.[101]

In fact, smuggling became prevalent as a social phenomenon in Kurdistan after the creation of Iraq, following the First World War.[102] It has continued to prosper there, under the aegis of the state rather than in opposition to it. If we merely stick to the recent period, the fraudulent importing of Iraqi fuel via Turkey, following the 1991 war in Kuwait, and in violation of United Nations sanctions, came about not only with the authorization and complicity of the authorities in Baghdad, anxious to find a way round the constraints of the embargo and the 'Oil for Food' arrangements, but also with the assent of those in Ankara, who saw it as a form of compensation for the economic and financial losses entailed by the conflict, officially estimated at 35–40 billion dollars, but more probably around 20 billion. From September 1994, Turkey thus smuggled in each year between 3 and 3.5 million metric tons of diesel and some 2 million tons of crude oil, either by road or, once the 'Oil for Food' programme had been set up in 1996, by pipeline. Thus it was that tens of thousands of lorries supplying the governorships of the Iraqi north with consumer products returned to Turkey loaded with diesel, at a rate of 4,800 litres per turnaround and 1.5 million metric tons per year. During the same period, private companies that had been granted official licences imported an extra 1.5 million metric tons of diesel, outside the United Nation's quotas, for TPIC, a branch of the national Turkish oil company (TPAO). Furthermore, in order to discharge their debt, Iraq delivered 2 million metric tons of crude oil to Turkey, which was over and above the quotas authorized on the Kirkuk-Ceyhan pipeline.

The Turkish state took pains to keep the upper hand politically and to profit from these flows of goods that would provide a living for some 500,000 people. From spring 2000 onwards, it thus forced the private transporters of contraband diesel to sell it to the depot of Silopi, near the frontier post of Habur, which enabled it to charge taxes on the fuel, but also to pick up a comfortable margin between a particularly advantageous purchase price and the price of resale to private or public redistributors, including the national company, Petrol Ofisi. As it happened, the private transporters managed blithely to ignore (or almost) these obligations, which penalized them financially, made them waste long hours waiting at the frontier post of Habur and limited their turnaround. By finding more points at which they could pass across the frontiers with Iraq, Iran and even Azerbaijan, they continued to supply directly the majority of the service stations in the south-east of Anatolia, even when the Turkish government slowed down semi-official fuel imports after autumn 2001, so as to bring pressure to bear on the Iraqi Kurdish parties which also drew revenue from them.[103] But this does not contradict the fact that the state is an agent, and sometimes even the initiator, of smuggling. Far from being the impotent spectator of such supposedly damaging activities, the state integrates them into its public policies. In 1992–3, Saddam Hussein, for example, deliberately used this process when buying wheat grown in the autonomous region of Kurdistan at a higher price than that which local authorities could offer, so as to maintain that region in its state of economic dependency (since he could not occupy it militarily).[104]

Fariba Adelkhah has shown how, in the case of Iran, smuggling and customs fraud with Dubai have to some extent played the role of a town-and-country planning policy by enabling the southern coastal regions to develop and thus match up to the pre-eminence of the northern provinces. Furthermore, the fraud has contributed to a certain cultural unification of society by making it easier to spread 'global' consumer goods on a national scale, beyond regional, ethnic or religious splits.[105] According to sources to which all concur, some of the principal institutions of the Islamic Republic are participants in these illicit flows of goods – which in any case are based on formal exchanges and supported by the 'frontiers', territorial or administrative, of the state: the Guardians of the Revolution, the Foundation of the Disinherited, and the services of the Guide of the Revolution which, between them, control this or that sector of fraudulent imports, 'launder' them by hiding their commercial value, or 'protect' the economic agents who take part in them, while the Central Bank operates on Dubai's money market and until 2003 benefited from the difference between the free price and the official price of the Iranian rial. It is generally impossible to tell the difference between the lucrative private motivations of authorities that indulge in these practices and their more general political considerations. A detour via the United Arab Emirates (or Cyprus) is indispensable as a way of making up for American sanctions. And, at Zahedan, fuel managers endeavour to limit the unauthorized export of petrol to Pakistan, which the price gap between the two countries has stimulated, by establishing a system of ration cards, but they do not intend to put a complete stop to a traffic which is known to be vital to the survival of numerous families and the social peace of the region.[106] It is also essentially for political reasons that Iran has tolerated the cabotage along its coasts of barges carrying Iraqi petrol exported outside the 'Oil for Food' programme and delivered to tankers off the coast of Dubai, even if these facilities have exacted a price. Finally, the intervention of the central bank on Dubai's money market attests first and foremost to its know-how, which analysts all recognize, and, second, to the influence of private interests. Nonetheless, the political economy of this transnational anchorage of the Islamic Republic in its regional or global environment is also propitious to the enrichment of individuals or families, which is revealed at regular intervals as a result of scandals and trials.[107]

Research carried out in sub-Saharan Africa confirms such conclusions.[108] In Cameroon and Chad, the administration, semi-public enterprises, local authorities, ministers and even the head of state – as has been proven in the case of Idriss Deby – are involved in smuggling and customs frauds which do not undermine the sovereignty of the state, or even the way the national space is structured.[109] The neighbouring regions from which these illicit flows of goods are organized are 'space-movements',[110] whose fleeting nature can be clearly read from the weakness of investments, whether in property or production, which they entail, from the precarious nature of the developed sites they shelter, from their contingency and dependence on the vagaries of regional commerce, and the ups and downs of politics and the transformations of road transport or other types of infrastructure. They do not constitute long-term poles of 'development' which would be capable of territorializing processes of primitive accumulation independent of national economies. They even tend to consolidate the territorial framework of the latter by bringing a greater administrative, police and political presence from the centre to the frontiers, even if only in the form of an increasing number of barrages of 'racket control', reinforcing the way the frontier is integrated into the rest of the state's space, by enriching the towns and cities in the hinterland. In short, the neighbouring regions are, in Central Africa, part of an 'internal recomposition of national territories' rather than a means whereby they are dismembered.[111]

The smuggling and fraud that flourish in these areas are, so to speak, the shadow cast by the actions of the public power. The 'beach *Ville*' (in Brazzaville) and 'Ngobila' (in Kinshasa), where the ferries dock that link the two capitals across the river Congo, and which are, as it were, the lungs of a fruitful commerce based on the increasing importance attributed to the shortages resulting from the Civil War, bear permanent witness to it. This is sometimes dramatic, when the capture of interests by the forces of order and the (ubiquitous) administrations entails the deaths of human beings. It is sometimes comical, as when ways of getting round the rules turn into slapstick comedy. Thus at the end of the 1990s, the handicapped used a regulation exonerating them from customs duty to turn their wheelchairs into vehicles overladen with several hundreds of kilos worth of merchandise, and they rented out their services to local traders.[112] The physical presence of the state, whose different services opened a large number of offices and dispatched many officials to the river ports, was in cahoots with the swarming crowd of merchants, 'mamans', illicit street vendors, porters, thieves and other 'floating populations'. The traffic follows the paths laid out by public policies and vice versa.

Cross-border commerce between Togo and Ghana is perhaps an even more interesting phenomenon, since it was accompanied by an irredentist Ewe movement that made use of the division of German Togoland between the United Kingdom and France at the end of the First World War. On the one hand, this demand, formulated by intellectuals and civil servants, misfired. On the other, smuggling constitutes a 'daily vote of confidence in the status quo' and reinforces the awareness of their respective differences among the inhabitants of Togo and of Ghana, since border communities play an active part in shaping national cultures and even the contours of the state as such.[113] And so it becomes easier to understand the non-existence or scarcity of separatist movements – and even civil war – to the south of the Sahara. The reproduction of frontiers inherited from colonization is not only the consequence of the *petitio principii* of the charter of the Organization for African Unity, adopted in 1963, and the destruction of the pan-African ideal by the puppets of imperialism. It rests on the social practices of the border populations themselves, which see in it opportunities as well as constraints. In this respect, smugglers are the first to validate and consolidate the 'territories' of the state, rather than signalling its 'end'. Their particular art is not a 'hidden transcription' of resistance to domination, but one contribution among others (however involuntary and unconscious) to the formation of the state.[114]

Europe had already provided a similar example. Daniel Nordman has established in detail how, in the case of France:

> [T]he existence of smuggling is at the exact place where the preoccupations of the state and obscure local activities come together. . . . It is in this relation that the state as such is constituted. Smuggling is naturally associated, in the minds of the administrators, jurists and historians, with the image of a state solidly entrenched within its frontiers, which it reveals, and which it contributes to defining and hardening.

A legendary person such as Mandrin, who smuggled into the kingdom of France skins and leather, grain, tobacco, gunpowder, lead and painted canvases, and into Savoy salt, colonial products and fabrics, underlined 'the spatial, territorial and indeed national image of the activity and the crime of smuggling, and made the relation between state frontier and economic infraction even more rigid'.[115] Furthermore, we see how the concretion of the state is interwoven with transnational logics, in accordance with a recurrent pattern that definitely needs to be brought to bear on the heart of an analysis of globalization.

Take the case of Libya.[116] The personal power of Colonel Gaddafi is based in particular on the tribe of the Qaddadfa in the region of Sebha, which is controlled on his behalf by the powerful governor General Abdel Hafiz Massoud, his cousin by marriage, and in addition a former commander of the Libyan expeditionary force to the Chad. The latter, as well as the main families in the said tribe, have control over the cross-border trade with Niger, whose main operators are the Toubou, a 'floating' and nomadic population living on horseback on the outer edges of different Saharan States. This trade consists in the export of subsidized Libyan products (pasta, oil, sugar, flour, tomato sauce, Qaryouni television sets) and the import of American cigarettes from Cotonou (a dozen or so lorries per week, each of them representing a profit of 165,000 euros) and female dromedaries (resold in herds of a thousand heads, costing 670 euros each). General Massoud and the leading members of the Qaddadfa community also supervise the arrival of some 5,000 sub-Saharan migrants per month; these provide a clandestine workforce that is locally at everyone's beck and call, and their transit northwards, or even to Europe, brings in new revenue (110 euros per passenger for the transfer to Tripoli, between 1,000 and 1,500 for the crossing to Italy). The political 'protection' of transnational flows of people and goods is simultaneously a source of accumulation, an element of negotiation in support for the central power, a way of preserving civil peace by co-opting or using the Toubou in this cross-border political economy, and an exercise in military and diplomatic sovereignty in so far as General Massoud is in charge of mediating between the Chad government and the rebellion of the Movement for Democracy and Justice in Chad (MDJC). It is evident that state power is not falling apart as a result of this illicit commerce, or because of the way society is organized by family lineage; rather, state power is strengthened by such processes.

But that can't be right, certain people will object. Does not the Libyan regime claim to be under the leadership of the 'Great Jamahiriya', explicitly denying that it is a state? But this would be to take at face value the daydreams of Gaddafi, and to underestimate the perception of other states in the international system which are not taken in – either by bombardments or sanctions or conferences. The same people will add: well, be that as it may, is it not true that tribal organization is the only factor that counts for anything? But this would entail forgetting that this is in no way antithetical to the formation of the state, as many studies in historical sociology or political anthropology have shown over and over again. It is merely one type among others of that hybridization of public and private by which sovereignty is exercised and capital accumulated.

The concrete political integration of societies stems in large part from the split and fragmentary workings of an interwoven network of personal and informal relationships – between and within families, merchants, religions, colleagues and other groups. The transnational extensions of these are essential. I spoke of Africa in terms of a 'rhizome state' to designate the 'protean multiplicity of networks, the subterranean stems of which link together scattered points in the society', and which close the feedback loop between society and postcolonial political institutions.[117] The notion would not be a bad way of describing the realities of *guangxi* China, or the Iran of the 'bond' (*râbeteh*), of the Turkey of the 'godfather' (*baba*). But the adventitious roots of such rhizome states, from which they secretly draw nourishment, frequently go deep down into the humus of the transnational 'second economy'. This has been shown to be true in the three countries I have just mentioned, in particular China, where the authorities are definitely not inclined to repress corporations that indulge in the manufacture of fake goods, or people-smuggling rings, and where the Army, the Customs and the Party are associated with various illicit activities.[118]

Another paradigm case is Touba, the holy city of the brotherhood of the Murids, and hence the capital of smuggling, fraud and Wolof emigration to Europe and North America. Touba is not the subversive Other of the state or the Senegalese political system. It finances its ruling class, provides it with most of its opportunities for enrichment, acts as a frame for its electorate and defuses the potential for social protest represented by a supernumerary population of unemployed young people. Dakar, with its pasteboard ministers, is merely its double, its astral body.

Ultimately, the state is indistinguishable from the informal or illicit activity of importation and re-exportation, as in Gambia, Togo, Benin, Equatorial Guinea, Burundi and Somalia, but also, to varying degrees, in the Baltic countries, Dubai, Lebanon, Cyprus, Afghanistan and Colombia. The word 'entrepôt' which economists use to describe this activity seems to be too polite and modest. It would be better to call a spade a spade, and a contraband state a contraband state, thus admitting that transnational commerce, however illegal it may be in the eyes of the law, does not necessarily contradict the processes of territorial sovereignty, or the ways in which the political dimension becomes autonomous – both of which lead to 'domination' or 'subjection'.

A very national 'international civil society'

This type of paradox is also found in the way that 'international civil society' is mobilized – a society which is also accused of undermining the mechanisms, legitimacy and demand for accountability of the public power.[119] Beyond the rowdy appearances of the demonstrations that now disturb the peace of mind of the mighty men of this world when they gather together, we need to ask a few questions about this 'agent' whom we have already met at work in the nineteenth century, in the last chapter, and who is now – so they claim – redefining the rules of the global game. Not without a certain theoretical or ideological confusion, the apology for 'civil society' has simultaneously presented itself as the key element of the 'minimum state' so dear to neo-liberals, of the anti-globalizing demands of leftist militants and of the new 'governance' to which has been given the responsibility, in the dreams of social democratic technocrats, for 'mastering' globalization. It has become the 'useful fiction'[120] par excellence of the double 'transition' in which the 1990s saw themselves reflected: the transition to the market economy, and the transition to democracy.

In so doing, it has not escaped a ridiculous anthropomorphism, and its success with such antagonistic ideological currents is in itself suspect. Diplomats, journalists, 'developers', philanthropists and, of course, NGOs invoke civil society as a divinity with a redemptive mission, and when the occasion arises they come out to meet 'her', consult 'her' or finance 'her', in spite of the fact that 'she' covers a heterogeneous mixture of organizations, movements and mobilizations which all pursue objectives that are no less disparate. The degree to which 'she' is institutionalized is also extremely variable. 'Civil society' is sometimes manifested in well-established transnational networks, especially in the domain of the defence of human rights or the protection of the environment, and sometimes in alliances or coalitions that are more specific and precisely delimited, such as the International Committee on Dams, Rivers and People.[121] Furthermore, civil society is not defined the same way in every country, and the transnational logic it is supposed to transmit in the eyes of its devotees has to compromise with different national identities. The French include only those NGOs that are voluntary associations; the Americans include businesses, consultancy firms and other stakeholders.[122] These differences of conception and method are obvious, and extend to the defence of the most universal and least disputable cause there is: that of human rights. The associative and militant tradition represented, for example, by the International Federation of Human Rights, French in origin, contrasts with the professionalized lobbying of the Human Rights Watch (the French equivalent is Reporters sans Frontières). A real competitiveness may ensue, or even on-the-spot conflicts, in spite of the common objectives and the several forms of cooperation that bring these agents together.[123]

Be that as it may, these approximations should not conceal the inanity of the concept of 'civil society' when it is misappropriated from one of the philosophical works from which it comes, and treated in abstraction from the concept of the state to which it refers. In this case, the fact that the error has been internationalized does not diminish its scope. And there is a certain incongruity in hearing the praises of 'international civil society' being sung by those who also report that the state has been rendered bankrupt by globalization. Resorting to this notion in the absence of any precise definition of the 'global state', or of any apprehension of the state's place in globalization, is a piece of theoretical nonsense.[124] More generally, 'civil society', reduced to a binary opposition with the 'state', is nothing other than a 'form of schematization proper to a particular technology of government', that of liberalism.[125] Not only can this disjunction not be seen as a 'historical and political universal which can enable us to scrutinize all concrete systems',[126] with all due respect to the advertising executives of today, but this dichotomy refers to a fallacious otherness – that of a 'state that holds power and exercises its sovereignty over a civil society which, in itself, is not the trustee of similar processes of power'.[127]

But 'civil society', however 'international' it may now be, is itself an asymmetric field of power in which the effects of competition, hierarchy or exclusion are intense, and which in simple terms reflects the global division of wealth and influence. We need only compare the North Atlantic NGOs with their equivalents in the South to become convinced of this, even though India, or various countries in Latin America, now find a place for dynamic associations of an international standard (while the converse is true of Japan or South Korea, which keep 'anti-globalization' movements at arm's length). The annual summits of the World Social Forum have nothing peaceful about them, for example, and are the site of fierce confrontations between movements of different origins and sensibilities, which are sometimes explicable as a result of a certain carnivalesque principle of inversion. 'If the Anglo-Saxons have imposed their liberal model, it is out of the question that they should also define the canons of anti-globalization', grumbled Bernard Cassen, the President of Attac, at Porto Alegre in January 2001; he was justifying the curbing of North American NGOs, an action to which he had resorted alongside his Brazilian hosts.[128] Likewise, the World Conference against Racism, Racial Discrimination, Xenophobia and Related Intolerance, in Durban, 2001, saw the NGOs that promote the defence of human rights tearing each other to pieces on the question of the Near East: they fell into a North–South divide, or at any event one of Arab countries versus the United States, and it ended in a fiasco for several of them, traumatized or discredited by the violence of the confrontation.

In particular, the constitutive organizations of 'civil society' are an essential part of 'governance' (or 'governmentality'), both national *and* global, of which they risk becoming mere cogs in the machine from the point of view of political co-option, economic accumulation, ideological legitimization or quite simply of foreign policy.

On the national level, NGOs become mere instruments in two ways. Sometimes this process is deliberate and highly conscious, or at least a twofold investment comes into play. On the one hand, they allow those who oppose or are independent of the circles of state power to mobilize symbolic, political and material resources so as to assert themselves as interlocutors of the latter, to build up their own influence or to accumulate wealth from their international supports and their position as intermediaries between their society and its external environment. It is not without interest to remember at this point a considerable proportion of development aid goes to NGOs and that, in the 1990s, they became major collectors of multilateral and bilateral credit. They thus offer tangible opportunities for *empowerment*, so long as this term is cleansed of its naively populist connotation. It is neither the 'people' nor their 'communities' that take control of their destinies, but well-defined individuals or groups that invoke the *manes* of the 'people' or the 'community' to legitimize their social and economic ascent. To run an NGO is to turn oneself into an advocate for collective ideals or interests, sometimes at the risk of one's liberty or one's life, but it can also, in other (or the same) circumstances, mean receiving gifts or advantageous loans, benefiting from customs duties exemptions or privileged tax deals, and being surrounded by the halo of international recognition. Never short of a pungent turn of phrase, the Cameroonians do not beat about the bush: they talk of 'good ways of putting pressure on western purses', of 'the latest trick of the trade ... for getting access to credit lines', of 'dummy companies behind which businessmen, but also and above all politicians, can hide', of 'preferential treatment, codes which enable certain people in the know to extort money'.[129] Thus, a certain development association that is well known in Dakar imports each year several dozens of vehicles: and you do not need to be much of an expert to guess that it resells them at a competitive price thanks to its customs exemptions.[130]

On the other hand, the supporters of state power, themselves conscious of the financial and ideological transformations which the international system has seen since the swing to neo-liberal policies in the 1980s, have drawn support from NGOs, or have quite simply created them, so as to make of them the instruments of political intervention and mobilization of international resources, particularly in the areas of development aid, pressure diplomacy and even intelligence and military operations. No offence to noble souls, but humanitarian impulses themselves have been 'nationalized, incorporated into the state, and above all militarized, leading some people to denounce the birth of a "military-humanitarian complex," '[131] and, rightly or wrongly, the reputation of an NGO such as International Alert, International Rescue Committee or Christian Solidarity has found itself sullied as a result.

GONGOS (government-oriented non-governmental organizations) are now an elementary piece of state engineering on the global stage, a central cog in global 'governance'. Tunisia is, from this point of view, a good example. There, the authorities have created an artificial 'civil society', setting up ever more 'RGOs' – i.e. 'really governmental organizations' – to please its western allies, but also to get its hands on the funds which the latter allocate to the said 'civil society'.[132] The grotesque distortion between the excessively police-like character of the regime and this piece of window-dressing, which makes it eligible (and how!) for finance from the Euro-Mediterranean Partnership, should not deceive anyone. This is not a case that simply tests certain norms to the limit, but is right at the heart of the matter. For, as it happens, the function of this smokescreen 'civil society' consists in disguising and discrediting a highly concrete expression of the Tunisian society or nation: that is, the Islamist sphere of influence or social movement, more or less politicized, which the Barcelona Process is trying to ward off, with its hand on its democratic heart as it pledges the values of the rule of law and 'good governance', but with the support of police cooperation.[133]

The constitution of such a block of NGOs placed at the service of an unlikely couple, openness together with stability, or vice versa, is also found in several other political societies, in the course of the change of scale that is inherent in globalization. From this point of view, those who hold authoritarian power, their organic auxiliaries, their foreign partners, multilateral backers, are like Monsieur Jourdain, who was speaking prose without knowing it: they are speaking the language of Gramsci without knowing it. They can sense that 'the state is simply an outer ditch', behind which stands 'a powerful system of fortresses and earthworks'.[134] In the 'transitional' situations of the 1990s, the combined efforts of political authorities and social elites that are generally described as 'moderate', but which could also be called 'conservative', created more and more associative fortresses behind which the structure of inequality is reproduced, decked out in an institutional finery that has hardly changed. In China, the hopes that some people had placed in 'civil society' when Tiananmen Square was occupied by students have misfired. Entrepreneurs had little sympathy for a movement which, by demanding democracy, threatened to shake the established order. In their minds, the categorical imperative of the 'market' seems to have completely disconnected from this demand: yes to 'reform' (*gaige*); no to 'transformation' (*gaizao*)! Even the denunciation of corruption and the emphasis laid on transparency aroused conflicting feelings in them, depending on the size and shape of the firm they managed, and for the most important of them, *guanxi*, or 'networking' with bureaucracy, seems to have comprised a more satisfactory solution to their practical difficulties than the adventure of political liberty and economic emancipation.[135] Other sectors of Chinese society did not show much solidarity with the protesters either, even if they did help them individually when they were hit by repressive measures. Nonetheless, the relative liberalization of the regime expressed itself, here as elsewhere, by the creation of a web of 'associations' or 'societies' (*shetuan*): nobody has claimed that these threatened the regime, but it is clear that it provided a means of pulling the wool over the eyes of foreigners and raising money from businesses, thanks in particular to their administrative connections. A far from negligible number of those in charge of them are in any case themselves bureaucrats or Party cadres.[136]

These links between the state apparatus and 'civil society' are also the rule in the very different context of sub-Saharan Africa. Either ministers found NGOs in their turn to dupe the givers of aid, or, on a more massive scale, civil servants take the initiative to build up rural development associations in their villages or original chieftainships. They are behaving as 'elites', as the term in use in French-speaking countries has it. The 'development brokerage' practised by these urban or urban–rural social categories, the 'stacking up' of administrative, associative, customary or entrepreneurial structures bequeathed by colonial and postcolonial history, are at the centre of the local political economy.[137] Seen from this angle, NGOs then participate directly in the production of social inequality in the crucible of the state. The ambiguity of the situation stems in part from the fact that 'the bureaucracy – however paradoxical this may seem – in many respects presents the characteristics of a social movement' whose progressive rise, since the period between the two world wars, 'has represented a sort of revolution . . . in favour of a non-negligible minority of "younger people" '. 'In a bizarre aberration, the possibilities of advance in civil society seem to be burdened right from the start by the fact that this process is controlled by the force that is least able to exercise power democratically' – this was an observation, and a prognosis, that could be made long before the political changes of the 1990s.[138]

It thus seems that the principle whereby the public and the private spheres overlap does not spare the world of so-called NGOs. Is this a youthful error, proper to states whose civil society is 'primitive and gelatinous', as Gramsci put it?[139] It is far from sure. The hybrid status of the International Committee of the Red Cross (ICRC), the tutelary jewel in the crown of humanitarian action, has been an illuminating precedent right from the start. Its mandate – to protect and assist the victims of armed conflicts – was conferred on it by states, by means of the four Geneva Conventions of 1949 and their additional protocols of 1977. These texts followed the first Geneva Convention of 1864, signed by twelve governments at the end of a diplomatic conference which the Helvetic Confederation had summoned to extend the private initiative of Henri Dunant and the Geneva Society of Public Utility. The ICRC remains a private organization, non-governmental in character, but it is different from NGOs properly speaking. It has, for instance, managed to have *accords de siège* in most of the countries in which it intervenes – agreements which are based on international law and grant it the privileges and immunities from which intergovernmental organizations generally benefit. Such an *accord de siège* has, furthermore, been signed with Switzerland itself, affirming the independence of the institution from the authorities in Berne. Nonetheless, the national anchorage of the ICRC is, so to speak, consubstantial, since its supreme organ, the Committee (or Assembly) is composed of between fifteen and twenty-five members, all of Swiss nationality. More than half its financing comes, furthermore, from states which have signed the Geneva Conventions.

The ambiguous nature of the ICRC is easily criticized by the hardline purists of humanitarian action. But these days, most of the big NGOs or western foundations also prosper in the interstices of public spending, living off subsidies, contracts or delegated funds granted to them by the authorities, and they claim less to take over from the state than to appeal to the latter in order to constrain it to take the causes they defend into consideration. Should the case arise, they see themselves being awarded, together with their equivalents in the South, various advantages granted by the nation-state or else by the multilateral system of which it is a part. They have thus become ubiquitous within the United Nations, to which 2,010 of them are accredited. John Ruggie, previously the Assistant Secretary-General, states that 'the UN would be incapable of doing what it does without the cooperation of the NGOs': 'One could not have better partners!'[140]

It is thus tempting to see them as having, at first glance, a function as tribunes, sometimes in the national framework and sometimes on the international scale. Michael Hardt and Toni Negri ironically call them 'the mendicant orders of the Empire'.[141] Occasionally, they are even its 'warrior orders', sheltering (more or less consciously) the plots of secret services and demanding, in the name of duty or the right to interfere, the military intervention of 'their' government – just like their ancestors who defended the case of slaves, Christians or national minorities.[142]

But it would be taking the shadow for the substance if we did not go further than this diagnosis. The forces of 'international civil society' are a 'powerful system of fortresses and earthworks', and as such they occupy above all a constitutive place not only in global 'governance' and its 'transactions', but of global 'governmentality', i.e. the relations of power that comprise globalization. On closer analysis, they are the privileged vehicles – sometimes in the literal sense of the word – of the 'actions' on which global 'action' is exercised. They are, in particular, one of the nodal points of what could be called 'glocalization', in which the 'local' and the 'global' are brought together, in the framework of public policies of 'sustainable development', environmental protection, humanitarian intervention, the promotion or defence of a whole series of 'human rights', whether individual or collective. From a neo-Foucauldian point of view, Michael Hardt and Toni Negri bring out more precisely how, on the most general level, the activities of these NGOs coincide with the activities of Empire 'beyond the political', in the area of bio-power, by satisfying the needs of life itself.[143] We will need to come back to this in a later chapter. For the time being, the essential thing is to grasp that the fibre of 'international civil society' is like the tendon of globalization: it ensures that the state is integrated into globalization and vice versa; it contributes to the engendering of social inequality on the planetary scale and to its organizational or political ramifications.

So it is that in Africa the NGOs and the problematics of 'civil society' which have been promoted by backers, by means of a twofold struc-tural adjustment to the market economy and democracy, have con-trived to bring about a multilateral version of the process of co-optation, the driving force behind the colonial and postcolonial 'passive revolu-tion'.[144] The international institutions of aid and development, in par-ticular the World Bank and the IMF, have taken over the 'transformist' ideology of exhausted one-party regimes by recruiting or financing the continent's counter-elites and assigning them to apolitical formulations of questions that are thoroughly political: those of the construction of the state, the way it is linked to the global economy, its social foundations and its relation with poverty. In a remarkable book on Lesotho, James Ferguson had already showed how the language of 'development' was thus an 'anti-politics machine'.[145] A fortiori, the moralistic celebration of 'good governance', of 'transparency' and 'market democracy', the puerile glorification of the informal sector as 'another path' for capitalist growth to take, the extolling of concrete society in the shape of its hypostasized form, 'civil society' – all these themes blunt the force of political critique and render the idea of revolution useless, at the same time as ideologically whitewashing the circulation of aid provided to regimes which could hardly be more 'political'.

In this situation, NGOs occupy a crucial place, and one that precedes the turn to neo-liberalism. The churches, which are, it must be remembered, transnational institutions, tended to form all by themselves the 'only' civil society, at least at the start of colonization.[146] They were one of the seedbeds for both nationalism and the state, in particular thanks to their work in health and education. In short, they were one of the cogs of the 'politics of the belly', defined as a historical configuration of governmentality.[147] They still are: witness their interventions (often courageous but, objectively, ambiguous and conservative) in different 'democratic transitions' throughout the 1990s.[148] Their revolutionary propensity was indeed reduced by the fact that the Holy See wished at any price to stave off the appearance of any African 'theology of liberation' or the arising of a sub-Saharan Père Aristide.[149]

The churches of the Christian establishment are these days flanked by various other forces which are their offspring, direct heirs or competitors. These several different associations, organizations, sects or churches, all purportedly 'independent', have joined in the confused task of state-formation: various activities have been delegated to them by the state, and to it they have often added a certain legitimacy, especially on the international scene. Rwanda, a very Catholic country, was a model of its kind, being controlled by foreign NGOs, and praised for the vigour of its 'civil society' before the tragedy of genocide exploded that particular myth.[150] Burkina Faso, which also basked in the glow of a flattering reputation, is its equivalent in West Africa – a fact which has hitherto evaded those who denounce the authoritarian character of the regime of Blaise Compaoré and his proven involvement in the conflicts of that region.

Nonetheless, the test case remains the way the mighty organization Oxfam, succumbing to an acute fit of 'Tanzaphilia', and blinded by the seductive experience (albeit one that was brutally interrupted in 1969) of the Ruvuma Development Association, made it possible to establish the officially conceived system of *Ujamaa*, and more specifically the coercive programme of 'villagization', with all that this involved in terms of the forced displacement of rural populations and the expulsion into the countryside of the unemployed or homeless of Dar es Salaam. In this way Oxfam became not just the propagandist of, but indeed 'the surrogate of the state', helping the latter to deprive peasants of their political power and representation.[151] The way in which 'international civil society' becomes compromised in the concrete exercise of domination can go very far. In the camp at Kakuma, in Kenya, which takes in Sudanese refugees and is at least partly under the control of the Sudanese People's Liberation Army, justice is administered by so-called 'traditional' magistrates. The latter hand down punishments involving whipping or detention in a prison built with the assistance of an international NGO, whose young guard brandishes a whip in full view of the numerous foreign visitors who supervise this masterpiece of humanitarian aid.[152] This is no doubt an extreme example, but it has the advantage of bringing out fully the involuntary collaboration of the 'NGO nebula' in global discipline.

In an incisive article on Egypt, Julia Elyachar establishes how there is cooperation between the NGOs which distribute 'micro-credit' and supervise the way it is paid back by its beneficiaries, the multinational institutions or bilateral backers which finance it at source, the banks which oversee its transfer, and the state which manages the Social Fund created at the demand of the World Bank to cover the finance needs of the informal sector and the so-called 'communitarian' community, imbued with values that for their part are described are 'cultural'. The author raises a provocative question: can NGOs 'be a new form of "indirect rule", since the native culture is yet again being mobilized in order to control the natives, but this time via international finance?' Indeed, the model of micro-credit 'has produced a new field of power, which makes light of the borders between states, multinational organizations and NGOs': these latter manage funds 'on behalf of an international finance which speaks the language of the market and of civil society'; where necessary, they contract with the multinationals, as in the case of the famous Grameen Bank of Bangladesh, which, in 1998, signed an agreement with the no less famous Monsanto to distribute its transgenic seeds and collect payments for it.[153]

The 'international civil society' on which so many neo-Habermasian hopes are placed would thus be less a vehicle of democratization or social justice than another form of the control or administration of the periphery by the centre of the global system of power and accumulation, as it were a new type of 'decentralized despotism'[154] on which the imperial regime of the foundational nineteenth century was built. It would be a way in which states become 'privatized'. As such, it would ensure there was a close link between concrete political societies and the processes of globalization, in counterpoint to reforms of economic liberalization, the traditional interplay of powers and the activity of different businesses. It would thus be imbued with the same ambivalence which characterized the 'dialogue'[155] between colonies and metropolises and marked the subsequent universalization of the state. It would in any event confirm that the formation of the latter definitely owes a great deal to transnational flows.

Transnational crime in the service of the state

And this indeed is what the analysis of 'transnational global criminality' has finally convinced us of. An entire literature denounces the proliferation of 'mafias' thanks to economic and financial liberalization, the narcotics rent and the revolution in telecommunications, as one of the main dangers with which democracy is confronted. The joint ventures established between the different national or ethno-national 'milieus' – for example between the Sicilian mafia, the *mafiya* of the CIS, Chinese Triads, Colombian cartels, and Nigerian drug-traffickers – are often cited as various manifestations either of a gigantic transnational plot against the legitimate sovereignty of the state, or, if not, of its mechanical erosion under the pressures of the market and the corruption of the latter.[156] The 'Prague Summit' between Russian and Italian associations of criminals in 1993[157] thus took on a symbolic dimension: at the apogee of globalization, gangsters from every country will soon be able to get together to sacrifice the virtue of the republic on the altar of crime.

But the best-informed investigations and analyses give the lie to such a fantasy, the grounds for which (in ideology or considerations of security) are sometimes perfectly clear.[158] Those who take part in 'transnational global criminality' do not constitute a homogeneous social category from the point of view of their internal organization, their cultural repertoires or their specializations, nor from that of their objectives or fields of activity. The latter, furthermore, remain as often as not national or local, and are far from being really 'globalized'.[159] In addition, there is nothing to indicate that the ratio between legal business and illicit business – since both are closely tied up with one another rather than being mutually exclusive – has increased drastically, and the estimates of 'gross criminal product' are not based on any proper methodology.[160] Finally, the major political phenomena that are generally correlated with this alleged increase in transnational criminality, in particular corruption and civil war, cannot be reduced to it. The former stems in the first place from the way the world market works, and depends on the initiative of the most highly reputed businesses or public administrations; the latter from social histories of such complexity that they are susceptible to contradictory scholarly interpretations, like the conflict in Sierra Leone; these histories cannot in any case be seen as simply the results of 'greed' or 'grievances' – *pace* Paul Collier, one of the court economists at the World Bank.[161]

In short, the 'Grand Narrative' of global transnational crime hardly stands up to an examination of the facts.[162] And where crime is at work, it does not necessarily undermine the state – of which it remains one of the functions. From this point of view, Susan Strange was wrong to rule out the hypothesis of a reconstruction, 'on a transational basis, [of] the kind of symbiotic coexistence of state and mafia power that survived so long in Italy, in China, in Colombia and other places'.[163] The liberalization of the Russian and sub-Saharan economies and their integration into the world market in the 1990s were a clear example of the alliance between political elites and national predatory elites on the one hand, and banks and international financial institutions on the other, under the gaze (whether self-serving, indifferent, or impotent) of the G7. The 'oligarchs' and their strong-man collaborators who benefited from the privatizations of the Yeltsin era or, on a smaller scale, the *feymen*, those crooks who prosper in the nooks and crannies of the authoritarian restoration carried out by the Cameroonian President Paul Biya, operate at the interface between the state and globalization, drawing their resources both from the support of personalities who are highly placed in the regime, and from their dubious activities abroad.[164]

Likewise, the American government was not averse to subcontracting its policy of containing the Soviet Union in Afghanistan to the Pakistani secret services, to local Islamist parties or military chiefs and to transnational Muslim networks, accepting as they did that this covert action would be financed not just by gifts from princely families in the Arabian peninsula or ordinary believers, but also by the opium trade.[165] In the labyrinth of this surrender of responsibility, the Bank of Credit and Commerce International (BCCI), founded in 1972 by a Pakistani financier as dodgy as he was charismatic, Agha Hasan Abedi, with the support of the sovereign of Abu Dhabi, Sheik Zayed, specialized in financial fraud to the detriment of its depositors, helped various heads of state to siphon off the resources of their countries, worked in tandem with Saddam Hussein and Manuel Noriega and managed to cash in on its influence in Washington or London, taking advantage of the blindness, tacit agreement or even active connivance of the American Federal Reserve, the Bank of England, the CIA and the City.[166] From a financial point of view, al-Qaida is the offshoot of this collaboration, which attests to the reconstitution of 'symbiotic coexistence', in its transnational dimension and global dimension, of the state and crime.[167]

The latter has for long been enrolled in the service of economic accumulation, political regulation or centralization, the social control of the poor, opponents or prisoners, the exercise of justice and coercion, the practice of war, and nationalist, revolutionary or democratic demands – as well as the repression of these latter. Figures such as the corsair, the pirate or the bandit – for example the Ethiopian *shifta*, the Iranian *gardan koloft* ('thick neck'), the Japanese *yakuza*, the Ottoman *celali* or *agha*, the Barbary Coast pirates of Algeria, the Sicilian *Mafioso* – are so many classic examples. Their heirs continue to be involved in this ambivalent commerce with the state, as is shown by the situations in (among other places) Japan, Italy or Turkey. But this does not mean they neglect the opportunities opened up by globalization, especially in the narcotics trade, the traffic of human beings or tobacco smuggling. The simultaneous inscription of crime in the national domain and in the process of globalization appears eloquently in the more or less enduring collaborations that are set up between the 'underworld', the secret services, the police, armies and their auxiliary forces, political elites and various businesses (air companies, ship-owners, refineries or cigarette manufacturers), especially when these collusions occur in the shadow of multilateral sanctions imposed in the name of peace or non-proliferation.

The drift into criminality of the Balkan economies, which has been in the news these last few years, is a result of nationalist mobilization, the creation of new states on the ruins of Yugoslavia, the intervention of different diasporas and measures taken by the United Nations or the European Union against warmongers. The differences in application of these sanctions from one country to another have enabled some of them, who had been spared or enjoyed a more favourable regime, notably in Macedonia or Montenegro, to set themselves up as intermediaries between the world market and Serbia, in tandem with, or in addition to, other states in the region – Greece, Bulgaria, Romania – which made it easier to get round the embargo on the authorities in Belgrade. The cooperation between the leaders (or some of their relatives), criminals, militia and nationalist parties of Montenegro, Serbia and Bosnia-Herzegovina made it possible for them to control the fraudulent import and re-export of cigarettes or the dispatching of clandestine immigrants from Turkey, Iran or China into the European Union via Croatia. The government elites of neighbouring countries, who were involved in all this trafficking, derived diplomatic influence with Serbia (and also Russia) from it, and returns in the form of commission or commercial profit. In Belgrade itself, the 'smuggling concession', in particular the smuggling of foreign currency, was an instrument both of self-financing for the security forces and of political vote-catching.[168] So Charles Tilly was quite correct when he foresaw that there was a potentially tragic analogy between war and state-formation on the one hand, and organized crime on the other.[169]

Nonetheless, the transnational hybridization of the state and crime is not restricted to the interplay of agents circumscribed by particular circumstances. It seems to be of a systematic order and constitutes one of the cogs in the interlocking machinery of state and world capitalism. It is in any case one of the elements of their geography. The circulation of illicit products or capital continues to be filtered by the state institution on which, here and there, it confers some of its vigour. What would have been the destiny of Cyprus if it had not benefited from the inflow of dubious investments from the Middle East (in particular Lebanon during the civil war) and from the Soviet Union, from the 1980s onwards, as well as from the revenue that was a by-product of frankly criminal activities such as the human trafficking of which it is one of the crossroads? It is indeed via the intermediary of the banks, the Stock Exchange, numerous offshore societies and the real estate sector of another state (in this case, Greece) that this money was definitively laundered in the eyes of the European Union, at the same time as the flow of capital or considerable sums of cash from Russia, Ukraine, Albania, Yugoslavia and other countries in the Balkans. The Greek economy itself profited en route, to a far from negligible degree. Looked at this way, belonging to the Union and entering Euroland – steps which could hardly be more honourable from the point of view of 'good governance'! – amount to gigantic operations of money-laundering. 'Borderline Europeanization', as Béatrice Hibou ironically calls it, placing the accent on the 'role of the margins' in the integration of the Old Continent and its relations with its environment.[170]

Likewise, it would be illusory to seek to explain the economic growth of Thailand, Singapore or South China, and the way power relations are established between political agents or between social groups that it has made possible, if we fail to take into account smuggling and fraud with Indonesia, or the contribution of illicit flows of goods, especially narcotics, from neighbouring Burma, and their transfer to markets which are represented by others and are defined by their respective bureaucracies, in particular their police and customs officers, namely Japan, the United States and Western Europe.[171]

'Neo-regionalism' often takes the form of such trading partners, bringing together 'vice' and 'virtue'. Thus Romain Bertrand points out that the 'escheated areas' of the archipelagos of Southeast Asia, made notorious by the affair of the 'Jolo hostages' in 2000, are closely linked with the 'real interests' of the states in the region, and in particular their 'privatization': 'These are expanses of territory in which [privatization] is in full swing – i.e. in which one can observe a surrender or discharge of royal prerogatives to "private" agents (Mafia networks, the main concessionary companies working in the sector of timber, hydrocarbon or minerals)', in other words, zones on which rests a whole swathe of the political economy of established regimes.[172] Bertrand justifiably compares them to the relatively inaccessible 'non-state spaces' such as mountains, swamps or the densest forests which, according to the anthropologist James Scott, have for centuries sheltered 'runaway' societies, peopled by fugitives and linked to kingdoms by a 'homeostatic mechanism':

> The mountains of Southeast Asia are 'anti-state', at least as much as 'non-state' or 'not-yet-state'. They are peopled, over long historical periods, by deserters, people evading tax and forced labour, refugees from slavery, those who have lost factional struggles and pariahs of every sort, not to mention religious dissidents, hermits, members of heterodox sects who, we might say, represent the 'organic intellectuals' of the margin, adding a symbolic dimension to the *practical* rejection of central power incarnated by these communities. The mountainous periphery of Southeast Asia is the negative of the society at the centre, in terms of ecology, religious practice, social structure. government and demography. And in particular thanks to its population of fugitives and dissidents.[173]

However, these areas of flight and dissidence have always had a synergetic relationship with the state and the economic world in which it is situated, as has been clearly shown by historians and anthropologists in the case of 'social banditry' in the Ottoman Empire or nomadism in the world of the Indian Ocean and Central Asia.[174] The same is true today.

In a more benign mode, attention has previously been drawn to the recurrent appearance of smugglers' states in Africa, which act as the commercial lungs of adjacent centres of (relatively) 'virtuous' commerce. Nonetheless, certain of them – in particular the Seychelles, Swaziland, Lesotho and Equatorial Guinea – make no bones about exploiting the lucrative seams of the international economy of crime, especially that of narcotics trafficking.[175] Furthermore, the coercive exploitation and fraudulent export of mineral, animal or human resources are in this case too closely interlinked with the political networks of the rhizome-state or armed movements which long to control it.[176] This is also the source of all the ambiguity of a city-state such as Dubai, praised for the competitiveness of its free zone and criticized for the opacity of its gold bazaar, which is alleged to have helped the activities of al-Qaida and facilitated the proliferation of Pakistan's nuclear technology.[177]

As a result, we can say that the regional or global structuring of the system of states coincides at least partly with the expansion of transnational relations, whether material or immaterial, informal or illicit – even, more precisely, that it emanates from them. It consists of an embedding of national formations within one another – formations whose interrelationships, both governmental and inter-societal, whether by means of businesses, banks and criminal networks or not, ensure that the legal and illegal spheres can both function by contributing on an equal footing to the crystallization of the state idea and its economy.

This obvious fact cannot be argued away by claiming that the examples mentioned are in some way evidence of the margins or dross of the process of globalization. For at its very heart, 'dirty money' serves the consolidation of the public power. In most western democracies, it finances the mechanisms of political representation. There is nothing merely anecdotal about this idea when we see how a boss such as Silvio Berlusconi, who made his riches in rather mysterious circumstances, can rise to be head of the Italian government and from that position arrange for his own impunity. In France, at least two men who had distinguished themselves in the functions of Minister of the Interior, and vigorously incarnated the 'sovereignist' trend, benefited from the largesse of 'rogue' states, or states notorious for their 'second economy' and transnational business networks that are often shady, not to say frankly criminal; and an oil company like Elf, one of the main national businesses, has long served as an arm of the foreign policy of the Élysée, as a cover for the secret services, as an interface with African regimes that are (to put it mildly) not entirely above suspicion, and, last but not least, as an instrument of illegal enrichment. In addition, the obsessional invocation and the orchestration of 'dirty money' (and its 'laundering') legitimize the ideological construction of that sociologically improbable category of 'transnational organized crime' which justifies the exorbitant reinforcing of police powers or of various repressive administrations to the detriment of people's liberties, on the false pretext of the fight against the 'mafia', and in spite of the fact that the new legislative texts, being quite superfluous, are ineffective against an enemy whose existence is far from being proven.[178]

The transnational ferment: the latest proofs

The favourite theorem of global studies thus turns out to be erroneous. Not only does globalization neither threaten nor erode the state: it actually produces it, and the transnational aspect is the leaven in the dough. This idea goes so much against the common view that it is probably not superfluous to illustrate it one last time with a few examples drawn from the latest phenomena of globalization.

The stupefying development of some seventy tax havens, through which half the world stock of money passes, and in which 20 per cent of the total private wealth (or 22 per cent of the foreign holdings of banks) resides, is often quoted as a factor of state depletion. But Ronen Palan has shown that 'the commercialization of sovereignty', in which offshore financial sites indulge, has been a progressive response on the part of certain states to the paradox of a 'growing economic integration within the context of political fragmentation', a defiant display in face of the contradictions 'of national sovereignty in the age of mobility of capital'. It has been a 'constant of the modern system of the state' and attests to the capacity of the latter to adapt to globalization – or even to create, 'as if by stealth', its infrastructure. It also intervenes in counterpoint to, and in support of, the big financial centres of London, New York and Tokyo, rather than taking their place. Thanks to the principle of fictitious residence, which has made it possible to dissociate the juridical domiciliation and the physical installation of an enterprise, a bank or an account, the City has thus become a major offshore financial centre, as a result of the launch of the eurodollar market in 1957.[179] The sponsorship of the Bank of England, and the role of the public power in the pursuit of this policy over forty years, have not however managed to shield the place from the poisoned profits of dirty money, as was shown by their involvement in the scandal of the BCCI or the circulation of the billions of dollars creamed off by the family of the late Nigerian dictator, Sani Abacha.[180] In reality, the financial offshore economy and the eurodollar market are merely the contemporary expressions of a centuries-old creative tension between the principle of the territorialization of political sovereignty and the logic of the deterritorialization of capital, which Marx, Weber, Braudel and Arrighi have all shown to be proper to capitalism and its relation to the state: Genoa and Venice are back in business.[181]

In a similar fashion, the flags of free registration, which the uproar created by the shipwreck of a few oil tankers has put in the spotlight, are the result of the public policies of states that are specialized in this service, such as Panama, Liberia, Greece, Cyprus, Malta, the Bahamas, the Honduras, Belize or, more recently, Cambodia and even Bolivia. The Cambodia Shipping Corporation, the flexibility of whose procedures for registering ships is common knowledge, was, for instance, created in 1994 to shelter North Korean boats judged to be undesirable in several ports.[182] The United States is today worried about a system which terrorist networks are suspected of being tempted to use. It is one of the ironies of history that the USA nonetheless had a direct responsibility for its establishment: it was the USA which helped Liberia to launch out on this activity during the Second World War so as to deliver weapons to Great Britain without infringing its official neutrality and to counterbalance the hegemony of Panama in this respect. It was also pressure from the USA which led to voting rights in the International Maritime Organization being made proportional to the tonnage registered, thereby rendering this UN-type institution immune to reform.[183] The USA was soon imitated by the United Kingdom and France, who opened their own 'second pavilions' – Gibraltar and the Kerguelen Islands respectively.

The political economy of flags of convenience is thus inseparable from the foreign policy of states and the commercial competition between nations, while at the same time it represents a major resource for countries on the periphery and one of the main ways they can become involved in the process of globalization. It also generates considerable profits for ship-owners or businesses which use their services and are not without influence on western movers and shakers. After all, the latter would need only to forbid flags of convenience from gaining access to European or North American ports to put an end to the system if they so desired.

Likewise, transnational or 'global' telecommunications businesses and the products they market are not as deterritorialized as Arjun Appadurai supposes.[184] The spread of Japanese pop culture in Southeast Asia and the East allows the Land of the Rising Sun to renegotiate its place within a continent that it has endeavoured to dominate in military terms, then on which it turned its back, in flight from its own past. The circulation of images and sounds, and the imaginary figures which this circulation transmits, are simultaneously vectors of regional globalization and modes of readjustment between the different states. The ascendancy of Japan over the media landscape gives it the opportunity to renew its links with Asia, by, among other things, importing the creations of Thailand, Taiwan, Singapore and Hong Kong, and confirming its technological, financial and cultural superiority over its neighbours. It is only a short step from the transnational to 'trans/ nationalism'.[185] The companies which draw their profits from the globalization of 'information' remain, in fact, bound to their original countries. The xenophobic rants of the newspapers and televisions in the Murdoch Group even remind us that they can soon sing the praises of the most hackneyed nationalism.

However, there is no example more instructive than the conflict between the United States, Afghanistan and Iraq in 2001–3, which gave rise to journalistic manoeuvres of this kind. The violation of American sanctuary by a transnational and widely dispersed terrorist group was supported by a state, Afghanistan – by two states, if we accept the claim made by the Bush administration (and so far unproven) that Saddam Hussein's regime was supporting al-Qaida. The wars that ensued were clearly wars between states, even though they were extended into police operations against the 'Arab' combatants, and Afghan armed movements, in particular the Northern Alliance, or the Kurdo-Iraqi peshmerga, were enrolled for the occasion. These wars were also accompanied by a considerable and at times tumultuous diplomatic activity, both bilateral and multilateral, within the United Nations, NATO and the European Union. They demonstrated the absolute military supremacy of the American 'hyperpower' and confirmed the radical asymmetry of the international system of states to the advantage of the latter by causing it to act in the modes of 'unilateralism' and 'pre-emption'. At the same time, they stirred up Arab nationalism. They provided a pretext for a return of national or multilateral administrations in the control of a certain number of international markets, starting with those of capital and transport. And the blurring of the distinction between 'organized transnational criminality' and 'international terrorism' – two equally confused notions – justified the questioning of essential public liberties.

In short, it is somewhat difficult to grasp how this sequence of globalization is supposed to have led to a 'retreat of the state' at the very time when the integration of the world economy continued, from financial crises to countries joining the OMC or the European Union, and when 'international civil society' showed itself to be mobilized as never before, either forming a front against the war, or becoming involved in anti-globalization movements. On the other hand, it is not in the least bit difficult to discern the way that transnational dynamics have been embedded within this unipolar configuration of the international system of states. From 1980, as we have seen, the State Department, the Pentagon and the CIA encouraged their Middle Eastern allies, in particular the Saudi monarchy and the Pakistani army, to finance and even arm Islamist parties and networks so as to help them to kick the Soviets out of Afghanistan, if necessary turning a blind eye to their drug-trafficking activities. To this end, both the United States and Great Britain, as well as the United Arab Emirates, Saudi Arabia and Pakistan compromised themselves in the transnational and fraudulent operations of the BCCI, and a certain Osama bin Laden was one of the instruments of this shadow war against the Soviet Union. Nonetheless, it would be wrong to limit this historical figure to a mere manipulation of secret services (or to its reversal by an Islamist ideology of direct action). Born into a prosperous family of Yemenite origin, making his fortune in Saudi Arabia, and well established in Geneva, the Public Enemy Number One of America enjoys an undeniable popularity among the transnational populations of the Gulf, and even beyond, in the *umma* as a whole, as a figure of political resistance to the 'arrogance' of the West, a model of social success in emigration, a re-inventor of the local repertoires of notoriety and a compromiser between the demands of globalization and those of faith.[185] This sequence of events, which has been at the top of the diplomatic and military agenda for more than twenty years, thus provides us with a striking summary of the fusion between the processes of formation of the state and those of globalization, on the basis of a systematic hybridization of the private and the public. In the Gulf, 'the terrorists constitute an alternative ruling class which proposes to conquer power in the oil zone'[187] by overturning the monarchies in whose bosom they were nourished. In America, the military project of the 'benevolent Empire' dear to Robert

Kagan does not exclude the personal interests of the neo-con movers and shakers in the profits to be made from war and reconstruction via the 'straddling' of the administration, the private sector and the various associations of 'civil society' such as the American Enterprise Institute.[188] The new international crisis in its turn makes it necessary to reformulate entirely the current debate on the place of the state in globalization.

Globalization: the motor of state-formation

The vacuous nature of the discussion comes to a large extent from the very weak definition of the state in which the theory of international relations and global studies remain caught. Most of the time, this definition remains narrowly institutional. The state is reduced to its 'foreign and security' policies, or its 'defence' policy, as has been said in Brussels, or to its most obvious economic roles. The definition thus remains shallow and normative, following the canons of 'good governance' and an 'international ethic' that have both been carefully depoliticized, or those of a supermarket Weberianism, holding forth about 'legal-rational' virtues. No consideration is taken of the 'integral state' of Gramsci, rooted in his 'civil society', nor of the complexity of power relations inherent in 'governmentality' as it is conceptualized by Foucault. The historicity of the situations being considered is completely sidelined. Hence the multiplication of misinterpretations, misdiagnoses and dead ends when it comes to the relation of the state to globalization, and most notably to transnational phenomena. The obscuring of the historical aspects of the social relations of power prevents us from understanding the economy of 'domination' or 'subjection', which involves political institutions or forces *stricto sensu* and a multiplicity of other phenomena, most often worldwide in scope. It forbids us to see something which otherwise is blindingly obvious: the 'event' of the state is the product of the 'event' of globalization.[189] The sequence of events that has lasted for two centuries and that we have taken as a yardstick of analysis confirms this decade after decade, and continent by continent.

Once again, sub-Saharan Africa provides us with proof, if not by a *reductio ad absurdum*, at least by a limit case. John Lonsdale has pointed out that its main distinct contribution to the history of mankind has been a reasonably peaceful way of living without the state,[190] in the sense that the kingdoms on the continent did not practise political centralization, tax collection, the militarization of war or a social and cultural polarization between the elites and the common people comparable with the logics of the great machines for dominating and killing that were prevalent in Europe or Asia. It was well and truly our foundational nineteenth century that implanted the state south of the Sahara as a system of territorial sovereignty that made politics autonomous. Globalization demanded it: the European powers, the United Kingdom first and foremost, passed from an 'imperialism of intention' to an 'imperialism of result' as soon as they discerned in the absence of centralized political formations one of the main obstacles to investment and occupied by force of arms the regions they had not managed to penetrate economically as much as they would have desired.[191] The scramble for Africa came about as a result of a multilateral conference, the Colonial Conference of Berlin in 1884–5, and rested on the systematic hybridization of private government and public government, which the Congo Free State and the concessionary companies took to an extreme level. The simultaneous intervention of European states, corporations, banks and churches made it impossible to separate the respective contributions of the two spheres, and it was revealing to see how the straddling of positions (especially those comprising salaried workers) of power or authority on the one hand and of the positions of accumulation on the other was right from the start at the basis of the 'politics of the belly', which had hitherto imposed itself as a historical configuration of governmentality.[192] Furthermore, grafting and state appropriation have been reinforced by transnational relations: not only those of smuggling, as we have observed, but also those of religious movements and multinational capital that have fitted into the territorial frameworks drawn up in Berlin or have emphasized the idea of the *ethnos*, an idea that comes before that of the nation. The role that pan-Africanism (whether cultural, intellectual or political in nature) played at the dawn of national self-assertion is also well known. This national self-assertion rests on the historical experience of Atlantic extraversion – and in particular on exchanges between the Creole Christian elites of the coast and on their relations with the Afro-American bourgeoisie or churches – rather than on any exclusive relation to the glebe of the hinterland.[193] Finally, the 'reverberation' effects between colonies and metropolises, and the interactions (aggressive or peaceful) between the different empires, or indeed, within the latter, between the different territories comprising them, all in turn contributed to the formation of the state. There are no two ways about it: the state has gone along with the process of the globalization of the continent. It is indeed the son of this process. A weakly child, perhaps, and at times a prodigal son, but blood is thicker than water.

This remains true in the period of economic and financial liberalization. The structural adjustment programmes are negotiated bilaterally between donors and sub-Saharan countries, with little consideration for the effects of synchrony or disjunction on the regional or world scale. As we have pointed out, indeed, they serve the hegemonic plans of national elites in that they depoliticize the domination they exert in the name of 'development' – a development that they hope, with a lofty cynicism or an unconscious candour, will be 'sustainable'. The postcolonial 'passive revolution' has become multilateral: this process, aided and abetted by international civil society, represents a real opportunity for the state, and not a threat. It may so happen that its attributes are whittled down by 'conditionalities' on the level of 'regional integration' and peer reviews, but this process of erosion is actually part and parcel of the way it is turned into an institution.

Historically, the sovereignty of the nation-state was actually the product of the whole set of relations between states and the constraints that bore down on the latter. There are no nation-states without a system of states, with all the limitations (de facto or de jure) on their sovereignty. The state does not come before the international system, it stems from it, and the way it is included within the system is less a form of alienation than a way for it to establish its power.[194]

Sub-Saharan Africa is no exception to this rule. And the fact that, in this part of the world, the state is 'weak' and subject to 'conditions' that affect the state's sovereign prerogatives is not an aberration from the norm. Giovanni Arrighi is right to point out the extent to which the notion of 'quasi-state' takes its guidelines from the exceptional case of France (whether absolutist or, later, republican). From this point of view, the United Provinces, and also Japan, South Korea, Taiwan, Singapore and Hong Kong also fall within this category.[195] The fact of the matter is that accession to national sovereignty is obtained via the immediate abdication of whole sectors of the latter. This was the case, for example, in 1919, when the promoting of the 'nationalities' of the Austro-Hungarian Empire into states was made conditional on their accepting the Fourteen Points of Woodrow Wilson, especially the principle of self-determination for 'minorities',[196] or even earlier, when the new Balkan States, in particular Greece and Romania, were placed under the 'collective protection' of the European Powers.

Admission to the UN or the European Union also depends on respect for supranational rules and regulations. This does not prevent it appearing as a necessary consecration of sovereignty, and even as a guarantee against external aggression. This paradox, a source of unease and misunderstandings, is particularly acute in Central and Eastern Europe. Entry into the Union ratifies the resurrection of the nation and procures an assurance of its perpetuation when confronted with Russian hegemony, while the European construction in the West rests more on the sense of a need to go beyond (or at least redraw) such national boundaries. The political tension that accompanies the process of enlargement stems in part from this discrepancy. But to the east of the Old Continent, there were more terrible contradictions. The globalization of the far reaches of Eurasia, in Central Asia and the Caucasus, under cover of their annexation by the Russian (and later Soviet) Empire, was the ruthless mechanism by which the nation was created; and the Stalinist theory of nationality, together with the deportations that came with it, played a significant part in this.

One of the results of the new theory of international relations has been that the latter can no longer be reduced to mere relations between states. Nonetheless, this theory has in general not realized that the logic of transnational relations, from society to society, also comprises the motors of state-formation, just as the system of states constitutes the international system. On the one hand, the synergy between global capitalism and state territorialization has become an obvious fact, thanks to historical sociology in its Marxist or Weberian form. Adam Smith himself was well aware that 'force' lay behind the establishment of the world market.[197] On the other hand, the transnational dimension of the international system is the soil from which the state grows. It is to a large extent by its intermediary that the two key ideas of the expansion and consolidation of the state have circulated: the notions (and the corresponding political engineering) of nation and reform. The Tanzimat of the Ottoman Empire, or their equivalents in Persia, Egypt and Tunisia, were a model of their kind. They were at one and the same time the expression of authoritarian reformist movements, of attempts at modernization 'from above', of which the military generally comprised the testing ground, and the end product of much more diffuse intellectual exchanges or cross-fertilization between peoples.[198]

In Europe itself, the 'Springtime of the Peoples', in 1848, was also an assertion of nationalism – of rival nationalisms, whatever the degree of transnational solidarity shown by the revolutionaries; it led to the forming of a Europe of nation-states.[199] During the century, the 'creation of national identities' was the object of thoroughgoing 'enterprises aimed at aiding in the creation of identity': these sprang up from the need to construct a language and a culture in the absence of a sufficient number of home-grown intellectuals. Serbia, Greece, Italy, Romania and Bulgaria benefited from these transfers of ideological technology from France, England or Germany. The universalism of Herder, the intellectual cosmopolitanism of the Brothers Grimm, legitimized this 'discovery of the national within the transnational' that was so obvious in the musical field, with itinerant figures such as Liszt, Chopin and, later, Bartók: As Anne-Marie Thiesse puts it:

> The second half of the [nineteenth] century sees the apogee of various forms of 'national music', composed according to the great international genres but with their own colouring, based on the reference to popular melodies that supposedly express the national genius and its several manifestations in culture, history or landscape.[200]

And this birth of the nation, aided by the forceps of culture, involves a process of reform. A reform of the state, but also a reform of bodies and minds, undertaken by the school system, youth movements, conscription and the churches – often, it has to be said, following transnational exchanges within the Old Continent, on both sides of the Atlantic, or within the framework of the colonial experience.

This transnational combination of nation and reform within the 'whole' state can also be found, finally, in China, when the Qing endeavoured to bring their country into the contemporary system of states following the disastrous Boxer Rebellion – a process that involved implementing the 'New Policy' (*Xinzheng*) in 1901–8. After the shock of their defeat in the Chinese-Japanese War of 1894–5, the Japan of the Meiji era served as both model and incubator.[201] The travels of students, writers and civil servants to the West, which influenced them greatly, also became more and more frequent.[202] Furthermore, the Chinese diaspora across Southeast Asia and America had a decisive influence in the growth and development of new ideas, in their financing and their concrete realization, in particular thanks to remittances and magazines from 'overseas' (*qiaokan*).[203] The case of China thus confirms that 'all good nationalisms have a transnational vision',[204] not the least of reasons for which is that they proceed from this vision. More generally, the 'cosmopolitan ideal' has come into being together with, and not in opposition to, the growth of the state.[205]

The place of migrations and telecommunications in the current phase of globalization has naturally intensified this bond between worldwide exchanges at a sub-state level and the formation of the state itself, including so-called 'long-distance' nationalisms.[206] Nonetheless, the phenomenon is much older, being concomitant with the emergence of the nation-state and the system of states that constitutes it. The classic example of Zionism attests to this.[207] And the fact that, these days, Islam is validating and reproducing the national framework as well as its ideology is a supplementary indication of the organic relation between the state and globalization.[208] The major Islamist parties, having been deployed by authoritarian or military regimes to stem the tide of leftist movements or street protests – for instance in Algeria, Egypt or Turkey – have become 'Islamo-nationalist', and taken up the torch of the struggle against the domination of western and Zionist imperialism, following the example of the Lebanese Hezbollah in Lebanon or the Palestinian Hamas and Jihad. The myth of the 'Green Internationale' has misfired, and the *raison d'État* soon overtook pan-Muslim revolutionary messianism in Iran, even before the Republic entered its Thermidorean phase.[209]

We can thus broaden our horizons somewhat and note that the change of scale of contemporary globalization, from the nineteenth to the twentieth centuries, simultaneously implies a series of effects of economic, financial, cultural and other kinds of globalization, the crystallization of a system of states across every continent, and the instigation of a logic of retrenchment of identities. The different versions of political culturalism, starting with nationalism, have been the commonest expression of this latter phenomenon.[210] From this point of view, A. G. Hopkins is right to bring out the symbiosis between the emergence of systems of states and an increasing cosmopolitanism that is demonstrated from the seventeenth and eighteenth centuries onwards.[211] Nonetheless, we need to complete the triangle and emphasize that the processes of closure – of territories, cultures and identities – have been the active principles of the changing of scale in societies and the increasing integration of the international system. And there is another paradox: the territorialization of sovereignty and the crystallization of particularist identities are at least partly produced in the 'open seas' of modernity (Arjun Appadurai) rather than in the hearts of societies – or, more exactly, in the relation between the latter and the high seas of globalization. The 'integral' state, in particular, is established by its frontier as much as at its centre.[212] In this respect, it consists in a configuration of global 'domination' or 'subjection' that cannot be reduced to the most explicitly political relations alone. It is rooted in the social realm and in the globalization of this latter.

One fundamental point remains to be resolved or at least identified. If we understand them in terms of combinations and permutations, are the 'global revolution', and the 'globality' that results from it, in Martin Shaw's terms, still organized around an asymmetrical structure of states, as he thinks? Or is the 'new global form of sovereignty' proper to 'Empire' now deprived of any centre: is it a pure post-imperialist regime of bio-power, exerted diffusely over the whole surface of the globe so that no territorial frontier can limit its reign, as Michael Hardt and Toni Negri claim?[213] Or, indeed, should the political realm now be understood as dissociated from sovereignty and the subject?[214]

The neo-Bukharinian insistence with which Martin Shaw endeavours to understand the way state, war and globalization are all interconnected is highly persuasive. The emphasis on the principle of reality when faced with the economy of desire and the nostalgia in which postmodern anthropology has sometimes indulged is very beneficial. The architecture of global statehood that he describes, in which the global-western state-conglomerate, quasi-imperial nation-states and (new) proto- or quasi-states all fit together, is quite effective in understanding the vicissitudes of the last decade, most notably the Iraq war of 2003.

The main fact to emerge from this sequence is the consolidation of a major asymmetry within the system of states, in the way the United States have irresistibly pulled ahead of the pack thanks to their absolute military primacy, their economic dynamism and their technological advances, especially in the domain of 'information'. On the other hand, however, Martin Shaw's (theoretically rather old-fashioned and naive) attachment to a political sociology of the agent is of little help when it comes to grasping globalization as global governmentality, and not just as the 'global revolution' of the system of states (and its wars).[215] The analysis of the relation between the 'integral' state and globalization presupposes that we have a better understanding of the social institutions that shape it and the modes of subjectivation that develop within them. Only on this condition can we avoid reducing globalization to a mere change of scale, as Martin Shaw invites us to do (without really furnishing himself with all the means necessary).[216] We need in particular to ascertain whether the 'withdrawal of faith [in the State]'[217] is actually real and whether the disconnection from the historical sites of political sovereignty or identification has been brought to completion. The implication of this is that we now need to question the social foundations of globalization.

3

The Social Foundations of Globalization

The usual view of globalization is that it involves dispossession, alienation and anomie. It comes from somewhere else and strikes communities of 'natives' or citizens hard. Basically, it is comparable to what the Iranian sociologist and philosopher Djalâl Al-e Ahmad called 'occidentalitis', a more or less untranslatable notion but one which referred to the idea of 'going jungle crazy', with sun-stroke and sudden illness.[1] In fact, it seems to be essentially deprived of any social base other than that of the little 'elite' of 'globapolitans',[2] of the 'cosmopolitan hyperbourgeoisie' of 'turbocapitalism' and the contemporary *compradores* of the latter, in particular 'globalized intellectuals' and 'experts'.[3] Thus the exploitation of the labour force which globalization entails is now effected less by the exhaustion of the latter than by its 'disaffiliation'[4] from the networks of which it is composed. In its extreme forms it seems to consist in the 'ever more drastic deprivation of links and the progressive appearance of an incapacity not only to create new links, but even to maintain the existing links (detachment from one's friends, the break-up of family ties, divorce, political absenteeism)', in short, in an 'absolute jettisoning' of the excluded individual.[5] As for the rest, globalization – so the claim goes – rests on the hazy, transnational, airborne group comprised of all those who read the weekend supplement of the *Financial Times*. And, indeed, there are two opposing forces struggling to reshape our world and our lives: globalization and identity.[6] Good Lord . . . !

Transnational historical fields

These populist definitions are extremely debatable in so far as they sympathize with mankind, and in particular individual nations, for having been deprived of their histories – and this seems quite unlikely. Not only have the formation and internationalization of the state over the past two centuries been achieved through the globalization of the social sphere and within the transnational dimension of the 'frontier', as we started to explain in previous chapters; these processes are still dependent on the historicity proper to the 'generalized mutual interaction' that characterizes globalization. In other words, globalization does not have to compromise only with the resilience of national or local political societies, proceeding by means of the 'reinvention of difference' in the now classic formulation of postmodern anthropology. In so far as globalization is an 'event', it is in itself a configuration of relational historicity. It takes the form of a series of transnational historical fields which we need to grasp in their wholeness, going beyond the analysis of mere relations between states (the focus of the classical theory of international relations), placing their trajectories back in the *longue durée* instead of concentrating simply on their supposed novelty, thus following the example of global studies, and taking into full account the social or cultural spheres, which most economists and specialists in 'geopolitics' tend to neglect. Once again, the historical sociology of the state turns out to be useful for performing this task.

The internationalization of the state and the setting up of a 'global-western state-conglomerate' on either side of the Atlantic, and indeed the Pacific, in accordance with the logic of the Trilateral Commission, have thus given rise to neo-Gramscian interpretations.[7] These even go so far as to put forward the hypothesis of the existence of a 'dominant transatlantic class', or of a 'postcolonial historical bloc' on the scale of the ancient empires.[8] We still need to re-establish the historicity of the 'domination', 'hegemony' or 'subjection' that such a configuration incarnates – a historicity of which the diplomatic or military machinations in which states as agents indulge comprise merely the surface foam and froth. As it happens, the transatlantic field constitutes an amazingly complex 'event'. This 'event' is at once political, military, economic and financial, since it has been at the epicentre of western capitalist expansion for five centuries as well as being the stage of many conflicts, including the two world wars. It is also an institutional 'event', since the transatlantic relation has been mediated via a dense tissue of businesses, banks, multilateral organizations, churches, associations, and university and other establishments, and it takes the form of a real supranational integration, thanks to the way sovereignty and law have been mutualized.[9]

It can, however, also be considered an 'event' on the level of civilization (for want of a better description); this enables us to account for the entire set of processes that for centuries have been shaping this common oceanic space in which we continue to live, without our being aware of its profound unity. There was in particular the 'Columbian exchange',[10] with the annihilation of whole populations in the Canaries or South America happening as a result of their vulnerability to illnesses brought by European conquerors, with the cross-breeding between non-indigenous and indigenous peoples or between the non-indigenous peoples themselves, and with the circulation of grain, seedlings and animal species on both sides of the ocean. This encounter was all the more complicated and ambivalent than historiography has long made out. For example, it is well known these days that rice-growing was implanted into America, especially the Carolinas and Georgia, from the West African coast, where it had long been practised. This transfer of seeds – and even more of agricultural expertise – and the adaptation of this cereal to the environment on the other side of the Atlantic, resulted from the activities of slaves themselves, in the interstices of the economy of deportation and plantation.[11] Generally, the Africans themselves played an active part in the emergence of a specifically Afro-American civilization, which initially found concrete expression in the crucible of the trading relations that were established between Europe and the sub-Saharan coastal regions, from the fifteenth century onwards, before developing into the tragic experience of slave-trading in the second half of the seventeenth century. The two best-known manifestations of this were of a religious kind – John Thornton compares the rise of Afro-Atlantic Christianity to that of Buddhism in China or the Indianization of Islam[12] – and musical in character, with the invention of jazz. This latter alone would be enough to demonstrate the importance of the African contribution to transatlantic civilization, and its appropriation by the whole set of peoples that it includes, so long as we remember that the creation of this artistic form also drew on European or Amerindian repertoires as well as on the cultural heritage of the slaves.[13] A two-way traffic of this kind can in any case be found between the Old World and Amerindians.[14] Joseph Roach, who has studied New Orleans and London, can thus speak in terms of a 'circum-Atlantic world' which was a veritable 'behavioural vortex': it was able to reproduce itself (often in a latent form) thanks to many memorializing practices – the very same ones that I referred to in the last chapter.[15] The place of the celebration of the dead, of carnival, dance, theatre, image, dream, and of the fantastical representation of the relation to the Other in the transmission of this oceanic memory, suggests the extent to which the vision of the theory of international relations remains too narrow.

As far as this precise and particular moment of our investigation is concerned, the essential point is to emphasize that the transatlantic historical field rested on identifiable types of political economy, i.e. on social relations of production, on social institutions, on exchanges of goods and services that may well, admittedly, have varied from one period or place to another, but which were no less concrete for all that, and in which different states took an active part through various 'discharges' or regulations, especially in the framework of the slave trade. It rested, for example, on privateering, piracy and slavery; on fortresses, missions, trading posts and plantations; on the trade in gold, silver, firearms, clothing, alcohol, tobacco, coffee or sugar.[16] The transatlantic historical field as such comprised a transnational social base that was interlinked both with the expansion of capitalism and with that of the system of states. In particular, the twelve million or so African slaves who were transported to the New World over 350 years of slave-trading, the hundreds of thousands of workers recruited under the system of indentured labour in India or China who took over from them in the nineteenth century, the fifty or so million European immigrants who, in successive waves, populated the two Americas or who, in lesser numbers, returned from them. But also, more specifically, the buccaneers, the *bandeirantes*, the trappers, the *trekboere*, the *pombeiros*, the 'burnt woods', the *gauchos*, the *vaqueros* and other cowboys who lived on the frontiers of transatlantic globalization. A particular place needs to be reserved for Jews and marranos, especially for the Portuguese 'New Christians' who were the kingpins of the transatlantic economy, forging the multireligious and multicultural conception of the *Naçao* in the shady milieu of ocean ports, and giving capitalist globalization two of its main thinkers: Spinoza and Ricardo.[17]

These are not, in this instance, merely gratuitous points, since the social relations inherent in the transatlantic civilization of the Modern Age of the Industrial Revolution are still making their unsettled presence felt at the heart of contemporary political modernity. As is well known, the Civil War was the pivot around which the state known as the United States of America was formed. Its human cost was terrifying: 620,000 dead – twice as many as the American losses during the Second World War. But its result meant that the unity of the country was 'axiomatic', whereas it might have remained 'problematic' or indeed broken up entirely, giving birth to a North American system of states similar to that of Europe.[18] It also opened up the path to the formidable economic growth and worldwide hegemony of the United States. At the same time, it continues to shape the political society of the US through a whole series of effects of memory and social enclaves. There are Americans who still weep when they make pilgrimages to the battlefields, and the race question, the rancour of the southern states towards the federal power, their attitude towards belligerence, the vigour of their fundamentalist or evangelical religiosity, the ideological weight of the religious right and its influence within the Bush administration, are all more or less the offshoots of this history. Now the American Civil War stemmed from the question as to how the Confederation (or the Union) was to be included within the transatlantic economy: what was at stake, in other words, were the problems of

PLEASE CHECK (✓) REASON FOR RETURN. THANK YOU.

- [ ] 1 Reject--no reason
- [ ] 2 Duplicate from another source
- [ ] 3 Damaged/defective
- [ ] 4 No to series (specify if subseries)
- [ ] 5 Out of scope/subject excluded
- [ ] 6 Sufficient coverage
- [ ] 7 Not on press list
- [ ] 8 Too expensive
- [ ] 9 Billing/shipping error

- [ ] 10 Wrong content level
- [ ] 11 Ordered in error
- [ ] 12 Poor quality
- [ ] 13 Specialized interest
- [ ] 14 Peripheral subject
- [ ] 15 Duplicated by YBP
- [ ] 16 Reprint
- [ ] 17 Too popular/low level
- [ ] 18 Narrow geographic area

Your reasons for returning this book will help us to assess your profile and recommend potential revisions to your approval plan.

Comments:

Init. 25

free exchange with Great Britain and the extension of slavery in the Midwest, soon to be colonized. In other terms, globalization, as a configuration of relational historicity, was the constitutive principle of the American state and its 'hyperpower', not an exogenous factor weighing down on the latter as if it came from elsewhere.[19]

On the other side of the South Atlantic, the consequences and the social memory of the slave trade likewise inform a number of splits or conflicts in the contemporary political scene. Apart from the fact that African nationalism was nourished by its exchanges with the Afro-American diaspora or with the Creole elites of the coast, as we have seen, the power relations between the postcolonial elites, the way these have been expressed in elections, and the various coups d'état or civil wars still all proceed, at least partly, from this history of extraversion.[20] The basic model implies an opposition between social groups that are accustomed to different types of transatlantic exchange and skill localized in the ports, and groups from the hinterland that have been deprived in educational and financial terms, but which have managed to acquire some chance of rising in the social scale thanks to a career in the military, administrative or political professions, or indeed in agriculture. Here and there, this kind of contradiction has occasionally been overcome at the ballot box. For instance, in Senegal, with the electoral victory of Senghor over Lamine Gueye in 1951, which sanctioned the rise of the 'peanut marabouts' and other 'bushmen' (broussards) to the detriment of the leading figures of the 'Four Communes', the citizens of which had enjoyed French civil rights since the nineteenth century. More often than not, it gave rise to compensatory political processes in the shape of particularly repressive one-party states, putsches or civil wars: this was the case in Guinea-Bissau, Sierra Leone, Liberia, Togo and Benin.

The case of Angola is a good example. While the three national liberation movements that, between 1960 and 1970, probably devoted more energy to tearing each other apart than kicking out the Portuguese colonizers cannot be reduced to mere terms in an ethnic or regionalist equation, it is clear enough that each of them was supported by a population or territory which occupied a rather singular position in regard to the slave economy of the seventeenth–nineteenth centuries: the National Liberation Front of Angola (FNLA) was the distant heir to the Kingdom of the Kongo, which had converted to Catholicism as early as 1491 and had played an active part in the slave trade, in partnership with Vili or Luandan merchants from the coastal area; the National Union for the Total Independence of Angola (UNITA) recruited mainly from these populations, in particular the Ovimbundu, whose ancestors had provided the slave trade with a reservoir of workers; the Popular Movement for the Liberation of Angola (MPLA) had inherited the mantle of the Luso-Africans, *metis* or *assimilados* from Luanda and

Benguela. These latter had acted as intermediaries and collaborated with the Portuguese colonial administrators and traders, before converting to the Marxo-nationalist creed in reaction to the discrimination that was hitting them and to the new challenge posed by European immigration. The postcolonial period is, if anything, even richer in examples of this kind. Right in the middle of the Cold War, the MPLA was appealing to Cuban troops to defend the American oil wells from which it drew the greater part of its revenue. And the UNITA fighters, encouraged by the intervention of the South African army, were co-opted by the United States and their regional allies as freedom fighters, notwithstanding the fact that they are the spokesmen of pro-indigenous and racialist demands that show little liking for the universal charms of market democracy, so far as we can judge from the methods of political control and repression within the movement. In short, the descendants of the slave traders have remained loyal to the *comprador* vocation of their ancestors, which they take up with a fine display of revolutionary logorrhoea and predatory zeal; and those whose forebears escaped deportation only thanks to the lucky chance of their existence tried to take their revenge, albeit in vain (they were defeated in 2002).

It is of course a little over-schematic to describe this whole process as a transatlantic western, a long civil war. Things are much more complicated.[21] Generally speaking, we should beware of the broad-brush historical frescoes in which geopolitical thinkers indulge. These simplifications give entire terraces packed with delighted business cadres the illusion that they now understand the situation. The tectonic reading of contemporary events in terms of the perpetuation of fractures between civilizations that have lasted for centuries – for example, the way the line of the iron curtain corresponded to the 'second serfdom' established in Eastern Europe in the sixteenth century, or the way the frontier of the Roman Empire in the East was later followed by the line along which Serbia and Croatia split when the former Yugoslavia collapsed, both of which have given rise to much discussion – is as seductive as it is misleading.

But this rapid sketch (or caricature?) of the civil war in Angola has no objective other than convincing the reader of a disturbing reality. The crisis of political representation on the Atlantic façade of the African continent, and the lack of state legitimacy that ensues, are less the product of a radical distortion between local societies and the open seas of globalization than a symptom of the effects of the latter within them and the many different practices of appropriation or instrumentalization to which it has given rise. Africans have been the active subjects of their progressive dependency and, if we are to believe the historians, they have taken a great deal of time to arrive at this result. They maintained the upper hand, including military dominance, in their relations with the Europeans into the middle of the nineteenth century, and it was only in the 1870s that the terms of the exchange started to work against them.[22] Their participation in transatlantic civilization pertained to a strategy of extraversion, by building up various different kinds of financial dependency of which the political economy is now made up.[23] It inspired veritable ideologies of appropriation, such as those of the 'Enlightenment' or of 'development' (olaju) in the Yoruba.[24]

However, it might be better to change the focus of the analysis if we wish to avoid the misunderstanding that consists in ascribing to the heritage of the slave trade an overdetermining weight in terms of the causality of contemporary conflicts.[25] We need merely to establish the way that history – more specifically Atlantic history – persists in ubiquitous ways in social relations. It continues to be very polemical, as was shown by the reception of the film Adanggaman (2002) by the Ivory Coast director, Roger Gnoan M'Bala.[26] Nonetheless, it contributes to the naturalization of the processes of globalization on the African continent.

Thus, on the coast of the Gulf of Guinea, the modern form of witch-craft known in Cameroon as ekong, which symbolically stages the way societies have become monetarized, or the capitalist accumulation which this latter produces, still refers, even today, to the traumatic experience of the slave trade. The person who is its target dreams that he has been tied up at the water's edge. He then realizes that he is being invisibly eaten by a relation who is consuming his vitality by enslaving him on the plantations of the dreaded Mount Koupé.[27] In fact, the historical experience of slavery was seen in these terms: captives deported overseas would be swallowed alive. They were convinced they were going to their deaths and that they would literally be devoured by the whites. The salted meat that the sailors ate, and their cooking oil too, were surely the sinister omens of this? Their cheeses were surely made from the brains of blacks they had taken prisoner, and their red wine was the blood of the latter? And their gunpowder must have been extracted from their bones. Each stage of the fateful journey – having to wait in the stinking warehouses of the coast or in the dismal holds of the vessels – revived these fears.[28] The fear of cannibalism never ceased to haunt relations between Africans and Europeans (in both directions, it goes without saying: there's always someone who's a bigger cannibal than you) – as witness the rumours and panics that were provoked at regular intervals, during the period of colonization, by the missionaries' campaigns of vaccination, pastoral work and Eucharistic rituals, or indeed the mysterious bureaucratic organization of wage labour and its use of machines, automobiles and electrical equipment.[29] This phobia led to the appearance of a new category of operators of the invisible, distinct from that of witches, namely vampires: they could use mechanized forms of transport and were perceived as internationalized, professionalized, controlled and merchandised.[30] Even in the 1970s – and everything suggests that the anecdote could be more recent – a French Jesuit who was visiting a far-flung suburb of Douala at night found himself suspected of dark designs.[31]

Likewise, in Lunda Norte, in Angola, the young men who are involved in the illegal diamond industry, the Bana Lunda, who come from the nearby Congo, compromise with a syncretistic cult of the Virgin Mary and the saints (*santu*) which was established thanks to the precocious (albeit relative) Christianization of the region in the seventeenth century along the old trading road where there was an exchange of, *inter alia*, textiles, guns, ivory, rubber, sacred objects and captives. The neo-Catholic fetish helps them to 'capture' the diamonds, as the hunting metaphor used in the region has it, and to grasp the dollarization of the local economy. This does not, however, prevent them from recognizing themselves in heroes of western imaginary, such as Buffalo Bill, Zorro, Rambo, Superman, Terminator, Godzilla or the Ninja Turtles. Indeed, the special forces or militia of different countries in Central Africa happily identify with these figures too.[32]

The impact of globalization on the intimate lives of societies and individuals on the Angola–Congo border is all the clearer in that these activities, whether economic, religious or playful, all relate to the accession of young men to the dignity of adult status, as we will be seeing in more detail later on: the ritual of social initiation melds into the (admittedly partial) appropriation of globalization. The latter has for several centuries contributed to shaping the *Weltanschauung* of the peoples of Central Africa, not only in their relations with foreigners, but also in their internal political organization – if, that is, we can distinguish between the two spheres. Their power relations, their conception of wealth or health, their understanding of kinship or the invisible, their grasp of democracy and authoritarianism, their commerce with God (and Satan): all espouse images and cults which the Atlantic history of their societies created.

In Sao Tomé, the annual representation of the *tchiloli* provides us with another fine example.[33] The original text of this theatrical form – 1,400 lines of verse in archaic Portuguese attributed to the poet from Madeira, Baltasar Dias – is one of the numerous avatars of the cycle of Charlemagne that the troubadours introduced into Portugal in the eleventh century. It seems to have been transplanted to Sao Tomé at the end of the sixteenth century, probably at the behest of the sugar manufacturers from Madeira, and within the context of the boom in sugar cane: around 1550 there were some 3,000 Europeans and *Filhos da Terra* (mixed race), 10,000 slaves and 60 mills on the island, which exported 12,000 tonnes of sugar per year to Lisbon and Flanders. But the contemporary *tchiloli* interlards the narrative of the 'tragedy of the

Marquis of Mantua and the Emperor Charlot Magne [*sic*]' with prose scenes written in contemporary Portuguese. The latter are an opportunity for modern personages with an array of telephones and typewriters, wearing military uniforms or three-piece suits (and not, like the members of the Court of Mantua or the imperial guards, French-style costumes), to recite a completely over-the-top juridical discourse in the form of pleas, the appearance of witnesses, displays of graphological expertise, and autopsies. The performance, partly danced to continental African music and with a choreography of European origin based on the style of a minuet or a ballet, is a celebration of justice. When the death sentence handed down to him in accordance with the Portuguese military code is announced, Prince Charlot, the son of Charlemagne, who stands accused of the murder of his friend Valdevinos, the nephew of the Marquis of Mantua (whose wife he had been lusting after) exclaims: 'In which country, even among those to which civilization has not come, has anyone ever been sentenced without being given a hearing? I do not accept this verdict as it goes against the most elementary principles of human rights'. To which the Emperor retorts (in Old Portuguese): 'I will punish the guilty man, be he rich or poor'. Whereupon he orders the execution of his own son, having been bedazzled by the 'experts'.

The *tchiloli* is generally agreed to be a critique of a colonial society whose history in Sao Tomé was particularly violent and tormented. In its performances during the second half of the twentieth century, Charlemagne seems thus to have incarnated the power of Lisbon, Prince Charlot the Portuguese governor, and the Court of Mantua the people of Sao Tomé. 'A crime initially brought about by concupiscence – that Portuguese colonial concupiscence which has created so many off-spring of mixed race – a friendship betrayed, and, throughout the play, subjects demanding justice, a justice that can be obtained from the master only against his own desires: the whole colonial drama is there'.[34] This reading is certainly relevant, so long as we go a little further. For the *tchiloli*, the characters in which, whether masked or not, have their faces covered in kaolin, is at the same time a variant of the cult of the dead, that key element in the 'circum-Atlantic performance'.[35]

The same goes for the rituals associated with the evoking of the Mami Wata, rituals the geographical distribution of which 'covers that of the slave trade down the Atlantic coast of Africa'[36] and which are specially widespread on the coastal region of the Gulf of Guinea and along the rivers, such as the Congo-Zaire or the Wouri.[37] The existence of this cult, attested ever since the eighteenth–nineteenth centuries, seems in fact to go back to the encounter between white and African traders in the fifteenth century. The image of the Mami Wata, hybrid spirits that are half-aquatic and half-terrestrial, and which assume the shape of mermaids, seems to mimic the prows of Portuguese ships.

The identity attributed to them is in any case that of 'foreign women' or even, more explicitly, of 'European women'. In fact, the Mami Wata are deemed to be detached from social links. Admittedly, they are 'mothers' (Mami), but without children or families, and free of any religious or ethnic identity. They consort with Christians as well as Muslims. They embody beauty, vanity, jealousy, sexuality (and sometimes homosexuality), romantic love and good luck – that which brings material and monetary wealth, not that of life, fecundity and health. They play a role as intercessors and give access to the resources of transatlantic trade, colonization, capitalism and desire emancipated from the moral rules of the established society. Their seduction is such that people are prepared to deliver their friends and families to their tender mercies.

So a Mama Wata supports the usual analogy between accumulation or success and the devouring of the other. She has something of the tropical or equatorial Faust about her. Nonetheless, more specifically, she in particular embodies an allegory of globalization, being a character of extraversion. She expresses Africa's twofold opening towards both East and West, especially within the multicultural framework of the Victorian Empire. At the start of the twentieth century, an exotic European image of the snake-charmer, drawn from the art of the circus (and you can hardly get more transnational than that), became widespread in the British colonies.[38] Encouraged by this initial success, the merchants and peddlers of Sind, who swarmed down the western coast of the continent, started to circulate, from the 1940s and 1950s onwards, an iconography of Hindu gods and goddesses, which gradually conferred on the Atlantic water spirits certain of their physical features and modes of dress. The synthesis between the Mami Wata and the Hindu pantheon was made even easier by the fact that the latter seemed to provide it with the keys to economic success: like the altars dedicated to the goddess Lakshmi, the 'tables' dedicated to the 'mother of the water' among the Ewe of Ghana or the Igbo of Nigeria are covered with merchandise, such as bottles of gin, packets of Uncle Ben's rice, crockery, mirrors, umbrellas, lamps, bars of Lux soap and sunglasses. This does not, however, exclude another latent syncretism between the representation of the Mermaid and that of the Virgin Mary, especially in the Congo Basin, Christianized as early as the fifteenth century.[39] Furthermore, commerce with this mythical creature is associated with the world of music and dance, and the creativity of the latter owes a great deal in turn to its exchanges with the Caribbean and North America.[40]

Mami Wata is the key that gives access to money and pleasure, and at the same time she dispenses political power. Marshal Mobutu, the man from the 'bend of the river'[41] who did not fail to take refuge on his yacht when things got difficult, had sacrificed to his mermaid several of his friends and family: his mother, his first wife, his uncle, one of his sons. The network of 'second offices' (*deuxièmes bureaux*) – the mistresses that come with the job, so to speak – merged symbolically into that of the 'water spirits' and contributed to the authoritarian and clientelist regulations of the single party. Politicians eager to preserve their jobs, or to 'defend' themselves from the attacks from the spirit world launched by their rivals, would resort to mermaids and their boas that disgorged 'silver money': 'Several times I have met and spoken with the mermaid in the bush, on the road . . . leading from Mount Ngafula to UNIKIN. It was here that I would meet the mermaid. Sometimes she came naked, sometimes she was clothed', admitted a former minister who regularly spoke with the chief of the Spirits and did not hesitate to sleep in a cemetery next to corpses or to share his bedroom with a big snake.[42]

On the same level as music, urban painting bears witness to the ubiquity of the intercession which Mami Wata offers to the Congolese, overwhelmed as they are by the change of scale in contemporary globalization. The latter, as a historical configuration of extraversion, is not foreign to them. On the contrary, it is the subject of their fantasies, their desires, their ambitions and their artistic creation. But it is also worth noting that Mami Wata, an icon of globalization, feeds (at least in the Congo) into the national imagination, at the same time as capitalist material culture and accumulation. She intervenes at the junction between the field of the state and that of the worldwide market of goods, capital, emotions and political ideas. She is an artistic and fantastical form, situated clearly within a chain of historical events, of the relational historicity inherent in the processes of globalization, so long as these are grasped in their *longue durée*.

From this point of view, there is nothing exceptional about the transatlantic area. The Chinese-Hindu-Muslim world economy in Asia has the same depth of field, one that is constitutive of the historicity of contemporary globalization.[43] It is hardly an epiphenomenon if the diasporas or merchant networks of Chinese, Indian or Iranian people maintain their galactic unity and their links with their lands of origin by means of funerary practices.[44] The cult of the dead structures Asian transnationalism just as much as it does the 'circum-Atlantic performance'. It is also in this respect that globalization is a memorializing experience, able to erect itself into a legitimate *Herrschaft* deprived of authority, even if it is at the price of a 'closure of narrative . . . placed at the service of the community's closure of identity'.[45]

The persistence of the regional past turns the contemporary experience of globalization into a veritable 'historical condition',[46] and not a mere moment of alienation. Thus, in Asia, the 'memory of trade'[47] is constructed out of items that were exchanged to a massive degree through the *longue durée* – the spices that Europeans hankered after (though their importance has perhaps been exaggerated), the sea products enjoyed by the Chinese, textiles, the manufactured goods produced by the Industrial Revolution from the nineteenth century onwards, slaves, sugar, and above all tea and opium – which continue to haunt the regional transnational imagination and condense particular fantastical figures. For example, the 'sea brides' who dwell in the depths of the Aru archipelago lavish pleasures and pearls on the sea-divers, in exchange for gifts of food, betel, tobacco, jewels and, above all, white crockery. They thereby help these divers to pay back their debts to the local traders, while also adding to their debts through their demands. They display the same ambivalence when they contribute to the success of their partner, with whom they have a monogamous relationship, while threatening to pursue him onto terra firma and if necessary 'eat' his friends and family, especially his children, when it comes to demanding their due. Like the African Mami Wata, which they actually resemble quite a lot, the 'sea brides' speak of the native identity and its inevitable relation to the Other within the centuries-old context of marine trade. They provide a form of mediation between the fishermen, who are torn between two poles of values and behaviour, the native 'Aru' repertoire and the extravert 'Malay' repertoire, and the traders and creditors, surreptitiously identified as 'Chinese', but acting as anchoring points in the 'Malay' world, however long they may have been established in the archipelago. Even the ocean depths themselves are affected by the processes of history. The joint venture between the 'Chinese' and the 'sea brides' seems to have supplanted the Arabic-Muslim traders and their prophets who all used to govern one level of the skin-diving industry, if we are to believe the ancients. As for the ships that imprison mysterious cargoes within their sides, which nurse all sorts of messianic hopes among those who wait for them (as in the 'cargo cults'), they are often described as *portugis* even if it is admitted that they are likely to be Spanish or English.[48]

The sea dispenses wealth, hope, desire and civilization, but it is also a source of violence and fear. It brought the devastation of the Second World War, just as it had brought colonial domination and exploitation. Furthermore, the predatory slave-trading of the Iranun and Balangingi which attacked and terrorized the greater part of the coasts of Southeast Asia, from the second half of the eighteenth to the middle of the nineteenth century, constituted a considerable 'traumatic event',[49] which right up to the present day has shaped the geographical implantation of populations along the coastal regions of the Philippines or the East Indies. Even today, parents appeal to the fear of 'pirates' when they are trying to get their youngsters off to sleep.[50] This fantastic tale has more important political repercussions, however. The contemporary representation of 'Islam', or 'piracy' or 'terrorism' and the social awareness of the recurrent conflicts tearing apart the south of the island

of Mindanao are the result of the unleashing of the slave-traders' raids
that were financed by the Sultanate of Sulu and of their belated eradication under the impact of Spanish, British and Dutch repression, at the
cost of the reification inherent in creating a 'foil' identity, that of
the 'Moro'. From this angle, state-formation in Southeast Asia needs
the same kind of analysis as the one we sketched for Angola, so long
as we bear in mind the limits of the exercise.[51] This formation is a direct
product of globalization – more precisely, of the habitual interlocking
of a whole series of factors that comprise this process: the intensification of China's external trade in the second half of the eighteenth
century and its increasingly international dimension thanks to the
trading rivalry between England, the Netherlands, Spain and other
western countries; the increasing demand for menial labour entailed
by this expansion, the development of new models of consumption,
the plantation economy and European imperial urbanization, with its
big building sites; the way the task of getting hold of this labour force
was delegated to Iranun and Balangingi maritime operators by the
Sultanate of Sulu and, in a less flagrant way, England; the suppression
of the 'discharge' of the slave trade in the middle of the nineteenth
century, within the context of eliminating privateering and piracy
across the planet in favour of a state monopoly on legitimate
violence.[52]

The 'historical condition' of contemporary globalization in Asia,
what Alf Lüdke would call its 'history of the everyday',[53] is thus also
part of a configuration of relational historicity that establishes it as an
'event'. Various ritual and fantastical narratives can be observed at
work here: these narratives are the object of interpretations, strategies
and social or political manipulations that for two centuries have interlocked with networks of trade or credit and have thus been involved
in the survival of empires and kingdoms, or in assertive nationalisms.
But over and above these narratives we can glimpse a more general
reality. Transnationalism has its own density. It was not born from the
ashes of the Cold War. It needs to be read across time, and gauged in
accordance with specific trajectories. In particular, the regional swarming of China, which has never been as closed off from its external
environment as the changing opinions of nationalist and liberal histo-
riographers has claimed,[54] and the economic supremacy of the United
Kingdom, a supremacy which it won thanks to its trade in two emblematic merchandises, tea and opium, were the main facts on the basis of
which the Asian transnational area was configured. However great the
importance of Calcutta, Shanghai, Tokyo or London with regard to the
globalization of that vast continent, Singapore and Hong Kong were
its key cities. Even apart from their financial, banking, industrial and
media roles (which are too well known to need highlighting), one
should mention elements that are secondary from the macro-economic

point of view, but as decisive as they are eloquent from the historical angle.

Thus Hong Kong was one of the main hubs of Chinese emigration in the second half of the nineteenth century and the start of the twentieth, thanks to the quality of the services procured by its specialized agents, especially in the field of information, the obtaining of banknotes, credit, passports, medical certificates or identity papers, transfers of funds, opportunities for smuggling, and offers of 'contractual' jobs overseas.[55] As for the free port of Singapore, founded in 1819, it was, over the next few decades, a commercial harbour for Iranun and Balangingi 'pirates', who here acquired the weapons they needed and sold slaves freshly captured on the shores and seas of the East Indies (or used Singapore as a staging post for their transport).[56] It is impossible to understand contemporary transnational relations in Asia and the part played in them (socially, culturally, economically and politically) by these two 'global' cities unless our analysis takes into full account events in the recent past – i.e. the foundational nineteenth century.

Transnationalism has often preceded, and then accompanied, the concomitant process of formation of colonial empires and, within them, of the nation-state. This has taken the minimal form of a regional integration that guarantees the close interrelation between specific territories and vaster (sometimes even 'global') economic and cultural fields. This remains the case even if we bear in mind the fact that the suffix 'national' is obviously anachronistic in the period before the appearance of the phenomenon of nationalism, colonialism or 'nativism' at the end of the nineteenth century. But this process more often aided and abetted the establishment of kingdoms and empires before the European imperial age, of which it was to some extent the social frontier. Now this latter became perpetuated within the gaps and crevices of western imperialism and the system of states that emerged from it, as the evolution of Southeast Asia and the Persian Gulf both demonstrate equally well. The trading in bags and bales, smuggling, banditry, piracy, migrations, religious syncretism, cultural cross-fertilization and ethnic meldings that flourish in them, in the gaps left by the plenitude of the state, are part and parcel of the continuity of an old history of 'generalized mutual interactions'.[57] The latest research emphasizes, moreover, the autonomy of these processes and these transnational spaces from European expansion. Of course, given the scale of the periodization I have adopted, the centrality of the colonial 'event' (one that was para-colonial in the cases of China, Siam, Persia and the Ottoman Empire) is undeniable. But this does not mean it was systematic.

Claude Markovits has thus shown how the Sindhi networks of Shikarpur and Hyderabad, which pre-existed the establishment of the Victorian Raj and were independent of it, were organized following their own specific parameters that were by no means dictated by the logic of the different political spaces over which they were scattered, finally came to terms with the establishment of a worldwide British Empire that had, after all, shaken their interests, and embodied a fascinating case of the way the local can become interlocked with the global while more or less short-circuiting the national authorities.[58] It is true that, since Partition in 1947, the Hindus of Sind have fled Pakistan and redeployed (in particular using Bombay as their base), and have shown a tendency to 'form a community' rooted in ethnic and religious identity, drawing closer to radical Hindu nationalism, if only so as to distinguish themselves from the Sikhs after the assassination of Indira Gandhi in 1984. Nonetheless, two main symptoms of globalization (on the one hand the functioning of a remarkably flexible economic network on the planetary scale, and on the other the mobilization of national identities and the formation of states on the ruins of a colonial empire) have in this example combined their energies in a local and partial way while never entirely coinciding for any length of time.

However, in the emigration of people from China, the 'disjunction' between these different levels (political and socio-economic) of globalization is probably less great these days, although the creation of the People's Republic made it seem more dramatic, from the seizure of power by the Communists in 1949 to Deng's reforms in 1978: the diaspora plays a major role in the rise of mainland China within the international system and the world economy, and, willingly or not, it provides its militaristic nationalism with the means for its ends, however much it may mistrust these. In the example of Iran, the effects of 'disjunction' between the national political domain and the expatriates are even more ambiguous and vary greatly from one place of settlement to another: the refugee community in California that settled there after the 1979 revolution nurses dreams of a *Reconquista*, which does not prevent it from indulging in frequent family visits, commercial exchanges and even economic or evergetic investments in the mother country; in Dubai and Tokyo, political susceptibilities are less immediately obvious, and there seems to be a proven collaboration between the authorities of the Islamic Republic and Iranian residents.[59]

We thus need to investigate, from one situation to another, the way in which we can see as an event the concrete relation at work between the historicity of the transnational field (or that of other effects of globalization, such as the establishment of the 'market') and the historicity of the process of state-formation. This is the only way in which we can leave behind misleading generalizations about globalization, notably as regards the 'rate of transnationalism' in the international system, from the end of the Cold War onwards. We have already seen how, for

global studies, this phenomenon has started to assume an unprecedented importance, and I would immediately cast some doubt on this
assertion, or at least on the universality of its relevance. In reality,
everything is a matter of historical contingency. Aihwa Ong is quite
convincing when she emphasizes the 'cultural logics of transnationality', the 'flexible citizenship' that stems from them, and the acceleration
of the Pacific Shuttle between Chinese-Asian societies and North
America. An increasing number of managers, technocrats and members
of the liberal professions circumvent the sphere of the nation-state so
that, paradoxically, they can maximize the fiscal, educational or health
gains they can obtain from it by localizing their investments, their
professional activities or their families on both sides of the ocean, while
escaping from the control of political authorities and their bureaucracies. Without questioning the sovereignty of the nation-state, they are
causing it to reform and 'recalibrate' itself depending on the zones in
which it is applied and exercised.[60]

But the fact remains that the detailed research carried out by Made-
line Hsu on the emigration into America of the natives from a city in
the south of China, Taishan, from the 1880s onwards, leads us to qualify
this perception of an increase in the activity of the Pacific Shuttle.[61] In
this precise case, the last decades have led to a fragmentation of the
transnational interface, and, in particular, to a disappearance of the
transoceanic public space that had been created by the publication of
various 'Chinese overseas magazines' (qiaokan) during the Republican
era, by the suspension of remittances and evergetic gifts, and by the
increasing rarity of family visits. The Japanese occupation of China, the
Civil War, the establishment of the Communist regime and the start of
the Cold War all cut off many of the links hitherto maintained between
Taishan and the west American coast over fifty years of emigration.
The new family groupings permitted by the adoption of a more liberal
legislation on immigration into the United States in 1965, and Deng's
opening of China, did the rest. The massive delocalization of people
from Taishan, more of whom these days live abroad than in their city
of origin, has sapped the 'transnational circuit of migration', and the
city councillors have drawn the inevitable conclusion, taking down the
sign at the coach station greeting the 'Chinese from overseas' returning
to their native land.[62] The growing number of Chinese and Koreans
settled in the United States who have the ashes of their ancestors transported so they can be buried in America, as they now think they will
never return to their homeland, suggests that the example of Taishan
is not exceptional.[63]

The sole general hypothesis from which we can start out is that
globalization, being a good 'night-time visitor', and interrelated
both with the state and with capitalism, has definitely proceeded by a
concatenation of its successive ages. The momentum of each of these

ages has proved to be cumulative rather than mutually exclusive. Tribal and knightly dynasties, nomadic societies, trading diasporas, thalassocracies, ancient techniques of trade and credit, the social institutions of former eras such as Islamic *vaqf* and bazaars, have often been reproduced under cover of the imperial expansion of the West which used them at the same time as it dominated, fought or marginalized them.[64] The change of scale unleashed in the nineteenth century did not start from a blank sheet. It re-used what was already there just as much as it created *ex nihilo*, and this is as true of the globalization of the social sphere, in particular via transnational relations, as it is of state-formation or the establishment of the capitalist mode of production.

However, though we may restore the historicity proper to 'generalized mutual interaction', we must not slip into mere historicism. Globalization is a production of History, and not just its reproduction, even if it is 'enlarged', as the Marxists would say. It is pushing us forward into a peculiar world. And it can be deciphered only in the light of the continuities from which it emerges, given that it cannot be reduced to the latter and that it is in itself the bearer of changes and even complete breaks. Already in the seventeenth and eighteenth centuries the mercantilist sugar plantations of Brazil and the Caribbean had prepared the way for the Industrial Revolution by inaugurating new methods of investment financing, unleashing capital and the management of units of production, merchandising the labour force, internationalizing it, and placing its disciplinary and total over-exploitation under the protection of the absolutist state, in an Atlantic replica of the 'second serfdom' which, from the sixteenth century onwards, vanquished the free peasantry of Eastern Europe.[65] The modern age reinvented an age-old form of labour, namely slavery, and thanks to this it brought about an unprecedented expansion of the economy of the Old Continent both towards the New World and towards Asia. It thus laid the foundations for a completely new mode of production. *Mutatis mutandis*, the same is true today, according to a different configuration, and with an equally uncertain outcome. It is indeed this indeterminate quality that we should draw on to grasp the historical trajectories of globalization, rather than lulling ourselves with an illusory rumination on what allegedly always stays the same.

The watershed between continuity and change is not to be drawn on the planetary scale, but at the level of local societies. A. Lakhsassi and M. Tozy, for instance, have shown how the system of the ancient social alliances of the *leff-s*, in the south-west of Morocco, structures the contemporary network of NGOs of development and their 'indirect administration' of this part of the Sheriffian kingdom.[66] Globalization, like state-formation, is first and foremost a matter of *terroirs*.[67] Parodying Giovanni Levi, while following his lesson in method, we need to talk about 'the globalization of the village' and write its discontinuous *microstoria*:

> In the long term, all personal and family strategies tend, perhaps, to appear so blunt that they melt into a common state of relative equilibrium. But the way each person participates in the general history, in the formation and modification of the structures that bear social reality, cannot be evaluated solely on the basis of perceptible results: during the life of every person, in a cyclical manner, there arise problems, uncertainties, choices, a politics of everyday life centred on the strategic use of social rules. . . . In the gaps between the normative systems already established or in the process of formation, groups and individuals develop their own significant strategy. This is capable of marking political reality with a durable imprint, not of preventing the forms of domination, but of conditioning and modifying them.[68]

The problem we are discussing is indeed that of the continuation of History, not that of its 'end', whatever sense (liberal or historicist) we naively give this term. By virtue of this fact, global Being-in-the-world is by no means in a state of weightlessness, cut off from its roots, isolated from its fellows and ancestors, dispossessed of its past and its identity, as too many books and lectures would have us believe. On the enlarged scale in which it is now at home, it continues to weave the web of its social relations and their meanings, in the classic expression used by Max Weber.

Indeed, those celebrated 'primordial identities', whose disappearance and unleashing are alternately bewailed by sovereignist lamentations, are the result of this change of scale and even, quite often, of the political and moral economies of extraversion that we have seen at work, notably in Africa and Asia. A plethora of anthropological and historical works has demonstrated that ethnicity and religious belonging were the results of the way societies were drawn into the maelstrom of globalization from the nineteenth century onwards and sometimes even from the Middle Ages or the early modern period – from their relation to the expansion of Christianity and Islam to the creation of the colonial state and the economic, cultural and political integration of its space, as well as to the internationalization of the economy.

'Tribalism' in Africa, 'communalism' and the caste system in India, and confessionalism in Lebanon are all textbook cases which it would be redundant to go over again, all the more so in that this effort would be pointless: there are none so deaf as culturalists who will not hear. But we also need to reflect on the ethnogenesis of peoples whom we will call 'vehicular' or 'transitive', and who dwell on the social frontiers and physical borders of regional systems of states, in the transnational dimension of the latter. The Iranun and the Balangigi of the 'Sulu zone' in the nineteenth century, the Orang Suku Laut of the archipelago of Riau-Lingga, off Singapore, and the Baluchi and Kurds are all of composite origin and constituted themselves as such (or were identified as such), over time, on the basis of their functions as participants in trading, smuggling, predatory or migratory activities.[69] Their identity is relational, being part of the social reality of the 'frontier', in line with the model of ethnogenesis in Africa established by Igor Kopytoff, who insists on the interaction between 'metropolises' and the 'frontier areas' to which they gave birth.[70]

With all due respect to the nativist clichés that the vogue for ecology has put back on the menu, the same applies also to societies that were long described as 'primitive' and these days are thought of in terms of 'communities of natives' or 'minorities', endowed with 'collective rights' in the great registers of the World Bank and International Civil Society & Co. Thus, in the Indonesian part of the island of Kalimantan, the Dayak Meratus, whom the regime of the New Order has been endeavouring to fix, within the framework of its twofold programme of 'managing isolated populations' and converting the latter to one of six religious affiliations approved by the administration, have long been integrated into various world markets for which they collect the produce of the forest thanks to their spatial mobility.[71] Their marginality was politically and religiously constructed in opposition to the local or regional domination of the system of Muslim states, and subsequently of the nation-state: the Dayaks still have no religion and, more specifically, exist outside Islam and its political sponsorship, though not outside regional political and economic relations.[72] Neither outside the state nor outside the market, they are, on the contrary, established by means of their relationships with them, into which they are subsumed. Constantly on the move but not, for all that, categorized as nomads, they do not correspond to the classical ethnography either of primitive peoples rooted in their native soil – or of a free-floating population. Their social practice of displacement, instead of being a symptom or a cause of their cultural restriction, as is asserted by the 'developers' of the central state, is a means for them to find a place within their environment and to negotiate with it.

Likewise, the Kabre in the north of Togo have forged their 'traditions' over three centuries of exchanges with the European presence on the coast and a colonial public policy that had delegated to the 'village community' the social reproduction of the labour force. The revival of rituals which has been witnessed over the last thirty years, the vigour of the economy of the gift, the conception of habitat, and the flexibility of social identifications and affiliations all bear witness to this positive inclusion of Kabre society in 'translocality', thanks to the experience of the exodus from the countryside and participation in a capitalist economy, and are not evidence of phenomena of resistance to a 'modernity' imposed from elsewhere.[73]

Finally, we may remember, state-formation and the crystallization of national consciousness are themselves phenomena that belong to social frontiers and physical borders which owe a great deal to globalization and the change of scale that it has represented over the last two centuries.[74] That the relation with the historical processes of globalization is probably the main source of the contemporary lines of political, social and cultural identification finally forces us to submit, willingly or not, to a little Copernican Revolution with respect to the holistic force of gravitation of the social sciences. Extraversion is the rule, so to speak, and endogenous evolution is an aberrant or phoney form of it. I am here following – as I have already stated – Michel Foucault's critique of the problematic of 'origin' (*Ursprung*); he replaces it by the concepts of 'provenance' (*Herkunft*) and 'emergence' (*Entstehung*).[75] So away with mythologies of identity and authenticity, the myth of the people, of self-sufficiency in food and other self-centred developments – away with these discourses of introversion which are merely malevolent variations on the old ideas of purity and thus pollution. They may have been, at the time of another change of scale (that of the passage from feudalism and absolutism to citizenship), factors of social emancipation and a broadening of intellectual horizons. But how can one be blind to the fact that they are now regressive and that the 'social contracts' they have legitimized have become obsolete, if not factors of enslavement?

We need to acknowledge the fact that historically the frontier is the centre, the Other is the Self and dispersion is unity. The initial standard can no longer be taken to be the absolutist or Jacobin state, and the nation stemming from it: France provided the model for this version, and sovereignist theory takes its temperature twice a day. It must boldly be those 'galactic'[76] expanses of which the Mediterranean, the 'Javanese crossroads' and the Caribbean are fantastical cultural expressions, sometimes irritating in their ideological silliness, but all the same not without meaning for those who seek to understand the global canvas of social relations. Here, the irony of globalization consists in the way it forces the historical sociology of the state to conceptualize the latter outside itself and in spite of itself.

The global web of social relations

At this point of our discussion, it appears that contemporary globalization rests on social relations imbued with their own historicity, that of transnational spheres of action that become interlocked with one another over centuries of commercial, religious and cultural exchanges, cross-breeding and, last but not least, periods (generally much shorter) of colonial occupation. From this point of view, the Americas present us with a particular case, thanks to the duration, the extent and the radical nature of political subjection found there. This subjection took the extreme forms of extermination, and the quasi-complete eradication of the native modes of social organization, plantation slavery, forced labour and racial discrimination.

The architecture of transnational historical fields is to some degree the societal façade of the hierarchical system of states which Martin Shaw has analysed. It now goes without saying that this architecture forms part and parcel of this system of states.[77] To take one of many examples, it is revealing to note how contemporary migrations – those transnational flows par excellence – continue so frequently to follow the pattern of relations between states and societies established in the era of (and within the framework of) western colonial empires. Migrations are historical processes and moments, as Saskia Sassen insists,[78] but their historicity is related to that of the world system of states.

We need to focus more specifically on these social relations that underlie globalization, to ascertain whether indeed the latter does not lie outside the societies which it subsumes and structures. Sticking to relatively strict criteria – and ignoring any question as to the extent of the dependency of the set of social relations of production with regard to the internationalization of the economy (an essential question, but one that goes beyond the competence of the present book) – it is easy to find populations whose economic reproduction and social existence are directly constructed on the interfaces of the 'generalized mutual interaction' that constitutes globalization, and more especially in its transnational dimension. We will here content ourselves with a summary and impressionistic typology in the form of a pyramid of operators of globalization.

At the top of the edifice we recognize the 'cosmopolitan hyperbourgeoisie': those who bewail the retirement of Concorde, the tightly closed circle of the G8, the major states and main global businesses, the stars of the jet-setting society, showbiz and the media. Their wealth and influence are enormous, but would not be enough to create a global world. From the point of view of the historical society of politics, things start to get serious at the middling levels inhabited by administrators, mandarins, the gentlemen of globalization, its organic intellectuals as well as its 'cultural intermediaries' who act as its 'traffic policemen', or its 'demiurges', to use the definition put forward by the historian of the French Revolution, Michel Vovelle.[79] The internationalization of the economy, education, health and leisure, the quest for 'global governance' or at any event a necessary regulation of the main sectors of activity or the worldwide techniques of communication, the 'new regionalization' of the international system, the expansion of religions on the planetary scale, the development of NGOs and media, have all given rise to what we will deliberately call a global 'middle class', accepting the debatable character of the notion which brings out the generality and banality of the phenomenon. Rightly or wrongly, it is taken for granted that the fate of capitalism and democracy, within the framework of the nation-state, lies in the hands of such an entity, however elusive it may be. Now, over the last two centuries, globalization has engendered a category of this type whose professional activity, spatial mobility and – a point to which I shall be returning later – economic ethos are defined by its parameters. This transnational 'middle class' has to some degree contrived to add itself to the networks of merchants, financers and transporters of the previous ages of globalization.

Without any attempt to be exhaustive, we can quote, in no particular order: international civil servants and diplomats; the civil servants of nation-states who are working for 'global governance'; the executives of businesses, banks, insurance companies, hotel chains etc., specializing in import and export, foreign markets or takeover operations; executives, technicians, shopkeepers and even certain qualified workers who have left their own countries more or less definitively; a great number of the executives or journalists on radio or television, and part of the press that now exists in a state of osmosis with the worldwide 'mediascape'; the staff (at least the airborne staff) of air companies; the missionaries of different religious affiliations or sects with a universal vocation who plough the furrows of the global marketplace of faith; and the militants of 'global civil society'. And a particular place must be found for 'communities of experts'. These latter, who have direct access to the hottest or most specialized files of globalization, such as the non-proliferation of weapons of mass destruction, the struggle against money-laundering, corruption or terrorism, the regulation of new technologies of information, energy, or the international financial system, or even the implementation of the programmes of structural adjustment of the IMF and the World Bank, are more often than not restricted in number, know each other personally, and share a social life and a common stock of knowledge that transcends national frontiers and affiliations, whatever the degree of loyalty civil servants may feel towards their administration and government. The influence of these 'communities of experts' over the way the world functions can be considerable, as has been demonstrated by the ambiguous collaboration between the Harvard Institute for National Development – in particular, Professors Jeffrey Sachs and Andrei Shleifer – and the 'dream team' of the reformers in Moscow round Yegon Gaidar and Anatoli Chubais in the 1990s: it is to this that we owe the strange ways Russia has effected its 'transition' to a 'market economy', entailing the 'siphoning off' of a considerable proportion of international financial aid.[80]

Generally speaking, the programmes of structural adjustment in Latin America and Africa, the liberalization of the economies of the former Soviet republics and the countries of Central and Eastern

Europe, Deng's reforms in China and the increase in the integration of worldwide exchanges that have resulted, have all entailed an at least partial substitution of managing elites by new categories of techno-crats. The latter draw their relative legitimacy and political resources from their privileged relation to the processes and institutions of glo-balization.[81] A similar analysis can be made of most public policies or sectors of activity. There is hardly any domain left in which the hierar-chy of decision-makers within organizations is not dictated by the types of competence, and the administrative and linguistic techniques required by rubbing shoulders with the people and procedures of glo-balization. The 'alternative' universe of NGOs is no exception.[82] Furthermore, the internationalization of university courses creates a circulation of young people that is not without its similarities to the transnational peregrinations of the quest for knowledge in the Europe of the Middle Ages, the Renaissance or the Enlightenment. Different forms of knowledge, the technologies by which they are acquired, spread and managed, have a worldwide scope, and their *literati* are inevitably in their image. The profession of IT specialists and the popu-larization of their art, which is comparable with a gigantic planetary movement for literacy, are enough to show that the 'information era' is evidently providing itself with the social strata capable of guarantee-ing its reproduction and expansion.

Then comes the vast army of the drudges of globalization, who delocalize their labour force by emigrating, or place it locally at the service of units of production and exchange that are directly integrated into the internationalization of industry or services: workers both male and female in special economic zones, free zones or 'corridors' aimed at satisfying the world market within the framework of trade within firms and in the shape of importing and re-exporting goods; women and children sent abroad to work as domestic servants, jockeys or slaves; workers both male and female, sometimes expatriated, in the international sex industry; legal or clandestine immigrants who sell their labour force in America, Europe, Japan or Australia, in the 'new industrial nations' of Asia, in the Persian Gulf, or quite simply in states that are less underprivileged than their own; the working classes of old industrial nations that are subject to the internationalization of produc-tion, and whose fate hovers uncertainly between intensified exploita-tion and dismissal.

As we have seen, it is almost whole societies or populations, 'tran-sient' or 'vehicular', which reproduce themselves or come into being, carried by the tides of globalization, in particular by transnational exchanges. They take on an ethnic, tribal or ethno-national configura-tion (as is the case of the Kurds, the Balutchis, the Pashtoons, the Touaregs, the Dioulas and the Hausa), or one that is national (the inhabitants of the warehouse-states of sub-Saharan Africa specialized in regional smuggling) or diasporic (such as the Chinese overseas, the Armenians or the Jews). In other cases, they are coming into being before our eyes, in the cross-border dimension of the international system, like the 'floating populations' of composite ethnic and national origin that have become specialized in highway robbery in North Cameroon, or the Hutu and Tutsi refugees resident outside Burundi and Rwanda.[83] It then becomes tricky to find the right term to describe them. The common denominator of these sets of people, and the important point for our purposes, is the 'flexible' and 'nomadic' character of their citizenship.[84] This conception can go together with a strong, even messianic, discourse of identity, as in the example of the Hutus and the Tutsis, but it is expressed in the instrumentalization and 'contextualization' of national affiliation, in accordance with changing circumstances. Holding several passports at once is an explicit symptom of this, a habit found in the Chinese diaspora, the cross-border Balutchi populations and the nebulous group of shopkeepers, traffickers and soldiers from West Africa.

We also need to take into consideration the seasonal or contract workers of globalization who draw part of their revenue, at one time of the year during a circumscribed phase of their existence, from economic activities that are integrated into the world market – for instance, temporary employees in the tourist sector; travellers who indulge in pavement selling; money-changers in the unofficial sector; the 'diggers' for diamonds, gold or other precious minerals; criminals, bandits, pirates and 'fighting customs officers' or other 'sobels' ('soldiers by day, rebels by night'), who operate in the grey areas of national sovereignty and pick up a share of the transnational manna by cutting off roads or seizing hostages; traffickers – in particular of drugs, illegal workers, stolen cars, counterfeit goods, or protected species – who transport, at every attempt, the illicit merchandise of the international economy (merchandise which may sometimes have an animal or human face).

This is not the whole story. If we ignore the sphere of production and the exchange of merchandise for that of consumption or affiliation (e.g. religious, cultural or ideological), the circle of social agents of globalization, whether permanent or working to contract, widens spectacularly. Indeed, it includes tourists travelling abroad for their holidays or for one-off journeys linked to a particular event such as a wedding, a funeral, the sales, an art exhibition or a music festival; members of different religions and universal sects organized into churches and multilateral or transnational communities, provided they form part of a circulation and social life that involve a supranational religious affiliation (for instance in the shape of pilgrimages, jubilees, retreats or celebrations); consumers and television spectators who are *au fait* with 'global' images and products; and even the pillaging soldiers or honourable citizens who lay their hands on towns and cities to get hold of the goods imported, as in most African countries over the past fifteen years or so, in Los Angeles in 1992 or Iraq in 2003.

Finally, if we turn to war, the conflicts that are most clearly linked (rightly or wrongly) with the 'event' of contemporary globalization, at least on the level of political representations – those of ex-Yugoslavia, Iraq, Afghanistan, Liberia, Somalia, Sierra Leone, the Great Lakes or Algeria – have spewed out onto the roads and seas millions of refugees for which the system of 'indirect rule' of globalization, namely the NGOs, endeavours to assume responsibility, in counterpoint with the traditional multilateral organization of the United Nations and bilateral forms of emergency aid.

What name are we to give to this human reality of globalization, unless we describe it in terms of social foundations? It comprises a mass phenomenon, even though this should not be exaggerated and even though we need to bear in mind this twofold warning: globalization is 'partial'[85] and, in so far as it prevails as a partial 'event', it is a 'partial condition'[86] in the sense that it excludes neither that of belonging to the state, nor that of being rooted in the local and that from this point of view it cannot be reduced to this zero-sum game. In particular, this human reality of globalization is not reducible to the anomic swarming of the 'multitude'. It is socially established in its relation to globalization – it both 'resists' it, as anti-globalization militants claim, but it also surrenders to it: and it would be idealistic to see this self-abandonment as merely the acceptance of a voluntary servitude.

Let us take the case of emigration. In many societies, the decision to emigrate is often taken within the family, and sometimes even at a family council, duly summoned for the occasion. It then gives rise to a thoroughgoing economic strategy on the part of the household: land, houses and herds are sold, so that the family's 'passage' can be financed. The motivation of the migrant, whether he has been designated as such or whether he is acting of his or her own volition, is social through and through. It is a matter of improving the fate of his friends and family, asserting his dignity and his maturity as an adult, and succeeding. The candidate for departure places his destiny in the hands of an often sophisticated social organization, for instance that of a merchant confraternity for the Murids of Senegal, or that of people-smugglers, sometimes at the cost of being temporarily dehumanized – a point to which I will need to return – but with the aim of re-establishing the social link with his original hearth and home. As soon as he arrives at his destination, the migrant sends a message back to his relatives, often in the form of a recorded cassette telling the epic tale of his journey, which he entrusts to an acquaintance who is returning to his village. This cassette will be listened to collectively by the family, then by the neighbours, and will give rise to a whole social narrative on the part of the listeners, extolling the self-abnegation and courage of the absent family member, stigmatizing the hard times they live in, asking questions about the mysterious West.[87] Later, the emigrant will endeavour to consolidate this still tenuous thread linking him to his family (or, in the case of the much more personal strategies of the Congolese *Sapeurs* or the *ghet-tomen* of the Ivory Coast, to his friends[88]), by sending money, showing solidarity with the new candidates for departure and the passing visitors, going back to stay in his country for a whole and to show off his success, and posing as an evergete or a 'Great Man'. The exorbitant place of the gift in the transnational economy of emigration is well known, especially as regards these journeys back home. This is not a sign of weakness in the social interaction inherent in globalization.

Likewise, transnational miners who exploit the resources of the African subsoil in lands adjacent to their own, in the course of journeys of greater or lesser duration, are not in a state of weightlessness, even if they too are emblematic figures of contemporary globalization, pointed at with accusing fingers by those who view 'blood diamonds' with contempt and associated with the sinister myth of wars that are presumed to be 'new' – even though they are authentic pioneers in the classic annals of the gold rush. On the borders of Angola and the Congo, the young 'diggers' who 'pick up' precious stones and dollars are integrated into the international monetary system via the greenbacks by means of which the transactions are effected. They work for the Antwerp market, and are unable to evade the monopolistic toils of the De Beers Company. At the same time, they are active in the transatlantic historical field, as I have already mentioned in my discussion of their commerce with the *santu* and the Mami Wata. They are subject to the ups and downs of Angolan and Congolese national policy, paying as they do a heavy tribute towards the war between the MPLA and UNITA, and the predatory activities of the forces of law and order in both countries. They compromise with local moral codes and reinvent them in the crucible of their social experience of the physical border and the social frontier.[89] In short, they are social agents fully involved in creating the social sphere, and this happens by virtue of their involvement in the processes of economic, monetary and cultural globalization in this part of Africa, not in spite of or in the margins of the latter. The same can be said of transient pavement sellers, male and female, and smugglers in the Gulf, or in Turkey: they are directly reliant on world markets and had already been severely hit during the Asian and Russian monetary crises of 1997–8; but their trading activities have a social background in their families, in the structures of the mafia or the different charities on which they rely, and in the ethical problems they raise by virtue of the way they get mixed up (whether in fact or fiction) with prostitution.[90]

The operators of 'globalization from below',[91] while being in direct contact with the processes of globalization, are integrated into the national political economies of which they remain, to a greater or lesser degree, the cogs, however transnational they may be. Money-changers in the streets, jewellers in the bazaars, ever ready to buy or sell currency, and the *bureaux de change* that proliferate in the cities are all clear examples of this. By definition, they too live on the pulsing energies of globalization, and some of its disjunctions that cause fluctuations in the value of the dollar, the euro or the yen. They also play on national regulations, especially in situations where a control of exchange rates or an official plurality of these is prevalent, and where the possibilities for black-marketing and speculation thus become systemic.

They are sometimes subject to repressive measures on the part of the authorities. These can take two forms. On the one hand, they actually work for some of these authorities. On the other, they provide a necessary service which the banking sector is incapable of satisfying. These characters from the 'unofficial' sector of the economy paradoxically confer on capitalism and the market a minimum of credibility in the countries where the central bank and the commercial banks have only an illusory credibility and where monetary depreciation is galloping. They are, in parallel, useful to those who hold power, since the primitive accumulation of this power proceeds notably from traffic in currency, from a privileged access to the most advantageous rates of exchange or from the invoicing of certain benefits and taxes at the most disadvantageous rates, as well as being useful to criminal circles, whose revenue or capital they can launder.[92]

Zaire provides us with a textbook case, at a time when the average rate of annual inflation was oscillating between 64 per cent (between 1975 and 1989) and 3,616 per cent (between 1990 and 1995). Monetary depreciation served as an instrument of fiscal extraction for the government and as a means of personal enrichment for Mobutu's nomenklatura. Its control of rates of exchange was, at all events, indispensable for Lebanese diamond traffickers and their political backers. In this context, and from the 1970s onwards, the 1,300 or so female foreign exchange dealers of the Ngobila beach, who were linked to the transnational smuggling trade with Brazzaville and the commerce of the 'fighters' in the interior of the country, as well as with the fraudulent export of precious stones, contributed decisively to the anchoring of the country in the international economy, under the self-serving protection of the state's leaders, of which they were sometimes suspected of being the 'offices'. Indeed, they sometimes indulged in implicit elective affinities with the mythology of Mami Wata thanks to their physical beauty and their reputation as 'free women' – i.e., single, divorced or widowed. Following the growing 'dollarization' and 'informalization' of the economy, the milieu of these foreign exchange dealers diversified. The currency market moved from Ngobila beach to the Avenue des Aviateurs, and then swarmed out into different parts of town. It unhesitatingly took the name 'Wall Street'. And it progressively started to evade the exclusive control of the women who had come together in the Moziki Sentiment Ngobila association and their 'NGOs' ('Nifty Girls' Organizations'), co-opting into its ranks students, ordinary town-dwellers obliged to find ways of getting by, and West African merchants, and the appearance of new functions that complement the money exchange operation itself, such as those of 'takers', 'shockers', 'rollages' or *atakulu*, which provide different kinds of door-to-door selling or beating of the clientele.[93]

The macroeconomic and macropolitical processes of globalization, such as programmes of structural adjustment and liberalization, monetary policies, the management of the external public debt and the institutionalization of regional integration, are, in short, taken over by social groups that subject them as far as they possibly can to their own strategies, or in any case to their need to survive, and that thus 'nationalize' or 'localize' them. The fluxes of globalization are inevitably filtered through the social sphere, i.e. through historicity. And the political economy of this 'formation' of the unity of the world turns out to be a complex matter. There is a strong temptation to read it in a naive and teleological way, celebrating the Wonderland of a hard, pure market. Or, conversely, to give it a cynical interpretation, emphasizing the way economic liberalization is hijacked by those who hold the reins of state power. Or indeed, to see it in a populist frame of mind, marvelling at the spirit of initiative of the 'voiceless', the benefits of development NGOs and the potential of the 'other path', that of the unofficial sector and micro-business.[94]

In reality, those who hold political power in the local or national arena are fully present in the practices of 'globalization from below'. They all 'get their cut' as people say in the Congo: highly placed officials get a share of the bribes paid to those lower in the hierarchy.[95] It is, for example, a matter of public knowledge that civil servants, the forces of law and order and the canton chiefs are in league with the 'road cutters' and other 'fighting customs officials' in the north of Cameroon.[96] But the way the state is involved is not just a matter of anecdotal villainy. It is, rather, a procedure by which it is actually produced, within the context of globalization that I have been analysing in the previous chapters.

To quote Janet Roitman:

> For many people, seizure is more than a brutal means of accumulation. In the Lake Chad basin, as in many other parts of the world, violent appropriation is a means of social ascent, but also of social security intrinsic in the set of relations that provide and guarantee economic security. The commercial–military relation is a site of transfers and redistribution; it is the domain in which forms of protection are created and

guaranteed; and it is also a mode of sociability in distant regions, supposedly marginal, which are starting to create specific forms of productivity. These days, seizure is both a means of overturning and of participating in the status quo established by certain obligations such as taxation and debt. It is a means of exercising power that involves practices of liberty and domination simultaneously. This makes sense if we consider, with Michel Foucault, that power relations are modified, reinforced and weakened *in the very way they are exercised*, given that practices of resistance are 'never external to power'. In other terms, practices of liberty and resistance are inherent in situations of power and emerge from within them.[97]

Likewise, the concrete implantation and functioning of capitalist business worldwide is supported by a composite social base, within which transnational bosses, executives and workers all rub shoulders, together with national political agents and the drudges or contract workers of globalization. To finance the distribution of their products, multinationals are resorting to microcredit, which is managed by NGOs.[98] The big American tobacco companies themselves supply the massive tobacco-smuggling trade in Africa and Europe, with the help of states such as Benin or Montenegro.[99] A Carrefour hypermarket in a suburb of Rio de Janeiro will hand over to the strong men of the neighbouring favela in the City of God any clients caught pinching goods; the latter will be beaten, have their heads shaved, or even be put to death, while in Columbia, Coca-Cola is accused of subcontracting the assassination of troublesome trade-unionists out to paramilitary groups.[100] And, in the Gulf of Benin, western oil companies cover, often against their will, fraudulent imports of merchandise and substantial thefts of crude oil – 100,000 barrels per day in Nigeria – at the same time as having to pay tribute to native lineages whose 'young men' (those aged from 16 to 40 or so) are organized into NGOs, in accordance with the canons of 'international civil society', but without being averse to violence.[101]

Nonetheless, I will not deny that the subaltern agents of globalization have their own autonomy – what I will provisionally call, following Anthony Giddens, their 'agency', i.e. 'the agents' own capacity for action'.[102] This latter capacity also seems to be a constituent element in the 'event' of globalization, its historicity. I do not here want to rehearse the complex debate that was opened up by the school of dependency, at the end of the 1950s, and the refutation of this current of thought in the works of those who refuse to think that the expansion of western capitalism across the world has made colonized peoples into passive observers of their own history.[103] For the time being, we need merely to observe a few concrete situations in which global 'governance' (or 'governmentality') is exercised.

Let us take, for example, the Thermidorean situations in which revolutionary strata have perpetuated themselves as professionalized political classes at the service of the state[104] and have consolidated their
domination, taking over the main channels of primitive accumulation
and, these days, confronting the twofold challenge of economic liberalization and the changing scale of globalization. Under this (Thermidorean) category, we find China and Russia, first and foremost, but also
the ex-Soviet republics or popular democracies of Central and Eastern
Europe, the countries of the former French Indochina, Iran and – by
extension – the regimes that emerged from nationalist movements with
revolutionary agendas or sensibilities which had adopted a 'socialist'
organization, or one that was in any case strongly *dirigiste* when it came
to the economy, like Indonesia, Egypt, Syria, Iraq, Algeria, Tunisia,
Angola, Mozambique and Ethiopia. Leaving Central Europe to one
side, it is not difficult to discern, in these situations, the capacity those
in power have to 'change everything so that everything will stay the
same', in the celebrated formula that Tomasi di Lampedusa lends to
his hero Tancredi in *The Leopard*. The logorrhoea of 'reforms without
change'[105] conceals the continuity of lines of domination and self-
serving activities, to the advantage of various hard cores of people that
are remarkably stable over time and barely even hidden by the fig
leaves of a highly influential private sector formed of paper tiger oligarchs, businesses, groups, conglomerates and bosses. The party, the
army, the secret services, the palace – depending on each particular case
– maintain control of cosmetic political transformations and economic
openness, in accordance with a logic that goes beyond the mere case
of Thermidorean situations in the strict sense of the term, and can be
found as much in the authoritarian situations of the 'market' as in
Morocco, Kenya, the Ivory Coast, Cameroon and even Thailand.[106]

All the same, these strategies of conservative modernization do not
eliminate all possibility of a society transforming itself and its relation
to globalization. The Chinese Communist Party will thus need to come
to terms with the diaspora, the particular features of Hong Kong and
Taiwan, the appearance of new forms of social and cultural mobility in
the towns, the problem of unemployment among workers, the rural
exodus of a massive peasantry, at the same time as it needs to respond
to the demands of the WTO of which it has become a member and the
rapid changes in its regional security environment – with the menace
from North Korea, the ineluctable rearmament of Japan and the military return of the United States to Asia.[107]

In the no less remarkable case of the Islamic Republic of Iran,[108] the
Thermidorean political class also intends to keep its hands on the illusory privatization of the economy. The latter is still 80 per cent controlled by the state, owing to the budgetary importance of oil revenues
and the absence of direct foreign investments. Its so-called 'private'

sector is completely dependent either on letters of credit and currency allocations from the Central Bank, given that there is no banking system worthy of the name, or on powerful 'foundations' inherited from the Revolution and in thrall to the regime, more particularly to its security services. Those in power are also actively involved in the flows of the 'second economy', which apparently represents between 20 and 40 per cent of the GDP, and particularly the transnational trade with Dubai and other neighbouring countries. Their 'father's sons' (*âghâ zadeh*: literally 'children of the Lord', the equivalent of the 'children of cadres' in the People's Republic of China) are not the last beneficiaries of liberalization measures, as the Karbastchi affair in 1998–9 and the Shahrâm Jazâeri Arab affair in 2002 started to reveal, before being suppressed in the name of 'the honour of the system'. Nonetheless, can this Thermidorean class be altogether sure, in the long term, about the activities in the bazaar, the different evergetic agents, and the networks of transient pavement sellers, all of which are (admittedly) consubstantially bound together, but tend to structure themselves into a real civil society? Or, indeed, can it be sure of the *vaqf* of Astan-e Qods in Mashhad that manages the sanctuary of the Eighth Imam and, fortified by its fabulous resources, has become a republic within the Republic, reigning without needing to share much of its power in the Khorassan and developing its own regional policies? Will it not need to compromise with the three million Iranians who live abroad, in accordance with the rules of 'flexible citizenship', and who hold considerable financial assets? And what about the weight of the clergy of Qom, who have long demonstrated their aloofness from an Islamic Republic that they had never wanted and who live on an equal footing in a specific transnational historical field: that of Shiism, which the fall of Saddam Hussein and the renaissance of the holy cities of Nadjaf and Kerbela have put back on the agenda?

The liberal and 'global' theme of reform in a Thermidorean situation is revealing in that it inescapably refers to the social and political spheres, and to their irreducible historicity – something whose shackles it claimed to have thrown off, as Fukayama thought. It then becomes less a matter of analysing the social foundations of globalization in terms of the static categories of 'classes' (or 'strata') than of seeing them from the dynamic point of view of processes of 'formation' of a contingent *Herrschaft*. Following the method of 'variable scales', it might be productive to change the focus of the analysis to bring out the discontinuous character of these processes and show, for instance, how globalization 'in the kolkhoz', in the former Soviet Asia, is being carried out in accordance with social and cultural practices rooted in local land, somewhere between gift and *qawm* (faction or clan).[109]

And yet, in the final analysis, it is really the genesis of the national system of inequality and domination that is in question, being linked as it is to both globalization and the expansion of capitalism. Thus, in sub-Saharan Africa, the overall pattern, over and above the historicity of individual areas of land, involves the establishment of a dominant class as part of a chain of events formed by the collaboration of a handful of social strata with the colonial state, their seizure of power when independence was achieved, their neo-mercantilist management of the private income economy and the pre-empting of its liberalization from the 1980s onwards.[110] If need be, war and crime can see to this.[111] But the different social groups that live on dependence income, exploiting it shamelessly in the upper echelons of the state, or cannibalizing it 'from below', are well and truly engaged in the 'formation' of an integral state whose random emergence remains inseparable from the history of globalization. The social foundations of the one are also those of the other.

Likewise, in Indonesia, the twofold dynamic of *Reformasi* and *Demokrasi* that was initiated in 1998 concerns both the exercise of universal suffrage, the safeguarding of national unity under the auspices of an army and a president who are both very punctilious on this issue, the re-establishment of the moral economy of power, in which the ordinary people in the suburbs and the villages can recognize themselves, and the renewal, or conversion, of part at least of the economic privileges of the New Order, under the gaze of the IMF and the World Bank and under the cover of interventions from the Indonesian Bank Restructuring Agency, operations to pay off the domestic debt and privatization measures.[112]

The trajectory of the former popular democracies of Central Europe is even more subtle. The recovery and guarantee of national sovereignty as a framework of 'domination' came about by joining the supranational institutions of the European Union and NATO. Unlike what happened in Russia, with its 'capitalists without capitalism', the 'transition' did not here turn out to benefit the Communist nomenklatura, but rather to benefit an alliance just between its technocrats and a new intellectual and political elite that was born from dissidence and universal suffrage. It led to a 'capitalism without capitalists', whose dominant class is still being formed. The old party cadres, for their part, have failed to transform themselves into an upper-middle class that would own the means of production, and are instead in a state of social decline.[113]

More generally, one of the modes of liberal, global 'governance' (or 'governmentality') – namely subcontracting out to private operators either the state's sovereign functions or, within multinational businesses, the activities that constitute the chain of production or commoditization – is evidence of the fact that intermediation has not ceased, over the last two centuries, to be a formality, with a crucial impact on globalization. The role of sponsors in the regulation of the labour market, immigration, credit, accommodation in the oil-monarchies of the Gulf; the inevitable importance of *dallal* in Iran or *waseteh* in Arab countries – i.e. 'intermediaries' – whenever one needs to carry out a piece of business; the importance too of 'gate-keepers' and 'front-men' who protect access to sub-Saharan markets; the intervention of people-smugglers in migrations; the development of business within firms and the interconnecting of international companies with the local fabric of small and medium enterprises; the delegating to NGOs of entire swathes of public policy; the 'privatization of the state' in the form of 'discharge', and all the effects of straddling that it entails; the cohort of brokers in finance, insurance and telecommunications – all of these have taken over from the *compradores*, the Christian missions and the system of indirect rule on which globalization has been built since 1800, within the framework of the expansion of capitalism and western imperialism.[114] Thus Tony Ballantyne suggests that we see the colonial empires as assemblages of networks that fit into one another.[115] This remains true of the contemporary 'Empire'.

The problem is thus no longer one of knowing whether globalization rests on a social basis – the facts are there, and one wonders why (and how) those who denigrate globalization can deny it – but of suggesting a problematization of its social foundations which will allow us better to understand it as an 'event' of subjection. Though the debate on how to describe transnational relations between social classes is premature and still very academic,[116] the question nonetheless remains of how to analyse the social inequality produced by the unity of the world – an inequality inherent in this unity. Not because a political critique of globalization needs to be populist, but because the historicity of a change of scale is necessarily linked, at least partly, with the emergence (or confirmation) of 'domination' (*Herrschaft*), as the formation of the nation-state within the crucible of the processes of globalization, for instance in Italy and Germany in the nineteenth century, or in Africa and Asia in the twentieth.

Globalization as networking?

These days, there is a broad consensus that globalization and the inter-mediations on which it rests consist in a systematic networking of social relations, of which the web of 'cyber-networks' is merely the paradigmatic tip.[117] In the domain of production, the vertical integra-tion of businesses (Fordist in type) is yielding to a horizontal integra-tion which, as we have seen, emphasizes trade within firms and subcontracting. Multinationals are more and more a matter of 'decentralized networks', being organized in semi-autonomous units by country, market, process and product, whether these chains of commodities are tied to the initiative of the producer (as in the auto-mobile, aviation, computer or electronics industries) or to that of the purchaser (as in the garment industry, shoes, toys and household equipment).[118] Veritable 'trans-enterprise' businesses are thus coming into being. As early as 1990, 30 per cent of the highly qualified person-nel in Silicon Valley were of foreign origin, and 25 per cent of the companies founded there between 1980 and 1998 – 29 per cent of those that had been set up between 1995 and 1998 – were being managed by Chinese or Indian Americans. The latter maintained links with their countries of origin. They readily subcontract out to these countries software, semi-conductors or personal computers. Comparable indus-trial interactions can be found between California and Israel and, increasingly, Mexico.[119] In the sphere of international trade, supply systems[120] are likewise being grafted onto informal chains of distribu-tion built on the example of the guilds and bazaars, and provided with transnational ramifications, or else conceptualized in the exclusively personal manner of 'relationships', as the Congolese put it.[121]

In the field of the international market of the labour force, analysts no longer emphasize the diasporas as much as they do the continuous circulation of people, money and information: so different settlements come to form a single community.[122] Informal systems of transfers of funds, such as the Chinese *jinshanzhuang* or the Islamic *hawilaad*,[123] are one of the most fascinating aspects of this networking. But there are also 'transnational families' and 'trans-villages' across whole seas and continents, and their interaction comes with a specific transnational autonomy, with an increase in the number of matrimonial and sexual alliances, lifestyles, the crystallization of public spaces, 'flexibility' of citizenship, economic investments and the taking over by the 'com-munity' of 'development', political mobilization and religious activ-ity.[124] This remains true even if the degree of the structuring, or indeed the institutionalization, of these 'circuits of migration' varies from one situation to another. Africanists, for instance, emphasize the contrast between the organization into fraternities or villages of migrations of Senegalese or Malians and the individualistic (albeit still socialized) character of the 'adventure' of young people from the Congo or the Ivory Coast.[125] The churches, too, fall into 'in networks'[126] and thus contribute to the social organization of migrations, given that their 'transnationalism', their 'multiculturalism' and their 'multilateralism' go back a long way, thanks to their universality: these days, the char-ismatic communities of African Christians residing in Western Europe claim to be evangelical and 'international' rather than African in the strict sense, whatever may be the intensity of their links with their countries of origin.[127]

Finally, I demonstrated in the last chapter that the combination of globalization and state-formation was mediated by various kinds of networking of which the Chinese *guanxi* provides us to some extent with the ideal type, but which is also found in the whole set of practices – memorializing, trading, associative, criminal, cultural or other – which guarantee that these two processes will be closely interlinked in the sphere of civil society and the globalization of this latter. The 'indirect rule' of global 'governance' (or 'governmentality'), in the Weberian mode of the 'discharge' of 'privatization', is clearly organized like a network, as is attested by the rhizomatic structure of the NGOs by which it is effectuated.

However, when all is said and done, this conceptualization in terms of 'networking' goes back a long way. The Manchester anthropological school resorted to it in the 1950s in its studies on urban life in Central Africa. Such a problematization these days needs to be complemented if we are to get beyond a redundant and really rather ideological formulation. As has been highlighted by Luc Boltanski and Ève Chiapello, the discourse of the network and the ethos attached to it are nothing other than the 'new spirit of capitalism'.[128] We do, however, need to consider the 'network' as a total social fact, in Mauss's sense, which we cannot reduce with impunity to any single one of its dimensions (e.g. economic, financial or numerical), or to any unambiguous effects from the point of view of the alienation which globalization supposedly brings with it.

For example, migration analysts do not merely look at the financial remittances that expatriate workers send home to their families or their regions. They also take into account the 'social remittances' which the latter repatriate in the form of the transmission of norms, practices and 'social capital', in an intentional way, via personalized relations, in contrast to the diffuse and anonymous circulation of global cultural fluxes.[129] This 'mutual interaction' must be grasped in its 'generality', since the latter is at the basis of its ambiguity. Thus, emigration has had widely different effects in the societies of the Maghreb and in Egypt. In the first case, it has facilitated the import of the West European model of conjugal relations and contraceptive practices, and the spectacular fall in the birth rate that has ensued. In the second, it has reproduced the conservative, pro-birth family model of the Arab countries of the Gulf, and has failed to encourage the take-off of demographic transition.[130]

A similar lack of predictability occurs in the political arena. Diasporas and 'transnational circuits of migration' sometimes feed into reformist, republican or democratic ideals, as in China at the start of the twentieth century, and sometimes radical nationalisms with a tendency to resort to violence, as in Ireland, Sri Lanka and Armenia. Liisa Malkki has thus shown how, in Tanzania, one and the same population of refugees (Hutu from Burundi) developed a very different political orientation depending on whether they lived in a camp or were scattered through the towns and villages.[131] And as I pointed out earlier, the aura of an Osama bin Laden and mullah Omar among the Balutchi emigrant community in Dubai and Oman is an expression of these ambivalences. These men leave their homeland in order to serve the 'honour' of their families, running the risk that they themselves will become 'corrupted' when they come into contact with the wicked order of the emirs and 'shuravi' ('Russian', 'Soviet') prostitution. They intend to benefit from, and even enjoy, globalization, while at the same time denouncing the arrogance and injustice of the Great Satan who presides over its destiny by bombing Muslims and delivering them over to the 'Jews'.[132] Diasporas are riven by this sort of contradiction. They pride themselves on their modernity and openness to the outside world, but they are often imbued with an implicit conservatism when it comes to marriage, sex or identity: 'If the Islamic Republic did not exist . . .' mocks Fariba Adelkhah with regard to the Iranians of California, even though they do not spare their criticisms of her, and many of them are political refugees who have fled the revolution or conscription, and what they imagine to be the obscurantism that prevails in their homeland.[133]

The diversity of social relations that are part of globalization leads us in particular to nuance and complicate the texture of different identities as it is frequently assigned to networks, with the aid of the vogue for multiculturalism and the theory of 'ethno-development'. It is true that many transnational trading circuits are ethnic, or else bearers (or even creators) of ethnicity, like, for instance, those of Nande, Hausa or Dioula shopkeepers in sub-Saharan Africa. Furthermore, diasporas are frequently defined by their ethno-national awareness, as with the Chinese, Tamil, Somali, Eritrean, Kurdish or Armenian communities scattered across the world. But this is not always really true, as Claude Markovits reminds us, as he 'deconstructs' the idea of an 'Indo-Pakistani' diaspora. In reality, the original land from which one comes – a province, a city – is often more influential and shaping than the subcontinental landmass, or even one's religious affiliation, be it Hindu, Muslim or Sikh.[134] The Chinese diaspora itself is far from being geographically undifferentiated. Most 'transnational circuits of migration' obey a principle of tightly circumscribed territorialization. If we just take the examples that we have already mentioned, the Sindhi trading circuits were historically based on Shikarpur and Hyderabad; Dominicans from the Bostonian suburb of Jamaica Plain live in osmosis with Miraflores, in San Domingo, their native city; and Taishanis from the west coast have remained faithful to their 'little native land' for as long as that had a demographic sense. But at the same time, strictly national affiliation, defined in terms of nationality and outside any ethnic characterization, remains an 'essential strategic element' for most migrants.[135]

Be this as it may, stato-national, ethno-national or ethno-regional identity is frequently assigned at a glance and by the (sometimes discriminatory) public policies of the host societies, rather than being naturally experienced as an inner feeling by the populations concerned. Chinatown, in San Francisco, is not the picturesque expression of Chinese identity within the encouraging framework of American multiculturalism. It is the fruit of the successive Exclusion Acts that Congress adopted from 1882 onwards in an attempt to try and stem the Asian presence on the west coast, and of the militant racism of part of the white population. These machines for manufacturing particularist mentalities forced migrants to rely on their local or family networks by making them even more dependent.[136]

Furthermore, the feelings (or representations) of ethnic, national or local belonging do not exclude other types of awareness or other splits within the networks. Migrants or transnational traders can also recognize themselves as having a religious identity – the Senegalese Murids, for instance, being essentially Wolofs who are very active in France, around the Mediterranean basin and, ever since the 1970s, in major North American cities such as New York, Atlanta, Cincinnati, Los Angeles and Washington; or Algerian Mozabites, who run a significant number of grocer's stores on the outskirts of Paris. Allegiance to an Islamic fraternity, in this case, goes with the devotion one bears to one's Holy City (Touba and Ghardaia respectively). At the same time, Islam is the universal religion par excellence, transcending the identity of individual traders and guaranteeing their business and the circulation of money by prescribing a very strict business ethos, one that includes in its remit peddlers and pavement sellers.[137]

Relations of patronage, sometimes expressed in the idiom of kinship or religion, also play an important role in the structuring of transnational networks.[138] But so do merely opportunistic relations and one-off collaborations. During a journey, the Iranian organization that has arranged a pilgrimage to the tomb of Zeynab in Damascus will use a large proportion of the customs allowance of other passengers in the coach to import goods for resale, and teachers behave in a similar way with their pupils when classes go on trips to the free island of Kish.[139] In Northern Rhodesia, Kenneth Kaunda, the future father of independence, who was at the time teaching at the school in Mufulira, also resorted to this subterfuge at the end of the 1940s as a way of indulging in the second-hand clothes trade with the Belgian Congo and in order to supplement the family income.[140]

Finally, the unequal relations of sex and generation are not absent from the social labyrinth of globalization. Aihwa Ong also emphasizes that the Chinese *guanxi* is a system of ethnic and family exploitation, disciplinary and sometimes violent, at the same time as it governs the business fraternity of diaspora entrepreneurs.[141] Conversely, a plethora of studies has shown how transnational commerce, either in bulk or carried out by transient pavement sellers, or even their function as money-changers, have enabled African women to meet the needs of their children and to assert themselves vis-à-vis their husbands, whether these be wage-earners or have been 'laid off'.[142] Likewise, in Iran, professional smugglers form 'caravans' of women to bring back merchandise from Dubai or the free zones, at a small cost and, above all, a growing number of these women take advantage of the system to indulge in pavement selling, using pilgrimage as their pretext: the transnational economy is a significant element in the transformation of the 'second sex' in the Islamic Republic.[143] As for young Africans, the economic 'adventure' of emigration (one that, in the case of Congolese *Sapeurs*, also involves a vestimentary adventure) is now their common means of gaining access to adult status, or even the standing of a 'Big Man', with all that this entails in terms of conflicts between age categories or between 'old' and 'young', 'big brothers' and 'little brothers'.[144]

So it is clear that network globalization does not merely express the complexity and diversity of pre-established social relations. It creates them. And it is in this way that it produces, rather than erodes, the social sphere. Tilo Grätz's investigations into the transnational networks of gold prospectors in West Africa is revealing in this context. The miners who have gathered in camps to 'dig' – outside the villages, in the north of Benin or in Burkina Faso – are young men of heterogeneous ethnic and national origins. Their social identities express this twofold experience of migration on the one hand and a particular line of trade on the other, one that is full of danger and unpredictability. It transcends, and indeed often challenges, the sense of ethnic belonging, or at any rate some of the moral imperatives associated with the latter in terms of respect – in cash terms – for seniority. The miners share an entirely new kind of transnational social life and solidarity, expressed in a specific habitus and ideology of 'friendship'.[145] These innovations are all the more noteworthy in that they accompany the perpetuation of an ancestral economic activity, namely gold mining, which has tied West Africa to Europe ever since Antiquity, first via the trans-Saharan route and later by way of the Atlantic seaboard.

The same ability to go beyond supposedly 'primordial' identities by setting up between them functional forms of cooperation and common lifestyles characterizes the majority of transnational economic circuits. Thus the Moroccan operators who established their pre-eminence over the Mediterranean area of *trabendo* – informal trade, more or less a form of smuggling – in the 1990s, starting from Marseilles, by taking advantage of the political problems of their Algerian competitors, work hand in hand with Turks from Brussels and Frankfurt, Pakistanis and Indians from London, Senegalese, Italians, Catalan and Andalusian gypsies, and Tunisians who open up new doors to them that enable them to make other connections with Libyans, Lebanese or sub-Saharans.[146] In a similar way, the West African pavement sellers of New York constitute a nebulous transnational and transethnic social grouping that, not content with freeing itself from the social divisions on the continent, does business with Taiwanese, Koreans, Chinese, Pakistanis, Indonesians, Afghans, Israelis and Arabs so as to feed the appetite of Afro-Americans for artefacts of Africanness, and (why not?) the similar tastes of Japanese tourists discovering Harlem.[147] As for the Château-Rouge district, in Paris, most of the shops there that sell African foodstuffs are run by Asians.[148]

In short, it is not merely in the upper 'globapolitan' sphere of capital and market forces, but also in its basement, that globalization comes into being historically by creating the social relations proper to it. Now, this global production of the social sphere, however much of a transnational network it might be, remains a spatial phenomenon. One of the main lessons of postmodern anthropology will have been to demonstrate how globalization is not so much tolling for the 'death of territories'[149] as reinventing them through the effects of 'glocalization', i.e. the compacting of the global and local dimensions, sometimes (though not necessarily) to the detriment of national intermediation.[150] Of course, globalization leads to a disconnection between the 'truth of experience' and the place in which this occurs,[151] by virtue of the new methods of communication and the importance they grant to the virtual dimension of social life. Migrations and diasporas are the main situations in which this phenomenon can be observed. Effective emigration is not the condition *sine qua non* of belonging to a 'transvillage' community because of the extent and density of 'social remittances'.[152] Thus, Fariba Adelkhah writes astutely of the way Iranian migrants 'go away without actually leaving', in so far as they remain attached to their families and their lands by means of many different affective, ritual or financial bonds, while, at the same time, their friends and family 'leave without actually going away', living 'in the fiction of a plan to emigrate which has little chance of coming to anything but enables them to reorganize their daily lives, especially in their family or professional lives':

> In other words, going away introduces into Iranian society a third principle in the process of production of status. Social distinction is now increasingly formed off shore. . . . Indeed, there are hardly any families that are not, directly or indirectly, affected by the phenomenon. What is at work here is a global reconstitution of the criteria of social classification, which follows the many different interactions between individuals or between (and within) families.[153]

But, at the same time, the processes of globalization manufacture locality itself. They do this, first, by making it technologically possible to accelerate or intensify the way emigrants can have a retroactive effect on their regions of origin. 'Transnational circuits' represent a decisive factor of reterritorialization, for instance in the form of 'transvillages'. They thereby modify the geography of the societies concerned by causing a qualitative mutation in their economic fabric, and even in their morphology. Very ordinary cities, such as Lâr, Grâsh, Evaz or Lâmerd in the south of Iran, had no national or regional profile, by Gulf standards, before the emigrants who left them reinvested massively in property, health and airports.[154] And, in south China, Taishan long prided itself on the exploits (perfectly vain, it has to be said) of its benefactor Chen Yixi (1844–1928) who made his fortune in Seattle and placed his competence and his money at the service of his home town, linking it to the sea by building a railway.[155] As a general rule, the original intentions of emigrants from Taishan (and of their relatives who stayed beyond) were local and conservative in nature. They wanted to preserve their families, clans and economic alliances and rise in the social hierarchy of the village, the district, the local area or the region.[156] But inevitably, their financial and social remittances modified the contours of inequality, the habitat, the educational opportunities, the transport system, the provision of energy, the industrial fabric and the cultural habits – and attracted bandits who were desirous in their turn to profit from the windfall of emigration. The absence of a great number of men also upset family patterns by creating new challenges to public morality and setting up their wives as heads of the household.[157] The reactivation and reinvention of the local sphere under the pressures of globalization can be summed up in terms of the Mafia godfather, who lives off the international economy of crime but, when on the run, takes refuge in his village. In any case, the entrepreneur who prospers in Silicon Valley behaves no differently. He stretches his evergetic wing over the city in which he met with his first successes. This leads Marc Abélès to speak of the 'provincialism of philanthropy' which flourishes at the centre of the 'new economy'.[158]

Furthermore, migrations leave a negative imprint in the urban space of industrial metropolises in a much more systematic way than one might deduce from the concentration of explicitly ethnic districts or the culinary multiculturalism of restaurants that cultivate an exotic aura. The female Filippino domestics in Rome, for example, meet up in 'pockets of gathering' to exchange information and food, at the risk of arousing the ire of the neighbours or the authorities – in particular at the EUR-Fermi metro station, the Mancini bus stop and round the Stazione Termini, until police harassment drives them under a motorway bridge, onto the banks of the Tiber or into a shack abandoned by Albanian refugees.[159]

In Tokyo, the park of Ueno, ideally situated on a metro line serving the Narita airport, was a prized refuge for Iranian immigrants who squatted in one of its avenues. The police eventually 'restored order'. But the park continues to provide a convenient meeting place at the foot of the statue of Saigo Takamori, at the exit of the JR station. 'It is dangerous to use this passage at night', one can read on the walls of a subway that leads to this station, written in Persian with a felt-tip pen. The Tehranese vendors of fake telephone cards (and various other services) operate illegally in the streets of the Shibuya district, and can easily be recognized so long as someone points them out to you. This whole little population also has its routines in the nightclubs, Turkish restaurants and pizzerias of Roppongi, whose proprietors or managers are also Iranians and affect the behaviour of 'thick necks', *gardan koloft*, but also of the *javânmard* (the man of integrity) that verges on caricature.[160] Even more remarkable, the Congolese in Paris have opened some sixty or so clandestine bars or *nganda*, often in squats. They get together there in the small hours to drink, eat, do 'bizness' (illicitly), take drugs, dance and indulge in ostentatious consumption.[161] Several hundred kilometres further north, in the multiethnic and multireligious district of Bijlmer, at the gates of Amsterdam, we find places of worship that Ghanaian Christians have secretly set up in the parking lots of big building blocks.[162]

There is thus a popular transnational territorialization whose spatial lines shape states and urban metropolises, in the shadow of the 'new geography of centrality',[163] no less territorialized, to which the latest period of globalization has given rise. In Manhattan, the 'pockets' in which West African pavement sellers gather – for instance Lexington Avenue and 42nd, Times Square and 34th, and Canal Street – are situated right in the heart of a major site of territorialization for finance, the 'Internet galaxy' and multilateral governance.[164] This spatial anchorage for the transnationalism of the 'lower classes' is not a mere juxtaposition or a residue of yesterday's world, one that is anachronistic and doomed to disappear. The 'new geography of centrality' encourages immigration, including (perhaps above all) clandestine immigration, since the enlarged reproduction of capital necessitates an abundant and cheap labour force, especially in textiles and the tertiary activities of unqualified services.[165] For its part, informal or criminal transnational trade is supported by the urban fabric of the industrial world. At the heart of the metropolises, whole districts have become specialized in this sort of exchange and afferent production, for instance 125th Street in New York (until the destruction of African Market in October 1994), the Sentier and Château-Rouge districts and certain streets in the 11th arrondissement in Paris, the Belsunce district in Marseilles, the Yeni-kapi and Laleli districts in Istanbul, or the Galerie d'Ixelles in Brussels. These are all places that are at one and the same time 'glocal' and transnational, thanks to the cooperation between ethnic or national trading networks that is becoming established there.

The 'new economy' itself, and the Internet, have their favourite territories, of which Silicon Valley has become the emblem. On the planetary scale, their indisputable centre is in the United States, thanks to the bandwidths available here and the number of websites registered. Then come, far behind the US, most of the countries in Western Europe and South Korea, with Japan rather curiously lagging behind. On the national scale, the territorialization of the Web is just as evident, benefiting as it does a few metropolises, or even (more precisely) certain of their districts: South of Market, in San Francisco; 'Silicon Valley' at the tip of Manhattan (at least before the attacks of 11 September 2001) and East Side, to the south of Central Park, in New York; Santa Monica, the Ventura Freeway Corridor and San Gabriel Valley in Los Angeles. Thus, in January 2000, the five main cities in the world, in which 1 per cent of the global population lived, were home to 20.4 per cent of Internet sites, and the first fifty of them, with 4 per cent of the world population, were the home of 48.2 per cent of them.[166]

The territorialization of the processes of globalization definitely thus engenders a transformation of the city, rather than its disappearance as was declared on the altar of the virtual and telecommuting.[167] The accelerating urbanization of the nineteenth century and the rise of new 'global' cities that enjoy a sometimes ephemeral moment of glory, such as San Francisco, Panama, Manaus, Singapore, Hong Kong, Shanghai and Baku, have all set things moving. These days, 'metropolitan regions' are emerging, interconnected by the worldwide links of the Internet, telephone, capital, and air and sea transport, whose nodal points they are: the Bay Area in San Francisco; the zone in South California that extends from Ventura to Orange County and now goes over the border into Mexico; the different conurbations on the East Coast; Greater London; the Paris-Île-de-France area; the 'Blue Banana' of the Rhine Valley and its extension across the Alps; the Tokyo-Yokohama-Nagoya axis that the Shinkansen bullet train is pulling southwards as far as Osaka, Kobe and Kyoto; the huge conglomeration of Hong Kong and the delta of the River of Pearls in South China; and the megalopolises of the countries that can optimistically be described as 'emerging'.[168] Here are being invented, amid suffering and a great deal of 'social energy',[169] lifestyles and activities to which the pessimism of those who look down on globalization does not do justice.

The 'limit-city' or *Edge City*, as the evocative title of a successful book from the beginning of the 1990s[170] puts it, is the 'new frontier' of globalization, on which the majority of the social relations constitutive of its historical regime of 'domination' or 'subjection' are being forged. It is a massively real phenomenon, from the triple point of view of economics, sociology and demography. It is just as clear that these social relations are starting to extend their grip across the whole planet, like a 'network', admittedly, but in ways whose tenor and complexity are not adequately expressed by this hackneyed term.

Once we have uttered the magic word three times and gambolled like a lamb in homage to a talented 'sovereignist' agent, we have not really said anything particularly meaningful. These celebrated networks are simultaneously places of 'agency' and places 'you can get by in' (as they say in Kinshasa), for the subalterns of globalization and the instruments of their exploitation or, indeed, exclusion, enslavement and degradation. They are the vehicles of strategic information, colossal financial flows and primitive accumulation. They are principles of deterritorialization and logics of territorialization. They are informal, but also compatible with a notable degree of institutionalization. They are at the antipodes of the juridical idea of the state and serve the cause of political centralization. They mark the age of 'disaffiliation' and yet they rest on the idea of 'confidence' and harbour strong ethical demands. Ironically, Susan Strange put us on guard against a concept (that of globalization) that could designate both Internet and the hamburger.[171] So what are we to say of a notion that claims to explain the organization of work in Microsoft, the pastoral idyll of Pentecostalism, and the coercive control of West African prostitutes in the rue Saint-Denis? *Pace* Manuel Castells (and many others), I am happy, in my quest for an understanding of the social foundations of the 'information era', to abandon portmanteau words and to return to the methods of the historical sociology of the political sphere.

4

Globalization and Political Subjectivation: The Imperial Moment (1830–1960)

It is now quite generally accepted that the formation of social inequality and political domination is not a matter just of the economic relations of exploitation or predation, but also of modes of existence that are spread by social groups, however these are conceptualized.[1] We also have a better understanding of the way the emergence of these modes of existence and the institutionalization of a central state power have been factors of individualization. Anyone who has read Tocqueville as well as Marx, Weber, Elias or Foucault should no longer be tempted to imagine the state, society and the individual as a zero-sum game. And yet it is this mistaken view in which people commonly get bogged down as soon as they start thinking about globalization. Globalization, not content with levelling off the state and gutting societies, is alleged to plunge the individual into moral and cultural destitution and complete anonymity. It is, so it is claimed, 'the enemy of Being'.[2] And this is understandable: is it not the vehicle (or the manifestation) of the expansion of capitalism, that principle of alienation? And that explains – tautologously – why your daughter suffers from anomie. All of which needs, of course, to be verified.

A question of method

Max Weber, for his part, did not ponder the factors that encouraged capitalist expansion in terms of 'causality', as is often held, so much as he questioned the development of a human type (*Menschentum*) created from 'components of religious origin and components of economic origin'.[3] He suggested that we identify, for a given religion, social levels whose life conduct played a particularly important role,[4] without defending the idea that the particular nature of any one religion is a function of the social situation cf the stratum that appears as its characteristic bearer (*Träger*). He thus rejected the idea of an ideology that would simply be a reflection of material or mental interests.[5] He drew attention to the role of social institutions (whether those of the state or others)[6] in the transmission of a precise 'method of life' or 'conduct of life' (*Lebensführung*), which could not merely be the *conscious choice* of each individual.[7] His main topic was thus the 'daily ethic' (*Alltagsethik*) – what he later called ethos, to bring out the fact that 'he is less interested in ideas in themselves than in their impact on social practices and the orientation they give to the way one leads one's life'[8] – and perhaps even more the processes of the way it is 'turned into a daily practice' (*Veralltäglichung*, infelicitously rendered as 'routinization' in the first translations into English and French).

Whatever people may have thought about this over the years, Weber's problematization of the 'way people live their lives' is perfectly compatible with the Marxist concepts of appropriation, or Gramsci's concepts of hegemony and common sense. But it may be the formulation of Michel Foucault which, at this point in our study, will be the most useful way of replying to our initial questions: do our belonging to the world, our constitution as 'moral subjects', proceed from a global governmentality, or are the processes of globalization irreducible to any idea of belonging, vectors of dispossession, harbingers of mere domination, exploitation without subjectivation? Is it only in the mode of resistance to globalization that the latter allows us to set ourselves up as 'moral subjects'?

We know that, at the end of his life, Foucault reviewed his work from a somewhat different angle. His intention, he claimed, had always been to conceptualize the very historicity of the forms of experience,[9] submitting his thinking on power to this objective, and focusing less on the constituted Subject than on the constitution of the Subject. It is not a question of saying that the Subject or the individual 'do not exist', which would hardly have any more sense than saying that they do 'exist' but that they are produced. And it is a question of investigating this historical process of production as the primordial 'event', instead of reifying the identity or subjectivity that it sets up. What counts is less the action of the Subject than the action that makes the Subject (and in which the Subject's action participates).

In other words, the important thing is to understand not what one is, but how one 'recognizes oneself' as a 'subject', in the twofold meaning of the word; the important thing is this 'hermeneutic of the Self'[10] that we see coming into being during Antiquity, but which of course takes different paths from one society or period to another. To do this, we should not analyse behaviour or ideas, societies or 'ideologies', but the 'problematics' through which being has to be thought and the practices on the basis of which they are formed.[11]

> There is no specific moral action that does not refer to a unified moral conduct; no moral conduct that does not call for the forming of oneself as an ethical subject; and no forming of the ethical subject without 'modes of subjectivation' and an 'ascetics' or 'practices of the self' that support them.[12]

Hence, for example, the project of restoring 'the whole rich and complex field of historicity in the way the individual is summoned to recognize himself as an ethical subject of sexual conduct', from classical Greek thought to the Christian doctrine and pastoralia of the flesh.[13] Hence also the way Foucault corrects himself when discussing the reworking of an ethic of self-control during the Hellenistic period and at the start of the Roman Empire:

> A growth of public constraints and prohibitions? An individualistic withdrawal accompanying the valorization of private life? We need instead to think in terms of a crisis of the subject, or rather a crisis of subjectivation – that is, in terms of a difficulty in the manner in which the individual could form himself as the ethical subject of his actions, and efforts to find in devotion to self that which could enable him to submit to rules and give a purpose to his existence.[14]

Gilles Deleuze summarized in lapidary (and quite Weberian) terms Foucault's problematic of subjectivation, seeing it as a production of modes of existence or styles of life.[15] He thereby brought out the extent to which this procedure is not a return to the subject, after an exaggerated emphasis had been placed on knowledge-power. A process of subjectivation is not to be confused with a subject (unless we see the latter as without any interiority or identity). Subjectivation has nothing to do with a person: it is, rather, an individuation, an event (a time of day, a river, a wind, a life): an intensive mode, not a personal subject.[16] To get his message across more clearly, and at the same time to deny that Foucault rediscovered the subject after killing off Man, Deleuze resorted to an illuminating metaphor: Foucault had not rediscovered subjectivity after denying it, and subjectivation has little to do with a subject. The subject is, rather, an electrical or magnetic field operating on the basis of intensities.[17] In short, there is no such thing as a subject: just a production of subjectivity,[18] akin to what Nietzsche understood by the invention of new possibilities of life.[19]

The notion thus possesses a critical normative dimension, and even a political dimension in so far as it designates the way individuals or communities become subjects, outside the establishment and its powers and norms – even if new forms of knowledge and power come into being in this process.[20] For Foucault, the problematic of subjectivation was thus closely linked to his political commitment to the cause of prisoners, homosexuals, Polish or Iranian demonstrators and, more generally, the recognition of the socially excluded as producers of 'lifestyles'.

This dissociation between the problematic of subjectivation and that of the subject is not a philosophical or ideological affectation. It is rooted in an entire intellectual quest in the western world, particularly in the empiricism of David Hume to which Deleuze's commentary on Foucault implicitly returns us, and in which subjectivity is essentially practical.[21] It is a proposition that Deleuze echoes in words that are now familiar to us: the spirit is not subject, it is subjected. Hence the 'splendour' of the anonymous One. Individuation is a mobile, supple process that takes place on the margins: intensities envelope and communicate with other intensities. The individual is not indivisible, and is not an I or a Self, but expresses, rather, pre-individual singularities.[22]

This Nietzschean way of seeing the individual not as an essential form but as a 'more or less composed form, i.e. a set of relations, made of movement and rest, speed and slowness, under which infinite numbers of parts belong to it', this way of discerning within it 'a collective', 'a pack', and identifying it with 'a power of being affected', this focus on working no longer on the individuality of different subjects but on *haecceities*, i.e. 'literally speaking, the fact of being this, the fact of being a "this", a degree of power',[23] will turn out to be of great use in helping us to understand globalization as a historical experience of subjection and as a 'partial condition'.[24]

We should be clear, all the same, that Max Weber means exactly the same thing when he refuses to see the way one lives one's life merely as the conscious choice of each individual,[25] and when he discerns in 'domination' (*Herrschaft*) 'the enigma of a servitude to which one voluntarily consents, and which is integrated by the subject as a component of its personal will'.[26] We could say, in terms that are derived partly from Hume and partly from Weber, that the 'man of daily life' (*Alltagsmensch*) is 'activated' by the principles of 'everyday ethics' (*Alltagsethik*) that constitute him as a moral subject and from which he forms his 'conduct of life' (*Lebensführung*). A same convergence brings Weber and Foucault together when the former sees 'social strata' (*Trägerschichten*) 'bear' (*tragen*) the 'conducts of life'[27] and the latter associates subjectivation with the 'self-affirmation' of a class, in this case the bourgeoisie.[28]

So it is now time to ascertain whether the social relations constitutive of globalization are part of the 'production of modes of existence or lifestyles' of which the social groups that we have identified in particular are the 'bearers', and to which various 'social institutions' of worldwide scope give rise. For several contemporary critics, there is no question of this. And yet, begging the question in this way means forgetting that, as we have seen, the subjectivation of men makes them 'subjects' in both active and passive senses;[29] they are 'moral subjects'[30] not in the mode of an unambiguous submission to an external rule, but in that of 'belonging'[31] to this rule: a 'mode of subjectivation' is the way an individual puts this rule into practice.[32] The concept of governmentality – in this case, 'global' – intervenes precisely at this intersection between the process of formation of domination or inequality, i.e., for instance, a social class or state, and practices of the self: governmentality, as we have seen, is the encounter between techniques of domination applied to others and techniques of the self.[33]

We can thus really speak of a 'global governmentality' – and of a global anonymous 'One', in all its 'splendour' – if we locate the processes of subjectivation, via practices of the self, which have for two centuries been supported by the change of scale and the expansion of capitalism, and if the 'lifestyles' which stem from it are 'borne' by social strata and social institutions constitutive of 'generalized mutual interaction', and thence a worldwide 'domination' (Herrschaft). To put it briefly, does globalization produce 'modes of subjection', and do we 'belong' to it?

Colonization as experience of subjectivation

The question is less silly than it may seem from a reading of the anti-globalization literature. And, at the risk of plunging Larzac into despair (in a famous statement, Sartre said he did not want to plunge Billancourt into despair – Billancourt being the site of the Renault factory) we will find the first evidence of this at the heart of the colonial enterprise, even though the latter was, by definition, a matter of military conquest, political exploitation, social and even racial degradation. The extent to which the 'colonial situation'[34] was a cruel and fertile laboratory for subjectivation, i.e. of a 'production of modes of existence or lifestyles', is paradoxical.

At the start, this was true for the colonizers themselves. Either they imposed 'conducts of life' on themselves, or – in the case of convicts, exiles, bankrupts, conscripts, the enlisted, and sons of good families who had gone to the bad and who were sent 'to the colonies' to redeem themselves or as a means of purifying the metropolitan social body – standards were imposed on them.[35] These 'lifestyles' soon became an integral part of colonial societies. As a result of their distance, the slowness of means of transport, the climatic and sanitary conditions, or quite simply of political and military vicissitudes, such experiences of subjectivation were radical, and often fatal. E. M. Collingham's laconic remark is true of most colonia possessions: the British experience of India was 'intensely physical'.[36]

Europeans were tormented by a phobia of insects, snakes, fever, miasmas of every kind, contagions, the cruelty of bandits and the sexuality of the natives.[37] At the start of the nineteenth century, up to 50 per cent of them died in the first year of moving overseas, the forts and missions were literally decimated, and towns like Luanda were nicknamed 'the white man's tomb'.[38] People had to wait until quinine was invented, vaccinations were made more generally available and the great campaigns to eradicate pandemics came into effect for western colonists, civil servants, soldiers and missionaries to have any hope of a decent life in the tropics. But the haunting fear of 'racial deterioration' in the harsh climates of Africa and Asia did not disappear, and a severe self-discipline in hygiene and food was necessary, one that would have turned into ascetic measures if there had not been a few added ingredients.

This discipline clearly represented a constrictive set of 'practices of the self'. The way the colonial adventure or the missionary vocation were turned into daily routines was based on a series of banal procedures that established a material, corporal and mental habitus among white people overseas: the daily ingestion of medicines, vaccinations, disinfection of the water, intensive use of showers and soaps, the deployment of mosquito nets, particular habits of clothing, specific architecture and furnishings. The discipline was also the fruit of public policies, initiated either by states or private individuals, and carried out by companies or congregations – public or private policies that regulated the sexual relations of their agents, access to European women in the colonies, the status of 'races', the granting of citizenship and many other domains in the life of the colonists, with the aim of building the latter into a middle or upper class, sometimes endowed with a neo-aristocratic ethos, and guaranteeing their symbolic pre-eminence by avoiding any failings that might have compromised it.[39] Apart from certain colonies, either designed to populate a country or create penitentiary colonies – for example Australia, Algeria, Angola and New Caledonia – poor or disreputable men were no more welcome than women or children. On all these levels, empires were at the tip of the 'bio-power' that liberalism was busy exploring in Europe itself.

In the dramatic crucible of these experiences of subjectivation, imperial 'traditions' were invented, of which the Dutch Indies and the Victorian Raj were two main sites.[40] Europeans in the colonies thereby turned themselves into 'moral subjects' of their own history, simultaneously positioning themselves vis-à-vis their often critical representations of the metropolis in prey to the decadence of the Industrial Revolution, materialism and communism, and vis-à-vis the savagery of the natives to whom they had come to deliver the liberating message of Civilization by means of the oblique path of conquest and coercion, in spite of the lukewarm idea they themselves had of the West. Europeans overseas thus made ethical choices about lucre or abnegation, the use of or abstention from violence, adhesion to universalistic conceptions of humanity or, on the other hand, ideas of racial hierarchy, the selection of their sexual partners or the option of chastity, or quite simply the choice of their daily material culture, whether they lived in western style or went native, *alla franca* or *alla turca*.[41]

What was at stake? Their reputations, the images they had of themselves, their honour, their modesty, their desire, their sexual, cultural or racial identity, their family ties, their national or 'European' awareness – or rather their awareness as 'Europeans' – and, more often than one might reasonably expect, their mental health or physical survival. Following these individual or collective itineraries, they developed an ethos in which they could recognize themselves – an ethos such as the 'Catonism' of the British civil servant,[42] the heroism of the French naval officer, the pioneer spirit of the Batavian planter, the redemptive path of the missionary, the sense of racial superiority of the 'working-class aristocracy' of the white miners in Northern Rhodesia or the Union of South Africa. Or, conversely, they failed to live up to these ideals or to the 'gaze' of their fellows, in the words of Georges Hardy, one of the theorists of French colonialism and the author of *Ergaste ou la Vocation coloniale*, published in 1929. Some endured the shame of a collapse of their sense of identity, vegetating in the despised condition of the 'little white man'. Others opted for racial betrayal, consorting not just with local whores but also with the very 'lifestyle' of the natives, or even transgressing heterosexual orthopraxis by taking (and getting others to take) their 'certificate in colonial studies', to use one of the French slang expressions designating masculine sodomy.[43]

Certainly, it might be conceded, that's the least one can expect from conquerors: courage and glory, in vain retribution for the suffering they inflict on the vanquished, and sometimes the moral perdition entailed by the intoxication of domination. But we need to add, in the second place, that the defeated are themselves abandoned to the Gallo-Roman syndrome. They brought a certain liking for (or at least granted certain attenuating circumstances to) the powers that had taken their historical destiny hostage, and stuck either to the form or to the spirit of the 'conducts of life' that the social institutions of colonization dispensed on them: the administration or the army, but also – and perhaps above all – the slave-trading post, the missionary base, the school, the hospital, the plantation, the factory, the mine, the concessionary company, even, in extreme cases, the forced labour site, the prison, or the concentration camp. These social institutions implemented discourses, procedures, regulations and prescriptions: in short, 'technologies of power' of which bodies were indeed the 'target':[44] sometimes imprisoned, stripped, chained, forced to work, beaten, deported, done to death; sometimes cared for, educated, dressed, fed and paid. These institutions thus harboured veritable 'cultures of the self' that enabled 'moral subjects' to be constituted and made it possible for the colonized to 'belong' to the colony by allowing the state to be grafted on and nationalism to be crystallized long before the political formation of the nationalist demand by so-called 'nationalist' parties.[45]

All too often, the 'discipline' inherent in the social institutions of colonization has been interpreted mechanistically, as an unequivocal cog in a totalitarian society.[46] But the 'microphysics of power' that such societies have deployed, without being in the least reluctant to use coercion, has offered a whole range of modes of subjectivation whose attraction has been underestimated thanks to the demands of political correctness. Many of the colonized have sincerely adhered to these 'conducts of life' that were simultaneously proposed to them and imposed on them. To deny this means listening to African voices 'without selves'.[47] It is to ignore countless eye-witness accounts and to abandon the attempt to understand how the European occupation perpetuated itself with such derisory military and administrative means. It also means reducing the collaboration of huge sectors of the native elites to self-serving motives or cultural 'alienation' and denying the truth of their Christian faith or their professional and social conscience, or indeed their attachment to the 'presence' of the colonizer, an allegiance that would be at the origin of so many tragedies in Indochina and Algeria.[48] What took place was a whole 'cultural process that aimed at creating a "moral" contract with the colonial order and its representatives, and inserted it into the native social temporality'.[49] It is just that this allegiance was a deeply ambivalent phenomenon, as one might expect.[50] Asians and Africans were able, in one and the same process, to take up a western 'conduct of life' and to reject European political domination, to find a way around the latter or even turn it to their own ends. The history of the nation-state, capitalism and Christianity to the south of the 35th parallel can more or less be summed up in terms of this antinomy.

The fantastical and sometimes hallucinatory character of the colonial situation did indeed stem from the ambivalence of the processes of subjectivation to which it gave birth. For example, African doctors, recruited not without difficulty due to the disgust felt for any contact with the sick, submitted to the rigorous discipline of Makerere University and then to great austerities, incarnated an ethos of devotion that aroused the admiration of patients and their families, and established them as 'pioneers of rationality' and universality, in spite of the recurrent corruption reigning in the hospitals, their personal enrichment and their self-serving participation in public affairs.[51] Likewise, in South Africa, the prestigious career of a nurse was synonymous with social dignity and a guarantee of financial income, the twofold dream of the petty bourgeoisie, which the mere fact of wearing the white uniform fully symbolized.[52]

But such nuptials between the colonized and the 'lifestyles' of the colonial regime had their counterparts in the nocturnal world. Medical 'technologies of power', and the modes of subjection they made possible, were major sites for the imaginary institution of colonial society, to adopt the words of Castoriadis. Western therapies were given a lukewarm reception: the ability of medical techniques to penetrate the skin (by injections or the use of scalpels) meant that these procedures were just as feared by the Africans as they were welcome to them.[53] The almost totalitarian vaccination campaigns and attempts to prevent the outbreak of a pandemic roused mixed feelings, ranging from a fetishistic infatuation to millenarian uprisings. The manipulation of blood and the most intimate kinds of bodily matter, which provide the operators of the invisible with a privileged field of activity, fed into many different rumours as to the vampire-like goings-on indulged in by European doctors and nurses and their native auxiliaries.[54]

Denunciations were uttered against the plots being hatched in the hospitals and dispensaries, but also in the public lavatories, use of which was forbidden or regulated in such a way that one could have no doubt as to what was being stored there: the bodies of the vampires' victims. And the priest who, in the 1930s, made available to the Catholic miners of the Mining Union of Upper Katanga, on the orders of his management, child care, the rudiments of family planning and scouting, was rapidly suspected of dark intentions from which only a strict bodily discipline afforded any protection: after 9 p.m. you could not allow yourself to go to the toilets, or to the 'City', a place of drink and perdition.[55]

The fantastical nature of the colonial processes of subjectivation did not prevent them from spreading, and sometimes even helped it. This was the case of the massive experience of subjection represented by the conversion of Africans to Christianity, with whole societies being turned upside down, as among the Beti of Cameroon and the kingdoms of the Great Lakes, or starting on the edges of the social order, as among the Yoruba.[56] The missionaries were deemed to have a certain affinity with the menacing nocturnal world, thanks to their skin colour and their commerce with God, their privileged (albeit sometimes hostile) relations with other white people, and their medical and educational activities. They were thus perceived as potential sorcerers or witches, an image that they have not entirely shaken off even now. Rituals such as that of the Eucharist or cults such as that of the Sacred Heart gave rise to terrible misunderstandings.[57] The devoutness of the priests was in no way above all suspicion – far from it. Referring to the period just after the war, a Mofu from the north of Cameroon relates the following:

People were running away. The Father said, 'Don't run away.' But they kept on running. They thought the white man ate people. But when they came up to him, he was full of smiles. People thought of him as a panther. People are frightened of the panther, but the panther is not frightened of people. He had hair on his body and his head: they said he came out of a cave like the monkeys, as we did not have body hair like him. Others said of him, 'He's a sorcerer who has come back to life. Now he is seeking to eat more people; but he's cunning: he binds their wounds, and then he eats the dressings. He cleans the wounds with cotton but he keeps the cotton.' People thought, 'He's going to make soup with it.' Parents told their children, 'He's a sorcerer who's coming back to life; don't go near him, he'll take your soul and you'll die. The whites are cunning. The first whites came with salt. When you taste the salt, you like it and tomorrow you'll have a bit more. This is their way of luring people so they can make off with them. Many people were lost after coming to get salt from the Whites. And now the Father comes with his pills. He's going to get you that way.' The sick were frightened of being eaten; so, instead of going to seek treatment, they preferred to die. When a patient came to get his wound treated, he would hold his hand in front of his face so that he wouldn't see the Father. The Father told a patient, 'You need to have your leg cut off.' But we thought: he's saying that so he can get the meat. So the patient preferred to die. The normal thing is to have black skin like us; you only have white skin when you graze yourself. People are really scared of the white man. When the Father was washing wounds, he didn't do it just any old how. People thought: there are a lot of dead people in his hut, he's going to make soup with it.[58]

At the same time, the missionaries inculcated in generations of Africans a 'culture of the self' with which many of the latter identified in their deepest being. Historians and anthropologists have established the trajectories that some of these Christian figures (or families) followed, and shown how conversion involved a complete transformation of bodily or practical practices, at the same time as it offered access to unprecedented knowledge and new professional statuses, whether waged or not.[59] If there was ever a social institution that dispensed 'conducts of life', it was indeed the mission, which acted by both retribution and coercion. Missions were generally implanted on the edge of town; they were often panoptic and all but totalitarian. Thus Chatelain, the founder of the Phil-African Mission in Angola, congratulated himself on the way he could 'oversee and master everything':[60] 'From my windows, on the upper storey of my new house, I can overlook the whole cultivated area; thanks to my binoculars, I can just see how people are working, and thanks to the foghorn I can give them orders without having to run up and down the furrows the whole time.' He was forever presenting himself as the incarnation of the Word that he taught; as he walked around, he would sing the canticles he had composed in Umbundu and was overjoyed when his flock started to sing them in turn.[61]

Nonetheless, the missionaries were not always content with just hymns and announcements on the *Urihorn*. Their holy wrath led them to discredit competing 'lifestyles', to destroy fetishes, to break up lubricious dances, to forbid the consumption of beer and tobacco, to assail the practice of clitoridectomy, to impose the wearing of dresses and regulate that of shorts or trousers, to recommend a petty bourgeois environment that discouraged promiscuity, to revile libertinage and to impose corporal punishment on the children entrusted to them.[62] The Christianization of Africa was an 'epic of the ordinary', an 'epiphany of the everyday', with all the joys and sorrows this brought with it.[63]

Most of these prescripts were taken up, often in an even harsher form, by the so-called 'independent' churches that proliferated in the wake of the 'North Atlantic' churches[64] and had broken off from the latter. Generally speaking, the Christian repertoire of subjectivation established a lineage and 'the leaf became soap', as the Yoruba proverb has it: just as the leaf that wraps the mixture of ashes and palm oil from which traditional black soap is made eventually dissolves, so individuals adapt in turn to their new environment and melt into it. In this case, the reciprocal assimilation of religions gave rise to a Yoruba 'cultural nationalism' whose Christian nationalism was the main institutional source, thanks to the way it was open to the African transnational elites on the West African coast.[65] This is no doubt an exceptional case, given the fact that a Christian presence antedates colonization. But however great the propensity of Africans to sin, the force of attraction of the Good News and the behaviour it lays down, in the rest of the continent, must not be underestimated, especially since it was a major influence, thanks to schooling, behind the 'lifestyle' of the nationalist elites which provided the backbone of 'domination' (*Herrschaft*) and seized power when independence came along. The constitution of the Christian 'moral subject' is at the heart of the governmentality of the belly that was established in a century of globalization and state formation.[66]

Even more generally, the indirect administration of the colonial empires took the form of a systematic process of assigning a sense of culture and identity. At the same time as it 'invented' and attributed ethnic or communalist identities, this administration imprisoned the natives in the artefact of a customary 'lifestyle'. The convergent intervention of 'traditional' jurisdictions and their jurisprudence, the vernacular pastoralia of the missions and the erudite labours of the colonial administration and its organic ethnologists reified these lifestyles. Nowadays it is accepted that the colonized soon made such culturalist processes of subjectivation their own. Together with the public policies of the European occupiers (or with the para-public policies of the social institutions that were entrusted with these 'discharges'), they started in turn to produce neo-traditional 'conducts of life', to 'make country fashion' as the Creole or pidgin expression has it.

These are 'lifestyles' that nationalist movements – for instance the BJP in India or Mobutism in Zaire – will be tempted, when the right time comes, to take over in an ideological fashion. So-called 'primordial' identities and the cultures they flaunt are also vehicles of subjectivation, which, as I have already emphasized, were yet again products of the colonial situation at the interface of state-formation and globalization. Let it be said in passing that this ought to dissuade us from interpreting them in utilitarian or instrumentalist terms, as might have happened with the encouragement of the problematic of the 'invention of tradition', to the great regret of those who created the concept.[67] Such lines of identification demarcate, even if only as 'illusions' (as in my *Illusion of Cultural Identity*), whole areas of subjection. Without himself resorting to this conceptualization, John Lonsdale has provided us with an erudite and illuminating demonstration of this process in the case of the moral economy of the Kikuyu in Kenya.[68]

In short, the colonial state and the social institutions that have been its 'powerful system of fortresses and earthworks' gave rise to 'moral subjects' who recognized themselves as being obligated to precise positive norms and social practices in everyday life (or rather in the way their existence was regulated in its everyday terms – *Veralltäglichung*). 'Social strata' (*Schichten*) have been constituted – civil servants, teachers, carers, business employees, traditional bosses, lawyers – who will 'bear' these 'conducts of life' and generally become, at least temporarily, the cornerstones of 'domination'.[69]

So both state-formation and the globalization of colonized societies seem inseparable from the rise of a particular 'type of person' (*Menschentum*) who was indeed made of religious and economic elements.[70] Naturally, in actual fact, this 'mode of subjection' took many forms as a result of the numerous religious, philosophical, political, social or material contradictions that divided the agents of colonization themselves or their auxiliaries and universal legatees. It has assumed many different shapes. It thus immediately found its limits – something which is completely ignored by the neo-Foucauldian theme (not always well understood) of 'discipline' in colonial or postcolonial situations. The phenomena of religious dissidence or of proliferation, the telescoping of the moral economies of one's *terroirs* or of transnational trading networks together with the bureaucratic and national ethos, doctrinal divergences that affect conditions of access to universality, have led to contradictions and convulsions. One and the same social institution has contrived to be the scene of antagonistic strategies on the part of different categories of agents, like the Christian churches in Africa which were imbued with the social ambitions of catechists or of women, often to the great chagrin of the white missionaries. Be this as it may, the production of 'lifestyles' in the framework of colonial empires was guaranteed thanks to the effect of miscellaneous 'components of religious origin and components of economic origin': by the different varieties of Christianity that differed in the way that they judged the ability of their faithful to gain, *de haute foi*, the bourgeois and monogamous respectability of Victorian morals, but also by the different trends of Islam whose theological, judicial, political and fraternity authorities were closely associated with the indirect administration of empires, or by the institutions of Hinduism and Buddhism, or even by trading networks and capitalist companies whose ethos and practices varied from one situation to another. Countries such as India, Indonesia and Nigeria exemplify the complexity of these 'religious encounters' and these joint ventures between local traders, transnational regional networks and European capitalists, in the domain of business. The irreducible plurality of the lines of subjectivation in a given historical situation does not guarantee the unity or coherence of the 'type of person' that was created by the colonial 'event'. This coherence thus remains subject to qualification and verification, if only because colonization was less a system or a structure than a contingency, subject to the vagaries of local circumstances and coming into effect in short stages, from one level to another, in accordance with unstable alliances, without any clear awareness or intention.[71] But it is no less obvious that the natives forged a 'culture of the self' through the traumatic experience of foreign occupation and that the imperial processes of subjectivation are part of a more general movement, corresponding to the period of two centuries that I have set out.

For in third place, colonization did not provide modes of subjection in the colonized societies alone. Thanks to 'reverberation' or 'refraction' effects that are now well understood by historians, it also contributed to shaping the 'conducts of life' of metropolitan citizens.[72] Circles of ideologists, such as the French Saint-Simonians of the nineteenth century, won over by the doctrine of *affamiliation* of Prosper Enfantin; social institutions such as the churches, freemasonry or trade unionism; political and military institutions such as, in France, parliament and the navy; literary or artistic milieus such as those of Algiers or Oran; 'transitive' or 'vehicular' peoples or social categories (diasporas, Creoles): all contributed to this surreptitious process of feedback.[73]

Colonization, as Foucault wrote (after pointing out that Blackwood's *Apologia pro regibus* had already in 1581 drawn up a parallel between the colonization of England by the Normans and that of North America by the English), transported European models to other continents, but colonial models were also brought back to the West: it was as if the West were colonizing itself.[74] Between the orientalist waves of the *chinoiseries* and other *japonaiseries* of the nineteenth century and the propagation of jazz in the twentieth century, between cubism and surrealism, the material and artistic cultures of the West have not ceased to define themselves vis-à-vis this imperial past, one that is constantly being re-actualized.

More precisely, a significant proportion of the subjectivation schemes to which westerners conform comes more or less from the colonial adventure – their national awareness to begin with, in the crucible of which their contemporary 'lifestyles' continue to be shaped, despite two centuries of globalization and fifty years of European construction. What would the fact of being British, Dutch, French, Portuguese or Spanish actually amount to if these countries had not thrown themselves body and soul into an imperial project? There is no doubt but that it would have been very different from what it is today. The very idea of the nation, its habitus, the polemical values to which it refers, its 'milieus' and its 'places of memory' (Pierre Nora) bear the (often traumatic) mark of conquest and decline. In the European single market of identity, we still find foibles that raise a smile or exasperate: 'Sebastianism' in Portugal, Victorian romanticism in Britain, the propensity to dispense civilization in France, nostalgia for the *tempo doeloe* (the 'good old days') of the East Indies in Holland. Conversely, Japanese, German, Italian or American national awareness would be quite different if the colonial epic of these countries had not stopped short. We can also wonder what the contribution of imperialism to the European idea itself has been, by means of the racial awareness of being a 'European' as opposed to one of the 'native' majority.

The painting and music of Westerners, their city life, their medicine, their hygiene, their conception of heroism, their representations of immigrants, their food, their sexuality are all implicitly marked by this historical experience of imperial society. The 'colonial encounter' did not simply influence the culture of the metropolises, in the form of a borrowing from other, exotic civilizations. It contributed to shaping it from within, being a time and place of intense innovation in every area of social life. It was, for instance, a major time for the growth of towns and cities in Asia and Africa, either by the reshaping of older cities, or by the creation of new ones. It thus fostered the advent of an original town and city civilization that invented its own material culture in terms of dress, food, body care, entertainment, artistic creation or political activity. But the 'total social fact' of the colonial, or para-colonial, city in Africa and Asia became interwoven with social change in Europe, America and even Japan. The simultaneous spread of imperial cooking and drinks – such as the 'rice table', curries, couscous, ginger ale and tea, but also beer, whisky, Portuguese red plonk, tomato sauce, Oxo cubes or tinned sardines – in the colonies and metropolises is an illustration of this form of 'mutual interaction', just as the expansion of England within the European system of states, from the Middle Ages onwards, led to the introduction of wines from Bordeaux, Porto, Madeira and Marsala into the dietary habits of its ruling classes and into the way they thought of such things as 'distinguished'. The emergence of a national or local habitus of food is almost always a case of extraversion.

Likewise, the modern housing estates and garden cities or new cities that have enfolded the historic centres of the Old Continent in their embrace ever since the Second World War are all new extensions of the ribbon development by which the colonial state endeavoured to channel the rural exodus of the natives and reduce the risk of epidemics. Ideologists of public health measures, and other progressive voices, set themselves within the great utopian tradition of the nineteenth century, and reforming French town planners, for instance, conceived and theorized their plans by simultaneously taking into account the demands of the Industrial Revolution in mainland France and those of the colonial conquest. Their careers have all encountered the paths of such men as Augagneur, Mayor of Lyons before his appointment as Governor General of Madagascar in 1905, Lanessan, General Governor of Tonkin from 1891 to 1894, Gallieni, and (in particular) Lyautey.

In Lyons, Tony Garnier's building (Garnier benefited from the explicit support of Herriot, the successor of Augagneur) became a landmark and was imitated in several Moroccan cities by his associate at the Villa Médicis, Henri Prost, to whom Lyautey had entrusted the urban planning of the new protectorate. In this domain as in others, the resident general deployed a neo-conservative method of government: authoritarian, centralized, rationalized and 'enlightened', whose message was addressed simultaneously to the counter-example of the colonization of Algeria and the decadent parliamentarianism of the metropolis. He himself, as a good dandy, played his role and displayed a para-aristocratic 'culture of the self' that amounted to a critique of bureaucratic mediocrity and fascinated a sector of French public opinion and administration. In opposition to the approach of the military engineers of the École polytechnique and the École des Ponts-et-Chaussées, he implemented the type of town planning of which the Musée social, created in 1894, a real 'community of experts' of republican and imperial French modernity, had laid the foundations. In 1931, the Conference on Town Planning in the colonies hailed him as the greatest town planner of modern times, while at the same time recommending the adoption of 'plans of redevelopment and extension' permitting both the respect for and the coexistence of the cultural habits of different 'races'.[75] During these years, Algiers had become the centre of passionate debates on town planning, thanks to its unbridled extension and the reaction against the neo-Moorish style that had prevailed there ever since the turn of the century. In this debate, Henri Prost took part, as did Le Corbusier, who advocated the radical redesign of the city.

Although Corbusier's plans were rejected, his disciples were active in the Town Planning Group of the Algerian region that was set up following the Second World War, even though it was one of their rivals, Fernand Pouillon, who was entrusted with the construction of the three cities designed for Muslim populations: Diar es-Saada, Diar el-Maçoul and Climat de France at Bab el-Oued.[76] This often highly polemical development of the colonial city, which had originally been inspired by the industrial city between the Saône and the Rhône, had an impact on metropolitan France in the shape of high-quality apartment blocks or high-density housing complexes during the period of national reconstruction, the baby-boom, the depopulation of the countryside, the massive arrival of immigrant workers and *pied-noir* refugees, and the 'Thirty Glorious Years' of French economic growth (1945–75). Thus it was that people could speak of the 'murder of Paris'.[77] Well, the murderers had learnt their lessons in Indochina, south of the Sahara and in the Maghreb; the first of them in particular, Paul Delouvrier, father of the 'new cities', who had been the delegate general to the government in Algeria, in charge of the Constantine Plan, from 1958 to 1961, before being appointed delegate general to the Region of Paris on his return to mainland France, then prefect of the Region of Paris in 1966, and so on. The contemporary town dweller and suburbanite who think they are a thousand leagues from the colonial political imaginary are well and truly the heirs of the colonial city.*

But it is within the domain of the socialization of children – so at the heart of the processes of subjectivation – that the imperial 'reverberation effect' between overseas possessions and metropolises has been most remarkable. The specialized press, cartoon strips, literature – or, more directly, family narratives and the sermons of missionaries back from abroad or passing through their native country – all transmitted the colonial *imaginaire*. One need only quote the work of Rudyard Kipling to bring to mind the central place of empires in the definition of the practices of the self of the child or teenager between the end of the nineteenth century and at least the middle of the twentieth. The scouting movement institutionalized this colonial *paideia* and had a certain influence on the construction of western masculinity between the Great War and the 1960s.

The itinerary of its founder, Baden-Powell, is a good example of this moment of imperial globalization. From 1876 to 1883 he travelled the world as an intelligence officer for Her Majesty, going successively to

---

* Admittedly, unrest in the suburbs in Autumn 2005 seemed to act as a reminder of this continuity, if we are to believe postcolonial studies. But the link between the political awareness of the young people in the big working-class estates and the colonial past has not been proven. The mobilization was social in nature – an act of protest – rather than being a matter of identity and 'postcolonial' self-assertion. [Author's note, 2007.]

India, South Africa, Russia, Germany, Malta and Dalmatia. In the following years, he fought successively against the Zulu, the Ashanti and the Matabele, then returned to India where he wrote *Aids to Scouting*. The Boer War brought him back to South Africa, where he distinguished himself at the Siege of Mafeking by his tenacity and the use of young boys as scouts and dispatch riders. His book became a bestseller, seducing British teenagers and educators. Promoted to lieutenant-general in charge of the Territorial Army, Baden-Powell drew on his personal experience in India and Africa and on his knowledge of initiation rites to launch the scouting movement in 1907–8. It was a runaway success both in England and throughout the whole empire. The pedagogy proposed – and set out in a second book, *Scouting for Boys* – was unambiguously based on the 'mode of subjection': it was a matter of 'shaping young men in the service of a social order',[78] at this precise moment of imperial expansion, the birth of an industrial, urban society and globalization. Baden-Powell wrote that he imagined every boy wanted to be useful to his country in one way or another, and the easiest way of doing this was to become a boy scout. A scout in the army, he continued, was generally a soldier chosen for his skill and his bravery – he could discover where the enemy was situated, and report back to his commander. But there are scouts in peacetime as well as in wartime, and they need the same qualities: these men, he adds, are at the frontiers of the world.[79]

Right from his first chapter, Baden-Powell sets up as role models the frontiersmen, pioneers and trappers of North America, explorers and missionaries of Asia, Australian colonists, and the police of the Canadian West and of South Africa. He does not fail to mention Kipling's Kim. But the scout is required, via an interactive pedagogy that emphasizes the importance of the imagination as well as obedience and service, a sense of chivalry, self-discipline and self-improvement:

1 A scout's honour is to be trusted.
2 A scout is loyal to his Queen, his country, his scouters, his parents, his employers, and those under him.
3 A scout's duty is to be useful and to help others.
4 A scout is a friend to all and a brother to every other scout, no matter to what country, class, or creed the other belongs.
5 A scout is courteous.
6 A scout is a friend to the animals and to all other created things.
7 A scout obeys the orders of his parents, patrol leader, or scoutmaster without question.
8 A scout smiles and whistles under all difficulties.
9 A scout is thrifty.
10 A scout is clean in thought, word and deed.[80]

The promise the boy makes, after a probationary period, marks the beginning of a path of initiation that makes scouting a 'rite of passage' (Arnold Van Gennep). This was all the more true in that it was accompanied, in the effective practice of the movement and in spite of its official prescriptions, by physical trials, or even by bullying and physical abuse that echo certain African rituals of adolescence. The basic organ of the institution, the 'patrol', 'makes it possible, from the point of view of education, to establish a subtle and powerful dynamism between constraint and liberty, teach-yourself methods and apprenticeship, individuality and collectivity'.[81]

Scouting benefited from a quite extraordinary degree of enthusiasm, with the exception of Germany where Anglophobia was the rule and where the *Wandervögel* already filled the slot, and it quickly became a transnational movement, simultaneously forming part of 'international civil society' and different national spaces, especially in virtue of its privileged relationship to the colonial venture and to nationalism, and due also to its ability to adapt to the religious particularities of its host societies. In France, for instance, its destiny was immediately linked to the Catholic Church, and its earliest promoters had often had overseas experience, like Father Sevin or General Guyot d'Asnières de Salins. Marshall Lyautey indeed, who became a fervent spokesman for the empire between the two world wars, became the honorary president of the movement. Scouting saw itself as a 'boy's complete upbringing', in Father Sevin's words.[82] With this aim in view, it inculcated 'techniques of the self' – initiatory stages, the pedagogic value of sport, the wearing of uniform, the development of one's powers of endurance and faculties of orientation by the practice of marching – and even an 'aesthetic of existence', illustrated by the often ambiguous drawings of Pierre Joubert in the press and scouting novels – that were all erected into 'a method of self-conquest', in the highly Foucauldian expression of the Jesuit Jean Rimaud, in 1933–4: 'In this painful and lasting state of fatigue [of adolescence], of uncertain and troubled thoughts, of resistance, and mistrust, the boy feels ill at ease. Hence a *need for escape*. . . . From the escapism that is a defeat, scouting must derive a method of self-conquest.'[83] As Christian Guérin remarks,[84] the strength of the movement was to transform this 'mode of subjection', one that was especially pernickety when it came to the inhibition and repression of sexuality – 'a scout is clean and pure in thought, word and deed' – into an enterprise of social liberation and the romantic sublimation of desire. There is a striking contrast between the celebration of the beauty of adolescents' bodies and souls in the literature and iconography of scouting, and the panoptic alarms of its highly Catholic leaders.

In spite of everything, people may think, even with a camp volant, the gravest of dangers is still there, namely the promiscuity of the almost always cramped tent, where boys sleep side by side. . . . The real degree of promiscuity depends a great deal on how many children are allotted to each tent. . . . Even then, every precaution must be taken and the strictest decency observed: scouts do not sleep in nightshirts, but in pyjamas, or remain fully dressed, and they slip into a sleeping bag before wrapping themselves up in their blankets. They wash outside the tent. There are in any case people keeping an eye on the tent. . . . We should also note that, because of the restricted dimensions of the tent, it is very difficult for any naughtiness to take place in it, without the complicity of at least several of those inside; in fact, they keep a mutual eye on one another. Finally, if the scoutmaster knows how to make his troop work hard, by the evening they will be so filled with a healthy exhaustion that, five minutes after the fires have been extinguished, they will all be fast asleep! . . . The ordinary life of the troop has allowed the scouts to discover the freedom of the camp gradually, and if the law is taken seriously and practised to a superhuman degree it will serve as a constant stabilizer that will always tend to put those adolescent souls back on their feet, however intoxicated (even physically) by this total absence of constraint that life in the open air creates.

So Father Sevin reassures himself, and he also recommends a few simple rules to the leaders:

11   [Do not camp] near a barracks, a military camp or a fort; the soldiers will enjoy 'initiating' your boys.
12   [Do not camp] for too long in the same place: movable camps are often better for soul and body. One of the dangers of the camp resides in the relations that are established between scouts and natives [note by J.-F. Bayart: These are the French 'natives', the peasants in the countryside where the camps are held]. . . .
14   It is forbidden to enter the tents during the day without the permission of the scoutmaster or the head of the tent.
15   Permission cannot be given for anyone to enter another's tent.
16   Siestas are taken in the shade, outside the tents. It should not last too long. Even then, demand dignity in dress. . . .
20   Do not allow two boys, even reliable ones, to share the same blanket. . . .
30   Letters are collected in the camp and taken to the post by a specially designated scout. Your boys should trust you so much that they spontaneously get into the habit of handing you their letters still open, so that you can always add a word or two to their families. . . .
37   Do not always send the same scouts for food: it is in this way that relationships develop. . . .
47   Do not imagine that everything is all right just because you do not see anything going amiss.[85]

Now, more than the knight of the Middle Ages, the tutelary figure of this 'mode of subjection' is the operator of imperial globalization: 'The model figure for the scout, in this sense, is the colonialist, the explorer, the missionary', continues Father Sevin.[86] As a corollary of this, Ernest Psichari justifies colonization in these terms: 'We come here to do some good among these cursed wastelands. But we also come to do ourselves some good. We want this great venture to serve our moral health and improvement.'[87] Even after 1945, the colonial situation was to provide French scouting with part of its ideology of subjectivation. One of the moral ideals offered to the emulation of adolescents would be that of the 'raider', the 'commando' – which raised a few problems when French parachutists distinguished themselves in the way we all know in Algeria.[88] The 'raider' mentality would be gradually abandoned in favour of that of the 'pioneer', and the movement would definitively break away with those nostalgic for the Empire in 1962 following the publication, in the collection 'Signes de Piste', of the novel *Aventures au Katanga*, hailing the combat of the 'Affreux', and prefaced by Colonel Trinquier.*

In Indochina, Algeria and other places, I knew young men capable of behaving like 'José' or Kamwania, the two heroes of the novel by J.-P. Jacques.

I have always noted that the absence of racism allows men of different races [*sic*], especially young men, to love each other and engage in a fraternal struggle against an enemy of civilization: communist materialism, or capitalist materialism, whether it comes from the East or the West.

I know that in Katanga, adolescents have performed, in the struggle against those rebelling against the authority of their country, and even the 'Blue Berets' who wanted to impose their power on their small land, actions worthy of those of the defenders of Budapest against the Soviet troops.

From the fifteen-year-old crusaders of the Middle Ages up to the young Vietnamese companions who have followed our soldiers into the rice paddies and mountains of Tonkin, and the young Muslims of Algeria who fought for France, young men have always provided models for adults and it has often been the former who have given the example on the field of sacrifice. . . .

Our young men instinctively realized that the battles that were being fought in Katanga were the same as those that we are fighting in Algeria, Laos or Angola. It is our freedom and our civilization that we are here defending.

I would have been proud to have José and Kamwania under my command. But I had their older brothers, in Indochina and Algeria –

---

* Roger Trinquier (1908–2000) was one of the main theorists of 'psychological warfare' and counter-guerrilla fighting in Algeria: his work was avidly read by many in the Republic of South Africa in the 1960s. [Tr.]

brave young men, who came from every race, but loved each other and fought for the same ideal.[89]

The author of the 'cult' series of *Prince Eric*, Serge Dalens (real name: Yves de Verdilhac) would take his radical interpretation of the scout 'mode of existence' by joining the National Front and becoming one of its dignitaries.

And indeed, the clearest demonstration of the influence of the colonial experience on the production of 'lifestyles' in the imperial metropolises was the enormous after-effect of decolonization. Not only was this experienced as a trial, or indeed a moral war, most particularly when it was accompanied by an armed struggle for national liberation, terrorist acts and their repression, if necessary by resorting to massacres and torture, as in Algeria. Not only did it profoundly divide the social institutions of the colonizing countries such as the armies, the churches, the universities, the youth movements, the trade unions, the political parties and the press, echoing at the heart of literary and artistic creation, as was demonstrated by the psychomachia of the confrontation between Sartre and Camus. But it also turned completely topsy-turvy the tangle of possible lines of subjectivation by transforming material culture and proposing new 'human types' with which one could identify.

In France, the independence of states in Indochina, Morocco, Tunisia and sub-Saharan Africa, and then Algeria, happened at the same time as the 'Thirty Glorious Years' and the slide into the consumer society, which was perceived as a desire for 'Americanization', to the sound of jazz and memories of the Liberation: 'American women have the best dressed hair in the world!' proclaimed the Helena Rubinstein ad in *Elle*, May 1955.[90] The 'mythologies' of the years 1950–60 were dominated by the cult of speed – the speed of the military and civil jet plane, the electric locomotive and the car, on the altar of which would be sacrificed, apart from the city of Paris, several literary celebrities – and by the rituals of cleanness, with the commoditization of washing machines, industrial detergents and cosmetic products, in tandem with the spread of a new code of bodily hygiene that was made possible by a material culture of more comfortable housing.

Drawing on the work of Henri Lefebvre and the writings of the Situationists, Kristin Ross believes that this shift in the field of subjectivation expresses a substitute form of the lost colonies and a 'colonization of everyday life': 'the effort that once went into maintaining and disciplining a colonial people and situation becomes instead concentrated on a particular "level" of metropolitan existence: everyday life'.[91] Magazines such as *Elle* and *Express*, the latter of which was edited by Hélène Lazareff, Françoise Giroud and Jean-Jacques Servan-Schreiber, embodied this new 'conduct of life' which rapidly found its 'human type': the 'young executive' living in Parly-II or the apartment blocks of Pouillon, Pont de Billancourt, playing tennis or going horse-riding, eating off meal trays at his workplace, waxing enthusiastic on reading *Le Défi américain* and seeing in Claude Lelouch's *Un homme et une femme* the *Romeo and Juliet* of his time.

However, all subjection remains incomplete. The consumerist dream had become a matter of everyday life with the coming of the end of the colonial epic and the change in scale of the Common Market. This led, in May 1968, to this phenomenon being questioned and an anti-lifestyle ideology being formulated. The 'young executive' became, for a number of young men, an object of derision, as did the positive heroes of colonialism or their feeble heir, the parachutist 'redneck' of *Le Grand Duduche*. The Netherlands, with the Provo movement, and Great Britain with its pop culture, had experienced comparable developments rather earlier.

Of course, the appearance of new 'modes of existence' in western countries, following the Second World War, cannot be reduced to the dislocation of the colonial empires. The United States, Germany, Italy and later on Spain experienced similar mutations in their schemes of subjectivation. The fact remains that in the old imperial metropolises the two 'events' seem inseparable. This delayed effect consolidates the hypothesis whereby globalization, here, in its colonial version, produces 'conducts of life'; while confirming the contribution of transnational flows to the processes of state-formation. Now the old colonial reverberations are persistent. Apart from the fact that they channel a notable proportion of contemporary migratory flows, as we have already seen, they define what geometers call 'fractals', i.e. 'non-entire borders'. Étienne Balibar notes this with respect to the relationship between France and Algeria, which comprise a set of 'one and a half': 'What we need to question is the idea that the dimensions of a sense of national belonging can necessarily be represented by whole numbers, such as one or two. . . . The fact that the nation was formed in the empire means that the empire remains present within nations. [92] . . . The relationship, often described as 'intimate' if not 'incestuous', between France and sub-Saharan Africa is another illustration of this.[93] It is in this respect that the most immediately contemporary experience of nation, belonging to the West or residing in the West, is sometimes described as 'postcolonial', especially in British cultural studies.[94]

Extraversion and coercion in imperial subjectivation

When it comes to understanding the current phase of globalization, there is a twofold advantage to be gained from considering processes of subjection in a colonial situation. It allows us to grasp how subjectivation can occur in a context of radical coercion, and simultaneously in a thirst for extraversion, without the latter necessarily being the 'false consciousness' of the former.

The fact bears repeating: colonization really and truly was a story of 'generalized mutual interaction', and not simply that of a vertical bipolar relation between metropolis and colonies. Within empires, and from one empire to another, 'knowledge-powers' circulated, with the Victorian Raj and the 'ethical' colonization of the East Indies providing models of administrative innovation. Religious institutions, migrations, the interplay of bureaucratic postings, the flow of business, intellectual and artistic quests all led to a huge intermingling of 'lifestyles' and moral or aesthetic reference points. The celebrated 'dialogue'[95] inherent in the imperial enterprise, which historians and anthropologists have been endeavouring to put together over the past twenty years, did not come down to a bilateral face-to-face between colonizer and colonized. It was less a duet than a polyphony, a series of improvisations on the modes of action available to historical societies when they were forced to 'encounter' one another and overlap with each other by the fact of empire. Colonization was thus a 'reinvention of difference' and not an act of cultural uniformity – in short, a founding moment in globalization.

To say that it was a regime of domination is a euphemism. It was literally conducted at gun point and with the lash of the whip. But it was, as such, still an experience of subjectivation. This was already true of the slave trade, even though it was evidently experienced in terror and humiliation. We need think only of the extreme violence of capture, the way people were torn away from their friends and families, stripped, chained, undernourished, whipped, worked until they dropped, suffered from sickness, forced to wait for ever in their own excrement and in the stench and darkness of the warehouse or ship, terrified that they might be executed from one moment to the next or even eaten, and branded with hot irons, while their companions in distress died or committed suicide: it is difficult to imagine more atrocious conditions than those of the slaves taken prisoner by the traders of the triangle of commerce on the Atlantic coasts, the warriors and traffickers of the Nile Valley or the Lake Chad basin, or even the Iranun and the Balangingi of Southeast Asia – apart, of course, from the conditions of the prisoners held in the death camps.

And yet, captivity gave rise to a painful process of self-reconstruction. The Portuguese Crown, for instance, stipulated that slaves were to receive a basic Christian education before being put on board ship at Luanda, and the King's officers saw to it that this was done. The catechism was taught them in Kimbundu, the lingua franca of the port, by other slaves who, more or less willingly, had gone over to the cause of the slave trade.[96] Likewise, the crews of ships scouring the shores of the Sulu Sea were not composed exclusively of sailors of Iranun or Balangingi origin, but also of captives who had been incorporated into these societies and had adopted the 'lifestyle' out of sheer despair, simply in order to survive.[97]

The figure of the 'renegade' symbolized this type of reversal in subjection, and it is well known how important it was in the history of buccaneering or at the apogee of the Sublime Porte. There even emerged from it a ruling elite of the Ottoman Empire, that of the Mamelukes. It had its equivalents in the Atlantic slave trade, in which the dissidence of the 'brown man' was not the sole repertory of subjectivation. Several slaves ended up 'belonging' to the social institution of the 'death road' and the plantation, if only by being Uncle Tom figures. In short, the historical experience of the Atlantic slave trade was the tragic source of 'lifestyles' which, as we have already seen, continue to vibrate in contemporary Africa and which have shaped the religious and cultural life, the civic activities and the social question in most of the countries of the New World. 'Afro-American civilization' has meaning only through the modes of subjection that it historically engendered. And right until the end of the nineteenth century, Christianity, a great dispenser of 'conducts of life' in the eyes of the Everlasting, was closely linked to slavery, whether it sanctioned it and to some extent 'whitewashed' it, or whether it impelled the European states to combat it, if necessary by the works of colonialism, and recruited the first members of its flocks among the captive, the fugitive or emancipated slaves.[98]

Now, we need to be clear that these coercive processes of subjectivation did not come about in spite of violence, but because of it. The Balangingi beat their prisoners with bamboos on their knees and elbows, and on the muscles of their arms and legs, so as to prevent them from running or swimming away, but also so as to convince them to turn their backs on their past, to abandon all memory of their families and to be satisfied with their condition now that it was freed of the weight of the Spanish *tributo*.[99] Likewise, the pains of the whip were the *sine qua non* of slavery, to use the expression of M. T. Taussig[100] – and also of the colonial situation. They were theorized and accepted in all good conscience. 'I have no hesitation in stating that I consider the use of the whip as absolutely indispensable', said Professor Louis Verlaine of the Colonial School of Angers. British bureaucracy responded in a paternalist fashion: 'I always treat my natives the same way as I treat children. I try to be gentle with them, to advise them and to guide them. But when kindness has no effect. you have to do the same as they do in the public schools, at home or throughout the empire: use the cudgel', declared a member of the Legislative Council of Kenya in 1941.[101] The application of corporal punishment was an everyday judicial or bureaucratic practice, and it was, as such, carefully codified and recorded. For example, colonial archives list 365 whippings in Zanzibar for the single year 1914 – one for every day of the year – to the detriment of thieves, drunkards, trouble-makers, the work-shy, and even native policemen guilty of negligence in performing their tasks.[102]

In Burundi the ruling no. 3/15 of 21 May 1917, relative to work discipline, laid down punishments of between four and twelve lashes applied to the small of the back; a later judicial ruling stated that this punishment should be immediately interrupted 'if a wound was produced or the prisoner fainted'; and a legislative ruling of 5 October 1943 limited the number of lashes to eight, exempting from this punishment old men, women, children and other categories of persons to be determined by the governor – basically, chiefs and deputy chiefs whose prestige was to be spared and whose powers were to be reinforced.[103]

But the whip was also an integral part of the 'private government' of many colonies. In the Bombay of the first half of the nineteenth century, it was permissible to send to the commissariat an employee bearing this note: 'Please flog the bearer', a sentence that was carried out there and then and without any further questions.[104] In the army or on the plantations, physical violence towards recruits or coolies was the order of the day until the twentieth century.[105] In Angola, the ferule (*palmatoria*) or 'child with five eyes' (*menino de cincos olhos*) – a bat of thick wood, pierced with five conical holes that sucked out and blistered the flesh on the palms of the hands and the soles of the feet to which it was administered – was present in all Portuguese homes and businesses. It was made abundant use of until 1961, together with the chicote (*chicote* or *cavalo marinho*): 'If the watchmen don't handle the whip well, it's their hands that start to swell under the lashes. Some even piss in their pants, I've seen the urine trickling down from their thighs when the *palmatoria* sings'.[106]

In most African societies, the use of the whip was an imported practice, constitutive of Atlantic civilization (or of the Indian Ocean): in short, one of the instruments of their globalization, and not an expression of their own spirit. Before the arrival of the Europeans (or of the Arab and Swahili traders), criminals and delinquents were more often than not punished by other means, and it was rare for children to be struck, except in the course of rituals of initiation or at the Koranic school.[107]

So the whip was a 'technique of the body', basically 'transatlantic' in nature, which asserted its presence in the social relations constitutive of globalization and in the processes of subjectivation to which they gave rise. Europeans themselves were punished by the whip or cane in schools and families. Coetzee remembers how pupils would be caned every day. Boys were ordered to bend over and touch their toes, before being caned. Coetzee shows clearly how this punishment, in

South Africa after the war, was an art and a profession, at the point of intersection between practices of the self and relations of power.

Each of the teachers in his school, men and women, has a cane and uses it at whim. Each of these canes has its personality, its character, one that is well known to the pupils, and is the object of endless discussions. As if they were thorough connoisseurs, the boys discuss the characteristics of the canes and the nature of the pain that they inflict, compare the arm and wrist technique of each of the masters who administrate the blows. Nobody mentions the shame there is in being summoned, forced to bend over and caned on the backside. . . . The bizarre thing is that just one hiding would be enough to break the malevolent spell that has him caught in a vice. He clearly realizes that if, one way or another, the punishment can be inflicted without his having time to stiffen himself into stone-like resistance, if the outrage to his body can happen really quickly, then the trial will forcibly turn him into a normal boy, and he will easily be able to join those who discuss the masters and their canes, and the degrees, the nuances of the sufferings they inflict. But by himself he is unable to cross this obstacle. It's the fault of his mother who never beat him. . . . He resents his mother for having turned him into something unnatural, something that has to be protected so that he can continue to live.[108]

Nonetheless, some Europeans were also whipped when they were adults: sailors, soldiers or convicted prisoners. In Angola – in 1841 and again in 1875 – prisoners were even whipped to death, with the help of up to a limit of 2,000 blows of the chicote.[109] And at the end of the nineteenth century, in the areas coloured pink representing the French Empire, the Companies of discipline – if we are to believe Georges Darien – subjected their soldiers to a whipping, among other punishments.[110]

The main point is that whites applied this punishment, or were present at it, either by professional obligation, or to pass the time of day and enjoy the show, or later on to wax indignant about it. Hallet, a subaltern colonial agent who arrived in the Belgian Congo shortly after the Second World War, recounts:

A Luba native was stretched out on the ground, his loincloth raised, exposing his entirely naked buttocks. A sturdy soldier was standing over him brandishing the *fimbo* – the deadly whip. . . . Each time the soldier lashed him with all his might, this *fimbo* would enter deeply into the muscles of the victim's buttocks, leaving red lines of blood that ran all down his thighs. . . . Then the victim got up unaided and staggered away.

'Wait a minute', cried the soldier. 'You forgot to say "thank you".' . . . I spotted Van Geel strolling down the steps of the shelter, imperturbably observing these proceedings. . . .

The next prisoner came before the man with the whip . . . the long row
of the Baluba waited in turn.[111]

Thanks to literary, pictorial or narrative depiction, the experience of
whipping finds its reflection in the colonial metropolises. In *A Child Is
Beaten*, Freud writes of the celebrated novel by Harriet Beecher Stowe,
Uncle Tom's Cabin, that it procures for its readers a 'masturbatory pleasure'. As for the abolitionist literature that flourished from the end of
the eighteenth century, dwelling as it did on the torments inflicted on
the slaves, it ensured that 'scenes that hitherto were confined to the
secrecy of the boudoir could circulate in the politically correct salons',
and to some extent it made respectable, or popularized, the themes of
Sadean or licentious literature that circulated illicitly or in restricted
circles of devotees.[112]

If one accepts that colonization also found expression in an economy
of desire, the image of the whip was a favourite fantastical expression
of this, which was echoed in various ways across western societies. So
did it merely happen by chance that the initiative of demanding 'that
corporal punishment be written into our laws to punish violent attacks
against persons and property' should have fallen to a retired naval
officer, a certain Dunoyer de Segonzac? The latter was convinced that
it was necessary to 'give a good drubbing' to young delinquents to
make them behave, and he started up a petition in the juries of several
assize courts in 1910. Various associations, as well as part of the press,
police officers, politicians, magistrates and doctors, all started to voice
their criticism of the 'mildness of sentences' and gravely wondered,
like Doctor Lejeune: 'Should hooligans be whipped?' The answer was
obviously 'yes'.

It is, so to speak, a theatrical penalty. . . . The executioner's movements,
the hiss of the instrument of flagellation, the muffled echo of the flesh
under the lash, all constitute a scene that terrifies the malefactor. . . .
There is no sight less beautiful than that of a person undergoing flagellation. Stripped naked, or almost so, the hooligan exposes his sickly,
degenerate anatomy; he shows himself just as he is, an inferior creature
whose existence in our great cities is tolerated only by our excessive
humanity. His hair, habitually so nicely pomaded, gets all tangled up
under the impact of the whipping, and his smooth-shaven face, usually
impudent and mocking, twists in the grimaces of a beaten child as that
cynical, mocking, creature is humiliated, begging like a coward to be
shown mercy. . . . The whipped man instinctively turns back into a slave,
one of the vanquished, and there is nothing better than to imprint this
sensation onto the bodies and minds of hooligans who think they are
free to do what they want. . . . The gang in which he was an influential
leader refuses to readmit him, the girls who provided for his existence
now refuse to be seen with a whipped man, and every day the hooligan

loses that aura of crime that comprised his strength and made him so redoubtable.[113]

At the time, the stigmatization of social and physical degeneration affecting city-dwellers was easily assimilated to that of primitive African, Arab or Asian customs, and vice versa.[114] To reduce the delinquent to the condition of a slave, even if only while he is being punished: this was the strange itinerary of subjectivation that certain Republican spirits enjoyed imagining, without them actually being followed by the government authorities and parliament. In any case, hooligans and the 'bat' d'Af' ('bataillons d'Afrique') were frequently associated in the press, in literature and in public statements. In Le Vagabond, déchet social (1910), Doctor Pagnier saw these battalions as the only possible salvation for young delinquents from the countryside – it being understood that the ne'er-do-wells of the cities were in his view irredeemably lost.[115]

In the colonies, the natives themselves seized on the whip and its associated mythology and likewise put it into practice. There is a great deal of evidence, literary and anthropological, that families supported the repressive fury of teachers in schools, seeing it as a guarantee of access to the knowledge and power of the white man – or an avatar of the traditional bastinado of initiation rituals.[116] In the Belgian Congo, the chicote was seen as a way of 'introducing people to civilization',[117] perhaps in accordance with a neo-Christian theme: the captivity of the Jews was the forerunner of the Promised Land, the whipping of Christ was the forerunner of the Resurrection, and the thongs of dried hippopotamus skin the harbinger of modernity and merchandise. A 'native' story from the same period as that of Hallet suggests in any case that the chicote belonged to the 'everyday reality' of colonial life.

> I was beaten with the chicote, forced to lie naked face down; I was given twenty-five lashes on the left buttock, and twenty-five on the right. It was a black policeman who hit me, while Bwana Kitoko kept count. When I got up, my backside was covered in blood. . . . He summoned me, I was beaten again, then sent to Kacya and so the whole affair concluded. *I continued to live with the Whites as I had done in the past.*[118]

The chicote later remained the 'justice of the peace' denounced by the *Moniteur du Congo* in 1885, and these days it is part and parcel of the nation's 'social memory'. One of the themes most often found in the urban painting of the Congo is the *Belgian Colony*, sometimes called *Whip*, which represents a 'native' agent whipping another African in front of a white man in uniform – a perfect echo of the scene described by Hallet in his memoirs, as described above. As Bogumil Jewsiewicki observes:

The image belongs to colonial popular culture (can we already speak of mass culture?) that blacks and whites have in common without, however, sharing it. First and foremost it is a question of political imaginings, but once the mental image had been fixed by a picture, it became a place of memory in which people can debate intensely the nature of political power.[119]

The social memory of the whip has been constantly updated. First, by the facts, since the chicote was still being used under Mobutu and, in 1997, was spectacularly rehabilitated by Laurent-Désiré Kabila as a means of political regulation and purification. As related by a Kisangani town councillor, elected in the wake of the city's capture by the rebels:

> The notorious *fimbo ya ujinga* (literally translated from the Swahili, it means 'the lash of stupidity', but we need to understand it as a whip that awakens people's consciences!) can reach everyone, for every sort of misdeed. Indeed, a person who has committed a misdemeanour (or is alleged to have done so) needs to be whipped in public to 'awaken' his conscience that years of Mobutism have put to sleep, since the ideological seminaries cannot in some cases achieve this.[120]

Ministers and senior civil servants did not escape this treatment, though they did not necessarily lose office as a result. They could be questioned, imprisoned, and beaten, and then go back to their desks as if nothing had happened.

As regards coercion, the armed movements that dominate the east of the country did not miss out on the action. According to one pygmy leader, a victim of the exactions of the 'Wipe the slate clean' movement (the fighters of Jean-Pierre Bemba's Movement for the Liberation of the Congo in September 2002), 'they came looking for money and pretty women. They whipped us a great deal. They also burned our hunting nets out of sheer malice.'[121] And the correspondent of the *La Croix-L'Événement* newspaper states that 'Commander Jérôme', the leader of the Armed Forces of the Congolese People, the puppet rebellion of Uganda in the gold-bearing region of Aru, has no qualms about taking over the Arab-Belgian heritage of the chicote:

> On this evening, it's party time at the place of the second-in-command of the FAPC, 'General Manu', who is celebrating his wife's nineteenth birthday with the other leaders of the FAPC. The whisky is flowing and speech follows speech, but the words do not cover the cries of terror of two naked men being whipped under the pouring rain in the back yard. 'They're soldiers of mine. They were impolite to the guests', explains Commander Jérôme.[122]

Then various painters came up with countless variations on the theme: *A whipping given by soldiers to a passer-by* (Burozi, Lubumbashi, 1997), *Caravan of slaves* (Bwaliya, Lubumbashi, 1995), *A flogging given as a punishment in prison* (Londe, Bunia, 1992) and, of course, the uninterrupted flood of pictures of the *Belgian Colony*, and depictions of the Christ-like martyrdom of Lumumba.[123] The Congo is a country in which the document (a gross forgery, in all probability) imputing to the latter the desire to set up a 'system of the whip' had appeared as an annex to a doctoral thesis in the 1980s, and been an object of debate when this latter was put online in 2001: it continues to fuel lively exchanges on the Internet.

To the President of the Provincial Government (all of them) except KATANGA

Subject: Measures of application of the first phase of the dictatorship . . .

(5) The establishment of the SYSTEM OF THE WHIP: give rebels ten lashes, morning and evening, for up to a limit of 7 successive days.

NB: Double the number of lashes if applied to Ministers, Senators and Members of Parliament; then, gradually lessen the number in accordance with the state of each individual;

(6) Make all the persons thus arrested feel a profound sense of humiliation, apart from the obligatory whipping described above.

For example: strip them in public and, if possible, in the presence of their wives and children. Make them carry a heavy burden and force them to go for a walk in this state.[124]

It is no exaggeration to say that in the Congo, the symbol of the whip, taken in its performative character, 'condenses' the historic awareness of the transatlantic space, economic exploitation, colonization, nationalism and state: in other words, the historic awareness of globalization itself as a mode of subjection. The governmentality of the belly is turned into the governmentality of the chicote, under the fearless gaze of Bula Matari, the fantastical representation of the state and the white man that has prevailed ever since the exploits of Stanley, Leopold II and the Kurtz of Joseph Conrad. But, over and above the single extreme case of the Congo, it is throughout the continent that political subjectivation is inseparable from the practice of the whip. Most armed movements there indulge in it to discipline their troops or terrorize civilian populations. And it goes without saying that police, prison guards and soldiers are not left out of the action. When identity is checked, taxes are levied or the countless illegal octroi 'barriers' set up for the benefit of the forces of law and order, the 'moral subject' of the state and of globalization is constituted 'on an everyday basis' (*alltäglich*) by having to submit to the harshest physical punishment. Thus, the 'translocality' studied by Charles Piot in the Kabre of Togo, on either side of the mountains of the north from which they come, and the towns of the south, where they work, is full of incidents of this kind.

> Vehicles with an excess of passengers were stopped by the forces of law and order during the night of last Sunday 14 March at one of the control points situated on the highway from Lomé to Kpalimé. Instead of imposing fines on the drivers, as the regulations demand ... our men in uniform gave the passengers and driver a very hard time, during which their buttocks were beaten with indescribable vigour using bludgeons, belts and other whips. You should have heard them screaming in pain and seen them twisting and turning in agony: then you would have appreciated just how sensitive adults are to such a treatment when they are forced to lie face down on the ground.... After this 'good hiding', everyone was ordered to get up and climb back on board.... The treatment had apparently been applied that night to every vehicle with an excess of passengers.[126]

So much for 'citizenship' and 'democratic transition' south of the Sahara. Pure domination? Without a doubt: but it is not without its own moral economy when one considers that the massive application of corporal punishment permits teachers not only to punish their pupils, but also to extort from them sexual favours or bribes,[127] given that the bosses of the street gangs and ghettos impose their authority on the 'sonny boys' by beating them up,[128] just as bosses do with their apprentices in workshops, and fathers with their women and children, given that discipline in refugee camps is maintained with the whip and financed by 'international civil society'.[129] Whipping is an everyday occurrence and a major procedure of the 'government' of contemporary Africa, as is shown by the satirical dialogue of a Cameroon newspaper concerning a pupil who had caught his deputy head assiduously courting a female classmate:

> 'The deputy head immediately summoned the kid to his office and forced him to choose between taking 70 strokes of the cane to the backside and immediate expulsion. Just for a smile!'
> 'And to pay for this eloquent smile, what did the boy choose?'
> '70 strokes on the backside, of course! You don't think he was going to lose his school year over such a little thing?'
> 'Why? In Cameroon there was a woman who died of a pistol shot since she refused to sit in the mud with her dress on.'[130]

Some people will see in this yet another sign of the archaic character of political domination in Africa and the avowed deficit of 'global governance' that afflicts it. But in Asia too, where British, Dutch, French and Japanese colonizers were not ungenerous with corporal punishment, the rattan is still a valued instrument of discipline and is even enjoying a new lease of life. In 1994, the sentencing of a young American, Michael Fay, to six blows of the cudgel for vandalism, threw a harsh light on the regular practice of flogging in Singapore.

In that global city, a thousand or so people – i.e. more than two per day – endure it each year as an additional punishment for various crimes or misdemeanours: rape, vandalism, exhibitionism or breaking the rules on immigration. The administration of the punishment is precisely codified. The rattan cane must measure five feet (1.6 metres) and be half an inch in diameter (13 millimetres). The caners, generally specialists in the martial arts, are provided by Indonesia, where the rattan stems fit the characteristics fixed by the penal code. The cane is soaked in water for several hours before the execution of the sentence so as to prevent the splices from muffling the effect of the blows. The caners train on dummies and practise breaking the skin of each of them while avoiding striking on already-opened wounds. According to a previous prison director, the caner 'does not merely use the strength of his arm, but the weight of his entire body. He swings on his feet to deliver the blow.' Thick layers of wadding are attached to the loins and the crotch of the prisoner: the rattan attacks just the posterior which starts to bleed at the third blow. A doctor ensures that the prisoner is conscious and brings him round if he has fainted so that the punishment can be pursued. The maximum number of blows laid down by justice is twenty-four, and only those aged between sixteen and fifty can have this sentence inflicted on them. The prisoner generally falls into a state of shock and is left with permanent scars [131]

Public opinion in Singapore was enthusiastically in favour of the bastinadoing of Michael Fay,[132] and neighbouring Malaysia immediately took advantage to extend the list of crimes that could be punished in this way.[133] It is remarkable that in Southeast Asia the whip, and many other forms of physical brutality too, are not mere instruments of political repression or economic predation, but 'legal rational' means of regulating the flows of globalization. In factories in the region, which are highly competitive and geared to the satisfaction of the world market, the workforce is regularly beaten, insulted and sexually harassed.[134] And, in Singapore or Malaysia, the law prescribes the rattan for illegal immigrants. In just one day (10 August 2002), five Indonesians and two Bangladeshis were sentenced to six blows for being without work permits, thanks to a new amendment of the Malaysian law on immigration.[135] In short, the bamboo educates the neo-Confucian 'moral subject', promotes 'Asian values' and coexists happily with the WTO.

Likewise, in Saddam Hussein's dictatorship, the whip presided over wage relations in the most modern sectors and those most directly included within the processes of globalization. Oudaï, the older son of the *raïs*, inflicted the *falaqa* – the bastinado on the soles of the feet, in accordance with a technique used in educational, police and judicial establishments (admittedly more local than colonial) – on the employees of his press group, in particular on journalists of the sports daily *Al-Baas al-Riadhi*, whose editor-in-chief relates:

> Two of his body guards always carried the necessary equipment with them. I underwent this punishment four times. The last time was a month before the start of the war, with three other employees. We had an article and were making up the pages but we hadn't noticed that the star chosen by the computer to indicate each paragraph was the star of David. I was given twenty lashes. . . . No one could escape. And the closer you were to him, the more you risked being beaten.

When Oudaï could not attend the punishment, he would listen to the cries of the tortured by telephone. Although the testimony does not make this clear, we can imagine that mobile phones have made this kind of broadcast easier, just as video made it easier at that time to film executions, tortures and *falaqa* for the information or pleasure of the leaders. As for unsuccessful competitive sportspersons, they were imprisoned not in a dungeon, but at the seat of the Olympic Committee.[136]

However, the contradiction or the paradox are merely apparent. Colonial coercion itself was a vehicle of extraversion. Either it made the internationalization and delocalization of the labour force easier, albeit in the form of slavery or its 'contractual' offshoots (indentured labour). Or it stimulated a desire for appropriation of the material culture and mental universe of the West. This appetite for the Other and the Elsewhere led to 'conducts of life' far beyond the circumscribed circles of the direct collaborators of colonial administration or the metropolitan capital, who recognized themselves in distinguished 'human types' such as doctors and male nurses, catechists, interpreters, houseboys, the 'civilized', the comprador. These subaltern social groups, dominated by the dominated, also contrived to be the 'bearers' (*Träger*) of the latter.

The same is true of the styles (the one cosmopolitan, the other localist) that James Ferguson identifies in the towns of Zambia.[137] These styles represent repertoires of 'performative competences' and as such are not merely 'received' or 'adopted' but, in particular, 'cultivated'. They are deployed in tension with one another, with the cosmopolitan style being less an adherence to the West than a distancing from the localist style. They enable town-dwellers to negotiate at one and the same time their relations with their families or villages of origin (or what are taken for such) and the demands of the external world. In this context, after the Second World War, westerns provided a 'cosmopolitan' material of subjectivation that was appreciated by women as much as men: certain female spectators at the very start of the 1960s explained how they liked cowboy films since they could learn the arts of self-defence from them (including against their husbands), as well as how to dress, ride horses and try to kill men.[138]

In the same period, the cultural movement known as *billism* swept across Léopoldville in the Belgian Congo. Young city-dwellers, identified with Buffalo Bill or Pecos Bill, accoutred themselves as cowboys, rode up and down the streets at the bars of their 'bicycle horses' shouting 'Bill oye!' as the passers-by replied 'Serumba!' These 'scourers of the Far West' lived in gangs in 'temples' or 'ranches', and met up in *nganda* (bars) where they contributed to the vitality of Congolese music. They practised rituals of initiation out in the bush, during which they acquired specific styles of combat (*bilayi*). 'Hard wood', 'strong wood' – they all placed the emphasis on physical strength, endurance, courage and violence. They used a particular slang, *hindubill*, the name of which placed them implicitly under the ambiguous patronage of Mami Wata. They represented at one and the same time a principle of social marginality or self-exclusion and a promise of emancipation from the declining colonial order. In fact, they played their role during the uprising and the pillaging of Léopoldville in January 1959, before fading away in front of other repertoires of subjectivation that they had in their own way heralded: those of the rebel and the soldier.[139]

As we saw in the last chapter, nowadays young 'diggers' of diamonds perpetuate their memory in a rather confused way by developing the same kind of positive norms, under cover of 'dollarization' and getting themselves called Zorro as well as Rambo, Superman, Terminator or Godzilla. *Mutatis mutandis*, this spread of the influence of the emblematic personage of the cowboy (and his traditional partner the Indian) is found in a great multitude of societies in the second half of the twentieth century: in Western Europe, of course, where the westerns provided whole generations with the formative plot-lines of their personalities, but also in Java, where certain dancers make up their faces to look like Redskins in homage to the films of the 1950s.[140]

This is just a creative derivation and not a 'westernization'. Its purpose is the development (playful, as it happens) of an 'aesthetic of existence'. The main thing is to accept that these interwoven and continual tensions between the terror of coercion and the desire for extraversion, between the moral imperative of the principle of independence and the appeal of the big wide world outside, which have characterized the history of globalization in the continents conquered by western powers, immediately form an equal part of the social relations which this latter has established. They have provided lavish ethical and imaginary raw material for the processes of subjectivation.[141]

Romain Bertrand has thus traced the 'moral history of a social elite' in Java, that of the *priyayi*, a category of the nobility that set itself up and asserted itself as 'cultural intermediaries', i.e. as 'brokers of morality' after the terrible war in Java. Their collaboration with the colonizer called for 'ethical recompositions':

> In short, only extraversion authorized the preservation and, in particular, the reinvention of the Perfect Tradition. . . . In the conditions of a crippling military defeat, the dilemma of the *priyayi* was not to 'remain Javanese' or to 'transform themselves into Dutchmen'. In reality it was a question of *appearing* Dutch so as to become Javanese.[142]

Nonetheless, the processes of subjectivation of the colonial era could only ever be creative of conflict. As Paul Veyne notes (he is here very close to Foucault):

> Culture is also a question of pride, of one's self-image, of aesthetics, if you will: in short, a question of the constitution of the human subject. And throughout the centuries, this subjectivity was a historical stake that was just as much a source of dispute as economic stakes or the division of power (in the sixteenth century, the revolt of educated Bible-reading Christians against the pastoral authority of the Church, caused more bloodshed than, three centuries later, the workers' movements).[143]

For about a century, the colonial embodiment of globalization was the stage on which such antagonistic forms of subjectivation were played out between colonizers and colonized, within the groups of the colonizers and the colonized, or in the very heart of each of the individuals or social groups that were protagonists of the 'colonial encounter', 'dismayed at not being two people,' like the hero of Cheik Hamidou Kane's *Aventure ambiguë*.[144]

This 'colonial encounter' involved flesh-and-blood creatures. This is why it was a cruel and passionate affair and often involved desire too: desire for power, for the body, for suffering, for death; desire for the Other or the Same. The desiring and fantastical nature of the colonial situation also explains why it was so frequently shaken by mimetic drives, by outbreaks of madness, by feelings of revulsion, by collective phobias, fears or hallucinations, both on the side of colonizers and that of the colonized. The great political, cultural or military battles of the imperial era concerned the 'constitution of moral subjects', at the same time as (or more than) the division of wealth and the distribution of power. The Mau Mau rebellion in Kenya, in the 1950s, was thus an 'internal ethnic war': its meaning was more moral than political, personal rather than structural.[145] In a more peaceful fashion, the social institution of Christian marriage and the phantasmagorical aspiration to a 'decent family life' that seemed to be sanctioned at the same time by the accelerated urbanization of Northern Rhodesia, thanks to the copper boom, concealed and depoliticized acute confrontational social relations in the Copper Belt between nationalists and colonial administration, miners and mining companies, villagers and town-dwellers, men and women, children and adults – confrontational relations that were readily resolved or rendered less acute in the practical transgression of the neo-Victorian model that was taken as a reference point.[146]

The colonizers themselves did not escape these violent tensions of subjectivation. In the nineteenth century, the British who served the Raj had to move from the Indianized mode of existence, which suited the East India Company, to an 'anglicization' of their bodily habits corresponding to the diffuse norms and expectations of the Civil Service: the *nabob* had to transform himself into a *sahib*.[147] And in the East Indies, *trekkers* (metropolitans there for a limited period) and *blijvers* (the colonists who were there to 'stay') clashed on questions of lifestyle, such as the hybridization of cooking or whether European women should wear the *sarong kebaia*, which, by leaving parts of the body uncovered, encouraged sloppiness or licentiousness, blurred the racial barrier between Whites and natives and damaged the 'spirit of society', as one French traveller observed.[148]

In the context of the change of scale entailed by globalization, the recurrent and creative tension between the pole of extraversion and that of native patterns of thought and behaviour was certainly the mainspring of most of these conflicts of subjectivation, as is suggested by the millenarian movements, the wars (or guerrilla wars) over dress codes in India, Southeast Asia or sub-Saharan Africa,[149] the jousting between native-based and universalist pastoralia within the missionary congregations,[150] or the crisis over clitoridectomy in Kenya between the two world wars.[151] What was in question, fundamentally, was politics (or the political dimension) as a 'way of being and living'.[152] As well as power and wealth, what was at stake was the definition of masculinity and femininity, and that of humanity as such; the bounds of intimacy; the shape taken by 'modernity' and 'tradition'; the representation of work, merchandise, money, the body; that of the nation; and, here or there, the fabrication of the 'New Man'.

Throughout the whole period I am considering here, in a colonial situation and, just as much, in extra-colonial or postcolonial contexts, such conflicts of subjectivation contrived to take a dramatic turn, of a binary kind, setting up the 'civilized' against the 'savages', 'foreigners' against 'native-born', 'revolutionaries' against 'counter-revolutionaries', or 'Aryans' against '*Untermenschen*'. The head-on collision was all the more bloody as a result, as is attested by the extermination of this or that native population or the 'Victorian Holocaust' that was brought about by the inhuman application of the economic laws of liberalism in the nineteenth century,[153] the collectivization of land in the USSR, the Shoah in Nazi Europe, the Cultural Revolution in China, that of the Khmer Rouge in Cambodia, or indeed the genocide of the Tutsis in Rwanda, if it is true that the denigration of the lifestyle of the majority of the population by an arrogant minority of 'the advanced' contributed to the murderous rage of 1994.[154] Nonetheless, most of the time, the production of modes of existence or lifestyles was segmentary, fragmentary, interstitial, diluted and frankly banal. It took the shape of slow processes of maturation, which long went unnoticed by contemporaries and suddenly erupted in brutal skirmishes whose immediate tenor did not always have an explicit meaning with regard to the subterranean processes of subjectivation. These gaps and delays, symptomatic of the effects of 'condensation' proper to the way the imagination works, are for instance striking in the case of antagonisms over dress code or hairstyle in the matter of different 'conducts of life'.[155]

To summarize: the *formation* of global 'domination' or 'subjection', in the course of the imperial experience, merged into that of transversal 'social strata', 'asserting itself' by means of 'conducts of life' which had a relative coherence and were more or less contradictory. However, these processes occurred in a state of ambivalence, especially in the equivocal atmosphere of the grey zone in which coercion and desire, imposition and appropriation meet. The 'social strata' on which globalization has rested for two centuries have been the 'bearers' of such 'human types', less via the linear and teleological *constructions* which the operators of the 'civilizing mission' indulged in (as did the agents of 'national liberation', the engineers of the 'revolution' and the adepts of 'transition') than in the cracks formed in the event of globalization, in accordance with the vicissitudes of cultural, social or global struggles, and in the mode of paradox.[156] There is no subjectivation outside of contingence.

5

Globalization and Political Subjectivation: The Neo-Liberal Period (1980–2004)

The joint formation of specific 'social strata' and 'lifestyles' that are part of the process of globalization, and are in both cases endowed with 'relative autonomy'[1] from the sphere of the nation-state, was by no means suspended as a result of the transformations in or the intensification of globalization after the advent of the neo-liberal era twenty-five years ago. Certainly, the *Ordoliberalen*, and Alexander von Rüstow in particular, argued for a *Vitalpolitik* of a kind that modelled the individual in accordance with the ethos and the structure of a business. In their writings, the spirit of enterprise was transmogrified into a total project of subjectivation, and life itself became a business enterprise.[2] It was this way of thinking that Margaret Thatcher and Ronald Reagan transformed into a programme of government, and which gradually spread throughout western countries, but also, to varying degrees, throughout the world. The globalization of the practices of political subjectivation is thus ongoing, and this is the case (with a few notable exceptions) within the same social institutions that the foundational nineteenth century had set up, conforming to the logic of concatenation that I have already identified, in other words (and the list is not exhaustive): businesses and banks; the Christian churches and the religious institutions of other beliefs; the organizations of 'international civil society': educational institutions; international, sports, professional, trade unions, political and other federations; and the 'communities of experts' that meet within the framework of independent authorities of regulation. The same kind of 'networks' or 'circuits' of merchandise and migrations of labour power, the same type of ethno-national diasporas are also continuing to mediate subjectivation in the transnational and 'glocal' dimension.

Social and technological changes can of course modify certain ways in which the modes of lifestyle are carried out. It appears to be quite clear that the media occupy a place in the spread of the latter that they did not have at the end of the nineteenth century, in spite of the industrialization of the written word and the image. Contemporary phone shops are not the exact equivalent of the *jinshanzhuang* of the Hong Kong of the Qing period, nor is Club Med the same as the spa towns of the 'Hundred Years' Peace'.[3] And football, a century ago, had not been raised to the level of a mass cult, as it now is. The fact remains that social relations across the world coincide, today as much as they did yesterday, with processes of subjectivation and are set up as 'modes of subjection'. As the latter dictate, the agents of globalization recognize themselves as 'belonging' to the observance of a 'conduct of life' whose 'conventions' sometimes assume the form of a stereotyped ritual,[4] and make it akin to the ethos of a 'status group' (*Stand*) the organization of which is necessarily 'societalized' (*vergesellschaftet*), even if it does not necessarily take the form of a grouping (*Verband*).[5]

Global social institutions and political subjectivation

The yuppies of high finance, the Chinese entrepreneurs of the transpacific diaspora, the 'communities of experts' of independent regulatory authorities or comparable professional groupings and federations, the now 'transnationalized' bazaar of cities such as Dubai or Istanbul: all correspond to a greater or lesser degree to this ideal type. In a looser, but also more massive, sense, multinational businesses, banks, churches and NGOs are established by means of shared aims or beliefs, 'ethical charters' that are enjoying an evident vogue, codes of dress and sometimes of uniform, and technical or professional prescriptions which are of course much more than that and work as positive norms, a whole host of performative rituals and specific idioms that make them into moral communities, even when they have no vocation other than that of the quest for profit, the conversion of souls or the tribune's traditional defence of the widow and the orphan. These social institutions tend to generate great amounts of scholarly literature, training seminars and other recollections whose main aim, often made explicit, is to consolidate their esprit de corps, their 'enterprise culture', their collective identity and the conduct, if not of life, at least of the behaviour that springs from this identity.

In spite of the triumph of financial capitalism, few of those who look down on the market economy and globalization would maintain these days that business executives or bosses, as individuals, are obeying a mere desire for gain. Never perhaps has Max Weber's remark on the 'irrational' aspect of 'this sort of life, where a man exists for the sake of his business, instead of the reverse',[6] been so relevant. And Marx had already understood the extent to which political economy was 'a truly moral science':

> Political economy, this science of *wealth*, is therefore at the same time the science of denial, of starvation, of *saving*. . . . This science of the marvels of industry is at the same time the science of *asceticism*, and its true ideal is the *ascetic* but *rapacious* skinflint and the *ascetic* but *productive* slave.[7]

Working for a business, after all, is a complete lifestyle. David Harvey already observed as much in the case of Fordism.[8] But the 'network company' of the 'information era' also has expectations of its employees, and these go beyond mere competence, productivity and punctuality. It counts on a certain type of habits of food and culture, sporting activities, fitness, presentation, extra-professional dress, family life: in short, a certain 'distinction' that naturally follows the kind of job in question, and does not (of course) exclude all transgression, but defines it as such. Even more relaxed wear is codified in the form of 'casual Friday'. The enterprise also makes it obligatory to read certain lifestyle manuals, comparable to those the Romans were so keen on in their quest to improve their own self-cultivation: 'management literature', that vehicle of 'the normativity of capitalism'.[9]

Now this process of the subjectivation of the 'young executive', springing, as did others, from decolonization, in metropolises as well as colonies, and the growing scope of economic and financial liberalization, has become transnational or global in step with the process whereby businesses changed their scale. The case of delocalization in India, with American call centres being outsourced, is perhaps too clear an example to be entirely representative.[10] It is still eloquent, in so far as telephone services aimed at the external market employ 110,000 people in this country, generate a business turnover of $1.5 thousand million, experienced a growth of 71 per cent in 2001–2 and, by 2008, should have a million employees. In a business such as Daksh e Services, established in a new town on the outskirts of New Delhi, the operators who work for the American company Sprint have to ensure that customers who telephone them for technical assistance are unaware that they are talking to Indian employees sitting thousands of miles away from their homes or offices These employees are given intensive training to enable them to create the illusion of proximity and pass themselves off as 'part-time Americans'. 'Every evening we go through a strange transformation. During the day we are Indians and at night we are Americans', one of them jokes. The staff of Daksh e Services take language classes to teach them to speak in different American accents, to abandon Indian idiomatic expressions or specifically English words, and to use Americanisms instead. They are also encouraged to 'imbue themselves in American culture', for instance by watching TV series. In the rooms of these operators, screens broadcast programmes from the other side of the Atlantic so that Indian agents will eventually be able to keep up a conversation with a garrulous customer who feels the need to chat about the weekend sports results. And each of the different offices is decorated with the colours of, and in the style of, the American state with which he is linked so that he will have 'a clearer idea of the people he talks to over the phone'. The spirit of enterprise is of course maintained by collective activities – for instance a footrace for 500 employees tied together by their toes – and 'American-style' group discussions in which everyone talks about him- or herself, their families, their sex lives and their opinions. Daksh e Services, or tele-subjection . . .

This may of course be the source of some affliction. But, for one thing, a business does not need to be transnational to develop such 'techniques of the self' as sales techniques or techniques of exploitation. Narrowly national and sovereignist capitalism has proved to be very competitive in this respect, and the cock-a-doodle-do or starry nights subjectivation of the Billancourt fortress, employees of Électricité de France, the miners' terraced houses of the Wendel family or Henry Ford's workers had no reason to envy the methods of the Indian tele-phone service companies. For another, the operators of Daksh e Services do not say they feel robbed of their 'identity' or their 'culture'. Doubtless, as a symptom of their extreme alienation, they claim to be happy in their open-space offices, with their wages and bonuses, the social life of the business and the mode of consumption that their profession makes available to them. As one 22-year-old employee concluded:

> For me, it's a great job. There are just young people here, you wear whatever you want, the atmosphere is relaxed and the hierarchy is much less in evidence than in the businesses I worked for previously. In addi-tion, there are some real possibilities for promotion. Before, I dreamed of going to the United States. Today, I have the impression I'm already there, even though I'm at home. I don't know what more I could ask for.

In fact, it hardly matters that the professional 'culture of the self', halfway between utilitarian instrumentalization and conversion to a dreamt-of identity, actually occurs by means of a spectacular practice of extraversion. We should merely note for now that contemporary globalized business produces 'conducts of life' that are 'made part of the everyday routine' and are the objects of an often extreme ethical discourse. This was already the case, against all expectations, of the

Bank of Credit and Commerce International (BCCI) which people compared to a 'secret society, with special rituals, jargon, and lore', closer to the Unification Church of the Reverend Moon than to Citibank or Barclays. The 'President and Founder', Abedi, prided himself on his philosophy:

> Hope is our vehicle. Hope is the experience of my being of future relationships. Hope is within possibility. Hope is moving into Relationships. The territory of Hope is Totality. Who hopes? Towards what does he hope? Into Totality – hope takes us into possibility. Into infinite relationship – like water. Hope is the Horizon.[11]

But the 'nouveaux riches' of Silicon Valley or Seattle, whose e-societies function in a network with Indian, Chinese, Taiwanese or Israeli subcontractors, are also eager, if belated, philanthropists:

> The philosophy of the new philanthropists is not aimed merely at rousing daydreams, but is more akin to an enterprise of internal and external regulation. Internal, with the setting up of an enterprise culture based on ethics. External thanks to philanthropic action, and with the explicit aim of forestalling possible problems arising from their numerical fracture.[12]

When it comes to the point, the philanthropic entrepreneur of bygone days makes way for the entrepreneurial philanthropist, anxious to fill the vacuum left by the withdrawal of the state under Reagan, but driven by a convergent ideology and concerned to 'make his gift a real investment', to devote himself, as a good 'social risk-taker' to 'philanthropic risk-taking' or venture philanthropy,[13] just as others dedicate themselves to venture capitalism. Even though the founder of eBay – Pierre Omidyar, of Iranian origin and a 'real *javânmard* of the Web', as Fariba Adelkhah drolly calls him[14] – is not himself a Muslim, his foundation is an example of transnational institutionalized evergetism, bringing with it a whole ethos of globalization. Sustained by the employees of this famous auction site for individuals, his foundation aims to 'help each one of us to rediscover the importance and the benefits of community in our lives', 'to make the community part of our lives'.[15] More concretely, it is based on a practical philosophy of commoditization that turns the consumer into an agent, and a 'moral' agent.

> Electronic commerce is, according to Omidyar and his emulators, inseparable from a certain spirit, in the Weberian sense of the term. It cannot flourish without becoming part of a communal environment. Here, philanthropy does not merely reinforce the image of the business, nor does it simply help to reduce the sense of guilt of the capitalists. It presents

us with a demonstration of the spirit of conviviality that also presides over transactions between eBay's customers. There is a new endorsement of the notion of commerce in the highest sense, one that cannot be limited to a purely economic relation between human beings. . . . In the first place, it is the very figure of the consumer that [eBay] is concerned to reshape, by treating him or her as an active player. . . . In the second place, the electronic market has everything to gain from greater transparency. . . . The use of information technology must enable information to be maximized and everyone to be offered control of the market. . . . The values of freedom and transparency that characterize the eBay model do not spring from excessive soft-heartedness, but have a precise function within the framework of the commercial system.[16]

It is true that eBay has been caught out red-handed in cases involving the commoditization of a few controversial products such as weapons, human organs, drugs, a false Rembrandt and the ova of a female model. But the website and its ethos ought to be able to remedy this. 'The site is created every day by its customers. They are the ones who exercise the most effective control. When something strikes them as dodgy, they contact us, we study the situation and we withdraw the object', says Pierre Omidyar in his own defence.[17] So eBay might be seen as e-subjection by peer review. The consumer's 'conduct of life', which the auction site claims to inculcate in its users, is thus no different from global commercial practice, which is the first vocation of the enterprise. It is consubstantial with it.

The entrepreneurial philanthropist of Silicon Valley thus prospers in the American institutional and fiscal tradition of charities, one which bears the stamp of Christianity. If need be, it can also form a synthesis between the latter and that of Islamic *vaqf* (Islamic religious property), as Fariba Adelkhah has shown in regard to Iranians in California:

The mode of organization of this Irano-Californian economy is something that might be called neo-*vaqf*: the Islamic *vaqf*, developing in an American cultural, juridical and fiscal environment, assuming an intercontinental dimension, directed by people with degrees and generally performing evergetic functions *en famille*. In a somewhat classic way, the social institution of the neo-*waqf* fills a whole series of functions other than evergetic or pious works: it enables the Irano-Californian operator to legitimize his relation with Iran in the eyes of a community that is always anxious not to consolidate the Islamic Republic, but also in the eyes of the American authorities keen to maintain their policy of sanctions on Tehranese; it provides the evergete/politician with a certain independence from the Iranian state; it provides the members of its family with jobs; it is a source of tax exemptions; it is a source of gifts that of course will be used to finance the cause advertised, but the management of which provides significant funds for other operations to be carried out; it does not prevent profits from being stored up as the benevolent acts are performed; it increases the social prestige and the relationship network of the benefactor; it eventually creates a capital of influence and recognition within Iran itself, including its provinces.[18]

In short, evergetism, 'this kind of civic patronage',[19] seems to be one of the most widespread transnational ethical repertoires, sanctifying or making respectable economic and financial globalization. The upper echelons of the 'globapolitan' world practise it on a grand scale, and it is the forest behind the tree of George Soros.[20] But what is of even greater significance here is the way that evergetic behaviour is 'borne' in the ordinary circuits of migration and trade. It is to some extent the common ethos of financial and social remittances that contribute to the transformation of 'transnational lifestyles', with their new cross-border family, and sexual, material, educational, university or religious habits.[21] At the same time, it can facilitate the integration of immigrant notables into their host society. These days, the Chinese overseas are perhaps less inclined to invest their philanthropy in their homeland, and in any case take great care to purchase 'symbolic capital' in western democracies, so as to gain racial and cultural acceptance throughout the world.[22] More generally speaking, evergetism plays a major role in the structuring of two central phenomena in contemporary globalization which I have already discussed: the reinvention of the local dimension and of tradition by the effects of 'glocalization', and the development of an 'international civil society' via the associative movement of NGOs and the whole range of religious institutions.

Evergetism is well and truly a 'culture of the self', a process of self-transformation. It is worth reminding ourselves at this juncture how, according to Mohamed Tozy, the Arabic word *Al-Ihsan*, 'benevolence', should be translated as 'gift of one's self'.[23] This is evidently the style of the 'man of integrity' (*javânmard*) in Iran, or the 'individuality of eminence' in Tamil Nadu, in India.[24] As soon as, on the ground, transnational or global social institutions, which provide an ethos in the image of religious enterprises or organizations, are closely interlinked with the 'mutual interactions' of international migrations and commerce, the economic evergetism of the notable, the businessman or the emigrant is easily superimposed on pious organizations. For example, on either side of the Persian Gulf, in the network of *hosseiniyeh* and sanctuaries that simultaneously proceed from the transnational dimension and are rooted in particular areas, like the cultic site dedicated to the *imam zadeh* Esmail, at Fasa, on the Bandar Abbas road, which owes its prosperity to the offerings of smugglers whose protector he is, or those which people from Grâsh and Lâr respectively have opened on the two shores of the cove of Dubai.[25]

Conversely, the religious believer now often sees him- or herself as an entrepreneur, even if he has not read the review *Ordo*. This is true of the Pentecostalists. They have professionalized the religious domain, developing a 'market communitarianism',[26] and preaching an unrestrained gospel of prosperity which hardly takes any account of the evangelical virtues of poverty.[27] Their theme of 'deliverance' from evil, which a growing number of religious movements in sub-Saharan Africa share (charismatic Catholics, Protestant churches, the so-called 'independent or 'African' churches and certain sects), appeals to the power of the Spirit to drive away Satan from the community and from the soul of each and every believer. It leads to the foundation of many different 'centres of evangelization and deliverance', of 'international biblical institutes', of 'sanctuaries of prayer', and of 'spiritual clinics', which skilfully use the names of international sponsors (mainly American) with a view to legitimizing their activities and raising funds, but they break free of 'denominational' ecclesial frontiers and function independently. Pentecostalism sings the praises of material success, a sign of sanctification and liberation from the feelings of jealousy that motivate witches. It emancipates the individual by hailing his personal ascent, blesses capitalist accumulation and the relation to merchandise, and 'armour-plates' believers against the menacing world of the invisible. In this respect, it inverts the 'equation that linked wealth to evil-doing and poverty to sanctity'.[28] Given the breadth of the religious movement that it represents, it embodies a veritable transnational ethical revolution whose 'elective affinities' with neo-liberalism suggest that it forms part of the emergence of a 'global governmentality', even if there is no question of seeing it as an 'expression' or a 'consequence' of the economic transformations of world capitalism. By means of 'assemblies of God', 'prayers for deliverance' and strategies proper to local religious entrepreneurs, skilled at instrumentalizing international religious cooperation in pursuit of their own individual interests, charismatic Christianity transmits 'conducts of life' that are often extraordinarily ritualized when it comes to habits of cuisine, clothes or bodily practices. These latter establish a lineage in African societies thanks to the intermediary of the native social strata that 'carry' them, while being strongly extraverted in the name of their fidelity to the Scriptures, as the Christian fundamentalism of the American Deep South interprets them. Thus, the Transcontinental Evangelistic Association, which had the wind in its sails in Monrovia in 1989, banished the use of percussion and dances in its celebrations, on the pretext that these practices were 'African', and replaced the drums by an organ, flutes and trumpets, which are more 'biblical'.[29] In this way, the charismatic 'conducts of life' occupy a political space which the mistakes of the 'democratic transition' had left vacant. When President Charles Taylor, against all likelihood, presented himself as a 'sacrificial lamb' on the day of his resignation, while the hall echoed with gospels, alleluias and glorias, and his official evangelic preacher exclaimed, 'I have a dream, you have a dream, the Liberians have a dream',[30] he knew that he was using a political language that was easier to hear, if not to believe, than that of democracy, and, no longer having the means to impose his 'style of death', he took his place in the framework of the 'lifestyle' that had dominated Monrovia for twenty or so years.

The diffuse social practices of global subjectivation

Over and above the social processes that are, properly speaking, made up of, inter alia, transnational religious movements, globalization ensures 'the production of modes of existence or lifestyles' of contemporary people in a diffuse fashion, thanks to the expansion of telecommunications, the mass media, travel and universal social practices of a cultural, sporting, sexual or other type. Relatively coherent 'conducts of life' – or, sometimes, conducts of 'segments of life', attached to a particular aspect of the lives of individuals, but in any case laden with a significant ethical or symbolical content, or one indeed that is erotic or pornographic, varying from one society to another – are spreading transversally across the world. Not only are 'new sorts of transnational and ethnicized subjectivity',[31] veritable transnational 'lifestyles', crystallizing out in migratory, trading or religious networks, for instance among the Chinese of the 'Pacific shuttle', among the Congolese of Paris, the West Indians of New York, the Iranians of California, and the Dominicans of Boston, and in permanent relation with their original societies.[32] Also, many 'cultures of the self' are being developed in the crucible of globalization without necessarily being dependent on 'social remittances' from precise transnational communities, families or 'villages', even if the latter contribute concretely to their reception, their deciphering and their reinvention on the local level.[33]

The world of football is an obvious example, and Christian Bromberger has provided us with a remarkable demonstration of how it transmitted complex ethical and civic models of action and identification, styles of play or spectator habits rooted in local or national realities, and an intense regional or global interaction thanks to the televised broadcast of the matches, the existence of a specialized press and iconography, and the travels undertaken by supporters.[34] There is no doubt about it: here is a global practice of subjectivation. There is no street on the planet where kids do not kick a football around, and every pavement, park or beach is capable of being transformed into a football pitch, provided with improvised goalposts in the form of tee-shirts, coats, satchels or tin cans. The other great disciplines, such as athletics, skiing, sailing and car racing, do not get left behind either. They too furnish moral guidelines in endurance, fair-play, technical mastery, the aesthetics of the body, and clothes. And if there is indeed a mass global narrative ethic, it is sport. Its circle of edification goes way beyond a mere audience of the 'cosmopolitan hyper-bourgeoisie' and transcends, at least partly or temporarily, the fault lines of identity or socio-economic circumstance by authorizing the most improbable communions, as in 1998, during the World Cup, when Iran met the United States and the French 'Blues' won, or every year when the New York marathon is run. The television viewer of international competitions is perhaps 'alienated', at least in the eyes of those who do not see this vogue for physical performance and playing games as anything other than a new 'opium of the people'. But is it therefore in a state of social dereliction?

Likewise, the globalization of sexual identities,[35] that of the representation of the desirable female body in the Miss World and Miss Universe contests, in shows, the media and advertising, and that of a 'gay' or 'lesbian culture' in the form of a transnational press, a style, night clubs and bars, universalize the way human beings have learnt to recognize themselves as subjects of a sexuality,[36] and the 'problematizations' associated with that process.[37] There is indeed a 'global sex', whose technology of globalization – the Boeing 747, the international telephone system, satellite television, video and the Internet – simultaneously encourages the expansion and relative autonomy of local, national or cultural fields of sexual practices.[38] Specialized publications, an international cinematographic or literary production, the birth of cybersex, a worldwide folklore of which Gay Pride events offer a brilliant illustration, all form part of this sphere proper to subjectivation on the level of desire and its satisfaction. The latter is undergoing a 'ritual stereotyping', one that is doubtless increasing thanks to the worldwide circulation of those who perform in it and the commoditization of social life. An observer of the homosexual striptease acts in Manila points out that the young male dancers turn out all to be wearing Calvin Klein underclothes when they drop their – no less inevitable – Levi Strauss jeans.[39] And on the screens of Star TV, MTV and KTV, disc-jockeys or actresses, who have to be Eurasian, give a desirable shape to the marketable and multicultural modernity of transpacific Asia.[40]

This does not, however, mean that what we are seeing is a uniformization of sexual practices and the way they are elaborated in people's imaginations. In this domain, as in others, globalization proceeds by a 'reinvention of difference'. Different sexual acts, the choice of one's partners, their affective construction or objectification as merchandise, the fetishistic folklore of pleasure, the ethical connotations of roles and positions in intercourse, are simultaneously a response to a general circulation of sexual repertoires and their expressions, and their creative hijacking under the pressure of local stories and depictions, or quite simply that of individual drives. In other words, 'global sex' is also material for 'glocalization' and deserves its own *microstoria*.

The debate on the historicity of homosexuality in Asia or Africa is an illustration of this, incorporating as it does the memory of the pre-colonial and colonial *imaginaire* of pleasure.[41] Writing on the categories of 'lesbi' and 'gay', which the mass media have introduced in Indonesia, Tom Boellstorff describes a culture of doubling, with lesbis and gays having their own dynamic, different from that we might expect from the use of these English words.[42] 'Gays' are distinguished from 'traditional' transvestite homosexuals, the *waria* or *banci*, who feel they have a woman's soul in a man's body and with whom they do not generally indulge in relations of pleasure. Nonetheless, their repertoire of sexual identification cannot be reduced to their supposed 'westernization'. It is in any case revealing that most of them are from humble backgrounds, do not speak English, have never travelled abroad and do not know any westerners.[43] Likewise, in Japan, the erotic genre known as YAOI, relating 'boy love' in the form of sexual or sexualized relations between young men and teenagers, to which several magazines, Internet sites and television programmes are dedicated, is well established in newsagents and on screens. It is highly prized by an audience of young women or schoolgirls, but it would cause a scandal in the United States or in Europe.[44] More generally, technologies of information, in particular email and the Web, facilitate the birth of virtual sexual 'communities' and create social bonds, especially in countries that repress certain practices of pleasure, such as Singapore or India.

In addition, the public policies of states or of multilateral organizations do regulate 'global sex'. NGOs are also taking an increasing interest in the matter. So sexuality gives rise to meta-discourses. The international coordination of the fight against AIDS has fed into and legitimized them. But the paranoid campaign against paedophilia, which is symmetrical with and comparable, in its fantastical character, to the denunciation of 'organized transnational crime', suggests that they are also tied up with the reinforcement of bureaucratic and disciplinary prerogatives.[45] The convergence of the state's policies of control with the normative intervention of 'international civil society' can again be seen in operation.

Furthermore, the political economy of 'global sex' has become inseparable from that of globalization in general, especially in the establishment of programmes of structural adjustment that have swollen the ranks of sex workers, the Malthusian compartmentalizing of migrations that has increased the amount of money to be made from their coercive exploitation, or the development of tourism that has increased the demand and facilitated the offer of *prostiturismo*. It is centred on the reterritoralization of globalization around the 'global cities' of sex (Bangkok, Pattaya and Phuket, which are mentioned often, indeed all too often in so far as the consumers here are first and foremost Thai[46]

– but also Tokyo, Dubai, Istanbul), around hubs of sex workers (as in the case of Cyprus, Greece and the states of the former Yugoslavia) and around countries that have, whether deliberately or not, developed this niche within the international economy (Gambia, Kenya, Senegal, the Philippines, Sri Lanka, Russia, Ukraine, Byelorussia, Turkey), or that have experienced a multilateral peacekeeping operation, such as Cambodia, Lebanon and Bosnia. 'Global sex' has finally become an element in the kit of the 'democratic transition'. The latter is now partly judged by the criteria of the promulgation of laws guaranteeing the equality of the sexes and of sexual practices, or stamping out the sexual mutilation of little girls (but not of little boys). The Republic of South Africa realized this clearly, decriminalizing homosexuality so as to mark the fact that it had emerged from the apartheid regime, while its neighbour Robert Mugabe associated sodomy with multiparty democracy so as to tar them with the same brush.[47]

Nobody would dream of underestimating the element of coercion in this moral and political economy of sexuality, or indeed the element of sheer symbolic violence inherent in the commoditization of relations of pleasure, even if the prostitute, whether male or female, is entirely consenting and is exercising his or her free will in full awareness of the situation. Aihwa Ong justifiably speaks in terms of 'new systems of sexual exploitation'.[48] The fact remains that venal love is the objective means, for many men and women, of entering the process of globalization and 'constituting themselves as moral subjects' by trading on their charms, given that this allows them to head off to town or emigrate, to negotiate their relations with their families or the people around them, to subsidize their parents or their children, or, like certain African businesswomen,[49] to initiate a process of primitive accumulation.

The 'historic condition' (P. Ricoeur) of international prostitution thus goes together with the invention or re-actualization of 'conducts of life' that are not lacking in notions of honour, modesty or intimacy, nor in family, religious or economic values. Several hundreds of thousands of Russian, Ukrainian and Byelorussian women have emigrated since 1989 to sell their bodies, some of them voluntarily, others falling prey to various stratagems.[50] They work in West Europe, Turkey, Dubai, Japan and China, and in the traditional places of pleasure in the rest of Asia. Although economists and political theorists prefer to hear nothing about them, they are a page of the history of the 'transition to the market economy' of the former Soviet republics, just as much as their Czech colleagues who offer themselves to tourists and German lorry drivers on the summer road to Prague. It would be somewhat cynical to deny them any ability to produce a relation to themselves in this world of subjection, and the dignity that proceeds from it. Georges Brassens has one or two powerful songs on this subject. This in no way attenuates the brutality of the situation to which they are subject, nor does it exclude the possibility and hope of other, definitely more desirable, 'lifestyles' in globalization. But it is all the more important to understand 'global sex' in terms of subjectivation in so far as the change of scale of the foundational nineteenth century had already led to an explosion of international prostitution in cities such as Vienna, Buenos Aires, Rio de Janeiro, Panama or San Francisco, before it did so in Tangiers, Havana, Shanghai, Berlin and Paris, followed by Hamburg and Amsterdam, at least in the *imaginaire*. Whether it intervenes as an opportunity or a threat, the globalization of sexual practices, whether venal or not, is inherent in the event and the era of globalization as I have described it, especially in the migrations it has caused, the invention of tourism and the recurrence of war.

In short, it would probably be impossible to find any more raw evidence of global processes of subjectivation, and thus of the emergence of a global governmentality, at the point of 'encounter between techniques of domination exercised on others and the techniques of the self', than the generalized sexual interaction and the transnational enjoyment of the body of the Other, even if the latter is imposed on or bought from that Other. The fact that it is sometimes a wretched process is irrelevant: the social experience of globalization remains a source of 'conduct of life'. The 'transient peoples' who draw their precarious existence from frontiers, like the Kurds and the Balutchis, have a prickly sense of ethics, even if it is the ethics of smuggling.[51] Likewise, the 'road cutters' whom Janet Roitman has been studying in the north of Cameroon wax indignant when she so much as dares to question their morality: 'You're insulting me! Let me tell you once and for all that, when there's a wage at the end of it, we're not thieves. I was working on the road.'[52] And this 'working on the road' is in line with the 'highway code' (of highway robbers, so to speak).

> The Koran governs the Islamic religion, the Bible governs Christianity, the Torah is for the Jews, and the highway code is for road users. . . . You can't take the Koran if you want to worship Jesus; you can't go to church with the highway code. If you use the Torah to maintain your motorbike, you'll have a wreck instead of a bike before long. . . . Let me tell you this: a trafficker who respects the government law can't succeed, since trafficking isn't governed by government law. It's governed by the law of the road. If you leave Nigeria with oil cans and stop off to see the customs officers and give them some money so you can go your way, they'll arrest you. They'll say there's something suspicious about you, you're not an ordinary trafficker! You're trying to tempt them, you must be a spy. But if you try and get away from them and they catch you out in the bush, well then you can negotiate, because you're within the normal order of the law of trafficking.[53]

As for the young Moroccans of Catalonia who sell a little hashish in Spain or France, brought back from a trip home to see their families,

and who manage to eke a living by straddling the Pyrenean border
between Barcelona and Perpignan, they interpret this 'lifestyle' as a
means of social participation, self-assertion and the invention of a
transethnic, national or religious social life, with an amoral lucidity that
gives considerable scope for the expression of ethical norms.

> You know, our little parcel of grass is a passport to freedom and peace,
> we can make loads of friends by handing out a few grams here and a
> few grams there, find a little job, some cool cafés where we can have a
> smoke together, like youngsters. We can live a bit like we never can in
> Perpignan. You're not a real criminal with five hundred grams and in
> any case you sell a hundred and you smoke a hundred. The real criminals
> get nabbed and they're not very popular. We don't belong to their world;
> they mean whores, violence, overdoses and the whole shebang. We want
> to be cool, and work normally, but with a nice lifestyle in town. It's a
> ticket for us to get back quietly into town, you see. Without the teaching
> assistants, the family, the teachers, the welfare assistants, the Kapos of
> the PAIO [Permanences d'accueil, d'information et d'orientation – offices
> in France that help young people to find jobs and cope with everyday
> problems: *Tr*.] and all that kind of stuff. *It's a way of life that really helps us
> become men with a bit of freedom. If you don't smoke hash, you can't understand
> the peace and quiet it gives us, as if we weren't Arabs any more, we're like all
> the good guys.*

So says Dalil, aged 19. And Loucine, aged 22, goes further:

> With my little packet of grass and kif, I can rustle up a little gang of
> friends, nice peaceful guys, even if I've often had to give everything away;
> it's been repaid to me a thousand times over by everything I know now,
> the places on the coast, the little towns, Barcelona, the villages, and so
> many cool friends, boys and girls, who don't want any racism or frontiers.
> *It's my answer, my kind of integration.* It's better than the way you have to
> integrate by taking useless training programmes, all the usual hassle with
> families, feeling lonely at work and in town, the idiot mugs of the Arab
> beardies and the pigs from the National Front in France. I've got plenty
> of friends in Perpignan who can understand that. . . . I don't know what'll
> happen to us in France, but now I know that I can live without violence,
> and even with pleasure, and that there are loads of us ready to spit on the
> stuff they brainwashed us with: trampling all over your friends to get
> some shitty job, having to live on your nerves every day for little bosses
> who piss on Arabs, and beating up your wife and children between four
> walls in the evening, that's what they call integration.[54]

These diffuse processes of subjectivation in globalization are not
brought about in spite of the latter in the shape of residual or playful
practices of resistance, flight or bypassing, and in the mode of what is
called, in crude and simple terms, the 'counter-cultures'. They spring

from its very historicity. They are its essence. So it is significant that the Internet, the technology par excellence of the 'information era', is first and foremost a 'cultural expression',[55] and not a mere means of communication, and that its technicians or users have formed 'communities'.

As such, the Web has given birth to moral figures – the hacker, the 'hacktivist', the cracker and the different varieties thereof: the 'warez dOOdz', the 'script kiddie' – who are locked in debate and conflict amongst themselves.[56] Its structural development has come about through a cultural movement, that of the *open source*, which has encouraged the communication of technical innovation in universities and impelled them to go online. The hackers form a 'status group' (*Stand*) that shares values of freedom and cooperation that subtend an 'economy of the gift':

> A hacker will post his or her contribution to software development on the Net in the expectation of reciprocity. The gift culture in the hacker world is specific vis-à-vis other gift cultures. Prestige, reputation and social esteem are linked to the relevance of the gift to the community. So, it is not only the expected return for generosity, but the immediate gratification of displaying to everybody the hacker's ingenuity. In addition, there is also gratification involved in the object of the gift. It not only has exchange value, but also use value. The recognition comes not only from giving but from producing a valuable object (innovative software).

This creation also produces an 'inner joy'. In short: There is a communal feeling in the hacker culture, based on active membership in a community, which is structured around customs and principles of informal social organization'. Nonetheless, the way in which it is ritually stereotyped, as Weber would say, is mainly virtual: 'serious hackers primarily exist as hackers on-line . . . the hacker culture, and its internal distinctions, are all about mental constructions and technological divides'.[57] These are no less real since, as Deleuze tells us, the virtual is not the opposite of the real, but of the actual, and the virtual is in itself fully real.[58]

'Human types' of globalization: main roles and American stars

Thus, contemporary globalization shapes 'human types' (*Menschentypen*) who are bearers of 'conducts of life', with which one can identify in accordance with one's condition, one's activity, norms, imaginary world and the constraints of one's family or other environment. Apart from the hacker, various emblematic figures immediately spring to mind. At the summit of the pyramid of globalization, the Magnate, the Big Boss, the Oligarch, the Star, more rarely the Manager (or his wife or daughter) present us with models of life that are popularized by the media and the material culture of consumption. They are objects of fascination or repulsion that stage – sometimes with a real sense of drama – some of the technical know-how and the moral qualities required by the period, as well as an 'aesthetic of existence' (Michel Foucault). Through the popular press, the television broadcasts for a large public or the specialized economic magazines aimed at the financial and business milieus; they throw up an incessant social commentary, one that can be laudatory, mimetic or polemical, and permits each and everyone to position themselves and to appropriate (or reject) fragments of the global Grand Narrative. In France, a character such as Jean-Marie Messier, the over-adventurous boss of the Vivendi group, acted as such an intercessor before transforming himself into a foil. The image (or in any case the function) of the saint is never far away, as the transnational cult of Diana, martyr of the Media and Speed (if not of a royal and Zionist plot) reminds us.

But we should immediately make room for another allegorical 'human type' of globalization that has been around for two centuries: the Reformer, the positive hero of society's adjustment to the change of scale, an often demonic Cincinnatus of economic liberalization, of state recovery and national regeneration. I have already in previous chapters shown how state-formation, in the framework of globalization, was supported by two great transnational ideas that were connected: the notions (and the corresponding political engineering) of nation and of reform, that have been active right across the planet, in an organic and ambiguous relation with the expansion of European imperialism. If we just stick to the Arab-Muslim world, sovereign figures such as those of the Ottoman Sultan Selim III (1789–1807), Muhammad Ali (1805–49) in Egypt, Ahmet Bey (1837–55) in Tunisia or Nasir al-Din (1848–96) in Persia immediately spring to mind. But they should not conceal a whole host of reformers, either frankly dissident, like Afghani (1838–97),[59] or critical, like the Young Ottomans in the second half of the nineteenth century,[60] or top civil servants of state, such as the Mameluke Khair ed-Din.

The latter (who lived c.1822–90), is especially emblematic for our purposes as he is a central reference point in the Maghrebi intellectual debate and was the author of an *Essay on the Reforms Necessary in Muslim States* published almost at the same time in Tunis, in Arabic, in 1867 and in Paris, in French, the following year, in a slightly different version, dictated directly in French rather than being translated from the Arabic.[61] The man of state, defender of 'liberal reforms among the Muslims, whom we see still groaning under the yoke of despotism',[62] poses unambiguously the question of globalization:

[T]hese days, with the rapidity of communications and the even more rapid means for transmitting thoughts, we need to consider the world as a set of nations that is, as it were, one single country inhabited by different races, in increasingly frequent contact with each other, having identical interests to satisfy, and contributing, albeit separately, to the common good.[63]

This theorist of good governance – literally, the Ottoman Tanzimat he appeals to are 'benevolent laws' – recommends to 'Muslim states' a strategy of extraversion; 'So what prevents us, these days, from taking from those who are strangers to our culture the knowledge whose importance and necessity are indisputable, so as to guard ourselves against all eventualities and procure our own good?'[64]

But Khair ed-Din, a court Mameluke of Circassian origin, brought up at the heart of the Ottoman Empire, is also of interest because of the ambiguities of his political itinerary. He arrived in Tunis at the age of 16, and was given a classical Arabic education, a modern training based on foreign languages and science, and military instruction dispensed by French officers. Then he entered the service of the beylicate of Tunis, over which the reformer Ahmed reigned. He thus belonged to a bureaucratic elite in virtue of his functions, one that was transnational by his Circassian birth and his early Ottoman education, and cosmopolitan by his competences, especially in languages, and his periods spent in Europe. He was Naval Minister of the beylicate from 1857 to 1862, then First Minister from 1873 to 1877. After his forced resignation under pressure from the court and the European powers, who were alarmed by his tacit nationalism and his rapprochement with the Ottoman Empire, he remained an influential personality. He was recalled to Istanbul and was even appointed Prime Minister cf the Sublime Porte (1878–9).

Throughout this both brilliant and frustrating career, he embodied the rigour of the state's growing importance and the integrity of its civil servants, when faced with the compromises and the wheeling and dealing of his predecessor, Prime Minister Mustapha Khaznadar, whom he held responsible for the financial shipwreck of the beylicate. This was a Manichean confrontation that he summarized in his treatise thus: 'To entrust the care of an establishment to those who desire its destruction is to create its most powerful cause of ruin.'[65] He became an apostle of economic openness and conservative liberalism, but ensured the absolute pre-eminence of state over society and of mortmain, trusting more to the 'sovereignty of reason' than to that of the 'people' – to use Guizot's terms, implicitly criticizing the parliamentarianism of the Young Ottomans and preparing the way ideologically for the authoritarian reformism of the Neo-destour party of Bourguiba. Faced with the clientelism of the big families, the deliquescence of the beylicate and the resistance of ordinary people, he drew a considerable proportion of his political resources and legitimacy from the support of the European governments, but he contradicted their ambitions and described their duplicity with a sharp political sense that is still of extraordinary relevance:

> In brief, it is indisputable that the policy of European governments, as far as the Muslim countries are concerned, is self-contradictory, and that the policy of some of them is in every respect the exact opposite of that of the others. For some of them support certain Muslim governments and are inclined to help them to introduce political institutions that are adapted to their social needs. Others are opposed to any reforms in one Muslim country, while insisting on their being applied in another, if this suits their political interests.[66]

In 1879, a Turk would cruelly sum up the Reformer's 'mission impossible' in a sentence that ought to be written in letters of gold as a preamble to all the programmes of structural adjustment put forward by the World Bank and the International Monetary Fund: 'Khair ed-Din is a magnificent Great Dane, but there are eighty of us street hounds, mangy if you like, but there are eighty of us; so we will eat him up.'[67]

This reformist vein persists in dominating the political landscape of the Muslim countries. It reached its heroic apotheosis with Mustapha Kemal, whose figure and heritage are even today points of 'fetishistic' crystallization on the part of secularists,[68] or of revulsion on the part of non-Turkish Islamists, always ready to denounce in the Salonican the accursed shadow of the *dönme*.[69] It also inspired the authoritarian nationalism of the Egyptian Young Officers, and Baathist parties in Syria and Iraq or the Pahlavi Empire, as well as projects for the liberalization and 'catching up' of economies, as these days in the states of the Maghreb, or indeed Islamists in so far as they are the universal legatees of nationalism and the spokesmen of an 'intellectual and moral reform', the very same which Afghani was inspired by Ernest Renan to promote: after all, in Iran, Ali Akbar Hashemi Rafsanjani, godfather of the Reconstruction movement, devoted a book to the Prime Minister of Shah Nasir al-Din, Amir Kabir.

The moral figure of the Reformer is of course not restricted to the historical aspects of the Arab-Muslim states. Let us take for example the somewhat hagiographic portrait of the 'young and brilliant Finance Minister which France has given to the Serbs' (*sic*), in *Le Nouvel Observateur*:[70]

> After ten years of the corrupt and authoritarian regime of Slobodan Milosevic, Boza the Flayer possesses all the qualities that the Serbs are voting overwhelmingly in favour of: honesty, authority and competence.

Indeed, you might say that the great treasurer of Belgrade has been preparing for this terrible mission all his life. His life resembles a fairy tale.
When, at the age of ten, Bozidar, who had been brought up by his grand-
parents, emigrated to France to join his mother, a seamstress, separated
from his father, he could hardly speak French. He was to become one of
the most brilliant products of the Republican school, a model of French-
style integration, an example of social success. First in his class, a brilliant
pupil at the Lycée Louis-le-Grand, two prizes at the *concours général*,* a
graduate of Sciences-Po, HEC, a doctorate . . . then an MBA, at Harvard
of course. Here he became the pupil of Jeffrey Sachs, the famous American economist, the guru of liberal reforms and mass privatization. Bozidar
was pulled into the adventure of the transition of East Europe. He became
director of privatizations in Poland, worked on the gigantic and controversial reform programme in Russia, advised the Romanian Prime
Minister.

And, further on:

Serbia was depressed and weary: he breathed his youth, his energy and
his enthusiasm into it. Today the Minister can line up trophies and economic figures in the same way that yesterday he collected diplomas:
monetary stability, reduced inflation, the convertibility of the dinar, the
cleaning up of the banking sector, economic growth at 6 per cent, the
reform of the labour code, etc. His country, which had only ever been
blacklisted, was given the Gold Medal of the transition by the European
Bank of Reconstruction. Bozidar was elected Man of the Year by the
Belgrade magazine *Vreme*. His successes came at a price. The associate
director of McKinsey is living off his savings as he earns less than 300
euros per month. Every day, he works late into the night. But the most
difficult thing, according to this diffident man who 'doesn't want to make
people who live in hovels cry', is the fact that his private life has 'suffered
terribly' from his Serbian venture. Separation from his wife, who is still
in France with his two children, has ended up in divorce. These days he
is alone, and this man without a party is getting more and more caught
in the cross-fire of ambitious people who are avidly in pursuit of power.
He is sometimes said to be on the verge of discouragement. But 'he
doesn't want to take his leave in midstream'. 'People write to me saying:
if you leave, our son will go off abroad too.' And so, he concludes, he is
not the master of his own destiny. And the assassination . . . of the reformist Prime Minister Zoran Djindjic was a terrible shock for him. In his
office he has put up a portrait of the assassinated head of government.
Bozidar remembers how, after he had delivered a funeral oration at the
funeral, he walked through a vast, silent crowd. He remembers those
hands stretched out, just to touch him, those hands 'which touched me
to tell me: stay here, carry on'. And so, in spite of the dossiers piling up

* An 'open competition' for high-school students in their final years – an avowedly
Republican and meritocratic institution. [Tr.]

and the killers on the prowl, and in spite of his bleeding paternal heart, Bozidar will continue to play the role of the flayer.

This fantastical figure of the Reformer, pathos-laden, 'strict but fair' and often vain, can be found in all western societies – especially in France, thanks to the weight of the state and the administration – in Japan, China, Indonesia, Russia, Latin America or sub-Saharan Africa. It arises at the point of synergy between the processes of formation of the nation-state and the demands of globalization. It constitutes a powerful vector of subjectivation at a time of economic liberalization, notwithstanding (or thanks to?) the ambivalence of its incarnations as illustrated by a Gaidar and a Chubais in Russia, a Tanri Abeng in Indonesia, or an Alassane Ouattara in the Ivory Coast.[71] The 'transactions' of reform, transition to the market economy, and globalization, are often 'tainted'.[72] Nonetheless, they still inspire activities that go beyond the confined circles of apparatchiks converted to neo-liberalism.

Thus in Indonesia, the 'movement for Reform' (*gerakan Reformasi*) in 1998 brought into the spotlight students whom it turned into heroes (*pahlawan*). With their jeans, their mastery of democratic jargon, their readings in political science and their mobile phones, they were the perfect players of change, acting out their roles in front of the cameras of foreign television channels. And yet, they presented to the Indonesians themselves – and to the country's real specialists – another face that confirmed the historicity of the global modes of subjection:

> [I]f we investigate the kind of language the students were using to communicate with the national public, if we bring out the historical resonances of their practices of protest, we see that their aim was less to make a complete break by importing political newspeak, than to affirm the continuity of their struggle (*perjuangan*) with the Physical Revolution of 1945–9, in other words with the egalitarian utopia of Sukarno. The repertoires of the different types of figure brought into play (that of the republican *pemuda* of anti-colonial struggle and that of ascesis) had the aim of 'making native' or 'renationalizing' a combat that might otherwise have been imputed by the authoritarian power to 'undesirable influences from abroad', i.e. delegitimized on the cultural level. The Indonesian student movement of 1998 was thus indeed a 'glocal' movement – in the sense that it combined the use of technologies and discourses characteristic of western 'modernity' with repertoires of action issuing from a local political history.[73]

From this point of view, the students are representative of a democratization that has extended the remit of many established interests, including those of the army, and whose moral economy re-employs cultural representations or pre-existing social memories, such as the practices of the invisible, the traumatic memory of colonization, the

Japanese occupation, the struggle for national liberation and the massacres of 1965–6, or the tension between the assertion of native values
and the strategies of extraversion.[74] In other terms, the 'human type' of
the Reformer, a transversal expression of the constraints of globalization, necessarily compromises with the vertical historicity of the societies which it attacks.

This is, a fortiori, the case of his twin brother, one who is nonetheless
often his enemy: the Nationalist. For, whatever the 'sovereignists' may
think, the Nationalist plays a role in the drama of globalization, so long
as one accepts that the state is the product of the latter. The Nationalist
has a complex relationship with the Reformer. Almost by definition, he
himself is a Reformer, whose ideal model is Mustapha Kemal, who is
influential far beyond the Arab-Muslim world. He is dedicated to the
'purification' and the moral reform of the nation, or to the political and
administrative reform of its institutions. As Khair ed-Din has shown
us, the Reformer is also a Nationalist, although his ideological and
practical positioning often obliges him to advance wearing a mask. The
relation each of these characters has with social inequality is also equivocal. On the one hand – the hand closest to their hearts – they serve
the general interest, the widow and the orphan. With the other – the
one that is reaching out for power – they work for the rise of a 'social
stratum' that 'bears' their 'conduct of life', and with regard to the
reformers one can repeat what nineteenth-century socialists said of
nationalists: they are 'petits bourgeois' with a hankering for domination (their own), even when their main spokesman is of lofty lineage.
However, the Reformer and the Nationalist are often opposed when it
comes to the how and the when of national sovereignty, especially at
times of economic liberalization. Questions of external trade, foreign
investment and currency are their usual bones of contention.

Be this as it may, the Nationalist in turn is a figure of subjectivation
– as Otto Bauer said in his own way[75] – and nationalism consisted, and
still consists, in a 'lifestyle' constitutive of a 'moral subject' which, as
we already know, drew on transnational loans so as better to manifest,
and often to invent, the soul of the People and to erect it to its status
as Sovereign. Complex matrices of self-formation, the different types
of clothing, eating and wearing one's hair, have close links with this
ideology-conduct of life. They are at the same time inseparable from
the cultural flows of globalization and the tension between nativist
ideology and extraversion. It would be superfluous here to rehearse
the well-known examples of the place that was occupied by clothes,
the way one had one's hair cut, the shape of one's beard and moustache, the definition and regulation of cookery or drink, especially
alcohol, in nationalist activity in Europe, North America, sub-Saharan
Africa, India, Indonesia and Turkey.[76] These cases also suggest,
more or less confusedly, that nationalism also has to do with a certain

conception of virility or, more precisely, of sexuality, if only because it is at least partly confused with the exercise of war.[77] 'We're the Right with balls. The others, Giscard and Barrot, are the wimpy Right', as the militants of the National Front elegantly put it, in the tranquil area of Haute-Loire.[78] And everyone knows that in northern Italy, 'the League's got a hard-on', in the words of Umberto Bossi.[79] Even in a country as puritanical as India, Hindu nationalist radicalism claimed it was breaking away from the effeminacy of old-style Hinduism, to which it opposes its martial vigour.[80]

A nationalist 'humanity' (*Menschentum*) thus came into being at the interface between the processes of globalization and the formation of a world system of states, a 'humanity' whose extremist leaders are happy to make a show of their elective affinities across the borders, like Jean-Marie Le Pen and Vladimir Zhirinovski. Its victims can be counted in their tens of millions over the last two centuries, but its force of seduction remains intact. It leads Tamil, Palestinian or Iraqi suicide bombers to the ultimate sacrifice. Less dramatically, it continues to demarcate the way the 'conduct of life' has become an 'everyday routine' for the vast majority of contemporaries, including in the United States or within the European Union. Although it is largely global in its forms, the material culture of mass consumption, grasped in its concrete practices and in its spirit, is still reliant on the national arena – to the reproduction of which it indeed contributes frequently.[81] The same can be said of the moral economy of citizenship, in the inner recesses of 'international civil society' whose organizations, although not governmental, are still national:[82] you can't get much more French than José Bové, unless (of course) you are a 'French doctor'!

In fact, it is far from certain that 'faith' in the state and the nation is on the decrease.[83] Peoples, and the individuals who comprise them, still worship their 'national heroes' who serve them as ethical beacons.[84] But the latter are not out of kilter with the change of scale represented by globalization. However national he may be, 'the hero seems to have the property of going beyond the very notion of identifying attributes, as he is defined by a more abstract capacity, he can subsume opposed attributes just as he can reconcile different scales of identification, from the local community to the nation and then the whole of humanity'.[85] Most of the time, it is his 'mediating capacity'[86] which is so exemplary, with the result that he can be enrolled into diametrically opposed causes, or, like Captain Dragan, commander of a special unit of Serbian troops in Krajina, base his stance on values of justice and universality without much of a link to the battle for identity whose cause he serves, combating 'without qualities'.[87] Some of the most 'national' heroes enjoy a recognition that transcends the frontiers of their social affiliation and are the object of baroque 'glocal' cults. Thus the Vietnamese, convinced that the holy man had stabbed a witch who might have eaten children's livers, venerate Yersin, the conqueror of the plague, and leave portions of 'Vache qui rit' cheese as offerings on his tomb.[88]

Other 'human types' throng into the intermediary storeys of globalization. One is the expert in his community, and quite often in his (television) set, who played a central role in the 'governmentalization' of western societies from the nineteenth century onwards, who is the best embodiment of their 'knowledge-power', and whom Michel de Certeau compared so felicitously to Felix the cat, who for a while now has been walking on air, high above the soil of science.[89] Then there is the great journalist or television presenter. And the preacher or the prophet, whether Christian or Muslim, so long as he too looks good on television. The 'NGO-ist', devoted to human rights, development, ecology, fair trade, humanitarian aid, the Good Samaritan of every emergency: not only has José Bové taken over from Asterix to defend the Gallic village against the 'Empire', becoming one of the champions of anti-globalization, somewhere between Mother Teresa, the Abbé Pierre and the agricultural leader Lee Kyung-hae, but also young French people 'pay particular homage . . . to all those anonymous heroes working in Third World countries, individually or within different associations'.[90]

'Human types' of globalization from below: the importance of bit players

Nonetheless, in the context of the highly normative debate on 'social disaffiliation' which is allegedly inherent in globalization, the main thing is to grasp that 'globalization from below' also forges 'human types', or contributes to producing them, by joining in 'lifestyles' that 'carry' various 'social strata' or events. We need to emphasize, first and foremost, that the 'lowest of the low', to use the expression from the Ivory Coast, are able to identify with models of life presented to them by the upper storeys of globalization. Bosses, politicians, princesses, show business stars and religious leaders all benefit, as is well known, from an almost universal aura, or are the object of a hatred of similar scale – which comes down to being the same thing from the point of view of the globalization of the processes of subjectivation. In short, Diana did not have to vegetate in the lower depths of 'generalized mutual interaction', any more than did Bin Laden, the man the Americans want dead but a valiant *sardar* of the global era in the eyes of the Balutchis and many other Muslims.[91] As for John Paul II, he is the idol of Catholic youth worldwide. Historians have long insisted on the way 'popular culture' and elite culture impact on each other. The same applies to the schemas of subjectivation that are produced by contemporary globalization.

All the same, more importance can be attributed, for the purposes of the present demonstration, to the emergence 'from below' of 'human types', or even heroes of globalization, who show off their ability to negotiate its pitfalls, embody itineraries of social ascent, set up new forms of solidarity and sociability, display moral and physical qualities appropriate to the change of scale which they face and are creators of a plebeian aesthetic of existence, sometimes constitutive of the way that age and gender are envisaged in their moral aspects. Footballers, and sportsmen and sportswomen more generally, are particularly representative of this type of 'moral subject'. When it comes to intermediation and ascension, both ethical and social, they have to some degree taken over from soldiers. Of modest extraction, they edify the 'lowest of the low' and encourage them to dream, while hoisting themselves up to the ranks of the 'highest of the high', not without impressing them with their performances, their valour and their other good qualities. But there are many other demotic heroes whom prejudice, the barriers of inequality, the ignorance of the situation and the lazy reluctance to imagine ambivalent phenomena all prevent one from identifying.

More than a century after the great trans-European and trans-oceanic movements of populations, and even though westerners cannot see the link between the epic of their ancestors and that of their contemporaries whom they repress and expel, the Emigrant remains the essential 'human type' of globalization. 'Migration is not merely determined by poverty and danger, as one often reads, it also belongs to an epic narrative borne by collective imaginings that turn the North into a place where heroes arise', writes Éliane de Latour with regard to the *ghettomen* of the Ivory Coast. The research carried out by Fariba Adelkhah into the Iranian diaspora, or by Justin-Daniel Gandoulou into the 'adventure' of the Congolese *Sapeurs* corroborate this epic dimension of expatriation.[92]

From day to day, the Emigrant negotiates the point of equilibrium between the moral imperatives of the society from which he has come and the demands of his new condition – as he does so, he is in danger, he suffers, he is hungry, and is trying to retain his dignity. In this respect, he plays a major role in the effective processes of 'glocalization': he brings about many different 'reverberation' effects between his own country and the country or the city to which he has moved. And, as we have seen, he develops a specific transnational 'lifestyle'. In Africa, Latin America, the Middle East, Asia, East Europe and (not so long ago) Italy, Greece and the Iberian peninsula, he plays out an exemplary destiny that is envied and feared. In collaboration with the people-smuggler, the professional 'agent' who alone can transform the desire for expatriation into a reality and holds the keys to the external world,[93] the Emigrant occupies a function of intermediation consubstantial with the very idea of a change of scale. So they are both by definition ambivalent characters who act on the basis of 'working misunderstandings'.[94]

Those who are left behind nurse towards those who leave ambivalent feelings of imitation and rejection, fall under the powerful influence of their extraverted customs and manners, while at the same time condemning their abandoning of local usages, and congratulate themselves on their generosity while condemning its limits. Sometimes quite reluctantly, emigrants are the heroes of one of the main social movements in these regions which comprise a reservoir of labour force: that of departure, which tends to assume a millenarian dimension, becoming a 'contemporary Mahdism in which awaiting the Messiah is more than anything the pretext for rearranging one's present time'.[95] Thus, at least 10,000 fake leaflets promising the possibility of financially very attractive emigration for men who agreed to marry an Iraqi war widow were sold in India during the years 1991–2, leading to a horde of candidates turning up at the gates of the Iraqi embassy in New Delhi.[96] And Lars Vilks, the Swedish artist and historian who, in 1996, created a virtual micro-nation on a rock in the Baltic Sea called Ladonia, was submerged with requests for naturalization from Pakistan, requests that led him to close his site *www.ladonia.net* in 2002.[97] The traffic in 'real fake passports' for virtual states is in any case quite common, as the 'republic' of Lomar or the 'principality' of Scaland have found out to their cost.[98] The messianic expectations aroused by departure exert a literally physical (and not just numerical) pressure, on the borders of countries that it would be nice to be able to call 'host countries'. Deserts and seas are crossed, ships, planes, trains and lorries are besieged and in Morocco, as previously in the German Democratic Republic, the last one to leave is invited to put out the light.

In the host society, the ambivalence of the Emigrant, who in the meantime has become the Immigrant (or, what is worse, the Illegal Immigrant, the Alien), is now reversed. The latter becomes a negative hero, a bearer of Otherness, of treacherous competition on the labour market, of odours and illnesses – fantastical perceptions which, we should hasten to emphasize, are not the exclusive property of westerners, but also characterize the way the 'Afghan' is imagined by Iranians or the 'Black' by people in the Maghreb. From the point of view of subjectivation, the Emigrant-turned-Immigrant is the anti-model, except for the fact that his zeal as a worker at everyone's beck and call, his kindness and simplicity, the sumptuous greeting that he has prepared for French friends visiting him on holiday back home in the village from which he comes, will all be tacitly hailed – or else he will be celebrated as the exploited victim of modern times, the anonymous Prince of the Multitude on whom will be brought to bear other messianic (or matrimonial) expectations.[99] In positive or negative terms, he intervenes in the antagonistic processes of subjectivation of the natives by fleshing out the definitions of citizenship, international solidarity or masculinity.

Be that as it may, the Emigrant and (much more than one would like to admit) the people-smuggler are themselves nascent 'moral subjects'.[100] They are obliged to reinvent their habitus completely, to overhaul their way of life and adopt new 'forms of life' (*Lebensform*) when it comes to food, clothing, furnishing, commensality, sexuality and language.[101] Their ethos is shot through with a contrast that would have delighted Marx. Their epic is aimed at achieving respectability. More often than not, the heroes of departure are constrained by circumstances and endure solitude, prison and even death to grasp the fantasy of a noteworthy (or at least ostentatious) success, by making a virtue (or an aesthetic) of necessity. As Fariba Adelkhah cruelly points out: '[Departure] is the vehicle of a petit-bourgeois aspiration, with fantasies of electrical household appliances, shiny cars, successful studies, happy marriages, and respectable lives. Its promised land is the hypermarket, its prophet Bill Gates, its archangel Leonardo Di Caprio and its scripture *Dallas*.'[102] This is a point confirmed by Éliane de Latour as far as the *ghettomen* of the Ivory Coast who have settled in Europe are concerned; she shows that the heroes of departure need more than anything else to be 'heroes of return' and speaks of the 'vital need for a sense of personal value and independence, the quest for exploits essential to one's self-fulfilment, the love of risk and splendour, all in order for one to have . . . a cosy place to call one's own.' 'I'm looking for a guaranteed life', says one. 'I'd like to have a settled, clean life, no more left-rights, that's it! Otherwise, what advice am I going to give my children later on?' confirms the other. The final word belongs to Zoom, an 'old father', and a drug dealer in Madrid: in his view, what one needs is to 'use your bit of imagination on the globality of things so that one day you can have your peace and quiet'.[103]

It is of no little interest that using 'your bit of imagination on the globality of things so that one day you can have your peace and quiet' may take the form of swindle, fraud or trafficking. The *ken* of the *keneurs* of the Ivory Coast, their 'kicks', their 'left-rights' which generally stop anyone from 'giving them grief' or physically assaulting them, the 'business', the ability to 'get by', and the 'co-op' of the Congolese 'movers and shakers' (who are also reluctant to resort to violence) are fully-fledged, albeit temporary, lifestyles. They enable delinquent young migrants to fulfil themselves and 'become someone'. They achieve social dignity by means of an extraversion of which travel is merely the instrument, and return the successful outcome, but also by means of skill, cunning and trickery. They are deceivers or tricksters, practising in their own way the *mètis* which, among the Greeks of

Antiquity, presided over all the activities in which powerful forces could be indirectly confronted and hijacked.[104] They take over the classic roles of the Hare, the Spider or the Smart Child in West African folk tales, that art of 'tactics' whose only place is the place of the 'other', and seizes on the wing a passing opportunity to achieve an 'operational performance'.[105]

By 'moving and shaking' things along, the young Congolese does not cease to formulate himself as a 'moral subject'. He is recompensed for the iniquity of colonization, he prepares his return as a hero or notable, and he amasses his treasure by pretence and patience, thereby showing how different he is from the 'Arab style of theft' (sic) that resorts to coercion rather than cunning.[106] He contributes to 'bearing' another 'human type' into globalization: that of the Crook. The Nigerian operators of the advance fee fraud known as '419' (in reference to the article of the penal code that makes it a crime), the Cameroonian feymen, the Mauritian tcheb-tchaba, the gorgui and other Senegalese moodu-moodu are doubtless the best representatives of the type. They embody a plebeian version of the project of subjectivation of the Ordoliberalen, according to whom existence itself become a piece of business and (why not?) of fraudulent business.[107]

It would be naive to imagine that we are here in the margins of globalization, if not anti-globalization, since we are not in a system of transparency (or of organized transnational crime). This is far from being the case. The '419' are now delocalized in the Republic of South Africa and in several West African countries, and they constitute one of the main sources of currency for Nigeria, after oil and indeed drugs, and their targets (and often their victims) are European or American businessmen and women, NGOs, and a whole host of western individuals.[108] Many readers will have received by fax or email these tempting offers to use their bank accounts as the hosts for enticing sums of money in return for commission – and the 'siphoning' of the said account for those who have yielded to the alluring temptation, sometimes paying an advance for the cost of the dossiers. As for the feymen of Cameroon, Radio-Trottoir and Radio-Couloir, its upper-crust sister, claim that they are not without their links to the political class of Yaoundé. In any case, the most mythical of them all, Donatien Koagne, rubbed shoulders with the staff of the South African ANC and with the turbaned heads of the Persian Gulf, and he brought down with him a woman civil servant of the Quai d'Orsay who was too candid, too zealous or too dedicated to other services of the Republic.[109]

The Crook works at the heart of the 'generalized mutual interaction' of credulity, in the milieus of migrants, whom he scours,[110] or with nice Europeans, whom he plucks.[111] He is part of a much more general economy of falsification devoted to fraud, faking, forgery, the fabrication of fake identity papers and fake attestations, and the swindling or pure pillage of public funds, in such a proportion that it is difficult to see in his twisted activities the mere dross of globalization, especially since government authorities and business milieus are to a greater or lesser degree associated with them too.

Fakes and forgeries represent, it seems, between 200 and 300 thousand million euros per year, in other words between 5 and 7 per cent of world trade, and they prosper in the shade if not of the complicity, at least of the indolence of the Chinese administration, the Russian bureaucracy, the Korean government, and several others.[112] Certain presidential regimes in Africa are no strangers to counterfeit currency.[113] Sagas such as those of Rafik Khalifa in Algeria, or Mikhaïl Khodorkovski in Russia, which became a scandal in 2003, also speak volumes from this point of view.[114] Aghan Hasan Abedi, the founder of the BCCI, was on the best of terms with the aristocracy of finance and the political classes of the 'free world'. Likewise, an internationally acclaimed singer such as the Congolese Papa Wemba organized a lucrative illegal immigration scam in Europe that is said to have transported some 200 fake musicians: it is almost an open secret and is not an isolated case in the small world of African showbiz.[115] For a significant and often 'respectable' proportion of humanity, globalization takes the form of a social experience of cheating. 'Moral subjects' are born from this process at the base of the pyramid as well as at its pinnacle, and political situations are quite burdened down by this 'regime of truth', like the Nigeria of the 1990s, the Russia of the reformers and oligarchs, or the states involved in smuggling.[116]

It is thus clear that the ambivalent – and often superimposed – figures of the Emigrant, the People-Smuggler and the Crook corroborate what we had started to sense in the previous pages. Transnational relations, migrations first and foremost, are major sites for ethical production and subjectivation. They are regulated in contradictory fashion by the repertory of confidence, guaranteed by decent people, to some extent the 'notaries' of expatriation and informal trade,[117] and that of deceit, of which many tricksters are operators. The stake of this contradiction or this tension is not the result of a Manichean struggle between Good and Evil, or the Licit and the Illicit, but the concrete exercise of social dignity, self-fulfilment, family solidarity, civic evergetism or religious good works. In short, the constitution of 'moral subjects', the emergence of problematizations and practices[118] in a given historical context, that of economic liberalization, state privatization and the generalized deregulation brought about by neo-liberal thinking, the internationalization of exchanges and the 'current situation' – i.e, as French-speakers in Africa put it, the '*conjoncture*' or crisis.

Global subjection, in this time of neo-liberalism, is occurring at the point of intersection between generalized transnational interaction and circumscribed historical *terroirs*. Filip de Boeck has thus analysed the boundary, at once geographical-political (the border) and socio-historical (frontier), between Angola and the Democratic Republic of the Congo, as a 'breach' in the Freudian and geological sense of the term – a volcanic rock composed of mineral fragments caught in solidified lava.[119] Every now and then this breach brings back to the surface a certain number of figures of subjectivation forged over history, which all refer to that of the mutant hero, an incarnation of the 'fetish': the hunter, the warrior, the soldier, the merchant, the chief, the saint – and even the cowboy, in so far as the imaginary theme of the Far West is very close to the hearts of young miners, who are often from urban backgrounds. To the eyes of the author, the lava of this frontier is far from being consolidated, and its fluidity allows the Bana Lunda who 'mine' in Angola to negotiate their identification with these models by means of various practices of the self, whether they have to do with sex, consumption, play or display.

The camps are highly organized, and in many respects form real social institutions, that are functionally differentiated. 'Arrivistes' ensure that order is maintained, in collaboration with the troops controlling the region of Lunda Norte. Diamond prospectors gather in 'stables' under the leadership of a 'compradore' or 'boss', who is often also the *dona moteur*, the owner of the boat and the oxygen equipment that enable the 'divers' (or *kazubuleurs*) to search under water. The profits are shared out between these roles, not forgetting the *lavador* who filters the stones and pebbles, nor of course the armed forces who dominate the zone. The clandestine miners who try to work independently of this organization – the *choqueurs* or 'shockers' – are pitilessly shot down. The camps are also the scene of 'mine weddings', which are sexual and economic associations, and they are linked to the Congo by means of trading and caravan networks composed of shopkeepers (*kamangistes*), porters (*pincheurs*) and intermediaries (*cocseurs*).

So they do not, properly speaking, form rural social institutions, and we should not take literally their geographical localization, within the borders of the nation-state. On the one hand, they are closely linked, on the economic and monetary front, to world markets, thanks to their 'dollarization' and the diamond export trade. On the other, the Bana Lunda are young pioneers, and the 'hunt' for precious stones and greenbacks is for them a way of 'capturing' the city of the whites, western modernity, the state-ruled space of the mythical figure of Bula Matari, so as to reshape them in their own terms, 'in a basically local perspective':

[P]assing over to Angola is the contemporary version of a strategy of self-realization or subjectivation that is much more ancient, like the hunter or the warrior, in so far as it constitutes a veritable rite of passage, modelled on the old *mukanda* circumcision ritual, to which the Bana

Lunda refer when they are discussing their experiences in the diamond-bearing field of Angola. As in the old *mukanda*, going to Angola imposes on you a suffering that you learn to endure: it fortifies you and hardens you physically, emboldens you and teaches you to 'put up with things'.[120]

The moral economy of the mining camp here intersects with the stratified repertoires of the cult of saints, rituals of lineage or royal societies, Mami Wata, the whip and the *billism* that we have already encountered in previous pages. Of course, as we have also seen, it frequently draws on the world market for imaginary figures so as to revitalize the tutelary models (perfectly interchangeable) of the hunter, the warrior, the merchant and the saint. But the mutability of these heroic guidelines, this borderline mode of subjection, shows the great stability, in the long term, of the ethical principles of subjectivation. Young adults become men at the price of the perilous practice of a cult of fecundity, prosperity and power that keeps up a necessary and troubled commerce with witchcraft, cannibalism, incest, homosexuality and death. The Angola–Congo frontier is in any case, in the literal sense, a space of death, infested with anti-personnel mines and fighters, not to mention the risks inherent in the diamond-prospecting trade itself.[121]

Though it may be peopled with the ordinary heroes of globalization, the frontier of the diamond-prospecting world and its associated mythology are not the product of a world without borders. On the contrary, it is rooted in individual local worlds, in line with the well-known logic of 'glocalization'. The Bana Lunda have been incorporated into economic and cultural globalization in such a way as to follow the historically signposted route of initiation by which they develop their masculinity or their social seniority. As such, it is fairly and squarely a matter of subjectivation.

This much is illustrated in turn by the gold prospectors of West Africa studied by Tilo Grätz.[122] In a completely different political context, their economic, professionalized and transethnic ethos, the way they take (and share) risks, finds its own style in a habitus and a semantic repertoire which exalt the qualities of endurance, solidarity in adversity, trust in teamwork, shared pleasures, and honour, and which celebrate an ideal of 'friendship' that is good news for the 'atmosphere'. Such an 'aesthetic of existence' amounts to a challenge to the moral economy of ethnicity and seniority. It is also a 'connection'[123] with cultural practices and models of identification that are urban and often come from outside Africa itself: the boxer Mike Tyson is venerated in discotheques, bars and small cinemas where videos are screened, as is the dissident singer from the Ivory Coast, Alpha Blondy. The miners' circuit of migration is here too akin to an initiation, a rite of passage to adulthood which globalization makes possible, instead of being an obstacle to it. We can deduce from this that the latter thus provides young Africans with a 'human type' different from that of the Crook or the Emigrant, though it does not thereby contradict them: the model of the Pioneer, operating at the interface of world markets and the societies of the sub-continent, sometimes but not always in the interstices of 'new wars' (or so-called 'new wars'). Now, the Pioneer, on his frontier, is obviously not a specifically African figure. For the last two centuries we have seen it haunting the moral imagination of the rush westwards in America, racial segregation in South Africa, the construction of the 'radiant future' in the USSR and China, the cruel mirage of 'French' and later socialist Algeria, the national project in Indonesia and, just for good measure, scouts in Western Europe.

The Pioneer rubs shoulders with another 'human type', one that is very much in vogue these days: the Fighter; indeed, in certain situations, the two meld together – for example on the twofold frontier, territorial and social, that unites (rather than it separates) Liberia and Sierra Leone. In their encampments, the young rebels of the different armed movements that are shedding so much blood in the region divide their time between diamond-prospecting, war, hunting, and consuming videos, drugs, alcohol and women. Rambo is their positive hero. He introduces them to the world, gives them different lessons on the way he works, provides them with schemes of action and survival, and allows them to hope for a possibility of reinsertion into society as veterans, as in *First Blood*.[124] The Congolese 'diggers' also have to compromise with the figure of the warrior and annex it to their imaginations, even if they are not themselves fighters.[125]

War in itself is a matrix of subjectivation. It subjects fighters, often forcibly enrolled in accordance with bureaucratic procedures or under threat of immediate execution, to 'conducts of life' that are experienced all the more intensely given that this latter – i.e. life – daily hangs by a thread. Thus, for the young Nuer of the SPLA, in Sudan, sexuality and marriage, for lack of power, emerge from the barrel of a rifle. Having a firearm and being able to use it properly have become emblems of virile power, beauty, strength and entry into adulthood. This entry has now become an inseparable item of the dowry: its appropriation by the group, the family or the community has modified the parameters of value formation for cattle and spears.[126] Likewise, the 'Maï Maï' of the Kivu admit that they are 'a bit superstitious':

> We believe in the powers of plants. But we could easily demonstrate that the leaf of a banana tree treated with sprinklings of our ritual water resists a bullet or a rocket. For a fighter the effect is the same, unless he has broken our code of conduct In this case, it goes without saying that he will fall at the first bullet. Furthermore, before our children go into

combat, our radars tell us who exactly has broken the rules and who is
thus doomed to die.

The 'code of conduct' in question forbids rape, theft and alcohol in
particular.[127]

It is by fire, blood and pillage that armed adolescents constitute
themselves as 'moral subjects' in sub-Saharan conflicts, at the cost of a
few eccentricities in their clothing and the cruelty that is mistakenly
seen as no more than a barbaric deviance. On the one hand, the history
of their country has left them with hardly any other 'modes of subjection', and those who are mainly responsible are not they themselves
but their leaders who for so long were pampered by 'world governance'. On the other, these soldiers in the flower of their age, and
sometimes still children, implement ethical codes, cosmogonic representations, native or foreign cultural repertoires and an 'aesthetic of
existence' whose fierce vacuity one may deplore, but which all build
them up into warriors or heroes, even if they are total idiots, where the
state and the 'current situation' give them no better choice than that of
being unemployed or delinquents.[128] From this point of view, war too
is a rite of passage, and this is how we need to understand the macabre
staging of certain enforced recruitments: the young captive is obliged
to massacre his whole family to make it impossible for him ever to
return to his village should he try to run away, and to render his new
condition irreversible; as a survivor of the butchery to which he has
submitted, he is reborn into a new identity, that of the fighter for whom
the armed movement is his whole family, and the leader a substitute
father-figure.[129]

In a less paroxystic way, urban militias have the same initiatory role
as people-smugglers, and grant their members the social status that is
otherwise denied to them. In Nairobi, for example, Mungiki, the Kikuyu
neo-prophetic sect has turned itself into a private security group, in
particular on collective taxi ranks and in property, actualizing the old
repertory of the moralizing warrior of society and protecting its recruits
from the sudden accusation of theft, which would immediately bring
mob justice down on their heads. 'As vigilantes, the faithful are in the
service of the local notables and thus are immediately integrated into
a relatively clear position for all the inhabitants in the neighbourhood'
– even if this means turning against their political and ethnic adversar-
ies the violence that was threatening *them*, indulging in the massacre
of other young men, as in Kariobangi, in March 2002, and getting
involved in the 'taxi war'.[130] Likewise, in Congo-Brazzaville, the phenomenon of the militia was historically the privileged framework of
socialization for many young men from the city, either in the context
of the 'revolution' of the 1960s, or in that of the civil war of the 1990s.
It was a major site of cultural extraversion, in which the forces of the

invisible, creativity in music, clothes and language could all flourish: from this base, successive generations endeavoured to assert themselves as a 'political age group' in the face of the domination and predation of the civil and military elite that emerged from the Congolese party of labour.[131]

There is in any case nothing exotic about this militarization of the process of subjectivation. In Europe, the Great War was in a similar way a school of heroism for children, adolescents and young men, though it was not outstanding in either intelligence or humanity.[132] And, for the young Iranian *bassidji* of the 1980s, the quest for martyrdom was first and foremost a 'construction of self' (*khodsâzi*), in the philosopher Ali Shariati's sense, in the horror of trench or marsh warfare, but also in a climate of adolescent mystical eroticism: 'It was then that I really grasped that the front was a school of self-identification', writes one of the characters of the literature of that conflict studied by Éric Butel.[133]

A comparable logic can be found, it appears, in the suicide attacks that certain armed movements now encourage. The Tamil Tigers, in Sri Lanka, make a point of rejecting this notion and prefer to speak of the 'gift of one's self' (*thatkodai*, rather than *thatkolai*, 'killing oneself'). Their martyrs, a good third of them women, are of course volunteers: they are given an intense physical and physiological training (a form of practice of the self), are invited to the table of the leader, Vellupillai Prabhakaran, for a last dinner, and sometimes have their deaths filmed for the edification of the masses. The iconography and the audiovisual production of the organization exalt their sacrifice. And the sacrifice gives rise to evergetic acts, such as the creation of an orphanage dedicated to the memory of Kantharuban Arivuchcholai, who blew herself up in 1991.[134] The Tigers reject any comparison with the Palestinian suicide attacks on the pretext that the latter are committed by desperate people. Nonetheless, this condescending attitude seems out of place since, in the eyes of radical Islamic militants too, 'Jihad is a way of life': 'When we look around and see the land stolen and dignity scorned, we are ready to give our blood and everything that we possess for the Jihad. . . . It is a matter of achieving the ecstasy of victory. . . . Your death is going to pass again and again before your eyes and you are going to live with it. Then you attain the greatest of secrets, that of life after death. You strike up a friendship with death', explain the leaders of the Jerusalem brigade (Sarava al-Qods), presenting themselves as 'martyrs who are still alive'. In fact, suicide attacks are the response to a redoubtable rational strategy:

> First of all it was a matter of causing the maximum number of deaths on the Israeli side. Then, of proving that the highly efficient security measures of the Zionist state can be overcome by striking at its heart. . . .

Finally, even if it happens that a bomb explodes without killing anyone, it still contributes to destroying the truce in force.[135]

However, the Fighter, like the celebrated fish, develops in the waters of the suffering of the civil populations of which he claims to be the dedicated servant. He is filmed, therefore he is, in the company of two other 'human types': the Refugee, who forms the transient population of the camps, that new social institution of globalization that is prospering on both sides of the state's borders and contributes to their validation; and the Disabled Person whose suffering, caused by his missing limb torn away by a bomb, a mine, or cut off by a machete – 'do you want a long sleeve or a short sleeve?' – reminds him that he is a bit player in a 'new war'. These two later 'human types', the Refugee and the Disabled Person, set themselves up as 'moral subjects' in line with their personal and collective tragedies as much as by the eye of the cameras and the bureaucratic evergetism of the 'international community'. They develop a transnational 'lifestyle (or of survival)'; they are obviously abandoned to their own unspeakable pain, but they are the objects of a knowledge-power on the part of the system of states and its non-governmental 'fortresses and earthworks'. This turns them into fully fledged agents in globalization, albeit in a negative guise: the Fighter fulfils himself thanks to their destiny – by global criteria, what would he be without them? – and sometimes lives off the alms that are granted to them; 'international civil society' has discerned in them the new abolitionist cause able to push forward the ideal of a global ethos of war, since a 'perpetual peace' is impossible; here the state finds a field of public policy and legitimation on the twofold level of its external influence and the satisfaction of its interior public opinion.

In short, the Fighter, grasped in his different variant forms (the Militiaman, the Martyr, the Soldier, the Commander, the Emir, the Blue Beret) and flanked by his victims (or his protégés), the Refugee and the Disabled Person, is a fully fledged 'human type' who is borne by 'social strata' to the four corners of the planet and in a dialogical relation with them. National, religious or ideological causes such as those of the Bosnians, the Afghans, the Chechens and the Karen, and historical or mythological characters such as Che Guevara, John Rambo, subcommander Marcos, commander Massud, the Ninja turtles, Carlos or Mohamed Atta have a worldwide aura. The 'cultures of the self' proper to different armed movements circulate around the globe, create hybrid forms, and unify the transnational genres of the militarization of social life and political suffering. It is quite remarkable that the new configuration of the global system of states is haunted by this figure of the Fighter in his most radical style, that of suicide attacks, from Manhattan to Madrid, Grozny, Jerusalem, Jakarta, Srinagar, Baghdad, Istanbul, Djerba or Casablanca.

However, the heroic character of the period must not be exaggerated, at the risk of falling into a twilight vision of globalization. This latter phenomenon can also be recognized, and much more frequently, in ordinary 'human types', dedicated to the priesthood of the everyday: the Salaried Employee, the hero of reconstruction and the economic miracle that is celebrated every Tuesday on a Japanese television programme, 'Project X: challengers';[136] the Working Man, and especially the Working Woman, from the outsourced factory in the free zones whose productivist asceticism reproduces the ethos of the family; the 'NGO-ist', who embodies, in the stench and noise of crowded city districts or the dust of villages, a haven of cleanness, silence, international competence and, *Insha'Allah*, petty-bourgeois devotion;[137] the well-informed Consumer who wonders 'What is the best item to choose?', as Lenin asked 'What is to be done?', and is now based on ethical criteria either of a social nature, in the name of fair trade, or of an environmental nature, impelled by ecological considerations; the Tourist with a yen for authenticity, who takes consolation from modern life by photographing the village, that familiar cultural figure of globalization which gave delight in succession to George Sand, Karl Marx, the preachers of the Basel Mission, Béla Bartók, ethnologists, colonial administrators and their nationalist successors, 'developers', revolutionaries of nativist tendencies, Liberation Theologians and Club Med.[138] It is indeed the rather banal grandeur of ordinary 'human types' which, in contrast, confers on other figures of globalization their epic character: the victim of the Crook or the Fighter is indeed that Mr Global Everyman whose ranks the Emigrant hopes so much to join, in his millenarian instincts.

Globalization, nation-state and individuation

The moral pantheon of globalization is indeed heavily encumbered, and this cannot fail to create differences of opinion between its divinities. The worldwide conflicts of subjectivation are legion, and attest to the tangibility of these processes, at the point of fusion of political societies and transnational exchanges. The social institutions of globalization – for instance, religious institutions or NGOs – are stirred by their own ethical debates which contribute to the transversal production of 'moral subjects'. The problems of marriage, homosexuality and paedophilia as they affect priests in the Catholic Church, and the way organizations that defend human rights take responsibility for 'positive' and 'negative' liberties, are among the symptoms of this. Even more significant is the fact that specific disputes arise from globalization itself and lead to transnational, transcultural and transreligious coalitions on the part of stakeholders. This is true of the (somewhat general) condemnation of sexual tourism and paedophilia, and the (much more polemical) condemnation of sexual mutilation, certain ways of fighting AIDS, the denial of rights to native minorities, and racism. The same is also true of the promotion of contraception or the recognition of homosexuality, which saw the establishment of a Holy Alliance between the Vatican, the (Protestant) Religious Right in America and certain influential Islamist voices at the International Conference on Population and Development, held in Cairo in September 1994 under the aegis of the United Nations.

Global campaigns aimed at eradicating political and moral ills are launched on a planetary scale, supported by international law, the more or less enforced conformity of national legislations with its positive norms, coercive state and inter-state policies, and even military interventions on a multilateral, bilateral or unilateral basis so as to bring to resipiscence those who are recalcitrant at the level of the state (or at levels lower than the state). Since the 11 September 2001 attacks, the 'war on terrorism' has thus become a gigantic bring-your-own-food party, where everyone brings to the table of repression his undesirable opposition.[139] Much earlier, the United States had unleashed a 'war on drugs', whose battle plans had always been infinitely variable, but which led the US to deploying military advisers in Columbia, to award *urbi et orbi* criticism and congratulations to the different states of the world, and to modulate their cooperation in accordance with this parameter.

Now most of these crusades lead to controversy or resistance. This is, by definition, the case with the repression of terrorism which is, for its authors, a just war, or even a holy war. The triumphant and provocative face of Amrozi bin Nurhasyim, one of those who carried out the bombing in Bali in 2002, is evidence of this. The attack on Iraq by the United States, Great Britain and Australia, in 2003, with the aim of containing the proliferation of weapons of mass destruction, itself profoundly divided public opinion in western countries, not to mention the Arab-Muslim or African world. Nor does the prohibition of narcotics engender any unanimous moral certainty, even though it has been at the heart of processes of globalization for two centuries. It was by force of arms that the United Kingdom made China open its market to the opium of the Raj, and, in their Asian colonies, the Netherlands and France entrusted to state-owned companies the monopoly for the commoditization of this product. Before they turned into a vice and a crime, drugs were an imperial manna.[140] These days, it is not just the young *keufeurs* of the suburbs who demand its legalization, but also *The Economist*, the organic weekly of good governance.

The development of 'moral subjects' on the world scale, on either side of transnational activities and public policies, has long been political and relatively autonomous from strictly national or local arenas. At the end of the nineteenth century, the Tsawa kings were prohibitionists and rebelled against the trade in alcohol with the support of non-denominational Christian missions and British temperance societies, but in opposition to the commercial and territorial ambitions of the British South Africa Company of Cecil Rhodes.[141] All the same, the global modes of subjection are not disconnected from historical societies. On the contrary, they find a good part of their truth in them. Globalization thereby produces 'lifestyles' that are one of the manifestations of its historicity, notably in terms of 'glocalization'. Posed in these terms, it thus tends to set itself up as a form of governmentality, where techniques of domination and techniques of the self overlap,[142] right into the deepest recesses of individuality.[143] It definitely goes far beyond a mere 'governance' whose theme, to tell the truth, is merely the expression of the neo-liberal project of subjectivation as conceptualized by Alexander von Rüstow and taken up by 'advanced liberalism'.[144]

Two points still need to be made on the subject of the emergence of this global governmentality. In the first place, the processes of political subjectivation continue to proceed largely from the sphere of the state, and they are no less 'global'. It should be emphasized from the outset that most transnational organizations or movements that work for the constitution of 'moral subjects' do not reject the state. Rather, they request its intervention to 'regulate', 'master' or curb globalization. This is the case of the anti-globalization movement, which put pressure on the prestigious assembly of the G8, on national governments or multinational and inter-state institutions. Their 'sovereignism' is often obvious. Likewise, human rights organizations appeal to public opinion on a national or transnational basis to force states to behave: democracies to boycott dictatorships and dictatorships to become more democratic. And French homosexuals in the transnational district of the Marais, in Paris, spray the walls with slogans for the eyes of the public powers: 'We are dying, you are doing nothing!' So nobody will be surprised to see, under other skies, the state implanting itself in neo-traditional rituals of initiation, as in Chad at the start of the 1970s and at present in Togo,[145] or in Uzbekistan taking a close interest in the rites of passage of birth, circumcision, weddings and funerals to regulate to its own advantage the moral economy of the gift that underlies relations between clientele.[146] I will return to this later: the question of subjectivation is too serious to be left to subjects!

In fact, most global institutions that are institutions of subjectivation are bureaucratic organizations in the Weberian sense of the concept. This is true of churches, businesses and even NGOs, sporting federations, youth movements or refugee camps, generally administered by disciplinary methods. Somehow or other, the militia themselves bureaucratize and militarize the rites of passage that were controlled, for example, by age groups or secret societies in African societies. As for gold-prospectors in Benin, they call each other 'President', 'brigadier', 'MD', 'ambassador', and 'Prime Minister' in their makeshift camps.[147] On this level as on others, it is in reality impossible to separate the processes of globalization from the processes of state formation. The latter are closely interwoven, when they do not simply meld together. The institutions or social practices that produce 'modes of existence or lifestyles' in the worldwide and transnational dimension are the very ones that have worked for the emergence of national 'domination'. The state, furthermore, is an active party in the work of subjectivation by means of its public policies. Even in this age of 'advanced liberalism', it is a legislative and regulatory agent of 'bio-power' and promotes a certain 'human type', like the 'benevolent' states of Asia which dispense lodging, healthcare, education, savings, credit and insurance, even if it means turning these weapons against dissidents or deviants and thereby submitting them more surely than if they were to resort to physical violence.[148]

Turkey is a textbook case of the way state subjectivation and transnational subjectivation are interwoven. In a very classic manner, its integration into the global system of states and what Mustapha Kemal called 'civilization', in the purest positivist vein, was mediated by the nationalism inspired simultaneously by the work of Durkheim and the 'identity assistance' of a certain number of transnational operators of the idea of nation, on the European scale. In itself, national awareness was in Turkey, as we have seen, a 'lifestyle' that found expression in a thoroughgoing Kemalist 'fetishism',[149] moulded by codes of dress and hairstyle and giving rise to a drastic reform of the language, a change in the mode of writing, a juridical revolution, the invention of a 'popular culture', the promotion of an ubiquitous state town planning, the inculcation of a rationalist official Islam and an ultranationalist vision of the world. Education, military service, the conduct of religious affairs – attached to the services of the Prime Minister – imposed the republican ethos in a systematic form, without stinting on coercive and disciplinary procedures, including in the national educational system and the army, where blows were frequent, not to mention the massive use of torture in police stations, the interrogation centres of the political police and prisons. There was something Soviet in the engineering of identity in the Kemalist utopia, and with good reason: certain of those who had conceived it were communists from the Kadro movement who had broken away from Moscow and been won over by the national revolution. These days, the nationalist ethos is nourished perhaps less by public policies than by the practices of 'civil society', often 'more statist than the state', as is indicated by the spontaneous farewell ceremonies when the conscripts leave, in the coach stations, or the patriotic transports that accompany *futbol* matches. In these expressions, it continues to lavish access to adult masculinity for adolescents of the *gecekondu* and the suburbs: young men show off their virility to one another and to the women who surround them by using the terms of state culture.[150]

The nationalist 'lifestyle' now has to face competition from the Islamic way of life that is 'borne' (among other social strata) by some inner migrants from Central or Eastern Anatolia who have settled in the cities of the West, emigrants from the European 'Blue Banana' and the manager class of small and medium-sized businesses (whose professional confederation is the MÜSIAD). The different demo-Islamic parties that have succeeded one another since the end of the 1960s have given this 'conduct of life' its parliamentary representation. From the point of view of historical sociology, they are situated in the wake of political formations that have fought for the favours of the provincial elites on which the Ottoman Empire rested, which the Kemalist regime had marginalized between the world wars, but had reintroduced themselves into the game thanks to the establishment of a multiparty system in 1945–6.[151] These days, Recip Tayyip Erdogan's Party of Justice and Development is the heir to Adnan Menderes' Democratic Party, Süleyman Demirel's Party of Justice or Turgut Özal's Party of the Motherland, more, perhaps, than it is the heir to Necmettin Erbakan, the historical leader of Turkish Islamic parliamentarianism. Nonetheless, the conflict of subjectivation that was provoked by the rise to power of this demo-Islamic trend tends to muddle these permanent lines and gives a dramatic turn to the alternating governments. Indeed, two lifestyles confront one another in battles over the wearing of the veil or the beard, over alcohol or education or the municipalization of the welfare state, even when the 'discipline of Islamic social life' was a principle of political centralization and universality under the Ottoman Empire[152] and these days provides the most dynamic sector of Anatolian capitalism with its economic ethos, and even though post-Kemalist Islam and the Kemalist ideology share a positivist and nationalist common ground.[153] It is also possible in Turkey to come across a 23-year-old imam requesting a divorce, arguing that his wife refuses to dress 'like a civilized woman' and persists in wearing the veil and mantle of Islam: 'I want a spouse who will suit the society in which we live.'[154] Mutatis mutandis, this twofold logic of contradiction and superimposition of different 'stylizations' of social attitudes already characterized the last decades of the Ottoman Empire when the two repertoires, alla franca and alla turca, coexisted in a state of confrontation in everyday and cultural life, for example when it came to dress codes or the performance of a particular musical genre.[155]

This polarization of modes of subjection is, in addition, inseparable from the event of globalization.[156] It involves, first and foremost, the Turkish populations that emigrated to Western Europe. It is mediatized by the commoditization of society and the new forms of sexuality that were brought about by the neo-liberal policy of Turgut Özal in the 1980s.[157] It makes the question of Turkey joining the European Union particularly complicated, in so far as, until the contrary is proved, the Party of Justice and Development seems to serve this cause better than did the secular parties. For twenty years it has taken part in the internationalization of the Turkish economy. It also tallies with its regional influence, since one of the components of the Islamic trend, the neo-confraternity of the Fethullahci, which acts by force of being exemplary (*tensil*) rather than by preaching and which trains English-speaking 'young saints' (*sakirt*), hosting them in small communities of six or seven students in its 'houses of light' (*isikevler*) or in its network of secondary schools and independent universities, has opened establishments in neighbouring Turkish-speaking countries.[158]

In short, the conflict of subjectivation between Islamic democrats and Kemalist secularists does not come down either to an alternative between the umma and the nation, or to a zero-sum game between the latter and globalization. It is a mainspring of the processes of subjectivation in the twofold dimension of nation and globalization. The Turks are situated in both of these, and continue to make the state the pivot of their 'constitution as moral subjects'. And the progressive deconfessionalization of successive Islamic parties demonstrates that the 'human type' of the democratic and prosperous Muslim can be an evolutionary driving force of subjectivation, particularly well adapted to the political and economic imperatives of globalization.

In a naturally very different context, we find in the Ivory Coast a rather similar combination of the processes of subjectivation, the transnational religious phenomenon and the national public debate. Historically, the country is a land of prophets. Prophecy has always been involved, on the one hand, in state-formation, following a trajectory of 'passive revolution' by co-opting, in particular, religious leaders, and, on the other hand, with the 'conduct of life' of the faithful and their individuation.[159] Ever since the end of the 1990s, as we know, a new type of evangelical priest has been occupying the foreground. Kacou Séverin, 'the prophet of all nations', who was killed in a road accident in 2001, was its most visible representative. He was the President of the Ivory Coast branch of the international Foursquare Evangelical Church, of American origin, whose West African seat was established in Nigeria; he had founded in tandem with this a Ministry for the Power of the Gospel that lay outside 'denominational' borders and had become a 'real international business', with its head office in Paris. He could thus dispense his message of 'deliverance' in the transnational sphere, as a good apostle of those 'Network Churches'[160] that were deemed to be the paragons of religious globalization. At the same time, he played an active part in national political life, prophesying the coup d'état of 1999, the failure of the provisional president, Robert Gueï, and the resurrection of the Ivory Coast thanks to the rise to power of a 'Christian' president. In his mind, subjectivation by fasting and prayer would be enough to deliver the nation from Satan and, as an additional bonus, from instability or the menace from abroad. André Mary summarizes the situation thus:

> With his qualities . . . as a priest, an exegete, a stage director and, very rapidly, a producer of cassettes, creator of sites and organiser of campaigns, Kacou Séverin appears as an entrepreneur, a businessman, managing his international network and his trips abroad, forever using his laptop . . . but he is also an inspired prophet, allowing people to see and hear an extreme sensitivity to the crisis in the country and the national drama that is being played out.[161]

Indisputably elected in disputable conditions in 2000, the new President, Laurent Gbagbo, is supported by the vitality of this charismatic movement of 'deliverance', whose importance for West Africa I have already emphasized, and has asserted that he is the spokesman of Ivory Coast nationalism and its 'second independence' from 'foreigners' and the old colonial power. The 'pasionaria' of this cause is his own wife, Simone, popular with the 'young patriots' and deeply religious. The heralds of this Christian or neo-Christian sensibility succeed one another in Abidjan, where they preach 'reconciliation' and often sanction the rather Islamophobic version that the head of state and, even more, his wife give of it, flanked by his *éminence grise*, the pastor Koré, a real Pentecostalist Rasputin.[162] The pastor Yonggi Cho, of the Yoido Full Gospel Choir of Seoul, and Tommy Lee Osborn, one of the leaders of the Gospel of Prosperity, thus rushed forward in 2001–2 to certify that 'the hand of God is on the Ivory Coast'.[163] In the minds of religious men, it is a self-evident truth that the country 'belongs to God' and that practices of 'deliverance' will bring it redemption. In the words of the successor of Kacou Séverin at the head of the Foursquare Church:

> All the problems that happen to a nation or a person always have a spiritual basis. The problems we experience every day are merely the result of what has already happened in the spiritual realm. Our contribution is to pray truly so that God will touch the hearts of each and everyone so that forgiveness will indeed be waiting for us.[164]

In most African countries, the field of political practices is in tension with that of religious practices, and the subjects of the state are 'subjects of God'.[165] The observance of a rule of faith, often very strict from the point of view of the 'practices of the self' that it demands in terms of food, clothes and sexuality and the giving of money to the church – 'Let us bind the demon of arrogance, let us bind the demon of carnal lust, let us bind the demon of drugs and tobacco,' the founder of the Gate of the Sheep enjoins her faithful, in Douala[166] – converges with 'belonging' to the nation as well as with a transnational 'conduct of life' generally borrowed from the North American evangelical or fundamentalist galaxy. Religious 'techniques of the self' support techniques of political domination. Thanks to the new means of communication, 'long distance' religious affiliation – to paraphrase Benedict Anderson when he talks of 'long-distance nationalisms' – turns out to be singularly propitious to this synergy.[167]

Over the past few years, there has been a lot of talk of 'God's revenge' (and of his decline).[168] But, as one would expect, the facts are more complex than rash generalizations would suggest. One of the central elements of the synergy between the processes of globalization and state-formation over the last two centuries has been the existence of religious life. Political centralization, in the context of globalization, i.e. the emergence of a global system of states, has often taken two paths: the path of collective or even mass conversion to a new faith, and the path of the bureaucratization of religious institutions, on the clerical model imported from the West and by means of transnational effects of dissemination or strategic imitation. This has been shown in numerous and very varied situations: for example, with regard to the spread of Shi'ism among the Arab tribes of Iraq, and the evangelization of sub-Saharan societies and the development within them of so-called 'independent' churches, the clericalization of the religious authorities of Shi'ism and Hinduism, or of the growing Islamic activity among the Balutchis after their effective incorporation into the Iranian state during the 1930s.[169] Syncretic movements such as the Bahai in Persia or the Taiping in China are also worth interpreting in this perspective. It was also in this respect that the nineteenth century was foundational for contemporary globalization, with Western Europe proving no exception to the rule.[170] The contemporary city is 'cultic', just as was the ancient city, if we are to believe François de Polignac: the religious dimension led to the creation of a society based on a cultic space in which (especially in the upsurge of religious activity in the eighth century) a collective system of representations was established.[171] The global city is still cultic thanks to the close interweaving of the 'cultures of the self', state-formation and the transnational religious phenomenon. Any differentiation of the processes of political subjectivation and the processes of religious subjectivation is not thereby annulled, as Fariba Adelkhah has shown in a subtle analysis of the Islamic Republic of Iran, in so far as the latter seems even to have reinforced the reciprocal particularization of the religious and political fields.[172] It is just that the two registers of subjectivation are forever intertwining, modifying the 'historical condition' of the Being-in-the-world conceptualized as production.[173]

Indeed – in second place – global governmentality, as an 'encounter between the techniques of domination over others and the techniques of the self' rests on religious, political or other practices of the self, which are a convergent response to a logic of individuation while remaining endowed with their own historicity, namely that of the society to which they 'belong'. In no case can the process of individuation be assimilated to the triumph of liberal 'individualism' or to cultural westernization. On the contrary, it draws its complexion from particular histories and cultural repertoires that cannot be dissolved in either the ideology of 'market democracy' or in the meta-discourse of identity and culture. There is no generic global human being,[174] nor any Christian, Islamic or neo-Confucian human being either. There are processes of individuation, historically situated, that enter into 'generalized mutual interaction'.

Writers such as Norbert Elias and Anthony Giddens rapidly identified a relationship between the change of scale of globalization and the transformation of the self.[175] And several 'transversal struggles',[176] such as the activities of the student, feminist or homosexual movements, brought the globalization of the processes of subjectivation into the spotlight at regular intervals (especially from the 1960s onwards). Nonetheless, the public debate relating to this phenomenon is finding it somewhat difficult to relate the concrete practices of individuation from one society to another in terms of their status as 'events', in this context of 'generalized mutual interaction'.

The heated discussion among homosexuals in Asia is interesting from this point of view. Some of them insist on their attachment to so-called traditional forms of homosexuality, in particular transvestism. Others feel that they have less in common with the latter than with the gays of Castro Street in San Francisco or the Marais in Paris. Dennis Altman highlights the fact that ' "modern" ways of being homosexual threaten not only the custodians of "traditional" morality, they also threaten the position of "traditional" forms of homosexuality, those which are centered around gender nonconformity and transvetism'. In his view, the title of the Indonesian review *Gaya Nusantara* (literally 'Indonesian style') 'captures this ambivalence nicely with its echoes of both "traditional" and "modern" concepts of nation and sexuality, but at the same time is clearly aimed at "modern" homosexuals rather than the "traditional" transvestite *waria*'.[177] The complex resources of individuation that certain Islamic practices procure within the context of a mass urban society (for instance the wearing of the veil or forms of social life linked to preaching)[178] or certain Communist 'penitential' procedures in a neo-orthodox Soviet society (such as self-criticism, denunciation, the purge, dissimulation)[179] also attest to the

irreducibility of this question of individuation to the liberal individualization which has, as a linear Grand Narrative, definitely been dis-
counted by philosophers and historians: one's relation to oneself is not
mere 'individualism'.[180]

We need to pick up Marx's recommendation and 'avoid once more
establishing "society" as an abstraction over the individual. The individual *is* the *social being*. His vital expression – even when it does
not appear in the direct form of a *communal* expression, conceived in
association with other men – is therefore an expression and confirmation of *social* life.'[181] Once this is accepted, individuation is inseparable
from 'being-in-society' and its relation to the civic community, as has
been magisterially demonstrated by Fariba Adelkhah and Mattison
Mines, respectively in the 'man of integrity' (*javânmard*) in Iran and the
'individuality of eminence' in South India.[182] Now, these days, 'social
being' is 'global'. I have pointed out precisely with respect to its transnational evergetism how the way it forms part of globalization and its
recognition as a moral subject of the latter were brought about in a
permanent negotiation between its often risky strategy of self-assertion
and its observance of an ethos of group, community or place. The
analysis of migrations and trading networks has much to tell us from
this point of view. The globalization of the social sphere is thus also,
indissolubly, the globalization of individuation in one's relation to the
social sphere. Philanthropy among American entrepreneurs of the 'new
economy' or among the magnates of the Chinese diaspora suggests that
this model of individuation on the basis of prestige – for example 'by
means of gifts that are skilfully made public'[183] – is prospering in the
heart of capitalism. In short, the notion of individualism is no more
appropriate to western societies than it is to African or Asiatic societies,
which are supposed (quite mistakenly) to be 'holistic'. The fact that the
one error is a mirror image of the other does not make it any more
acceptable.

Once individuation is realized *urbi et orbi* via this participation in
both the social and the global spheres, it refers to the 'historical condition' of the agent or, we should rather say, the process of subjectivation
that we are examining. In other words, it inevitably leads to a 'reinvention of difference'. Not a difference between one 'culture' or 'civilization' to another, as so many commentators and ethno-psychiatrists
would like. But between one historical situation and another, which is
completely different. The implantation of psychoanalysis in an America
struggling with the crazy Puritanism of 'civilized morals' illustrates
remarkably well this historicity of the transnational processes of subjectivation in the mode of individuation. Its introduction into the United
States coincided with the moral revolution and the overcoming of traditional forms of modesty.[184] However, the rejection of the excessively
puritanical lifestyle that had imposed itself, at least on the east coast,

nudged Freudianism towards a therapeutic practice and an ideological discourse of moral hope that had little to do with the original work of the master. The transatlantic spread of a repertory (or an engineering) of subjectivation did not lead to a uniformity of the processes of subjectivation on either side of the ocean. And conversely, the importing into Europe in the 1960s and 1970s of American reference points in the sphere of the 'counter-culture', music and dance, sexual and narcotic practices, and the demand for women's and homosexuals' rights, did not lead to an 'Americanization' of the processes of subjectivation on the Old Continent, however great the degree of 'transversality' of these 'struggles'.

Likewise the communist, who – as Oleg Kharkhordin as shown – was a neo-orthodox figure of individuation in Russia (and the pitiful collapse of the Soviet Union should not lead us to forget that the communist was a fundamental 'human type' of globalization in the twentieth century), experienced many reincarnations in the different parts of Europe, in China, Vietnam, Cambodia, Cuba, Ethiopia and Angola. From the agents of the Comintern to the Khmer Rouge, or even from the apparatchiks of the Chinese Communist Party to the Red Guards, from the Italian Eurocommunist to his or her French comrade, from Che Guevara to Laurent Kabila – such contrasts![185] And in Africa we have seen this logic of individuation assuming the different faces of the Prophet,[186] the Emigrant, the Crook, the Pioneer or the Fighter. It is worth betting that the 'human type' which neo-liberalism is working on will turn out to be just as varied.

The generality of the process of individuation results simultaneously from the expansion of capitalism – more precisely from the principles of investment, of the wage, and (as we shall see in the next chapter) of consumption – and anthropological mutations entailed by globalization over the past two centuries in regard to 'bio-power' (Foucault) and 'self-reflexivity' (Anthony Giddens). All the same, it by no means produces a homogenization of 'lifestyles' even though the practices of subjectivation are spreading across the world. Only those readers most resistant to speech-act theory and the description of the historical sociology of the state will find this surprising or paradoxical. For reception is creation, and unity is heterogeneity. The historical, social and cultural material reworks this general movement of individuation from one situation to another and 'generalized mutual interaction', far from levelling the landscape of the world, proceeds (as is worth repeating) by highlighting singularities.

In this case, the relation between globalization and the logic of individuation makes a difference and supports the hypothesis of the emergence of a planetary governmentality. Foucault emphasized how discipline manufactures individuals.[187] He put forward this analysis of 'bio-power' in the context of the liberal nation-state of the nineteenth century. The remark is still relevant on the scale of contemporary global subjection by means of the transversal processes of subjectivation that I have mentioned. We should also remember that these processes cannot be seen in abstraction from the context of the nation-state, nor do they render its own 'discipline' obsolete. They are closely interwoven with it, supported by it, take over where it leaves off and complete it, as we have observed in the case of Turkey and the Ivory Coast. Throughout the period we are considering, it would be pointless to see globalization as the opposite of the individualizing power of the state; Tocqueville had already intuitively seen this power at work, and he foresaw that it would be able to accompany the universalization of democracy. It is well and truly the global system of states (as a product of globalization) that is 'a modern matrix of individualization', to use Foucault's terms.[188] The power that it exercises, however, is never anything other than an 'action on actions'; actions that reshape the logics of individuation from one society to another, and from one social stratum to another, by conferring on them their truth and their historicity.

It is well known that it was indeed Foucault's aim to conceptualize 'the very historicity of forms of experience'.[189] This intellectual project is still a burning issue, so long as we take care to emphasize the concrete practices of appropriation of globalization that are constitutive of its subjection. Meanwhile, we can view as futile any attempt to identify a global 'human type', and as self-evident the 'moral' character of globalization when grasped at the level of its social basis.

6

The Global Techniques of the Body

The 'conducts of life' engendered by globalization, the 'types of human-ity' that are 'borne' by various different 'social strata' in this historical context, give rise, by definition, to practices of appropriation. For an ethos, or a habitus, is an activity of appropriation: a 'having with the value of being'.[1] Globalization then presents itself as 'an event of appro-priation constitutive of the event of existing'[2] and no longer as an event of dispossession. Still, we need to bear in mind the fact that this ethos is subjection. Man is the master of his creation, but appears as its slave, said Marx.[3] Only by emphasizing this paradox can we dismiss both the gloomy apprehension of globalization to which the heritage of the Frankfurt School condemns us, quick to denounce the commoditiza-tion of the world, and the playful interpretation proposed by one type of postmodernist anthropology, according to which 'where there is consumption there is pleasure, and where there is pleasure there is agency'.[4] Marxist cynicism still remains the best introduction to the global experience of subjectivation.

> Man appropriates his integral essence in an integral way, as a total man. All his *human* relations to the world – seeing, hearing, smelling, tasting, feeling, thinking, contemplating, sensing, wanting, acting, loving – in short, all the organs of his individuality, like the organs which are directly communal in form, are in their *objective* approach or in their *approach to the object* the appropriation of that object. This appropriation of *human* reality, their approach to the object, is the *confirmation of human reality*. It is human *effectiveness* and human *suffering*, for suffering, humanly con-ceived, is an enjoyment of the self for man.[5]

If we are to understand global governmentality as an encounter between techniques of domination over others and techniques of the self, we need first to analyse the relation to merchandise: its consumption, but also the 'techniques of the body'[6] which consumption activates without our generally being aware of the fact. It is now accepted that these practices of 'material culture' – as the hallowed expression has it (but could we imagine a 'culture' that would not be 'material'?) – are about creation, rather than simply reproduction: daily life is something to be invented in a personal way.[7] Thus 'things matter',[8] and they matter even more than the way they are used, which needs to be analysed in itself: things form a repertoire which users draw on tactically, forming their own sentences from a pre-existing vocabulary and syntax.[9] Consumption, even mass consumption, is by virtue of this a factor of individuation.[10] As an ad for the eau de toilette 'Allure' from Chanel puts it, 'Allure Makes the Man'. Thus Daniel Miller speaks of 'objectification' to designate this process by which one finds self-realization in the objects that one acquires and consumes[11] – or indeed that one transmits from generation to generation.[12]

Merchandise and subjectivation

Material culture is a vehicle of subjectivation in so far as it contributes to the constitution of moral subjects and the production of social relations. This is evident in the case of habitat, a principal site of the memory, creative imagination, distinction, fabrication, and reproduction of family relations, social life and exclusion, demarcating the spheres of private and public, defining intimacy, modesty and purity, social success and personal fulfilment.[13] In this respect, it is the first matrix of the moral economy to which we 'belong'. After all, don't people say that houses have a soul?

Likewise, food – and more particularly certain ingredients such as sugar, alcohol, stimulants and, in bygone days, spices – imply a self-relation, the conception one has of one's body, the way one represents one's aesthetic and one's desire, as well as one's identification with a social milieu thanks to the machinery of distinction, and to an ethnic, religious or national community by means of taboos and the way food is prepared. Thus it comes with a strong set of moral,[14] but also aesthetic, connotations: cookery is an art, almost an erotic art. The worldwide saga of the great French chefs demonstrates that its exercise intervenes at the intersection of individual venture and collective experience. It simultaneously rests on its commoditization and on the pleasure, both personal and social, that it procures. It depends on, and exists in a state of tension with, local territory, the national sphere and the big wide world of globalization. The chef is one of the 'human types' of globalization: as a capitalist entrepreneur, reliant on the bank, he dispenses dreams and enjoyments; as a man of money, he erects gastronomy into an ethos and a 'vocation' (*Beruf*), as a national hero, he waves the flag of his part of the world and travels the place of the planet from Tokyo to New York; as a universal (and how!) legatee of cultural memory, he is a creator; while despising income taxes, he doesn't refrain from dreaming up a dinner for the French President; in his broken English he defends the idiosyncratic identity of French culture, but adopts exotic flavours; as a magician of the ephemeral, he gives it a fixed form in frozen dishes. The epic of French cuisine alone is an example of subjectivation in globalization and its relation with the body and merchandise.

Nonetheless, technological innovations and the most common consumer products also have a considerable degree of elasticity that simultaneously authorizes the individuation of their users or consumers and their social participation: as Marx comments, the only intelligible language we speak is the language of our objects as they relate to one another.[15] Studies on the spread of the telephone or the commoditization of tupperware boxes in the United States have thus confirmed that the world of merchandise and technology was the devoted servant of being-in-society, rather than its implacable adversary. It reproduces and reshapes relations of kinship, friendship, sex or gender instead of levelling them off or segmenting them by condemning the consumer to 'disaffiliation'.[16]

The effective use of merchandise also implies its cultural and social 'authentification' in the dimension of the *imaginaire*, as happened with the Orientalist vogue of the nineteenth century and the subsequent trade in Asian craft objects or curios, in which Sindhi merchants specialized from the 1860s onwards, first in Egypt, with the development of tourism, then at the interface of the Far East and the main places of transit, vacation or residence in the imperial or global market, especially in the Canaries, Gibraltar, Panama and the Caribbean.[17] Consumption can even be accompanied by its poetic exaltation and sexualization, as witness the work of the anonymous and volunteer rhymers who celebrated the Congo Soap made by the Établissements Vaissier Frères de Roubaix, between 1880 and 1900:

> When my mouth on your mouth
> Gives you a burning kiss,
> When we roll on your bed
> In intoxicating bliss,
> It's the Congo I can savour,
> When my mouth is on your mouth.[18]

Capitalism rests on the interweaving of desire, exploitation and violence as Marx perceived, long before Freud, and that he summed up as the process whereby one person fleeces another while procuring pleasure for that other.[19] Thus, at the turn of the millennium, the fashion for 'glamour', as the rap suburbs of Los Angeles have relaunched it, is titillating the senses of the consumer, and quite happily indulges in exaggeration and vulgarity,[20] and *IDEAT*, a 'lifestyle magazine' that deals with 'deco trends, fashion mind, passion culture!', has given itself a subtitle that is utterly unambiguous: 'There is plenty here to give you pleasure.'

The specialists of distribution have been deliberately playing this card for the past twenty years or so, and are putting their money on the 're-enchantment of bodily activity and commercial spaces' via 'fun shopping' and 'retailtainment'. 'Warehousing' must to their minds be a source of hedonistic and playful gratification. Lush, the British cosmetics chain, has opened *Cosmic Delis*, organized on the model of 'old-style' cheese shops or groceries, in which beauty products are partly manufactured on the spot by saleswomen dressed in overalls and sold in the form of food products, in any shape or form, in small pots or tomes of cheese. As two researchers from the École supérieure de commerce de Paris comment: 'By trying to give an extra meaning to the meanings that cosmetics usually generate, the probability of purchase is increased, and by transporting the customer into such an original universe, he or she is given an experience that makes the high prices more acceptable.'[21] Conversely, 'the success of shops giving discount or hard discount comes from a dramatization of . . . disenchantment'.[22] When confronted by this lumpen-competition and the challenges of e-commerce, shopping malls transform themselves into 'spaces of conviviality and desire', where shop signs enable their customers – sorry, their 'visitors' – an 'unforgettable life experience', and where the act of selling (and buying) is set up as an 'art of living', supported by restaurants, hairdressing and massage salons and crèche facilities.[23] Malls such as those of Pentagon City in Washington, of Bloomington in Minnesota, of West Edmonton in the state of Alberta, Canada, of Dubai in the United Arab Emirates, or, more modestly, of the Sénart Square in the Paris region, are all famous examples, and they enjoy a huge vogue. The West Edmonton Mall is the foremost tourist site in Canada, beating even the Niagara Falls, and the computer supermarket Surcouf, in avenue Daumesnil, Paris, is the fourth such site in France. The London sales (and, increasingly, the Paris sales too) are a high point of European leisure life, while every year the Dubai Shopping Festival attracts some 2.8 million visitors, who are treated to parades, fireworks, lotteries and, of course, special offers.[24]

More commonly, the consumer indulges in a weekly (or even daily) 'fun shop', making his purchase in the supermarkets, meeting friends there and 'chilling out', like the 'mall rats' of Moscow.[25] As one thing leads to another, the shopping mall becomes a 'new urban space', 'one of the few places where a real social mix still exists', declares

Jean-Michel Silberstein, the CEO of the National Centre for Shopping Malls. This is confirmed by the sociologist Samuel Bordreuil:

> It is a space that brings together groups belonging to at least three gen-
> erations, a wider spread than one finds in many other urban spaces, or
> spaces where urban people hang out. There is a real presence of the
> 'seniors' in particular, but also of children who find themselves much
> less 'out of place' there than in other urban spaces.

As an extension, or even substitute form, of the city, the shopping mall now offers, apart from administrative or public services (such as electric and gas showrooms and post offices), various games, artistic activities or shows.[26]

Finally, hedonism becomes the foremost motivation or pretext for frequenting a shop, where you play a role for others and yourself, where, from adolescence onwards, you are initiated into the world of merchandise by cruising the shelves with bands of girlfriends, where you look after your body in 'beauty spaces'. In America and Europe, spas and healthcare facilities are becoming more and more numerous in big shops, perfumeries or ready-to-wear stores.[27]

But it is probably in the districts of Omotesando, Roppongi, Aoyama or Shibuya in Tokyo that the theatre of consumption is at once the most refined and the most playful. Here, the big luxury brands are opening commercial spaces the design of which they entrust to architects, artists, graphic designers or other famous names in the world of design: Jun Aoki for Louis Vuitton in Omotesando and Roppongi Hills; Jacques Herzog and Pierre de Meuron for the epicentre of Prada in Aoyama; Ettore Sottsas, Ron Arad, Toyo Ito, Andrea Branzi, Sol LeWitt, Louise Bourgeois or Takeshi Murakami for the layout and decoration of 'Planet 66' (roku-roku), the 'city within the city' that the magnate Minotoru Mori set up in Roppongi Hills.[28] These places, with their extremely sophisticated minimalist decor, are designed to provide the backdrop for a 'selling ceremony', to use the expression of Yves Carcelle, the president of Louis Vuitton,[29] which is aimed at a feminine clientele avid for famous, high-quality products, as well as for impeccable service. The presentation of the items, the body language of the personnel, the wrapping – all are extraordinarily stylish, and the after-sales services are staggering (Hermès employs seven fine leather craftsmen for this purpose) and become more and more personalized.[30]

The passion that Japanese women show for imported quality bags and shoes can be partly explained by socio-economic reasons. Young women generally continue to live with their parents before getting married and so can spend the majority of their wages on consumer goods. In addition, they are staying single for longer than before, and are even giving up the idea of getting married so that they can preserve their freedom; furthermore, they usually have only one or two children, which means they can soon return to the pleasures of consumption. As a consequence of this, the acquiring of luxury products does not have anything like the same social meaning that it has in Western Europe. Specialists speak of a market of some fifty million potential buyers, as opposed to five in France. It is not rare for a girl from the Land of the Rising Sun to have several big brand handbags, while her French equivalent would find it unthinkable to have even one: a third of Japanese women possess a Louis Vuitton, and 20 per cent of them a Gucci.[31]

Here, however, we need to remember the irreducible factor of the happiness procured by the contemplation or acquisition of merchandise, its reinterpretation in line with native codes of play, its display for the purposes of seduction, competition or ostentation. How else can we understand the fetishistic cult that the Japanese have developed for Vuitton bags, one that is the pretext for several mythical tales, in which the fine leather craftsman from the Ardèche copied Japanese motifs, or the Crown Prince Hiro Hito himself had set his heart on a suitcase made by the said craftsman during a stay in Paris? Be this as it may, visiting the elegant boutiques of Omotesando or Roppongi Hills on a Saturday afternoon is a cultural habit of teenagers and young couples. The way they dress is an opportunity to show an often exuberant creativity that defies the canons of western elegance and assumes the form of a real movement in popular culture, or at least a middle-class culture, as in the very 'in' district of Shibuya: the women known as 'Shibuyettes' have set the tone for a transnational, picturesque and provocative street fashion, whose temple is block '109', not far from the J.R. station, which is all the rage in Asia, and which has been taken over by the juvenile style *kawaï* (cute, childish). Likewise, women love to meet up at midday in restaurants where they promote a 'crossover' cuisine and the consumption of wine. Here as elsewhere, the practices of material culture consume forms of cultural assertion that resort to the symbolic resources of extraversion – here perhaps more than elsewhere, in so far as 'strategic hybridization' has long been a key element in Japanese national identity.[32] Carrefour has learned this lesson the hard way, by placing local products on its shelves, as dictated by its traditional approach to foreign markets: its clientele in Tokyo stayed away in droves, since they had been expecting imported products.[33] On the other hand, the so-called 'entertainment' restaurants of the UG chain Growing Up owe their phenomenal success to their outrageously exotic decors: the Buttu Trick Bar, with its monumental meditating Buddha; the Elephant Café, with its neo-Thai style; Bobby's Café, a parody of Europe as seen by Americans; the Aladdin, with its Arab atmosphere; and, above all, the Christon café in the night-life district of Kabukicho, in Shinjuku, 'a restaurant with the image of a church', which Philippe Pons describes in these terms:

> In the filtered light shed by the candles on the tables and mural wall lights held by chubby little cherubs, the decor appears to be that of a church. One whole side of the room is occupied by a majestic altar in gilded wood, six feet high, with a statue of the Christ of compassion with candles burning before him. On either side are alcoves with big colourful wooden statues of Mary and the saints. Here, a tabernacle; there, an embroidered chasuble lit up in a display case; and over there, a private salon decorated with a mural painting of the Last Supper; and then there are other display cases in which are shown statues of biblical characters and religious objects, plaster figurines representing the Holy Family. . . If you look up, you can see crosses hanging from the chandeliers and huge gargoyles holding up the ceiling. At the entrance, the menu looks like a Bible on a lectern.

The chain justifies itself thus:

> It was never our intention to shock anyone. We simply wanted to innovate on the style of the western restaurant by creating an unexpected decor. Priests have told us that, in the final analysis, it's just like for a wake; you eat and drink, and God would be happy to see young people having fun![34]

By breaking away from neo-Taylorist productivism, the 'ten lost years' of the economic crisis have paradoxically boosted this society's capacity for cultural imagination, and especially that of its younger generation, 'who skilfully wed inventiveness, underground, commercialization and new media'.[35]

Even better, e-commerce, throughout the world, is deterritorializing the hedonism of the market. The world leader for Internet auctions – eBay – which has thirty-seven million active users, thus makes the spirit of collection and the spirit of lucre work for it, in the name of shared pleasure: 'I started just for fun, and I go on for fun, it's like playing shops. . . . It's all in the suspense, the pleasure of seeing the money rise at a dizzying pace', explains one retired Belgian woman, now making the most of the Internet niche for contemporary Japanese knickknacks – erotic mangas, dolls or Buddhas – that her son, who has settled in Tokyo, brings back for her.[36] And Arjun Appadurai has suggestively shown how the 'huge economy of gifts in the United States' leads the consumer to fantastical practices.

> Reading the gift catalogue proceeds from what I consider to be the 'pornography of recent capitalism', in so far as the catalogues are often read merely to sense the intense pleasure of objects (and bodies) that they

enable you to gaze on. Above all, they enable individual subjects to imagine presents they might give or receive from other people in an economy that might be called an economy of 'prosthetic' gifts, in which the number of relations imagined and evoked in the secrecy of one's living room far exceeds the real presents given by real people to other real people. Of course, the existence of a huge real market of gifts lying in the market place gives a firmer base to the prosthetic, libidinous market of imagined relations and possible pleasures. Looking for presents always has this quality, but the world of gift catalogues has [a] secret, pornographic dimension, like other contexts such as the teleshopping networks where you can buy from home.[37]

Nonetheless, the erotic pleasure of the act of buying, often masturbatory in type, excludes neither frustration nor theft and its repression. 'When a patrol comes across a *beur rmiste* all kitted out in Ralph Lauren and with Weston shoes, they are surely entitled to entertain some doubts', a duty policeman wisely points out; he works in a working-class suburb of Toulouse, where a black market economy based on theft and resale is flourishing, and where youth riots break out from time to time.[38] Shopping malls, the 'garnisons-entrepôts'[39] of industrial societies, are under constant surveillance, which is delegated to private security firms, or even, in some countries, to criminal gangs, in line with the logic of 'discharge', and they are in this respect one of the social institutions on which global 'governmentality' rests, somewhere between pleasure and coercion. They are also fragments of public space in which social groups can measure up each other, in symbolic and sometimes physical violence; the places where hatred (as in the film *La Haine*) is just as prevalent as friendlier forms of social life.[40]

The globalization and appropriation
of merchandise

It is a truism, but it is still worth emphasizing, that globalization, in changing the scale of capitalism, consisted in the vast spread (and thus the appropriation) of merchandise. The clientele of the Établissements Vaissier Frères saw it clearly:

> Before embarking on board the Equator
> For the state of Congo of which he is the Governor
> The illustrious de Brazza slipped into his case
> The precious agent that charms and civilizes:
> The soap, I mean, of the famous inventor.[41]

The globalization of goods and products; the globalization of their techniques of production and use: this twofold phenomenon characterized the expansion of international exchanges from before the foundational nineteenth century. Foreign objects often entered countries earlier than did foreigners themselves.[42] One need think only of the trade in spices, stimulants, narcotics or sugar cane to grasp immediately that the transformations of 'material civilization' (Fernand Braudel) were at the heart of processes of subjectivation, for example by giving rise to new forms of social life, by arousing furious moral polemics or by modifying the representations and practices of relations between genders.[43]

The Industrial Revolution and its consequences naturally intensified and broadened the mediation of merchandise and technology in the processes of globalization.[44] But this mediation was constitutive of generalized mutual social interaction, instead of being its negation. It was part of the constitution of 'moral subjects' through many different 'practices of the self' and the way that different 'conducts of life' were made an everyday reality. An Iranian joke sums the situation up nicely. It makes fun of the propensity shown by the people who live in the city of Abadan to make Ray-Ban glasses one of their emblems of identity: 'The Iraqis took me prisoner', says one. 'During my detention, I underwent physical tortures and psychological tortures. I was beaten. That wasn't so bad. The worst was when they took off my Ray-Bans and smashed them in front of my eyes.'[45] There could be no better expression of the way subjectivation, however local, passes via consumption, however global.

It was mainly because of merchandise and its relation to the body that the colonial moment was a moment of subjectivation. This was true of the millenarian movements of the nineteenth century or the start of the twentieth century, which were at times an eschatological expectancy, on the model of the Cargo cult, and at times a massive rejection of the white man's merchandise. The same was true of the imaginary developments of globalization; the 'sea brides' of the Aru archipelago and the African Mami Wata, whom we have already encountered in a previous chapter, govern its Faustian acquisition, just as the male witch consents to devour those close to him, invisibly, so as to procure it. It is true, above all, of Christianity. Conversion to the Christian faith was, inseparably, a way of joining the material culture of which it was the harbinger. Either it was imposed by missionaries, in particular when it came to clothes, in the name of a certain conception of modesty, as in the Pacific islands and sub-Saharan Africa, where people had hitherto gone naked. Or the faithful themselves embraced it because they saw it as a means of reversing (to their own benefit) the lines of social inequality, an opportunity to succeed economically, or quite simply a matter of desire, since, as Marx says, every product is a bait for the other person and his money and every need, real or virtual, is a weakness that will draw the fly to the glue.[46] From this point of view,

Christianization indubitably contributed to the universal exploitation of man's social essence,[47] by establishing this equation between religious practice and the commoditization of exchange, and by placing it at the heart of social relations between natives and foreigners or among the natives themselves.

The act of believing contrived to become a synonym for receiving or buying an article of goods, and the art of preaching became akin to the art of being the most generous with one's gifts or the best equipped to compete in business. In the Aru archipelago, a man explained to an anthropologist how great his perplexity had been in the 1970s: Muslims had told people to join them, as had Protestants, trying everything in their power: only under Van Lith, a Catholic missionary, had this become possible. Van Lith captured people's hearts with crates of clothes and hand-outs of trousers, skirts, shirts, sweaters and oil.[48] The gift was always an element in the 'contract of implantation' of missionary stations, which could not fail to leave certain preachers feeling uneasy: 'The people seem really pleased to see us coming, but their thoughts are fixated more on the fabrics and glass jewellery than on the Word of God,' complained the pastor Arthur Grandjean, in Mozambique.[49]

But over and above the mere strategy of seduction represented by the distribution of gifts to the flock one hoped to conquer, a whole pastoral tradition had built up an equivalence between the development of trade and the spreading of the Christian faith.[50] Merchandise in itself was a vector of civilization and a virtuous (or, more precisely, Victorian and bourgeois) lifestyle.[51] Preaching and trade thus went together, not without some ambiguity, even if the missionaries generally abstained (but not systematically) from selling items such as firearms, munitions and alcoholic drinks. Here or here, the men of God indulged all the more easily in the exchange of merchandise in that they benefited from customs exemptions or dispensations from the usual rules on the part of the colonial authorities, and created trading companies, following the example of the Mission of Basel. The pastoral tour of duty became a mercantile expedition, as in the Mission philafricaine du Suisse Chatelain, in Angola, at the start of the twentieth century: its 'missionary chariots' dispensed 'the "good news" to the crowds which would cluster round the wagon for trade', and its 'traffic will attract around the evangelist thousands of blacks who would never come simply to hear evangelical songs, and even less for any sort of preaching whatsoever':

> After announcing our arrival with blasts on the horn, or rather the *Urihorn*, like our old Swiss friends from the Waldstätten, I immediately unwrapped my cheap junk and started to call for maize, beans, flour, manioc and sweet potatoes. My junk included, as far as possible,

everything that the natives could desire, except for schnapps. So as to get 50 francs' worth of maize and beans, you have to go for a discount (and even more) in merchandise. There's no harm in my giving you an idea, just this once. This time I had: sugar, salt, oil, dried meat, soap, padlocks, locks, spades, hoes, axes, brass wire, traps for rats and wild beasts, knifes at various prices, pen-knifes, forks, spoons, plates, cups, pots, bowls, gold-plated nails, shirt and jacket buttons, ten kinds of glass beads, rings, necklaces, ear rings, belts, cotton fabrics and handkerchiefs of every colour, blankets, shirts, trousers, jackets, hats, powder, lead, capsules, flint, medicines, paper, mirrors, needles, thread, matches, bracelets, mouth organs, and the 'et caetera' that I can't remember just now: a complete bazaar, as you can see.[52]

Still, we need to understand that the missionaries were not simply indulging in cynical utilitarianism. They instrumentalized merchandise, admittedly, in order to place it at the service of their religious plans, riding on the supposedly infantile cupidity of their neophytes. In this respect they were being faithful to the old adage which says that the Lord moves in mysterious ways. But they felt some compunction about doing this, and they found it very difficult to get the right balance between their desire to bring their flock to the point where they could share the universal petty bourgeois lifestyle and their irritation at seeing them desert their African identity so as to espouse the trinkets of urban modernity. Thus, some of them waxed indignant that their pupils wished to wear shorts rather than the so-called traditional fabric.[53] In addition, most missionaries themselves 'belonged' to this Victorian vision of civilization, respectability, decency, 'Christian providence' and its material manifestation (Christian welfare). Their fetishistic attachment to glass and to optical goods – especially to mirrors, which they gave as presents and sold left, right and centre – betrayed their blind adherence to the ideology, the 'conduct of life' and the material culture of industrial globalization at the end of the nineteenth century.[54] In short, conversion to the Scriptures was at the same time the appropriation of the 'Enlightenment' of the West – to use the Yoruba notion of *olaju*[55] – and of the material lifestyle which accompanied this Enlightenment in terms of clothing, architecture, bodily hygiene, medicine and, soon thereafter, diet. It was a way of seeing 'the everyday as epiphany', 'an epic of the ordinary', as Jean and John Comaroff put it.[56] In extreme cases, conversion to Christianity required possessing western merchandise – so Christianity itself was produced via consumption.[57] And the 'human type' that it thus promoted occupied, at least in sub-Saharan Africa, a decisive place within the process of globalization, in so far as Christian elites tended to merge with the nationalist elites who governed the state.[58]

These days, Christianity still has a close link with merchandise. The Word is a 'Prosperity Gospel', especially when it is delivered by charismatic movements that no longer revere the virtues of evangelical poverty, value individual success and set themselves up as real enterprises in the hands of the businessmen of faith.[59] West African Pentecostalism, for instance, 'defetishizes' merchandise by laundering its possession.[60] It demands loud and long that it be included in globalization, since it wants to be 'international' and 'global' much more than 'African'; it legitimizes the consumption of imported goods, which represents the main form of the region's participation in planetary exchanges, if we take into account the collapse or stagnation of its productive activities and the fall in its exports, but which is also the object of an obstinate moral suspicion. Is not the possession of money and foreign objects always potentially a sign of witchcraft, especially when it comes with an aura of mystery? Is the consumption of others not always, in itself, an action that participates equally in the world of money and of technology, as is proved day after day by the magical multiplication of banknotes by various *marabouts* (or presidents, skilled in the ways of hyper-inflation!), the exploitation of zombies on the plantations of Mount Koupé in Cameroon, the way Liberian fighters imagine their enemies' hearts as their 'motors', which it is a good idea to ingest so as to 'armour' themselves, or the motorized, mechanized, electrified vampires of East Africa?[61] For Pentecostalists, prayer extracts capitalism from the disquieting world of the invisible and makes it possible for its material culture to be appropriated in a permissible form. *Mutatis mutandis*, pilgrimage plays the same role for Muslims, in so far as it is also an act of consumption: there is no *hajj* without purchases, and so without a trip to the bazaar or the travel agency, following the classical formula of 'pilgrimage and tourism', which indeed are the words explicitly adopted by certain administrative forms at customs or immigration services.[62]

Nonetheless, consumption remains a highly contested and polemical moral issue. In Africa, as we have seen, it appears to be a prologue to the subjectivation of the young man as he is transformed into a mature and dignified adult, via the initiatory ritual of emigration or the adventure of being a pioneer. It is essentially through consumption – whether this be ostentatious, redistributive, festive, or conjugal and familial – that the individual gains access to maturity and masculinity, as is attested by the 'diggers' and '*Sapeurs*' of the Congo, the *ghettomen* of the Ivory Coast, or, on a more austere level, Muslim traders and expatriate workers.[63] Consumption has its own value and suffices to demarcate the respective spheres of social success or failure. As one Burkinabé migrant states, 'When I came back from the Ivory Coast, I stopped at Ouagadougou to buy my bike, a six-battery radio, and some suits. That's what we were after: that's all it is.'[64]

The dramatic corollary of this orientation towards the fulfilment of material desires is the terrible degradation inflicted on the illegal immigrant brutally expelled from Europe without even a bag of personal effects. One result has been real mutinies on board the charter flights requisitioned for this purpose by the French police, and violent confrontations on their landing at Bamako airport, not to mention the suicides and shipwrecks of individual travellers. The appropriation of merchandise also seems to be one of the moral mainsprings of the mobilization of young fighters in civil wars such as those of Somalia, Liberia or Sierra Leone. In any case, it contributes to the 'aesthetic of existence' of armed fighters, always very careful about the way they dress and greedy for signs of distinction borrowed from 'global' fashion.[65] Finally, the desire (or need) for merchandise underlies the rush for commodities that causes such turmoil in Africa – the fact that smuggling is so common, as are customs fraud and transient pavement sellers, is to some extent a homage on the part of vice to the virtue of trade. The appetite for material goods also at regular intervals inspires the military – or even ordinary citizens – to raid towns. The systematic and festive pillaging of Kinshasa, in September 1991, still constitutes a prime example. But one cannot disguise the recurrence of this practice of 'door-to-door vaccination' – to use the grim expression of the aptly-named campaign to 'Wipe the slate clean' in the Congo, in 2002–3 – in most sub-Saharan countries, the minute political circumstances lend themselves to it.[66]

The fact remains that, at the same time, other social movements reject (often violently) the possession of consumer goods of western origin, following the example of certain rebellions which execute their owners or users.[67] Furthermore, ancestors forbid this or that product for a variety of reasons, and the way in which the invisible realm is imagined interferes with the way the material culture of capitalism is envisaged: the first tins introduced into Rhodesia were suspected of containing human meat taken from workers in mines, factories and farms, or indeed from the victims of European medicine.[68] In addition, the massive production of fakes or counterfeit money subverts the order of merchandise.

This order is thus clearly the field of sharp conflicts of subjectivation in globalization, and these conflicts are not found only in sub-Saharan societies or in poverty-stricken economies. Maoist China turned material culture into a thoroughly political question by subjecting its population to a very strict regime of prescriptions and interdicts: any transgression of these was severely punished. The 'Dengist' reforms, the prospect of belonging to the WTO and the subsequent rise in imports have rapidly propelled China towards a consumption of merchandise in which practices of extraversion are commonplace. These days, a rite of passage such as marriage is happy to borrow from the western repertory of wedding-related activities, which sometimes leads to tensions with the Party, or even with the religious authorities in the case of the Hui, the Muslims.[69] In Shanghai, Villa d'Roma (*sic*), the first Chinese agency for pseudo-Christian weddings, thus offers different combinations of 'ready-to-marry' ceremonies for young 'with-it' couples, costing from 730 to 7,000 euros and celebrated in a chapel, 'a jewel of ecclesiastical fakery' – with the exception that the most blatantly Christian signs have had to be suppressed following intervention on the part of the Bureau of Religious Affairs.[70] More generally speaking, items such as luxury cigarettes or expensive liquors, and certain leisure activities of foreign origin such as bowling, are still objects of mistrust in the infinitely variable climate of the denunciation of 'corruption', even though they also have their place in the formation and hierarchization of business networks (*guanxi*).[71]

In other climes, in Afghanistan, the Taliban have deployed a nit-picking and iconoclastic zeal towards products or appliances judged to be 'non-Islamic', thereby pushing to an extreme a religious susceptibility that had already been demonstrated by Iranian revolutionaries at the start of the 1980s or the more radical militants of the Islamic Salvation Front in Algeria. And in India, Bal Thackeray, the leader of the ultranationalist party of Shiv Sena, made this martial-sounding declaration in 1995: 'We will not allow Kentucky Fried Chicken to penetrate Maharashtra. . . . We will not let our people be poisoned and succumb to cancer.'[72] In the same period, a rumour was going round the country that statues of the elephant god were drinking the milk offered to them, and this unleashed a real collective fever among devotees or the curious. Nonetheless, it did not escape the notice of certain of the latter that 'Ganesh preferred to drink milk rather than Coca-Cola'.[73]

In the so-called consumer societies themselves, consumption can sometimes turn out to be polemical, especially when it is linked with globalization. The individual or collective appropriation of brand names, especially among teenagers and young adults, can be a means of social self-affirmation, individuation, cultural creativity and even political protest, as was once the case in the Soviet Union or the popular democracies, but it is also something that can lead to discredit or relativization among part of the public, as is currently the case in Asia.[74] The reception of foreign mass media images, thanks to satellite television, video, the Internet or the good old cinema, can cause irritation or scandal to sovereignists, culturalists or the religious. Everyone remembers how the installation of the first satellite dishes in the suburbs of metropolitan France aroused a certain anxiety in the middle of the 1990s: could the Republic – '*une*', '*indivisible*' and '*laïque*' – allow itself to cultivate a double, televisual allegiance amongst its immigrants?[75] After all, the French fiercely defend their 'cultural exception' against American invasion. But the governments of Malaysia, Singapore and China also keep a watchful eye on the preservation of their 'identity' and their 'values', which are supposedly 'Asiatic', while the Japanese have compared the impact of satellite television on their society to the sudden appearance of Admiral Perry's fleet.[76] For different reasons – cultural, social, political or dietary – Coca-Cola, the Big Mac, Nike trainers, audio-visual products and the Islamic veil have all become central and fraught themes in the public debate on the effects of globalization.

McDonald's, the paragon of planetary food provision, even has the privilege of being the target of an annual protest campaign, every 16 October, in particular in the United States and Australia. In this latter country, the firm, which controls 42 per cent of the fast-food market and is developing a highly aggressive commercial policy by contributing to the private financing of schools and offering 'happy meals' to the most deserving blond-haired blue-eyed kids, at the cost of an inexorable rise in their obesity, is arousing increasing criticism on the part of public opinion and the authorities. Citizens are even mobilizing in an attempt to stop new restaurants opening and are endeavouring to promote Mac-Free Zones. José Bové is clearly not the only person to resist, and his publicity stunts need to be seen in their effective context: in Europe, France is the country where the chain registers its best results![77] Likewise, the clothing and footwear industries, accused of exploiting the Third World labour force, are the object of boycott appeals on the part of NGOs that have an anti-globalization sensibility. And the Bratz doll – made by the Irano-American Isaac Larian – which can be found in Hispanic, white, black, mixed-race or Jewish versions and has dethroned Barbie, with 150 million models being sold in 2003, has caused a scandal. 'Bratz dolls seem to live on the pavement. They are provocative figures who seem to be waiting for their pimp who must be somewhere around in his limo, snorting coke', moaned the *Daily Telegraph* – an opinion echoed by feminists: 'My generation had enough problems with Barbie and all the social conservatism she represented. Now here are we with Bratz, who loves to go skiing in cut-off shorts with her navel on display. What kind of message do you think Bratz is sending our daughters?'[78]

So the globalization of consumption is riven by conflicts. However, the splits that result cannot be reduced to a simple alternative between the adepts of globalization and its opponents. The Catholic Church does not condemn the mobile phone, but just its sacramental or religious use. Reacting to the increasingly frequent use of the short message service for penitential purposes, the secretary-general of the Episcopal Conference of the Philippines deems that 'technology does of course enable one to gain time, but in no case should it lead to the disappearance of human contact, the seal of confession . . . no one can pray, or fast, or give alms by SMS.'[79]

A consumer can reject a brand for political reasons, while remaining faithful to a certain type of product. After their Revolution, the Iranians continued to be great devotees of Coca-Cola, of which they drink different ersatz versions, since there is no trading agreement between the firm in Atlanta and local manufacturers. Their Zam-Zam has contrived to make a noteworthy breakthrough in the Gulf following the intervention of the United States in Afghanistan and Iraq and the alignment of the Bush administration on the policies of Ariel Sharon in the Near East: Arab consumers were keen to express their disapproval by giving up Coca-Cola, but not soda. A French-Tunisian, Taoufik Mathlouti, plunged into the breach, launching his Mecca-Cola, stating that he would give 10 per cent of profits to charities and 10 per cent to activities in favour of Palestinian children.[80] He was rapidly imitated by Qibla-Cola Company.[81] A few months later, right in the middle of a diplomatic and strategic wrangle between Washington and Ankara, the Turks flocked to buy Cola-Turka, adverts for which used New York images for the evident purpose of identification, with plenty of jeans and cow-boy hats in evidence, at a time when – and this shows up the ironies of the marketplace – Coca-Cola was setting its ads in the centre of Istanbul, against a background of Turkish music.[82] So we can apply what Roger Chartier says about 'intellectual objects' to merchandise: 'It is . . . the relations to objects that constitute the latter, in a specific way that follows assemblages and distributions that are always highly individual.'[83] It is also in this sense that Michel de Certeau spoke of consumption as 'another production'.[84] One immediate corollary is that seeing the globalization of merchandising as a process that imposes cultural uniformity, in the form of the 'Americanization' or 'McDonaldization' of the world, is a huge mistake.

Merchandise and the reinvention of difference

No society holds a monopoly over the production of the objects or practices of consumption that set the tone for the whole planet when it comes to commercialized subjectivation or the commercialization of subjectivation. The domination of the United States is merely relative. The contribution which Europe has made to the globalization of material culture is far from negligible, in particular in the areas of haute couture, ready-to-wear garments, perfumery, cosmetics, food, design, furnishing, cars and tourism. The way that the consumption of wine, beer, certain liquors, espresso coffee, French bread and cheese has gradually become universal (to go no further than the most trivial aspects of everyday existence) is one symptom among others. At the 2002 finals, it was a team of three Japanese who won the fifth World Cup in baking at Villepinte, and the French came fourth (after the United States and Belgium), not even getting a place on the podium.[85] The Japanese are now at the cutting edge of innovation when it comes to bread – they have become devotees of the stuff, even if they do flavour it to their own particular taste, for example adding cuttlefish ink. And the declining fortunes of Beaujolais Nouveau, after thirty years of a wild success story in the export market, are due less to the global inadequacy of this particular plonk than to the worldwide increase in the number of vineyards and the ensuing global overproduction (of the order of forty million hectolitres): French wine is a victim of the seductive impact it had on the market and what Catholics would call its inculturation, not of the disaffection or cultural resistance of consumers on other continents.[86]

The influence of Japan is increasingly evident.[87] Apart from the role it has played in reinventing the motorbike, transforming the car and innovating in the field of electronics and photo accessories, its pop culture – a product of the world of mangas, video games, cartoons, pop music and TV soap operas – attests to the way it has become a trans-Asiatic reference point of subjectivation: the 'J-sense'. And this is now being addressed to westerners. Launched in 1974 as an 'inexpensive little gift that brings a smile to the lips and facilitates human relations', in the words of Sanrio, the 'Hello Kitty' kitten, for instance, has met with worldwide success, and its brand name is found in countless variants as the emblem of different objects or services. Shin-Chan pencils, Astro Boy and Pokemon are up there with it. Western businesses are drawing a lesson from this and, in turn, are playing on the J-sense to seduce the consumers of Asia or elsewhere: L'Oréal and Coca-Cola have both, in different Asian countries, sold products specially designed for the Japanese market; McDonald's has given away Hello Kitty models to its customers; Louis Vuitton has called in graphic artist Takeshi Murakami and reprised the theme of cherry trees in blossom in a spring collection called 'Cherry Blossom'.[88] Furthermore, what has been called Japan's 'return to Asia' in the 1990s is interwoven with the dynamism of other regional cultural poles and the way the relationship between Asia and the West is being reconfigured. From this point of view, Hong Kong occupies a key place, being a financial centre but also a major site of creativity in television, music and cinema, as well as a beacon of fashion. A singer such as Dick Lee, in search of 'WEAST' (a fusion of West and East), a director such as Wong Kar-wai, or an actor such as Leslie Cheung are among the most eloquent representatives of this pan-Asian globalization, in which the consumer finds both an appreciable proportion of his or her moral and aesthetic reference points and a cultural exemplification of 'flexible citizenship'.[89]

Even countries such as India or Egypt are not secondary emitters of global items. It is through their images that emigrants working in the Gulf experience globalization and constitute themselves as 'moral subjects' within it.[90] In Abu Dhabi, the Thuraya company, whose main shareholder is Etisalat, the public company for mobile telephones in the United Arab Emirates, has developed an original technology for satellite telephone links, that enables the user to link up to the terrestrial mobile phone networks when these cover the territory in which he or she is, and which automatically disables the apparatus when an excessive temperature threatens to melt its electronic circuits. It won a commercial victory during the Iraq war in 2003.[91] And the Oman group Zubeir Furnishing, whose workforce is largely Indian, stole a march on western operators on the markets for the furnishing of international hotels such as the George V in Paris and the Marriott hotels in the United Kingdom. As for Africa and Latin America, they have inspired several fashions in music and other audio-visual media, as well as clothes and food, which have been taken up across the world, especially in North America and Western Europe.

In short, the globalized world of merchandise is polymorphous and is affected by the same 'reverberation' effects that we previously detected in colonial empires. The commercial ventures of the Japanese cosmetics company Shiseido, which in the 1980s shouldered its way into the very exclusive club of worldwide brands, is a good example from this point of view. The business was founded in 1872 to promote western medicine in a country that was still dominated by Chinese medicine. Thanks to the help of Japanese artists who practised European techniques of painting, it imposed an original design that combined elements of Art Nouveau and Art Deco with the native style. One of these designers, Yamana Ayao, drew some of his inspiration from Aubrey Beardsley, who himself borrowed from the Japanese repertory of prints (*ukiyoe*). Art Nouveau in France was also derived from the vogue for things Japanese at the end of the nineteenth century. In the 1980s, Shiseido again drew on this history of cultural interaction by entrusting Serge Lutens with the task of renewing the brand style. With this aim in mind, the latter, boosted by his 'emotional kinship' with the business – in the words of its president, Fukuhara Yoshiharu – turned less towards its own syncretic tradition than towards the depiction of Japan in Roland Barthes's *Empire of Signs*. He thus managed to get first French, and later European, consumers to accept the idea that the brand was 'Japanese without being Japanese, and western without being western'. This marketing success drew on a whole century of intense artistic exchanges between the two countries.[92]

In addition, the consumption of global merchandise proceeds by creative derivation and the 'reinvention of difference'. However 'one-dimensional' they may be from the point of view of the messages they convey, information technologies are themselves the bearers of diversity. The Internet favours a polyglot world: it enables languages that are relatively little spoken to continue to be written down, now that they are free from the costs of paper and distribution.[93] The international chain CNN, a symbol of the cultural imperialism of the USA, broadcasts in twenty-two different versions, one of them in Turkish and two in German, and it is linguistically 'de-Americanized'.[94] Above all, the process whereby merchandise is appropriated by being consumed recreates that merchandise. Igor Kopytoff analyses the effectiveness of the process of commoditization in terms of 'the cultural biography of things', which is to some extent a way of making of it an 'event'.[95] The cultural biography of one and the same Mercedes Benz saloon will be different in Africa and in Germany, since the social act of acquiring it, the commercial relation between seller and buyer, the number and kind of passengers, the concrete way the car is used, and its maintenance, will not be the same in the two countries, let alone the state of the roads. The itinerary of a bottle of Guinness in Cameroon is quite different from that of its equivalent in Ireland.[96] As for Zimbabweans, they have long used toothpaste to soothe, staunch and protect their wounds, at the same time as using it to brush their teeth.[97] Over and above the illusion of uniformity engendered by the homogeneity and omnipresence of global brands, the consumption of their products is differentiated from one society to another, from one period to another, from one category of consumers to another. It is subject to enunciative practices.

Global firms themselves play, without a second thought, the card of 'glocalization' via the intermediary of the system of franchises. The managers of Coca-Cola, for instance, reject the accusation that is often laid against them of indulging in the 'Coca-colonization' of the planet.

> 'It's wrong because all the thing wants to do is to refresh you, and it is willing to understand your culture, to be meaningful to you and to be relevant to you. Why is that called Coca-colonization?'
> 'Because values are being imposed from somewhere external . . .'
> 'I don't think they are. I don't think that's true. I think that friendship was there, is there, and will be there forever. It was there before Coke. If Coke disappears, friendship will always be there. What Coke does is it treats friendship accordingly. In Japan, that means one kind of thing, and in Brazil, another. And Coke acknowledges those differences, but Coke stands for friendship. So, what's wrong with that? I mean, I don't think that that's an imposition of a value. I don't think that Coca-Cola projects. I think that Coca-Cola reflects.'[98]

Likewise, McDonald's, which now defines itself as a 'worldwide multilocal business', has started to adapt its hamburgers to the culinary habits or 'traditions' of some of its markets. In France, the firm that now promotes Asterix has, since 1997, included on its menu the McDeluxe, 'in French taste': it has a sauce with a base of 'old-style' mustard and pepper, instead of the usual sweet and sour seasoning, 113 grams of minced beef, a thicker slice of tomato, a slice of cheddar, fresh onions and, 'for the first time', a 'whole lettuce leaf, not one cut up into little pieces'.[99] Greek customers, in turn, are sold souvlaki-style hamburgers, and the Big Mac has a halal version in Muslim countries, a kosher version in Israel and a vegetarian variant in India. Only the French fries are universal![100]

The great dilemma in the marketing of global brands, in fact, lies in the decision whether to make a definite choice or to compromise between several possible market approaches. They can try to stick to their cultural or social particularities, or foreground the identity and the dreams proper to their society of origin, like Tommy Hilfiger, Polo Ralph Lauren, Wrangler or Marlboro, who endeavour to sell the American values and symbols of the Far West, the Deep South or New England, or indeed to claim a multicultural and multiracial universalism by flattering and pandering to the desires of a deterritorialized youth, like Levi's, Nike, Microsoft, Playstation or Benetton.

However, businesses are merely registering, in each case, this obvious truth stated by Michel de Certeau: consumers themselves weave the web of the meaning of what they buy. Frequently cited ethnological investigations have established the extent to which the appropriation of the most emblematic imported products of globalization – Daniel Miller speaks in terms of 'meta-merchandise'[101] – was not experienced in terms of the alienation or dispossession of identity and culture. Drinking Coca-Cola in Trinidad or eating a McDonald's in Eastern Asia does not mean surrendering one's specific identity to the hegemony of America.[102] This consists in being-in-society, in being in *your* society, and re-employing the repertory of commoditization for one's own ends and in accordance with one's own codes. As in the case, for example, of Greek families that use empty bottles of Coca-Cola to burn oil, in the little oratories that, along the roadsides, celebrate the memory of accident victims or give thanks for their survival. Just as economic and financial liberalization remains dependent on the political societies to which it is applied, so transnational mass consumption has its own particular historicity within each of them.

Claude Lévi-Strauss brought this out very forcefully in the case of the execution of Father Christmas by the children of Catholic youth clubs in Dijon, on 24 December 1951, on the instigation of Catholic authorities anxious to struggle against the 'paganization' of the 'feast of the Saviour's birth'. For the anthropologist, the unprecedented extent of this new ritual of Father Christmas was a 'direct result of the influence and the prestige of the United States of America'. Nonetheless, he immediately adds that usage extrapolates what was already there – in this case, rites of passage and of initiation and an ancient form of the cult of the dead.[103] These days, those who view Christmas with disfavour are to be found rather in the ranks of the anti-capitalist or anti-globalization extreme left, hostile to consumer society, than in the

Church. But for the majority of the French population, of whatever religious or ethnic origin, the festival, having once been pre-Christian or neo-Christian, seems to have become a national celebration of the family and of childhood, in a sort of potlatch of spending. And, for immigrants, it is the proof that they are indeed in France: 'A photo with Father Christmas is a symbolic photo of being in France', which is then sent 'to the folks back in the village', 'back home', as a shopkeeper from Sarcelles observes.[104]

Mutatis mutandis, the same applies to a product such as a McDonald's hamburger.[105] The historicity of its mass consumption, for example in eastern Asia, stems from the way that families have been restructured within the context of strong economic growth and opening up to the West, or indeed forming a hybrid composite with the West as in Hong Kong or Japan. McDonald's burgers provide busy city-dwellers, especially young people and women, with havens of peace and sociability that have little to do with the original concept of fast food. Of course, the meals are prepared quickly and delivered to the customers just as rapidly. Nonetheless, the latter take their time eating them. Students linger in McDonald's to chat or to work; women like meeting there, where they are safe from masculine predators and the collateral effects of alcohol consumption; children celebrate their birthdays there; yuppies ostentatiously frequent them; and lovers dine out in style there, in a corner of the restaurant that is generally reserved for them. The commercial space of the restaurant simultaneously becomes a place of social participation in public space, especially for women, who turn it into a place to go and socialize, or for students who can read there as if they were in a library, and also a place of practices that are usually associated with private space, especially for the children who have their parties there or for teenagers anxious to escape from the promiscuity of their cramped lodgings. As such, McDonald's is indeed a place in which 'moral subjects' come into being.

Aunty McDonald, a character created in Beijing to look after children, herself serves those whose birthday it is – they will previously have received, over the public announcement system, the personal congratulations of Uncle McDonald, in Chinese and in English. Children without siblings draw a sense of personal importance and gratitude from this. Likewise, the egalitarian character of the service (or rather the absence of service) and the food on offer allows one to avoid losing face. All the customers are treated equally, and the prices of the different meals on offer are sufficiently similar to exclude the risks of ostentatious competition when ordering, or of embarrassment when having to pay the bill. Finally, the chain offers conditions of hygiene, both in the selection and preparation of products and in the toilets, which are in themselves a real field of subjectivation, at least in Peking.

Karen Tranberg Hansen has shown how buying and wearing second-hand clothes imported from the West, thanks to the collaboration of charities and specialized commercial enterprises, support, in a country such as Zambia, self-formation and create an 'aesthetic of existence', here too in accordance with a logic of 'the reinvention of difference'. This is a question of much more than a mere cheap imitation of western fashions. Local cultural norms of decency and sexual decorum[106] intervene in the individual's choices as he ferrets around amid the bundles of clothes. So second-hand clothes are as much a matter of desire as of need. More generally, the incorporation of European clothes into the 'lifestyle' of Zambians was, right from the start, a way of conceptualizing their social status and their ethnic identification, i.e. their own 'belonging', in a critical relation with the West.[107]

This recourse to extraversion, which involves the purchase of 'new' clothes taken from bundles opened in situ, so as to avoid any suspicion of 'third-hand' second-hand clothes that have already been worn by Zambians,[108] is expressed in incongruous, baroque ways: men can decorate their outfits with women's clothes and, conversely, the latter do not hesitate to deck themselves out with items of masculine clothing. In short, 'the consumption of clothes constitutes a good observatory for examining the way young women and young men experiment with the possibilities and constraints of moving into their adult condition in a poor country such as Zambia'.[109] Second-hand clothes, like the 'gear' (sape) worn by Congolese people, give to those who select and wear them the power to imagine their social dignity and to seize their chance.

Merchandise and political subjectivation

Political subjectivation, in the strict sense of the term, itself resorts to the mediation of merchandise, and to this end globalization provides it with useful resources, both on the symbolic level and on the material level. In Turkey, the confrontation between secularists and Islamic democrats that I have already mentioned does not transcend material culture and its political economy. It adopts its forms and merges into them. Yael Navaro-Yashin goes so far as to maintain that secularist and Islamist identities in Turkey are manufactured products, although they are not naturally experienced as such, but as quasi-primordial identities.[110] In fact, the democratic-Islamic party of Tayyip Erdogan, the AKP, and the business milieus that are close to it, grouped together in the MÜSIAD, are to be found among the heirs (and the beneficiaries) of the period of deliberate liberalization presided over by Turgut Özal during the 1980s, who himself was close to the brotherhood of the Nakshibendi, and shared many of its ideas. So there is a 'green' capitalism, with its yuppies, directly integrated into industrial globalization and underlying the conservative and Islamic liberalism of the government for which the AKP now bears the electoral torch. One of its main productions is Islamic female apparel, with its different components, from the *pardösüs* in silk, an overcoat which with women students cover themselves, to the different varieties of scarf such as the *türban*. Now the Islamic veil, the *pardösüs*, and the Islamic, 'covered' woman (*tesettür*) proceed from the order of merchandise. They give rise to effects of fashion (*moda*), whatever the pious traders may say. They are presented at the time of *defile*. They constitute a market. They have their own commercial brands. And, in fact, they are commercialized: on the informal market of the Topkapi district, in Istanbul, whose modesty is in contradistinction to the pride of the shopping malls which spread during the 1980s, in accordance with a kind of psychomachia, but also in the big store of Tekbir, Inc., in the Fatih district, whose television screens continuously show the collections of the brand, one of the very foremost in the Islamic garment industry. Beneath its deceptive appearances of fundamentalist retraction, this is not very far removed from globalization. For one thing, certain Muslim clothes are imported, and ostentatiously sold as such so as to bring out their chic and their high quality: the foreign textile industry is placed in the service of the faith and the constitution of an Islamic 'moral subject', with its own 'aesthetic of existence', in this case one that is neo-Ottoman in character. For another, Turkish businesses export *türban* and *pardösüs* to Western Europe, to the Middle East and even to Asia, either via duly recorded commercial exchanges, or via the intermediary of pavement trading that flourishes in the districts of Yenikapi or Laleli, in Istanbul.

At the other end of the ideological spectrum, Özal's policy of openness has also given a boost to the rising power of companies such as Mudo, Yargici or Zeki Trico, which offer their clientele the trappings of 'modernity' and 'civilization', in explicitly neo-Kemalist terms – and in polemical response to Islamic fashion. Furthermore, the 'fetishism' that continues to celebrate Atatürk, and is even intensifying as the democratic-Muslim current becomes more established on the political scene, has its own palette of accessories, busts, photos and badges, which all enable the secularists to demonstrate their difference, and their resistance, clearly.[111] But, in contrast to these explicitly political emblems, what is essential lies in their support for mass consumption, whose doors the shopping malls have opened both to them and to other Turks. For in commercial spaces such as Galleria, Akmerkez, Capitol, Bauhaus or Carrefour, on the European and Asian banks of Istanbul, people can 'experience civilization', as the daily paper *Hürriyet* puts it[112] – a 'lifestyle' which extols national identity via the appropriation of foreign codes of clothing, food, architecture and so on.

This has always been one of the constitutive paradoxes of Kemalism. In order to invent politically a national popular culture, one that is Turkish and Anatolian, and to reject the multicultural cosmopolitanism of Constantinople, Kemalism turned towards the universal engineering of 'westernization'. A move to hats or, at least, caps; to the musicological researches of Béla Bartók, for instance; and to the transnational and transideological architecture of the Modern movement whose precepts had been spread by the annual meetings of the Congrès International d'Architecture Moderne (CIAM) since 1928. The 'New Architecture' was greeted in Ankara as the advent of the 'city of the future', in its Manichean struggle with the 'city of the past', Istanbul, and as an expression of the 'new truth' that was being spread across the world. It saw itself without hesitation as being in the service of 'a transformation of civilizations' (*inkilap*) and of the 'revolution' (*devrim*) being carried out by the state, and as an instrument of 'inner colonization' (*iç kolonizasyon*) of Anatolia. In its 'model villages', peasants were to learn how to sleep in beds, and use tables and chairs. The 'New Architecture' did not in fact entirely conceal the interest it showed in French or Italian colonial town planning in Northern Africa. In the towns, cubic houses and apartments immersed town-dwellers into the new Republican 'lifestyle', with its emphasis on family values and hygiene. The fact remains that the enterprise soon ran up against its economic limits, and architecture became less 'new' than 'national' from the end of the 1930s onwards, when the utopian and revolutionary spirit started to run out of breath.[113]

The entry of Turkey into the world of globalized mass consumption, from the 1980s onwards, has modified the terms of this question. The relationship to merchandise has to some extent become more democratic, however great may be the financial difficulties of the majority of households and the heavy tribute paid to recurrent inflation. The frequenting of shopping malls has thus become, for women, a way of playing a social part in the public space and renegotiating their economic power within the family.[114] The mass market is now shared, albeit in a conflictual way, whereas in the first decades of the Republic, the majority of the population was excluded from the sphere of merchandise. Struggles for subjectivation thus represent a conversation that is intensely national,[115] one that draws its nourishment from Turkey's new involvement in the processes of globalization and the contradictory appropriation of the material culture of capitalism. In other terms, the militant commitment of an Islamic sort does not here amount to a rejection of this culture, a rejection which the Afghan Taliban preached; and commoditization is neither a disenchantment of the political sphere nor a dissolution of national identity. It also appears that it cannot be dissociated from its relation to the body: from the way in which the body is dressed, but also fed, looked after, washed and moved. The national conversation about political subjectivation partly bears on the conception of beauty, health and psychological and physical equilibrium that the social agents create for themselves, in reference at once to more or less reinvented native cultural repertoires, and to imported knowledge or fashions.

The neo-liberal moment in which we are living does indeed have its peculiarities from this point of view, when it comes to medical expertise, leisure, sport, hygiene and cosmetics. But the globalization of practices of the self, when grasped in the twofold dimension of their commoditization and their relation to the body, is an old business. Communism and fascism, which both influenced the Kemalist experience, were thus transnational movements of political subjectivation that participated in the formation of national 'dominations' and, at the same time, of a system of nation-states whose absurd and bloody apogee was the Second World War. They brought into play 'aesthetics of existence' that in actual fact partly overlapped with one another.[116] These had their own material culture – an architecture, a habitat, a way of dressing, fine arts and music, and their corporal canons, directly associated with a representation of the moral economy of masculinity and femininity. *Rank und schlank*, 'slim and tall', as Hitler professed; what he had in mind – as did all the racists of his period – was the Greek statuary which the priest Johann Joachim Winckelmann, Prefect of Pontifical Antiquities, had popularized at the end of the eighteenth century.[117] This ideal of the virile and muscular beauty of *ephebes* – which presented itself as, in principle, hostile to democracy (imagined as decadent, pacifist and 'potbellied') via a whole series of practices both physical and material: very short trousers and very short hair, bare legs and torso, military and gymnastic exercises, the cult of masculine comradeship and strength, the celebration of the flag and of speed – spread the fascist 'new man' throughout Europe and beyond it, by tending to replace the class war with the war between the generations, at least on an aesthetic and symbolic level.[118]

Nonetheless, this repertoire of subjectivation went beyond the fascist movement alone. It could be found in the Soviet Union and in the nationalist or socialist parties of the whole world – in Turkey, in Israel, in India[119] – and also in the democracies themselves, however 'potbellied'. Thus, scouting adopted many of these elements without automatically incurring the suspicion of being sympathetic to fascism (or communism), even though it has regularly been accused of this, and the ideological drift of certain of its spokesmen could indeed provide material in support of the allegation.[120] Likewise, Edda, Mussolini's elder daughter, was the talk of the town when she went cycling in public, but this was forty years after the Victorian 'new women', and – as I will be showing later – nearly sixty years before the female cyclists of Chitgar Park in Tehran.[121]

In other words, globalization, apprehended as a historical experience of subjectivation, has over the past two centuries broadly become
identical with the expansion of merchandise and – it should now be
added – with the spread of the techniques of the body that this expansion produces. The 'objectification', individuation and constitution of
'moral subjects' enabled by consumption are all effected via the mediation of these latter. And, conversely, all these 'transformations of civilization', in Braudel's sense of the term, have supplied 'matter for
politics' – in the most material sense.[122] Thus in Germany, the malaise
of the *Ossies*, ever since reunification, has inspired their *Ostalgie* for the
old material culture of the former GDR, as so amusingly depicted in
the *Goodbye Lenin!* of Wolfgang Becker, seen by six million people
during the very first months after it came out: the pickled gherkins of
the Spreewald, Gold coffee and Florena soap are all rehabilitated; the
food industry has launched pizzas to suit *Ost*-German tastes; Ossiver-
sand, a mail order service for the Länder of the East, saw its turnover
increase by 300 per cent in 2002; a Centre for the Documentation of
Everyday Life in the GDR was opened at Eisenhüttenstadt, containing
some 80,000 objects: it is visited by 10,000 tourists per year.[123]

Soviets plus electrification: indeed, Lenin's vision was clear and
acute, since the generalization of artificial light was doubtless one of
the great changes in the processes of subjectivation which the founding
nineteenth century introduced.[124]The democratic-Islamists of the AKP,
in Turkey, were equally far-sighted, since they made the electric light
bulb the emblem of their party. But the essential change still lies in the
future, with part of Southeast Asia becoming affluent and 1.2 billion
Chinese erupting into the world of merchandise – and its techniques
of the body.[125] It should now be easier to understand why it is possible
to speak of the emergence of a global 'governmentality', and not simply
of a global 'governance'. The practices of appropriation of globalization, the 'actions' on which the 'action' of the state or the market are
based and the great labour of subjection are all written into the flesh
of beings-in-society (and in globality). This is what now needs to be
clarified.

Globalization in movement

The processes of political subjectivation by means of the use of merchandise are indeed incarnated in techniques of the body that need to
be grasped as such. Not in the terms of semiology, as people have
abundantly tried to do over the past few decades, but in accordance
with those of a motor praxeology. It was the techniques of the body,
said Mauss, that counted: the body as our first and most natural
technical object. Mauss thus underlined the role of education in the

acquisition of these ways of being by doing.[126] He was close to those of his contemporaries who were musicians, painters, doctors, historians, ethnologists or pedagogues and who, for some thirty or so years, had taken an interest in the 'music of gestures', to use the expression of the Swiss writer Émile Jacques-Dalcroze (1865–1950), and gave to rhythm and vibration their 'physical and corporeal substrate'.[127] It then becomes important to analyse the way that 'embodied motor practices are objectified': 'So what makes material culture is all material objects, of whatever kind, manufactured or not, living or not, whose static and dynamic aspects are more or less incorporated into motor practices.'[128] For Halbwachs, man is an animal who thinks with his fingers, and Mauss adopted this view.[129] He wrote, for example, that sexual techniques and morality were closely related.[130]

Understand in this way, material culture is action, in other words gestures and movements, more often than not unconscious or at least automatic, and this action contributes to the constitution of 'moral subjects', including in the political sphere. In other words, subjection can be grasped only in the movements of the body that set it in motion, and these latter are in thrall to the materiality of objects. Let Alain Corbin demonstrate this to us with regard to an anonymous clog-maker from the first half of the nineteenth century, in the Perche region; his account is worth quoting at length:

> We can, without much risk of error, view the technical, gestual and somatic culture of Louis-François as being largely the product of this art of clog-making. This involved a good knowledge of different woods, of their essence and their age. Louis-François had to be able to analyse in depth the odours of fresh wood, measure the consistency and the hardness of the balls, take into account their colour and design, predict the extent to which they would shrink on drying, weigh up at a glance, and by listening to its sonority, the quality of a new clog.
>
> He had to be able to manipulate an extensive range of cutting, piercing and scraping tools, with their many different shapes: straight, tapering, curved. Given the permanent risk of cuts, he had probably adopted the habit, from youth onwards, to grow a skin thick enough to tolerate this pain. His trade had taught him the mastery of a series of gestures which doubtless governed his behaviour in everyday life. It had led him to acquire strength in his wrist, precision in his moves and sharpness of vision. Throughout his life, he was obliged, day by day, tirelessly to manufacture a particular shape in space. . . . The essential thing, no doubt, if we are to understand Louis-François Pinagot, lies in the intuitive grasp he must have had of the relations between clogs and rural civilization; or, if you prefer, the perception of peasant life as it is signified by the wearing of clogs. Let us dwell for a while on what wearing clogs actually meant within this society and thus on the importance the clog-maker assumed in the social imaginary.

Clogs impose a repertoire of gestures, a somatic rhythm, a form of behaviour. They prevent you from walking in a free and easy way and from running. They weigh you down. They stop your feet from bending. On the other hand, they stabilize them, on most kinds of terrain, by imposing a dragging gait. They protect your feet from bumps, accidents, burns. They shelter them from water, mud and snow. In winter, the straw you stuff clogs with keeps your feet warm. In summer, you put bracken in, and this, being lighter, is refreshing. Clogs harden the soles of the feet, whose nakedness (unlike shoes) they liberate. But clogs are also a tool. When you dig, you push down on your clog; and a simple push will be enough to disperse the earth in a compact mound.

The countryside and its empty spaces are filled with the echo of clattering clogs as they mark the presence of other people and of oneself. It is clogs which give their rhythm to dances and, if necessary, cover the noise of inopportune voices. It is no accident if folksongs mention clogs so often. Clogs enable you to gain time. Unlike boots, so difficult to put on and even more difficult to pull off, they can be slipped on without you having to bend forward or sit down. Furthermore, they are easy to clean. They enable you to go into the garden, to the well, to the barn, to the stable without getting your feet dirty – if indeed this is something clog-wearers are particularly worried about. On occasion, clogs can constitute redoubtable weapons. . . .

Clogs constitute one of the decisive markers of the identity of the person whose presence they reveal. Placed outside a door, they can signal the presence of an unwanted guest as well as that of a beloved person. In the countryside, 'you were announced by the noise of your clogs'; old people were recognized by their slow steps, young people by their quicker steps, and weary labourers returning from the harvest by their dragging gait. Not forgetting the difference – picked up straightaway – between the hasty busyness of feminine clogs and the tranquil heavy tread of masculine clogs. In short, just as much as the song of the labourer in the fields, just as much as the noise of those familiar voices, whose meaning it was not even necessary to perceive to feel assured of a certain person's presence, the rhythmic clop of clogs here contributed to the very sound of one's environment. During the series of arson attacks that marked the year 1830 in Lower Normandy, a man presumed to be guilty was condemned to death because one of the witnesses claimed to have recognized the sound of his steps.

Clogs are an intimate part of the peasant's universe. . . . This value as a token of identity leads us to keep the clogs of the dead neatly lined up; even more than the dead person's clothes, they have the aura of one last memory of that person's presence.[131]

We simply need here to replace the clog by the computer, the clog-maker by the computer technician, and, lo and behold, we have an idea of the incorporation of the material culture of the most immediately contemporary globalization in a series of motor conducts of life that such and such a 'type of person' 'bears' in everyday life. For the past two centuries, globalization has thus consisted in transformations in the sphere of objects and techniques that were simultaneously revolutions in motor activity. Not only have shoes, whether for wear in town, when walking, or for playing sport, replaced clogs, but engines have supplanted vehicles drawn by animals, and pedestrians have become drivers – and even started to fly like Icarus. The artificial production of light thanks to electricity and infrared rays has completely transformed ways of being social, or moving from place to place, and of fighting. Optics, especially photography and the procedures that relate to it, such as cinema or video, and the various methods of recording sound have also modified their relation to other people, to space, and to time. In short, the changing scale of capitalism and the state has had as its cornerstone a mutation in the habitus, but less the habitus as understood by Bourdieu as the one imagined by Mauss: the set of techniques of the body, the *hexis* of Aristotle – 'acquired' habits and 'faculties' – that present themselves as 'montages' of a physical, psychological and sociological nature, set up by the social authorities.[132]

The emergence of liberal, imperial or neo-liberal governmentality from the nineteenth century onwards thus rested on a 'microphysics of power', which, as Foucault showed, was immediately objectified and put to work in architectural and urban spaces. Disciplinary control imposes a relation between a single gesture and the overall posture of the body, and defines the way the body relates to the objects around it.[133]

Foucault refers here to an instrumental way of coding the body, whose obligatory syntax of manoeuvres, so dear to the military theorists of the eighteenth century and a veritable propaedeutic for the democratic infantry of the two following centuries, would be the quintessence.[134] Indeed, this disciplinary society is based on a material culture that is described at length in *Discipline and Punish*: the panoptic architecture and arrangement of prisons, and of military, educational and hospital institutions, and even that curious steam contraption for the swift correction of little boys and girls depicted in a late eighteenth-century engraving – all that great transfer to things and to space of the task of controlling souls, bodies and desires[135] is the object of precise descriptions and reproductions.

Of course, the thesis of such a 'political anatomy', in its unambiguous aspects,[136] was soon to raise several objections, in particular from Michel de Certeau.[137] But it was soon tempered by Foucault himself, when he refined his problematic of subjection in his last writings. The techniques whereby others are dominated then became similar to the techniques of self-domination, since they are both techniques of the body, such as diet or sexual acts, closely associated with the exercise of the civic capacity depending on whether they are experienced as 'active' or 'passive'.[138]

The formidable analysis of Subordination in the 'Patient Infantry-man' that we find in the work of the Polish novelist Józef Wittlin is a good demonstration of this, precisely in a situation of 'time–space compression', that of the unleashing of the First World War. The hero, Piotr Niewiadomski, the son of a Polish father and a Hutsul mother, is a porter in a railway station on the Ruthenian borders of the Austro-Hungarian Empire. 'It's all starting up!' Mobilization – which in itself is a whole programme of movement – brings him, amid the ruffled roar of a bogie, to the heart of a 'strange church of a railway', the Budapest station, where 'great luminous clocks indicated the sacred time, the time of railway timetables'. From here he is transferred, with his com-panions, to the 'depot', some way from a small Magyar town, between the municipal abattoir and the cemetery, as if 'they were deliberately billeting men who would have to march to their deaths next to the temples of death, so that they could tame it in time'. In this border ter-ritory, the chief warrant officer Bachmatiuk has for sixteen years been greeting the new classes of conscripts who 'emerged from his hands really transformed into human marvels'.

> And all of a sudden, the civilians realized that the host of the depot was fear. Fear was managing this whole sharecropping farm of death, it was to fear that they had been led by the oath they had solemnly sworn the Emperor. Fear, yes fear, transformed living men into rigid squares, into rhythmic columns. These fine marches, these splendid processions, were the products of human fear. One day fear would make these disciplined detachments emerge from the walls of the Farkas and Gjömeky brasserie, it would make them leave Hungarian land and send them off to encoun-ter death, far, far away. The fear of something more terrifying and more powerful than the officers, the sergeant-majors, perhaps even than the Emperor and than death itself. They still did not know the name of this divinity, but they could already feel its sharp claws. They still did not know Subordination, and yet its icy breath was already freezing them.

In the depot, the new recruits learn from the men of the marching battalion that 'the cult of Subordination demanded numerous practices and numerous ritual gestures', such as 'snapping into a posture of immobility and bowing to strangers because the latter wore shin-ing stars':

> The men of the marching battalion had up until then frolicked freely with the civilians [the new conscripts, still in civvies], taking advantage of the truce that had been concluded between themselves and fear. All of a sudden, they started to rise to their feet, to stand upright, to adjust their kepis, to do up their buttons, to chuck their lighted cigarettes to the ground. Their faces were transformed into dead maggots, their torsos grew rigid, their eyes glazed over. Like puppets, they turned their heads

left, right, left, right. The stars hypnotized them from afar, and the soldiers' hands shot up to their kepis and smacked into their peaks. After
a certain number of seconds laid down by the regulations, they fell back.
Their limbs relaxed, and their deadly tension left them. The hypnosis of
the stars had ceased. The men transformed into wood came back to
themselves as if from a distant journey into the beyond. Fear sweated
out from every pore. It communicated itself to the civilians. But these
latter did not shift from where they were. The stars did not as yet exercise
any murderous fascination on them. Their civilian costume acted like a
protective suit of armour.

Subordination rests on the transcendence of the regulations, something that is perfectly well mastered by the chief warrant officer
Bachmatiuk:

[E]ven though he knew off by heart those ancestral books about the soldier's life, and even though he understood their infallible and indeci-
pherable contents better than anyone else in the depot, he never stopped
reading and rereading them, discovering new truths and new revelations
each time. . . . Understanding and plumbing the Regulations means, does
it not, living strictly in accordance with each of them, performing literally
and blindly each of their paragraphs, each point in them? By night and
by day, in times of peace and of war, by land, sea and air? O supreme
perfection, you were the dream of Rodolf Bachmatiuk! . . . He dreamed
of perfection like a man who is still far away from it. He was unaware
that he had possessed it for a long time already. For through what, if not
through perfection, was he able to awaken such fear? He petrified not
only the soldiers, but the officers too, especially the reserve officers. They
diligently avoided putting their foot in it – heaven forbid! – when he was
around. . . . In the history of Subordination, it rarely happens that it is
not the subordinate who is afraid of his superiors, but the converse. The
officers were afraid of him, oh yes they were, because in his eyes he
incarnated all the virtues, and nothing is as alarming as virtue. . . . He
did everything to perfection: shooting, sounding the bugle, playing the
drum, he could strip a machine gun and put it back together again in
just a few minutes. Squatting down, placing one knee on the ground,
getting the right posture, shouldering arms, grasping a rifle by the butt
– all these actions had to be performed just the way that Bachmatiuk did
them. He was the perfect illustration of the correct position.

This practice of the military persona and its techniques of the body
enables the chief warrant officer to fashion the 'Patient Infantryman'
in the image of the Regulations, to inculcate a total and physical
'conduct of life' in him, and to constitute him as a 'moral subject':

His words had a terrible power. When he shouted, 'I'll make a man of
you, lad!', the unhappy creature to whom he was addressing these words
felt that he had before him a real creator; he felt that very soon some

frightening, extreme, original things would happen, that very soon the creation would begin. God the Father no longer counted for anything, since the tanned and hairy little finger of the chief warrant officer dispensed a current capable of killing anything that was alive, and of summoning it back into life.

And, right at the end:

> [S]uddenly, fear swept across all these men. Up until then, fear had been outside them, but now it had settled inside them. It penetrated into their bodies from the prickly fibres of their uniforms. They all felt that this uniform, with its whiff of malt, condemned them to death. A miracle happened: into this undisciplined mass, Subordination entered. It slipped into their bones, mingled with their marrow and stiffened their movements. It transformed their very voices.
>
> Until late that evening, in the camp, the NCOs taught them how to march, how to fold their greatcoats, how to make their beds. They also taught them new manners. To the question, 'What's your name?', the recruits had to answer, '*Landszturminfanteryst* so-and-so, company such-and-such, X regiment of King N . . .'. This was how incorporation was achieved.
>
> Was the man who went off to sleep that night on his bedstead between Bryczynski, the manservant of a count, and the Styrian minor Guglhupf, still Piotr Niewiadomski? No, he was no longer our old acquaintance from the station at Topory-Czernielica, nor was he Piotr Niewiadomski, the son of Wasylina, brother of Paraszka, a woman of easy morals, but *Landszturminfanteryst* Piotr Niewiadomski. And there was a great difference.[139]

'Incorporation' into the global way of the world is thus achieved at the confluence of matter and the body. As everyone knows, the 'Patient Infantryman' has been a fundamental 'human type' of globalization ever since the nineteenth century, and Max Weber emphasizes how he contributed to the furthering of democracy.[140] Somehow or other, he continues, tightly buttoned into his uniform, to play the main roles, on both sides of the front line of 'good governance'; patrolling in Iraq, carrying out peacekeeping operations, but also crushing the demonstrations on Tiananmen Square. The instrumental coding of the body[141] of which he is the bearer is still relevant, as has been demonstrated by *Beau Travail*, Claire Denis's film on the Foreign Legion, or the performance of the suicide of ex-chief warrant officer Pierre Chanal, presumed guilty of the murder of three hitch-hikers.

The latter, under arrest in a 'maximum security cell' in a Rheims hospital, and placed under suicide watch with checks every quarter of an hour, managed to kill himself thanks to his 'extreme technical skill', his 'infallible rigour', which had been acknowledged during the trial by his former companions in arms who were called as witnesses, and which had been inculcated in him by his training in the 'neutralization of sentries'.

> According to the first indications of the inquiry, the chief warrant officer seems to have concealed two blades in the stiff label of a pair of trousers. . . . On Tuesday, after the visit of the clerk of the court, who left at 22:50, the former soldier managed to bring them out and hide them in his bed. Then, under his sheets, Chanal cut the elastic of his jogging trousers to make two garrottes, so as to accelerate the rate of haemorrhage. Then, with his left hand, after two attempts, he slit his left femoral artery. 'We found two blades between his thighs, under the sheet, the one covered in blood and the other clean', stated Vincent Lesclous, Attorney-General of Rheims. Chanal had folded his blanket over his thighs; the investigators believe this was in order that 'the guards behind the window would not see the bloodstain'. A puddle 40 centimetres in diameter, invisible from the surveillance hatch, was found under the bed. Chanal had taken into account the time that elapsed between each round of surveillance: according to the doctors, this 'technique' allowed him to die in five or seven minutes.

So ran the account in *Libération*. 'The work of a real pro,' commented the Attorney-General.[142]

The 'Patient Infantryman' is flanked by other professionals of violence or coercion – police, militia, private security guards, prison screws – who are also in charge of the general subjection, and also by the professionals in health, education, food provision, transport and commerce, who, in their turn and always in uniform, incarnate and inculcate motor practices of a commercial, technical, hygienic or moral order. One can extend to the whole realm of globalization the remark made by E. M. Collingham on the Victorian Raj: it is an intensely physical experience.[143]

The industrialization of the food industry, the commercialization of cheap oils, the increase in the consumption of sugar, the spread of public transport and passive leisure, and the mechanization of work have thus led to a 'worldwide epidemic of obesity', according to the World Health Organization. The number of overweight people is said to have passed from 200 million in 1995 to 300 million today, including 115 million in the developing countries. Apart from the physical appearance and the mobility of the populations concerned, this affects their health, since the increase in body fat is a cause of diabetes or of cardiovascular illnesses, diseases that affect the muscles and bones, and even cancer.[144]

We still need to realize that subordination is action and that the techniques of the body that are constitutive of globalization are modes of appropriation of the latter, in so far as they are practices of subjectivation. The styles of command and obedience are 'lifestyles' and 'aesthetics of existence', and are fashioned from the flesh. And, as is to be expected, this relation to the body cannot be separated from the relationship with merchandise. Norbert Elias has shown how the 'sociogenesis of the state' since the Middle Ages came with a 'process of the civilization of manners' which involved table manners, the codification of natural functions and the spread of self-control. The same applies these days to globalization, on the one hand, since this latter coincides with the formation of the state, and, on the other, because it transmits specific techniques of the body that are dictated by technological innovation, the intensification of transport and telecommunications, the reign of merchandise or the spread of transnational cultural practices. In these concrete procedures of subjection, suffering is indissolubly linked with pleasure, and discipline with resistance, thus rendering equally vain the normative discourses that liberals and anti-globalization militants exchange.

The globalization of gestures

Let us examine, for instance, how global social institutions regulate the movements of the body. This, as the example of Charlie Chaplin shows, has been the case in factory or workshop labour since Taylorism; certainly, the disciplinary condition (often prison-like in its severity) remains the rule in many branches of the web of industrial production that is deemed to characterize the 'information era'. Workers, especially female ones, in sweatshops are producing for 18 hours a day, and sometimes, in periods when the economy is overheating, for 24 hours at a stretch, snatching a brief rest in dormitories set up in free zones or close by, so as to favour the 'flexibility' of their timetables. Their lives are closely surveyed, including their natural functions, with threats of financial or even physical punishments. They are frisked to prevent them from stealing, sexually harassed and deprived of their freedom of movement, at risk of their lives as a result of fire – as was proved by the death of 188 women workers in the Kader factory in Thailand, and of 87 employees of the Zhili Toy Factory in China, all of whom were shut up together in padlocked premises.[145] Industrial globalization is that of bodily techniques in relation to their productivity.[146] The fact remains, as I have already said, that factory work, however harsh it may be in practice, is a response to a moral economy of duty and desire: a duty towards your family, to whom you can send a little money, and a desire to procure for yourself certain of the items that you are helping to produce, and to return to your village or to your local district, having managed to put a penny or two aside.

In a very different disciplinary genre, the global implantation of the scout movement, sometimes in a coercive context of colonization, coincided with training in a particular physical culture which dispenses a transnational savoir-faire in rituals, games, sporting exercises and camping, and which simultaneously institutionalizes projects of moral or political subjectivation proper to each of the societies concerned. In the Algeria of the 1930s, for instance, the movement was attractive to nationalist adolescents, 'thanks to its ability to articulate modernism, especially the values of nature, the body (shorts were shocking for the traditional representations of decency associated with clothes), of technology, and an attachment to the cultural heritage of the Arab and Muslim world', and because of its tendency 'to express a progressive cultural patriotism aligned with a moral structure, associating the desire for renewal of the *nahda*, and an ethical ideal of the regeneration of society through its young people, and the regeneration of its young people through a healthy life, freed from the corruptions of the city (alcohol, kif, prostitution)'.[147] The way scouting engineers the body, when associated with the way the global religious organizations, both Christian and Muslim, on which the movement depends, carry out the same function, has often been the matrix of this synergy between nationalism, reform and the constitution of 'moral subjects' that we have uncovered in several situations.

Likewise, international hotels have spread through the whole planet, at the nodal points of the process of globalization, a relative homogenization of the material frame of a certain number of bodily functions, and have thereby shaped the way they are performed.[148] Not only in the conception of bathrooms and toilets, beds and spaces for rest and relaxation, but also in the provision of food: the technique of the buffet enables one to limit time-wasting and misunderstanding between the staff and the customers who do not have the same dietary habits and do not necessarily speak the same language, even if it is just a different kind of English that they speak; it enables the traveller to judge the dishes on an individual basis and to compose his meal in a simulacrum of abundance, transforming into freedom the self-service that is imposed, and it has the advantage of reducing the staff costs as well as problems of communication.

Of course, this hotel discipline is quickly subverted, and the noble objective that is assigned to the employees, 'to serve the needs of everyone', as the attractive formula of one French chain puts it, sometimes takes strange routes. Thus, in the Gulf, it is not beds that are rented out to princes and other sheiks, but bedrooms into which their retinue can pile, without the management knowing how many are there. Likewise, the TV dinners of room service are not taken away as soon as the meal has been eaten, for fear of intruding on the wives, but at the end of the stay, once the rooms are empty.[149] Nonetheless, once this element of 'difference' has been identified, it really is a relatively precise and consistent form (*Gestalt*) of hygiene, food provision and sleep that is dispensed in a commercial fashion. But now, this is something that is bought and evaluated, even if some details are criticized. Apart from a few dissatisfied customers, the traveller is reassured by the standardization of the space and the services that are generally billed at a high price and is happy, as regards a change of the cultural or hedonistic scene, with a few artificial touches of local colour that the management throws in for him, a decorative pattern here, a local dish there – as he is pleased to enjoy a comfort and smooth-tongued amiability that are beyond reproach.

For technical, financial and – these days – security reasons, air companies have gone much further in the exploration of the Marxist analysis of the link between enjoyment and suffering. Thirty years after their irreversible 'disenchantment', the result of the way air transport became available to the masses, these companies persist in distilling dreams and fantasies of luxury, while they now sell nothing but displacement and have admirably interiorized the definition of globalization as 'time–space compression' – being more successful in the compression of space than that of time.

Far from being a dreamlike experience, as the advertising suggests, air travel is an elaborate ritual of a disciplinary and even ascetic type: stereotypical procedures of embarkation and disembarkation, the continual need to have your safety belt attached, periods of prostration in cramped seats, the ingestion of food arranged with millimetric precision on a tray, having to go without tobacco, the strict regulation of opportunities to go to the toilet.[150] As is often the case with rituals, this is all accompanied by mystifications, for example in the case of timetables or the quality of the allowances, and practices of inversion or excess, especially when it comes to buying duty-free merchandise or consuming alcohol. It has become so severe and constraining that passengers now have to undergo physical exercises, take special food and observe dress codes during flights so as to avoid problems in blood circulation: they must not wear trousers that are too tight, they must stretch their legs regularly, and must make movements that will keep thrombosis and phlebitis at bay, drink a lot of water, and abstain from alcohol.

It goes without saying that the attacks of 11 September 2001 have made the cult of the plane even more rigid. Travellers have submitted to the observance of the new rules without too much shilly-shallying, and have even anticipated them and modified their behaviour or the way they dress in consequence. They wear 'post-11 September' shoes which are easy to take off at control points and do not have any metal tips, clothes without metal buttons, and bras that do not have stiff supports. When they can, they take off medical supports that might lead to humiliating body searches, including fixtures designed to prevent incontinence. They present the security agents with their X-rays before going through the security gates when their bones are supported by surgical pins. They abstain from drinking coffee or water before taking the shuttle between New York and Washington, since any movements within the cabin are forbidden when flying over the federal capital, and punishable by a fine of 10,000 dollars.[151] Furthermore, passengers, at least those travelling to or from the United States, are now filed and scrutinized by the American police, who, if there is the least doubt about them, interrogate them or have them interrogated in their airport of embarkation, as was illustrated by the way the American administration behaved in the case of the Air France flights over Christmas 2003, with the cancellation of several flights.[152] Soon, biometric technology, which is already being tested by the SAS at Umea airport, 645 kilometres north of Stockholm, will be adding its bit and inculcating new attitudes or new gestures when it comes to facing the cameras that will identify faces, or placing one's finger in the scanners.[153] There is no doubt that passengers will acquire the automatic responses required, just as they have been broken in to the frisking and the systematic passage of their luggage through the X-ray machines.

Most global social institutions are developing their own body style in the transnational dimensions, reproduced more or less unconsciously by their members and generally spotted by outsiders, who are irritated or amused by them. The compunction of the Catholic priest, the preaching of the Protestant missionary dispensing the Word from his perch in his chariot at the start of the twentieth century, the televisual gesticulations of the charismatic pastor, the 'similarity in the expression of affliction [among Pentecostalists], translated by the symbolism of the possessed body of the afflicted faithful who are cured by exorcism',[154] the rhythm of the ablutions or the hand rapidly passed through the beard of the Muslim believer, the various tics of the executives of multinational businesses, international organizations or NGOs, the austere and sublime fidelity of the Communist militant dedicated to internationalism: all are (or have been) easily observable demonstrations of this. But we also need to take into account the protean revolution of positions and movements engendered by the industrial or postindustrial revolution in peace as in war, at work as at play, in the private sphere as in the public space.

Several techniques of the body have become universalized and are pursuing their development on the planetary level, via several different effects of transversal diffusion, recomposition and reverberation. This is the case with quick meals, not only in public transport, but also in self-service restaurants, offices and even at home. This applies to the use of the knife and fork in Asia too, and to chopsticks in the West. It applies to the way vehicles are driven, cameras manipulated, sounds or images are received by the media, or a telephone number is dialled. It applies to travelling by bicycle, a mode of locomotion whose importance with regard to globalization has been grossly underestimated. It applies to the syringe, which holds no more mysteries for nurses, diabetics, junkies, curers, witches, vampires and DIY fanatics on all five continents. It applies to the way computers are used: the computer mouse has completely transformed the motor functions of the hand, at the cost of various pathological problems, and the discipline of which presupposes an obedience to the ergonomic prescriptions that are dispensed by the contemporary offshoots of the old lifestyle manuals. As Compaq tells its customers:

> At your work desk, you run a certain number of far from negligible risks of bodily injury. We recommend that you read and follow the recommendations contained in this manual *Security and Ergonomy at Your Work Desk* so as to reduce as much as possible all risks and to improve your working comfort. . . . In the following pages, you will find a description of a correct arrangement for your work desk, the position of your body while working at a computer and healthy working habits.

Quite apart from the universalization of the gestures of western medicine, the techniques of the dressing, presentation, maintenance and enjoyment of the body tend to become globalized. Procedures of washing, intimate hygiene, shaving, the regulation of fecundity, protection against sexually transmitted diseases, plastic surgery, tattooing, piercing, cutting or branding, gymnastics, body-building and body art, relaxation treatments, cosmetics and perfumery, underclothes and bathing costumes and sportswear all tend to become homogenous on a planetary scale thanks to the industrialization of their production, merchandising and international commoditization. Thalassotherapy has thus become a must of global tourism, and spas an almost obligatory service of luxury hotels. In all metropolises, boutiques for tattooing and piercing, fitness clubs and beauty institutes are becoming ever more common.

The cosmetics industry alone is now worth $160 billion per year, and Americans are spending more on their beauty than on their education. Businesses such as L'Oréal, Elizabeth Arden, Helena Rubinstein, Revlon, Estée Lauder, Nivea and Shiseido have become economic giants whose activities have recorded an impressive growth for more than a decade.[155] Their products are omnipresent on the surface of the globe, are the object of frenzied smuggling activities and are shamelessly copied by fakers.

Applying hair cream, make-up, perfume and gel, taking a shower and cleaning your teeth are now daily actions for hundreds of millions of people, although hundreds of millions of their contemporaries are deprived of these activities for lack of resources. Of course, this global convergence of the material culture of the body is not the same as a

uniformization. Its concrete usage gives rise to different social imaginary meanings since, here as elsewhere, consumption is another form
of production.[156] In his remarkable social history of soap in Zimbabwe,
Timothy Burke ironically emphasizes how the Africans took the gospel
of merchandise into their hearts but soon started to interpret it in their
own ways, if only because the needs of hygiene interfered with the
representations of the invisible.[157]

Nonetheless, the repertoires of gestures and the movements that are
associated, so to speak, mechanically with the practices of the body, are
circumscribed. There are not all that many different ways of shampoo-
ing, using an electric razor, using a spray, slipping on a pair of pants,
or putting on a condom. A South African marketing specialist, who
graduated in 'Bantu Studies' from the University of Witwatersrand, put
it very clearly in 1960: 'Marketing creates needs and sells solutions to
problems. It is better to sell categories of products than brand names:
to sell ways of cleaning one's teeth than mere toothbrushes and toothpaste.'[158] And these new ways of doing old things have to be learned
from one's family, at school or by watching television. 'We are the new
pupils, we're dirty, we don't know how to wash, we aren't clean', sang
the new pupils in a Rhodesian religious school in the 1930s.[159] In two
centuries, globalization has thus seen the emergence of what might be
called transnational 'motor genres', in allusion to the 'discursive genres'
that Bakhtin described when designating 'relatively stable types of
statement'.[160]

These 'motor genres' are the object of types of behaviour and narratives of support or rejection, of negotiation, adaptation and derivation
which sometimes unleash 'transversal struggles' for subjectivation, and
in any event contribute to the constitution of 'moral subjects'. Sculpting
your body, marking your skin, moving in accordance with stereotyped
techniques which, nonetheless, give rise to performances of personal
style, or can indeed be practised in intimacy or solitude, at the cost of
physical pleasure and pain – this all amounts to constructing one's self
in relation to the Other.[161] Thus, in France, several hundreds of men per
year have their penises surgically lengthened or thickened because
they suffer from 'locker-room syndrome'. 'It's a real torture for me to
take a shower with my sports partners', confides one of the candidates
for the operation. Certain psychotherapists associate this complex with
the disappearance of explicit rites of passage and the erosion of social
sites where masculinity can be affirmed.[162]

Likewise, the way one treats one's hair transmits an idea of virility
and forms part of the way we recognize ourselves as subjects of sexuality,[163] or indeed as the subject of God when religious orthodoxy, in
particular in the case of Islam and Judaism, pays particularly scrupulous attention to it. These days, shaving your head, the length of your
beard and moustache, shaving your torso, armpits, legs and even your

pubic hair and testicles for the adepts of the G-strings and fine lingerie that have been made fashionable by the Hom company, signal in France a complex metamorphosis in the nature of masculinity.[164] And this latter owes a great deal to the globalization of images and merchandises on which it is based, while being historically situated. It is clear that when a young Frenchman has excess hair removed, this is quite different from the way it is prescribed by Islam for his Afghan contemporary. The Taliban insisted on checking – so it is said – that armpits and even pubic hair were shaved when they were inspecting the militia.[165] In the West, hair is the object of fashion and marketing, as well as being a pretext for desire and fantasies, and it has its transnational models, from Fidel Castro and 'Che' to Barthez and Zidane, as well as its brands. The redefinition of virility is also linked to the increasingly frequent recourse to plastic surgery and methods of corporeal modification, such as stretching, scarring, branding, the trimming and decoration of the teeth, and subcutaneous implants. All of these methods are generally imported from the United States and borrowed from the global repertoire of sado-masochism.[166] It echoes the progressive development in the way homosexuality is represented; it has been de-dramatized, made commonplace and 'ordinary' by European, American and Asian cinema, advertising in international magazines, trans-societal practices such as wearing ear-rings and boys kissing each other, or the transformation of Gay Pride marches into multicultural popular spectacles. Meanwhile, it also turns out that the 'reverberation' effects are frequent in the material culture of the body. Massages, whose origins (at least in fantasy) are perceived to lie in Asia or the East, are progressively becoming part of the habits of western menfolk in ways that are both de-medicalized and de-sexualized, either in beauty parlours and thalassotherapy centres, or even in the with-it or (as in Spain) frankly specialized bars that are opening up in big cities. Let's not forget, after all, that 'shampoo' comes from the Hindu word shâmpo, 'to massage': the hybridization of the techniques of the body on a planetary scale is an old business that industry, in this case the cosmetics industry, has taken over, and that confirms the logic of globalization by concatenation.

The redevelopment of virility and its gestures is obviously indiscernible from a linked process as regards femininity. The changes in relations between 'genders', in the labour market and within the family, have occurred alongside the development of new techniques in lingerie, intimate hygiene and contraception, not to mention the appropriation by the 'second sex' of bodily practices that were previously reserved for men, such as the different sporting disciplines, the consumption of alcohol and tobacco or the private rituals of skin incision.[167] These transformations are taking place right across the world. Taking one year with the next, it is now the case that women in every continent go swimming and bike riding, drive cars, wear trousers, bras and shorts, take the pill and wax their bodies, whatever may be the pockets of political or cultural resistance, the differences in time frame or the repertoires of reinterpretation from one society or social category to another. And the commoditization of the body is a vector of subjectivation. A business such as La Perla is well aware of this, having 'managed to make its presence felt in an increasingly competitive domain: that of seduction', thanks to the 'wave of chic porn' of 2000, during which there flourished in the western press provocative ads sometimes with a lesbian flavour and sometimes a sado-masochistic tinge – the woman Ungaro and her dog, the Rochas woman wearing a necklace, the duet of lascivious girls from Dior – 'putting back into the saddle lust, cock-teasers and sex that isn't exactly safe'.[168]

Of course, this style of femininity and spectacle of desire, albeit on glazed paper, has its limits. It is unlikely to convince all the puritanical masses of Asia or the Middle East, and even in the West, it arouses indignant reactions in the name of decency or the equality of the 'genders'. But the fact remains that this last argument is defeated by the increasing, and often highly ambivalent, eroticization of the masculine body in adverts, that Japan is contributing actively to spreading its own tastes amongst its neighbours, that the best is still to come given the transformation of China, and that funny things can happen under the hijab. Already, anti-aging creams have seen a 40 per cent per year increase in sales in India, and the middle classes of countries such as China, Russia and South Korea are important markets for the beauty industry.[169]

As far as can be judged, we are thus almost certainly participating in the globalization of the parameters of desire and sexual gestures, following the same logic of the historical concatenation of behaviour, the spread of bodily motor behaviour and their reinvention in difference that we have already seen at work when we discussed the transnational practices of homosexuality and prostitution. Sex tourism, the press and pornographic programmes broadcast by satellite all contribute to it at the same time, and this has doubtless spread the frequency of kissing, fellatio, heterosexual anal penetration and condoms, in a way which even eroticizes the latter.[170] It is also likely that the disfavour in which intercourse with an uncircumcised person, either male or female, judged to be immature, is held in the societies that value this ritual mutilation is gradually weakening or has already been overcome.[171]

As for masturbation, it has won (or won back) the right to exist after two and a half centuries of paranoid stigmatization. One trend in feminism has recommended it as a practice of sexual autonomy. Gay milieus have resocialized it in their meeting places. Sex shops and e-business sell considerable numbers of sex toys, a major proportion of which are designed for solitary pleasure. The proliferation of porn magazines, digital messages and websites has given respectability (especially on the Web) to onanism, which continues to be judged vulgar or immoral by certain people, but can no longer be considered entirely 'shameful' given that it is so ubiquitous, thanks to its commoditization. In 2002, in the USA, the sex shops Good Vibrations sponsored a 'National Masturbation Month', with posters in support, and an information campaign put out by the South African government, rather drolly titled 'Join the Arm Struggle' in allusion to the armed struggle against apartheid, proclaimed 'Masturbate, don't rape!'[172] Even the Catholic Church has made its aggiornamento on this subject. Pius XII still felt that sexual self-gratification was 'intrinsically and seriously sinful'. At the start of the 1990s the Catholic psychotherapist and theorist Domenico Barrila eventually admitted that masturbation was 'an important stage in the adolescent's development', so long as it had 'as its objective a better understanding of, or a desire to get closer to, the opposite sex', and that it represented, in the contrary case of being 'an affirmation of one's egotism', nothing more than a 'minor vice (*vizietto*)'.[173]

Furthermore, the AIDS pandemic on every continent has shaped a global experience of sexuality now dominated by the spectre of death and the demand for protection. Once again, the responses to this challenge vary. Some people endeavour to prevent and to cure, while others deny the obvious. From the point of view of subjection, this is not the essential point, which lies rather in the common framework that henceforth encloses the conflicts of subjectivation relative to the sexual techniques of the body. The Catholic Church's opposition to condoms, for example, is a dialectical element in the spread of their use and moral economy. It brings together other beliefs, other values and other fears too, relative to fidelity, trust, responsibility, freedom and pleasure.[174]

The same applies to anal sex, which, in certain societies or certain social categories, can be dissociated from homosexual feelings even when it is performed between boys, and which nonetheless has a dialogical and more or less critical relation to transnational gay practices. The Indonesian street children who frequently indulge in it are described in the conservative press either as the victims of paedophiles, or as depraved perverts. They devote a great deal of their own time to convincing themselves that they are not queer and are not yielding to pederasty even when they have to offer themselves to the older friend who protects them, and when they sell their charms to adults. They use homophobic language. Nonetheless, they accept *sodomi* as a normal means of obtaining emotional comfort, physical pleasure, a guarantee of security, an income and material advantage. Their carnal relation with other boys or men, whether Indonesian or foreign, is experienced as a sexuality of survival, pleasure, accident, or even as a romance or a rape, but not as anything 'gay'.[175] In a similar fashion, the *muzhik*, i.e.

the 'lad', the 'bloke' who, in Russian prisons, carries out an 'abasement' (*opouskanie*) of other detainees by reducing them to the status of passive homosexuals, is essentially indulging in a demonstration of power and authority, even if it gives him satisfaction.[176] In this case, as so often, the 'queer' is the other man, the one you possess.

The senses of globalization

In short, the fact that the gestures of sexuality have become universalized does not signify their uniformity, through the destruction of its historicity or of the singularity of desire, but the formation of a global level of governmentality, relatively highly integrated, in which 'actions' are performed on 'actions' and the techniques of the domination of others are interwoven with the techniques of the self, in a mixture of violence and pleasure.

This is accompanied by conflicts in subjectivation that are all the harsher in that the immediate impact of globalization resides in the fact that it is a revolution in one's five senses, as Marx realized: 'Man is therefore affirmed in the objective world not only in thought but with *all* the senses.'[177] The work of Alain Corbin has highlighted the sensory transformations which accompanied industrialization and urbanization in France in the nineteenth century. Scientific research and technical innovations in the domains of optics and the reproduction of sound were the source of a profound renewal in artistic creation, as was shown by a remarkable exhibition called 'The Origins of Abstraction' held in the Musée d'Orsay in 2003–4, showing how this trend was a synaesthetic experience.[178] Likewise, after the Second World War, the 'Thirty Glorious Years' of French prosperity turned the material and sensory culture of metropolitan France upside down. Jean-Jacques Salgon, from the Ardèche, recalls:

> Whole days in yellow-and-green. Those two colours, in successive layers, extended their dominion ever further each day: no surface with the vocation of being painted on could have escaped them. . . . You cannot imagine how great was my surprise on the day when my father installed in the kitchen cupboards with sliding doors – we were starting to call them 'elements' – that he had just made himself: they were white. I was dazzled. We had just entered the modern era.[179]

The celebration of hygiene and cleanliness, with the help of many washing and beauty products, was also addressed to the senses.[180] If we stick to the most recent period of globalization, the 'transition' to a market economy and democracy was also a matter of 'smells, sights and sounds', as Christoph Neidhart has shown in relation to Russia.[181]

And, as we have already observed in Egypt, 'international civil society', in 'developing countries', is also an odourless, antiseptic realm of silence that contrasts with the noise, dust and sweat of the workshops.[182]

Thus, the different ways people dress, within the context of the internationalization of commerce and clothes manufacture, imply the sense of touch. Silk, cotton and nylon were the textile matrices of globalization, and provided people with tactile impressions, and also with symbols of purity, cleanliness, gentleness and sensuality, as inspired by political movements, as happened in India with the Swadeshi nationalist campaign in 1905–8.[183] These days, the constitution of 'moral subjects' remains a problem of the epidermis. The new fine masculine lingerie, which both reveals and transmits a reformulation of the idea of virility, appeals to materials hitherto reserved for women, such as tactel or polyamides, contact with which provides you with a sensation that is different from that given by cotton and can lead to a certain sense of unease in the consumer.[184] In addition, for the last twenty years, globalization has taken the form of another tactile revolution: that brought about by the keyboards of bureaucratic work which everyone uses, from secretary to boss, from worker to artist, from employee to school pupil. We can thus fill out the identikit portrait of globalized man: apart from the fact that he enjoys electricity, he can type and – though this may change under the impact of the 'sexy seductive line' of Hom clothes[185] – he has cotton underwear, whatever social class he may come from (more or less). This doesn't amount to much, you may say. True. But it is a relatively recent phenomenon and, as Gombrowicz has been telling us for a long time, 'you have no idea of the way you can, with these little details, become really big'.

When it comes to taste, spices (in bygone days) and sugar and salt (today) are the object of debate: their consumption has sexual connotations or is accused of every ill.[186] In addition, background music has imposed itself in most public places, as the insipid sound canvas of globalization, while noise has become a subject of strong feelings among those who live near airports, in city centres or in big apartment blocks. It has been claimed that the preaching of Protestant missionaries at the end of the nineteenth century privileged hearing over sight, in opposition to the solemn ceremonies of the Catholics or the independent churches.[187] Perhaps. But the eyes did not wait for long before taking their revenge. Globalization has given a large proportion of humanity access to reading and has stuffed it with images, initially printed (these played a great role in conversion to Christianity, in the clericalization of Hinduism or Shiism, and in the vitality of the cult of Mami Wata) – and later broadcast. Everyone knows what place is occupied these days by television, video and multimedia in everyday life, and also – as is only right and fair – in charismatic preaching. In short, visual conflict is ubiquitous. Apart from the fact that the audiovisual media are polemic in spite of their propensity to be insipid and infantile, industrial creams that lighten the complexion are, at the same time, desired and criticized in Africa.[188]

Finally, the sense of smell has not ceased to mediate the process of globalization over the last two centuries. It was, in particular, a crucial fantasmatic element in colonial racism or nationalist passion: the native and the enemy both stink.[189] An unfortunate declaration made by Jacques Chirac a few years ago demonstrated that the representation of the Other continues to pass through the nose. The other's cooking, his habits – we no longer are to say 'his body' – offend the delicate nostrils of local people. The sense of smell is also at the heart of the practices of the self that are developed on a mass level by the flourishing cosmetics industry, and this happens in a more complex way than is commonly believed. The Japanese, who are very fond of French or Italian leatherwork, do not like their perfumes, which they judge to be vulgar, only good for Westerners who have bad breath. Likewise, in Africa, Christians were often reproached for smelling bad when they washed with imported soap.[190] These days, air pollution in cities, and even more the tobacco habit, cause major conflicts in the sense of smell. Smoking provokes moral hatred in the non-smoker towards the smoker and swiftly unleashes his wrath. The increasingly systematic nature of the measures to ban smoking in America and Europe, on the joint initiative of public authorities and private organizations, together with the extent of the individual or collective resistances entailed by the latter, in terms of smuggling or the transgressing of regulations, confirm that globalization does indeed relate to the emergence of a governmentality at the interface of self and others. The 'governance' of the common public goods that the air and our lungs have become, via the edicts laid down by legislative bodies and community directives, is directly related to our senses in society.

At this point of the argument, it will come as no surprise if I remark how greatly the state remains caught up, via its public policies, in the regulation of techniques of the body and of the senses that these policies activate, and how the state relies to a great extent on the indirect administration provided by NGOs and business. In the colonial period, it already demarcated the sphere of 'civilization' and raised the barriers of the racial segregation that protected this civilization by means of discriminatory measures in the domain of consumption: certain cosmetics, certain clothes were restricted to the 'natives' and carried warnings of the type *For Natives Only* or *Not for European Consumption*.[191] These days, state intervention in the rationing, allocation or taxation of consumption as 'enjoyment' – oh liberalism, what crimes are committed in thy name! – is one of the fields on which are decided battles of subjectivation. Should fat people, or at least their favourite food, be taxed? 'If people want to eat their way to grossness and an early grave, let them', says *The Economist* in peremptory tones.[192] Should tobacco be completely banned from bars and restaurants, as was done by the Irish government, following the lead of the city authorities in New York, or is it preferable that it lets those who so wish smoke a cigar or pipe or cigarette after dinner, as the ex-mayor of that city gravely recommended on the public radio station RTE?[193] Should narcotic orgasm be criminalized, at the cost of a huge and expensive mobilization of police and military forces, the incarceration of tens of thousands of individuals and the execution of several hundred of them, or would it be reasonable to legalize drugs and emphasize prevention and education?

There is indeed a state interventionism underlying consumption and its relation to the body. But to infer from this interweaving of the state and its system of indirect administration in the regulation of the senses a supplementary argument asserting that globalization is a total regime of unequivocal domination, operating through consent and obedience, is a step that I prefer not to take. For the last two centuries, the global techniques of the body have been 'forms in which human beings have "appropriated" their world – and have thereby constantly transformed it'.[194] They have been an action, in the proper sense of the term, by which globalization has been carried out on a day-to-day basis.

The world in movement

Even beyond the everyday economy of motor actions of which this globalization is made, and that I have in part described, the political or cultural movements that have 'borne' the lifestyles constitutive of subjection on the planetary scale have often been, quite simply, different forms of movement. It is particularly striking to see the extent to which dance has supported globalization, either playfully or critically, for the past two centuries, by incorporating its horizon into a kind of behaviour that could hardly be more active in the sense of bodily movements. In Africa, during the colonial period, troupes of dancers seized entire regions, adopting the uniforms of the colonial army and administration. They formed part of a bureaucratization in the imaginary life of the town-dwellers who indulged in them, getting them to take up gestures, physical attitudes and bodily techniques such as marching in step, processions, saluting and shouting out orders or reports, all of which are part of the baggage of bodily movements on the global scale.[195] It was partly thanks to this type of choreography that sub-Saharan societies acquired the bases of the Subordination inherent in the behaviour of the 'Patient Infantryman', whether the latter was enrolled in the army, an employee in the administration or recruited into a private enterprise. Furthermore, ever since colonial urbanization, young people have negotiated their relation to cultural extraversion in the bars and nightclubs of towns and cities or mining posts, to the sound of rumba, 'high life' or other more recent styles, relentlessly jiggling around, night after night. Even in the chiefdoms in the countryside, dances, sometimes masked, are a technique (one that is simultaneously ritualized, politically controlled and socially or culturally creative) that enables people to grasp what is at stake in globalization, at the price of open tensions or conflicts between those in authority and the subordinate categories who contest the monopoly of extraversion claimed by the former.[196] There is no technique of the body that intervenes more significantly in Africa's relation to the rest of the world, except perhaps football, or the religious gestures of Christianity and Islam.

But one can also see troupes of dance theatre in Bali, in the courtyards of temples or on village squares, casting a philosophical derision on the terrible attack of 12 October 2002 in Kuta.[197] And in the French provinces, troupes of majorettes, built up from the 1960s on the American model, took up baton-throwing in their parodies of military parades, a figure that seems to have been imported into the United States from Siam, the islands of Samoa, and even Arabia, in the 1930s.[198] Dance and choreography have for two centuries been global practices of subjectivation whose importance cannot be underestimated. Not only have they been instrumentalized to explicitly political ends, especially in totalitarian or authoritarian regimes, but they have also foregrounded the 'aesthetic of existence', the diffuse and spontaneous adoption of styles of dress, the interaction between 'genders' and the definition of femininity or masculinity, the staging and sometimes also the keeping at bay of eroticism, the stimulation of the consumption of certain products such as alcohol, tobacco or narcotics. In the slang of Shanghai, the social life of the disco provides one with an opportunity to 'enter' (literally to 'rise in') society; it is a moment of 'self-merchandising' in which you sell yourself on the jobs and marriage market, within the highly competitive context of 'transition'.[199] It is by indulging in entrechats that most of the 'human types' of globalization have changed level, by learning about, and inventing, the city to the rhythms of the waltz, the tango, the Charleston, the paso doble, rock, the samba, disco and techno music, and dancing their way round the planet.

Indeed, most of these dance movements are resolutely transnational. Either they developed as a result of multiethnic and multicultural cohabitation and the displacements of refugees and emigrants – such as rebetiko and the zeibekiko that accompanies it – who were born in Constantinople and the Ottoman ports of Asia Minor, and later in the islands of the Aegean Sea and the Piraeus, following the exchange of populations in 1923, and in the industrial centres of America, where expatriate Greek workers had concentrated.[200] Or they took advantage of a worldwide fashion and were reinterpreted in accordance with local canons, such as the tango, of which the musicians of the Eastern Mediterranean, among many others, have created some colourful versions. In dance, the appropriation of globalization is something immediate and voluptuous. It also happens in the *longue durée*, since this cultural practice, providing its habitués with a kinaesthesic vocabulary[201] represents a 'milieu of memory', propitious to the transmission of history and its traumatic events, as we have learnt from what happened on the Atlantic coasts, notably in Sao Tomé. In short, the cabarets, balls, bars, nightclubs and taverns really are social institutions open to the 'high seas' of modernity and providers of subjectivation, in sensuality and joy, to be sure, but also in sexual rivalry, in a concern for one's honour, in doubt, outrage, frustration and shame, or, as often as not, in fisticuffs.[202]

More or less the same could be said of sport. I have already mentioned how greatly it contributed to the subjectivation of our contemporaries. By definition, sport means acquiring the techniques of the body, from childhood onwards. In addition, it is shared with others, way beyond the circle of those who practise it, thanks to the building of ever more gigantic stadiums and especially thanks to the televised transmission of the events. A great deal has been said about its contribution to political domination, and its links with nationalism are no secret. Nonetheless, it is irreducible to the mere notion of the control or the domestication of the body. It is one element in the formation of the state and the global system of states, and for all the reasons I have dwelt on at length, it cannot be disassociated from global subjection, in both senses of the word.

It is revealing that sport plays such a major role in extraversion. Arjun Appadurai, for instance, has shown how the export of cricket, so typically British and Victorian, seduced a great variety of social categories in India, provided the colonial 'dialogue' with a preferred syntax and, as it became more and more Indian, and less Victorian, fed into the way masculinity and the 'erotics of the nation' were imagined.[203] The Indo-Pakistanis who settled in Kenya, indeed, transmitted their passion for this sport to the Luo, one of the main ethnic groups in this country. Kenneth Odhiambo, the first African player in the Kenyan team, recalled how they played for pleasure and the chance to tour the world – but also for economic gain.[204]

There is an even more thought-provoking example: the martial arts known in Japan by the name *budo*, such as judo and aikido, are in reality a 'modern invention' that goes back to the last decade of the nineteenth century, a hybrid form of tradition and modernity. The way it is taught is now completely different from the hermetic procedures of initiation and has mobilized the rationalist resources of western science and pedagogy, even the spirit of commoditization, since the pupil has become a customer or even a consumer. In the view of some promoters of this renovation, a technique of the body such as judo was no longer a martial art but an entire way of life, designed to educate a 'new type of citizen' – sport, in fact, in the universal sense of the word, which indeed was eventually adopted during the Olympic Games of 1964, after a period of disgrace and banishment following its ideological recuperation by militarism.[205]

In fact, the so-called Asian martial arts have spread throughout the world as practices of the self and now constitute one of the great narratives of subjectivation relayed by the cinema. The agents in kung fu films from Hong Kong and Taiwan speak to Asia, and an audience beyond it, of justice and fraternity; their leaping exploits tell of a world different from the brutal world of the capitalism of tycoons and their sidekicks – *A Better Tomorrow*, as the title of John Woo's trilogy puts it.[206] In the suburbs of Paris, Thai boxing, prized by young Arab and African immigrants, gives them an opportunity 'to be treated with consideration and perceived, at the other side of the world, as really foreigners, and thus to feel really French' when they go for training in Bangkok.[207] But in Iran too, it was his gold medal at the Olympic Games in Melbourne, 1956, in other words his elevation to the world stage, that consecrated the wrestler Takhti as the prototype of the 'man of integrity' (*javânmard*). As a brochure produced by the Organization of Civic Education proclaims:

> Takhti has often climbed onto the podium, he has often looked up at the sky, he has become a credible and respectable figure in world sport. But what distinguished him and gave him his authenticity were his qualities as a hero, a *javânmard*, and his simplicity. What makes a hero or a sportsman are not his rippling torso nor his muscular arms, but his elevated ethical and human qualities. These are what make the difference between the champion (*qahramân*) and the true hero (*pahlavân*).[208]

The most global of sports, football, also proposes a similar synthesis between the moral repertoires of historical societies and a transnational technique of the body, whose market for competitions, players and images is increasingly internationalized.[209]

If we accept that the global techniques of the body are active practices of subjection – i.e. of the constitution of 'moral subjects' taking part in the emergence of a governmentality, and not just of passive and conformist behaviour in thrall to a transcendent order or one imposed from outside – if we see globalization as a form of immanence, we can only refuse to reduce it to a process of dispossession or alienation of identity, culture and sovereignty. Several anthropological studies, for instance, have shown how the reception of images, whether televised or broadcast in some other way, is equivalent to the way the spectator transforms (as a function of his personal expectations) the moral economy to which he feels he 'belongs', and the field of family, social or even political forces in which he situates himself.

Often harshly criticized, the melodramas and other soap operas that circulate round the planet, such as the American series *Dallas* and *Dynasty*, the Japanese *Oshin*, *Tokyo Love Story* or *101st Proposal*, the Indian *Hum Log* or the Mexican *telenovelas*, thus provide their large audiences with plot-lines into which they can project themselves in the intimacy of their imaginations and through conversations with parents, neighbours or colleagues, friends, travellers and the users of public transport, all of which are fostered by these broadcasts. It has sometimes happened that television spectators themselves celebrate the happy and unhappy events that punctuate the plot-lines of these soap operas: the heroine's wedding, the death of the patriarch become part of their own lives, and are honoured with a family meal or a hand-out of sweets in the neighbourhood. Identifying with one or another of these characters, and rejecting others, are ways of accepting or denying certain values, and initiating oneself in global material culture. One might go so far as to say that the heroes, positive or negative, of these deliberately edifying audiovisual productions are 'human types' that 'bear' 'conducts of life'. And this is not the least of the processes of subjectivation, especially when it comes to the family, in the contemporary world. Melodramas are veritable social phenomena, capable of paralysing whole cities, shaping transnational spaces, acting as the carriers of women's self-assertion against men, and imposing themselves as categorical ethical references.[210] These empirical facts have led to a modification of Habermas's pessimism vis-à-vis the mass media. Do not the latter extend and democratize the public space rather than ruining it, especially in places where the liberal bourgeoisie does not politically dominate society?[211]

Likewise, consumption, with its stereotypical gestures of acquisition – pushing your trolley down the aisles, placing your purchases on the conveyor belt at the check-out and wrapping them up as fast as you can in plastic bags that won't open, pinching things without getting nabbed – is a practice of the self, since, as Marx comments, to need something is irrefutable proof that the thing in question is part of *my* being, and its appropriation is my *own* being in its most particular properties.[212] The acquisition of merchandise is a way of composing your 'aesthetic of existence', here again with its values, and even its 'conduct of life'. Even the ascetic, the puritan, the communist or Maoist militant express themselves through a material culture, however elementary and stripped-down it might be, that a few years of economic liberalization are often enough to rehabilitate, as is attested, we have seen, by *Ostalgie* in Germany, but also the yuppie cult for the Great Helmsman in China. 'Since it coincides with Mao's birthday, come in disguise, and we'll eat the kind of food they ate during the Cultural Revolution, it'll be a hoot', a young woman of Beijing puts in her invitation to a flat-warming party.[213]

In particular, the global techniques of the body, in so far as they comprise motor activities, frequently enable the 'moral subject' whom they help to set up as a citizen, to evolve in the public space, to redefine the relations between the latter and the private sphere. The use of cosmetics is an everyday illustration of this. First, because it relates to the way the body is staged on the public space, opening the door to innumerable micro-negotiations cf the frontier between the latter and the private sphere: a woman will not put on make-up in public, but she will do so when she is going to appear in public and she might reapply lipstick in the café or the bus, between meetings. Second, because the practices of the body that are linked to beauty products are also capable of turning their back on the public space and devoting themselves to the demarcation of intimacy: the man who shaves his pubic area to show off his fine lingerie is aiming to please his sexual partner rather than his colleagues, and if he is going to visit his family or his friends, he can easily not shave without being accused of being negligent or committing a faux pas. The often polemical dimension of cosmetics, especially make-up, proceeds in fact from their privileged relation to the demarcation of the private and public spheres.

There are, of course, more dynamic motor activities than these. In her fine monograph on Minot, in the Côte d'Or, Yvonne Verdier brought out very subtly the way in which boys were more likely than girls to be given 'objects relating to mobility, bicycles and even, these days, mopeds'.[214] Women's access to the public space did indeed presuppose a modification in their techniques of the body, the way they dress, and their financial resources, as I mentioned above. This process was naturally quite different from one social milieu to another. In France, processions of majorettes (and it is difficult to think of a more striking example of movement in public), thus played a pre-eminent role in the social visibility of a category of girls who had little in the way of economic and cultural capital.[215] Women of the bourgeoisie or middle classes affirmed themselves through other repertoires of motor activity. In a given society, and now throughout the world, there nonetheless exists a common economy whereby the 'second gender' can gain access to the public space. It rests on transformations of material culture, some of them of a general kind (the development of the wage-earning labour force, certain social laws, the revolution in public transport and the media, for example) while others are proper to their sex (new types of intimate hygiene or new kinds of lingerie that are better adapted to professional life and exercise, the appropriation of trousers or the two-wheeler), as well as on the unprecedented kinds of mobility that these developments make available to them, in the city, the country and the world. It is no accident if, in several countries, women drivers are simultaneously socially distinguished and an object of political or social polemic, or at least of macho jokes.

For Fariba Abdelkhah, it is just this civic capacity for movement that represents a crucial stake in the mobilization of women in Iran, one that wearing the hijab has paradoxically extended. Faezeh Hachemi, a reformist deputy, states:

> Rationally speaking, I cannot accept that the hijab should be obligatory. But I think that, in the context of our society, the hijab has been rather positive for women. The reason is simple. Eighty per cent of the people in our society are traditionalists or religious women, if we except the north of the city of Tehran. The obligation to wear the veil has created a sort of trust between women and society. It has enabled women and girls to take part in social activities. It is this that has enabled women to participate more generally in society, including in out-of-the-way places.[216]

The presence of women in the revolutionary demonstrations of 1978–9, their activities in support of the front-line combatants during the war with Iraq, their growing involvement in informal trade or the jobs market, their trips to the provinces or the local region for religious, family or tourist purposes, have progressively brought them out onto the political stage of the Islamic Republic.[217] In an emblematic fashion, the conflicts provoked by their sudden emergence on the electoral stage have frequently been closely associated with this freedom of movement. Indeed, Faezeh Hachemi presented herself, in 1996–8, as one of the leading figures in Islamic feminism, less, no doubt, as the daughter of her father, who was President of the Republic at the time, than through her independent style and her 'youthful Islamic chic': 'In a certain way, Faezeh Hachemi, by insisting on the practice of sport or on new forms of the hijab that are better adapted to modern, active life, as well as to contemporary tastes, vaguely sensed the importance of movement, of "circulation", in the transformation of the feminine condition.'[218]

The bully-boys of Ansar-e Hezbollah, feeling nostalgic for the revolution and opposed to this kind of new openness, realized what was at stake when a judicial decision turned out not to be in their favour. They attacked women cyclists in one of the parks that the reformist mayor of Tehran, a close friend of Faezeh Hachemi, had opened to them, and smashed the marble skating rink at Ispahan.[219] In small provincial towns, the limitations of the campaigns conducted by candidates often result from the problems of visibility in the strict sense of the term – shopkeepers refuse to stick their posters up in their shop windows – but they also have to do with the difficulties of going round canvassing from door to door and talking personally to the electors.[220]

Generally speaking, the public space is produced and explored by people just walking about. Hegel grasped the importance of these wanderings for the French Revolution; other examples include the civic ceremonies of the Florentine Renaissance, the imposing marches of the Iranian Revolution, all those processions and demonstrations, all those military parades, that impose a rhythm on the social, religious and political life of the city. 'On 1 March, everyone against Le Pen: let's march!' was the headline in *Libération* on 30 April 2002. But there are also ostentatious ways of walking about, through which one can appropriate space and matter in order to make an exhibition of oneself, like the dandies of Brazzaville. A Congolese *Sapeur* explains:

> Once I'm all togged up, I feel so much at ease with myself that nothing else exists around me. I'm like floating on air. And then I can go places I don't usually hang out in. I can walk a really long way, since it's a way of getting people to see me. It's as if I were gliding over the whole world. In general, it's public places I go to, since it's all about looking good, getting others to see you; dance halls, cafés, the main avenues, the big crossroads, and so on.[221]

If we think about it, it's on this level that, every day, a link is forged between the practices of material culture and the formation of the public space, as described by contemporary anthropologists: for example, by means of going out with your family or a gang of your mates and strolling round the shopping malls. As everyone knows, Jürgen Habermas ascribes a significant place to public places of consumption or entertainment – cafes, restaurants, salons, theatres – in the emergence of *Öffentlichkeit*, a point which historians have largely confirmed. But you have to *go* to the café, the restaurant, the theatre, the cinema or the supermarket before you can *be* there and say as much on your mobile phone to the person calling you: 'I'm in the Flore, come and *join* me.' You *go* into town, you *go out* into the street, either to shop, while away the time, protest or rebel. And 'the position of your arms and hands while you walk forms a social idiosyncracy, and not just a product of some mysterious, purely individual mechanisms, almost entirely purely psychological'. So 'you can recognize at a distance the way an Englishman or a Frenchman walks' given that such styles circulate from one society to another. During the interwar period, Marcel Mauss noted:

> I was ill in New York. I asked myself where I had seen ladies who walked the way my nurses did. . . . I finally realized that it was in the cinema. When I returned to France, I noticed that this gait was very frequent, especially in Paris; the girls were French and this was the way they too walked. In fact, American styles of walking were, thanks to the cinema, starting to reach us.[222]

So there is a historical aspect to the way we walk which is not far removed from the changing scale of globalization. It was the genius of Jacques Tati to have grasped on the screen, especially in *Playtime*, this relation between the way one walks (in this case, the way M. Hulot walks) and globalization.

Public, commercial, cultural, social or political space is movement – by definition, so to speak. These days, what is one of the main techniques of the body by which the western town-dweller appropriates this space? The jogging that you practise instead of (and at the same time as) going to church on a Sunday morning, or between two meetings during your business trips, as institutionalized by great rituals, such as the New York Marathon: Mauss also emphasized the historicity of these techniques.[223] As is repeated ad nauseam, modern man is in a hurry. But this haste comes with its own moral economy. It can shock, and infringe the rules of sociability or the expectations of affection, when it takes the form of boorishness. It can even cause disquiet: in Africa, town-dwellers who walk too quickly are often suspected of being thieves, and are lynched, just like the poor devils in Indonesia who drift around in public space without a roof over their heads and try to run away when you question them.[224]

So it is only logical that colonial, authoritarian or totalitarian regimes should have endeavoured to limit movement or to ban it altogether by bringing people together in one rural habitat, regulating the trips they can take, forcing them to seek authorization before they are allowed to move house, or imposing interior passports. This is still a major issue on the scale of globalization. The coercive division of the international jobs market makes the 'democratization of the frontier' one of the burning demands of our time.[225] And the most coherent essay on anti-globalization, *Empire*, deems that, through circulation, the multitude actively reappropriates space, establishing a counter-imperial ontology.[226]

The global political techniques of the body

At all events, what we are seeing is the emergence of political techniques of the body, whether global or 'glocalized', which justify an in-depth analysis of the motor praxeology of globalization. On the coast of China, karaoke bars are places where young women can distance themselves from communist forms of social life and take up the 'family romance' of transnational capitalism, while in Italy, politicians, especially those of Forza Italia, are taking over this Japanese means of expression in the wake of the extraordinary success of a particular TV presenter, Fiorello.[227] Ever since the summer of 2003, flashmobs, summoned by emails, have been growing ever more numerous in the public places of great western cities. Thus, on 2 July, at 7 pm, 200 people gathered in the mezzanine of the Hyatt hotel in New York and clapped loudly enough to raise the roof for fifteen seconds. On 24 July, a similar troupe imitated animal cries under the walls of the Museum of Natural History in Central Park, while in Rome, customers burst into a Megastore asking for an imaginary book. On 7 August, in London, a group intoned the letter 'O', without consonants, in a furniture shop. On 13 July, in Montreal, children floated plastic ducks in a fountain and made them quack. It seems that the first 'instant crowd' in France gathered on 28 August, between 7:15 and 7:18 pm, under the Louvre Pyramid: 500 people suddenly stood stock still, fell to the floor, picked themselves up, turned to the main door and applauded.[228]

Up until now, these flashmobs have had no explicit political purpose. 'It's just for pleasure, for the futile, absurd, amusing and ephemeral side of it all. Lying under the Pyramid was pleasant and we couldn't have done it if we'd been alone. It's a way of re-appropriating the city. We're "space invaders".'[229] But for an author such as Howard Rheingold, they prefigure the next social revolution – and smartmobs will be its protagonists.[230] Meanwhile, the 'transversal struggles' of globalization rely on particular forms of expression such as streaking, a way of disturbing official ceremonies while not wearing any clothes.

In the last ten years or so, the classic exercise of demonstrating in the streets has become internationalized, and this has seriously constrained the stiff and starchy arrangements of G8 summits or multilateral institutions, to such an extent that they have forced the organizers to hold them in places difficult to reach and easy to control. From this point of view, anti-globalization protest has unquestionably managed to reconfigure the public space worldwide, by combining the resources of transnational globalization and the national or local repertoires of the political technology of the body. Thus the South Korean militant peasant Lee Kyung-hae, who committed suicide on 10 September 2003, on the very first day of the Ministerial Conference of the WTO in Mexico, stabbing himself through the heart – with a Swiss knife – placed at the service of a certain global cause a mode of political denunciation endowed with a strong symbolic historicity, if we are to believe the evidence provided by his companions. As the trade unionist Jung Kwang Hoon explained:

> Lee used his body to show our sufferings. It's difficult for Westerners to understand. But in Korea, the history of social struggle is marked by a certain tradition: we use our bodies and can mutilate ourselves to express a political cause. Lee was very strong-willed. To show his determination, he struck his body in a symbolic place: his heart.

And the style of Lee Kyung-hae's diary leaves little doubt as to the 'glocal' dimension of his gesture:

When we learnt of the possible consequences of the Uruguay Round, our innocent little hearts were plunged into a saucepan of boiling tears. We couldn't sleep, and we decided to come to Geneva to meet the former director of the WTO. We spoke sincerely but prudently to him of our difficulties. Of course, our request was cordially rejected in diplomatic terms. Our voices were too small and timid to pierce the great wall facing us. Then, all at once, I was sent off on a journey in my imagination: I suddenly saw a crowd of my peasant comrades on strike in the street. Unconsciously, my hand, holding a knife (a Swiss army knife, I think) was cutting into my abdomen. I immediately regretted this uncontrolled action, carried out when I was over-agitated.[231]

Even more tragically, the spread of suicide attacks, following the example set by the Tamil Tigers, and taken up by radical Islamic militants, demonstrates the extent to which the global political techniques of the body are of a nature to weigh on the definition of public space. The systematization of security measures that it has entailed now conditions people's daily circulation and submits them to a new discipline of screening and frisking every time they enter public places or public transport. It represents a spectacular change in the 'microphysics of power' that has been imposed over the last twenty years without arousing any real opposition.

Suicide attacks are, of course, an extreme technology of the body. It is worth recalling that it takes the form of a labour of subjectivation that intervenes, here too, at the interface between a global mode of action and local and national political or cultural repertoires. To the great confusion of the Japanese, those who carry out these attacks are called kamikazes, though it should be borne in mind that the Japanese pilots of the Second World War drew part of their courage in Christian representations of self-sacrifice and philosophical concepts of 'the general interest' imported from the West and subordinated to the objectives of militarist nationalism, and were in no way the pure products of an eternal home-grown tradition.[232] These days, the Islamic terrorists of al-Qaida who offer up their own (and others') lives on the altar of the anti-imperialist struggle grow less from the national soil (unlike their Palestinian equivalents) than from the transnational dimension of the world system of states. Olivier Roy emphasizes the degree to which they come from the West, if we include those who are members of the 'second generation' of immigration, and take over the social processes characteristic of North American or European societies, such as individuation, sectarian religious behaviour, militant commitment and the use of the Internet for propaganda or organization purposes.[233] As a political technique of the body, the suicide attack is a radical act whereby certain people can appropriate globalization. It reached its (perhaps provisional) apogee in the destruction of the World Trade Center. The world has never been quite the same since then, and, as everyone knows, the shockwave has not been completely absorbed, especially from the point of view of the reinforcement of political and police control to the detriment of public liberties.

Nonetheless, we need to avoid any holistic and unequivocal apprehension of global subjection and its overthrow. World governmentality, which the techniques of the body and transnational commoditization and conducts of life are progressively allowing to emerge, at the interface of the system of states, is less panoptic than kaleidoscopic. It rests on a 'microphysics of power' that is neither total nor overdetermining. It is still an arena for 'transversal struggles', as Foucault put it, which treat the reality of political action as an art of the possible. It is, above all, contradictory and based on the principle of incompletion, even when it turns violent.

As we have seen, whipping as a punishment is a political technique of the body constitutive of globalization, less as an archaic survival than as the arrangement of new forms of domination, for example in the Islamic Republic of Iran, which is a modern regime that has broken away from the classic conception of religion held by the clerical establishment, or in that of the armed movements that are the protagonists of the 'new wars', or indeed the industrial authoritarian regimes of Southeast Asia and the 'thuggish' despotism of Saddam Hussein. Nonetheless, at the same time, the disfavour into which corporal punishment has fallen, and the way it is increasingly becoming illegal, even within families, are becoming elements of a global 'governance' which the various associations, parliaments, administrations, law courts and supreme courts of justice of more and more western countries are concerned to see is respected. We need to add that, in these societies, the erotic, sado-masochistic practice of flagellation seems to be spreading or increasing in visibility and respectability, both among homosexuals and heterosexuals, via the press, the Internet and the advertising industry. 'Babette: to be bound, whipped and sometimes stirred', proclaimed a publicity campaign for Candia of a semi-skimmed cream a few years ago[234] – it is starting to become clear that a technique of the body, even a coercive and summary one, is capable of gaining disparate or conflicting meanings within the framework of global governmentality, and inevitably leads to a debate or a conflict in subjectivation.

While British human rights organizations denounce cruel and inhumane punishments, and a group of teachers, civil servants, lawmakers and magistrates is tempted to criminalize physical punishments meted out to children, a reality show on Channel 4, *That'll Teach 'Em*, anxious to 'start a debate on education', gets together some thirty or so schoolchildren in a 1950s-style boarding school and submits them to its discipline, its material culture, and its training techniques, from caning and hitting the fingers with a ruler to uniforms in prickly synthetic fibre, gym lessons in the rain and at daybreak, recitations learnt off by heart and the awful food of the post-war years. Some of them crack, while others (and sometimes the same ones) just love the experience. As Holly writes to her parents, three weeks after she burst into tears in front of the TV cameras:

> The teachers are strict, but fair so long as you obey the rules. In fact, it's really great. I'm ashamed I was so stupid. I'm much happier now. We've been taught to knit and sew. You won't recognize me when I come home: I've learnt to be graceful, elegant and tidy. We're also being taught to stand upright and walk properly.[235]

Perhaps it is now easier to see why we should not restrict the historicity of contemporary subjection within a false alternative, asking ourselves 'whether the subject is active or passive,' when subjectivity is basically a *practice*:

> The subject is the mind activated by principles, and the notion of activation avoids the alternative. To the extent that principles sink their effect into the depths of the mind, the subject, which is this very effect, becomes more and more active and less and less passive. It was passive in the beginning, it is active in the end. This confirms the idea that subjectivity is in fact a process, and that an inventory must be made of the diverse moments of this process . . . the subject is an imprint, or an impression, left by principles, that it progressively turns into a machine capable of using this impression.[236]

If we think about the processes of subjectivation as a 'production of modes of existence or lifestyles', in the modes of 'activation' of the 'One' rather than the 'I' or the 'Me', as Gilles Deleuze put it, and if we analyse global governmentality in terms of *haecceities*, i.e., 'literally speaking, the fact of being this, the fact of being a "this", a degree of potentiality';[237] if we accept that the individual is not the indivisible, and that individuation forms internal multiplicities;[238] if we take as our object modes of operation and schemes of action, rather than the subject as their author or vehicle[239] – then we can grasp that, yes indeed, 'It's all starting up!' as Józef Wittlin put it, and has been for the last two centuries: 'it' travels by train and plane, 'it' marches along, 'it' makes war, 'it' makes things, 'it' sells and 'it' buys, 'it' taps away at the keyboard, 'it' enjoys and 'it' suffers.

This general starting up which was brought about by the changing scale of capitalism and the state, from the nineteenth century onwards, is globally ours. It is history, and thus appropriation. But the latter is much too disordered and segmented to be subsumed into yet another Grand Narrative, whether it be the liberal version (governance) or the radical version (anti-globalization). Globalization is globally ours, but in a fragmentary, momentary way, in 'intensities'. And the conflicts of subjectivation or the political disputes that it opens up tear us apart inside, instead of opposing to the market and to globalization, in an extraneous relation, those already constituted forces or principles such as the state, identity, sovereignty. Globalization preoccupies us, frightens us, wounds us, since it divides us in our flesh, in our desire, and not just in our ideas. None of us is either for or against it. It inhabits and subjects us. Indeed, though he is master of his creation, man appears as its slave, as Marx put it.

Once this has been established, the study of the techniques of body by which we constitute ourselves as 'moral subjects' of globalization leaves us with a paradox. The latter is deemed to be all acceleration and urgency.[240] Nonetheless, it inculcates a huge discipline of waiting in us. Queuing is one of the procedures that it has systematized throughout the world, even among people who are most recalcitrant to this exercise. In Hong Kong, for example, people never used to wait patiently in a line until they were served, in banks, restaurants or at the counters of transport companies until the 1970s. Together with the landing stages of ferries and taxi ranks, McDonald's taught them this way of doing things, and its consumers now send rough-mannered continentals packing when they try and push in.[241]

People used to make fun of the queues in Soviet Russia. But perhaps they were an avant-garde socialist contribution to globalization? For we are forever lining up, in an increasing number of places and on an ever growing number of occasions, to gain access to the benefits of the society of commoditization: in the self-service café; in restaurants, before the maître d' can take us to our seats; in airports, to check in and then hand over our luggage; in the plane, to sit, go to the toilet, disembark; in the cinema, since certain Parisian cinemas have invented the double queue, one to buy tickets and the other before the doors open; at the Sainte-Geneviève library, on the Place du Panthéon, or the library of the Georges-Pompidou Centre as we wait for a free seat; outside museums, especially when there is an exhibition on; at the doors of department stores, on the first day of the sales; on the pavement outside consulates or prefectures to obtain a visa or a travel permit; and at the check-out of supermarkets. The queue has become so prevalent in our everyday lives that we no longer pay any attention to it. From the point of view of the 'microphysics of power', it is to some extent the airlock into globalization. But the latter is not situated on the margins of the process. It is at its heart, it is constitutive of it. We queue in the most luxurious places in New York, or at dawn in the rue du Faubourg-Saint-Honoré, outside the British Embassy, a stone's throw away from the Elysée. We do it on a weekly basis at the Carrefour or Leclerc supermarket so as to procure the goods we cannot live without. We do it whenever we have to take that means of transport that has brought about 'time–space compression': the aeroplane. Even Mohammed Atta had to queue to buy his cutters and climb into one of the fateful flights that was to destroy the World Trade Center. Just as do 'travel for the sake of it' and the sense of 'urgency', so such a discipline of waiting seems inherent to the 'regime of historicity' that characterizes the current moment of globalization.[242] It is part of its governmentality and reveals its fundamental contradiction, between the liberalization of the international markets of capitals and goods on the one hand, and the coercive division of the labour market on the other. There is every likelihood that we will see emerging from the outer shadows of these 'zones of waiting' unprecedented conducts of life, new lines of political subjectivation, and original techniques of the body.

Conclusion: When Waiting is an Urgent Matter

As we have seen, having to stand in line, as a technique of the body, stylizes man's 'historical condition' in the situation of globalization. In this 'regime of historicity', in this 'way of being in time',[1] the only urgent thing is indeed to wait, and *Godot* is the only worthwhile manifesto. Taken in all their diversity and sometimes their contradictions, the processes of globalization create states, and even, to an increasing degree, 'states of emergency' or 'of exception', which are states in which peoples are stockpiled and forced into latency. Not that the latter are excluded or marginalized properly speaking, as is often said. It is at the heart of the reactor of globalization that they wait. They proceed from it and participate in its reproduction. Let the reader judge from a few facts.

Global Godot

The attacks of 11 September 2001 and the 'worldwide war on terrorism' that they legitimized have led the United States to authorize the Attorney-General to detain any alien suspected of endangering national security (the 'Patriot Act' of 26 October 2001) and to subject non-US citizens to special jurisdictions making it possible for them to be placed in 'indefinite detention', following the details set out in President Bush's 'Military Order', dated 13 November 2001. 'Prisoners taken on the battlefield' and 'illegal enemy combatants' are nameless and outside the law. On the one hand, the category to which they are assigned has no juridical existence, either international or American. On the other, they are dumped, for an indefinite period of which the only thing one can be sure is that it will be long, in extraterritorial places – the bases at Guantanamo in Cuba, or Bagram in Afghanistan, different centres of detention scattered around the planet[2] – that lie outside all legislation, but not all regulation, which are not all made known to the public and which harbour anonymous men accused of crimes that are not divulged, or even known to their gaolers.

As Giorgio Agamben comments:

> Not only are the Taliban captured in Afghanistan unable to enjoy the status of prisoners of war as defined by the Geneva Convention, but they do not correspond to any case of imputation fixed by American laws: neither prisoners nor defendants, but mere 'detainees', they find themselves subjected to a pure de facto sovereignty, a detention that is not only indefinite in the temporal sense, but indeed in the more real sense of escaping completely from the law and any form of judicial control. With the detainee of Guantanamo, bare naked life is found at the most extreme level of indefiniteness.[3]

In fact, there is a striking contrast between the absolute panoptic character of the way the camp is set out – cages of meshed wire which do not allow the least bodily intimacy ('every cell is observed by one of my men on average every thirty seconds', states Colonel Jerry Cannon, commandant at Camp Delta[4]) – and the opacity of a condition of imprisonment the reasons for which the identity of the subjects and the length of detention are all kept secret and not even known to the authorities who set up the camps. If we are to believe the International Committee of the Red Cross, the 660 or so detainees of Guantanamo are 'left to their own devices, without prospects, unable to count the days to a particular date, whether it be the date of their indictment, their trial or their liberation'.[5] They live in a state of despair and are prone to strongly suicidal thoughts.[6] Most of them are barely in their twenties, sometimes they are minors, and they are deprived of the freedom to die as well as of the freedom to live.

But the uncertainty of their interrogators is equally great. Joseph Lelyveld, one of the veterans of American journalism, worries:

> [T]he American officials who, in Afghanistan, sorted the prisoners were obsessed by the fear they might allow someone important to escape, and had – thanks to the language barrier – only a vague idea of the identity of these prisoners: men who, in certain cases, had been handed over to them in exchange for money with the assurance that they were really, authentically dangerous or 'interesting' from the information point of view, in exactly the same way that a carpet that attracts your attention on the legendary frontier of Afghanistan may turn out to be really, authentically rare.[7]

And indeed, everyone knows that providing fake suspects was a profitable bit of trafficking for the different politico-military entrepreneurs who were fighting the Taliban and saw the American intervention as a divine surprise.

This condition of indefinite waiting was based on an emergency. It was one of 'an ever more frequent resort to the paradigm of emergency as a system of government',[8] of the state of emergency that the above-mentioned texts de facto established, but also in the hastiness dictated by the urgency of circumstances. It is above all a physical condition: the prisoners are given a beating when they are captured and, according to certain witnesses, on their arrival at Guantanamo; their beards and hair are forcibly shaven; they are blindfolded; they are forced to kneel; they are chained up; they are deprived of sleep; their natural functions have to be carried out in full view of the guards and the other detainees; their movements are restricted, as they are locked into cells of 2.07 by 2.43 metres, and they are allowed out only twice a week, each time for just fifteen minutes. This is, quite deliberately, a condition of degradation and animalization. 'We were like animals. If we were men, why put us in a cage?' as an ex-detainee asks.[9] But it is, at the same time, a global condition, since it is right at the heart of the international 'agenda' of the greatest power in the world. And also because its material culture and the techniques of the body that the latter induces are those of the neo-liberal moment of subjection.

Camp Delta was constructed by a subsidiary of Halliburton, Vice-President Dick Cheney's old company, and the same company that is prospering in liberated Iraq. The labour force that built it came from India and the Philippines to keep costs down, though these in fact rose to $9.7 million. The cell blocks were assembled from metallic containers used in maritime transport – and some of the detainees had already had a chance to make the acquaintance of this technology of imprisonment, prized by General Rachid Dostom, one of the USA's local allies, in Afghanistan. The prisoners 'queue up for the interrogations',[10] unable to queue up in the 'only McDonald's in Cuba', the 'Downtown' one, as the commercial area of Guantanamo base is ironically called.[11]

Some might be tempted to see the camp of the 'battlefield prisoners' as having a merely symbolic meaning, one that is admittedly tragic and scandalous, or justified, but infinitesimally small. They would be wrong. Guantanamo is a microcosm of globalization, including in the relation the detention camp establishes between the off-shore principle and the sovereignty of the state at its most absolute. President Bush's 'Patriot Act' and 'Military Order', in fact, struck at several ordinary immigrants, who were merely not quite in line with the regulations, and at American or western citizens, by withdrawing from them the decrees of habeas corpus.[12] They turned upside down the ways people travel round the world, imposed unprecedented procedures of control, discipline and repression, reshaped the techniques of the body linked to travel, and broadened and intensified the grip of 'bio-power'.[13]

Above all, they represent the quintessence of a second, more ordinary condition of waiting, that which regulates international migrations. The major disjunction between the coercive restriction of these migrations, and the liberalization of the circulation of capital, goods and images, has led to the creation of other populations without any rights, and other zones of detention, some of them administrative, at the gates of the industrial states, others social, in the cities or the buffer regions that serve as approach ramps to the mirage of their prosperity. To the south of the United States and Europe, Mexico, the Maghreb, Turkey and the Balkan countries are well-known thresholds in which vegetate emigrants using them as stop-off points, waiting in a permanent state of stand-by, and cities such as Tangiers, Tetuan or Istanbul are veritable hubs from which pioneers in search of 'adventure' set off.

Nonetheless, these marches should not conceal two facts. The migrations between southern countries themselves, either on a temporary or permanent basis, are just as massive. The poorest states export their labour force to the regional poles of growth or passage: West African countries to the Ivory Coast, Nigeria, Morocco or Libya; those of the Horn of Africa to Djibouti; Zimbabwe and Mozambique to the Republic of South Africa; Indochina and Burma to Thailand, Singapore and Malaysia; North Korea to China and Russia; and China to South Korea. Meanwhile, the Arab monarchies of the Gulf and Israel import workers from the whole world. In fact, you can always find someone who is poorer or richer than you are. Egypt and Jordan, for instance, have become notable countries of immigration, and even Pakistan may appear as an Eldorado for the women of Bangladesh or Burma. In addition, the pile-up of migrants does not merely happen on the frontiers or at the gates into industrial societies, but also at their very heart, in police detention centres or humanitarian centres such as the one that the Red Cross ran at Sangatte, or even, in a diffuse way, in certain districts or certain ports that are well known to the authorities.[14] Nobody, indeed, is more visible, and sometimes ostentatiously so, than the illegal immigrant.[15]

These new 'floating populations' – to borrow the expression used in French colonial administration – are in a situation of permanent waiting: waiting for a people-smuggler, a job, papers, waiting to be expelled or to return. The time they have to wait will be all the longer as they are tending to become ever younger. The immigration of minors, whether spontaneous or controlled by criminal gangs, is on the rise: teenagers from the Maghreb or Africa hidden in lorries or aircraft underbellies, gypsy kids forced into begging or prostitution, jockeys or domestic servants from the Indian sub-continent and the south-east of Iran, 'mules' for the traffic in heroin, 'little maid servants' from the Ivory Coast, young workers from the fields and the towns – they are all now part of the social landscape of the industrial metropolises, the petromonarchies or the plantation regions.[16] At the same interminable tempo as that of several first-rate films, such as *Blissfully Yours* (2002) by Apichatpong Weerasethakul, *De l'autre côté* (2002) by Chantal Ackerman, *Histoires de vies brisées (Les 'double peine' de Lyon)* (2001) by Bertrand Tavernier, or the disappointing *In this World* (2003) by Michael Winterbottom, the 'floating populations', of all ages, are deprived of rights and of social dignity. 'A zone without rights unworthy of our country', in the words of the report of the Médecins du Monde organization on the ZAPI ('Zone d'attente pour personnes en instance' (*sic!*) [Waiting Zone for Persons Waiting – *Tr.*] – at Roissy-Charles-de-Gaulle airport, where the dirtiness of the buildings, the insults, the humiliations, the brutalities, the violation of legal prescriptions and regulations supposed to protect foreigners when they are called in for questioning, are the daily lot (*Veralltäglichung*).[17] After they disembark, and even before they have to face the police controls and the holding centre, those who are asking for political and economic asylum – and who is in any position to distinguish between them?[18] – can stagnate for a shorter or longer time in the installations of the international zone. Someone who is often in the place testifies:

> In airport 2A, I met several foreigners when I visited. They said they'd been there for more than two weeks. In 2B I saw twelve people who had been waiting on blue seats, opposite the police office, for four or six days. These people do not exist while they wait. The places where they have to wait are well known. The foreigners told me that they were, at best, fed by the people who worked as cleaners. An African explained to me that they would ferret in the dustbins of the cafeteria. Another told me that he came every day to ask the policeman to register him as an asylum seeker. They told him, 'Stay there, you have to wait.' ... On another occasion, I discovered that some ten or so people had been waiting for over ten days.[19]

Are these mere blunders, ascribable to a police that is still in thrall to colonial memories, riddled with racism, intoxicated by twenty years of an exorbitantly security-focused political discourse and sure of its own impunity? Things are more complicated than that. For one thing, the status, if one can call it that, of illegal immigrant belongs to the social foundations of globalization and is one of the far from negligible sources of capitalist accumulation on the world scale, as we saw in an earlier chapter. For another, it is no more enviable in countries other than France. In Switzerland, the Federal Office of Refugees sends Africans who are not authorized to stay back to Abidjan and sub-contracts their return home to their countries of origin to the authorities and lawyers of the Ivory Coast, outside any juridical framework.[20] Twice a month, a night train, loaded with a thousand or so illegal immigrants, travels from the retention camp in Lindela, South Africa, to the frontier with Zimbabwe.[21] Massive expulsions, rising to tens of thousands of individuals, or even pogroms of illegal immigrant workers, are current to the south of the Sahara and in Libya. And the *Herald* sums up the destiny of immigrant workers to South Korea in these terms: 'Dirty work, bad pay and no defence.'[22] Even before the Patriot Act, an American delegation could express satisfaction at the good upkeep of the ZAPI at Roissy-Charles-de-Gaulle, in comparison with the way illegal immigrants were treated in the United States.[23] Waiting in uncertainty, dirt and stench are an everyday experience in globalization, the equivalent, in advanced capitalism, to the confinement of slaves in the entrepôts of the mercantile period, and the demotic parallel to the aeroplane passengers waiting for an eventual take-off.

Waiting is in no way external to globalization. It is a constitutive practice of it, now that the border is an 'institution' (as Etienne Balibar calls it). At the limits, it is a whole region that might be living in a state of expectancy, like the states to the north of Mexico, that country 'so close to the United States, so far from God', and the place where migrants congregate, as well as the 'coyotes' who are to 'get them across the border', the female workers on the *maquiladoras* specialized in exports, and which experienced such a transient boom, and where people are still yearning for the results of an inquiry that would finally elucidate the unpunished murders of at least 370 female workers, servants or students since 1993 in just one city, Ciudad Juarez.[24]

Perhaps it is now easier to understand what Fariba Adelkhah understood by the 'madhi-like dimension of emigration'.[25] And indeed, waiting is consubstantial with emigration. Fawzi Mellah, who has travelled between North Africa and Europe for the purposes of research, says:

> So we had to wait. Wait. An illegal immigrant spends over half his time (of his life?) waiting for something. The reply of a people smuggler. Arrival in an improvised or unknown port. The goodwill of a contact. The chance to meet a friend. The benevolence of an employer who will let you moonlight. An amnesty. A presidential election. The coming to power of the Left – any Left. The departure of this same Left from power. A demonstration of intellectuals. The occupation of a church. Expulsion . . . In short, I said above that you couldn't talk about the future to people who experience life as a temporality made of little immediate futures; I will now add that, as well as that, there cannot be any question of the future for people who spend most of their time waiting for something to happen.[26]

And 'in Tangiers, you live clutching your mobile phone waiting for the announcement that the money that will enable you to cross the sea has been transferred to your bank'.[27]

For all that, globalization is in synergy with other ways in which populations are stocked up. To begin with, that of the common law prison population that is forever increasing and growing younger all the time, including in western countries, and whose sentences are lengthening. In France, the average length of detention has doubled in twenty-five years, even without the principle (adopted from the United States) of automatic 'minimum' sentences in the case of repeated offences.[28] In the present neo-liberal period, prison does seem to be a coherent political response to the social question.[29] And it is obvious that neither in Russia nor in China has the 'transition to a market economy' led to the dismantling of the gulag or of the 'forgotten archipelago'.[30] But what do prisoners do, in their cells or dormitories, except count the days that separate them from their liberation?

Secondly, the canalizing towards countries that are reservoirs for the huge army of refugees that the First World War first threw out onto the roads of Europe,[31] of which the Second World War swelled the ranks, and which has been renewed by the various conflicts, operations of ethnic cleansing, and even genocides. The number of the 'victims of forced displacements' is today as high as 50 million, according to the United Nations High Commission for Refugees, of which 12–18 million are refugees in the strict sense of the term, i.e. forced to live outside their own countries. This figure was just over 1.5 million at the start of the 1950s. As a result, 'the characteristic – the only one, no doubt – which unifies this whole population scattered across the planet' is that 'the displaced and the refugees are for a while set outside the *nomos*, the ordinary law of human beings'. 'Their existence is based on the loss of a *place*, to which were attached attributes of identity, relation and memory, and on the absence of a new social *place*. . . . For the vast majority, which has to survive, is forced to wait, displacement represents a brutal entry into a condition of hanging around at borders.'[32]

This state is indisputably a 'state of insecurity' whose everyday existence (*Veralltäglichung*) is woven through with corporal punishments, sexual aggression, armed robbery, confrontations between the refugees themselves or between refugees and local populations.[33] It is thus that the camp of canvas tents has become a new global social institution, able to welcome each and every kind of detainee, as in Guantanamo, when the first 'prisoners of the battlefield' arrived at X-ray, the homeless results of an earthquake who are aided by the emergency services of the whole world, or, in this case, civilians fleeing combats and massacres. A refugee camp can shelter several tens of thousands of people – or even 750,000, like the humanitarian conurbation of Goma, in Kivu, between 1994 and 1996 – and begin to look like a town without ever actually becoming one, because of its precarious nature.[34] Surviving in a state of suspense, its inhabitants are not thereby cut off from the rest of the world. They have complicated relations with the natives who, sometimes, have an even lower standard of living, and can sell their services to some of the better-off among the refugees.[35] The media, NGOs, the aid of the United Nations, the World Bank, the European Commission or foreign states help them to stay part of the processes of globalization, even if only as assisted victims or as consumers of images. As they wait in the camps, they cannot work, and so cannot afford to buy much, but 'the video shops are permanently full, showing Indian or American films, or pre-recorded sports events from across the world'.[36]

Finally, the synergy of the global system of states and the internationalization of economies has led to the incorporation of 'minorities' and 'native peoples' into the interplay of the worldwide market and national domination by forcing them, sometimes at gunpoint, into a situation of 'interior colonialism', while involving them in commercial exchanges, mining or forestry activities, smuggling artworks or animal species, the vigilance of 'civil society', and the curiosity of tourists.[37]

Once again, what emerges from these notations is that violence and power are inherent to the 'historical condition' and the 'regime of historicity' of contemporary globalization. As governmentality, the latter is akin to a configuration of bodily constraint, either in the form of forced recruitments or the trafficking of human beings, something which is rising to a spectacular degree,[38] or via the retention, expulsion, incarceration, confinement to camp or industrial discipline of the free zones, which are, to some extent, institutionalized and legitimate versions of these traffickings.

It is of course not a question of seeing globalization as the ultimate or exclusive reason behind all the effects of population flow, and the ways people are forced to wait, but of accepting that it sits easily with the most hackneyed procedures of subjection and puts them together with the most sophisticated technologies of 'bio-power'. The expulsions of illegal immigrants are carried out with physical vigour, prison overpopulation makes prison conditions even more degrading, and corporal punishment and brutality are commonplace in the centres of detention or correction reserved for children and adolescents of the United States or Mexico, even if we restrict ourselves just to the heart of the international system.[39]

The relation between constraint and globalization is clear when these establishments are delocalized, like vulgar industries or bank accounts. Not far from the formidable penitentiary market created by the policy of 'zero tolerance' towards delinquents, are not the Caribbean countries poised to transform themselves into free zones of education, paradises of punishment? The home at Tranquility Bay in Jamaica, specialized in behaviour-modification programmes for American teenagers, and managed by the World Wide Association of Speciality Programs and Schools (WWASPS), based in Utah, is an outpost among

others of these new social institutions, famous for the polemic that
raged as a result of the ill-treatment to which it subjects its 300 board-
ers, aged from 12 to 19 years.[40] Likewise, in France, the Vagabondage
association, which had been entrusted with young people in difficulty
by the child welfare services and the *département* council of Finistère,
organized sessions of 'breakdown treatment' in Zambia. One of the
children in its care died there of an epileptic fit after three days of
torture during which he had spent a whole night tied, naked, to a post
in a pigsty, had his head plunged into the filthy farm water, and was
beaten by his schoolmates and sprinkled with their urine.[41] This is one
form the transational subjectivation of western youth can take, at a time
when the tender-hearted folk of Northern Europe are waxing indignant
at the idea that anyone might raise their hand to their offspring.

The 'event' of globalization has also entailed or reproduced the
enslavement of children imported into the Arab countries of the Gulf,
Southeast Asia, Africa or indeed Western Europe, and forced to do the
sexual bidding of their masters, carry out domestic chores, work in
industry, cottage industries or agriculture, beg, perform in camel races,
or prostitute themselves.[42] Scotland Yard has even dismantled in
London a ring of young Africans who had been reduced to servitude
and were used in social security benefits frauds; the gang had been
guilty of at least one ritual murder of a boy aged between 4 and 7 from
the south-west of Nigeria.[43] It is improbable that a candid aspiration to
'good governance' and 'transparency' can deal with this hardly hidden
face of globalization – especially since (as is worth repeating) the
authoritarian regulation of population flows does not seem to be an
epiphenomenon of the latter, but rather one of its mathematical functions. Historians will not be in the least surprised to see neo-liberalism
resorting to force, and the latter disguising itself in the trappings of
emancipation. The formation of the state and that of the world market
of goods and capital, the Grand Narrative of the nation, have resorted
to similar pretences. And from this point of view, the nineteenth century
was indeed foundational – its laissez-faire led to the extermination
of the Indians in North America, organized the mass famines of the
Victorian period in Asia and supported colonial conquest from the
Cape to Hanoi, or at least accepted it.

Globalization as a liminal condition

It thus turns out to be true that the essential paradox of globalization
lies in this contradiction between economic and financial openness on
the one side, and, on the other, the coercive compartmentalization
of the international labour market and the obstacles placed in the way
of the circulation of people. Waiting is something that happens when

these processes intersect, at the ticket windows of air companies, in the squalid hotels of people-smugglers or in the temples of commercial consumption. So the important thing is to gain a better understanding of the relation between globalization and this 'regime of historicity' of waiting and to reach a precise conceptualization of the latter.

For some years, it has been customary to take up the idea of the *limen*, which the anthropologist Victor Turner had himself borrowed from the discussion of rites of passage in the ethnological work of Arnold Van Gennep.[44] This reference is all the more tempting in that the 'adventure' of emigration or mining is consciously associated with the experience of initiation among young Africans and that, pretty much across the world, the epic of expatriation or the less romantic epic of entering the job market confer the social status of an adult, open the path to marriage, procure an aura of respectability, or even notability – in short, they sanction a change of state. In fact, the itinerary of migrants, especially when they are illegal immigrants, corresponds to the three phases of the rites of passage: that of 'separation', that of the margin or *limen*, and that of 'aggregation'. The person leaving tears himself away from his family and his home territory, entrusts himself life and limb to successive people-smugglers, and re-establishes communication with his family once he has arrived safely at his destination by sending them a cassette narrating his epic.[45] The well-named moment of 'passage' is a passage across a threshold, and the emigrant abandons himself to it as he waits, confined, in fear, thirsty, hungry and suffering, before being reborn as an immigrant vis-à-vis the host society, and as a man of honour, if not a notable, vis-à-vis the society he has left behind. There is nothing lacking from the rituals of initiation: they are accompanied by both blows and lies.

When I telephoned the contact I had, I was told to meet up outside my hotel. Two men pulled up in a car, I got in with them, they took me to a cafeteria. There we sat down and, ten minutes later, the agent arrived: young, very well dressed, very chic and elegant, loaded with mobile telephones and accompanied by four bodyguards, all Kurds. He got to the point straightaway, asking me what I wanted. I said, 'To go to Europe', and he replied, 'I can get you there via Italy, by ship or lorry.' He paused, looked thoughtful, and then added, 'But what *you* need is the ship. Take the ship', making it sound obvious, like a solution that was thoroughly well adapted to my case, and like a gift he was making me by advising me to make this choice. I asked for some more details, whether it was an ordinary ship. He replied, 'Of course! It's a very good ship, it carries travellers, tourists. You'll see, it's really fine. I guarantee it!' A week later, encouraged by a hail of blows from the sticks of the people smugglers who hit people to make them embark more quickly, I climbed up the gangway of an old cargo ship that was practically a wreck and found myself, a few moments later, shut up in a hold, together with some 450 other people. We sailed out to sea, only to be caught up by the Turkish police a few hours later.[46]

Victor Turner sees millenarian movements as liminal experiences – these are movements that we have seen flaming up throughout our two centuries of globalization, the pilgrimages that turn the commerce between believers and God and merchandise into a spectacle, or the hippie movement of the 1960s, which is an example of a 'transversal struggle'.[47] Nonetheless, the danger of such a reading would be to indulge complacently in an effect of fashion or vocabulary, artificially to impose on the analysis in terms of the historical sociology of the political a demonstration of anthropological or ethnological order, or, even worse, to take over as one's own the functionalist vision from which the latter does not always manage to escape. It is easy to see, for instance, how a neo-liberal doctrinaire that has converted to postmodernism, during an evening drinking bout, could impassively explain the processes of 'transition' to the market economy and democracy in accordance with the three phases of Van Gennep. The first of these would be 'separation' from mercantilist or socialist state control, at the price of a political crisis, by withering away or by revolution, and of a financial crisis due to runaway debt. The second would be precisely the liminal period of 'passage' through the processes of structural adjustment and the ascetic nature of the reforms. The third would be that of 'integration', by full market freedom, the establishment of 'good (and transparent) governance', the recovering of stability, and reincorporation into the international economy and 'community'. One can also see the advantages the immigration services might be able to draw from Turner's concept if they took it into their heads to read him: surely it is normal and legitimate to subject migrants to invisibility, savagery, insults, blows, nudity, lack of food, sexual abstinence, arbitrary punishment and the anonymity that go with the *limen*, satisfying themselves with the solidarity and sense of *communitas* that their lack of individual identity will bring about in them?

Unless we abandon ourselves to an eschatology of globalization, the rebirth of the world from its margins and its zones of retention cannot be considered as complete, although social youngsters have historically been eminent focuses of subjectivation. You may recall how, for Foucault, this notion designates, in particular, the way individuals or communities constitute themselves as subjects. This may happen in the margins of current forms of knowledge and power, even though new forms of knowledge and power may arise precisely in these margins. So, according to Deleuze, subjectivation always comes out of time, in a sort of fold – and it is often not the masters but the socially excluded among whom subjectivation occurs, in lamentation as well as in exaltation.[48] Thus, freedmen in Ancient Rome, and slaves or fugitives in the

Africa of the nineteenth century, were the main 'bearers' of the Christian lifestyle.[49] As for the Iranun who scoured the seas of Asia, they had forged their ethos as pirates in the necessity of a panic-stricken exodus, following a terrible eruption of the Maketering volcano that ravaged their lands, around 1765.[50] Their lifestyle and death, in the interstices of the world economy, was that of refugees, as we would say these days. The same is true today in the lower depths of 'globalization from below'.[51] But we should beware of not jumping out of the frying pan into the fire, from stigmatizing the new 'dangerous classes' who live in the suburbs in a state of illegal immigration, if we are to believe the 'securocrats' of every sovereignist hue, to extolling them naively as a deterritorialized, desiring 'multitude' subverting 'Empire'.[52]

It goes without saying that the liminal experience produces subjectivation. Among other evidence, the anthropological research and the film, *Bronx Barbès* (2000), which Éliane de Latour devoted to the 'ghettos' of the big cities of the Ivory Coast, attest to it.[53] The trans-ethnic ethos (one that is extravagantly globalized in its imaginary dimension) of the *warrior* and his renown, as cultivated by *old fathers* and their *sons* in their thirst to *be really stylish,* is at once separate from the particularist style of village life, described as 'ethnic', claims to be universal, and demands the right to respectability – the respectability that comes with money, clothes and fatherhood.

From this point of view, the term 'ghetto' should not cause confusion. A ghetto is not a dismal dungeon in which 'ghetto people' simply vegetate. It is a meeting place for young people, one that is flanked by public space and is still tightly inserted into it. It is, for instance, localized near a crossroads or a market. It is perfectly visible and recognized for what it is, even though some of its activities are invisible and illegal. It is in permanent interaction with its immediate environment. It is also open to the world in which nicknames, fashion and the odyssey of emigration allow one to appropriate.

> At first glance, the street presents you with an image of liberty, universality, invention. It picks up the last cultural quivers of the planet. It fills you with desire, offering as it does an apparently unconstrained new life, linked to celebration and pleasure, to a solidarity that has been won back as if in some utopia, to the desire for domination, for escaping from one's lot in life.[54]

The experience of the ghetto really is a liminal experience in the sense that it strips the recipient of his former skin by giving him a new name, a new look, a new knowledge, that of the 'sciences' (i.e., the sciences of the art of theft). In addition, it starts out from the old technique, partly initiatory, partly colonial, partly Houphouetist, of a beating. 'When a *son* arrives, you knock him about a bit with sticks, a few kicks, to turn him into an animal. Maybe you see something that's really hard to do, you send him to do it, he goes off all by himself, and comes back with what you asked him for', explains one denizen of the ghetto.[55] And if all goes well, it leads to the creation of a different 'moral subject'.

> When I was a kid, coming back from a hold-up with my money – maybe as much as 2 or 3 million – there were some *big brothers* who robbed me blind. They took everything. The lot. They gave me nothing. After, when I plucked up my courage a bit, they stopped mugging me. When you mug me, I'll get out my pistol, you've been a fucking idiot and I'll fill your feet full of lead. That's the way I used to live. After, they respected me. They didn't dare any more. Ah, I was stronger now! That's when I became a real lad![56]

The experience of the ghetto is also a liminal experience because it is experienced as temporary. The global 'human types' that it venerates are not just the combatants, sportsmen or gangsters of myth, but also self-made bosses. 'I want to be a businessman, manage apartment blocks, companies, taxis, have a lot of money.'[57] Basically, these *warriors* are soft-hearted.

> I dream of living a really luxurious life and giving some stuff to my Mum 'cos my father is already dead and I've only got my mother left. She's far away, in Mali. I dream of before her death: even if it's just a little place, I'm going to do it so she can rest there. I'm thinking of all of that, the future of my children, my little brothers and my little sisters.[58]

They even have a 'blue flower' side, with their 'go' or their 'love' that they carefully distinguish from their 'bit of skirt' with whom they are not in love – even if the beloved was conquered by rape, sometimes collective.

> I take you by force because I love you. I can't waste my time courting you, no, I'll take you by force and then, when we've made love, I'll take you and sit you down and then I'll talk to you. 'Ah, *li'l sis*, sorry, the truth is I'm a big *fan of yours.*' . . . I rape her by myself or not. We raped a girl, there were seven of us, then she became my girlfriend. Ah, that's love all right![59]

In addition, we have seen how the 'diggers' for diamonds or gold, in Angola or West Africa, cultivated a 'lifestyle' and an 'aesthetic of existence' that were quite comparable. Nonetheless, the liminal situations created by globalization are capable of creating a great variety of processes of subjectivation, whose social and political orientations can pull in opposite directions. Born from the 'transversal struggles' of post-1968, the charismatic community of Sant'Egidio aims to be an experience of the 'suburbs', dedicated to serving the poor. 'The suburbs of life, the suburbs of the world, since the centre has either disappeared or else it is open to only a few. But in each suburb, the centre is reborn when we bring together the community of brothers when we celebrate the Eucharist', states its founder, Andrea Riccardi.[60] This movement, multinational and heavily involved in inter-religious dialogue, ecumenism and the promotion of peace, accepts globalization as the framework of subjectivation while inviting us to 'read the parable of the Good Samaritan on the level of the whole world and not just our local streets'.[61] Now it so happens that it has a very high profile in the towns of the Ivory Coast where it helps prisoners and AIDS sufferers and is endeavouring to facilitate the reconciliation between the government and the rebels and to act as a counterweight to Pentecostalist and somewhat Islamophobic radicalism. In other words, there are several ways of being liminal, and the conclusions that one draws from it as regards the stakes of globalization are variable, since a desire to observe the conventions or to act rebellious does not always lie where you would expect. The sole common denominator of the liminal condition is that it manufactures social relations, whether temporary or hierarchical, and that it is irreducible to the idea of 'disaffiliation', even in those places of 'bare life', refugee camps.[62]

Indeed, another paradox lies in the fact that being forced to wait on the threshold of the globe is a form of movement rather than stagnation, and of subordinate integration rather than exclusion or marginality. The 'floating' and transitive populations of the frontier are in a state of permanent displacement – as nomads, smugglers, bandits, sailors or woodcutters.[63] This is also, by definition, the case of the illegal immigrant, whatever he may be waiting for. Even more important, movement in the liminal situation remains closely interwoven with the state. The latter contributes, for example, to regulating the very way it breathes, even if only by constraining it and obliging the 'floating populations' either to accept its laws, or to find a way round them. But, over and above that, it participates in the definition of the liminal practices of subjectivation, for instance in the development of identities and of ethnic, religious or national types of habitus among immigrants, via its public policies.[64] Its role as an intermediary between the liminal condition and globalization is more ambivalent than is generally thought. An air company such as Air Tchad, under the control of the President of that country, has drawn substantial profits not just from smuggling, but also from the conveyancing of illegal immigrants expelled from Saudi Arabia.[65] Anxious to avoid a massive, uncontrolled immigration from Asia, the Russian administration is collaborating with the authorities in Pyongyang to enrol and train North Korean workers in Siberia, following procedures that are reminiscent of the indentured labour of the second half of the nineteenth century.[66] And when the director of Black Hawk Down filmed in the Sidi Moussa district of Salé, in Morocco, as he felt that the architecture there resembled that of the Mogadishu of Operation Restore Hope, and needed to employ black bit players, he found them waiting for their *patera* and obtained safe conduct for them from the Moroccan authorities for the duration of the shoot.[67]

The state is involved in the governing of the liminal condition – directly, in the case of the prison population, even though it tends to 'delegate' this to the private sector. Or via the 'indirect administration' of NGOs and enterprises to which it hands over a number of its prerogatives in the domains of social policy, public aid to development, humanitarian action, and the control of migration.

The liminal experience is bureaucratized in various different ways. The same is true of immigration, which is marked out by the 'rational-legal' procedures of the police and the air companies, or of the refugee camps, which are administered. One might even say that a large part of the experience of waiting constitutes the liminal experience in the product of bureaucratic action: having to queue at check-in desks or police controls; hoping for a cargo vessel that can escape or negotiate with the diligence of coastguards; hoping for the right to asylum which civil servants can take months or years to refuse; having to queue, yet again, at mealtimes in front of the steaming saucepans of humanitarian administration in the camps or the detention centre at Sangatte. Yes, liminal time is bureaucratic, and it secretes bureaucratic imaginings. In their encampments, set apart from the villages, African 'diggers' – as we have seen – are very keen on titles that belong to the world of the state or business, as well as on nicknames drawn from the world of sport or war, and in breakaway Congo-Kinshasa, the way the period is represented in apocalyptic terms means that it is Satan who hands you your laissez-passer.[58]

This correspondence between the bureaucratic order of things and the liminal condition reaches its climax in one last paradox. There are 'national-liminal' situations of which the state is the receptacle or the matrix. Once again the synergy between the state and the processes of globalization is evident. Waiting reproduces and legitimizes the national consciousness. It may even be exacerbated in the form of a radical or frankly millenarian nationalism, as among Palestinians or the Hutu of Burundi residing in refugee camps in Tanzania.[69] More frequently, waiting finds its natural framework in the national consciousness. Most African societies have thus subsided without too much fuss into the envelope of the state, in 'expectations of modernity' and in immediate circumstances of poverty.[70] In the same way, the exodus of some 10 per cent of the Philippines population, with the encouragement of the public power that sees in this a means of pacifying the social crisis and boosting the country's economy, has in no way altered the sense of belonging to the nation found among immigrants.[71]

But it is also perfectly possible to say that the global system of states engenders these 'national-liminal' situations through its unequal and hierarchical regulation of economic wealth or that of diplomatic action. We have found that, in this area too, the only urgent activity is often that of waiting. For some 50 years, certain states have been decomposing – Afghanistan, Iraq, Burma, Cambodia, North Korea, Congo-Kinshasa, Algeria – as have certain nationalist demands – think of the Palestinians, the Kurds, the Chechens, the Burmese minorities – as the result of calculations that are rational if not always very intelligent on the part of the local political authorities, whether in the region or the world.[72] Neither China nor South Korea desires the collapse of the Pyongyang regime, and they are ready, as are many others, to finance its survival. The status quo in Burma is just as convenient in the eyes of other ASEAN states, and it has the merit of acting as a buffer zone between the respective regional ambitions of Beijing and New Delhi. The support that was long given to the Khmer Rouge by countries anxious to check the ambitions of Vietnam was of the same kind. The United States are eager to safeguard the useful fiction of a vague recognition of the Palestinian cause as they are unable with complete impunity to countenance its eradication. They did more than a little to stoke the fire of the civil war in Angola from 1961 to 2001 before betraying their man, Jonas Savimbi. The same went for Sudan, until the government in Khartoum saw the error of its ways. As for the Algeria of the generals and their 15 or 20,000 disappeared, everybody expresses admiration for its organized stagnation – so long as this remains anti-Islamicist.

As is to be expected, liminal nations hang about or complain in the antechamber of the world without knowing when, or even if, the usher will let them in. The cynicism of their leaders is of little help to them. One month after the earthquake in Boumerdès, in 2003, a disillusioned civil servant stated: 'The earthquake has torn the Vale: Algeria is appearing in its nakedness. It has been a disaster area for 40 years. Now we have the corresponding status, that's all.' This did not prevent one of his colleagues from flying into a rage against a woman who had put up three breeze blocks under a sheet metal roof, in a shanty town, in order to flee the carnage, and who now had the nerve to ask to be rehoused: 'She is putting on an act, saying to herself: "Great, there's been an earthquake, I can make the most of it." But how can she be a victim since she didn't have anywhere to live before? Look at the way she's strutting around. It's a real paradise for her here.' In the refugee camp nicknamed 'Guantanamo', the survivors stayed huddled close to their tents:

I could wait to be relodged more comfortably with a member of my family. But if anything happens and you're not there, you can lose everything. The authorities tell themselves: that person doesn't need anything. We stay here, it's like queueing, making sure we won't be forgotten as always happens when things get handed out.

A black joke among the 'Hittists', whose block of flats collapsed leaving nothing but a hole, summarizes the reef on which the Algerian struggle for national liberation has foundered: 'Before, they said we had our backs to the wall. But there isn't any wall now. So our backs are to the void.'[73] The same applies to many nations, forced up against the void in the world's limbo.

And yet the antechamber is not cut off from the rest of the apartment. The proprietors, the visitors, the delivery man are forever crossing it this way and that, showering people with kind words or asking for a few little favours from those who are patiently putting up with their difficult situation. National liminal situations are an essential part of globalization. They now attract the solicitous attentions of the 'American hyper-power' which is resolved to track down its enemies in 'whatever dark corner of the universe', and is obsessed with the 'caves' in which lurk terrorists or arms of mass destruction.[74] They receive international aid and are integrated into the 'indirect administration' of globalization thanks to the intervention of NGOs and the presence of multinational businesses. To a greater or lesser extent, they appropriate universal material culture, they remain caught up in international commercial exchanges as long as they have at their disposal natural resources and they are also associated with international monetary system thanks to the 'dollarization' or, more rarely, the 'euroization' of their economy.[75] They invest their holdings in offshore financial institutions. They affect, albeit with a certain amount of reticence and deceit, to submit to the prescriptions of neo-liberal 'good governance' by consenting to programmes of structural adjustment and privatizations which, all things considered, broaden the circle of liminal populations, and the biggest 'rogues' among them even use the sanctions affecting them to perpetuate themselves via economic liberalization, as did Saddam Hussein in Iraq.[76] It is no more than natural justice if they have an impact on global configurations. They export refugees, like those from Afghanistan and Iraq – in the 1990s, the two main suppliers of refugees – not only to their immediate environment, but also to Western Europe and Australia. They shelter terrorists, criminals, illicit capital and narcotics traffickers. They endanger the security of the well-off and their neighbours. They provide the world with its new map of dreams and nightmares. In short, they contribute to the historicity of globalization.

They thereby remind us that globalization is a matter of contingency and thus historical sociology. There is no systematic model of the national-liminal situation. There are situations, diverse and contrasting, which corroborate the fact that globalization rests on disjunctions. In this way, the Burmese military, having held on to power in spite of the opposition's electoral victory in 1990, has become a pariah of the international system. The United States and the European Union have applied sanctions to it and most western investors will look twice before moving in or setting up shop there. Nevertheless, Burma gives rise to intense dramatic activity. Its neighbours continue to do business with it and even, in the case of China, to court it. The Secretary-General of the United Nations has sent a special representative whose task, worthy of Sisyphus, is to initiate the process of transition between the junta and Aung San Suu Kyi, the leader of the opposition and winner of the Nobel Peace Prize. The United Nations Development Programme, various NGOs and the International Labour Organization, are also active there. Above all, Burma, as a pariah state, is, in spite of itself, a cog in the wheel of the emergence of an international judicial system. Although it seems improbable that an oil company deliberately resorted to forced labour in a country where the cost of labour is among the lowest in the world, NGOs have brought lawsuits against Total in France, Belgium and the United States. American lawyers are working on the evidence of Burmese refugees in Thailand, various foundations have agreed to pay their fees, 'international civil society' is stretching its wings and the Yadana gas pipeline has become one of the targets of choice for anti-globalization. Furthermore, Burma is still part and parcel of the world economy. Less in fact thanks to its gas, which is exported to neighbouring Thailand for the satisfaction of its own market, than to the traffic in opium and meta-amphetamines, the trade in precious stones or subcontracting in the garment industry, on the initiative of mainly Chinese businesses which are anxious to get round the quotas imposed by the European Union. Thanks to its two holdings, the junta has set itself up as a partner of a limited but lucrative stock of foreign investments in favour of the apparent liberalization of the country's economy. The country also welcomes some 120,000 tourists a year and exports its labour force into the regions in the shape of wage-earners, refugees or prostitutes. On the other hand, apart from its debt, it is disconnected from the international financial system and, since it does not have normal access to the Internet, it is turning its back on 'the information era'.[77]

The liminal condition is different in different parts of the world. The ruling elite of the MPLA in Angola reigns over a country in ruins and infested with landmines, where some 10 per cent of the population are 'displaced persons' as a result of the civil war. Social indicators are overwhelmingly negative and contrast cruelly with oil revenue and the extravagant way of life of the regime's nomenklatura. Nonetheless, western governments are striving to outdo each other in their indulgence towards the authorities in Luanda who control significant natural wealth, in particular hydrocarbon, in the good old Atlantic zone, far from the turmoil of the Middle East. They even went so far as to accept the military presence of Angola in the two Congos and its highly undiplomatic pressures on Zambia when the latter was consenting more or less willingly to grant transit facilities to UNITA. Foreign companies have obviously not allowed themselves to fall behind, and the substitution of NGOs to the state in the social or humanitarian domain completes the way the country is caught up in globalization.[78]

In the limbo of the international system, the same causes do not always have the same effects. The discriminatory gaze of central states shapes the category of 'rogue states' by making it legitimate and acceptable, or scandalous and punishable, to keep different populations waiting. But whatever the case, free riders are still part of the game – contrary to what is often believed.

Plenum and void in global governmentality

The heterogeneous nature of the liminal condition makes it completely impossible to indulge in any populist daydreams about the way the 'damnés de la terre' will contribute to the salvation of mankind. The 'multitude' is no more anti-globalization than it was revolutionary in previous times. But by making globalization part of its everyday practices, it participates in its uncertainty. It is here that the concept of 'governmentality' is fruitful, since right from the start it posits the idea that power is an 'action on actions', at the interface, as I have said, of 'techniques of the self' and 'techniques of domination exerted on others'. It condenses that subtle tension between servitude and consent that we have discovered again and again in the course of our discussions and that is rather drolly summarized by two quotations extracted from the world's chattering classes. Highlighting the various consultations he held with his allies, the then American Secretary of State, Colin Powell, defended himself against the charge of unilateralism: 'If I spend so much time on these contacts, it's because I think that the United States is the dominant power, but that it needs other powers to follow it.'[79] And Miuccia Prada echoes his words in reference to four 'test perfumes': 'I love them. They are really very good. They have been developed in complete liberty with the team that followed me to the letter.'[80]

Above all, the concept of 'governmentality' restores the element of indeterminacy found in globalization as a whole. The synergy that we have seen at work between globalization and state-formation, the techniques of the body that transport its appropriation, must not dissuade us from seeing our time in its incompleteness and its fragility. Global government is not absolute, or, if it is, it is within the limits of the genre. So-called 'systemic' risks result from its zones of ungovernance, something which financial crises bring out at regular intervals. Not only is the market in capitals forever staggering on the edge of the precipice; not only does the Phoenix of protectionism never cease to rise from its ashes; not only does international law include leakages and suffer from numerous aporias in domains that are as essential as those of the establishment of property; not only does the system of states get bogged down in the proclamation of liberty and the daily ways this is slanted; not only is the Internet riddled with viruses; not only is air traffic control deficient over a large part of the African continent; not only is it perfectly possible that a nuclear accident or a series of explosive attacks on industrial installations or transports of hydrocarbon might happen: in addition, globalization remains at the mercy of Dame Nature who, in alarming ways, reminds it of her presence.[81]

Even without having to make any pronouncements on the tangibility of the danger represented by global warming, we can see that the pandemics of AIDS and malaria, the terrifying outbreaks of Ebola, Sars and bird flu, mad cow disease, and the capacity of viruses to mutate, all suggest that globalization proceeds from the unpredictability of life, in which we participate. Historically, globalization has been dependent on nothing more than a mosquito, as is proved by the difficulties of the colonial conquest of sub-Saharan Africa or the rise of malaria in Egypt during the Second World War as a result of the irrigation of the Nile, the revolution in transport, the circulation of populations and troops, and military difficulties.[82] Over the centuries, globalization has been played out between plague and cholera, between smallpox and syphilis, and the unity of the world was consummated in death: for example the death of 3 million Indians in the West Indies between 1494 and 1508 under the impact of 'Columban exchange', or of 14 million people during the Spanish flu in 1918, straight after a conflict that had bled Europe white.

It would be wrong to conclude simply with obvious facts if the latter were not sometimes obliterated and sometimes rendered purely imaginary in the public debate. The question of the future of globalization and the transformations it is introducing into the way the world works is unaffected. But it cannot be answered in the millenarian terms of anti-globalization or neo-liberalism.

Like all changes of scale, the one that we have been producing over the past two centuries constitutes a complex 'event' that can be better grasped as a negative, in its incompletion and on its 'frontiers', rather than in the majesty of its plenitude. Peter Brown has already demonstrated as much with regard to the Christianization of the Roman

Empire and its boundaries.[83] The same applies to globalization across the ages as to Chinese painting. The Plenum constitutes the visible aspect of the structure, but it is the Void that structures the way it is used.[84] Also, the work operates through the gaps in it, gaps which are constitutive of it. 'The *there is* and the *there is not* engender each other', says the *Laozi*.[85] And, continuing the analogy:

> [T]he mountain in the rain or the mountain in fine weather are, for the painter, easy to depict . . . but the fact that from fine weather [it] tends to rain, or that from rain [it] tends to return to fine weather . . . when the whole landscape is lost in confusion: emerging-immersing itself, between *there is* and *there is not* – that is what is difficult to depict.[86]

There is no doubt about it: the meteorology of our period is mixed up. This is neither the place nor the time to ask whether the social sciences, like western painting – at least until 'the origins of abstraction'[87] – have become locked in a problematic of presence and absence which prevents them from grasping the 'emerging-immersing itself', the 'between *there is* and *there is not'*, even if the concepts of governmentality and subjectivation do indeed enable us to apprehend the ambivalence of the social by doing away with the presence (or absence) of the Subject, and thus of many other things too.

I need merely emphasize, with the 'Patient Infantryman' that 'things are astir'. And emphasize the necessity – the 'urgency'? – of a political ethics of cosmopolitanism and re-employment, at a time of universalization by means of the reinvention of difference. For, essentially speaking, the 'event' of globalization appears, as you will have understood, as the systematization of the historical experience of extraversion. However, nowhere can one see clearly emerging any transnational movement of political subjectivation similar to that represented by nationalism, socialism, communism or fascism in the nineteenth and twentieth centuries. It is doubtful whether the lukewarm movement of 'market democracy' can take their place for long, and violent action, as a 'new possibility of existence', has a limited but intense power of seduction.

Contemporary globalization has sometimes been compared to the Hellenistic world. Not without reason. Just as 'Rome is the people whose civilization was that of another people, the Greeks', and just as it contributed to the harmonization of the Mediterranean in Latin,[88] so we need these days to discover how to be European under America, to parody the title of a scholarly work,[89] or how to be American while remaining European. This is a mere manner of speaking, of course, since the dilemma also raises itself for the Chinese, Japanese, the Africans and the whole 'caravan of peoples', as the Arabs put it in the nineteenth century. 'When the struggle with the United States is over and all Americans are dead I'd like to go into business. I'm sure that my English will be very useful to me' – this was the dream of a pro-Taliban demonstrator in Peshawar, in September 2001.[90]

The historicity of globalization, via its appropriation by the masses, is no longer in doubt. Nevertheless, the question remains as to the nature of this historicity, taking into account the formidable asymmetry that has become established between the United States and the other parts of the planet. In the next decades, the synergy between the formation of the system of states and globalization may lead either to the emergence of a competitive configuration of power, more or less low-key – the celebrated 'multipolar' world so dear to French diplomacy – or to the widening and tightening of an imperial grip that would no doubt be more territorialized than Toni Negri and Michael Hardt have suggested, and that several European leaders seem ready to endorse so as to participate in it more fully. In the second case, the historicity of most societies, including that of the Old Continent, would become (or would become again) colonial or quasi colonial in type and would be based essentially on the art of 'tactics', without any 'place of its own' being set up (as Michel de Certeau would put it). One consequence among others would be a change in its cognitive status and the social sciences would then be transformed into colonial studies, or even into 'colonial science'. And are we so far from that, now that universities and research institutions have been turned into the financial vassals of the priorities decided by the government, the institutions of Bretton Woods, the European Commission or the marketplace, and dedicated to the celebration of 'governance' or 'international civil society', now that calculation has replaced thinking, and NGOs have replaced laboratories?

These days, we are living in a time of co-optation rather than of critique, and this does not make lucidity or imagination any easier. The 'reinvention of difference', underlying globalization, is not necessarily incompatible with the 'one-dimensional' nature of the latter, whose advent was announced by Marcuse. The dilemma affects the capacity of societies to create their own history or to see themselves being brought to heel by the 'local'.[91]

Of course, everyone pretends to be aware of what is at stake, however he formulates it and whatever may be the political response he brings to this dichotomy. But, obsessed as we are by diplomatic and military manoeuvres, questions of security, financial issues, the combats of industrial titans and the spectre of 'civilizations', we ascribe little importance to the desires and sufferings that circulate round the world's limbo. Intoxicated by speed, we neglect waiting. This is to forget that History often moves forward only by stealth.

Notes

Preface

1 Taking Bayart at his word, I have simply used 'globalization' to translate both French words *globalisation* and *mondialisation*. [Trans.]
2 This work was financed by the Centre d'études et de recherches internationales de Sciences Po (Paris), as a 'special project'.

Chapter 1 Two Centuries of Globalization: The Changing Scale of State and Capitalism

1 See in particular the concept of 'bio-power' in Michel Foucault; or in A. Giddens, *The Consequences of Modernity* (Stanford: Stanford University Press, 1990) and *The Transformation of Intimacy. Sexuality, Love and Eroticism in Modern Societies* (Stanford: Stanford University Press, 1992).
2 D. Harvey, *The Condition of Postmodernity. An Enquiry into the Origins of Cultural Change* (Cambridge, MA: Blackwell, 1990), p. 240. See also Giddens, *The Consequences of Modernity*.
3 R. Robertson, *Globalisation. Social Theory and Global Culture* (London: Sage Publications, 1992), pp. 8ff. See also P. Anderson, *The Origins of Postmodernity* (London: Verso, 1998).
4 D. Harvey, *Spaces of Hope* (Berkeley: University of California Press, 2000), p. 13.
5 S. Strange, *The Retreat of the State. The Diffusion of Power in the World Economy* (Cambridge: Cambridge University Press, 1996), p. xiii.
6 Karl Marx, *Manifesto of the Communist Party* (1848). Cf. the commentary in Harvey, *Spaces of Hope*, ch. 2.
7 *The Economist*, 2 February 2002.
8 M. Castells, *The Internet Galaxy: Reflections on Internet, Business, and Society* (Oxford: Oxford University Press, 2001), p. 1.

9   Ibid., pp. 240ff, based on the work of M. Zook (<www.zooknic.com>).

10 M. Castells, *The Information Age: Economy, Society and Culture*, vol. I, *The Rise of the Network Society* (Cambridge, MA and Oxford: Blackwell, 1999), p. 154.

11 E. Cohen, *L'Ordre économique global. Essai sur les autorités de régulation* (Paris: Fayard, 2001), pp. 77ff.

12 P. Jacquet, J. Pisani-Ferry and L. Tubiana, 'Rapport de synthèse: les institutions économiques de la globalisation', in *Gouvernance globale, Conseil d'analyse économique* (Paris: La Documentation française, 2002), p. 53.

13 J. Sgard, 'Qu'est-ce qu'un droit de propriété international?', in *Gouvernance globale*, pp. 417–29.

14 J. Sgard, *L'Économie de la panique. Faire face aux crises financières* (Paris: La Découverte, 2002).

15 S. Sassen, *Globalization and its Discontents. Essays on the New Mobility of People and Money* (New York: The New Press, 1998).

16 Friedrich Engels and Karl Marx, *The First Critique of Political Economy*.

17 K. H. O'Rourke and J. G. Williamson, *Globalization and History. The Evolution of a Nineteenth-Century Atlantic Economy* (Cambridge, MA: The MIT Press, 1999).

18 A. Appadurai, *Modernity at Large. Cultural Dimensions of Globalization* (Minneapolis: University of Minnesota Press, 1996).

19 Castells, *The Information Age*; M. Shaw, *Theory of the Global State. Globality as an Unfinished Revolution* (Cambridge: Cambridge University Press, 2000); M. Hardt and A. Negri, *Empire* (Cambridge, MA, and London: Harvard University Press, 2000).

20 Robertson, *Globalisation*, p. 8.

21 E. Balibar, *Nous, Citoyens d'Europe? Les Frontières, l'État, le peuple* (Paris: La Découverte, 2002), pp. 165–66 (my italics).

22 Ibid., p. 168. Cf. also M. Kaldor, 'Nations and blocs: towards a theory of the political economy of the interstate model in Europe', in A. Hunter (ed.), *Rethinking the Cold War* (Philadelphia: Temple University Press, 1998), pp. 193–212; and Shaw, *Theory of the Global State*, pp. 117ff.

23 Robertson, *Globalisation*, p. 6. Cf. also Shaw, *Theory of the Global State*, and Balibar, *Nous, Citoyens*.

24 F. Braudel, *La Dynamique du capitalisme* (Paris: Arthaud, 1985), p. 78.

25 P. Anderson, *Passages from Antiquity to Feudalism* (London: New Left Books, 1975), and *Lineages of the Absolutist State* (London: New Left Books, 1974).

26 Max Weber, *Economy and Society* (Berkeley: University of California Press, 1978), pp. 353–4; Karl Marx, *Capital*, book I; G. Arrighi, *The Long Twentieth Century. Money, Power and the Origins of Our Times* (London: Verso, 1994), pp. 12ff.

27 M. Weber, *The Religion of China: Confucianism and Taoism*, trans. and ed. Hans H. Gerth (New York: Macmillan, 1964), p. 324; F. Braudel, *A History of Civilizations*, trans. Richard Mayne (London: Penguin, 1995), pp. 45–6.

28 In this case, the term 'transnational' is obviously anachronistic. I am using it for comparative purposes.

29 J. Rosenau, *Along the Domestic-Foreign Frontier. Exploring Governance in a Turbulent World* (Cambridge: Cambridge University Press, 1997); Frederic

Jameson, 'Postmodernism, or the cultural logic of late capitalism', *New Left Review*, 146, 1984, pp. 53–92 (for the concept of *postmodern hyperspace*).

30 To adopt the striking metaphor of A. R. Zolberg, 'L'influence des facteurs "externes" sur l'ordre politique interne', in M. Grawitz and J. Leca (eds), *Traité de science politique* (Paris: PUF, 985), vol. I, pp. 567–98.

31 Appadurai, *Modernity at Large*.

32 G. Salamé, *Appels d'empire. Ingérences et résistances à l'âge de la globalisation* (Paris: Fayard, 1996).

33 Z. Laïdi, *Le Sacre du présent* (Paris: Flammarion, 2000); P.-A. Taguieff, *L'Effacement de l'avenir* (Paris: Galilée, 2000).

34 P. Veyne, *Writing History: Essay on Epistemology*, trans. Mina Moore-Rinvolucri (Middletown, CT: Wesleyan University Press, 1984).

35 M. Foucault, 'Nietzsche, genealogy, history', in *Essential Works of Foucault, 1954–1988*, trans. Robert Hurley et al., vol. 2, *Aesthetics* (London: Penguin, 1998), p. 374.

36 Ibid.; M. Henry, *Marx: A Philosophy of Human Reality*, trans. Kathleen McLaughlin (Bloomington: University of Indiana Press, 1984).

37 Foucault, 'Nietzsche'.

38 Hardt and Negri, *Empire*.

39 B. Berman and J. Lonsdale, *Unhappy Valley. Conflict in Kenya and Africa* (London: James Currey, 1992), p. 5.

40 D. Held et al., *Global Transformations. Politics, Economics and Culture* (Stanford: Stanford University Press, 1999), p. 414.

41 G. Hopkins (ed.), *Globalisation in World History* (London: Pimlico, 2002).

42 Ibid. See also the works of Fernand Braudel, Perry Anderson and the French Marxist anthropologists on capitalism.

43 Ibid.

44 This follows the periodization and terminology of Hopkins (ed.), *Globalisation*.

45 G. Frank, *Global Economy in the Asian Age* (Berkeley: University of California Press, 1998).

46 K. Polanyi, *The Great Transformation* (Boston, MA: Beacon Press, 1957).

47 V. Harlow, *The Founding of the Second British Empire, 1763–1793* (London: Longman, 1952 and 1964) and T. Ballantyne, 'Empire, knowledge and culture: from proto-globalisation to modern globalisation', in Hopkins (ed.), *Globalisation*.

48 M. Davis, *Late Victorian Holocausts. El Niño Famines and the Making of the Third World* (London: Verso, 2001), pp. 216ff.

49 O'Rourke and Williamson consider that the lowering of transport costs from 1860 onwards was one of the decisive factors of globalization, much more important than the liberalizing of external trade (*Globalization and History*, ch. 3).

50 Quoted by E. J. Hobsbawm, *The Age of Capital, 1848–1875* (Paris: Fayard, 1978), p. 64.

51 Ibid., p. 63.

52 K. Starr and R. J. Orsi (eds), *Rooted in Barbarous Soil. People, Culture and Community in Gold Rush California* (Berkeley: University of California Press, 2000).

53 The notion of 'transnational circuit of migration' was introduced by R. Rouse, 'Mexican migration and the social space of postmodernism', *Diaspora*, I (1), Spring 1991, pp. 8–23, and put to superb use by M. Y. Hsu, *Dreaming of Gold, Dreaming of Home. Transnationalism and Migration between the United States and South China, 1882–1943* (Stanford: Stanford University Press, 2000).

54 O'Rourke and Williamson, *Globalization and History*, p. 120; N. Foner, *From Ellis Island to JFK: New York's Two Great Waves of Immigration* (New Haven: Yale University Press, 2000); M. Wyman, *Round Trip to America: The Immigrants Return to Europe, 1880–1930* (Ithaca: Cornell University Press, 1993).

55 Held et al., *Global Transformations*, ch. 6; S. Sassen, *Guests and Aliens* (New York: The New Press, 1999).

56 Hobsbawm, *The Age of Capital*.

57 F. Cooper and A. L. Stoler (eds), *Tensions of Empire: Colonial Cultures in a Bourgeois World* (Berkeley: University of California Press, 1997); J. and J. Comaroff, *Of Revelation and Revolution*: I, *Christianity, Colonialism and Consciousness in South Africa*; II, *The Dialectics of Modernity on a South African Frontier* (Chicago: University of Chicago Press, 1991 and 1997), as well as *Ethnography and the Historical Imagination* (Boulder: Westview Press, 1992); E. Hobsbawm and T. Ranger (eds), *The Invention of Tradition* (Cambridge: Cambridge University Press, 1983); G. W. Johnson (ed.), *Double Impact: France and Africa in the Age of Imperialism* (Westport: Greenwood Press, 1985); A. L. Conklin, *A Mission to Civilize. The Republican Idea of Empire in France and West Africa, 1895–1930* (Stanford: Stanford University Press, 1997); E. F. Irschick, *Dialogue and History: Constructing South India, 1795–1895* (Berkeley: University of California Press, 1994); M. Foucault, *Society Must Be Defended. Lectures at the Collège de France, 1975–76*, ed. Mauro Bertani and Alessandro Fontana; trans. David Macey (London: Allen Lane, 2003), p. 58.

58 P. Duara, *Rescuing History from the Nation. Questioning Narratives of Modern China* (Chicago: University of Chicago Press, 1995), p. 164.

59 Davis, *Late Victorian Holocausts*, p. 139.

60 Hannah Arendt, *L'Impérialisme* (Paris: Fayard, 1982).

61 J. D. Y. Peel, *Religious Encounter and the Making of the Yoruba* (Bloomington: Indiana University Press, 2000), pp. 189–90.

62 J. N. Rosenau and E.-O. Czempiel (eds), *Governance without Government: Order and Change in World Politics* (Cambridge: Cambridge University Press, 1992).

63 Polanyi, *The Great Transformation*, p. 29.

64 Ibid., p. 62.

65 See the table in Held et al., *Global Transformations*, pp. 44–5.

66 C. Charle, *La Crise des sociétés impériales* (Paris: Le Seuil, 2001), pp. 33 and 163. See also chapters 4 and 5.

67 N. Harper, 'Empire, diaspora and the languages of globalism, 1850–1914', in Hopkins (ed.), *Globalisation*, p. 144.

68 These terms have been used by Africanist anthropologists on the subject of lineage societies incorporated into empires: cf. for example R. Horton, 'Stateless societies in the history of West Africa', in J. F. A. Ajayi and

M. Crowder (eds), *History of West Africa* (New York: Columbia University Press, 1976), vol. I, pp. 72–113.

69 B. Anderson, *Imagined Communities. Reflections on the Origin and Spread of Nationalism* (London: Verso, new edn, 1991).

70 J. E. Thomson, *Mercenaries, Pirates, and Sovereigns. State-Building and Extra-territorial Violence in Early Modern Europe* (Princeton: Princeton University Press, 1994), especially pp. 86–8 and pp. 147ff.

71 Hobsbawm and Ranger (eds), *The Invention of Tradition*.

72 J.-F. Bayart, *The Illusion of Cultural Identity*, trans. Steven Rendall, Janet Roitman, Cynthia Schoch and Jonathan Derrick (Chicago: University of Chicago Press, 2005).

73 Polanyi, *The Great Transformation*, pp. 189–90 and 261–2.

74 I am here following the analysis by Arrighi in *The Long Twentieth Century*, which is broadly inspired by the work of Fernand Braudel.

75 M. Mann, *The Sources of Social Power*, II: *The Rise of Classes and Nation-States, 1760–1914* (Cambridge: Cambridge University Press, 1993).

76 Hobsbawm, *The Age of Empire*.

77 Charle, *La Crise des sociétés impériales*, p. 205.

78 G. Hopkins, 'The "New International Economic Order" in the Nineteenth Century: Britain's First Development Plan for Africa', in R. Law, *From Slave Trade to "Legitimate" Commerce. The Commercial Transition in Nine-teenth Century West Africa* (Cambridge: Cambridge University Press, 1995), pp. 240–64.

79 P. W. Schroeder, 'The risks of victory. An historian's provocation', *The National Interest*, Winter 2001–2, pp. 22–36.

80 Cf. Held et al., *Global Transformations*, passim.

81 E. J. Hobsbawm, *Age of Extremes: The Short Twentieth Century, 1914–1991* (London: Michael Joseph, 1994).

82 Polanyi, *The Great Transformation*, p. 248.

83 Hobsbawm, *Age of Extremes*.

84 Ibid.

85 A. Vichnevski, *La Faucille et le rouble. La Modernisation conservatrice en U.R.S.S.* (Paris: Gallimard, 2000); D. Kharkhordin, *The Collective and the Individual in Russia. A Study of Practices* (Berkeley: University of California Press, 1999).

86 As does F. Cooper, 'What is the concept of globalisation good for? An African historian's perspective', *African Affairs*, 100, 2001, pp. 183–213.

87 M. Foucault, *The History of Sexuality*, vol. 2, *The Use of Pleasure*, trans. Robert Hurley (London: Viking, 1986), p. 11.

88 Ibid., p. 6.

89 J.-F. Bayart, 'L'énonciation du politique', *Revue française de science politique*, 35 (3), June 1985, pp. 343–72, and *The Illusion of Cultural Identity*, pp. 134ff.

90 J. Clifford, *The Predicament of Culture. Twentieth Century Ethnography, Literature and Art* (Cambridge, MA: Harvard University Press, 1988), p. 15.

91 Giddens, *The Consequences of Modernity*.

92 F. Jameson, 'Cognitive mapping', in C. Nelson and L. Grossberg (eds), *Marxism and the Interpretation of Culture* (Urbana, IL: University of Illinois Press, 1988), p. 349.

93 Appadurai, *Modernity at Large*.
94 G. Deleuze, *Difference and Repetition*, trans. Paul Patton (London: The Athlone Press, 1994), pp. 178–9.
95 Bayart, *The Illusion of Cultural Identity*.
96 M. de Certeau, *The Practice of Everyday Life*, trans. Steven Rendall (Berkeley: University of California Press, 1984), p. 15.
97 I am here extending the conceptualization that I developed in *The Illusion of Cultural Identity*, chs 3 and 4.
98 P. Veyne, *La Société romaine* (Paris: Le Seuil, 1991), pp. 145–7.
99 Polanyi, *The Great Transformation*, pp. 22 and 108–9.
100 B. Badie, *L'État importé. Essai sur l'occidentalisation de l'ordre politique* (Paris: Fayard, 1992).
101 Polanyi, *The Great Transformation*, p. 130.
102 M. Gluckman, *Order and Rebellion in Tribal Africa* (London: Cohen & West, 1963).
103 A. Appadurai, 'Disjuncture and difference in the global cultural economy', *Public Culture*, 2 (2), Spring 1990, pp. 1–24, repr. in *Modernity at Large*, ch. 2. Appadurai situates these disjunctions between the different 'landscapes' of globalization: ethnic, media, financial, ideological, etc.
104 O'Rourke and Williams, *Globalization and History*, ch. 10 and pp. 286–7.
105 B. Hibou and L. Martinez, 'Le Partenariat euro-maghrébin: un mariage blanc?', *Études du CERI*, 47, November 1998, and, under the general editorship of B. Hibou, 'Les faces cachées du Partenariat euro-méditerranéen', *Critique internationale*, 18, January 2003, pp. 114–78.
106 G. Deleuze and F. Guattari, *What is Philosophy?*, trans. Hugh Tomlinson and Graham Burchell (New York: Columbia University Press, 1994), p. 98.
107 G. Deleuze, *Negotiations, 1972–1990*, trans. Martin Joughin (New York and Chichester: Columbia University Press, 1995).
108 Veyne, *La Société romaine*, ch. 1; Peel, *Religious Encounter*, pp. 241ff.
109 P. Veyne, *Did the Greeks Believe in Their Myths? An Essay on the Constitutive Imagination*, trans. Paula Wissing (Chicago: University of Chicago Press, 1988).
110 Deleuze, *Negotiations*.
111 Bayart, *The Illusion of Cultural Identity*, ch. 4.
112 Quoted in *Gouvernance globale*, p. 13.
113 Foucault, 'The techniques of the self'.
114 M. Foucault, *History of Sexuality*, vol. 1, *The Will to Knowledge*, trans. Robert Hurley (London: Penguin, 1990), p. 60.
115 P. Macherey, 'Pour une histoire naturelle des normes', in *Michel Foucault philosophe. Rencontre internationale. Paris, 9, 10, 11 janvier 1988* (Paris: Le Seuil, 1989), p. 209.
116 Foucault, *History of Sexuality*, vol. 2, *The Use of Pleasure*, p. 27.
117 Foucault, 'The subject and power', in *Power*, vol. 3 in *Essential Works of Foucault 1954–1984*, ed. James Faubion, trans. Robert Hurley et al. (London: Penguin, 1994), p. 341.

Chapter 2   The State: A Product of Globalization

1 M. Weber, *The Religion of China: Confucianism and Taoism*, trans. and ed. Hans H. Gerth (New York: Macmillan, 1964).
2 This is a hypothesis that Max Weber in no way rejects, introducing precisely this distinction between 'creation' and 'appropriation' (ibid.). W. Schluchter emphasizes that his Eurocentrism is heuristic, not normative: see *Paradoxes of Modernity. Culture and Conduct in the Theory of Max Weber* (Stanford: Stanford University Press, 1996, pp. 109–10). We can here recognize the terms of the debate between Bertrand Badie, *L'État importé. Essai sur l'occidentalisation de l'ordre politique* (Paris: Fayard, 1992) and myself, *The State in Africa. The Politics of the Belly*, trans. Mary Harper, Christopher and Elizabeth Harrison (London: Longman, 1993) and, under my editorship, *La Greffe de l'État* (Paris: Karthala, 1996).
3 On Soviet decolonization, see O. Roy, *La Nouvelle Asie centrale ou la Fabrication des nations* (Paris: Le Seuil, 1997) and the ongoing work by T. Gordadze, in particular 'Les nouvelles guerres du Caucase (1991–2000) et la formation des États postcommunistes', in P. Hassner and R. Marchal (eds), *Guerres et sociétés. État et violence après la guerre froide* (Paris: Karthala, 2003), ch. 13; 'La réforme du passé. L'effort historiographique de construction de la nation géorgienne', *Revue d'études comparatives Est-Ouest*, 30 (1), 1999, pp. 53–80; 'La Géorgie et ses hôtes ingrats. Conflits politiques autour de l'autochtonie', *Critique internationale*, 10, January 2001, pp. 161–76. For a more general problematization, see also J.-F. Bayart (ed.), *La Greffe de l'État*, and the idea of colonial nationalism in B. Anderson, *Imagined Communities. Reflections on the Origin and Spread of Nationalism*, new edn (London: Verso, 1991), ch. 10, so long as it is broadened and the analysis enriched by including the ambivalence and complexity of the interactions between the agents of colonization and the colonized society (as is done by example by R. Bertrand, who deploys it critically with respect to Java: *État colonial, noblesse et nationalisme à Java. La Tradition parfaite* (Paris: Karthala, 2005)).
4 R. H. Jackson, *Quasi-States: Sovereignty, International Relations, and the Third World* (Cambridge: Cambridge University Press, 1990).
5 See in particular, selected from a vast and often redundant bibliography, K. Ohmae, *The End of the Nation-State* (New York: Free Press, 1995) and *The Borderless World* (New York: Harper Business, 1990); B. Badie, *La Fin des territoires. Essai sur le désordre international et sur l'utilité sociale du respect* (Paris: Fayard, 1995); J.-M. Guehenno, *La Fin de la démocratie* (Paris: Flammarion, 1993); Manuel Castells, *The Information Age: Economy, Society and Culture*, vol. 2, *The Power of Identity* (Maiden, MA; Oxford, Blackwell, 1997); M. Van Creveld, *The Rise and Decline of the State* (Cambridge: Cambridge University Press, 1999). There is a detailed and nuanced overview of the destiny of the state in globalization in D. Held et al., *Global Transformations. Politics, Economics and Culture* (Stanford: Stanford University Press, 1999), pp. 436ff.
6 S. Strange, *The Retreat of the State. The Diffusion of Power in the World Economy* (Cambridge: Cambridge University Press, 1996).

7 B. Badie, *Un monde sans souveraineté. Les États entre ruse et responsabilité* (Paris: Fayard, 1999), p. 178.

8 Ibid., pp. 181 and 183.

9 Z. Laïki, *Un monde privé de sens* (Paris: Fayard, 1994), p. 207.

10 K. Postel-Vinay, *Corée, au coeur de la nouvelle Asie* (Paris: Flammarion, 2002), p. 189.

11 M. Castells, *The Power of Identity*, p. 70. On all these points, see too K. Ohmae, 'The rise of the region-State', *Foreign Affairs*, 72 (2), Spring 1993, pp. 78–87.

12 J. Harding, 'The Mercenary Business', *London Review of Books*, 1 August 1996; D. Shearer, *Private Armies and Military Interventions* (Oxford: International Institute for Strategic Studies, 1998); W. Reno, *Warlords, Politics and African States* (Boulder, CO: Lynne Rienner, 1998); P. Chapleau and F. Misser, *Mercenaires S.A.* (Paris: Desclée de Brouwer, 1998); F. Misser and O. Vallée, *Les Gemmocraties. L'Économie politique du diamant français* (Paris: Desclée de Brouwer, 1997); G. Mills and J. Stremlau (eds), *The Privatisation of Security in Africa* (Johannesburg: The South African Institute of International Affairs, 1999); J. Cilliers and P. Mason (eds), *Peace, Profit or Plunder? The Privatisation of Security in War-Torn African Societies* (South Africa: Institute for Security Studies, 1999). For the notion of an 'economically oriented war', see also Max Weber, *General Economic History*, trans. Frank H. Knight (New York: Collier Books, 1961). The reports of the British NGO Global Witness on Cambodia and Angola have contributed to publicizing the debate, which nonetheless rapidly tended to focus on 'blood diamonds' (see for example I. Smillie, L. Gberie and R. Hazleton, *The Heart of the Matter. Sierra Leone, Diamonds and Human Security* (Ottawa, Partnership Africa Canada, January 2000). Apart from the conflicts in Angola and Sierra Leone, that in Congo-Kinshasa is often cited as the archetype of 'economically oriented war'. (Cf. in particular the *Rapport du Groupe d'experts sur l'exploitation illégale des resources naturelles et autres richesses de la République démocratique du Congo* (New York: United Nations, 16 January 2001).

13 Max Weber, *General Economic History*; M. Foucault, *Society Must Be Defended*; A. Giddens, *The Nation-State and Violence* (Berkeley: University of California Press, 1987); C. Tilly, *Coercion, Capital and European States, A.D. 990–1990* (Oxford: Blackwell, 1990); M. Shaw, *Theory of the Global State. Globality as an Unfinished Revolution* (Cambridge: Cambridge University Press, 2000).

14 K. J. Holsti, *The State, War, and the State of War* (Cambridge: Cambridge University Press, 1996), ch. 2; M. Van Creveld, *The Transformation of War* (New York: Free Press, 1991); M. Kaldor, *New and Old Wars: Organized Warfare in the Global Era* (Cambridge: Polity, 1999).

15 P. B. Evans, 'Transnational linkages and the economic role of the State: an analysis of developing and industralized nations in the post-World War II period', in P. B. Evans, D. Rueschemeyer and T. Skocpol (eds), *Bringing the State Back In* (Cambridge: Cambridge University Press, 1985), ch. 6; A. Ong, *Flexible Citizenship. The Cultural Logics of Transnationality* (Durham: Duke University Press, 1999), ch. 8; K. Iwabuchi, *Recentering Globalization.*

Popular Culture and Japanese Transnationalism (Durham: Duke University Press, 2002).

16 See in particular R. Marchal and C. Messiant, 'Les guerres civiles à l'ère de la globalisation. Nouvelles réalités et nouveaux paradigmes', *Critique internationale*, 18, January 2003, pp. 91–112, and Hassner and Marchal (eds), *Guerres et sociétés*.

17 S. Heydemann (ed.), *War, Institutions and Social Change in the Middle East* (Berkeley: University of California Press, 2000); A. Forsberg, *America and the Japanese Miracle. The Cold War Context of Japan's Postwar Economic Revival, 1950–60* (Chapel Hill: University of California Press, 2000); M. Woo-Cunings, 'National security and the rise of the developmental state in South Korea and Taiwan', in H. Rowen (ed.), *Behind East Asian Growth* (London: Routledge, 1998); P. Grosser, 'Histoire de la guerre froide ou histoire des vainqueurs?', *Critique internationale*, 12, July 2001, pp. 71–2, in a critique of G.-H. Soutou, *La Guerre de Cinquante Ans. Les relations Est-Ouest, 1945–1990* (Paris: Fayard, 2001).

18 L. Martinez, *The Algerian Civil War 1990–1998*, trans. Jonathan Derrick (London: Hurst, 2000).

19 G. Dorronsoro, *La Révolution afghane* (Paris: Karthala, 2000), pp. 32–3 and 299, in an interpretation that is contested by Olivier Roy.

20 'For the first time in independent Africa, a country, Zimbabwe, is intending to transform another country, the Democratic Republic of Congo, into an economic colony', declares John Makumbe of the University of Zimbabwe (*Marchés tropicaux et méditerranéens*, 15 October 1999, p. 2101). Comparable accusations have been levelled at Rwanda. For a nuanced judgement of the 'economic orientation' of Zimbabwe's military involvement in the Democratic Republic of Congo, see M. Nest, 'Ambitions, profits and loss: Zimbabwean economic involvement in the Democratic Republic of the Congo', *African Affairs*, 100 (400), July 2001, pp. 469–90.

21 D. M. Tull, 'A reconfiguration of political order? The state of the state in North Kivu (DR Congo)', *African Affairs*, 102 (408), July 2003, pp. 429–46.

22 P. Mathieu and A. Mafikiri Tsongo, 'Guerres paysannes au Nord-Kivu (République démocratique du Congo), 1937–1994', *Cahiers d'études africaines*, 105–52, XXXVIII-2–4), 1998, pp. 385–416; J.-L. Pabanel, 'La question de la nationalité au Kivu', *Politique africaine*, 41, March 1991, pp. 32–40.

23 R. Paris, 'Echoes of the *Mission civilisatrice*: peacekeeping in the post-cold war era', in E. Newman and O. Richmond (eds), *The United Nations and Human Security* (London: Macmillan, 2001).

24 B. von Krusenstjern and H. Medick (eds), *Zwischen Alltag und Katastrophe. Der Dreissigjährige Krieg aus der Nähe* (Göttingen, Vandenhoeck and Ruprecht, 1998), reviewed by O. Christin in *Le Monde*, 30 October 1998; C. Gantet, 'La guerre des cannibales. Représentations de la violence et conduite de la guerre de Trente Ans (1618–1648)', in Hassner and Marchal (eds), *Guerres et sociétés*, ch. 1.

25 P. Richards, *Fighting for the Rain Forest. War, Youth and Resources in Sierra Leone* (Oxford and Portsmouth: James Currey, Heinemann, 1996), pp. 25ff and 104; K. Peters and P. Richards, 'Jeunes combattants parlant de la

guerre et de la paix en Sierra Leone', *Cahiers d'études africaines*, 150–2, XXXVIII (2–4), 1998, pp. 581–617.

26 S. E. Hutchinson, *Nuer Dilemmas. Coping with Money, War, and the State* (Berkeley: University of California Press, 1996), p. 355.

27 Ibid., pp. 51, 108 and 140.

28 Ibid., p. 110.

29 Ibid., pp. 354–5.

30 For contradictory interpretations of the relation between war and the state in Africa, see Hassner and Marchal (eds), *Guerres et sociétés*; C. Clapham, 'Guerre et construction de l'État dans la Corne de l'Afrique', *Critique internationale*, 9, October 2000, pp. 93–111; R. Marchal, 'Atomisation des fins et radicalisme des moyens. De quelques conflits africains', ibid., 6, Winter 2000, pp. 159–75; J.-F. Bayart, 'La guerre en Afrique: dépérissement ou formation de l'État?', in *Esprit*, 247, 1998, pp. 55–73.

31 To use the apt expression of R. Bertrand in *État colonial*.

32 M. Castells, *The Internet Galaxy: Reflections on Internet, Business, and Society* (Oxford: Oxford University Press, 2001), p. 1.

33 E. Cohen, *L'Ordre économique global. Essai sur les autorités de régulation* (Paris: Fayard, 2001), p. 278. See also *Gouvernance globale* (Conseil d'analyse économique: Paris, La Documentation française, 2002); R. B. Hall and T. J. Biersteker (eds), *The Emergence of Private Authority in Global Governance* (Cambridge: Cambridge University Press, 2002); Z. Laïki, 'L'État global-isé', *Esprit*, 288, October 2002, pp. 136–57.

34 C. Chavagneux, 'Réglementation prudentielle: le forfait de la BRI?', *Revue d'économie financière*, 60, n.d. (2002), pp. 47–58.

35 *Le Monde*, 25 March 2003, pp. ii–iii.

36 *La Croix-L'Événement*, 7 February 2003, pp. 12–13.

37 B. Hibou and M. Tozy, 'De la friture sur la ligne des réformes. La libérali-sation des télécommunications au Maroc', *Critique internationale*, 14, January 2002, pp. 91–118, and B. Hibou, 'Les enjeux de l'ouverture au Maroc. Dissidence économique et contrôle politique', *Les Études du CERI*, 15, April 1996.

38 D. L. Wank, *Commodifying Communism. Business, Trust and Politics in a Chinese City* (Cambridge: Cambridge University Press, 1999); Y. Chevrier, 'L'empire distendu: esquisse du politique en Chine des Qing à Deng Xiaoping', in Bayart (ed.), *La Greffe de l'État*, ch. 9; F. Mengin and J.-L. Rocca (eds), *Politics in China. Moving Frontiers* (New York: Palgrave, 2002).

39 K. Erwin, 'Heart-to-heart, phone-to-phone. Family values, sexuality and the politics of Shanghai's advice hotlines', in D. S. Davis (ed.), *The Consumer Revolution in Urban China* (Berkeley: University of California Press, 2000), pp. 145–70; C. R. Hughes, 'Pourquoi Internet ne démocratisera pas la Chine', *Critique internationale*, 15, April 2002, pp. 85–104; *Le Monde*, 29 December 2000, p. 15; *Libération*, 22 July 2002, p. 7.

40 'The big plus of cable is the way that the government can both control the programmes and get money out of it', declared Andy Lai, the representa-tive of Euro-RSCG in Hong Kong (*Media-Asia's Media and Marketing News-paper*, 9 December 1994).

41 C. R. Hughes, 'Pourquoi Internet'.

42 J. Sgard, *L'Économie de la panique*, p. 272, my italics. See also B. Hibou's work on Morocco, Tunisia, sub-Saharan Africa, Greece and Portugal, quoted in the course of this chapter.

43 J. Sgard, *L'Économie de la panique. Faire face aux crises financières* (Paris: La Découverte, 2002), p. 232.

44 B. Hibou (ed.), *Privatising the State* (London: Hurst, 2004), as well as (also edited by Hibou), 'La privatisation de l'État', *Critique internationale*, 1, Autumn 1998, pp. 128–94, and 'L'État en voie de privatisation', *Politique africaine*, 73, March 1999, pp. 6–121. The concept of 'delegation' (*Verpachtung* or *Überweisung*) is taken from M. Weber, *General Economic History*. I am grateful to D. M. Tull (University of Hamburg) for his comments on the concept of 'delegation'.

45 K. H. O'Rourke and J. G. Williamson, *Globalization and History. The Evolution of a Nineteenth-Century Atlantic Economy* (Cambridge, MA: Harvard University Press, 1999).

46 K. Polanyi, *The Great Transformation* (Boston, MA: Beacon Press, 1957); J. E. Thomson, *Mercenaries, Pirates, and Sovereigns.* (Princeton: Princeton University Press, 1994); G. Arrighi, *The Long Twentieth Century* (London: Verso, 1994); D. Dessert, *Argent, pouvoir et société au Grand Siècle* (Paris: Fayard, 1984). This problematization owes a great deal to my reading of this last work, as well as to my reflections on Africa and its 'politics of the belly'.

47 P. Minard, *La Fortune du colbertisme. État et industrie dans la France des Lumières* (Paris: Fayard, 1998), pp. 257f.; S. L. Kaplan, *Le Pain, le peuple et le Roi. La bataille du libéralisme sous Louis XV* (Paris: Perrin, 1986), and *La Fin des corporations* (Paris: Fayard, 2001); F. Crouzet, *De la supériorité de l'Angleterre sur la France. L'Économique et l'imaginaire, XVIIᵉ–XXᵉ siècle* (Paris: Perrin, 1985); J. Brewer, *The Sinews of Power. War, Money and the English State, 1688–1783* (London: Routledge, 1994); I. Wallerstein, *The Modern World-System*: II, *Mercantilism and the Consolidation of the European World Economy (1600–1750)* (San Diego, CAL, and London: Academic Press, 1980).

48 S. Khilnani, 'La "société civile", une résurgence', *Critique internationale*, 10, January 2001, pp. 38–50; M. Foucault, *Power*, vol. 3 in *Essential Works of Foucault 1954–1984*, ed. James Faubion, trans. Robert Hurley et al. (London: Penguin, 1994), pp. 290–1; Z. A. Pelczynski (ed.), *The State and Civil Society. Studies in Hegel's Political Philosophy* (Cambridge: Cambridge University Press, 1984).

49 X. Bougarel, *Bosnie: anatomie d'un conflit* (Paris: La Découverte, 1996); F. Debié, 'Balkans: une criminalité (presque) sans mafias?', *Critique internationale*, 12, July 2001, pp. 6–13.

50 Fédération internationale des droits de l'homme, Human Rights Watch, *Aucun témoin ne doit survivre. Le génocide au Rwanda* (Paris: Karthala, 1999), p. 18. Cf. also C. Vidal, 'Questions sur le rôle des paysans durant le génocide des Rwandais tutsi', *Cahiers d'études africaines*, 150–2, XXXVIII, 2–4, 1998, pp. 331–45.

51 P. Uvin, *Aiding Violence. The Development Enterprise in Rwanda* (West Hartford: Kumarian Press, 1998), p. 67.

52 Ibid.

53 Bayart, *The Illusion of Cultural Identity*, trans. Steven Rendall, Janet Roitman, Cynthia Schoch and Jonathan Derrick (Chicago: University of Chicago Press, 2005); P. Geschiere, 'Le social standardisé: l'État contre la communauté?', *Critique internationale*, 1, Autumn 1998, pp. 60–5.

54 See for example Africa Watch, *Divide and Rule. State–Sponsored Ethnic Violence in Kenya* (New York: Human Rights Watch, 1993); C. Thomas, 'Le Kenya d'une élection à l'autre. Criminalisation de l'État et succession politique (1995–7)', *Les Études du CERI*, 35, December 1997; D. M. Anderson, 'Vigilantes, violence and the politics of public order in Kenya', *African Affairs*, 101 (404), October 2002, pp. 531–55; H. Maupeu, 'Mungiki et les élections. Les mutations politiques d'un prophétisme kikuyu (Kenya)', *Politique africaine*, 87, October 2002, pp. 117–37. See also R. Bertrand, 'Les virtuoses de la violence. Remarques sur la privatisation du maintien de l'ordre en Indonésie contemporaine', *Revue Tiers Monde*, XLIV (174), April–June 2003, pp. 323–44.

55 See, for various examples, B. Hibou, 'De la privatisation des économies à la privatisation des États. Une analyse de la formation continue de l'État', in Hibou (ed.), *La Privatisation des États*, pp. 26ff; R. Banégas, 'De la guerre au maintien de la paix, le nouveau business mercenaire'; Bertrand, 'Les virtuoses de la violence'.

56 Sources: interviews with the author; law no. 97/021 of 10 September 1997.

57 R. Banégas (ed.), 'L'Ouganda, une puissance régionale?', *Politique africaine*, 75, October 1999, pp. 5–90.

58 J. Roitman, 'The Garrison-Entrepôt', *Cahiers d'études africaines*, 150–2, XXXVIII-2-4, 1998, p. 314, and 'La garnison-entrepôt: une manière de gouverner dans le bassin du lac Tchad', *Critique internationale*, 19, April 2003, pp. 93–115; Richards, *Fighting for the Rain Forest*, pp. 13–14.

59 *Africa Analysis*, 15 October 1999; *Le Figaro*, 14–15 August 1999; *Libération*, 26 February 1999.

60 See the book by David Osborne and Terry Gaebler that has been influential in American and British political circles, *Reinventing Government* (Reading: Addison-Wesley, 1992).

61 Global Coalition for Africa, International Alert, *The Privatization of Security in Africa. Summary Report*, Washington, Overseas Development Council, 12 March 1999. The gathering brought together representatives of private security companies such as Sandline International or MPRI, universities, experts, functionaries of the World Bank, members of NGOs sometimes known for their dealings with secret service circles or private protection, and members of the western military.

62 C. Parenti, *Lockdown America. Police and Prisons in the Age of Crisis* (London: Verso, 1999), chs 5 and 11.

63 *Africa Confidential*, 39 (10), 15 May 1998; E. Leser, 'L'armée américaine fait de plus en plus appel au secteur privé', *Le Monde*, 11 February 2003, p. 18; A. de La Grange, 'Le marché florissant de la privatisation des guerres', *Le Figaro*, 2 April 2002, p. 4; J.-D. Merchet, 'Prestataires de guerre', *Libération*, 3 November 2003, pp. 42–3; House of Commons, *Private Military Companies: Options for Regulations* (London: The Stationery Office, 2002); P. W. Singer, 'Corporate warriors. The rise of the privatised military industry

and its ramifications for international security', *International Security*, 26 (3), Winter 2001–2, pp. 186–220. On the exemplary case of the American–British occupation of Iraq, see 'The military can't provide security. It had to be outsourced to the private sector and that was our opportunity', *Financial Times*, 30 September 2003, and 'L'Irak, nouveau filon des sociétés privées de sécurité', *Le Monde*, 27 December 2003.

64 Sources: interviews with the author.

65 *Le Monde*, 13 March 2003, 1 October 2003, 19 December 2003; *Libération*, 9 May 2003.

66 A. Riccardi, *Sant'Egidio. L'Évangile au-delà des frontières. Entretiens avec Dominique Chivot* (Paris: Bayard, 2001).

67 <http://www.law.harvard/Programs/PON>; J. Cana, 'La privatisation de la diplomatie: une expérience caucasienne', *Critique internationale*, 1, Autumn 1998, pp. 169–78; interviews with the author in Geneva (October 2001 and June 2002).

68 Thomson, *Mercenaries*.

69 A. W. McCoy, *The Politics of Heroin. CIA Complicity in the Global Drug Trade* (New York: Lawrence Hill Books, 1991); R. Reeve and S. Ellis, 'An insider's account of the South African Security Forces' role in the ivory trade', *Journal of Contemporary African Studies*, 13 (2), 1995, pp. 227–44; S. Ellis, 'Africa and international corruption: the strange case of South Africa and Seychelles', *African Affairs*, 95, April 1996, pp. 165–96, and 'The historical significance of South Africa's Third Force', *Journal of Southern African Studies*, 24 (2), June 1998, pp. 261–99.

70 H. Bozarslan, *Network-Building, Ethnicity and Violence in Turkey* (Abu Dhabi: The Emirates Centre for Strategic Studies and Research, 1999), and 'Le phénomène milicien: une composante de la violence politique dans la Turquie des années 1970', *Turcica*, XXXI, 1999, pp. 185–244.

71 F. Ocqueteau, *Déclin de l'état wébérien et recompositions des fonctions policières dans les sociétés de la modernité tardive* (Paris: Université de Paris–I–Sorbonne, 2002).

72 Parenti, *Lockdown America*; J. Allen and H. Als, *Without Sanctuary. Lynching Photography in America* (Santa Fe: Twin Palms Publishers, 2000). See also F. Zimring, *The Contradictions of American Capital Punishment* (Oxford: Oxford University Press, 2003), and 'Aux États-Unis, la peine de mort est héritière d'une justice "privée" ', *Libération*, 28–9 June 2003, pp. 44–5 (on the link between 'vigilantism' and the death penalty in America).

73 Sources: interviews with the author.

74 F. Ocqueteau, *Déclin*.

75 L. Rouban, 'Les États occidentaux d'une gouvernementalité à l'autre', *Critique internationale*, 1, Autumn 1998, p. 134.

76 Ibid., p. 149.

77 Hibou, 'Retrait ou redéploiement de l'État?'

78 Shaw, *Theory of the Global State*, p. 82.

79 Ibid., pp. 116–33 and 228ff.

80 Smillie, Gberie and Hazleton, *The Heart of the Matter*, pp. 38ff.

81 For instance, the two well-known internationalists, R. O. Keohane and J. S. Nye, Jr., in an extremely banal article: 'Globalisation; what's new? What's not? (And so what?)', *Foreign Policy*, Spring 2000, pp. 104–19.

82   C. Gantet, 'Le "tournant westphalien". Anatomie d'une construction historiographique', *Critique internationale*, 9, October 2000, pp. 52–8; A. G. Hopkins, 'Introduction: globalisation – an agenda for historians', in A. G. Hopkins (ed.), *Globalisation in World History* (London: Pimlico, 2002), p. 24; Shaw, *Theory of the Global State*, pp. 30–1.

83   Z. Laïdi, *Le Sacre du présent* (Paris: Flammarion, 2000).

84   E. Hobsbawm and T. Ranger (eds), *The Invention of Tradition* (Cambridge: Cambridge University Press, 1983); A. Smith, 'The nation: invented, imagined, reconstructed?', *Millennium*, 20 (3), Winter 1991, pp. 353–68; T. Ranger, 'The invention of tradition revisited: the case of colonial Africa', in T. Ranger and O. Vaughan (eds), *Legitimacy and the State in Twentieth-Century Africa. Essays in honour of A. H. M. Kirk-Green* (London: Macmillan, 1993), pp. 62–111; Bayart, *The Illusion of Cultural Identity*, pp. 56ff.

85   F. Jameson, *Postmodernism, or the Cultural Logic of Late Capitalism* (Durham: Duke University Press, 1983); R. Rosaldo, 'Imperialist nostalgia', *Representation*, 26, 1989, pp. 107–22.

86   Anderson, *Imagined Communities*, pp. 178ff.

87   J.-P. Warnier (ed.), *Le Paradoxe de la marchandise authentique. Imaginaire et consommation de masse* (Paris: L'Harmattan, 1994) and *Authentifier la marchandise. Anthropologie critique de la quête d'authenticité* (Paris: L'Harmattan, 1996). See below, ch. 6.

88   P. Novick, *L'Holocauste dans la vie américaine* (Paris: Gallimard, 2001).

89   G. Hermet, *Les Désenchantements de la liberté. La Sortie des dictatures dans les années 90* (Paris: Fayard, 1993); 'Mémoire, justice et réconciliation', ed. P. Hassner, *Critique internationale*, 5, Autumn 1999, pp. 122–80.

90   *Le Monde*, 9 April 2003.

91   B. Anderson, *The Spectre of Comparisons. Nationalism, Southeast Asia and the World* (London: Verso, 1998), ch. 3.

92   E. Buch, *La Neuvième de Beethoven. Une histoire politique* (Paris: Gallimard, 1999), ch. 7.

93   On these points, see P. Ricoeur, *Memory, History, Forgetting*, trans. Kathleen Blamey and David Pellauer (Chicago and London: University of Chicago Press, 2004).

94   *Libération*, 17 February 1992, p. 41.

95   M.-R. Trouillot, *Silencing the Past. Power and the Production of History* (Boston: Beacon Press, 1995), pp. 17ff.

96   Ibid.

97   E. Moosa, 'Truth and Reconciliation as performance: spectres of eucharistic redemption', in C. Villa-Vicencio and W. Verwoerd (eds), *Looking Back Reaching Forward. Reflections on the Truth and Reconciliation Commission of South Africa* (The Cape: University of Cape Town Press, 2000), p. 116, quoted by B. Jewsiewicki, 'De la vérité de mémoire à la réconciliation. Comment travaille le souvenir?', *Le Débat*, 122, November–December 2002, p. 63. See also S. Ellis, 'Vérité sans réconciliation en Afrique du Sud', *Critique internationale*, 5, Autumn 1999, pp. 125–37.

98   Z. Laïdi, *Le Sacre du présent*, p. 156.

99   A. Huyssen, 'Present pasts: media, politics, amnesia', *Public Culture*, 30, 2000, p. 26.

100 'Negroes are Anti-semitic because They're Anti-white', *New York Times*, 9 April, 1967, see <http://www.nytimes.com/books/98/03/29/specials/baldwin–antisem.html?_r=1&oref=slogin>. Quoted by P. Novick, *L'Holocauste dans la vie américaine*, p. 277. See also the work by the Israeli historian Idith Zertal and her interview: 'Ce lien exclusif entre la Shoah et l'État d'Israël est désastreux', *Libération*, 20–1 September 2003, pp. 42–3.

101 See for example, on the subject of Afghanistan, M. Wrong, 'Smugglers' bazaar thrives on intrepid Afghan spirit', *Financial Times*, 17 October 2001; 'Feeding the enemy. Commerce across the front line', *The Economist*, 10 November 2001; F. d'Alançon, 'Les trafiquants pachtouns se disputent Spin Boldak', *La Croix-L'Événement*, 3 December 2001; A. Rashid, *Taliban. Militant Islam. Oil and Fundamentalism in Central Asia* (New Haven: Yale University Press, 2001).

102 M. M. van Bruinessen, *Agha, Shaikh, and State. On the Social and Political Organization of Kurdistan* (Utrecht, Rijksuniversiteit, 1978, pp. 239ff).

103 Sources: interviews with the author; H. Bozarslan, 'Kurdistan: économie de guerre, économie dans la guerre', in F. Jean and J.-C. Rufin (eds), *Économie des guerres civiles* (Paris: Hachette, 1996), pp. 140ff; P. Robins, *Suits and Uniforms. Turkish Foreign Policy since the Cold War* (London: Hurst, 2003), p. 333; *Le Monde*, 26 March 2003; *La Croix-L'Événement*, 6 February 2003; *Le Figaro*, 26–7 October 2003.

104 D. McDowall, *A Modern History of the Kurds* (London: I. B. Tauris, 1996), p. 383.

105 F. Adelkhah, 'Le retour de Sindbad: l'Iran dans le Golfe', *Les Études du CERI*, 53, May 1999.

106 Sources: interviews with the author (in Zahedan, November 2002).

107 F. Adelkhah, 'Le maire, le ministre, le clerc et le juge', in J.-L. Briquet and P. Garraud (ed.), *Juger la politique. Entreprises et entrepreneurs critiques de la politique* (Rennes: Presses universitaires de Rennes, 2002), pp. 123–37.

108 J. MacGaffey (ed.), *The Real Economy of Zaire. The Contribution of Smuggling and other Unofficial Activities to National Wealth* (London: James Currey, 1991); B. Hibou, *L'Afrique est-elle protectionniste? Les chemins buissonniers de la libéralisation extérieure* (Paris: Karthala, 1996).

109 K. Bennafla, *Le Commerce frontalier en Afrique centrale. Acteurs, espaces, pratiques* (Paris: Karthala, 2002), J. Roitman, 'The Garrison–Entrepôt'; B. Hibou, *L'Afrique est-elle protectionniste?*; C. Arditi, 'Du "prix de la kola" au détournement de l'aide internationale: clientélisme et corruption au Tchad (1900–1998)', in G. Blundo (ed.), *Monnayer les pouvoirs. Espaces, mécanismes et représentations de la corruption* (Paris: PUF, 2000), pp. 249–67.

110 K. Bennafla, quoting F. Braudel, *Le Commerce frontalier*, p. 98.

111 Ibid., passim, especially p. 339. See too, for a more political interpretation, J. Roitman, 'Le pouvoir n'est pas souverain. Nouvelles autorités régulatrices et transformations de l'État dans le bassin du Lac Tchad', in B. Hibou (ed.), *La Privatisation des États*, ch. 5, and, for a remarkable ethnography of trade on the borders of Zaire, J. MacGaffey (ed.), *The Real Economy of Zaire*.

112 AFP, 25 September 1999.

113 P. Nugent, *Smugglers, Secessionists and Loyal Citizens on the Ghana-Togo Frontier* (Athens and Oxford: Ohio University Press and James Currey, Legon, Sub–Saharian Publishers, 2002), pp. 232–3 and 5.

114 P. Nugent, *Smugglers*, in a critique of J. C. Scott, *Weapons of the Weak: Everyday Forms of Peasant Resistance* (New Haven: Yale University Press, 1985), and *Domination and the Arts of Resistance: Hidden Transcripts* (New Haven: Yale University Press, 1990).

115 D. Nordman, *Frontières de la France. De l'espace au territoire. XVIe–XIXe siècle* (Paris: Gallimard, 1998), pp. 349–50. Peter Sahlins has also shown that, in the valley of la Cerdagne, national awareness, Spanish and French, crystallized on either side of the border, following an autochthonous process, rather than being inculcated by the centre of each of the two states: *Boundaries. The Making of France and Spain in the Pyrenees* (Berkeley: University of California Press, 1989).

116 Sources: interviews with the author in Tripoli (in June 2002 and February 2003). See too K. Bennafla, *Le Commerce frontalier en Afrique centrale*, pp. 44ff.

117 Bayart, *The State in Africa*, pp. 270ff.

118 W. Zafanolli, 'L'économie parallèle en Chine: une seconde nature?', *Revue d'études comparatives Est-Ouest*, 14 (3), September 1983, pp. 103–52, and 'De la main visible à la main fantôme: la réforme chinoise à l'épreuve de l'économie parallèle', *Revue Tiers Monde*, XXVII (108), October–December 1986, pp. 897–921; J.-L. Rocca, *L'Empire et son milieu. La Criminalité en Chine populaire* (Paris: Plon, 1991), as well as 'Corruption and its shadows: an anthropological view of corruption in China', *China Quarterly*, 130, June 1992, pp. 402–16, and 'The rise of the social and the Chinese State', *China Information*, XVII (1), 2003, pp. 1–27.

119 See for example H. Védrine, 'La diplomatie au service de la démocratie', *Le Monde*, 22 January 2001, pp. 1 and 15, and 'Refonder la politique étrangère française', *Le Monde diplomatique*, December 2000, p. 3, and C. Tréan, 'Hubert Védrine, les ONG et les droits de l'homme,' *Le Monde*, 3 January 2001, pp. 1 and 15.

120 A. Przeworksi, *Democracy and the Market, Political and Economic Reforms in Eastern Europe and Latin America* (Cambridge: Cambridge University Press, 1991), pp. 66–7.

121 W. F. Fisher, 'Grands barrages, flux mondiaux et petites gens', *Critique internationale*, 13, October 2001, pp. 123–38.

122 B. Pouligny, 'Acteurs et enjeux d'un processus équivoque. La naissance d'une "internationale civile" ', in ibid., pp. 164–76.

123 Sources: personal survey (2001); J.-F. Bayart, *Rapport au ministre des Affaires étrangères sur le dispositif français en matière de promotion de la démocratie et des droits de l'homme* (Paris: Ministère des Affaires étrangères, January 2002).

124 R. Germain and M. Kenny, 'The new Gramscians', *Review of International Studies*, 24 (1), 1998, pp. 3–28; Shaw, *Theory of the Global State*, p. 89.

125 M. Foucault, *Résumé des cours, 1970–1982* (Paris: Julliard, 1989), p. 113.

126 Ibid, p. 113.

127 'Entretien avec Michel Foucault', in Foucault, *Dits et écrits, 1954–1988*, vol. 4: *1980–1988*, p. 89.

128 Quoted by L. Caramel, 'Les réseaux de l'antiglobalisation', *Critique internationale*, 13, October 2001, p. 161.

129 Survey carried out in Cameroon by the newspaper *Dikalo*, 27 June 1996, quoted by B. Hibou, 'Le capital social de l'État falsificateur, ou les ruses de l'intelligence économique' in J.-F. Bayart, S. Ellis and B. Hibou, *The Criminalisation of the State in Africa* (Oxford: James Currey, 1999).

130 Sources: interview with the author.

131 G. Salamé, *Appels d'empire. Ingérences et résistances à l'âge de la globalisation* (Paris: Fayard, 1996), p. 127.

132 B. Hibou, 'Les marges de manoeuvre d'un "bon élève" économique: la Tunisie de Ben Ali', *Les Études du CERI*, 60, December 1999; S. Khiari, *Tunisie: le délitement de la cité. Coercition, consentement, résistance* (Paris: Karthala, 2003).

133 B. Hibou and L. Martinez, 'Le partenariat euro-maghrébin: un mariage blanc?', *Les Études du CERI*, 47, November 1998; B. Hibou (ed.), 'Les faces cachées du Partenariat euro-méditerranéen', *Critique internationale*, 18, January 2003, pp. 114–78; O. Lamloun, 'L'indéfectible soutien français à l'exclusion de l'islamisme tunisien', in O. Lamloun and B. Ravenel (eds), *La Tunisie de Ben Ali. La Société contre le régime* (Paris: L'Harmattan, Les Cahiers de Confluences, 2002), pp. 103–21.

134 A. Gramsci, *Note sul Machiavelli, sulla politica e sullo Stato moderno* (Turin: Einaudi, 1966), p. 68, trans. H. Portelli, English translation in *Selections from the Prison Notebooks*, pp. 237–8.

135 Wank, *Commodifying Communism*, pp. 180ff.

136 X. Lü, *Cadres and Corruption. The Organizational Involution of the Chinese Communist Party* (Stanford: Stanford University Press, 2000), pp. 214–15. For a critique of the use of the concept of 'civil society' in relation to China, see also the pioneering works of Yves Chevrier, in particular: 'Une société infirme: la société chinoise dans la transition "modernisatrice" ', in C. Aubert et al., *La Société chinoise après Mao. Entre autorité et modernité* (Paris: Fayard, 1986), pp. 229–315; 'L'économie urbaine' and 'La société urbaine', in M.-C. Bergère, L. Bianco and J. Domes (eds), *La Chine au XXe siècle*, II: *de 1949 à aujourd'hui* (Paris: Fayard, 1990), pp. 181–238; 'L'empire distendu: esquisse du politique en Chine des Qing à Deng Xiaoping', in Bayart (ed.), *La Greffe de l'État*, pp. 263–395; '*Tenants of the house*: privatisation de l'État et construction du politique', in B. Hibou (ed.), *Privatising the State*, pp. 245–317. See also the useful overview by F. Mengin and J.-L. Rocca (eds), in *Politics in China*.

137 T. Bierschenk and J.-P. Olivier de Sardan (eds), *Les Pouvoirs au village. Le Bénin rural entre démocratisation et décentralisation* (Paris: Karthala, 1998); T. Bierschenk, J.-P. Chauveau and J.-P. Olivier de Sardan (eds), *Courtiers en développement. Les Villages africains en quête de projets* (Mainz and Paris: APAD and Karthala, 2000); J.-P. Chauveau, 'Question foncière et construction nationale en Côte d'Ivoire. Les enjeux silencieux d'un coup d'État', *Politique africaine*, 78, June 2000, pp. 94–125.

138 J.-F. Bayart, 'La revanche des sociétés africaines', *Politique africaine*, 11, September 1983, p. 120, reprinted in J.-F. Bayart, A. Mbembe and C. Toulabor, *Le Politique par le bas en Afrique noire. Contributions à une problématique de la démocratie* (Paris: Karthala, 1992), p. 97.

139 A. Gramsci, *Note sul Machiavelli*, p. 68.
140 *Le Monde*, 5 February 2001, p. 2.
141 M. Hardt and T. Negri, *Empire* (Paris: Exils Éditeur, 2000), p. 63.
142 Salamé, *Appels d'empire*, ch. 4; F. Vergès, *Abolir l'esclavage: une utopie colo-niale. Les Ambiguïtés d'une politique humanitaire* (Paris: Albin Michel, 2001).
143 Hardt and Negri, *Empire*, p. 382.
144 On the interpretation of the 'politics of the belly' in Gramscian terms of 'passive revolution', see Bayart, *The State in Africa*, ch. 7.
145 J. Ferguson, *The Anti–Politics Machine. 'Development', Depoliticization and Bureaucratic Power in Lesotho* (Cambridge: Cambridge University Press, 1990).
146 J. and J. Comaroff, *Of Revelation and Revolution*, II: *The Dialectics of Moder-nity* (Chicago, University of Chicago Press, 1997), p. 385.
147 J.-F. Bayart, 'Les Églises chrétiennes et la politique du ventre: le partage du gâteau ecclésial', *Politique africaine*, 35, 1989, pp. 3–26, and 'Fait missi-onnaire et politique du ventre: une lecture foucaldienne', *Le Fait mission-naire*, 6, September 1998, pp. 9–38.
148 P. Gifford, *African Christianity. Its Public Role* (Bloomington: Indiana Uni-versity Press, 1998); F. Constantin and C. Coulon, *Religion et transition démocratique en Afrique* (Paris: Karthala, 1997); S. R. Dorman, ' "Rocking the boat?": Church NGOs and democratization in Zimbabwe', *African Affairs*, 101 (402), January 2002, pp. 75–92.
149 G. ter Haar, *Spirits of Africa. The Healing Ministry of Archbishop Milingo of Zambia* (London: Hurst and Co., 1992).
150 Uvin, *Aiding Violence*, pp. 163ff.
151 M. Jennings, ' "Almost an Oxfam in itself": Oxfam, *Ujamaa* and develop-ment in Tanzania', *African Affairs*, 101 (405), October 2002, pp. 509–30, and especially pp. 512 and 530.
152 J. Crisp, 'A State of insecurity: the political economy of violence in Kenya's refugee camps', *African Affairs*, 99 (397), October 2000, pp. 603–4.
153 J. Elyachar, 'Finance internationale, micro–crédit et religion de la société civile en Égypte', *Critique internationale*, 13, October 2001, pp. 139–52 (especially pp. 141, 148 and 151). The author uses the notion of 'indirect rule' in the sense given to this phrase by M. Mamdani, in *Citizen and Subject: Contemporary Africa and the Legacy of Late Colonialism* (Princeton: Princeton University Press, 1996).
154 Mamdani, *Citizen and Subject*.
155 E. F. Irschik, *Dialogue and History: Constructing South India, 1795–1895* (Berkeley: University of California Press, 1994).
156 See, from among an immense literature, and in very different genres: Strange, *The Retreat of the State*, ch. 8, and ibid., *Mad Money. When Markets Outgrow Governments* (Ann Arbor: University of Michigan Press, 1998), ch. 7; also, J. de Maillard, *Le Marché fait sa loi. De l'usage du crime par la globalisation* (Paris: Fondation du 2 mars, Mille et Une Nuits, 2001).
157 S. Handelman, *Comrade Criminal. Russia's New Mafia* (New Haven: Yale University Press, 1995), p. 257.
158 See for instance the work done by the Institut de criminologie de Paris, Université de Paris-II-Panthéon-Assas, and in particular the works in the

collection 'Criminalité internationale' (Paris: Presses universitaires de France), general editor Xavier Raufer.

159 D. Gambetta, *The Sicilian Mafia. The Business of Private Protection* (Cambridge, MA: Harvard University Press, 1993); F. Varese, *The Russian Mafia. Private Protection in a New Market Economy* (Oxford: Oxford University Press, 2001).

160 G. Favarel-Garrigues, J. Cartier-Bresson, H. R. Friman et al., 'Mafias, banques, paradis fiscaux: la globalisation du crime', *L'Économie politique*, 15, 3rd trimester, 2002, 112 pp.

161 R. Marchal and C. Messiant, 'De l'avidité des rebelles. L'analyse économique de la guerre civile selon Paul Collier', *Critique internationale*, 16, July 2002, pp. 58–68. On the war in Sierra Leone, see the (often rather polemical) debate between P. Richards, *Fighting for the Rain Forest*, and the different contributors to 'Lumpen Culture and Political Violence: the Sierra Leone Civil War', *Afrique et développement*, XXII (3–4), 1997, as well as M. C. Ferme, *The Underneath of Things. Violence, History, and the Everyday in Sierra Leone* (Berkeley: University of California Press, 2001), and 'Liberia, Sierra Leone, Guinée: la régionalisation de la guerre', *Politique africaine*, 88, December 2002, pp. 5–102. On the case of Liberia, see also S. Ellis, *The Mask of Anarchy. The Destruction of Liberia and the Religious Dimension of an African Civil War* (London: Hurst, 1999).

162 R. T. Naylor, *Wages of Crime. Black Markets, Illegal Finance, and the Underworld Economy* (Ithaca: Cornell University Press, 2002).

163 Strange, *The Retreat of the State*, p. 121.

164 Sgard, *L'Économie de la panique*, ch. 4; S. Handelman, *Comrade Criminal*; V. Volkov, *Violent Entrepreneurs. The Use of Force in the Making of Russian Capitalism* (Ithaca: Cornell University Press, 2002); J. R. Wedel, 'Tainted transactions. Harvard, the Chubais clan and Russia's ruin', *The National Interest*, Spring 2000, pp. 23–34; D. Malaquais, 'Arts de feyre au Cameroun', *Politique africaine*, 82, June 2001, pp. 101–18.

165 A. W. McCoy, *The Politics of Heroin*.

166 *The BCCI Affair*, A Report to the Committee on Foreign Relations, United States Senate, by Senator Kerry and Senator Hank Brown, Washington, December 1992; P. Truell and L. Gurwin, *False Profits. The Inside Story of BCCI, the World's Most Corrupt Financial Empire* (Boston: Houghton Mifflin Co, 1992).

167 *Le Monde*, 25 September 2001, p. 5.

168 F. Debié, 'Les relations internationales illicites dans les Balkans occidentaux: État, criminalité et société', *La Revue internationale et stratégique*, 43, Autumn 2001, pp. 102–11.

169 C. Tilly, 'War making and state marking as organized crime', in P. B. Evans, D. Rueschemeyer and T. Skocpol (eds), *Bringing the State Back In*, p. 186.

170 B. Hibou, 'L'intégration européenne du Portugal et de la Grèce: le rôle des marges', in S. Mappa (ed.), *La Coopération internationale face au libéralisme* (Paris: Karthala, 2003), pp. 87–134, and 'L'historicité de la construction européenne: le secteur bancaire en Grèce et au Portugal', *Les Études du CERI*, 85–6, April 2002; S. Raffy, 'Prostitution: les nouvelles filières de l'esclavage', *Le Nouvel Observateur*, 25 November 1993, pp. 12–31.

171 McCoy, *The Politics of Heroin*; P. Phongpaichit, S. Piriyarangsan and N. Treerat, *Guns, Girls, Gambling, Ganja. Thailand's Illegal Economy and Public Policy* (Chiang Mai: Silkworm Books, 1998); W. G. Huff, *The Economic Growth of Singapore. Trade and Development in the Twentieth Century* (Cambridge: Cambridge University Press, 1994), esp. pp. 280–1; S. Mydans, 'Thai sex king sees staid new world', *International Herald Tribune*, 31 July 2003, pp. 1 and 5; F. Bobin, 'A Ruili, le trafic d'héroïne birmane prospère avant que la drogue ne parte vers l'Occident', *Le Monde*, 10 January 2003, p. 4; personal observation (Kunming and Chinese–Burmese border, September 1993).

172 R. Bertrand, 'L'affaire de la prise d'otages de Jolo; un exemple de criminalisation du politique en Asie du Sud-Est', *Revue internationale et stratégique*, 43, Autumn 2001, pp. 40–7, as well as ' "Asal Bapak Senang": Tant qu'il plaît à Monsieur. Le gouvernement pastoral comme matrice et alibi de la privatisation de l'État en Indonésie', in Hibou (ed.), *Privatising the State*, ch. 9.

173 J. C. Scott, 'La montagne et la liberté, ou pourquoi les civilisations ne savent pas grimper', *Critique internationale*, 11, April 2001, pp. 86–104 (especially 103–4). The expression *non-State spaces* is taken from Anna Tsing (*In the Realm of the Diamond Queen: Marginality in an Out-of-the-Way Place* (Princeton: Princeton University Press, 1993).

174 K. Barkey, *Bandits and Bureaucrats. The Ottoman Route to State Centralisation* (Ithaca: Cornell University Press, 1994); M. E. Meeker, *A Nation of Empire. The Ottoman Legacy of Turkish Modernity* (Berkeley: University of California Press, 2002); K. N. Chaudhuri, *Asia Before Europe. Economy and Civilisation of the Indian Ocean from the Rise of Islam to 1750* (Cambridge: Cambridge University Press, 1990), ch. 9.

175 See for example J. Roitman and G. Roso, 'Guinée équatoriale: être "off-shore" pour rester "national" ', *Politique africaine*, 81, March 2001, pp. 121–42; D. B. Coplan, 'A river through it: the meaning of the Lesotho–Free State border', *African Affairs*, 100 (398), January 2001, pp. 81–116.

176 Bayart, S. Ellis and B. Hibou, *The Criminalisation of the State*.

177 *Le Monde*, 23 October 2002, p. 3; ibid., 26 February 2003, p. 12; ibid., 19–20 October 2003, pp. 12–13; *International Herald Tribune*, 18 February 2002, pp. 1 and 7, and 13 February 2004, p. 2; R. Marchal (ed.), *Dubaï, cité globale* (Paris: CNRS Éditions, 2001).

178 M. L. Cesoni (ed.), *Criminalité organisée: des représentations sociales aux définitions juridiques* (Geneva, Brussels and Paris: Georg, Bruylant and LGDJ, 2004); G. Favarel–Garrigues, ' "Crime organisé transnational" et lutte anti–blanchiment', in J. Laroche (ed.), *Globalisation et gouvernance globale* (Paris: IRIS, PUF, 2003), pp. 161–73, and 'La création d'un dispositif institutionnel anti–blanchiment en Russie', in G. Favarel-Garrigues (ed.), *Criminalité, police et gouvernement en Russie post–communiste* (Paris: L'Harmattan, 2003).

179 R. Palan, 'Paradis fiscaux et commercialisation de la souveraineté de l'État', *L'Économie politique*, 15, 3rd trimester 2002, pp. 79–96 (passim), and 'Tax havens and the commercialization of State sovereignty', *International Organization*, 56 (1), Winter 2002, pp. 153–77, as well as *The Offshore World*.

Sovereign Markets, Virtual Places, and Nomad Millionaires (Ithaca: Cornell University Press, 2003).

180 *The BCCI Affair*; P. Truell and L. Gurwin, *False Profits*; M. Roche, 'La City a aidé à blanchir les "fonds sales" du dictateur nigérian Sani Abacha', *Le Monde*, 25 October 2000, and J.-C. Buhrer, 'Des banques suisses accusées d'avoir accepté des fonds détournés au Nigeria', *Le Monde*, 6 September 2000.

181 For a comparison between the eurodollar market and medieval fairs in their relation with political sovereignty, see J. G. Ruggie, 'Territoriality and beyond: problematizing modernity in international relations', *International Organization*, 47 (1), 1993, pp. 139–74; Arrighi, *The Long Twentieth Century*, pp. 80ff.

182 *La Croix-L'Événement*, 7 February 2003, p. 12.

183 *The Economist*, 18 May 2002, p. 71; *Le Monde*, 25 May 2002, p. 4.

184 A. Appadurai, *Modernity at Large*.

185 K. Iwabuchi, *Recentering Globalisation*, pp. 52–6 and 78–84.

186 This was remarkably brought out by F. Adelkhah several months before 11 September 2001 in 'Qui a peur du mollah Omar? L'économie morale du "talébanisme" dans le Golfe', *Critique internationale*, 12, July 2001, pp. 22–9.

187 Interview with E. Hobsbawm, *Libération*, 20 September 2001.

188 P. Krugman, 'Cronies reap Iraqi contracts', *International Herald Tribune*, 1 October 2003; D. Jehl, 'Firm offering business advice on Iraq has ties to Bush', *International Herald Tribune*, 1 October 2000; E. Leser, 'Des sociétés proches de l'administration Bush se créent pour le marché irakien', *Le Monde*, 14 October 2003; 'The military can't provide security. It had to be outsourced to the private sector and that was our opportunity', *Financial Times*, 30 September 2003.

189 A. G. Hopkins reaches a similar conclusion by other means: 'Either way, the nation-state, and not just the Westphalian state, needs to be placed at the centre of the history of globalisation, and this means, minimally, taking a fresh look at the nineteenth century' ('The history of globalisation – and the globalisation of history?', in Hopkins, *Globalisation*, p. 30).

190 J. Lonsdale, 'States and social processes in Africa: a historiographical survey', *African Studies Review*, XXIV (2–3), June–September 1981, p. 139.

191 A. G. Hopkins, 'The "New International Economic Order" in the nineteenth century: Britain's first Development Plan for Africa', in R. Law (ed.), *From Slave Trade to "Legitimate" Commerce. The Commercial Transition in Nineteenth Century West Africa* (Cambridge: Cambridge University Press, 1995), p. 248. See also the renewed debate on British imperialism, harbingered by the publication of the two volumes by P. J. Cain and A. G. Hopkins, *British Imperialism* (London: Longman, 1993), in particular R. E. Dumett (ed.), *Gentlemanly Capitalism and British Imperialism. The New Debate on Empire* (Harlow: Addison Wesley Longman Ltd., 1999).

192 J.-F. Bayart, *The State in Africa*, and 'Africa in the world: a history of extraversion', *African Affairs*, 99 (395), April 2000, pp. 217–67; G. Kitching, *Class and Economic Change in Kenya. The Making of an African Petite-Bourgeoisie* (New Haven: Yale University Press, 1980), which relies in particular on the unpublished works, difficult to obtain, by M. P. Cowen.

193 On all these points, see for example the dazzling demonstration by J. D. Peel, *Religious Encounter and the Making of the Yoruba* (Bloomington: Indiana University Press, 2000), pp. 189, 280, 284, 303–4. But the case of the Marxo-compradore nationalism of the MPLA, in Angola, is just as instructive: cf *infra*, ch. 3, pp. 139ff.

194 Apart from the works of Max Weber and Otto Hintze, see A. Giddens, *The Nation-State and Violence*, ch. 10 (esp. p. 263); J. Thomson, *Mercenaries*, pp. 16–17.

195 Arrighi, *The Long Twentieth Century*, pp. 76 f. It is worth remembering that the notion of 'quasi-state' comes from Jackson, *Quasi-States: Sovereignty, International Relations and the Third World*.

196 Holsti, *The State, War and the State of War*, pp. 53ff.

197 Arrighi, *The Long Twentieth Century*, pp. 19–20.

198 S. Mardin, *The Genesis of Young Ottoman Thought. A Study in the Modernization of Turkish Political Ideas* (Princeton: Princeton University Press, 1962); D. Kushner, *The Rise of Turkish Nationalism, 1876–1908* (London: Frank Cass, 1977); F. Georgeon, 'La montée du nationalisme turc dans l'État ottoman (1908–1914). Bilan et perspectives', *Revue du monde musulman et de la Méditerrannée*, 50 (4), 1988, pp. 30–44; 'La Révolution française, la Turquie et l'Iran', *Cemoti*, 12, 1991; J. R. I. Cole, *Modernity and the Millennium. The Genesis of the Baha'i Faith in the Nineteenth Century Middle East* (New York: Columbia University Press, 1998); M. Bayat, *Iran's First Revolution. Shi'ism and the Constitutional Revolution of 1905–1909* (New York: Oxford University Press, 1991) and *Mysticism and Dissent. Socioreligious Thought in Qajar Iran* (Syracuse: Syracuse University Press, 1982); Khayr ed–Din, *Essai sur les réformes nécessaires aux États musulmans, présenté et annoté par Magali Morsy* (Aix-en-Provence: Édisud, 1987); K. Fahmy, *All the Pasha's Men. Mehmed Ali, his Army and the Making of Modern Egypt* (Cambridge: Cambridge University Press, 1997).

199 Hobsbawm, *The Age of Capital, 1848–1875*, p. 103.

200 A.-M. Thiesse, *La Création des identités nationales. Europe, XVIIIe–XXe siècle* (Paris: Le Seuil, 1999), pp. 83ff and 180ff.

201 P. Duara, *Rescuing History from the Nation. Questioning Narratives of Modern China* (Chicago: University of Chicago Press, 1995), pp. 159ff.

202 P.-E. Will, 'L'ère des rébellions et de la modernisation avortée', in M.-C. Bergère, L. Bianco and J. Domes (eds), *La Chine au XXe siècle*, vol. I: *D'une révolution à l'autre, 1895–1949* (Paris: Fayard, 1989), pp. 69ff; Y. Chevrier, 'Des réformes à la révolution (1895–1913)', in ibid., p. 87–121; W. Meissner, 'Le mouvement des idées politiques et l'influence de l'Occident', in ibid., pp. 326–56.

203 H. van de Ven, 'The onrush of modern globalisation in China', in Hopkins (ed.), *Globalisation*, pp. 167–93. See, for example, Hsu, *Dreaming of Gold* for the case of the city of Taishan.

204 Duara, *Rescuing History from the Nation*, p. 13.

205 Hopkins, 'The history of globalisation', p. 25.

206 Anderson, *The Spectre of Comparisons*, ch. 3.

207 See for example J. S. Migdal, *Through the Lens of Israel. Explorations in State and Society* (Albany: State University of New York, 2001), and *State in Society. Studying How States and Societies Transform and Constitute One*

Another (Cambridge: Cambridge University Press, 2001); Z. Lockman, *Comrades and Enemies. Arab and Jewish Workers in Palestine, 1906–1948* (Berkeley: University of California Press, 1996).
208 O. Roy, 'Moyen-Orient: faiblesse des États, enracinement des nations', *Critique internationale*, 4, Summer 1999, pp. 79–104, and *L'Islam globalisé* (Paris: Le Seuil, 2002); G. Salamé, 'Islam and the West', *Foreign Policy*, 90, Spring 1993, pp. 22–37.
209 F. Adelkhah, J.-F. Bayart and O. Roy, *Thermidor en Iran* (Brussels: Complexe, 1993); O. Roy, *L'Échec de l'islam politique* (Paris: Le Seuil, 1992).
210 Bayart, *The Illusion of Cultural Identity*, part 1.
211 Hopkins, 'The history of globalisation', pp. 24ff.
212 On the model of what is proposed by, for example, I. Kopytoff, *The African Frontier. The Reproduction of Traditional African Societies* (Bloomington: Indiana University Press, 1987), or B. Hibou, with her notion of 'borderline' Europeanisation (art. cit.). I have for my part tried to show how the state in Africa corresponds to a principle of incompletion (*The State in Africa*) and how this ambivalence is constitutive of the political (*The Illusion of Cultural Identity*).
213 Shaw, *Theory of the Global State*, passim; Hardt and Negri, *Empire*.
214 J.-L. Nancy, *La Création du monde ou la Globalisation* (Paris: Galilée, 2002), pp. 164ff.
215 'Globality is not the result of a global teleology or a global spirit. It is, however, the outcome of the conscious and intentional actions of many individual and collective human actions': Shaw, *Theory of the Global State*, p. 17.
216 Ibid., pp. 80ff.
217 Van Creveld, *The Rise and Decline of the State*, pp. 408ff.

Chapter 3   The Social Foundations of Globalization

1 D. Al-e Ahmad, *L'Occidentalite. Gharbzadegui* (Paris: L'Harmattan, 1988).
2 M. Castells, *The Power of Identity* (Maiden, MA; Oxford, Blackwell, 1997).
3 P.-A. Taguieff, *L'Effacement de l'avenir* (Paris: Galilée, 2000), passim; Z. Bauman, *Globalisation: the human consequences* (Cambridge: Polity, 1998), pp. 6ff.
4 R. Castel, *Les Métamorphoses de la question sociale* (Paris: Fayard, 1994).
5 L. Boltanski and E. Chiapello, *Le Nouvel Esprit du capitalisme* (Paris: Gallimard, 1999), pp. 450–451.
6 Castells, *The Power of Identity*.
7 R. Cox, *Production, Power and World Order: Social Forces in the Making of History* (New York: Columbia University Press, 1987); S. Gill, *American Hegemony and the Trilateral Commission* (Cambridge: Cambridge University Press, 1990) and (ed.), *Gramsci. Historical Materialism and International Relations* (Cambridge: Cambridge University Press, 1993).
8 K. van der Pijl, *The Making of the Transatlantic Ruling Class* (London: Verso, 1984) and *Transnational Class Formation* (London: Routledge, 1998); J.-F. Bayart, *The State in Africa*, tr. by Mary Harper, Christopher and Elizabeth Harrison (London: Longman, 1993), ch. 7.

9   M. Shaw, *Theory of the Global State* (Cambridge: Cambridge University Press, 2000), pp. 116–33 and 228ff.

10 A. W. Crosby, *The Columbian Exchange: Biological and Cultural Consequences of 1492* (Westport: Greenwood Press, 1972).

11 J. A. Carney, *Black Rice, The African Origins of Rice Cultivation in the Americas* (Cambridge, MA: Harvard University Press, 2001).

12 J. Thornton, *Africa and Africans in the Making of the Atlantic World, 1400–1800*, new edn (Cambridge: Cambridge University Press, 1998), p. 235.

13 D.-C. Martin, 'Filiation ou innovation? Le dilemme des origines dans les musiques afro-américaines', Pointe-à-Pitre, colloquium on 'La Caraïbe face au monde', 28–30 July 1986, and 'Filiation or innovation? Some hypotheses to overcome the dilemma of Afro-American music's origin', *Black Music Research Journal*, 11 (1), Spring 1991.

14 S. Gruzinski, *La Pensée métisse* (Paris: Fayard, 1999) and *La Guerre des images de Christophe Colomb à Blade Runner, 1492–2019* (Paris: Fayard, 1990).

15 J. Roach, *Cities of the Dead. Circum-Atlantic Performance* (New York: Columbia University Press, 1996).

16 See for example P. D. Curtin, *The Rise and Fall of the Plantation Complex. Essays in Atlantic History*, new edn (Cambridge: Cambridge University Press, 1998); S. W. Mintz, *Sweetness and Power. The Place of Sugar in Modern History* (New York: Viking Penguin, 1985); J. C. Miller, *Way of Death. Merchant Capitalism and the Angolan Slave Trade, 1730–1830* (Madison: University of Wisconsin Press, 1988).

17 See for example N. Wachtel, *La Foi du souvenir. Labyrinthes marranes* (Paris: Le Seuil, 2001); J. I. Israel, *Diasporas within a Diaspora: Jews, Crypto–Jews and the World Maritime Empires (1540–1740)* (Leiden: Brill, 2002).

18 D. Reynolds, 'American globalism: mass, motion and the multiplier effect', in A. G. Hopkins (ed.), *Globalisation in World History* (London: Pimlico, 2002), p. 247.

19 I should also mention that celebrated (and controversial) thesis of Frederick Jackson Turner who, in 1893, ascribed a decisive influence on the American 'national character' to the idea and the experience of the 'frontier'. 'The significance of the frontier in American history', in R. A. Billington (ed.), *Frontier and Section: Selected Essays* (Englewood Cliffs: Prentice Hall, 1961, pp. 28–36).

20 Bayart, *The State in Africa*, pp. 182ff and 'Africa in the world: a history of extraversion', *African Affairs*, 99 (395), April 2000, pp. 217–67 (more especially pp. 231ff).

21 The thesis by Didier Péclard can be consulted (Paris: IEP, 2004); see also his 'Savoir colonial, missions chrétiennes et nationalisme en Angola', *Genèses*, 45, December 2001, pp. 114–33, and the remarkable work by Christine Messiant, especially 'Angola, les voies de l'ethnicisation et de la décomposition. 1. De la guerre à la paix (1975–1991): le conflit armé, les interventions internationales et le peuple angolais. 2. Transition à la démocratie ou marche à la guerre? L'épanouissement des deux partis armés (mai 1991–septembre 1992)', *Lusotopie* 1–2, 1994, pp. 155–210, and 3, 1995, pp. 181–212; and *1961. L'Angola colonial. Histoire et société. Les*

prémisses du mouvement nationaliste (Basel: P. Schlettwein Publishing, 2006), as well as J. C. Miller, *Way of Death*.

22 J. Thornton, *Africa and Africans in the Making of the Atlantic World, 1400–1800*; Miller, *Way of Death*, chs 2, 3 and 4.

23 Bayart, *The State in Africa* and 'Africa in the world'; B. Hibou, *L'Afrique est-elle protectionniste? Les chemins buissonniers de la libéralisation extérieure* (Paris: Karthala, 1996).

24 J. D. Y. Peel, *Ijeshas and Nigerians. The Incorporation of a Yoruba Kingdom, 1890s–1970s* (Cambridge: Cambridge University Press, 1983), and *Religious Encounter and the Making of the Yoruba* (Bloomington: Indiana University Press, 2000). See also J. Dunn and A. F. Robertson, *Dependence and Opportunity. Political Change in Ahafo* (Cambridge: Cambridge University Press, 1973).

25 I am here referring to J. Revel (ed.), *Jeux d'échelles. La Micro-analyse à l'expérience* (Paris: coll. 'Hautes Études', Gallimard and Le Seuil, 1996). As Ricoeur comments, a change of scale means that events unnoticed on the macrohistoric level can become visible: *Memory, History, Forgetting* tr. Kathleen Blamey and David Pellauer (Chicago and London: University of Chicago Press, 2004).

26 *Libération*, 23 July 2002, p. 6.

27 E. de Rosny, *Les Yeux de ma chèvre. Sur les pas des maîtres de la nuit en pays douala (Cameroun)* (Paris: Plon, 1981); P. Geschiere, *Sorcellerie et politique en Afrique. La Viande des autres* (Paris: Karthala, 1995).

28 Miller, *Way of Death*, ch. 11.

29 L. White, *Speaking with Vampires. Rumor and History in Colonial Africa* (Berkeley: University of California Press, 2000); B. Weiss, *The Making and Unmaking of the Haya Lived World. Consumption, Commoditization, and Everyday Practice* (Durham: Duke University Press, 1996), ch. 8.

30 White, *Speaking with Vampires*, p. 29, on East Africa.

31 Rosny, *Les Yeux de ma chèvre*.

32 F. De Boeck, 'La frontière diamantifère angolaise et son héros mutant', in J.-F. Bayart and J.-P. Warnier (eds), *Matière à politique. Le pouvoir, les corps et les choses* (Paris: Karthala, 2004), ch. 3.

33 Source: *Internationale de l'imaginaire*, 14, Spring 1990, and performances of the *tchiloli* at the Maison des cultures du monde, Paris.

34 C. Valbert, 'Le tchiloli de Sao Tomé, un exemple de subversion culturelle', in ibid., pp. 36–7.

35 Ibid., pp. 43–4; J. Roach, *Cities of the Dead*.

36 F. De Boeck, 'La frontière diamantifère angolaise', p. 106.

37 H. J. Drewal, 'Mami Wata shrines: exotica and the construction of self', in M. J. Arnoldi, C. M. Geary and K. L. Hardin (eds), *African Material Culture* (Bloomington: Indiana University Press, 1996), ch. 13; B. Jewsiewicki, *Mami Wata. La Peinture urbaine au Congo* (Paris: Gallimard, 2003).

38 P. Jacob, *La Fabuleuse Histoire du cirque* (Paris: Le Chêne, 2002).

39 B. Jewsiewicki, *Mami Wata*, pp. 120ff.

40 Ibid.; S. Bemba, *50 ans de musique du Congo-Zaïre (1920–1970)* (Paris: Présence africaine, 1984).

41 V. S. Naipaul, *A Bend in the River* (London: Deutsch, 1979).

42 *La Cité africaine* (Kinshasa), week of 29 July to 8 August 1991. See also B. Jewsiewicki, *Mami Wata*.

43 K. N. Chaudhuri, *Asia before Europe. Economy and Civilization of the Indian Ocean from the Rise of Islam to 1750* (Cambridge: Cambridge University Press, 1990).

44 M. Y. Hsu, *Dreaming of Gold* (Stanford: Stanford University Press, 2000), p. 9; F. Adelkhah, 'Le retour de Sindbad', *Les Études du CERI*, 53, May 1999, pp. 47–8.

45 On this relation between *Herrschaft* and memory, see Ricoeur, *Memory, History, Forgetting*.

46 Ibid.

47 P. Spyer, *The Memory of Trade. Modernity's Entanglements on an Eastern Indonesian Island* (Durham: Duke University Press, 2000).

48 Ibid.

49 M. Vovelle, *Idéologies et mentalités* (Paris: François Maspero, 1982), pp. 321ff.

50 J. F. Warren, *Iranun and Balangingi. Globalisation, Maritime Raiding and the Birth of Ethnicity* (Singapore: Singapore University Press, 2002), p. 23, ch. 11 and pp. 388ff.

51 See for example R. Bertrand, 'Chroniques d'une guerre morale. Subjectivation par l'ascèse et formation de l'État à Java', in Bayart and Warnier (eds), *Matière à politique*, ch. 2.

52 Warren, *Iranum and Balangingi*; Thomson, *Mercenaries*.

53 A. Lüdtke (ed.), *Histoire du quotidien* (Paris: Éd. de la Maison des sciences de l'homme, 1994).

54 Hsu, *Dreaming of Gold*, pp. 8ff; H. van de Ven, 'The onrush of modern globalisation in China', in Hopkins (ed.), *Globalisation*, pp. 167–93; P. Duara, *Rescuing History from the Nation. Questioning Narratives of Modern China* (Chicago: University of Chicago Press, 1995).

55 Van de Ven, 'The onrush of modern globalisation', pp. 174ff.; Hsu, *Dreaming of Gold*, pp. 31ff.

56 Warren, *Iranun and Balangingi*, pp. 186ff.

57 Apart from the works already mentioned, see, on the Gulf, H. Fattah, *The Politics of Regional Trade in Iraq, Arabia and the Gulf, 1745–1900* (Albany: State University of New York Press, 1997); F. Adelkhah, 'Le retour de Sindbad'; and on the 'ideology of staying on the frontier' and of travelling in the construction of Islam in the Middle Ages, H. Touati, *Islam et voyage au Moyen Âge* (Paris: Le Seuil, 2000), ch. 6.

58 C. Markovits, *The Global World of Indian Merchants, 1750–1947. Traders of Sind from Bukhara to Panama* (Cambridge: Cambridge University Press, 2000).

59 See the ongoing research by F. Adelkhah, in particular 'Le retour de Sindbad', and 'Les Iraniens de Californie: si la République islamique n'existait pas . . .', *Les Études du CERI*, 75, May 2001.

60 A. Ong, *Flexible Citizenship* (Durham: Duke University Press, 1999).

61 Hsu, *Dreaming of Gold*, which explicitly reproaches Aihwa Ong's 'formidable monograph' with not 'historicising' the experience of the Chinese overseas in the 1990s (p. 8).

62 Ibid., pp. 179ff.

63 *International Herald Tribune*, 16 July 2002.
64 See the chapters by C. A. Bayly, A. K. Bennison, R. Drayton and T. Ballantyne in Hopkins (ed.), *Globalisation*; the works by Africanist Marxist theorists on the articulation of modes of production in the 1970s and 1980s; Bayart, *The State in Africa*, pp. 133ff.
65 R. Drayton, 'The collaboration of labour: slaves, empires and globalisations in the Atlantic world, c. 1600–1850', in Hopkins (ed.), *Globalisation*, pp. 98–114; P. Anderson, *Lineages of the Absolutist State* (London: New Left Books, 1974); Curtin, *The Rise and Fall of the Plantation Complex*.
66 A. Lakhsassi and M. Tozy, 'Segmentarité et théorie des *leff–s*: *tahuggwatt-aguzult* dans le Sud-Ouest marocain', *Hespéris–Tamuda*, XXXVIII (2000), p. 201: 'Far be it from us to claim that the *leff–s* are still functional, or that they are undergoing any renewal of vigour. We merely wish to suggest that the logics of the way the memory of a group is structured often lie outside the understanding of the agents. The protagonists of the current political situation are in the process of re-elaborating new reference points when they foreground the "legendary solidarity of the Soussi" in the service of a "new dynamic and entrepreneurial society"; but their quest for the original tradition is still determined on one level by old logics and old reflexes, even if these logics no longer have any basis in the real.'
67 Bayart, *The State in Africa*, Conclusion.
68 G. Levi, *Le Pouvoir au village. Histoire d'un exorciste dans le Piémont du XVIIᵉ siècle* (Paris: Gallimard, 1989, pp. 12–13).
69 Warren, *Iranun and Balangingi*; C. Chou, *Indonesian Sea Nomads. Money, Magic and Fear of the Orang Suku Laut* (London: Routledge, 2003); P. C. Salzman, *Black Tents of Baluchistan* (Washington: Smithsonian International Press, 2000); M. van Bruinessen, *Agha, Shaikh and State: On the Social and Political Organization of Kurdistan* (Risjwijk: Europrint, 1978).
70 I. Kopytoff (ed.), *The African Frontier* (Bloomington: Indiana University Press, 1987).
71 A. L. Tsing, *In the Realm of the Diamond Queen: Marginality in an Out-of-the-Way Place* (Princeton: Princeton University Press, 1993).
72 Ibid., p. 43.
73 C. Piot, *Remotely Global. Village Modernity in West Africa* (Chicago: University of Chicago Press, 1999).
74 T. M. Wilson and H. Donnan (eds), *Border Identities. Nation and State at International Frontiers* (Cambridge: Cambridge University Press, 1998); P. Sahlins, *Boundaries: The Making of France and Spain in the Pyrenees* (Berkeley: University of California Press, 1999); D. Nordman, *Frontières de la France. De l'espace au territoire, XVIe–XIXe siècle* (Paris: Gallimard, 1998); Bayart, *The Illusion of Cultural Identity*.
75 M. Foucault, *Dits et écrits, 1954–1988*, vol. 2: *1970–1975* (Paris: Gallimard, 1994), pp. 141 and 144.
76 S. J. Tambiah, *World Conqueror and World Renouncer: A Study of Buddhism and Polity in Thailand against a Historical Background* (Cambridge: Cambridge University Press, 1976), ch. 7 and 8, and *Culture, Thought and Social Action: an Anthropological Perspective* (Cambridge, MA: Harvard University Press, 1985), ch. 7; E. Leach, *Political Systems of Highland Burma* (London: Bell, 1954).

77 Shaw, *Theory of the Global State*.
78 S. Sassen, *Guests and Aliens* (New York: The New Press, 1999).
79 M. Vovelle, *Idéologies et mentalités*, pp. 163ff.
80 J. R. Wedel, 'Tainted transactions. Harvard, the Chubais clan and Russia's ruin', *The National Interest*, Spring 2000, pp. 23–34.
81 Y. Dezalay and B. G. Garth, *La Globalisation des guerres de palais. La Restructuration du pouvoir d'État en Amérique latine, entre notables du droit et "Chicago Boys"* (Paris: Le Seuil, 2002); X. Lü, *Cadres and Corruption. The Organizational Involution of the Chinese Communist Party* (Stanford: Stanford University Press, 2000); D. L. Wank, *Commodifying Communism*; G. Eyal, I. Szelényi and E. Townsley, *Making Capitalism without Capitalists. Class Formation and Elite Struggles in Post-Communist Central Europe* (London: Verso, 1998).
82 J. Elyachar, 'Finance internationale', *Critique internationale*, 13, October 2001.
83 J. Roitman, 'La garnison-entrepôt', *Critique internationale*, 19, April 2003, pp. 93–115, and *Fiscal Disobedience. An Anthropology of Economic Regulations in Central Africa* (Princeton: Princeton University Press, 2004); L. H. Malkki, *Purity and Exile. Violence, Memory, and National Cosmology among Hutu Refugees in Tanzania* (Chicago: University of Chicago Press, 1995).
84 A. Ong, *Flexible Citizenship*; M. Joseph, *Nomadic Identities. The Performance of Citizenship* (Minneapolis: University of Minnesota Press, 1999); P. Cheah and B. Robbins (eds), *Cosmopolitics. Thinking and Feeling beyond the Nation* (Minneapolis: University of Minnesota Press, 1998).
85 J. Sgard, *L'Économie de la panique* (Paris: La Découverte, 2002).
86 S. Sassen, 'Spatialities and temporalities of the global: elements for a theorization', *Public Culture*, 12 (1), Winter 2000, p. 215.
87 S. Laacher, 'Partir pour le bout de la terre', *Critique internationale*, 19 (April 2003), pp. 157–70; F. Adelkhah, 'Partir sans quitter, quitter sans partir', ibid., pp. 141–55.
88 E. de Latour, 'Héros du retour', *Critique internationale*, 19 (April 2003), pp. 171–89; J.-D. Gandoulou, *Entre Paris et Bacongo* (Paris: Centre Georges-Pompidou et Centre de création industrielle, 1984), and *Dandies à Bacongo. Le Culte de l'élégance dans la société congolaise contemporaine* (Paris: L'Harmattan, 1989); J. MacGaffey and R. Bazenguissa-Ganga, *Congo-Paris. Transnational Traders on the Margins of the Law* (Oxford: James Currey, 2000).
89 Boeck, 'La frontière diamantifère angolaise', ch. 3.
90 Adelkhah, 'Le retour de Sindbad'; C. Hann and I. Beller-Hann, 'Markets, morality and modernity in north-east Turkey', in Wilson and Donann (eds), *Border Identities*, pp. 237–62.
91 A. Tarrius, *La Globalisation par le bas. Les Nouveaux nomades de l'économie souterraine* (Paris: Balland, 2002).
92 See for example T. Hodges, *Angola from Afro-Stalinism to Petro-Diamond Capitalism* (Oxford and Bloomington: James Currey and Indiana University Press, 2001), pp. 115ff; F. Debié, 'Les relations internationales illicites dans les Balkans occidentaux: État, criminalité et société', *Revue internationale et stratégique*, 43, Autumn 2001, pp. 102–11, and 'Balkans: une crimi-

nalité (presque) sans mafias?', *Critique internationale*, 12, July 2001, pp. 6–13.

93 T. de Herdt and S. Marysse, 'La réinvention du marché par le bas et la fin du monopole féminin dans le "cambisme" à Kinshasa', Leuven, *Conférence internationale sur "L'argent feuille morte? L'Afrique centrale avant et après le désenchantement de la modernité*, 21–2 June 1996.

94 The Peruvian economist Hernando De Soto has developed the idea of the 'other path' of development, that of the informal sector, with regard to Peru, and this approach met with a large audience in the years 1980–90, especially within the World Bank.

95 J. MacGaffey (ed.), *The Real Economy of Zaire. The Contribution of Smuggling and other Unofficial Activities to National Wealth* (London: James Currey, 1991), p. 76.

96 J. Roitman, 'La garnison-entrepôt', pp. 97–8.

97 Ibid., my italics.

98 J. Elyachar, 'Finance internationale', pp. 141 and 148.

99 *Le Figaro*, 19 July 2001; *Libération*, 10 October 2003, pp. 2–4; S. Véran, 'La guerre des cartouches', *Le Nouvel Observateur*, 18 December 2003, pp. 86–90.

100 *Libération*, 6 February 2001; *Le Monde*, 8 and 13 February 2001; and *Libération*, 21–2 July 2001.

101 *Le Figaro*, 4 August 2003; M. Watts, 'Economies of violence: governmentality, governable spaces and oil in the Niger Delta, Nigeria', SSRC, Workshop on *Resources: Conceptions and Contestations*, Katmandu, 3–12 January 2003; J. Roitman and G. Roso, 'Guinée équatoriale', *Politique africaine*, 81, March 2001, p. 126; J. G. Frynas, 'Political instability and business: focus on Shell in Nigeria', *Third World Quarterly*, 19 (3), 1998, pp. 457–78, and *Oil in Nigeria. Conflict and Litigation between Oil Companies and Village Communities* (Münster: LIT Verlag, 2000), as well as 'Corporate and State responses to anti–oil protests in the Niger Delta', *African Affairs*, 100 (398), January 2001, pp. 27–54; C. Gore and D. Pratten, 'The politics of plunder: the rhetorics of order and disorder in Southern Nigeria', ibid., 102 (407), April 2003, pp. 211–40.

102 J.-P. Olivier de Sardan, 'Les trois approches en anthropologie du développement', *Revue Tiers Monde*, XLII (168), October–December 2001, p. 739; A. Giddens, *Central Problems in Social Theory. Action, Structure and Contradiction in Social Analysis* (London: Macmillan, 1979).

103 M. Sahlins, 'Cosmologies of capitalism: the "trans-pacific sector of 'the world system' " ', *Proceedings of the British Academy*, 74, 1988, pp. 2–3, quoted (and criticized) by T. Asad, *Genealogies of Religion. Discipline and Reasons of Power in Christianity and Islam* (Baltimore: Johns Hopkins University Press, 1993), p. 3. For my position on this subject, see J.-F. Bayart, *L'État au Cameroun* (Paris: Presses de la Fondation nationale des sciences politiques, 1979), and *The State in Africa*.

104 According to the definition given by B. Baczko, 'Thermidoriens', in F. Furet and M. Ozouf (eds), *A Critical Dictionary of the French Revolution*, trans. Arthur Goldhammer (Cambridge, MA, and London: Belknap Press of Harvard University Press, 1989).

105 M. Tozy, *Monarchie et islam politique au Maroc* (Paris: Presses de Sciences-Po, 1999).

106 See for example, apart from the vicissitudes that have befallen the 'oligarchs' in Russia and the Khalifa group in Algeria, to which I shall be returning in ch. 5, Y. Chevrier, 'De la révolution par le communisme', *Le Débat*, 117, November–December 2001, pp. 92–113; B. Hibou and M. Tozy, 'De la friture', *Critique internationale*, 14, January 2002, pp. 91–118; B. Hibou, 'Les enjeux de l'ouverture', *Les Études du CERI*, 15, April 1996, and 'Les marges de manoeuvre', *Les Études du CERI*, 60, December 1999; S. Heydemann, 'D'Assad à Assad. La politique syrienne n'est pas un théâtre d'ombres', *Critique internationale*, 9, October 2000, pp. 36–43; Bayart, *The State in Africa* and 'Africa in the World'.

107 F. Mengin and J.-L. Rocca (eds), *Politics in China. Moving Frontiers* (New York: Palgrave, 2002); D. S. Davis (ed.), *The Consumer Revolution*; M. Dutton, *Streetlife China* (Cambridge: Cambridge University Press, 1998).

108 Sources: research trips (1991–2002); F. Adelkhah, *Being Modern in Iran*, trans. Jonathan Derrick (New York: Columbia University Press, 2000), and 'Le maire, le ministre, le clerc et le juge. Le judiciaire et la formation du politique en République islamique d'Iran', in J.-L. Briquet and P. Garraud (eds), *Juger la politique. Entreprises et entrepreneurs critiques de la politique* (Rennes: Presses universitaires de Rennes, 2001), ch. 6, and her two studies 'Le retour de Sindbad' and 'Les Iraniens de Californie'; see also F. Adelkhah, J.-F. Bayart and O. Roy, *Thermidor en Iran* (Brussels: Complexe, 1993); A. Ehsteshami, *After Khomeini. The Iranian Second Republic* (London: Routledge, 1995).

109 O. Roy, 'En Asie centrale: kolkhoziens et entreprenants', in J.-F. Bayart (ed.), *La Réinvention du capitalisme* (Paris: Karthala, 1994), ch. 3; B.-M. Pétric, *Pouvoir, don et réseaux en Ouzbékistan postsoviétique* (Paris: PUF, 2002).

110 Bayart, *The State in Africa* and 'Africa in the world'; Hibou, *L'Afrique est-elle protectionniste?* (Paris: Karthala, 1996).

111 J.-F. Bayart, S. Ellis and B. Hibou, *The Criminalization of the State in Africa* (Oxford and Bloomington: James Currey and Indiana University Press, 1999); R. Marchal and C. Messiant, *Les Chemins de la guerre et de la paix. Fins de conflit en Afrique orientale et australe* (Paris: Karthala, 1997).

112 *International Herald Tribune*, 3 October 2003, p. 15; 'Friends and family', *The Economist*, 18 October 2003, pp. 77–8; R. Bertrand, 'La politique du Fmi et l'Indonésie de Suharto', *Esprit*, 242, May 1998, pp. 47–57, and *Indonésie: la démocratie invisible. Violence, magie et politique à Java* (Paris: Karthala, 2002).

113 G. Eya, I. Szelényi and E. Townsley, *Making Capitalism* (London: Verso, 1998).

114 F. Adelkhah lies behind this remark, having drawn my attention to the systematic nature of intermediation in Iran and the United Arab Emirates.

115 T. Ballantyne, 'Empire, knowledge and culture: from proto-globalisation to modern globalisation', in Hopkins (ed.), *Globalisation*, p. 133.

116 See for example Cox, *Production, Power and World Order*; Gill (ed.), *Gramsci, Historical Materialism and International Relations*; L. Sklain, *Sociology of the*

Global System (New York: Wheatshea, 1991); S. G. McNall, R. F. Levine and R. Fantasia, *Bringing Class Back In: Contemporary and Historical Perspectives* (Boulder: Westview Press, 1991).

117 M. Castells, *The Internet Galaxy* (Oxford: Oxford University Press, 2001).

118 M. Castells, *The Rise of the Network Society* (Cambridge, MA and Oxford: Blackwell, 1999), p. 192.

119 Ibid.

120 B. Fine and E. Leopold, *The World of Consumption* (London: Routledge, 1993).

121 See for example K. T. Hansen, *Salaula. The World of Secondhand Clothing and Zambia* (Chicago: University of Chicago Press, 2000); MacGaffey and Bazenguissa-Ganga, *Congo-Faris*.

122 R. Rouse, 'Mexican migration and the social space of postmodernism', *Diaspora*, I (10), Spring 1991, p. 14; Hsu (*Dreaming of Gold*) follows just this conceptualization.

123 Hsu, *Dreaming of Gold*, pp. 35–40 and 150–1; R. Marchal, 'La Somalie, nouvelle cible de "Justice illimitée?" ', *Politique africaine*, 84, December 2001, pp. 155ff.

124 P. Levitt, *The Transnational Villagers* (Berkeley: University of California Press, 2001); Ong, *Flexible Citizenship*, pp. 127ff.

125 C. Quiminal, *Gens d'ici, gens d'ailleurs* (Paris: Christian Bourgois, 1991); MacGaffey and Bazenguissa-Ganga, *Congo-Paris*; E. de Latour, 'Héros du retour', *Critique internationale*, 19 (April 2003), and 'Du ghetto au voyage clandestin: la métaphore héroïque', *Autrepart*, 19, 2001, pp. 155–76.

126 A. Colonomos, *Églises en réseaux. Trajectoires politiques entre Europe et Amérique* (Paris: Presses de Sciences-Po, 2000).

127 G. ter Haar, *Halfway to Paradise. African Christians in Europe* (Cardiff: Cardiff Academic Press, 1998).

128 Boltanski and Chiapello, *Le Nouvel Esprit du capitalisme*.

129 Levitt, *The Transnational Villagers*, ch. 3.

130 Y. Courbage, 'Migration internationale et transition démographique au Maghreb', in R. Benhaïm, Y. Courbage and R. Leveau, *Le Maghreb en suspens* (Paris: CERI, 1994, pp. 9–28).

131 Malkki, *Purity and Exile*.

132 F. Adelkhah, 'Qui a peur du mollah Omar?', *Critique internationale*, 12, July 2001.

133 Adelkhah, 'Les Iraniens de Californie'.

134 Markovits, *The Global World of Indian Merchants*.

135 Latour, 'Héros du retour', p 183; A. Sayad, *La Double Absence* (Paris: Le Seuil, 1998), p. 19.

136 Hsu, *Dreaming of Gold*, ch. 3. See also R. Kastoryano, *La France, l'Allemagne et leurs immigrés: négocier l'identité* (Paris: Armand Colin, 1996).

137 P. Stoller, *Money Has No Smell. The Africanization of New York City* (Chicago: University of Chicago Press, 2002), ch. 3; C. Anta Babou, 'Brotherhood solidarity, education and migration: the role of the *dahiras* among the Murid Muslim community of New York', *African Affairs*, 101 (403), April 2002, pp. 151–70; *International Herald Tribune*, 29 July 2003, p. 2.

138 MacGaffey (ed.), *The Real Economy of Zaire*, pp. 30ff.
139 Adelkhah, 'Le retour de Sindbad', and her video film *Bons Baisers de Damas* (Paris: CERI, FNSP, 2004).
140 Hansen, *Salaula*, p. 71.
141 Ong, *Flexible Citizenship*, pp. 116ff.
142 MacGaffey (ed.), *The Real Economy of Zaire*, ch. 7; A. P. Cheater, 'Transcending the State? Gender and borderline constructions of citizenship in Zimbabwe', in T. M. Wilson and H. Donnan (eds), *Border Identities*, pp. 191–214; A. Lambert, 'Les commerçantes maliennes du chemin de fer Dakar–Bamako', in E. Grégoire and P. Lazabée (eds), *Grands Commerçants d'Afrique de l'Ouest. Logiques et pratiques d'un groupe d'hommes d'affaires contemporains* (Paris: Karthala, 1993), ch. 1; J.-Y. Weigel, '*Nana* et pêcheurs du port de Lomé: une exploitation de l'homme par la femme?', *Politique africaine*, 27, September 1987, pp. 37–46; E. Ayina, 'Pagnes et politique', ibid., pp. 47–54.
143 F. Adelkhah, 'Iran: femmes en mouvement, mouvements de femmes', in M. Bennani–Chraïbi and O. Fillieule (eds), *Résistances et protestations dans les sociétés musulmanes* (Paris: Presses de Sciences-Po, 2003), ch. 6, and the aforementioned film, *Bons Baisers de Damas*.
144 M. Samuel, *Le Prolétariat africain noir en France* (Paris: François Maspero, 1978); MacGaffey and Bazenguissa-Ganga, *Congo-Paris*.
145 T. Grätz, 'Gold trading networks and the creation of trust: a case study from Northern Benin', *Africa* 74 (2), 2004, pp. 146–72.
146 A. Tarrius, *Fin de siècle incertaine à Perpignan* (Canet: Llibres del trabucaire, 1997), pp. 105ff.
147 Stoller, *Money Has No Smell*, ch. 4.
148 MacGaffey and Bazenguissa-Ganga, *Congo-Paris*, p. 73.
149 B. Badie, *La Fin des territoires. Essai sur le désordre international et sur l'utilité sociale du respect* (Paris: Fayard, 1995).
150 See for example B. Meyer and P. Geschiere (eds), *Globalization and Identity. Dialectics of Flow and Closure* (Oxford: Blackwell, 1999). The concept of 'glocalization' comes from the language of Japanese marketing (*dochakuka*, i.e. 'global localization'): R. Robertson, *Globalisation, Social Theory and Global Culture* (London: Sage, 1992), pp. 173–4.
151 Following the now classic formula of F. Jameson, 'Cognitive mapping', in C. Nelson and L. Grossberg (eds), *Marxism and the Interpretation of Cultures* (Urbana: University of Illinois Press, 1988), p. 349.
152 Levitt, *The Transnational Villagers*, p. 11.
153 Adelkhah, 'Partir sans quitter', pp. 151ff; Hsu makes a similar remark: Taishan is defined by absence, that of the emigrants (*Dreaming of Gold*, p. 17).
154 Adelkhah, 'Le retour de Sindbad'.
155 Hsu, *Dreaming of Gold*, pp. 47ff.
156 Ibid., pp. 17–18.
157 Ibid., ch. 4.
158 A. Abélès, *Les Nouveaux riches. Un ethnologue dans la Silicon Valley* (Paris: Odile Jacob, 2002), p. 94.
159 R. S. Parrenas, *Servants of Globalization. Women, Migration and Domestic Work* (Stanford: Stanford University Press, 2001), pp. 206ff.

160 Source: observations made by Fariba Adelkhah in Tokyo (March–April 2003). On the figure of the *javânmard*, see her *Being Modern in Iran*, ch. 2.
161 MacGaffey and Bazenguissa-Ganga, *Congo-Paris*, pp. 142ff.
162 G. ter Haar, *Halfway to Paradise*, p. 40.
163 S. Sassen, *Globalisation and its Discontents* (New York: The New Press, 1998), p. xx.
164 Stoller, *Money Has No Smell*.
165 Ibid.; Sassen, *Globalisation and its Discontents*.
166 Castells, *The Internet Galaxy*, ch. 8, as well as the cartography of Matthew Zook (<www.zooknic.com>).
167 Castells, *The Internet Galaxy*, ch. 8.
168 Castells, *The Rise of the Network Society*, p. 407.
169 M. Le Pape, *L'Énergie sociale à Abidjan. Économie politique de la ville en Afrique noire, 1930–1995* (Paris: Karthala, 1997).
170 J. Garreau, *Edge City: Life on the New Frontier* (New York: Doubleday, 1991).
171 S. Strange, *The Retreat of the State* (Cambridge: Cambridge University Press, 1996), p. xiii.

Chapter 4 Globalization and Political Subjectivation: The Imperial Moment (1830–1960)

1 E. P. Thompson, *The Making of the English Working Classes* (London: Victor Gollancz, 1963).
2 D. Le Breton, 'La globalisation, ennemie de l'être', *Libération*, 8 August 2003, p. 11.
3 See M. Weber, *The Sociology of Religion*, trans. Ephraim Fischoff (London: Social Science Paperbacks, 1971). [However, references are, at the author's suggestion, to the French translation, *Sociologie des religions* (Paris: Gallimard, 1996), by Jean-Pierre Grossein – Tr.] Grossein translates both *Menschentyp* and *Menschentum* by 'type d'homme', 'type of man (or person)', and explains: *Menschentum* 'does not designate humanity as the set of human beings, but humanity in its qualitative aspect, referring to specific human qualities'. He indicates that *Menschentum* does not appear in Germany until the nineteenth century, when it is detached from *Menschheit* (*Sociologie des religions*, p. 122).
4 *Sociologie des religions*, p. 333.
5 Ibid., p. 335.
6 Ibid.
7 Ibid., p. 142, my emphasis.
8 J.-P. Grossein, 'Présentation', in ibid., p. 106.
9 M. Foucault, Preface to *Ethics*, vol. 1 in *The History of Sexuality* in *Essential Works of Foucault 1954–1984*, ed. James Faubion, trans. Robert Hurley et al. (London: Penguin, 1994), p. 200.
10 M. Foucault, *The History of Sexuality*, vol. 2, *The Use of Pleasure*, trans. Robert Hurley (London: Viking, 1986), p. 6.
11 Ibid.

12 Ibid, p. 28.
13 Ibid., p. 32.
14 M. Foucault, *The History of Sexuality*, vol. 3, *The Care of the Self*, trans. Robert Hurley (London: Allen Lane, 1988), p. 95, my italics. See also M. Foucault, 'L'Herméneutique du sujet', in *Cours au Collège de France*, 1981–1982 (Paris: Gallimard and Le Seuil, 'Hautes Études', 2001).
15 G. Deleuze, *Negotiations, 1972–1990*, trans. Martin Joughin (New York and Chichester: Columbia University Press, 1995).
16 Ibid.
17 Ibid.
18 Ibid.
19 Ibid.
20 Ibid.
21 G. Deleuze, *Empiricism and Subjectivity: An Essay on Hume's Theory of Human Nature*, trans. Constantin V. Boundas (New York and Oxford: Columbia University Press, 1991).
22 G. Deleuze, *Difference and Repetition*, trans. Paul Patton (London: The Athlone Press, 1994).
23 G. Deleuze, lecture given on 15 February 1977.
24 S. Sassen, 'Spatialities and temporalities of the global: elements for a theorization', *Public Culture*, 12 (1), Winter 2000, p. 215.
25 M. Weber, *Sociologie des religions*, p. 142, my emphasis.
26 This is the interpretation put forward by P. Bouretz, *Les Promesses du monde. Philosophie de Max Weber* (Paris: Gallimard, 1996), p. 253.
27 Weber, *Sociologie des religions*, pp. 279 and 333–5; see also Grossein's commentary, ibid., p. 67, n. 3.
28 M. Foucault, *History of Sexuality*, vol. 1, *The Will to Knowledge*, trans. Robert Hurley (London: Penguin, 1990).
29 Ibid.
30 Foucault, *The Use of Pleasure*.
31 This is the interpretation put forward by P. Macherey, 'Pour une histoire naturelle des normes', in *Michel Foucault philosophe. Rencontre internationale. Paris, 9, 10, 11 janvier 1988* (Paris: Le Seuil, 1989), p. 209.
32 Foucault, *The Use of Pleasure*, p. 27.
33 M. Foucault, 'Technologies of the Self', in *Ethics*, p. 225.
34 G. Balandier, *Sociologie actuelle de l'Afrique noire. Dynamique sociale en Afrique centrale*, new edn (Paris: PUF, 1971), ch. 1.
35 See for example the evidence in G. Darien, *Biribi*, new edn (Paris: Le Gadenet, Jérôme Martineau, 1966).
36 E. M. Collingham, *Imperial Bodies. The Physical Experience of the Raj, c. 1800–1947* (Cambridge: Polity, 2001), p. 1.
37 M. van Woerkens, *Le Voyageur étranglé. L'Inde des Thugs, le colonialisme et l'imaginaire* (Paris: Albin Michel, 1995); D. Arnold, *Colonizing the Body. State Medicine and Epidemic Disease in Nineteenth-Century India* (Berkeley: University of California Press, 1993).
38 P. D. Curtin, *Disease and Empire. The Health of European Troops in the Conquest of Africa* (Cambridge: Cambridge University Press, 1998); J. D. Y. Peels, *Religious Encounter and the Making of Yoruba* (Bloomington: Indiana

University Press, 2000), pp. 219ff; J. C. Miller, *Way of Death. Merchant Capitalism and the Angolan Slave Trade, 1730–1830* (Madison: University of Wisconsin Press, 1988), ch. 9.

39 J. Clancy-Smith and F. Gouda (eds), *Domesticating the Empire. Race, Gender, and Family Life in French and Dutch Colonialism* (Charlottesville: University Press of Virginia, 1998).

40 E. Hobsbawm and T. Ranger (eds), *The Invention of Tradition* (Cambridge: Cambridge University Press, 1983); D. Cannadine, *Ornamentalism. How the British Saw their Empire* (London: The Penguin Press, 2001); R. Bertrand, *État colonial, noblesse et nationalisme à Java. La Tradition parfaite* (Paris: Karthala, 2005).

41 Clancy-Smith and Gouda (eds), *Domesticating the Empire*; R. Aldrich, *Colonialism and Homosexuality* (London: Routledge, 2003); J. Bulmer, *The White Tribes of Africa* (New York: Macmillan, 1965); Bertrand, *État colonial*, ch. 8.

42 B. Berman and J. Lonsdale, *Unhappy Valley. Conflict in Kenya and Africa*, vol. II, *Violence and Ethnicity* (London: James Currey, 1992), pp. 234–5.

43 Aldrich, *Colonialism and Homosexuality*, p. 1, and *Barrage contre le Pacifique* by Marguerite Duras, translated into English as *The Sea Wall*, as well as Jean Hougron's cycle of novels, *La Nuit indochinoise*, on the world of the 'white folks' in French Indochina.

44 Foucault, *The Care of the Self*, p. 116.

45 I am here drawing on the ideas of Benedict Anderson in the second edition of his celebrated book, *Imagined Communities* (London: Verso, 1991).

46 The essay by Timothy Mitchell, *Colonising Egypt* (Berkeley: University of California Press, 1991), often quoted, sometimes falls into this misapprehension.

47 L. White, *Speaking with Vampires. Rumor and History in Colonial Africa* (Berkeley: University of California Press, 2000), pp. 67–8.

48 J.-P. Sartre's preface to F. Fancn, *The Wretched of the Earth*, trans. Constance Farrington (London: Penguin, 1967), is a particularly condescending example of this egregious error.

49 A. Mbembe, *La Naissance du maquis dans le Sud-Cameroun (1920–1960). Histoire des usages de la raison en colonie* (Paris: Karthala, 1996), p. 284.

50 J.-F. Bayart, *The Illusion of Cultural Identity*.

51 J. Iliffe, *East African Doctors. A History of the Modern Profession* (Cambridge: Cambridge University Press, 1998).

52 M. Egli and D. Krayer, ' "Mothers and daughters": the training of African nurses by missionary nurses of the Swiss Mission in South Africa', *Le Fait missionnaire* (Lausanne), 4, March 1997, pp. 7–135.

53 White, *Speaking with Vampires*, p. 99. See also J. D. Y. Peel, *Religious Encounter and the Making of the Yoruba* (Bloomington: Indiana University Press, 2000), pp. 219ff.

54 Ibid., ch. 3.

55 Ibid., pp. 285–6.

56 P. Laburthe-Tolra, *Vers la Lumière? Ou le désir d'Ariel. A propos des Beti du Cameroun. Sociologie de la conversion* (Paris: Karthala, 1999); H. B. Hansen, *Mission, Church and State in a Colonial Setting. Uganda, 1890–1925* (London: Heinemann, 1984); Peel, *Religious Encounter*.

57 J.-F. Bayart, 'Les Églises chrétiennes et la politique du ventre: le partage du gâteau ecclésial', *Politique africaine*, 35, 1989, p. 25; F. Raison–Jourde, *Bible et pouvoir à Madagascar au XIXe siècle. Invention d'une identité chrétienne et construction de l'État* (Paris: Karthala, 1991), pp. 587ff.

58 As reported in B. de Dinechin and Y. Tabart, *Un Souffle venant d'Afrique. Communautés chrétiennes au Nord–Cameroun* (Paris: Le Centurion, 1986), pp. 77–8.

59 See for example T. Ranger, *Are We Not Also Men? The Samkange Family and African Politics in Zimbabwe, 1920–64* (London: James Currey, 1995).

60 This is the phrase used by M. de Certeau, *The Practice of Everyday Life*, trans. Steven Rendall (Berkeley: University of California Press, 1984).

61 D. Péclard, 'Ethos missionnaire et esprit du capitalisme. La Mission philafricaine en Angola, 1897–1907', *Le Fait missionnaire* (Lausanne), 1, 1995, pp. 39–40 and p. 37, note 69. See too, by the same author, ' "Amanha para ser homem". Missions chrétiennes et formation du sujet colonial en Angola central au XXe siècle', *Politique africaine*, 74, June 1999, pp. 113–29.

62 On the use of whips in schools, in establishments or during cleansing campaigns, or quite simply in domestic relations on the missions, see for example N. R. Hunt, *A Colonial Lexicon of Birth Ritual, Medicalization and Mobility in the Congo* (Durham: Duke University Press, 1999), pp. 94–5, 136 and 150; on the coercive imposition of a 'lifestyle' by fundamentalist Protestant missionaries, see in particular W. James, *The Listening Ebony. Moral Knowledge, Religion and Power among the Uduk of Sudan* (Oxford: Clarendon Press, 1988), pp. 207ff.

63 J. and J. Comaroff, *Of Revelation and Revolution*, II: *The Dialectics of Modernity* (Chicago, University of Chicago Press, 1997), pp. 29–35.

64 A. Mbembé, *Afriques indociles. Christianisme, pouvoir et État en société postcoloniale* (Paris: Karthala, 1988).

65 Peel, *Religious Encounter*, ch. 9.

66 J.-F. Bayart, *The State in Africa. The Politics of the Belly*, trans. Mary Harper, Christopher and Elizabeth Harrison (London: Longman, 1993), and 'Les Églises chrétiennes et la politique du ventre: le partage du gâteau ecclésial', *Politique africaine*, 35, 1989.

67 T. Ranger, 'The invention of tradition revisited: the case of colonial Africa', in T. Ranger and O. Vaughan (eds), *Legitimacy and the State in Twentieth Century Africa. Essays in Honour of A. H. M. Kirk-Green* (London: Macmillan, 1993), pp. 62–111. See also the critique of the notion by A. Smith, 'The nation: invented, imagined, reconstructed?', *Millennium*, 20 (3), Winter 1993, pp. 353–68.

68 Berman and Lonsdale, *Unhappy Valley*.

69 See for example the work done by R. Bertrand on the *priyayi* of Java: *État colonial*, and 'L'ascèse pour la gloire. Trajectoires notabiliaires de la noblesse de robe de Java (XVIIe–XIXe siècles)', *Politix*, 17 (64), 2004, pp. 17–44.

70 Weber, *Sociologie des Religions*, p. 138.

71 F. Cooper, *From Slaves to Squatters. Plantation Labour and Agriculture in Zanzibar and Coastal Kenya, 1890–1925* (New Haven: Yale University Press, 1980, pp. 56–57), and F. Cooper, A. F. Isaacman, F. E. Mallon, W. Roseberry and S. J. Stern, *Confronting Historical Paradigms. Peasant, Labor and the*

Capitalist World System in Africa and Latin America (Madison: University of Wisconsin Press, 1993), especially chs 2 and 3.

72 See for example J. and J. Comaroff, *Of Revelation and Revolution,* and *Ethnography and the Historical Imagination* (Boulder: Westview Press, 1992); F. Cooper and A. L. Stoler (eds), *Tensions of Empire: Colonial Cultures in a Bourgeois World* (Berkeley: University of California Press, 1997); T. Ranger, 'The invention of tradition in colonial Africa', in Hobsbawm and Ranger (eds), *The Invention of Tradition,* pp. 211–62; A. L. Conklin, *A Mission to Civilize: the Republican Idea of Empire in France and West Africa* (Stanford: Stanford University Press, 1997); G. W. Johnson (ed.), *Double Impact: France and Africa in the Age of Imperialism* (Westport: Greenwood Press, 1985); J.-P. Dozon, *Frères et sujets. La France et l'Afrique en perspective* (Paris: Flammarion, 2003); N. Bancel, P. Blanchard and F. Vergès, *La République coloniale. Essai sur une utopie* (Paris: Albin Michel, 2003).

73 See for example Dozon, *Frères et sujets;* E. Temime, *Un Rêve méditerranéen. Des saint–simoniens aux intellectuels des années trente* (Arles: Armand Colin, Fondation nationale des sciences politiques, 1974); M. Diouf, 'The French colonial policy of assimilation and the civility of the originaires of the Four Communes (Senegal): a nineteenth-century globalisation project', *Development and Change,* 29 (4), October 1998, pp. 671–96.

74 M. Foucault, *Society Must be Defended. Lectures at the Collège de France, 1975–76,* ed. Mauro Bertani and Alessandro Fontana; trans. David Macey (London: Allen Lane, 2003).

75 P. Rabinow, *French Modern. Norms and Forms of the Social Environment* (Chicago: University of Chicago Press, 1989), passim (especially ch. 9); J. R. Horne, 'In pursuit of Greater France: visions of empire among Musée social reformers, 1894–1931', in Clancy-Smith and Gouda (eds), *Domesticating the Empire,* ch. 2.

76 Exhibition 'Alger, paysage urbain et architectures' (Paris, Cité de l'architecture et du patrimoine, 2003); E. de Roux. 'Comment s'est bâtie Alger la Blanche', *Le Monde,* 19 August 2003, p. 20.

77 L. Chevalier, *L'Assassinat de Paris* (Paris: Calmann-Lévy, 1977).

78 C. Guérin, *L'Utopie Scouts de France* (Paris: Fayard, 1997), p. 45. The following pages are mainly based on this work.

79 Quoted in ibid., my italics.

80 Quoted in ibid., p. 48. English version at <http://www.geocities.com/Heartland/Flats/3201/sctlws.html>.

81 Ibid., pp. 53–4.

82 Quoted in ibid., p. 97.

83 Quoted in ibid., p. 159, my italics.

84 Ibid., pp. 98–9.

85 Quoted in ibid.

86 Quoted in ibid., p. 101.

87 E. Psichari, *Terres de soleil et de sommeils* (Paris: Calmann–Lévy, 1908), quoted in Bancel, Blanchard and Vergès, *La République coloniale,* p. 90.

88 Guérin, *L'Utopie Scouts de France,* pp. 335ff.

89 Quoted in ibid., pp. 409–10.

90 K. Ross, *Fast Cars, Clean Bodies, Decolonization and the Reordering of French Culture* (Cambridge, MA: The MIT Press, 1996), p. 80.

91 Ibid., p. 77.
92 E. Balibar, *Droit de cité*, new edn (Paris: PUF, 2002), pp. 76 and 80.
93 Bayart, *The State in Africa*, pp. 241ff and *La Politique africaine de François Mitterrand* (Paris: Karthala, 1984).
94 Cf. A. Ong, *Flexible Citizenship. The Cultural Logics of Transnationality* (Durham: Duke University Press, 1999), pp. 32–3, for a critical presentation of this approach.
95 E. F. Irschick, *Dialogue and History. Constructing South India, 1795–1895* (Berkeley: University of California Press, 1994).
96 Miller, *Way of Death*, pp. 402ff.
97 J. F. Warren, *Iranun and Balangingi. Globalisation, Maritime Raiding and the Birth of Ethnicity* (Singapore: Singapore University Press, 2002), ch. 11.
98 See for example Peel, *Religious Encounter*.
99 Warren, *Iranun and Balangingi*, p. 318.
100 M. T. Taussig, *The Devil and Commodity Fetishism in South America* (Chapel Hill: University of North Caroline Press, 1980), p. 42.
101 L. Verlaine, *A la recherche de la méthode de colonisation* (1924), quoted in L. Zoumenou, *Un Précurseur du mouvement démocratique et panafricain en Afrique noire française: Kojo Tovalou Houenou (1887–1936)* (Paris: Institut d'études politiques, 1985), p. 265; Berman and Lonsdale, *Unhappy Valley*, I: *State and Class*, p. 107.
102 Cooper, *From Slaves to Squatters*, p. 120.
103 Texts quoted by J. Gahama, *Le Burundi sous administration belge. La Période du mandat, 1919–1939* (Paris: Karthala, 1983), pp. 308–9.
104 Collingham, *Imperial Bodies*, p. 109.
105 Ibid., pp. 141–4.
106 Pepetela, *Yaka* (Brussels: Les Éperonniers, 1992), pp. 127–8. See too R. Pélissier, *La Colonie du Minotaure. Nationalisme et révoltes en Angola (1926–1961)* (Orgeval: Pélissier, 1978), p. 131.
107 F. Bernault (ed.), *Enfermement, prison et châtiments en Afrique du XIXᵉ siècle à nos jours* (Paris: Karthala, 1999); Gahama, *Le Burundi sous administration belge*, pp. 308–9.
108 J. M. Coetzee, *Boyhood: Scenes from Provincial Life* (London: Secker and Warburg, 1997), ch. 2.
109 J. Vansina, 'L'enfermement dans l'Angola ancien', in Bernault (ed.), *Enfermement, prison et châtiments*, p. 86.
110 Darien, *Biribi*.
111 J.-P. Hallet, *Le Congo des magiciens* (Paris: La Table ronde, 1967, p. 34), quoted in B. Jewsiewicki, *Mami Wata. La Peinture urbaine au Congo* (Paris: Gallimard, 2003), p. 95. In 1908, a Belgian procurator appointed to a post in the Congo had produced similar evidence: cf. A. Hochschild, *Les Fantômes du roi Léopold II. Un holocauste oublié* (Paris: Belfond, 1998), pp. 147ff.
112 F. Vergès, *Abolir l'esclavage: une utopie coloniale. Les Ambiguïtés d'une politique humanitaire* (Paris: Albin Michel, 2001), p. 123.
113 M. Perrot, 'Dans la France de la Belle Époque, les "Apaches", premières bandes de jeunes', in *Les Marginaux et les exclus dans l'histoire* (Paris: U.G.E., 1979), pp. 401–3.
114 J. and J. Comaroff, *Of Revelation and Revolution*, and *Ethnography and the Historical Imagination*.

115 Perrot, 'Dans la France de la Belle Époque', p. 407, note 37.
116 P. Laburthe-Tolra, *Initiations et sociétés secrètes au Cameroun. Essai sur la religion beti* (Paris: Karthala, 1985); W. Soyinka, *Aké. Les Années d'enfance* (Paris: Belfond, 1984), p. 312.
117 Jewsiewicki, *Mami Wata*, p. 93.
118 Ibid., p. 96, author's emphasis. See also Hunt, *A Colonial Lexicon*, pp. 94–5, 136, 150.
119 Ibid., p. 98. On the continuity of the use of the whip in the east of the Congo, from the period of Arab-Zanzibari slavery to the nineteenth century, to the Congo Free State and the Belgian Congo, see Hunt, *A Colonial Lexicon*, p. 95.
120 A. Maindo Monga Ngonga, *Voter en temps de guerre. Kisangani (RD Congo), 1997. Quête de légitimité et (con)quête de l'espace politique* (Paris: L'Harmattan, 2001), pp. 73–4.
121 J.-P. Rémy, 'Actes de cannibalisme au Congo', *Le Monde*, 27 February 2003, p. 13.
122 A. de Mun, 'Le "commandant Jérôme" fait régner une drôle de paix à Aru', *La Croix-L'Événement*, 23 December 2003, p. 7.
123 B. Jewsiewicki et al., *A Congo Chronicle. Patrice Lumumba in Urban Art* (New York: Museum for African Art, 1999).
124 Quoted by Jewsiewicki, *Mami Wata*, p. 97.
125 In Freud's sense of the term: see J.-F. Bayart, *The Illusion of Cultural Identity*, trans. Steven Rendall, Janet Roitman, Cynthia Schoch and Jonathan Derrick (Chicago: University of Chicago Press, 2005), pp. 190–2.
126 *La Tribune africaine* [Lomé], 63, week of 23–8 February 1999. See also C. Piot, *Remotely Global*, pp. 40ff on the Kabre diaspora and the ceaseless circulation of vehicles between the mountains of the North and the coastal towns.
127 C.-M. Toulabor, 'La violence à l'école. Le cas d'un village au Togo', *Politique africaine*, 7, September 1982, pp. 43–9.
128 M. Sow, *Su Seruf Sedder. L'Échec* (Dakar: Enda, 1984), pp. 47–8, in which we see Maba, the ringleader of a street children's gang, beating one of his 'protégés' with a belt.
129 J. Crisp, 'A state of insecurity: the political economy of violence in Kenya's refugee camps', *African Affairs*, 99 (397), October 2000, pp. 603–4.
130 *Le Messager* (Douala), 146, 24 October 1988. The dialogue alludes to a police 'blunder' that occurred during one of those systematic 'raids' to which the inhabitants of the different districts in town are subjected, during which they are forced to sit in the mud.
131 R. Franklin, 'Singapour menace du bâton un Américain', *Libération*, 21 April 1994, p. 19; *The Economist*, 12 March, 1994, pp. 69–70.
132 Ong, *Flexible Citizenship*, p. 79.
133 *The Economist*, 9 April 1994, p. 68.
134 D. Harvey, *Spaces of Hope* (Berkeley: University of California Press, 2000), p. 44; Ong, *Flexible Citizenship*, p. 223; P. P. Pan, 'A new syndrome faces China's laborers: "overwork death" ', *International Herald Tribune*, 14 May 2002, p. 8.
135 *The Economist*, 31 August 2002, p. 44.

136 J.-F. Perrin, 'Ma vie au service d'Oudaï, un cauchemar', *Libération*, 25 November 2003, p. 11; C. Ayad, 'Les écrans de l'horreur font fureur. Les films de torture fascinent les Irakiens. Ainsi que les prêches islamistes et les films pornos', in ibid., 2 November 2003, p. 6: 'In another film, the recruits have to endure, one after the other, the torture of the *falaqa*'.

137 J. Ferguson, *Expectations of Modernity. Myths and Meanings of Urban Life on the Zambian Copperbelt* (Berkeley: University of California Press, 1999), ch. 3.

138 Quoted in ibid., p. 181.

139 F. De Boeck, 'La frontière diamantifère angolaise et son héros mutant', in J.-F. Bayart and J.-P. Warnier (eds), *Matière à politique. Le pouvoir, les corps et les choses* (Paris: Karthala, 2004), pp. 120ff.

140 'Javanese in step with Americana', *International Herald Tribune*, 30 July 2003, p. 9.

141 See for example, in addition to the Africanist studies already mentioned: S. Gruzinski, *La Guerre des images de Christophe Colomb à* Blade Runner, *1492–2019* (Paris: Fayard, 1990); C. Duverger, *La Conversion des Indiens de Nouvelle-Espagne* (Paris: Le Seuil, 1987); A. L. Tsing, *In the Realm of the Diamond Queen: Marginality in an Out-of-the-Way Place* (Princeton: Princeton University Press, 1993); P. Spyer, *The Memory of Trade. Modernity's Entanglements on an Eastern Indonesian Island* (Durham: Duke University Press, 2000).

142 Bertrand, *État colonial*, p. 253, and 'Chroniques d'une guerre morale'.

143 P. Veyne, *La Société romaine* (Paris: Le Seuil, 1991), pp. 307–8.

144 C. H. Kane, *L'Aventure ambiguë*, new edn (Paris: U.G.E., 1979), p. 164.

145 Berman and Lonsdale, *Unhappy Valley*, p. 246. See also all of chs 11 and 12.

146 Ferguson, *Expectations of Modernity*, ch. 5.

147 Collingham, *Imperial Bodies*.

148 Bertrand, *État colonial*, ch. 8, and 'La rencontre coloniale, une affaire de moeurs? L'aristocratie de Java face au pouvoir hollandais à la fin du XIXe siècle', *Genèses*, 43, June 2001, pp. 32–52.

149 E. Tarlo, *Clothing Matters. Dress and Identity in India* (London: Hurst, 1996); Bertrand, *État colonial*; Bayart, *The Illusion of Cultural Identity*, pp. 220ff.

150 J. and J. Comaroff, *Of Revelation and Revolution*.

151 Berman and Lonsdale, *Unhappy Valley*; J. Spencer, *KAU. The Kenya African Union* (London: KPI, 1985).

152 C. Meier, *La Naissance du politique* (Paris: Gallimard, 1995), p. 179. The author here criticizes the instrumental concept of political rights found in M. Finley.

153 M. Davis, *Late Victorian Holocausts. El Niño Famines and the making of the Third World* (London: Verso, 2001).

154 P. Uvin, *Aiding Violence. The Development Enterprise in Rwanda* (West Hartford, Kumanian Press, 1998), pp. 128ff.

155 Bayart, *The Illusion of Cultural Identity*, ch. 4.

156 Weber, *Sociology of Religion*; E. Troeltsch, *Protestantism and Progress: The Significance of Protestantism for the Rise of the Modern World*, trans. W. Montgomery (Philadelphia: Fortress Press, 1986); M. Foucault, *Dits et écrits*, vol. 2, p. 148; vol. 4, pp. 228–32.

Notes to pp. 163–168   331

Chapter 5 Globalization and Political Subjectivation: The Neo-Liberal Period (1980–2004)

1 In the sense in which Nicos Poulantzas defined 'relative autonomy' – in this case, that of the capitalist state from the bourgeoisie – as a specific functioning of the latter vis-à-vis class struggle, *Political Power and Social Classes*, ed. and trans. Timothy O'Hagan (London: Verso, 1978).

2 See for example C. Gordon, 'Governmental rationality: an introduction', in G. Burchell, C. Gordon and P. Miller (eds), *The Foucault Effect. Studies in Governmentality* (Chicago: University of Chicago Press, 1991), pp. 41ff; N. Rose, *Powers of Freedom. Reframing Political Thought* (Cambridge: Cambridge University Press, 1999), pp. 137ff.

3 On waterside cities as 'global cities', see E. Hobsbawm, *The Age of Capital, 1848–1875* (Paris: Fayard, 1978), pp. 241ff.

4 M. Weber, *Sociologie des Religions*, trans. Jean-Pierre Grossein (Paris: Gallimard, 1996), p. 378, author's italics.

5 Ibid., p. 377.

6 M. Weber, *The Protestant Ethic and the Spirit of Capitalism*, trans. Talcott Parsons, intro. by Anthony Giddens, 2nd edn (London: Allen and Unwin, 1976), p. 57.

7 K. Marx, *La Première Critique de l'économie politique. Les manuscrits de 1844* (Paris: UGE, 1972), p. 172.

8 D. Harvey, *The Condition of Postmodernity. An Enquiry into the Origins of Cultural Change* (Cambridge, MA: Blackwell, 1990), pp. 125 and 136ff.

9 L. Boltanski and E. Chiapello, *Le Nouvel Esprit du capitalisme* (Paris: Gallimard, 1999), pp. 93ff.

10 Source: P. Prakash, 'Inde, la voix de l'Amérique', *Libération*, 20 January 2003, pp. i–iii. See also 'Offshoring', *The Economist*, 13 December 2003, pp. 65–7; J. Auray, 'L'Inde, paradis de la délocalisation high-tech', and 'Une spécialisation sur fond d'inégalité', *Alternatives économiques*, 220, December 2003, pp. 13–15; P. Prakash, 'Le succès de l'Inde lui monte aux cerveaux', *Libération*, 6 January 2004, p. 18; E. Leser, G. Macke and M. Roche, 'L'Inde met ses cerveaux au service de l'industrie occidentale', *Le Monde*, 9 December 2003, p. 17.

11 P. Truell and L. Gurwin, *False Profits. The Inside Story of BCCI, the World's Most Corrupt Financial Empire* (Boston: Houghton Mifflin Co., 1992), pp. 21ff, and 419ff.

12 M. Abélès, *Les Nouveaux Riches. Un ethnologue dans la Silicon Valley* (Paris: Odile Jacob, 2002), p. 169.

13 Ibid., pp. 191, 193 and 207.

14 F. Adelkhah, 'Les Iraniens de Californie: si la République islamique n'existait pas . . .', *Les Études du CERI*, 75, May 2001 p. 36. *Javânmard* is the 'man of integrity' who practises the gift of self, especially in the form of evergetic acts (see F. Adelkhah, *Being Modern in Iran*, trans. Jonathan Derrick (New York: Columbia University Press, 2000), ch. 2).

15 Quoted in Abélès, *Les Nouveaux Riches*, p. 153.

16 Ibid., pp. 151–2.

17 Quoted by L. Mauriac, 'Ebay version France, gare aux enchères', *Libéra-tion*, 5 October 2000, p. 28–9.

18 F. Adelkhah, 'Les Iraniens de Californie', pp. 34–5.

19 P. Veyne, preface to G. Degeorge, *Palmyre, métropole caravanière* (Paris: Imprimerie nationale, 2001), p. 36.

20 G. Soros, *The Alchemy of Finance. Reading the Mind of the Market* (London: Weidenfeld and Nicolson, 1987).

21 A. Ong, *Flexible Citizenship. The Cultural Logics of Transnationality* (Durham: Duke University Press, 1999).

22 Ibid., p. 107.

23 M. Tozy, *Monarchie et islam politique au Maroc* (Paris: Presses de Sciences–Po, 1999), pp. 196ff.

24 Adelkhah, *Being Modern in Iran*; M. Mines, *Public Faces, Private Voices. Community and Individuality in South India* (Berkeley: University of California Press, 1994).

25 F. Adelkhah, 'Le retour de Sindbad: l'Iran dans le Golfe', *Les Études du CERI*, 53, May 1999, pp. 40ff.

26 A. Colonomos, *Églises en réseaux. Trajectoires politiques entre Europe et Amérique* (Paris: Presses de Sciences-Po, 2000), pp. 125 and 140.

27 R. Marshall-Fratani, 'Prospérité miraculeuse: les pasteurs pentecôtistes et l'argent de Dieu au Nigeria', *Politique africaine*, 82, June 2001, p. 24–44; A. Mary, 'Prophètes pasteurs. La politique de la délivrance en Côte d'Ivoire', *Politique africaine*, 87, October 2002, pp. 79ff; B. Meyer, 'Commodities and the power of prayer: pentecostalist attitudes towards consumption in contemporary Ghana', in B. Meyer and P. Geschiere (eds), *Globalization and Identity. Dialectics of Flow and Closure* (Oxford: Blackwell, 1999), pp. 151–76.

28 Mary, 'Prophètes pasteurs', p. 81.

29 P. Gifford, *Christianity and Politics in Doe's Liberia* (Cambridge: Cambridge University Press, 1993), pp. 293–4.

30 *Libération*, 12 August 2003.

31 Ong, *Flexible Citizenship*.

32 Ibid.; Adelkhah, 'Les Iraniens de Californie'; P. Levitt, *The Transnational Villagers* (Berkeley: University of California Press, 2001); R. S. Parrenas, *Servants of Globalisation. Women, Migration and Domestic Work* (Stanford: Stanford University Press, 2001); J. MacGaffey and R. Bazenguissa–Ganga, *Congo-Paris. Transnational Traders on the Margins of the Law* (Oxford: James Currey, 2000).

33 I am here drawing on the distinctions introduced by Levitt in *The Trans-national Villagers*, pp. 11 and 63ff.

34 C. Bromberger, *Le Match de football. Ethnologie d'une passion partisane à Marseille, Naples et Turin* (Paris: Éd. de la Maison des sciences de l'homme, 1995); B. Buford, *Among the Thugs* (New York: Vintage Departures, 1993).

35 D. Altman, *Global Sex* (Chicago: University of Chicago Press, 2001), pp. 86ff.

36 M. Foucault, *Power*, vol. 3 in *Essential Works of Foucault 1954–1984*, ed. James Faubion, trans. Robert Hurley et al. (London: Penguin, 1994), p. 327.

37 M. Foucault, *The Use of Pleasure*, vol. 2 in *The History of Sexuality*, trans. Robert Hurley (London: Viking, 1986); author's italics.

38 C. Berry, F. Martin and A. Yue (eds), *Mobile Cultures. New Media in Queer Asia* (Durham: Duke University Press, 2003); Altman, *Global Sex*.

39 Altman, *Global Sex*, p. 58.

40 Ong, *Flexible Citizenship*, pp. 166–8.

41 Altman, *Global Sex*, p. 88; T. Boellstorff, 'I knew it was me: mass media, "globalisation" and lesbian and gay Indonesians', in Berry, Martin and Yue (eds), *Mobile Cultures*, pp. 21ff.

42 Ibid., p. 22.

43 Ibid., pp. 30–1. See too D. Oetomo, 'Coming out as a homosexual', *Review of Indonesian and Malaysian Affairs*, 37 (1), 2003, pp. 159–67.

44 M. McLelland, 'Japanese Queerscapes: global/local intersections on the Internet', in Berry, Martin and Yue (eds), *Mobile Cultures*, pp. 52ff.

45 See for example Altman, *Global Sex*, pp. 145ff.

46 Ibid., p. 107.

47 See for example C. Durton and M. Palmberg, *Human Rights and Homosexuality in Southern Africa* (Uppsala: Nordiska Afrikainstituet, 1996).

48 Ong, *Flexible Citizenship*, p. 21.

49 J. MacGaffey, *Entrepreneurs and Parasites. The Struggle for Indigenous Capitalism in Zaire* (Cambridge: Cambridge University Press, 1987), ch. 7.

50 'Alerte sur une croissance globale des trafics d'êtres humains', *Le Monde*, 17–18 August 2003, p. 2.

51 P. C. Salzman, *Black Tents of Baluchistan* (Washington: Smithsonian Institution Press, 2000).

52 J. Roitman, 'La garnison-entrepôt: une manière de gouverner dans le bassin du lac Tchad', *Critique internationale*, 19, April 2003, p. 101.

53 Ibid., p. 110. Cf also J. Roitman, *Fiscal Disobedience. An Anthropology of Economic Regulation in Central Africa* (Princeton: Princeton University Press, 2005).

54 Quoted in A. Tarrius, *Fin de siècle incertaine à Perpignan* (Canet: Llibres del trabucaire, 1997), pp. 131–2, my italics.

55 M. Castells, *The Internet Galaxy: Reflections on Internet, Business, and Society* (Oxford: Oxford University Press, 2001).

56 Ibid.; P. Himanen, *The Hacker Ethic and the Spirit of the Information Age* (New York: Random House, 2001); *Libération*, 13 August 2001, pp. 2–4; A. Nivat, 'Saint–Petersbourg, cité pirate', *Libération*, 27 February 2001, p. 29; Y. Eudes, 'Piratage informatique, spécialité du Palais de la créativité à Moscou', *Le Monde*, 1 March 2002, p. 34.

57 Castells, *The Internet Galaxy*.

58 G. Deleuze, *Difference and Repetition*, trans. Paul Patton (London: The Athlone Press, 1994). On the 'virtual communities' of web–surfers, see Castells, *The Internet Galaxy*.

59 N. R. Keddie, *An Islamic Reponse to Imperialism. Political and Religious Writings of Sayyid Jamal ad-Din 'al-Afghani'*, new edn (Berkeley: University of California Press, 1983).

60 S. Mardin, *The Genesis of Young Ottoman Thought. A Study in the Modernization of Turkish Political Ideas* (Princeton: Princeton University Press, 1962).

61 Khayr ed-Din, *Essai sur les réformes nécessaires aux États musulmans*, presented and annotated by Magali Morsy (Aix-en-Provence: Édisud, 1987).

62 Ibid., p. 142.

63 Ibid., pp. 83–4.
64 Ibid., p. 89.
65 Ibid., p. 139.
66 Ibid., pp. 127–8.
67 Quoted by Magali Morsy in ibid., p. 55.
68 On Kemalism as a form of 'fetishism', see Y. Navaro-Yashin, *Faces of the State. Secularism and Public Life in Turkey* (Princeton: Princeton University Press, 2002), ch. 6.
69 G. Kepel, *Le Prophète et Pharaon. Les mouvements islamistes dans l'Égypte contemporaine* (Paris: La Découverte, 1984), pp. 119–120. The *dönme* are the followers of the Jewish prophet Shabbetai Zevi (1626–76): they converted to Islam and are suspected of having maintained their original faith – in short, they are the Ottoman equivalent of the marranos.
70 J.-B. Naudet, 'Bozidar Djelic, l'écorcheur préféré des Serbes', *Le Nouvel Observateur*, 7 August 2003, pp. 4–5.
71 See for example the autohagiography by T. Abeng, *Indonesia, Inc. Privatising State-Owned Enterprises* (Singapore: Times Academic Press, 2001).
72 J. R. Wedel, 'Tainted transactions. Harvard, the Chubais clan and Russia's ruin', *The National Interest*, Spring 2000, pp. 23–4.
73 R. Bertrand, 'Les *pemuda* en politique. Les répertoires d'action des marches protestataires des étudiants en Indonésie en 1998', *Le Mouvement social*, 202, January–March 2003, p. 43 and pp. 50–1.
74 R. Bertrand, *Indonésie: la démocratie invisible. Violence, magie et politique à Java* (Paris: Karthala, 2002).
75 O. Bauer, *La Question des nationalités et la social-démocratie* (Paris: Études et documentations internationales – Arcantère Éditions: Montreal, Guérin Littérature, 1987), I.
76 J.-F. Bayart, *The Illusion of Cultural Identity*, trans. Steven Rendall, Janet Roitman, Cynthia Schoch and Jonathan Derrick (Chicago: University of Chicago Press, 2005), ch. 4; E. Tarlo, *Clothing Matters. Dress and Identity in India* (London: Hurst, 1996); J. Willis, *Potent Brews. A Social History of Alcohol in East Africa, 1850–1999* (Oxford: James Currey, 2002); E. Akyeampong, *Drink, Power, and Cultural Change. A Social History of Alcohol in Ghana, c.1800 to Recent Times* (Portsmouth: Heinemann, 1996); J. Crush and C. Ambler (eds), *Liquor and Labor in Southern Africa* (Athens: Ohio University Press, 1992).
77 See for example G. L. Mosse, *Nationalism and Sexuality. Middle-Class Morality and Sexual Norms in Modern Europe* (Madison: University of Wisconsin Press, 1985), and *L'Image de l'homme. L'invention de la virilité moderne* (Paris: Abbeville, 1997); S. Walby, 'Woman and nation', *International Journal of Comparative Sociology*, XXXIII (1–2), 1992, pp. 81–100; L. Braudy, *From Chivalry to Terrorism. War and the Changing Nature of Masculinity* (New York: Alfred A. Knopf, 2003); R. Aldrich, *Colonialism and Homosexuality* (London: Routledge, 2003).
78 *Libération*, 26 April 1993, p. 10.
79 Quoted in M. Avanza, *L'Art identitaire. L'Unione Padane Artisti (UPART), une association d'artistes indépendantistes dans l'Italie du Nord* (Paris: EHESS-ENS, 1999), p. 100.

80 C. Jaffrelot, *Les Nationalistes hindous. Idéologie, implantation et mobilisation des années 1990* (Paris: Presses de Sciences-Po, 1993).

81 Adelkhah, 'Le retour de Sindbad'.

82 B. Pouligny, 'Acteurs et enjeux d'un processus équivoque. La naissance d'une "internationale civile" ', *Critique internationale*, 13, October 2001, pp. 163–76.

83 M. Van Creveld, *The Rise and Decline of the State* (Cambridge: Cambridge University Press, 1999), pp. 408ff.

84 Thanks to Thorndike Gordadze for initiating me into the theme of 'national heros', a field in which he is an expert. See for example his 'La Géorgie et ses "hôtes ingrats" ', *Critique internationale*, 10, January 2001, pp. 161–76.

85 P. Centlivres, D. Fabre and F. Zonabend (eds), introduction to *La Fabrique des héros* (Paris: Éditions de la Maison des sciences de l'homme, 1998), p. 4.

86 Ibid.

87 I. Colovic, 'Le capitaine Dragan, nouveau guerrier serbe', in ibid., pp. 115–24.

88 C. Colombani, 'Saint Yersin de Nha Trang', *Le Monde*, 28 December 1991, pp. 9 and 11.

89 M. de Certeau, *The Practice of Everyday Life*, trans. Steven Rendall (Berkeley: University of California Press, 1984).

90 A. Muxel, 'Les héros des jeunes Français: vers un humanisme politique réconciliateur', in Centlivres, Fabre and Zonabend (eds), *La Fabrique des héros*, p. 87.

91 F. Adelkhah, 'Qui a peur du mollah Omar? L'économie morale du "talebanisme" dans le Golfe', *Critique internationale*, 12, July 2001, pp. 22–9.

92 Adelkhah, 'Les Iraniens de Californie' and 'Le retour de Sindbad'; J.-D. Gandoulou, *Entre Paris et Bacongo* (Paris: Centre Georges-Pompidou et Centre de création industrielle, 1984), and *Dandies à Bacongo. Le Culte de l'élégance dans la société congolaise contemporaine* (Paris: L'Harmattan, 1989).

93 S. Laacher and L. Mokrani, 'Le passeur et son passager, deux figures inséparables', *Plein Droit*, 55, December 2002.

94 In the helpful formulation of F. A. Salamone, 'The social construction of colonial reality: Yauri emirate', *Cahiers d'études africaines*, 98, XXV-2, 1985, pp. 139–59. On the ambivalence of the relations between the 'people smuggler' and the illegal immigrant, see the evidence provided in F. Mellah, *Clandestin en Méditerranée* (Tunis: Cérès Éditions, 2000).

95 F. Adelkhah, 'Partir sans quitter', *Critique internationale*, 19 (April 2003), p. 154.

96 *Libération*, 25–6 April 1992, p. 18.

97 O. True, 'Le pays virtuel qui attire 3,000 réfugiés', *Libération*, 14 March 2002, p. 29.

98 Ibid.

99 J. Harding has clearly brought out this ambivalence in the figure of the Immigrant in *The Uninvited. Refugees at the Rich Man's Gate* (London: Profile Books, 2000).

100 Thanks to Smaïn Laacher for drawing my attention to the 'moral' dimension of the people-smuggler.

101 M.-P. Julien, 'Sujets chinois de la République française', in J.-F. Bayart and J.-P. Warnier (eds), *Matière à politique. Le pouvoir, les corps et les choses* (Paris: Karthala, 2004), ch. 7.

102 Adelkhah, 'Partir sans quitter', p. 154.

103 E. de Latour, 'Héros du retour', *Critique internationale*, 19 (April 2003), pp. 188 and 172.

104 M. Detienne and J.-P. Vernant, *Cunning intelligence in Greek culture and society*, trans. Janet Lloyd (Chicago and London: University of Chicago Press, 1991).

105 Certeau, *The Practice of Everyday Life*; D. Paulme, *La Mère dévorante. Essai sur la morphologie des contes africains* (Paris: Gallimard, 1976), passim.

106 MacGaffey and Bazenguissa-Ganga, *Congo-Paris*, pp. 52–9.

107 A. Apter, 'IBB = 419: Nigerian democracy and the politics of illusion', in J. L. and J. Comaroff (eds), *Civil Society and the Political Imagination in Africa. Critical Perspectives* (Chicago: University of Chicago Press, 1999), ch. 10; D. Malaquais, 'Arts de feyre au Cameroun', *Politique africaine*, 82, June 2001, pp. 101–18; Z. Ould Ahmed Salem, ' "Tcheb–tchib" et compagnie. Lexique de la survie et figures de la réussite en Mauritanie', ibid., pp. 78–100; C. Coulon, 'La tradition démocratique au Sénégal. Histoire d'un mythe', in C. Jaffrelot (ed.), *Démocraties d'ailleurs* (Paris: Karthala, 2000), pp. 86ff.

108 Apter, 'IBB = 419', J. L. and J. Comaroff (eds), *Civil Society*, ch. 10.

109 *Libération*, 14 and 15 November 1998; Malaquais, 'Arts de feyre'.

110 Based on fieldwork by F. Adelkhah in Tokyo and Dubai (source: interviews).

111 See for example P. Tourancheau, 'Roulé dans la farine des billets noircis, Michel a cru à la multiplication de sa fortune, l'arnaque lui a fait perdre 15,000 euros', *Libération*, 11 May 2003, p. 15.

112 *Le Monde*, 20 June 2003; R. Werly, 'Faux et usage de faux en Corée du Sud', *Libération*, 27 May 2002, p. 25; V. Brunschwig, 'Le piratage cinématographique est devenu une affaire de grand banditisme', *Le Monde*, 25 August 1999, p. 26; *Libération*, 9 March 2004, pp. 6–8.

113 Source: interviews with the author.

114 On the Khalifa affair, see F. Aubenas and J. Garçon, 'Khalifa, les dessous d'une débâcle', *Libération*, 3 April 2003, pp. 26–7 and 7–8 June 2003, p. 21; *Le Monde*, 21 March 2003, p. 18; *Le Figaro*, 26–7 April 2003, p. 9. On the Youkos affair, see N. Nougayrède, 'La mutation d'un oligarque', *Le Monde*, 21 November 2003; C. Freeland, 'Falling tsar', *FT Weekend*, 1–2 November 2003, pp. W1–W2.

115 Sources: interviews with the author; *Le Figaro*, 21 February 2003.

116 J.-F. Bayart, S. Ellis and B. Hibou, *The Criminalization of the State in Africa* (Oxford and Bloomington: James Currey and Indiana University Press, 1999); Apter, 'IBB = 419'.

117 A. Tarrius, *La Globalisation par le bas. Les Nouveaux nomades de l'économie souterraine* (Paris: Balland, 2002), pp. 46ff.

118 Foucault, *The Use of Pleasure*.

119 F. De Boeck, 'La frontière diamantifère angolaise et son héros mutant', in J.-F. Bayart and J.-P. Warnier (eds), *Matière à politique. Le pouvoir, les corps et les choses* (Paris: Karthala, 2004).

120 Ibid., p. 119.

121 F. De Boeck, 'Domesticating diamonds and dollars: identity, expenditure and sharing in Southwestern Zaire (1984–1997)', in Meyer and Geschiere (eds), *Globalisation and Identity*, pp. 177–209.

122 T. Grätz, 'Gold trading networks and the creation of trust: a case study from Northern Benin', *Africa* 74 (2), 2004, pp. 146–72.

123 J.-L. Amselle, *Branchements. Anthropologie de l'universalité des cultures* (Paris: Flammarion, 2001).

124 P. Richards, *Fighting for the Rain Forest. War, Youth and Resources in Sierra Leone* (Oxford and Portsmouth: James Currey, Heinemann, 1996), pp. 55ff, 87ff, 105ff.

125 De Boeck, 'La frontière diamantifère', pp. 108ff and 123ff.

126 S. E. Hutchinson, *Nuer Dilemmas. Coping with Money, War and the State* (Berkeley: University of California Press, 1996), pp. 149ff.

127 L. Tormaquenaud, 'Une guérilla de voisinage', *Libération*, 29 May 2000, p. 10. See also F. van Acker, K. Vlassenroot, 'les "Maï-Maï" et les fonctions de la violence milicienne dans l'est du Congo', *Politique africaine*, 84, December 2001, pp. 103–16.

128 Richards, *Fighting for the Rain Forest*, passim; R. Marchal, 'Les *mooryan* de Mogadiscio. Formes de la violence dans un espace urbain en guerre', *Cahiers d'études africaines*, 130, XXXIII-2, 1993, pp. 295–320; S. Ellis, *The Mask of Anarchy*; 'Disciplines et déchirures', *Cahiers d'études africaines*, XXXVIII (2–4), 150–2, 1998; 'RDC, la guerre vue d'en bas', *Politique africaine*, 84, December 2001; 'Lumpen culture and political violence: the Sierra Leone civil war', *Afrique et développement*, XXII (3–4), 1997.

129 Apart from the titles mentioned in the previous note, see C. Geffray, *La Cause des armes au Mozambique. Anthropologie d'une guerre civile* (Paris: Karthala, 1990).

130 H. Maupeu, 'Mungiki et les élections. Les mutations politiques d'un prophétisme kikuyu (Kenya)', *Politique africaine*, 87, October 2002, pp. 132–3.

131 P. Bonnafé, 'Une classe d'âge politique. La JMNR de la République du Congo-Brazzaville', *Cahiers d'études africaines*, VIII (3), 31, 1968, pp. 327–68; R. Bazenguissa-Ganga, 'Milices politiques et bandes armées à Brazzaville. Enquête sur la violence politique et sociale des jeunes déclassés', *Les Études du CERI*, 13, April 1996.

132 S. Audoin-Rouzeau and A. Becker, *14–18, retrouver la guerre* (Paris: Gallimard, 2000); M. Eksteins, *Rites of Spring. The Great War and the Birth of the Modern Age* (Boston: Houghton Mifflin, 1989).

133 E. Butel, *Le Martyre dans les mémoires de guerre iraniens. Guerre Iran–Irak (1980–1988)* (Paris: INALCO, 2000), p. 608.

134 *International Herald Tribune*, 15 January 2003, p. 2.

135 *Libération*, 28–9 July 2001, pp. 5–6.

136 'The salaryman as Japanese hero', *International Herald Tribune*, 22 August 2003.

137 J. Elyachar, 'Finance internationale, micro-crédit et religion de la société civile en Égypte', *Critique internationale*, 13, October 2001, pp. 139–52.

138 Bayart, *The Illusion of Cultural Identity*, pp. 69ff.

139 J.-F. Bayart, B. Hibou and S. Khiari, 'Les régimes autoritaires libérés des conditionnalités', *Critique internationale*, 14, January 2002, pp. 7–11.

140 T. Brook and B. Tadashi Wakabayashi (eds), *Opium Regimes. China, Britain, and Japan, 1839–1952* (Berkeley: University of California Press, 2000).

141 N. Parsons, *King Khama, Emperor Joe and the Great White Queen. Victorian Britain through African Eyes* (Chicago: University of Chicago Press, 1998).

142 Foucault, *Power*, p. 225.

143 M. Foucault, *Abnormal: lectures at the Collège de France, 1974–75*, ed. Valerio Marchetti and Antonella Salomoni; general eds, François Ewald and Alessandro Fontana; trans. Graham Burchell (London: Verso, 2003).

144 Rose, *Powers of Freedom*, ch. 4.

145 C. Piot, *Remotely Global. Village Modernity in West Africa* (Chicago: University of Chicago Press, 1999), p. 91.

146 B.-M. Pétric, *Pouvoir, don et réseaux en Ouzbékistan postsoviétique* (Paris: Presses universitaires de France, 2002).

147 Grätz, 'Gold trading networks'.

148 Ong, *Flexible Citizenship*, pp. 201ff.

149 Navaro-Yashin, *Faces of the State*, ch. 6.

150 Ibid., p. 121.

151 M. E. Meeker, *A Nation of Empire. The Ottoman Legacy of Turkish Modernity* (Berkeley: University of California Press, 2002).

152 Ibid.

153 P.-X. Jacob, *L'Enseignement religieux dans la Turquie moderne* (Berlin: Klaus Schwarz Verlag, 1982).

154 *Libération*, 6 May 1993.

155 A. Kudsi Erguner, 'Alla turca – alla franca. Les enjeux de la musique turque', *Cahiers de musiques traditionnelles*, 3, 1990, pp. 45–56; P. J. Dorn, 'A la turka / à la franka: cultural ideology and musical change', *Cahiers d'études sur la Méditerranée orientale et le monde turco-iranien*, 11, 1991, pp. 51–9.

156 D. Kandiyoti and A. Saktanber (eds), *Fragments of Culture. The Everyday of Modern Turkey* (London: I. B. Tauris, 2002); C. Keyder (ed.), *Istanbul between the Global and the Local* (Lanham: Rowman and Littlefield Publishers, 1999).

157 Navaro-Yashin, *Faces of the State*, ch. 3; Kandiyoti and Saktanber (eds), *Fragments of Culture*.

158 B. Balci, *Missionnaires de l'islam en Asie centrale. Les Écoles turques de Fethullah Gülen* (Paris: Maisonneuve et Larose: Istanbul, Institut français d'études anatoliennes, 2003).

159 M. Augé, *Théorie des pouvoirs et idéologie. Étude de cas en Côte d'Ivoire* (Paris: Hermann, 1975); J.-P. Dozon, *La Cause des prophètes. Politique et religion en Afrique contemporaine* (Paris: Le Seuil, 1995); J.-F. Bayart, *The State in Africa. The Politics of the Belly*, trans. Mary Harper, Christopher and Elizabeth Harrison (London: Longman, 1993), ch. 7.

160 Colonomos, *Églises en réseaux*.

161 Mary, 'Prophètes pasteurs', p. 77.

162 R. Banégas and B. Losch, 'La Côte d'Ivoire au bord de l'implosion', *Politique africaine*, 87, October 2002, pp. 139–61.

163 Quoted by Mary, 'Prophètes pasteurs', p. 85.

164 Ibid., p. 87.

165 This was the title ('sujets de Dieu') given by Didier Péclard and Ruth Marshall–Fratani to the number of the review *Politique africaine*, 87, October 2002.

166 E. de Rosny, *Étude panoramique des nouveaux mouvements religieux et philosophiques à Douala* (Douala: Centre spirituel de rencontre, 2000), p. 20.

167 P.-J. Laurent, 'Effervescence religieuse et gouvernance. L'exemple des Assemblées de Dieu du Burkina Faso', *Politique africaine*, 87, October 2002, p. 114.

168 G. Kepel, *La Revanche de Dieu. Chrétiens, juifs et musulmans à la reconquête du monde* (Paris: Le Seuil, 1991).

169 Y. Nakash, *The Shi'is of Iraq* (Princeton: Princeton University Press, 1994); F. Raison-Jourde, *Bible et pouvoir à Madagascar au XIXe siècle. Invention d'une identité chrétienne et construction de l'État* (Paris: Karthala, 1991); J. D. Y. Peel, *Religious Encounter and the Making of the Yoruba* (Bloomington: Indiana University Press, 2000); A. Appadurai, *Conflict and Worship under Colonial Rule: a South Indian Case* (Cambridge: Cambridge University Press, 1981); Jaffrelot, *Les Nationalistes hindous*; Salzman, *Black Tents of Baluchistan*.

170 E. R. Wolf (ed.), *Religious Regimes and State-Formation. Perspectives from European Ethnology* (Albany: State University of New York Press, 1991); C. Maire, *De la cause de Dieu à la cause de la nation. Le jansénisme au XVIIIe siècle* (Paris: Gallimard, 1998).

171 F. de Polignac, *La Naissance de la cité grecque* (Paris: La Découverte, 1984), pp. 154–5. I have used this model myself, in J.-F. Bayart (ed.), *Religion et modernité politique en Afrique noire. Dieu pour tous et chacun pour soi* (Paris: Karthala, 1993), and Bayart, *The Illusion of Cultural Identity*, pp. 253ff.

172 Adelkhah, *Being Modern in Iran*.

173 M. Henry, *Marx, I: Une philosophie de la réalité* (Paris: Gallimard, 1976), p. 109.

174 Marx, *La Première Critique*, p. 244.

175 N. Elias, *The Society of Individuals*, ed. Michael Schröter, trans. Edmund Jephcott (Oxford: Basil Blackwell, 1991); A. Giddens, *Modernity and Self-Identity. Self and Society in the Late Modern Age* (Stanford: Stanford University Press, 1991), and *The Transformation of Intimacy. Sexuality, Love and Eroticism in Modern Societies* (Stanford: Stanford University Press, 1992).

176 Foucault, *Power*, p. 329.

177 Altman, *Global Sex*, p. 8. See also Oetomo, 'Coming out'.

178 Adelkhah, *Being Modern in Iran*, and P. Haenni and T. Holtrop, 'Mondaines spiritualités . . . "Amr Khâlid "shaykh" branché de la jeunesse dorée du Caire', *Politique africaine*, 87, October 2002, pp. 45–68.

179 O. Kharkhordin, *The Collective and the Individual in Russia. A Study of Practices* (Berkeley: University of California Press, 1999).

180 M. Foucault, *Dits et Écrits, 1954–1988*, ed. Daniel Defert and François Ewald (Paris: Gallimard, 1994), vol. 4, p. 653.

181 Marx, *La Première Critique*, p. 249.

182 Adelkhah, *Being Modern in Iran*; Mines, *Public Faces, Private Voices*.

183 P. Brown, *Power and Persuasion in Late Antiquity: Towards a Christian Empire* (Madison: University of Wisconsin Press, 1992), p. 126.

184 N. Hale, *Freud and the Americans: the beginnings of psychoanalysis in the United States, 1876–1917* (New York: Oxford University Press, 1971), p. 25.

185 Che noted his disappointment at the 'lifestyle' of Laurent Kabila in his diary; see P. I. Taibo, F. Escobar and F. Guerra, *L'Année où nous n'étions nulle part. Extraits du Journal de Ernesto Che Guevara en Afrique* (Paris: Métailié, 1995).

186 J. Thornton clearly brings out the element of individual performance in the man of religion in ancient Africa, who was often suspected of being a 'deceiver': *Africa and Africans in the Making of the Atlantic World, 1400–1800* (Cambridge: Cambridge University Press, 1992), pp. 246–8.

187 M. Foucault, *Discipline and Punish. The Birth of the Prison*, trans. Alan Sheridan (Harmondsworth: Penguin Books, 1979), p. 53.

188 M. Foucault, 'The subject and power', in *Power*, p. 334.

189 Ibid., *Ethics*, p. 200.

Chapter 6   The Global Techniques of the Body

1 J.-L. Nancy, *La Création du monde ou la Globalisation* (Paris: Galilée, 2002), p. 36.

2 J.-L. Nancy, 'Un sujet?', in A. Michels, J.-L. Nancy, M. Safouan, J.-P. Vernant and D. Weil, *Homme et sujet. La Subjectivité en question dans les sciences humaines* (Paris: L'Harmattan, 1992), p. 55.

3 K. Marx, *La Première Critique de l'économie politique. Les manuscrits de 1844* (Paris: UGE, 1972), p. 201.

4 A. Appudarai, *Modernity at Large. Cultural Dimensions of Globalization* (Minneapolis: University of Minnesota Press, 1996), p. 7. See also C. Breckenridge (ed.), *Consuming Modernity. Public Culture in a South East Asian World* (Minneapolis: University of Minnesota Press, 1995).

5 Marx, *La Première Critique*, p. 242–3.

6 M. Mauss, *Sociologie et anthropologie* (1950) (Paris: PUF, 1980), pp. 368–9 and 384.

7 M. de Certeau, *The Practice of Everyday Life*, trans. Steven Rendall (Berkeley: University of California Press, 1984).

8 D. Miller (ed.), *Material Culture. Why some Things Matter* (Chicago: University of Chicago Press, 1998).

9 Certeau, *The Practice of Everyday Life*.

10 D. Miller, *Modernity. An Ethnographic Approach. Dualism and Mass Consumption in Trinidad* (Oxford: Berg, 1994); D. Davis (ed.), *The Consumer Revolution in Urban China* (Berkeley: University of California Press, 2000); X. Liu, *In One's Own Shadow. An Ethnographic Account of the Condition of Post-Reform Rural China* (Berkeley: University of California Press, 2000); O. Kharkhordinh, *The Collective and Individual in Russia. A Study of Practices* (Berkeley: University of California Press, 1999), pp. 340ff.

11 D. Miller, *Material Culture and Mass Consumption* (Oxford: Blackwell, 1987).

12 L. de Courcy, 'Les objets de famille ont une âme', *La Croix-L'Événement*, 5 December 2001, pp. 13–15.

13 E. Mueggler, *The Age of Wild Ghosts. Memory, Violence and Place in Southwest China* (Berkeley: University of California Press, 2001), pp. 52ff; J. Sand, 'At home in the Meiji period. Inventing Japanese domesticity', in S. Vlastos

(ed.), *Mirror of Modernity. Invented Traditions of Modern Japan* (Berkeley: University of California Press, 1998), ch. 13; C. Piot, *Remotely Global*, ch. 5; D. Malaquais, *Architecture, pouvoir et dissidence au Cameroun* (Paris: Karthala, 2002).

14 S. W. Mintz, *Tasting Food, Tasting Freedom. Excursions into Eating, Culture and the Past* (Boston: Beacon Press, 1996), in particular ch. 5, 'Sugar and morality'.

15 Marx, *La Première Critique*, p. 210.

16 C. Fischer, *America Calling: A Social History of the Telephone to 1940* (Berkeley: University of California Press, 1992), and *To Dwell among Friends* (Berkeley: University of California Press, 1982); A. J. Clarke, *Tupperware. The Promise of Plastic in 1950s America* (Washington: Smithsonian Institution Press, 1999); N. Woolsey Biggart, *Charismatic Capitalism. Direct Selling Organizations in America* (Chicago: Chicago University Press, 1989).

17 C. Markovits, *The Global World of Indian Merchants, 1750–1947. Traders of Sind from Bukhara to Panama* (Cambridge: Cambridge University Press, 2000), pp. 116ff, 122–3, 141–2, 150–1, 197, 240–1, 280ff; B. Spooner, 'Weavers and dealers: the authenticity of an oriental carpet', in A. Appadurai (ed.), *The Social Life of Things. Commodities in Cultural Perspective* (Cambridge: Cambridge University Press, 1986), ch. 7; M.-P. Julien, 'Devenir fabricants de meubles laqués chinois pour acquérir des modes d'habiter français', in J.-F. Bayart and J.-P. Warnier (eds), *Matière à politique. Le pouvoir, les corps et les choses* (Paris: Karthala, 2004), ch. 7. On the theme of authenticating merchandise, see J.-P. Warnier (ed.), *Le Paradoxe de la marchandise authentique. Imaginaire et consommation de masse* (Paris: L'Harmattan, 1994), and J.-P. Warnier and C. Rosselin (eds), *Authentifier la marchandise. Anthropologie critique de la quête d'authenticité* (Paris: L'Harmattan, 1996), as well as P. Chaudat, *De la cuve au palais. Le système d'approvisionnement des vins d'Arbois (Jura)* (Paris: Université René-Descartes, 1997).

18 M. Angenot, *L'Oeuvre poétique du Savon du Congo* (Paris: Les Cendres, 1992), p. 45.

19 Marx, *La Première Critique*, p. 170.

20 See for example 'Style 5. Glamour spécial mode été 2001', supplement to *Libération*, 10 March 2001.

21 O. Badot and M. Dupuis,'Le réenchantement de la distribution', <www.le–sechos.fr/cgi–bin/btnimpr.pl>, 2003, p. 1.

22 Ibid., p. 2.

23 Remarks made by professional people and reported by B. Grosjean, 'Les centres commerciaux misent sur le rayon plaisir', *Libération*, 28 August 2002, pp. 2–4.

24 Ibid.; Badot and Dupuis, 'Le réenchantement'; G. Biassette, 'Le "mall" de Washington, condensé de rêve américain', *La Croix-L'Événement*, 3 September 2003, p. 28; L. Lutaud, 'Dubaï se rêve comme La Mecque globale des soldes', *Le Figaro-Entreprises*, 20 January 2003, pp. 18–19; 'In this world, shopping can be an art', *International Herald Tribune*, 12 December 2002, p. 18.

25 S. Tavernise, 'In Moscow "mall rats", signs of improving times', *International Herald Tribune*, 6 February 2003, p. 2; M.P. Subtil, 'Les Moscovites découvrent les hypermarchés', *Le Monde*, 15–16 December 2002, p. 12.

26 M. Mermoz, 'Un nouvel espace urbain', *Alternatives économiques*, 205, July–August 2002, pp. 52–5.

27 For Paris, see V. Lorelle, 'Services "bien-être" ', *Le Monde*, 13 December 2003, p. 24.

28 Interview with Jun Aoki, *Axis* (Tokyo), 102, March–April 2003, pp. 58–63; *The Japan Architect*, 48, Winter 2003, pp. 30–3; 'Miuccia Prada, retour à Tokyo', *Le Figaro*, 3 July 2003, p. 17.

29 Quoted in M. Alessandri, 'Roppongi Hills, la cité globale', *Le Nouvel Observateur*, 25 September 2003, p. 42.

30 Sources: interviews and personal observation, Tokyo, April 2003; N. Forestier, 'Les petites marques du luxe commencent à souffrir sur le marché japonais', *Le Figaro-Économie*, 8 October, 2003, p. ix.

31 Forestier, 'Les petites marques du luxe'.

32 K. Iwabuchi, *Recentering Globalisation. Popular Culture and Japanese Transnationalism* (Durham: Duke University Press, 2002), p. 53.

33 Sources: interviews with the author, Tokyo, April 2003.

34 P. Pons, 'Les églises-cafés de Tokyo, "c'est quand même mieux que McDo!" ', *Le Monde*, 28 November 2002, p. 37. See also, on the Global Dining restaurant chain, *The Economist*, 28 September 2002, p. 73.

35 P. Pons, ' "Cool Japan": le Japon, super-puissance de la pop', *Le Monde*, 19 December 2003, p. 20.

36 Quoted by M.-D. Arrighi, 'eBay, une souris . . . et des sommes', *Libération*, 17 November 2003, pp. 42–3.

37 A. Appadurai, 'Les choses à venir. Les régimes émergents de la matérialité', *Bulletin du CODESRIA* (Dakar), 3–4, 1999, p. 45.

38 G. Laval, 'Frimes bizness: à la Reynerie, à Toulouse, une minorité vit de la fauche', *Libération*, 26 January 1999, p. 14.

39 J. Roitman, 'La garnison-entrepôt: une manière de gouverner dans le bassin du lac Tchad', *Critique internationale*, 19, April 2003, pp. 93–115, and 'The Garrison-Entrepôt', *Cahiers d'études africaines*, 150–2, XXXVIII-2–4, 1998, pp. 297–329 (with reference to North Cameroon). There is an obvious analogy with the excessively high-security shopping malls of South Africa.

40 As witness Jean-Michel Silberstein, director of the CNCC, quoted by M. Mermoz, 'Un nouvel espace urbain', p. 53.

41 Angenot, *L'Oeuvre poétique du Savon du Congo*, p. 69.

42 S. Gruzinski, *La Pensée métisse* (Paris: Fayard, 1999), p. 25 (with respect to Amazonia); P. Spyer, *The Memory of Trade. Modernity's Entanglements on an Eastern Indonesian Island* (Durham: Duke University Press, 2000), pp. 14ff.

43 C. A. Bayly, ' "Archaic" and "modern" globalisation in the Eurasian and African area, *c.*1750–1850', in A. G. Hopkins (ed.), *Globalisation in World History* (London: Pimlico, 2002), pp. 53ff; S. W. Mintz, *Sweetness and Power. The Place of Sugar in Modern History* (New York: Viking Penguin, 1985).

44 See for example B. Orlove, *The Allure of the Foreign. Imported Goods in Postcolonial Latin America* (Ann Arbor: University of Michigan Press, 1997).

45 Joke overheard in Dubai, in February 2002, in the company of Fariba Adelkhah.

46 Marx, *La Première Critique*, p. 169.

47 Ibid.
48 Quoted by Spyer, *Memory of Trade*, p. 103.
49 Quoted by N. Monnier, 'Stratégie missionnaire et tactiques d'appropriation indigènes: la Mission romande au Mozambique, 1888–1896', *Le Fait missionnaire* (Lausanne), 2, December 1995, pp. 61–2.
50 R. Elphick and R. Davenport (eds), *Christianity in South Africa. A Political, Social and Cultural History* (Berkeley: University of California Press, 1997), pp. 36, 109, 340–1; J. D. Y. Peel, *Religious Encounter and the Making of the Yoruba* (Bloomington: Indiana University Press, 2000), p. 129.
51 J. L. and J. Comaroff, *Of Revelation and Revolution. II: The Dialectics of Modernity* (Chicago, University of Chicago Press, 1997), in particular pp. 218ff.
52 Quoted by D. Péclard, 'Ethos missionnaire et esprit du capitalisme. La mission philafricaine en Angola, 1897–1907', *Le Fait missionnaire* (Lausanne), 1, May 1995, pp. 76 and 80–1.
53 T. Ranger, *Dance and Society in Eastern Africa. 1890–1970. The Beni Ngoma* (London: Heinemann, 1975), pp. 127 and 131–2; T. Burke, *Lifebuoy Men, Lux Women. Commodification, Consumption, and Cleanliness in Modern Zimbabwe* (Durham: Duke University Press, 1996), p. 102.
54 J. L. and J. Comaroff (eds), *Of Revelation and Revolution*, I: *Christianity, Colonialism and Consciousness in South Africa* (Chicago: University of Chicago Press, 1991), pp. 185ff.
55 J. Peel, *Religious Encounter*, and *Ijeshas and Nigerians. The Incorporation of a Yoruba Kingdom, 1890s-1970s* (Cambridge: Cambridge University Press, 1983).
56 J. L. and J. Comaroff, *Of Revelation and Revolution*, II: *The Dialectics of Modernity*, pp. 29ff.
57 B. Meyer, 'Commodities and the power of prayer: pentecostalist attitudes towards consumption in contemporary Ghana', in B. Meyer and P. Geschiere (eds), *Globalisation and Identity. Dialectics of Flow and Closure* (Oxford: Blackwell, 1999), p. 156.
58 J.-F. Bayart, 'Les Églises chrétiennes et la politique du ventre: le partage du gâteau ecclésial', *Politique africaine*, 35, 1989, pp. 3–26.
59 G. ter Haar, *Halfway to Paradise. African Christians in Europe* (Cardiff: Cardiff Academic Press, 1998); A. Corten and R. Marshall-Fratani (eds), *Between Babel and Pentecost. Transnational Pentecostalism in Africa and Latin America* (London: Hurst, 2001).
60 Meyer, 'Commodities', pp. 151–76.
61 L. White, *Speaking with Vampires. Rumor and History in Colonial Africa* (Berkeley: University of California Press, 2000); B. Weiss, *The Making and Unmaking of the Haya Lived World. Consumption, Commoditization and Everyday Practice* (Durham: Duke University Press, 1996); R. L. Swarns, 'A vampire hysteria swoops down on the villages of Malawi', *International Herald Tribune*, 15 January 2003
62 See in particular the video film made by Fariba Adelkhah, *Bons baisers de Damas* (Paris: CERI, 2004), which deals with the pilgrimages made by Iranians to the holy places of Shi'ism in Damascus.
63 J. MacGaffey and R. Bazenguissa-Ganga, *Congo-Paris. Transnational Traders on the Margins of the Law* (Oxford: James Currey, 2000), ch. 3.

64 Quoted by P.-J. Laurent, *Une association de développement en pays mossi. Le Don comme ruse* (Paris: Karthala, 1998), p. 91.

65 R. Marchal, 'Les *mooryan* de Mogadiscio. Formes de la violence dans un espace urbain en guerre', *Cahiers d'études africaines*, 130, XXXIII-2, 1993, pp. 295–320; S. Ellis, *The Mask of Anarchy. The Destruction of Liberia and the Religious Dimension of an African Civil War* (London: Hurst, 1999), p. 122; P. Richards, *Fighting for the Rain Forest. War, Youth and Resources in Sierra Leone* (Oxford and Portsmouth: James Currey, Heinemann, 1996), pp. 28 and 54.

66 J.-P. Rémy, 'Actes de cannibalisme au Congo', *Le Monde*, 27 February 2003, p. 13; Marchal, 'Les *mooryan* de Mogadiscio'; R. Devisch, 'Frenzy, violence and ethical renewal in Kinshasa', *Public Culture*, 7 (3), Spring 1995, pp. 593–629; Ellis, *The Mask of Anarchy*; R. Bazenguissa-Ganga, 'Milices politiques et bandes armées à Brazzaville. Enquête sur la violence politique et sociale des jeunes déclassés', *Les Études du CERI*, 13, April 1996.

67 R. Doom and K. Vlassenroot, 'Kony's message: a new *koine*? The Lord's Resistance Army in Northern Uganda', *African Affairs*, 98 (390), January 1999, p. 5–36.

68 Burke, *Lifebuoy Men*, pp. 161–2 and 179.

69 M. Gillette, 'What's in a dress? Brides in the Hui quarter of Xi'an', in Davis (ed.), *The Consumer Revolution*, ch. 4; see also D. Davis and S. Harrell (eds), *Chinese Families in the Post-Mao Era* (Berkeley: University of California Press, 1993).

70 F. Bobin, 'À Shanghai, le mariage branché parodie les rituels chrétiens', *Le Monde*, 5 February 2003, p. 25.

71 G. Wang, 'Cultivating friendship through bowling in Shenzhen', and D. L. Wank, 'Cigarettes and domination in Chinese business networks. Institutional change during the market transition', in Davis (ed.), *The Consumer Revolution*, chs 11 and 12.

72 *Libération*, 4 October 1995, p. 10.

73 *Le Monde*, 23 September 1995, p. 5. See also L. Caramel, 'À Bombay, Coca-Cola est érigé en symbole de ces multinationales accusées de pollution', ibid., 22 January 2003, p. 4.

74 'Who's wearing the trousers?', *The Economist*, 8 September 2001, pp. 27–30; K. Go, 'Asia goes mad for culture beauty', *Financial Times – Weekend*, 1–2 November 2003, p. W10; 'The Japanese don't buy it. They are tiring of luxury-brand goods', *International Herald Tribune*, 27–8 September 2003, pp. 1 and 7; Forestier, 'Les petites marques', p. ix.

75 D. Rouard, 'Les paraboles de l'exil', *Le Monde*, 29–30 December 1996, p. 8.

76 Iwabuchi, *Recentering Globalisation*, p. 4.

77 'La crise du modèle McDonald's', *Le Monde*, 16 October 2002, p. 18; 'Le fast-food est atteint par la crise de la restauration', *Le Monde*, 21 March 1997, p. 24.

78 A.-C. Poirier, 'Barbie peut aller se rhabiller', *Libération*, 30 December 2003, p. 20.

79 *Libération*, 5 March 2003, p. 12.

80 S. Michel, 'La guerre de Coca-Cola en Iran', *Le Figaro*, 15 February 2001; P. Claude, 'Les combats de Mecca-Cola', *Le Monde*, 5 February 2003, p. 14; *Libération*, 15 August 2003.

81 *Libération*, 5 February 2003.

82 *La Croix-L'Événement*, 21 July 2003.

83 R. Chartier, *On the Edge of the Cliff: History, Language, and Practices*, trans. Lydia G. Cochrane (Baltimore, MD, and London: Johns Hopkins University Press, 1997), p. 130.

84 Certeau, *The Practice of Everyday Life*, p. 214.

85 *Libération*, 20 May 2002.

86 J.-Y. Nau, 'Les vins de Beaujolais traversent une grave crise d'identité', *Le Monde*, 20 November 2003, p. 12. See for example Y. Zhao, 'China slowly acquiring taste for Western wines', *International Herald Tribune*, 31 December 2003 and 1 January 2004, pp. 1 and 4.

87 Iwabuchi, *Recentering Globalisation*.

88 B. Pedroletti 'Le Japon, nouvelle référence du consommateur asiatique', *Le Monde*, 7–8 December 2003, p. 14; Pons, ' "Cool Japan" ', pp. 1 and 20.

89 Iwabuchi, *Recentering Globalisation*; A. Ong, *Flexible Citizenship. The Cultural Logics of Transnationality* (Durham: Duke University Press, 1999).

90 F. Adelkhah, 'Qui a peur du mollah Omar? L'économie morale du "talebanisme" dans le Golfe', *Critique internationale*, 12, July 2001, pp. 22–9.

91 C. Ayad, 'Thuraya, l'autre téléphone arabe', *Libération*, 20 October 2003, pp. 42–3.

92 T. Aoki, 'Aspects of Globalisation in Contemporary Japan', in P. L. Berger and S. P. Huntington (eds), *Many Globalisations. Cultural Diversity in the Contemporary World* (Oxford: Oxford University Press, 2002), pp. 77ff.

93 G. Nunberg, 'Languages and language communities in the age of electronic discourses', in D. Lacorne and T. Judt (eds), *Language, nation and state: identity politics in a multilingual age* (New York: Palgrave Macmillan, 2004), conclusion.

94 *The Economist*, 13 April 2002, p. 13.

95 I. Kopytoff, 'The cultural biography of things: commoditization as process', in Appadurai (ed.), *The Social Life of Things*, ch. 2.

96 'The road to hell is unpaved', *The Economist*, 21 December 2002, pp. 65–7.

97 Burke, *Lifebuoy Men*, p. 206.

98 Quoted by W. M. O'Barr, 'The airbrushing of culture. An insider looks at global advertising', *Public Culture*, 2 (1), Autumn 1989, p. 15.

99 'McDonald's lance le hamburger "au goût français" ', *Le Monde*, 21 March 1997, p. 24; 'Avec des restaurants moins uniformes, la France tire la croissance du groupe en Europe', *Le Monde*, 16 October 2002, p. 18; L. Le Vaillant, 'Fast France', *Libération*, 25 November 1999; 'Delicious irony', *The Economist*, 27 April 2002, p. 63.

100 J. L. Watson, 'Introduction: transnationalism, localization, and fast foods in East Asia', in J. L. Watson (ed.), *Golden Arches East. McDonald's in East Asia* (Stanford: Stanford University Press, 1997), pp. 24–5.

101 D. Miller, 'Coca–Cola: a black sweet drink from Trinidad', in D. Miller (ed.), *Material Culture*, p. 170.

102 Ibid.; Watson (ed.), *Golden Arches East*.

103 C. Lévi-Strauss, *Le Père Noël supplicié* (Pin-Balma: Sables, 1996), pp. 15, 17, 18, 21. Thanks to Romain Bertrand for bringing this text to my attention. It was first published in *Les Temps modernes* in 1952.

104 A. Chemin, 'Comment Noël, fête chrétienne, devient un rite national', *Le Monde*, 24 December 2002, p. 8.

105 Watson (ed.), *Golden Arches East*, passim.

106 K. T. Hansen, *Salaula. The World of Secondhand Clothing and Zambia* (Chicago: University of Chicago Press, 2000), p. 6.

107 Ibid., pp. 51–2; J. Ferguson, *Expectations of Modernity. Myths and Meanings of Urban Life on the Zambian Copperbelt* (Berkeley: University of California Press, 1999).

108 Hansen, *Salaula*, pp. 182–3.

109 Ibid., p. 227.

110 Y. Navaro-Yashin, *Faces of the State. Secularism and Public Life in Turkey* (Princeton: Princeton University Press, 2002), p. 79, in a chapter explicitly titled: 'The market for identities: buying and selling secularity and Islam'.

111 Ibid., pp. 85ff.

112 Ibid., p. 91.

113 S. Bozdogan, *Modernism and Nation Building. Turkish Architectural Cuture in the Early Republic* (Seattle: University of Washington Press, 2001), passim, and especially pp. 101, 174, 193ff. See also the 49 numbers of the trimestrial *La Turquie kémaliste* published between 1933 and 1948, various photos from which are reprinted in *'La Turquie kémaliste'. The Atatürk Era. A New Turkey and a New Generation* (Istanbul: Ray Sigorta, 1998).

114 A. Durakbasa and D. Cindoglu, 'Encounters at the counter: gender and the shopping experience', in D. Kandiyoti and A. Saktanber (eds), *Fragments of Culture. The Everyday of Modern Turkey* (London: I. B. Tauris, 2002), ch. 3.

115 J. B. White, *Islamist Mobilization in Turkey. A Study in Vernacular Politics* (Seattle: University of Washington Press, 2002), p. 53.

116 G. L. Mosse, *La Révolution fasciste. Vers une théorie générale du fascisme* (Paris: Le Seuil, 2003).

117 E. Pommier, *Winckelmann, inventeur de l'histoire de l'art* (Paris: Gallimard, 2003); G. L. Mosse, *L'Image de l'homme. L'invention de la virilité moderne* (Paris: Abbeville, 1997).

118 Mosse, *La Révolution fasciste.*

119 C. Jaffrelot *Les Nationalistes hindous. Idéologie, implantation et mobilisation des années 1990* (Paris: Presses de Sciences-Po, 1993); W. Laqueur, *A History of Zionism* (London: Weidenfeld and Nicolson, 1972); Mosse, *L'Image de l'homme.*

120 C. Guérin, *L'Utopie Scouts de France* (Paris: Fayard, 1997).

121 Mosse, *La Révolution fasciste*, p. 81; N. Parsons, *King Khama, Emperor Joe and the Great White Queen. Victorian Britain through African Eyes* (Chicago: University of Chicago Press, 1998), pp. 18–19; F. Adelkhah, 'La question féminine, angle mort de la démocratie islamique en Iran', *Politix*, 13 (51), 2000, p. 146.

122 Bayart and Warnier (eds), *Matière à politique.*

123 F. Chapta, 'La vie en rose version "Ostalgie". En Allemagne, la nostalgie de la RDA envahit la culture et la consommation', *Libération*, 12 August 2003; R. Bernstein, 'In East Germany, a wave of nostalgia for the good old days', *International Herald Tribune*, 12 January 2004, p. 3.

124 D. Roche, *Histoire des choses banales. Naissance de la consommation, XVIIe–XIXe siècles* (Paris: Albin Michel, 2000); S. Delattre, *Les Douzes Heures noires. La nuit à Paris au XIXe siècle* (Paris: Albin Michel, 2000).

125 'China's consumer class keeps growing', *International Herald Tribune*, 16 December 2003, p. 13; 'Asia's consumers: a billion boomers', *The Economist*, 11 October 2003, p. 66.

126 M. Mauss, *Sociologie et anthropologie*, pp. 372 and 384, author's italics.

127 A. Pierre, 'La musique des gestes. Sens du mouvement et images motrices dans les débuts de l'abstraction', in *Aux origines de l'abstraction, 1800–1914* (Paris: Réunion des Musées nationaux, 2003), p. 85.

128 J.-P. Warnier, *Construire la culture matérielle. L'Homme qui pensait avec ses doigts* (Paris: PUF, 1999), pp. 26 and 81. Thanks to Jean-Pierre Warnier for bringing to my attention this issue of motor praxeology as we were working on *Matière à politique*. See also D. Harvey, *Spaces of Hope* (Berkeley: University of California Press, 2000).

129 Quoted in Warnier, *Construire la culture matérielle*, p. 21.

130 Mauss, *Sociologie et anthropologie*, p. 383.

131 A. Corbin, *Le Monde retrouvé de Louis-François Pinagot. Sur les traces d'un inconnu (1798–1876)* (Paris: Flammarion, 'Champs', 2002), pp. 118–121.

132 Mauss, *Sociologie et anthropologie*, pp. 363–69 and 384. See also P. Bourdieu, *Le Sens pratique* (Paris: Minuit, 1980), pp. 111–34.

133 M. Foucault, *Discipline and Punish. The Birth of the Prison*, trans. Alan Sheridan (Harmondsworth: Penguin Books, 1979).

134 Ibid.

135 M. Foucault, *Abnormal: lectures at the Collège de France, 1974–75*, ed. Valerio Marchetti and Antonella Salomoni; general eds, François Ewald and Alessandro Fontana; tr. by Graham Burchell (London: Verso, 2003).

136 Foucault, *Discipline and Punish*.

137 Certeau, *The Practice of Everyday Life*.

138 Foucault, *History of Sexuality*, vol. 2, *The Usage of Pleasure*; vol. 3, *The Care of the Self*.

139 J. Wittlin, *La Saga du patient fantassin*, tr. into French from the Polish by A.-C. Carls (Montricher, Noir sur Blanc, 2000), pp. 27, 179, 187, 189, 197, 211–12, 238–40, 270. See also the comparative considerations of Marcel Mauss on marching in the French and British infantry during the 1914–1918 war (*Sociologie et anthropologie*, p. 367).

140 M. Weber, *General Economic History*, trans. Frank H. Knight (New York: Collier Books, 1961).

141 Foucault, *Discipline and Punish*.

142 M. Pivois, 'Chanal se condamne à mort', *Libération*, 16 October 2003, p. 15.

143 E. M. Collingham, *Imperial Bodies. The Physical Experience of the Raj, c.1800–1947* (Cambridge: Polity, 2001), p. 1.

144 C. Galus, 'L'obésité s'étend désormais aux pays en voie de développement', *Le Monde*, 15 October 2003, p. 25; 'Spoilt for choice. A survey of food', *The Economist*, 13 December 2003; M. Perez, 'Obésité: Washington tente de peser contre l'OMS', *Le Figaro*, 22 January 2004, p. 12.

145 B. Manier, 'Dans l'enfer des sweatshops', *Alternatives économiques*, 197, November 2001, pp. 40–2; O. Aubert, 'Le paradis du thon free tax', ibid.,

pp. 63–5; P. P. Pan, 'A new syndrome faces China's laborers: "overwork death" ', *International Herald Tribune*, 14 May 2002, p. 8; Ong, *Flexible Citizenship*, pp. 78 and 223; Harvey, *Spaces of Hope*, p. 44.

146 Mauss, *Sociologie et anthropologie*, p. 374.

147 O. Carlier, *Entre nation et jihad. Histoire sociale des radicalismes algériens* (Paris: Presses de Sciences-Po, 1995), p. 49.

148 See for example A. J. Wharton, *Building the Cold War: Hilton International Hotels and Modern Architecture* (Chicago: University of Chicago Press, 2001).

149 Sources: interviews with the author, Mascate, February 2002.

150 It is still worth noting that 'air companies are rediscovering first class', *Le Monde*, 28–9 December 2003, p. 10.

151 K. Zernike, 'A very different world for travelers. Two years after attacks, airports and passengers have changed', *International Herald Tribune*, 12 September 2003, pp. 1 and 5; J. Sharkey, 'Shoe inspections leave passengers ready to revolt', *International Herald Tribune*, 27 June 2003, p. 9.

152 *Le Monde*, 27 December 2003, p. 20.

153 *International Herald Tribune*, 12 September 2003, p. 2.

154 P.-J. Laurent, 'Effervescence religieuse et gouvernance. L'exemple des Assemblées de Dieu du Burkina Faso', *Politique africaine*, 87, October 2002. p. 114.

155 'The beauty business. Pots of promise', *The Economist*, 24 May 2003, pp. 69–71.

156 Certeau, *The Practice of Everyday Life*, p. 11.

157 Burke, *Lifebuoy Men*, p. 165. See also pp. 50–1.

158 Quoted in ibid., p. 127.

159 Ibid., p. 41.

160 J.-F. Bayart, *The Illusion of Cultural Identity*, trans. Steven Rendall, Janet Roitman, Cynthia Schoch and Jonathan Derrick (Chicago: University of Chicago Press, 2005), p. 170. I introduced this 'fundamental distinction': 'To my mind, discursive limits – which I will also call repertoires – are not limited to explicit discourses, whether oral or written, but extend to other means of communication, whether gestual, musical, or vestimentary'.

161 F. Borel, *Le Vêtement incarné. Les Métamorphoses du corps* (Paris: Calmann–Lévy, 1992); D. Le Breton, *La Peau et la trace. Sur les blessures de soi* (Paris: Métailié, 2003).

162 F. Deschamps, 'Pour quelques centimètres de plus', *Libération*, 6 November 2003, p. 27.

163 M. Foucault, 'The subject and power', in *Power*, p. 326.

164 J.-M. Normand, 'L'homme prend son poil au sérieux', *Le Monde*, 19 November 2003, p. 27; M. Ecoiffier, 'Pour les hommes qui n'ont pas froid aux fesses: le string masculin aguicheur fait un tabac au rayon lingerie', *Libération*, 17 December 2003, p. 27; R. Lecadre, 'Des dessous masculins gainant pile-poil', *Libération*, 27 January 2004, p. 28.

165 'À Kaboul, hors la barbe point de salut. Après les femmes voilées, les pilosités mâles sont devenues l'obsession', *Libération*, 21 May 1997, p. 14.

166 J.-Y. Nau, 'L'homme illustré', *Le Monde*, 28 August 1991, p. 13; P. Krémer, 'Tatouage et piercing, "nouveaux marqueurs identitaires" pour les jeunes',

ibid., p. 8; M. Coutty, 'Chirurgie esthétique: les hommes aussi', ibid., 12 January 2001, p. 25; C. Vincent, 'Ados à fleur de peau', ibid., 9 July 2003, p. 25; Le Breton, *La Peau*.

167 Le Breton, *La Peau*.

168 C. Mabrut, 'La Perla, l'éveil des sens', *Le Figaro*, 19 December 2002, p. 19.

169 'The beauty business', p. 70.

170 D. Altman, *Global Sex* (Chicago: University of Chicago Press, 2001), pp. 76 and 107.

171 On the disgust which such sexual relationships can arouse and the conflicts of subjectivation that ensued in Kenya, see L. White, *The Comforts of Home. Prostitution in Colonial Nairobi* (Chicago: University of Chicago Press, 1990), pp. 107ff; B. Berman and J. Lonsdale, *Unhappy Valley*, II, *Violence and Ethnicity*, pp. 388ff and 456ff; J. Spencer, *KAU*.

172 T. W. Laqueur, *Solitary Sex. A Cultural History of Masturbation* (New York: Zone Books, 2003), pp. 79ff and 362ff.

173 *Libération*, 17 January 1994, p. 23.

174 J. Mossuz-Lavau, *La Vie sexuelle en France* (Paris: La Martinière, 2002), pp. 266–85.

175 H. Beazley, 'The sexual lives of street children in Yogyakarta, Indonesia', *Review of Indonesian and Malaysian Affairs*, 37 (1), 2003, pp. 17–44.

176 Y. Vavokhine, *Qui sont les vrais "moujiks" dans les sociétés russo–soviétiques et leurs établissements pénitentiaires?* (Paris: École doctorale de l'Institut d'études politiques de Paris, 2002). Thanks to Gilles Favarel-Garrigue for bringing this work to my attention. See also L. Fourchard, 'La prison entre conservatisme et transgression: le quotidien carcéral en Haute-Volta, 1920–1960', in F. Bernault (ed.), *Enfermement, prison et châtiments en Afrique du XIXe siècle à nos jours* (Paris: Karthala, 1999), p. 280.

177 Marx, *La Première Critique*, p. 244.

178 Musée d'Orsay, *Aux origines de l'abstraction*, in particular the chapters by Marcella Lista and Pascal Rousseau.

179 J.-J. Salgon, *07 et autres récits* (Lagrasse: Verdier, 1993), pp. 104–5.

180 K. Ross, *Fast Cars, Clean Bodies. Decolonization and the Reordering of French Culture* (Cambridge: MIT Press, 1996).

181 C. Neidhart, *Russia's Carnival. The Smells, Sights and Sounds of Transition* (Lanham: Rowman and Littlefield Publishers, 2003).

182 J. Elyachar, 'Finance internationale, micro-crédit et religion de la société civile en Égypte', *Critique internationale*, 13, October 2001, pp. 145–6.

183 C. A. Bayly, 'The origins of swadeshi (home industry): cloth and Indian society, 1700–1930', in A. Appadurai (ed.), *The Social Life of Things*, pp. 285–321; E. Tarlo, *Clothing Matters. Dress and Identity in India* (London: Hurst, 1996).

184 Ecoiffier, 'Pour les hommes'; Lecadre, 'Des dessous masculins'.

185 This is the expression used by Dominique Raffali, managing director of Hom and the designer of this collection, ibid.

186 'Spoilt for choice'.

187 J. L. and J. Comaroff, *Of Revelation and Revolution*, II: *The Dialectics of Modernity*, pp. 71–2.

188 Burke, *Lifebuoy Men*, pp. 188ff.

189 S. Audoin–Rouzeau and A. Becker, *14–18, retrouver la guerre* (Paris: Galli-mard, 2000), pp. 124 and 168.

190 Burke, *Lifebuoy Men*; N. R. Hunt, *A Colonial Lexicon of Birth Ritual, Medi-calization, and Mobility in the Congo* (Durham: Duke University Press, 1999); M. J. Hay, 'Hoes and cloth in a Luo household: changing consumption in a colonial economy, 1906–1936', in M. J. Arnoldi, C. M. Geary and K. L. Hardin (eds), *African Material Culture* (Bloomington: Indiana University Press, 1996), p. 254.

191 See for example Burke, *Lifebuoy Men*, chs 1, 2 and 3.

192 *The Economist*, 13 December 2003, p. 11.

193 *International Herald Tribune*, 19 September 2003.

194 K. Marx, quoted by A. Lüdtke (ed.), *Histoire du quotidien* (Paris: Éd. de la Maison des sciences de l'homme, 1994), p. 6.

195 See in particular Ranger, *Dance and Society*.

196 N. Argenti, 'La danse aux frontières. Les mascarades interdites des femmes et des jeunes à Oku', in Bayart and Warnier (eds), *Matière à politique*, ch. 5, and '*Kesum–Body* and the places of the gods: the politics of children's masking and second–world realities in Oku (Cameroon)', *The Journal of the Royal Anthropological Institute*, 7 (1), March 2001, pp. 67–94.

197 R. Jenkins, 'Balinese theater softens pain of bombing', *International Herald Tribune*, 15 October 2003, p. 22.

198 S. Darbon, *Des jeunes filles toutes simples. Ethnographie d'une troupe de major-ettes en France* (Jean-Michel Place, n.d. [1995]), pp. 51ff.

199 J. Farrer, 'Dancing through the market transition. Disco and dance hall sociability in Shanghai', in Davis (ed.), *The Consumer Revolution*, pp. 242 and 245.

200 G. Holst, *Road to Rembetika. Music of a Greek Sub–Culture. Songs of Love, Sorrow and Hashish* (Athens: Denise Harvey and Co., 1975); E. Petropoulos, *Songs of the Greek Underworld. The Rebetika Tradition* (London: Saqi Books, 2000).

201 J. Roach, *Cities of the Dead. Circum-Atlantic Performance* (New York: Colum-bia University Press, 1996), pp. 26–7.

202 See for example J. K. Cowan, *Dance and the Body Politic in Northern Greece* (Princeton: Princeton University Press, 1990).

203 Appadurai, *Modernity at Large*, ch. 5.

204 'Luo tribe makes Kenya's team a family business', *International Herald Tribune*, 26 February 2003, p. 17.

205 I. Shun, 'The invention of the martial arts. Kano Jigoro and Kodokan judo', in Vlastos (ed.), *Mirror of Modernity*, ch. 11.

206 Ong, *Flexible Citizenship*, pp. 161ff.

207 D. Lepoutre, *Coeur de banlieue. Codes, rites et langages* (Paris: Odile Jacob, 1997), p. 260.

208 Quoted by F. Adelkhah, *Being Modern in Iran*, trans. Jonathan Derrick (New York: Columbia University Press, 2000), pp. 125–8 and 199ff. See also P. B. Zarrilli, 'Repositioning the body, practice, power and self in an Indian martial art', in Breckenridge (ed.), *Consuming Modernity*, ch. 8.

209 C. Bromberger, *Le Match de football. Ethnologie d'une passion partisane à Marseille, Naples et Turin* (Paris: Éd. de la Maison des sciences de l'homme, 1995); P. Boniface (ed.), *Géopolitique du football* (Brussels: Complexe, 1998).

See also, for rugby, the interview with Pierre Villepreux, former trainer of the French team, who insists on the 'way the game has become standardised': 'globalisation entails uniformisation', *Libération*, 7 October 2003, p. iii.

210 W. Dissanayake (ed.), *Melodrama and Asian Cinema* (Cambridge: Cambridge University Press, 1993); S. Dickey, *Cinema and the Urban Poor in South India* (Cambridge: Cambridge University Press, 1993); P. Mankekar, *Screening Culture, Viewing Politics. An Ethnography of Television, Womanhood and Nation in Postcolonial India* (Durham: Duke University Press, 1999); W. Armbrust, *Mass Culture and Modernism in Egypt* (Cambridge: Cambridge University Press, 1996); Adelkhah, *Being Modern in Islam*, pp. 137–89; F. D. Ginsburg and L. Abu-Lughod (eds), *Media Worlds. Anthropology on a New Terrain* (Berkeley: University of California Press, 2002); Iwabuchi, *Recentering Globalisation*; T. Liebes and E. Katz, 'Six interprétations de la série *Dallas*', *Hermès*, 11–12, 1992, pp. 125–44.

211 D. F. Eickelman and J. W. Anderson (eds), *New Media in the Muslim World. The Emerging Public Sphere* (Bloomington, Indiana University Press, 1999); Ong, *Flexible Citizenship*, pp. 158ff.

212 Marx, op. cit. *La Première Critique*.

213 P. Haski, 'Révocul par-dessus tête pour les 110 ans de Mao en Chine. Nostalgie, populisme ou exorcisme, le Grand Timonier est très tendance', *Libération*, 26 December 2003, p. 9.

214 Y. Verdier, *Façons de dire, façons de faire. La laveuse, la couturière, la cuisinière* (Paris: Gallimard, 1979), p. 192.

215 Darbon, *Des jeunes filles*.

216 Adelkhah, 'La question féminine', p. 154, note 19. Thanks to Fariba Adelkhah for drawing my attention to this relationship between movement and the public space.

217 F. Adelkhah, *La Révolution sous le voile. Femmes islamiques d'Iran* (Paris: Karthala, 1991), and *Being Modern in Iran*.

218 Adelkhah, 'La question féminine', pp. 145–6 and 154.

219 Adelkhah, *Being Modern in Iran*, p. 46. See also the cycling adventures of Adelkhah in *La Révolution sous le voile*, p. 247.

220 Adelkhah, 'La question féminine', pp. 155–6.

221 Quoted in D. Gandoulou, *Dandies à Bacongo. Le Culte de l'élégance dans la société congolaise contemporaine* (Paris: L'Harmattan, 1989), p. 97. For other African examples, see Bayart, *The Illusion of Cultural Identity*, pp. 229ff.

222 Mauss, *Sociologie et anthropologie*, p. 368.

223 Ibid.

224 Sources: interviews with Fr Eric de Rosny; Swarns, 'A vampire hysteria'; R. Bertrand, *Indonésie: la démocratie invisible. Violence, magie et politique à Java* (Paris: Karthala, 2002), pp. 85ff.

225 E. Balibar, *Nous, citoyens d'Europe? Les frontières, l'État, le peuple* (Paris: La Découverte, 2001).

226 M. Hardt and T. Negri, *Empire* (Cambridge, MA, and London: Harvard University Press, 2000).

227 Ong, *Flexible Citizenship*, p. 156.

228 J.-M. Normand, 'L'attroupement-éclair, un étrange rituel urbain', *Le Monde*, 17 September 2003, p. 27; <parismobs.free.fr>.

229 Quoted in F. Roussel, 'Avec le flashmob, devenez un pro du foule-contact', *Libération*, 23 January 2004, p. 26.

230 H. Rheingold, *The Virtual Community. Homestealing on the Electronic Frontier* (Cambridge, MA: MIT Press, 2000).

231 D. Bornstein and M. Temman, 'Contre l'OMC jusqu'à la mort', *Libération*, 23 September 2003, pp. 24–5.

232 E. Ohnuki-Tierney, *Kamikaze, Cherry Blossoms and Nationalism. The Militarization of Aesthetics in Japanese History* (Chicago: University of Chicago Press, 2002). This interpretation is admittedly criticized by M. Sleeboom (*IIAS Newsletter*, July 2003, p. 35).

233 O. Roy, *Globalised Islam: The Search for a New Ummah* (London: Hurst, 2004).

234 M. Mermoz, 'Les femmes ne veulent plus être des poupées', *Alternatives économiques*, 202, April 2002, pp. 40–3. See also P. Sabatier, 'À New York Sado et Maso vont au resto', *Libération*, 28 July 1998, p. iv; C. Dutilleux, 'Le Brésil entre instit' fouetteuse et curé swingeur', ibid., 26 March, 1999, p. 34; S. Davet, 'La Jackass attitude débarque en France', *Le Monde télévision*, 14 February 2004, p. 6.

235 'Ça vous apprendra', *Libération*, 15 August 2003, p. 13. See also 'Des écoles catholiques britanniques défendent les châtiments corporels', *La Croix-L'Événement*, 2 February 1999, p. 11.

236 G. Deleuze, *Empiricism and Subjectivity: An Essay on Hume's Theory of Human Nature*, trans. Constantin V. Boundas (New York and Oxford: Columbia University Press, 1991), pp. 117 and 127.

237 G. Deleuze, lecture given on 15 February 1977, and *Difference and repetition*, tr. by Paul Patton (London: The Athlone Press, 1994).

238 Ibid.

239 Certeau, *The Practice of Everyday Life*.

240 Z. Laïdi, *Le Sacre du présent* (Paris: Flammarion, 2000); P.-A. Taguieff, *Résister au bougisme. Démocratie forte contre globalisation techno–marchande* (Paris: Mille et Une Nuits, n.d. [2001]).

241 J. L. Watson, 'Introduction: transnationalism, localization, and fast foods in East Asia', in J. L. Watson (ed.), *Golden Arches East*, pp. 28–9.

242 F. Hartog, *Régimes d'historicité. Présentisme et expérience du temps* (Paris: Le Seuil, 2003).

Conclusion

1 F. Hartog, *Régimes d'historicité. Présentisme et expérience du temps* (Paris: Le Seuil, 2003).

2 J. Risen and T. Shanker, 'Secret universe holds US terror suspects. Detainees are spread across the world', *International Herald Tribune*, 19 December 2003, p. 5.

3 G. Agamben, 'L'état d'exception', *Le Monde*, 12 December 2002, p. 16. See also the F.-A. Mann address given in London on 25 November 2003 by Johan Steyn, judge at the appeal court of the House of Lords: 'Guantanamo Bay: the legal black hole', ibid., 10 December 2003, pp. 1 and 14.

4 P. Gélie, 'Voyage dans les geôles de Guantanamo', *Le Figaro*, 9 December 2003, p. 2,

5 Declaration by Christophe Girod, representative of the ICRC in Washington, *Le Monde*, 19–20 October 2003, p. 1. The camp held up to 680 detainees before the freeings in summer 2003.

6 Evidence gathered by C. Gall and N. A. Lewis, 'Freed Guantanamo captives tell of suicidal despair', *International Herald Tribune*, 18 June 2003, pp. 1 and 4; P. Cochez and M.-F. Masson, 'Des parents racontent les silences de Guantanamo', *La Croix-L'Événement*, 16 October 2003, pp. 4–5; M.-F. Calle, 'Le calvaire d'un captif de Guantanamo', *Le Figaro*, 20 June 2003, p. 4; F. Chipaux, 'Un Pakistanais libéré de Guantanamo raconte sa détention', *Le Monde*, 9 November 2003, p. 4.

7 J. Lelyveld, 'Retour à Guantanamo', *Le Monde*, 9 November 2002, p. 14.

8 G. Agamben, 'Europe des libertés ou Europe des polices?', *Le Monde*, 4 October 2002, p. 16.

9 *Le Monde*, 9 November 2002, p. 4.

10 Witness Mohammed Sanghir, ibid.

11 Lelyveld, 'Retour à Guantanamo', pp. 14–15.

12 *International Herald Tribune*, 19 December 2003 and 29 September 2003; J. Crowley, 'Triomphe des sécuritaires', and D. Sabbagh, 'Vers une relégitimation du "profilage ethnoracial"?', *Critique internationale*, 14, January 2002, pp. 29–38.

13 See also the reasons for which Giorgio Agamben now refuses to visit the United States: 'Non au tatouage biopolitique', *Le Monde*, 11–12 January 2004, pp. 1 and 10.

14 C. Roitman and H. Sabéran, 'Clandestins coincés aux ports d'exil', *Libération*, 26 February 2003, pp. 16–17; S. Laacher, 'Partir pour le bout de la terre', *Critique internationale*, 19 (April 2003), pp. 157–70.

15 J. MacGaffey and R. Bazenguissa-Ganga, *Congo-Paris. Transnational Traders on the Margins of the Law* (Oxford: James Currey, 2000), p. 27.

16 N. Revise, 'Les enfants étrangers, forçats da la Thaïlande', *Libération*, 25–6 May 2002, p. 20–1; C. Rotman, 'Des mineurs clandestins à Marseille. Entre deux rives', *Libération*, 24 January, p. 46; S. de Royer, 'Ces victimes de la traite des mineurs étrangers', *La Croix-L'Événement*, 6 March 2003, p. 6; M.-C. Tabet, 'Des centaines d'enfants en perdition à Calais', *Le Figaro*, 8–9 November 2003, p. 8; A. Baker, 'A 12-years-old "mule" on drug run to US', *International Herald Tribune*, 13–14 April 2002; N. Bonnet, 'Pérou: l'exploitation des enfants dans les mines. Travailler et mourir pour quelques paillettes d'or', *Le Monde*, 29 August 1991, and 'Pérou: les enfants martyrs de la ruée vers l'or', *Libération*, 17 and 18 August 1991; A. Boher, 'Côte d'Ivoire/Mali: les enfants-esclaves vont rentrer chez eux', *La Croix-L'Événement*, 11 September 2000, p. 9, and C. Holzbauer, 'Le rêve d'émigrer des enfants maliens tourne à la tragédie', *La Croix-L'Événement*, 23 January 2002, pp. 12–13; J. Rueff, 'Planteur ivoirien cherche jeune esclave', *Libération*, 5 September 2000, p. 12, and 'Les enfants esclaves, une plaie africaine', *Libération*, 20 March 2002, p. 8; T. Kouamouo, 'Confusion au Bénin après le retour d'un navire soupçonné de transport d' "enfants-esclaves" ', *Le Monde*, 18 April 2001, p. 3; T. Oberlé, 'Les enfants-esclaves de l'eldorado ivoirien', *Le Figaro*, 4 July 2001.

17 S. Zappi, 'Deux rapports dénoncent les violences policières en zone d'attente', *Le Monde*, 7 March 2003, p. 6. See also S. Zappi, 'La Cimade s'inquiète de la hausse spectaculaire du nombre d'étrangers placés en centre de rétention', *Le Monde*, 2 December 2003, p. 12.

18 'Construire un récit. Entretien avec Dominique Noguères, avocate spécialisée dans le droit des immigrés', *Critique internationale*, 19, April 2003, pp. 191–6.

19 Remarks reported by C. Rotman, 'Le huis–clos de la zone d'attente de Roissy. Témoignage de l'intérieur', *Libération*, 22 October 2002, pp. 18–19.

20 *Courrier international*, 486, 24 February 2000, pp. 46–7.

21 M. Wines, 'Zimbabweans on the night train back to nowhere', *International Herald Tribune*, 24 September 2003, p. 2.

22 D. Kirk, 'Dirty work, bad pay and no defense', *International Herald Tribune*, 31 May 2002, p. 2.

23 Source: interview with the author, Paris 1998.

24 On the murders of Ciudad Juarez, see *Le Monde*, 24–5 August and 2 October 2003; *International Herald Tribune*, 13 August 2003; *Libération*, 23 December 2003. On the region, see the film *De l'autre côté* by Chantal Ackerman, as well as her presentation in *Le Monde*, 26–7 May 2002, p. 30; D. Bornstein, 'Pauvres, mais trop chers', *Libération*, 8 August 202, pp. 14–15; 'Special report: the US–Mexican border. Between here and there', *The Economist*, 7 July 2001, pp. 29–32.

25 F. Adelkhah, 'Partir sans quitter, quitter sans partir', *Critique internationale*, 19, April 2003, p. 155.

26 F. Mellah, *Clandestin en Méditerranée* (Tunis: Cérès Éditions, 2000), pp. 50–1. See also J. Harding, *The Uninvited. Refugees at the Rich Man's Gate* (London: Profile Books, 2000).

27 L. Barros, M. Lahlou, C. Escoffier, P. Pumares and P. Ruspini, *L'Immigration irrégulière subsaharienne à travers et vers le Maroc* (Geneva: BIT, n.d. [2003]), p. 34.

28 *Le Monde*, 10 April 2003.

29 C. Parenti, *Lockdown America. Police and Prisons in the Age of Crisis* (London: Verso, 1999).

30 J.-L. Domenach, *Chine: l'archipel oublié* (Paris: Fayard, 1992).

31 H. Arendt, *L'Impérialisme* (Paris: Fayard, 1982).

32 M. Agier, *Aux bords du monde, les réfugiés* (Paris: Flammarion, 2002), pp. 55–6. See also pp. 93–5.

33 J. Crisp, 'A state of insecurity: the political economy of violence in Kenya's refugee camps', *African Affairs*, 99 (397), October 2000.

34 M. Agier, *Aux bords du monde*, p. 79 and pp. 111ff.

35 Crisp, 'A State of insecurity'.

36 Agier, *Aux bords du monde*, p. 112 and 93–4.

37 A. Ong, *Flexible Citizenship. The Cultural Logics of Transnationality* (Durham: Duke University Press, 1999), pp. 35, 223–4 and 231; A. L. Tsing, *In the Realm of the Diamond Queen: Marginality in an Out-of-the-Way Place* (Princeton: Princeton University Press, 1993).

38 J.-P. Stroobants, 'Alerte sur une croissance globale des trafics d'êtres humains', *Le Monde*, 17–18 August 2003, p. 2; 'Desperate cargo', *The Econo-*

mist, 2 March 2002, p. 59; 'A cargo of exploitable souls', *The Economist*, 1 June 2002, p. 48.

39 'Tallulah tales', *The Economist*, 19 April 2003, pp. 41–2; M. Jordan, 'Mexican children riot over detention conditions', *International Herald Tribune*, 6 November 2002, p. 2.

40 T. Weiner, 'Storm rages over Caribbean center for teenagers', *International Herald Tribune*, 18 June 2003, p. 2.

41 J. Coignard, 'Un camp "éducatif" sans garde-fous', *Libération*, 29 April 2003, p. 17.

42 S. Sengupta, 'Bangladesh's stolen lives. Servitude and sex slavery await children abroad', *International Herald Tribune*, 30 April 2002, pp. 1 and 4; N. Wood, 'A trade in children flourishes in Albania', *International Herald Tribune*, p. 3; M. Bran, 'Les Tsiganes handicapés, de Roumanie à l'Europe des riches', *Le Monde*, 13 July 2002, p. 2.

43 J. Duplouich, 'Scotland Yard révèle l'ampleur du trafic d'enfants africains', *Le Figaro*, 30 July 2003, p. 4; *Le Monde*, 31 July 2003; C. Boltanski, 'Un tronc nommé Adam', *Libération*, 16 February 2004, pp. 38–9.

44 V. Turner, *The Ritual Process. Structure and Anti–Structure* (Ithaca: Cornell University Press, 1st edn 1969, new edn 1977), ch. 3.

45 Laacher, 'Partir'.

46 As reported in ibid., p. 164.

47 Turner, *The Ritual Process*, pp. 111–12, and *Dramas, Fields, and Metaphors. Symbolic Action in Human Society* (Ithaca: Cornell University Press, 1st edn 1974, new edn 1987), pp. 196–7 and passim.

48 G. Deleuze, discussing the work of Foucault, in *Negotiations, 1972–1990*, trans. Martin Joughin (New York and Chichester: Columbia University Press, 1995).

49 P. Veyne, *La Société romaine* (Paris: Le Seuil, 1991), ch. 1, and *Roman Erotic Elegy: Love, Poetry, and the West*, trans. David Pella (Chicago and London: University of Chicago Press, 1988), p. 31; J. D. Y. Peel, *Religious Encounter and the Making of the Yoruba* (Bloomington: Indiana University Press, 2000), pp. 241ff.

50 J. F. Warren, *Iranun and Balangingi. Globalisation, Maritime Raiding and the Birth of Ethnicity* (Singapore: Singapore University Press, 2002), pp. 45ff and 126ff.

51 Tarrius, *La Globalisation*.

52 Hardt and Negri, *Empire*.

53 E. de Latour, 'Métaphores sociales dans les ghettos de Côte d'Ivoire', *Autrepart*, 18, 2001, pp. 151–67, and 'Du ghetto au voyage clandestin: la métaphore héroïque', *Autrepart*, 19, 2001, pp. 155–76, as well as 'Héros du retour', *Critique internationale*, 19, April 2003, pp. 171–89. The terms in italics that follow are in Nushi, the street language of the Ivory Coast.

54 Latour, 'Métaphores', p. 153.

55 Ibid., p. 156.

56 Ibid.

57 Latour, 'Du ghetto', p. 173.

58 Latour, 'Métaphores', p. 152.

59 Ibid., p. 164.

60 A. Riccardi, *Sant'Egidio. L'Évangile au-delà des frontières. Entretiens avec Dominique Chivot* (Paris: Bayard, 2001), p. 26.

61 Ibid., pp. 48–9.

62 Agier, *Aux bords du monde*, pp. 97ff, 119ff; H. Englund, *From War to Peace on the Mozambican–Malawi Borderland* (Edinburgh: Edinburgh University Press, 2002).

63 J. Roitman, *Fiscal Disobedience. An Anthropology of Economic Regulation in Central Africa* (Princeton: Princeton University Press, forthcoming); Tsing, *Diamond Queen*, pp. 123ff; Adelkhah, 'Partir'; P. C. Salzman, *Black Tents of Baluchistan* (Washington: Smithsonian International Press, 2000).

64 Apart from the vast literature on the 'invention' of ethnicity, on 'communalism' and confessionalism, see D. Lacorne, *La Crise de l'identité américaine. Du melting-pot au multiculturalisme* (Paris: Fayard, 1997); R. Kastoryano, *La France, l'Allemagne et leurs immigrés: négocier l'identité* (Paris: Armand Colin, 1996), and M. Y. Hsu, *Dreaming of Gold, Dreaming of Home. Transnationalism and Migration between the United States and South China, 1882–1943* (Stanford: Stanford University Press, 2000).

65 K. Bennafla, *Le Commerce frontalier en Afrique centrale. Acteurs, espaces, pratiques* (Paris: Karthala, 2002), pp. 301ff; interviews with the author (1995).

66 J. Brooke, 'Russia turns to North Korea for cheap labor', *International Herald Tribune*, 20 May 2003, p. 2.

67 Barros et al., *L'Immigration*, p. 39.

68 F. De Boeck, 'Dancing the Apocalypse in Congo: time, death and double in the realm of apocalyptic incertitude', *Bulletin des séances de l'Académie royale des sciences d'outre-mer*, 47, 2001, pp. 58ff; T. Grätz, 'Gold trading networks and the creation of trust: a case study from Northern Benin', *Africa* 74 (2), 2004.

69 L. H. Malkki, *Purity and Exile. Violence, Memory, and National Cosmology among Hutu Refugees in Tanzania* (Chicago: University of Chicago Press, 1995).

70 J. Ferguson, *Expectations of Modernity. Myths and Meanings of Urban Life on the Zambian Copperbelt* (Berkeley: University of California Press, 1999).

71 L. Carroué, 'Philippines: la grande braderie de main–d'oeuvre', *Alternatives économiques*, 215, June 2003, pp, 62–5; R. S. Parrenas, *Servants of Globalization. Women, Migration and Domestic Work* (Stanford: Stanford University Press, 2001).

72 See for example G. Salamé, 'Une déraison politiquement correcte', *Critique internationale*, 2, Winter 1999, pp. 6–14.

73 F. Aubenas, 'Algérie: l'aide inhumanitaire', *Libération*, 4 July 2003, pp. 10–12.

74 D. Lacorne, 'États-Unis: surveiller et punir tous les "coins noirs" de l'univers', *Critique internationale*, 17, October 2002, pp. 16–24. The expression comes from President Bush, who was addressing the officers of West Point (p. 19).

75 B. Théret, 'La dollarisation: polysémie et enflure d'une notion', *Critique internationale*, 19, April 2003, pp. 62–83; J. Marques-Pereira and B. Théret, 'La couleur du dollar. Enquête à La Havane', *Critique internationale*, 17, October 2002, pp. 81–103; H. Smith, 'La Corée du Nord vers l'économie

de marché', *Critique internationale*, 15, April 2002, pp. 6–14; F. Debié, 'Balkans: une criminalité (presque) sans mafias?', *Critique internationale*, 12, July 2001, pp. 6–13.

76 F. Rigaud, 'Irak: le temps suspendu de l'embargo', *Critique internationale*, 11, April 2001, pp. 15–24.

77 Source: research trip (November 2003).

78 See the remarkable article by C. Messiant, 'La Fondation Eduardo dos Santos (FESA). À propos de l'"investissement" de la société civile par le pouvoir angolais', *Politique africaine*, 73, March 1999, pp. 82–102, and the narrative of P. Rosa-Mendes, *Baie des Tigres* (Paris: Métailié, 2001), as well as T. Hodges, *Angola from Afro-Stalinism to Petro–Diamond Capitalism* (Oxford: James Currey, 2001).

79 Interview in *Libération*, 18–19 May 2002, p. 7.

80 *Le Figaro*, 3 July 2003, p. 17.

81 On globalization as a 'risk society', see U. Beck, *La Société du risque. Sur la voie d'une autre modernité* (Paris: Flammarion, Aubier, 2001), and A. Giddens, *Modernity and Self-Identity. Self and Society in the Late Modern Age* (Stanford: Stanford University Press, 1991).

82 P. D. Curtin, *Disease and Empire*; T. Mitchell, *Rule of Experts. Egypt, Techno–Politics, Modernity* (Berkeley: University of California Press, 2002), ch. 1.

83 P. Brown, *The Rise of Western Christendom: Triumph and Diversity*, AD 200–1000 (Malden, MA and Oxford: Blackwell, 1996), and *Authority and the Sacred: Aspects of the Christianisation of the Roman World* (Cambridge: Cambridge University Press, 1995).

84 F. Cheng, *Vide et plein. Le langage pictural chinois* (Paris: Le Seuil, 1979), p. 30.

85 F. Jullien, *La Grande Image n'a pas de forme, ou du non-objet par la peinture* (Paris: Le Seuil, 2003), passim, especially pp. 101 and 131.

86 Qian Wenshi, quoted in ibid., p. 19.

87 Musée d'Orsay, *Aux origines de l'abstraction, 1800–1914* (Paris: Réunion des Musées nationaux, 2003).

88 P. Veyne, preface to the key work by P. Green, *Alexander to Actium: the Hellenistic age* (London: Thames and Hudson, 1993).

89 S. Goldhill (ed.), *Being Greek under Rome. Cultural Identity, the Second Sophistic and the Development of Empire* (Cambridge: Cambridge Universirty Press, 2001).

90 *Libération*, 14 September 2001.

91 I am drawing on the terms used by T. Asad, *Genealogies of Religion. Discipline and Reasons of Power in Christianity and Islam* (Baltimore: Johns Hopkins University Press, 1993), pp. 1–24.

Index